Game Theory and Society

T0298661

The progress of society can only happen through interpersonal cooperation, because only cooperation can bring about mutual benefit, thus bringing happiness to each person. This should be our collective rationality, but we often see it conflicts with individual interests, which leads to the so-called "Prisoner's dilemma" and does not bring happiness to all.

From a game theoretical perspective, this book addresses the issue of how people can cooperate better. It has two objectives. The first is to use common language to systematically introduce the basic methodologies and core conclusions of Game Theory, including the Nash equilibrium, multiple equilibriums, dynamic games, etc. Mathematics and theoretical models are used to the minimum necessary scope too, to make this book get access to ordinary readers with elementary mathematical training. The second objective is to utilize these methods and conclusions to analyze various Chinese social issues and institutional arrangements, with a focus on the reasons people exhibit non-cooperative behaviors as well as the institutions and cultures that promote interpersonal cooperation.

In addition to economics, specialists in sociology, law, history, politics and management will also be attracted by this book for its insightful analysis on the issue of cooperation in these fields. Also, readers curious about Chinese society will benefit from this book.

Weiying Zhang is a Professor of Economics at Peking University. His research interests include Applied Game Theory, information economics, corporate governance, Chinese economic development, and reform.

China Perspectives

The *China Perspectives* series focuses on translating and publishing works by leading Chinese scholars, writing about both global topics and China-related themes. It covers Humanities and Social Sciences, Education, Media, and Psychology, as well as many interdisciplinary themes.

This is the first time any of these books have been published in English for international readers. The series aims to put forward a Chinese perspective, give insights into cutting-edge academic thinking in China, and inspire researchers globally.

For more information, please visit www.routledge.com/series/CPH

Existing titles in economics:

Internet Finance in China
Introduction and Practical Approaches
Ping Xie, Chuanwei Zou, Haier Liu

Regulating China's Shadow Banks
Qingmin Yan, Jianhua Li

Internationalization of the RMB
Establishment and Development of RMB Offshore Markets
International Monetary Institute of the RUC

The Road Leading to the Market
Weiying Zhang

Peer-to-Peer Lending with Chinese Characteristics
Development, Regulation and Outlook
P2P Research Group Shanghai Finance Institute

Forthcoming titles in economics:

Tax Reform and Policy in China
Gao Peiyong

China Economic Transition Research
Zhao Renwei

Contents

Game Theory and Society

Weiying Zhang

Routledge
Taylor & Francis Group

LONDON AND NEW YORK

The Chinese edition is originally published by Peking University Press in 2013

British Library Cataloguing-in-Publication Data
A catalogue record for this book is available from the British Library

Library of Congress Cataloging-in-Publication Data
A catalog record for this title has been requested

ISBN: 978-1-138-57345-1 (hbk)
ISBN: 978-0-367-53679-4 (pbk)

Typeset in Times New Roman
by Apex CoVantage, LLC

Contents

Figures

Tables

Foreword to the Chinese edition

(1)

The main question throughout this book is: How can humanity cooperate better?

Society is formed by individuals. It exists because of people, and yet also exists for people. As rational individuals, each one of us has our own personal interests and pursues our own happiness. This is entirely natural and no force can change it. However, the progress of society can only happen through interpersonal mutual cooperation. Only cooperation can bring about mutual benefit, thus bringing happiness to each person. This should be our collective rationality, but we often see that decisions based on individual rationality conflict with collective rationality. This leads to the so-called "Prisoner's Dilemma" and does not bring happiness to all.

In addition to individual interests, another important obstacle for human cooperation is our limited knowledge. At present, even though human knowledge of the laws of nature has increased dramatically, our understanding of humanity itself is not even sufficient enough to allow us to understand the best way to pursue happiness. It is relatively easy to get the average person to accept knowledge from the natural sciences, but very difficult when it comes to the social sciences. We are short-sighted, arrogant, narrow-minded, presumptuous, and often do not know where our true interests lie. It is precisely because of our ignorance that so many conflicts exist in human society. That which appears to be conflicts of interest are often actually conflicts of ideas. In reality, most shameless actions that harm others for the benefit of oneself in essence are also the result of ignorance. Those that harm others mistakenly believe that they are maximizing their own happiness, but often harm themselves as well. Some people have good hearts – they are always thinking of others' happiness – but because of ignorance, they have brought about huge amount of disasters upon humanity. A classic example of this is the planned economy.

Luckily, as the only rational animal on this earth, humans not only have the natural ability to create, they also have the ability to learn. Over the long span of our history, humanity has invented various technologies, institutions, and cultures to overcome the Prisoner's Dilemma and continuously move toward cooperation. Only then did humanity progress. Speech, writing, property rights, currency, prices, corporations, profit, laws, social norms, values, moral standards, even clocks, computers, and the Internet are examples of inventions that humanity uses to escape the Prisoner's Dilemma and realize cooperation. Of course, every time that cooperation brings about progress, a new Prisoner's Dilemma appears. The Internet provided humanity with a wider scope of cooperation, but it also provided new opportunities for fraudulent behavior. The history of human civilization is simply the history of creating Prisoner's Dilemmas and then escaping them.

Human cooperation and progress cannot be separated from the contributions of some great thinkers. During the Axial Age over 2,000 years ago, there appeared a number of great thinkers, such as Confucius, Sakyamuni, Aristotle, Christ, etc. They took it as their duty to change an immoral world into a moral world and created the cornerstone for human civilization. Their thinking reduced humanity's ignorance and became the pillar of later thought. Even today, they influence our behavior and way of life.

If we begin counting at the year Adam Smith published *The Wealth of Nations*, the history of economics is only 236 years long. However, economics has made a tremendous contribution to the increase in humanity's cooperative spirit and morality. Adam Smith showed that, with the assumption that people are rational, the market is the most effective means of interpersonal cooperation. Today, we can see that in the countries that truly respect the ideas of Adam Smith and implement the market economy, people's cooperative spirit and morality are much higher than in countries without a market economy.

Since the middle of the twentieth century, perhaps the most outstanding accomplishment within the entire field of social sciences has been the development of Game Theory. Game Theory studies the way in which rational people make decisions in interactive environments. The full name of Game Theory is "Non-Cooperative Game Theory". This type of name can easily lead to misunderstandings for non-specialists, such as incorrectly thinking that it teaches people how to not cooperate. This is unfortunate. In reality, Game Theory focuses on ways to promote human cooperation. The Prisoner's Dilemma Model provides us a means of thinking about ways to overcome the Prisoner's Dilemma. Only by understanding why people do not cooperate can we find the most effective means of promoting cooperation.

The greatest difference between economics and sciences like sociology, psychology, and ethics is its assumption that humans are rational. Game Theory maintained this assumption. This assumption is often criticized, and certain scholars from other fields and social activists blame the behavior that harms others for personal benefit and lapses in morals on economists' assumption that humans are rational. They believe that economists encourage people to become bad. This is a great misunderstanding. Both historical fact and logical analysis prove that the assumption of "altruism" is more likely to lead people to behave badly than is the opposite. Dictatorship has thrived in China for over 2,000 years. An important reason for this is because we assume that the emperor is a "sage" ("*shèngrén*") and the bureaucrats that govern the country are "virtuous ministers" ("*xián chén*"). If in the beginning we assumed that the emperor was a rational person and selfish, then perhaps China would have implemented democracy and the rule of law early on. The countries that implemented the democratic system first were precisely the countries that early on did not view the king as a sage and did assume that bureaucrats would take any chance to pursue their own interests.

Of course, the assumption that people are rational is not without its pitfalls. In reality, people are not as rational as they are in the assumptions of economics. However, I still believe that only with the assumption of rational humans as our foundation can we understand the importance of institutions and cultures in humanity's escape from the Prisoner's Dilemma. Advancing social cooperation and promoting human progress cannot place its hopes on denying the rationality of humans. Instead, we must improve institutions so that mutual cooperation becomes the best choice of rational people.

(2)

This book has two objectives. The first is to use common language to systematically introduce the basic methodology and core conclusions of Game Theory. The second is to utilize these methods and conclusions to analyze various social issues and institutional arrangements (including culture). We will focus especially on the reasons people exhibit non-cooperative behavior as well as the kinds of institutions and cultures that promote interpersonal cooperation.

This book is separated into 14 chapters. Chapter 1 discusses the two basic issues that society faces: Coordination and cooperation. The key to coordination is forming consistent expectations. The key to cooperation is providing right incentives. Then, we will briefly introduce the concept of the rational person assumption, criticisms of it, and the appropriate use of this assumption. Last, we will discuss evaluations of individual behavior using social standards. We will use numerous examples to show how a Pareto optimum can appear in actual institutional arrangements.

Chapter 2 will formally introduce Game Theory. We will introduce the basic ideals of Game Theory. We will discuss the contradictions between individual rationality and collective rationality leading to the Prisoner's Dilemma and from this foundation introduce the Nash equilibrium. The Nash equilibrium is the most important concept for predicting how people formulate decisions and the consequences of decisions in an interactive situation. We will also prove that private property rights and the law can assist in resolving the Prisoner's Dilemma by aligning individual and collective rationality.

Chapter 3 discusses multiple equilibriums. In reality, there often exist multiple Nash equilibriums in a game. When multiple equilibriums exist in the same game, the way in which participants coordinate expectations becomes the key to cooperation. We discuss how institutions and cultures coordinate predictions to help people select certain Nash equilibriums. This includes coordinating conflicts between different cultures. We also discuss the issue of institutional path dependency.

Chapter 4 introduces dynamic games. The most important concept of dynamic games is non-credible threats and commitments. Non-credible threats means that the optimum is different before and after the fact, meaning sometimes a Pareto optimum cannot be realized. Commitments turn non-credible threats into credible ones, which instead benefit social cooperation. We also discuss the commitment function of constitutional government and the democratic system.

Chapter 5 discusses the issue of bargaining. Bargaining is the combination of cooperation and competition. We introduce the axiomatic approach and strategic approach to bargaining, the Nash Bargaining Solution to the axiomatic approach, and the Refined Nash Equilibrium of the strategic approach. The result of bargaining with complete information is certainly a Pareto optimum, but incomplete information may inhibit a Pareto efficient allocation. This chapter also discusses social norms in bargaining.

Chapter 6 discusses repeated games. It proves that repeated games cause participates to heed long-term interests and thus escape singular game Prisoner's Dilemmas and realize cooperation between rational people. We discuss the psychological and institutional elements of decisions to cooperate and how certain social norms within greater society overcome second-order Prisoner's Dilemmas. These theories are very important for understanding the value of organizations and institutions in society.

Chapter 7 explores the ways in which incomplete information leads to the appearance of reputation mechanisms. From ancient times until the present, the reputation mechanism has been one of the most important protections of social cooperation. When information is incomplete, people have an incentive based on their own interests to establish a reputation to willingly cooperate. It is precisely because people care about reputation do we see mutual trust. We utilize the reputation mechanism to explain certain interesting phenomena in reality and discuss how reputation is built.

Chapter 8 discusses how adverse selection with asymmetric information can obstruct cooperation. It also discusses the market and non-market mechanisms that resolve adverse selection. Brand names are a type of reputation mechanism that is important for the realization of valuable cooperation. They are the most important component of the market system. There is good reason for government regulation as a form of non-market institution to resolve adverse selection, but in many cases, it not only is ineffective, but can instead seriously damage the market's reputation mechanism.

Chapter 9 discusses the ways in which one party with private information communicates that information via certain signals to a party without it. Many behaviors in social life function to transmit signals and aid in resolving the problem of adverse selection. Considerable space was allocated to discusses how social norms like gift exchanges signal willingness to cooperate. Of course, this kind of social norm may lead to wasteful behavior.

Chapter 10 discusses the way a party without private information can obtain another party's private information via mechanism design. The key to mechanism design is making people tell the truth. We prove that when a type of institution causes the cost of telling a lie to be higher than telling the truth, then people will tell the truth. No matter if we are discussing the transaction of private goods or the provision of public goods, institutions that lead to telling the truth improve efficiency and create a win-win situation. This chapter also discusses the contradiction between equality and efficiency in the allocation of income caused by asymmetric information, as well as the selection mechanism for university professors.

Chapter 11 discusses moral hazard and the design of incentive mechanisms. The source of moral hazard (corruption) is related to the information asymmetry about the actions of people involved. We analyze the ways in which the optimal incentive mechanism balances insurances and incentives, the main element in determining the strength of incentives, and the difficulty of incentivizing multiple tasks. We rely on the "corruption equation" to analyze the causes of official corruption and means to resolve it.

Chapter 12 discusses the basic concepts of evolutionary games and how cooperation under repeated games can become a type of evolutionarily stable equilibrium. We also analyze the spontaneous evolution of institutions and why social norms like the first-on rule of property rights is respected. In contrast with the previous chapters, this chapter abandons the assumption of complete rationality and assumes that people's rationality is limited. People's actions are a process of learning, imitation, and adaption. However, our basic conclusion is the same: Under repeated games, cooperation can appear as the equilibrium result.

Chapter 13 uses the foundation established in the preceding chapters to undertake a systematic analysis of laws and social norms that act as rules of the game. We discuss the complementary nature and supplementary nature between law and social norms and the differences and similarities between the two. We touch upon the ways laws and social norms incentivize people to cooperate, coordinate people's expectations, and transmit private information. We discuss the reasons people respect or violate social norms and the social conditions needed for laws and social norms to play a role.

Chapter 14 discusses institutional entrepreneurs' role in creating rules of the game for society. We discuss the risks faced by institutional entrepreneurial innovation and the elements that determine success or failure. It returns to the Axial Age to examine the five basic "ways" ("*dào*") established by the great thinkers of that time to advance human cooperation and establish a harmonious society. We analyze the ways in which these ways aided humanity in escaping the Prisoner's Dilemma. We prove that the basic conclusions of these ways align with Game Theory. We also analyze Confucian culture as a combination of law and social norms as well as the ways in which it coordinates expectations, mediates conflicts, and incentivizes people's cooperative spirit. We also point out that the main fault in Confucian culture is that it never found an institutional means to restrict the monarch. The type of institutional means to do this is constitutional government and democracy.

To systematically introduce the basic methodology and core conclusions of Game Theory, there is no choice but to spread discussion of related social issues throughout various chapters, so readers interested in a specific issue (such as government action, university governance, social norms, etc.) may feel that the narrative is rather disorderly. However, my main objective is to allow the reader to grasp the methods of analysis, instead of knowing about a specific viewpoint. Thus, I believe that the reader will be understanding of the arrangement of chapters.

The audience for this book includes specialists and non-specialists with under-graduate or above training in social science fields such as sociology, law, history, politics, economics, and management. I also believe that this book is suitable as extracurricular reading material for students of the sciences and engineering. Of course, the reader must be curious about social issues.

Because of the theoretical rigor and need to save space, there is no choice but to use some mathematical formulas and graphs in this book. However, to the greatest extent possible I limited the use of mathematics to the minimum necessary scope. There should not be any issues for a person with elementary mathematical training to read this book. This book does not require the reader to first have training in economics.

I would like to especially point out the fact that even those with a solid training in economics can also gain from reading this book. Today's specialized training helps students grasps some complex methods of technical analysis, but also leads them to not see the forest for the trees. They lack an overall grasp of social issues.

My hope is that reading this book not only increases readers' knowledge, but also increases readers' cooperative spirit and makes their lives more plentiful.

(3)

This book developed from my lecture notes and recordings for a general course titled "Game Theory and Society" for undergraduates at Peking University. From the time that I first formulated my writings until the formal publication, eight years have passed. Many people contributed to this book appearing for readers in its current form. For that, I am grateful.

First, I must thank Dr. Yong Wang at the Economic Research Institute of Tsing-hua University. He and the others mentioned below spent a significant amount of time and energy editing the recordings and lecture notes into the first manuscript. After that he alone spent a large amount of time editing and revising to create the second manuscript (the first eleven chapters). This saved me a tremendous amount of time. During the finalization of the manuscript, he also was responsi-ble for designing the charts, supplementing and verifying the reference materials, editing the index, and providing recommendations on content revisions. He was my most important partner in writing this book. Without his assistance, there is no doubt that the publication of this book would have been delayed much longer.

I want to especially thank Dr. Feng Deng at the Peking University School of Law. He participated in the draft organization of Chapter 13 and 14 and made important contributions to the content of these two sections. His rich knowledge of law and history complemented my original viewpoints and corrected some of my limited understandings. He added valuable recommendations right up until the very last manuscript.

In addition to Wang and Deng, I would like to thank Hao Wang, Miaojun Wang, Juzheng Yang, and Bo Long for their contributions to the first draft.

Professor Xiao-ping Chen at the University of Washington made numerous valuable recommendations on the contents of Chapter 1 and Chapter 14. Most of her recommendations were included in the final manuscript and improved the content of these two chapters.

Mr. Zhongqiu Yao, Chairman of the Unirule Institute of Economics, and Mr. Rui Peng, who pursued his master's degree under my supervision, made valuable recommendations on Chapter 14. I admire Zhongqiu Yao's interest in Confucian culture and Rei Peng's faith in Christianity.

Of course, if there are any mistakes within the book, the responsibility lies solely with me and none of the people mentioned above.

Xiaoli Fang, who graduated with an undergraduate degree from the Peking University Guanghua School of Management in 2000, and Yanan Li, who graduated with an undergraduate degree from the School of International Relations in 2000, took on the work of organizing fifteen lecture recordings. Although I do not know where they are now, their contributions will not be forgotten.

I also must thank my teaching assistants for the course "Game Theory and Society" between 2004 and 2010. They are: Miaojun Wang, Hu Zhang, Juzheng Yang, Yuli Wu, Jiasheng Yong, Weilin Liu, and Qi Duan. Without textbooks, they meticulously edited handouts, homework, and quizzes as well as took on extracurricular tutoring. They made important contributions to the success of this book.

Over the span of seven years, over 2,000 undergraduates have taken my "Game Theory and Society" course. Their applause at the end of each class will be a lifelong memory. Interacting with them has not only been an important opportunity to learn, but also very enjoyable. I want to thank them for taking that course. I want to deeply apologize to them for the inconvenience brought about by not having a textbook to teach from. I hope the publication of this book can make up for this.

I would like to thank Ms. Junxiu Lin at Peking University Press for her patience and supervision. This book became part of Peking University Press' publication plan six years ago, but I did not predict that it would be delayed until today. The main reason was that before December of 2010 I did administrative work, so I could not focus my full attention to it. Beginning in the spring of 2011, I took my sabbatical, so I could concentrate my efforts on completing this task. Of course, publishing late has its benefits. I believe that if this book had been published a few years earlier, the content would not be as complete as it is now, although there is still room for improvement.

Over the last few years, friends and colleagues provided care and assistance. They make my life and writings full of enjoyment. I cannot possibly list all of their names, but I know they will not have any complaints, because the best requital I can give them is to remain true to myself and passionate towards liberty and truth.

It goes without saying that the greatest source of energy has been the understanding and love of my family. They lessened my troubles and increased my happiness, which was vital to completing this book.

I am thankful for the seriousness and perfectionism of Yan Zhang, the Lead Editor.

Writing this book brought me happiness, and I hope it brings happiness to the reader!

Weiying Zhang
January 5, 2013

1 Individual rationality and social cooperation

Coordination and cooperation are the two primary issues faced by human societies that affect the interests of each member of society. Aligned expectations must be formed to resolve the coordination issue. The incentive mechanism must overcome the misalignment between individual rationality and collective rationality to resolve the cooperation issue. The basic function of social institutions is to coordinate expectations and promote cooperation, thus resolving the conflicts caused by the "Prisoner's Dilemma" and unaligned expectations.

Game Theory is a tool for analyzing interactive decision-making. It studies how people in societies act, how people coordinate with each other, how social institutions evolve, and how to better design institutions to realize cooperation. Game Theory assumes that people are rational. Although this assumption is a bit extreme, Game Theory built on the rationality assumption still provides a good analytical tool to predict people's behavior and evaluate institutions. It is precisely economist's rationality assumption that promotes the human cooperative spirit and increased moral standards, not the contrary.

All men created equal means each person is the best judge of his own happiness. This point applied to economics is the utilization of the Pareto efficiency criterion to judge whether a person's behavior is proper or not and should be incentivized (or sanctioned). The Pareto criterion means a person implementing an action that does not harm the interests of others is proper, otherwise it is improper. Under the equality of opportunity premise, a Pareto optimal satisfies Rawls's social justice requirements and thus is a collective rationality standard.

This book's title is *Game Theory and Society*. The hope is to emphasize the ways in which to utilize Game Theory methodology to analyze social issues and analyze the types of institutions that assist interpersonal coordination and cooperation. The goal is to make human life happier.

Section one: basic issues of society

In the book *Robinson Crusoe*, English novelist Daniel Defoe told the story of a seafarer named Robinson Crusoe who, because of an accident at sea, lived alone on an island for twenty years. Every day on the island, Crusoe had to consider the amount of time he would allocate between farming, hunting, and fishing. This is a classic resource allocation problem. The issues faced by Crusoe are the same issues we as individuals face: With limited resources and time, how do we decide to produce (or purchase) different items so that we can obtain the most satisfaction from economic activity?

As for the resource allocation problem, economists have already undertaken profound systematic research. The basic conclusion reached is that if in each additional application of resources the marginal return of production declines,[1] then the optimal allocation of resources must satisfy the condition that the last unit of resources will create the same gain no matter what application it is used for. Thus, the marginal contribution of each application must be equal. In economics, this is called the equi-marginal principle.[2]

However, the vast majority of us do not live on an isolated island like Crusoe. Instead, we live in groups, so not only are each person's choices limited by resource restraints, but are also limited by restraints from the choices of others. If we say that the main issue faced by each individual[3] is the resource allocation problem, then what is the main issue faced by society? In other words: What is the basic issue faced by a society?

To answer this question, we must first clarify the meaning of "society". We use the word "society" almost every day, such as "contemporary society", "social issues", and "underground societies", but what is society?

This is a question that each of us can grasp, but not explain clearly. In different contexts, the meaning of the word "society" is different. The basic concept refers to a group in contrast to an individual. American biologist Edward O. Wilson defined "society" as a group of similar individuals that is formed through mutual cooperation.[4] More simply, we can define society as interaction and interdependence between a group of individuals. When each person makes a decision, consideration must be given to personal choices and the choices of others. Because no person's choices are given, the results of each person's decisions will be influenced by the decisions of others. This type of interaction within a group will determine the social attributes of each individual. The social attributes of a person mean that one person's choices are not entirely something that person can decide. A person's choices are influenced by social values and cultural factors. Concepts like virtue and vice, right and wrong, and fairness only have meaning when humans are members of society. Our language, manners, cuisine, and clothing all indicate that humans are social animals.

One example using language would be a student of mine that did not turn his homework in on time. My teaching assistant asked him the reason, and he replied that he got sick because of a lack of moral character. When my teaching assistant reported this to me, I did not understand the connection between lacking moral character and getting sick. My assistant explained to me that among young people, "moral character" ("*rénpǐn*") meant "luck" ("*yùnqì*"), not "moral conduct" ("*pǐnxíng*"). I asked him how "moral character" would come to have this meaning among young people. He said he did not know, but because everyone else spoke like that, he did, too.

In Game Theory, a person doing something because everyone else is doing it is called herd behavior. Herd behavior does not only exist for language, but also manners, clothing, cuisine, investment, etc. Herd behavior can be considered an obvious reflection of people's social attributes.

From the above descriptions, we could consider society as an interdependent group. From there, we can ask again: What is the basic issue faced by society?

Perhaps each reader will have a different understanding of this issue. Academic circles also have different viewpoints. Traditionally, economists focused on the issue of efficient allocation of social resources. Sociologists focused on the issue of interests between different members of society. Jurists focused on the issue of how individuals undertake responsibilities and duties. These understandings make sense from certain perspectives, but from the perspective of interpersonal interaction, there are two most basic issues of society: The coordination problem and the cooperation problem.[5] Because in most practical issues these problems are often combined together, people often believe that they are the same problem. Actually, the coordination problem and cooperation problem are vastly different, so separating them is extremely important.

1.1 The coordination problem

What is the coordination problem? Below, we use traffic as an example. This example is a pure coordination problem because conflicts of interest do not exist.

For two people considering which side to travel one, each person has two choices: The left or the right. If their choices are not compatible, meaning one person chooses to travel on the left side and the other on the right side, at some point they will run into each other. If their choices are compatible, meaning they both choose to travel on either the left or the right, they can proceed unhampered. We can explain this using Figure 1.1.

In the figure, the numbers represent the benefit each of the two people gain from making each choice. The first number represents the benefit for Pedestrian A, and the second number represents the benefit for Pedestrian B. If both people chose to travel on the left (the top left corner) or travel on the right (the bottom

	Pedestrian B	
	Travel on the left	Travel on the right
Pedestrian A — Travel on the left	1, 1	−1, −1
Pedestrian A — Travel on the left	−1, −1	1, 1

Figure 1.1 Traffic Game

right corner), then each will proceed unhampered, so we can say that their payoff is 1. If their choices are incompatible, meaning Pedestrian A chooses to travel on the left but Pedestrian B chooses to travel on the right (the top right corner) or the other way around (the bottom left corner), then they will bump into each other, so we can say that their payoff is −1.

The reader should note that this figure assumes that under each situation, both parties obtain the same benefit from each, either 1 or −1. In some cases, this assumption is untrue because one person may fare worse than the other in the collision or because one person may benefit more from proceeding unhampered. However, by assuming that their benefit is the same and that the benefit of complementary action is higher than the benefit of contradictory action we can depict the essence of the coordination problem. The essence is that both benefit from coordinated interaction and both lose from uncoordinated interaction.

The core of the coordination problem is the way in which people anticipate other's actions. The most direct method of understanding expectations is mutual communication and exchange. For example, if Pedestrian A and Pedestrian B travel on foot, when they approach each other, they can communicate via language or hand signals to coordinate each other's actions.

Communication is the exchange of information and knowledge between people. To make the correct predictions, the people involved must grasp relevant knowledge. This includes knowledge about the scope of behavior, the other party's special characteristics, and the other party's expectations about one's own knowledge. This is known as higher-order knowledge.[6] In China, there is a saying "to enter the village and adapt to the customs". When people go to other parts of the country to take care of matters, they often must understand the way local people get along with each other to adjust their own behavior. This knowledge of customs and social norms is extremely important for resolving the coordination problem. In some parts of northeastern China, when toasting someone else, it is considered polite to finish the alcohol in your own glass before the person being toasted. In Henan, however, the other person should be allowed to drink first. When a northeasterner and a Henanese drink together, how should they display respect? Depending on their location, they should become accustomed to the local custom to resolve the coordination problem.

Knowledge about the other party's special characteristics is also extremely important for resolving the coordination problem. In the traffic example given above, if one of the people involved is blind and the other finds this out, they will coordinate with the blind person by changing their own choices. For new drivers, putting a sticker that indicates as so on the back of their car warns others that they are not accustomed to driving, which helps coordination. In many situations, coordination means that different people should respect different rules. At that point, understanding the special characteristics of others is even more important. In ancient China, traveling officials banged on gongs to clear the streets. It was a way to communicate their special status so that others could adjust their behavior.

Grasping higher-order knowledge of other's expectations about one self is also very important. In the traffic example we observed, Pedestrian A's decision to keep to the left or right must consider Pedestrian B's expectation of Pedestrian A's decision. If Pedestrian A believes Pedestrian B will expect Pedestrian A to keep to the left, Pedestrian A's best choice is to keep to the left. If Pedestrian B predicts that Pedestrian A will keep to the left, but Pedestrian A mistakenly believes that Pedestrian B predicts he will keep to the right so that Pedestrian A chooses to keep to the right, then there will be a collision. This shows that the coordination problem not only requires expectations to be consistent, but also that expectations about expectations are consistent. In reality, this requires the ability to correctly predict other's behavior to be quite high. Because of differences in the structure of knowledge, beliefs, and biases, it is very difficult to correctly judge other people's intentions, while at the same time it is difficult to know other people's expectations of our judgments. At this point, there will be a failure of coordination. Many conflicts in human society are not conflicts of interest, but instead of misunderstandings or incorrect expectations.

Generally speaking, because of the various types of knowledge required to make correct predictions, we often have too little knowledge, or no usable knowledge at all. As for knowledge about norms, when traveling to the unfamiliar, we often find that we have difficulty completely grasping the local customs. In daily interaction with friends, we often also find out that close friends sometimes surprise us. This means that we have not completely grasped all of our friends' special characteristics. Of course, sometimes we will have too much knowledge that our minds cannot comprehend, so we are at a complete loss at what to do. Another situation that causes us to be unable to form correct expectations is our failure to use knowledge. In real life, we often discover that we know something, but when making decisions, because of various reasons, including forgetfulness, we do not correctly utilize this information.[7]

In any case, communication is costly. If the cost of communication is high, or even impossible, how can coordination happen? Imagine two people are driving fast and their point of contact is around a curve. Before contact, they cannot see each other, but once they come into contact, it is already too late to communicate. This type of situation in which coordination via communication is difficult is common in reality. After all, communication requires certain prerequisites, such as language, ideas, and knowledge; otherwise, it is ineffective.[8]

For the traffic issues we observed, one of the means to resolve this issue is to establish traffic rules. For example, in China, the law states that we drive on the right, but in England and some other countries, they drive on the left. Why is it that laws can resolve the coordination problem? The reason that laws and formal institutions can resolve the coordination problem is that they aid people in correctly judging (or predicting) other people's behavior. For example, when the traffic laws dictate that people drive on the right, each driver will anticipate that other drivers will drive on the right, so driving on the right is everyone's best choice. Of course, in many situations, the formation of expectations relies on the authority behind laws. The existence of authority means that when someone violates the law, they will be punished. When it is expected that everyone else will respect authority or abide by the law, then abiding by the law becomes each person's best choice. As soon as the law loses authority, it cannot play a coordinating role because at that point, people lose the ability to predict other's behavior. The significance of this is that an important reason people are willing to accept authority is to better coordinate. Conducting an orchestra is a classic example. In reality, this is the reason that during an emergency situation, such as a serious traffic jam, people will follow the guidance of a volunteer that orders people about.

We can see that in order to resolve the coordination problem, people must all be able to correctly predict the actions of others. In order to make correct predictions, people must communicate, grasp, and correctly apply relevant information. Some clear rules are also necessary. Communication and rules both play a role in coordinating predictions. The relative advantage and importance of the latter depends on the specific issue. In reality, in a situation with clear rules and rules that are in play, we can rely on rules to predict other's behavior. In a situation with unclear rules and rules that are not in play (including different people's different perceptions of rules), communication is more important.

1.2 The cooperation problem

Below, we examine society's other basic problem: The cooperation problem. Human progress is almost entirely the result of cooperation. The larger the scope of cooperation, the faster social progress is. Without sophisticated and large-scale cooperations, humanity today would still be living as hunter-gatherers.

For simplicity, let us examine a society composed of two people, A and B. In some activity, each person can choose to cooperate or not with the other person.[9] If both people chose to cooperate, each person can enjoy the benefits of cooperation, known as cooperation dividends. If both people chose to not cooperate, thus falling into what Hobbes called the "war of all against all",[10] then both people will suffer. If one person chooses to cooperate, but another person chooses not to cooperate, one person will suffer losses and the other will benefit. We can explain this using Figure 1.2.

As the figure shows, if both parties cooperate, the payoff for each person is 3. If neither of them cooperates, their payoff is zero. If one person chooses to cooperate but the other person chooses not to, the person that cooperates will receive a payoff of −1 and the person that does not cooperate will receive a payoff of 4.

		B	
		Cooperate	Does not cooperate
A	Cooperate	3, 3	−1, 4
	Does not cooperate	4, −1	0, 0

Figure 1.2 The Cooperation Dilemma

Obviously, from the perspective of both people's total benefit, otherwise known as collective rationality,[11] choosing to cooperate is most optimal. In that case, their total payoff is 6, but in other choice combinations, the highest total payoff is only 3. However, will this kind of social optimum appear? Do not forget that we assume that only two people exist in this society, so the most optimal benefit for both people is also the social optimum.

If each person made choices based on their own interests, perhaps the socially optimal result would not appear. Each person will understand that if the other person chooses to cooperate, but he does not, then the payoff will be 4. If he chooses to cooperate, the payoff will be 3. At this point, choosing to not cooperate is better than choosing to cooperate. If neither party chooses to cooperate, then the compensation for both is zero. If only one person chooses to cooperate, the payoff for that person is −1. At this point, choosing to not cooperate is still better than choosing to cooperate. Therefore, regardless of the other person's choice, the best choice for each is to not cooperate. If each person is self-interested and rational, the end result will be that both parties choose not to cooperate, and each person's payoff is zero. This example shows that sometimes individual rationality is not aligned with collective rationality, meaning conflict exists between individual rationality and collective rationality. This is what we refer to as the cooperation problem (or cooperation dilemma).

In real life, there are similar situations. Economists and other social scientists describe the conflict between individual rationality and collective rationality as the Prisoner's Dilemma. The existence of the Prisoner's Dilemma poses an important question to us: If cooperation dividends exist for society, how do we obtain them? In other words, if collective rationality is the goal we would like to achieve, then how do we realize it via the choices of individuals?[12] In the discussions later in this book, we will see that many social institutions and cultures evolved as solutions to the Prisoner's Dilemma.

Careful consideration will show that the essence of the cooperation problem is an incentive problem. If we want to realize collective rationality via the rational choices of individuals and obtain cooperation dividends, we must incentivize and induce individual behavior. These incentives and inducements are often in material form, such as rewards for cooperation and punishments for non-cooperation. This will cause the benefit of cooperation to be larger than the benefit of non-cooperation, thus incentivizing people to cooperate. Obviously, the prerequisite for implementing material rewards is a third party that is not limited by resources so that enough wealth is available to institute rewards. Another prerequisite is that the third party has enough information and the ability to recognize who chose cooperation and who chose non-cooperation and then fairly implement rewards and punishments.

As we can see, implementing material incentives places a relatively high requirement on the third party's wealth, information, abilities, and fairness. In many instances, these four qualities are hard to achieve. Sometimes not even a third part exists, or a third party exists that lacks the material wealth or information and ability to implement rewards and punishments. In this circumstance, incentivizing cooperative behavior often relies on non-material means. In actuality, we can see that in many countries, mainstream values have confirmed the value of cooperative behavior.[13] Even in some subcultures, such as organized crime, self-sacrificial behavior is held in esteem. Under the influence of these values, not only will people obtain material benefit, but also spiritual rewards. Similarly, non-cooperative behavior will also cause the allure of material benefit to decrease. The reason spiritual rewards can play a role is because of the human pursuit of honor.[14] If we can commend cooperative behavior and denounce non-cooperative behavior, then if people pursue honor, to a certain degree people will be incentivized to choose cooperation. This shows that through the influence of culture and formation of values we can shape people's inner spiritual power. We do not need to rely on the supervision of third parties, thus reducing a large amount of transaction costs and can promote cooperation at a low cost.

1.3 The intersection of coordination and cooperation

In the previous sections, we discussed the two categories of basic issues faced by society: Coordination and cooperation. In reality, the coordination problem and cooperation problem are interconnected and influence each other. Most issues are actually the combination of the coordination problem and the cooperation problem.

Imagine a narrow bridge that only one car at a time can pass through. Two cars approach from different directions. If one car goes through first and the other yields, the first driver receives payoff 2 and the other driver receives payoff 1. If both cars try to cross the bridge at the same time, both receive payoff −2. If both cars yield, both of them also receive payoff −2. This is demonstrated in Figure 1.3.

This is a classic example of a coordination and cooperation problem. Cooperation means that one person crosses first and the other yields, which is better than both of them crossing or yielding at the same time. However, if their expectations are not aligned, the cooperative result will not appear. If A incorrectly believes that B will yield, but B also incorrectly believes that A will yield, then neither will be able to cross. The difference between this and the first example (the pure coordination problem) is that even if cooperation is better for both of them, each person hopes the other will yield, so a conflict of interests exists. In reality, traffic

	B	
	Go through first	Yield
A Go through first	−2, −2	2, 1
Yield	1, 2	−2, −2

Figure 1.3 Coordination and Cooperation

congestion is the end result of a failure to coordinate and cooperate. Perhaps some issue conflicted with people's expectations, such as road maintenance. When cars that should have kept on the right now have to keep to the left, people reduce their speeds in order to readjust. If everyone cooperates by alternating use of the left lane, gridlock will not appear, but wait times will increase. If no one is willing to cooperate, no one can move. Without cooperation, the situation is worse.

Sometimes, even with aligned expectations, if individual interests and collective interests are not aligned, then cooperation will fail. Bank runs happen when everyone expects a bank to fail, so they rush to withdraw their deposits in a panic. The result is that banks that originally would not have failed now fail, and also impact other banks, harming the interests of all depositors. In the end, each person's expectations are correct.[15]

In the second half of 2003, severe acute respiratory syndrome (SARS) broke out in China. It was followed by Bird Flu in 2004. These were both coordination and cooperation problems. On the one hand, localities did not report cases of SARS because they worried it would impact local business investment and tourism. However, if every locality conceals the fact, the result will be a disaster affecting all of society. On the other hand, because hospitals did not coordinate on isolation, disinfection, and treatment, hospitals became the biggest transmitters of the disease.

On the one hand, a difference exists between the mechanisms that play a role in the coordination problem and the cooperation problem. On the other hand, they also influence each other. Therefore, resolving the two basic social issues of cooperation and coordination requires seeking out different methods for different circumstances. Generally speaking, the larger the scale of society, the harder it is to resolve these two issues. From our prior analysis we know that correct expectations are required to resolve the coordination problem, which requires a grasp of relevant information and rules. Obviously, in a small-scale society, the amount of interaction is relatively limited, and the amount of relevant information to grasp is relatively limited. This makes it relatively easy to make correct predictions, so it is relatively easy to coordinate. For example, it is very easy for family members to coordinate. After dinner, the person responsible for the dishes does the dishes, and the person responsible for mopping does the mopping. If we organize a twenty- or thirty-person band for a performance, without a relatively long period of practice, they will not be in sync. As the number of people increases, the difficulty of coordination increases. From the perspective of cooperation, as the number of participants increases, individual cost and benefit become asymmetric, and values become diverse. Sometimes, there are different understandings of what behavior constitutes cooperative behavior (i.e. Chinese nod their heads to indicate agreement, whereas Japanese nod their heads to indicate understanding). This necessarily causes cooperation to be more difficult. If we cannot rely on the power of internal consciousness or material appeal, the advancement of cooperation relies on the existence of a third party with substantial resources, access to information, strong judgment, and a sense of justice. With the increase in the number of people, the requirement for the third party to satisfy these four aspects increases.

For example, as the number of people increases, it is more difficult for the third party to identify the people that choose not to cooperate.

Above, we assumed that the coordination problem and cooperation problem are given, but in terms of the long-term development of human society, both are the result of human choice. Modern society is a division-of-labor society. The division of labor is an important endogenous driver of coordination and cooperation. Humanity divides labor in order to cooperate and the division of labor also makes coordination more important. On his isolated island, Robinson Crusoe did not have to coordinate with anyone, but he also did not have the opportunity to obtain the benefits of the division of labor. The division of labor increases production efficiency, but if producers and consumers cannot effectively coordinate their actions, the division of labor will not produce the effects of cooperation. The way in which producers anticipate customer demand is itself a coordination problem. The failure to anticipate means the products produced by producers do not truly have value. In serious circumstances, this will lead to an economic crisis. Similarly, if links in the value chain of the production process cannot effectively coordinate, an increase in the productivity of one link not only will not increase human welfare, it will result in wasted resources. After the division of labor, each person only grasps partial information, so coordination becomes more difficult. Dispersed information also means that fraud is harder to discover, which also increases the difficulty of cooperation.[16]

Today's division of labor is a global division of labor. Basically, the production of every product is the result of cooperation on a global scale. Coordinating the actions and promoting cooperation between different nations, peoples, production methods, and values is a formidable task. In this process, increasing understanding between countries is without a doubt important. On the one hand, this can be used to grasp relevant information and form correct expectations about other's behavior. On the other hand, understanding other's interests is beneficial to cooperation. From this perspective, we can easily understand the need for organizations like the United Nations, World Trade Organization, World Bank, World Health Organization, etc. In reality, the objective of all of these organizations is to coordinate the behaviors of various nations and promote cooperation between various nations.

1.4 Formal institutions and informal institutions

Coordination requires alignment of expectations. Cooperation requires alignment of individual and collective interests. If both of these are satisfied, the ideal result will appear. For example, if each person expects that other people will be honest, and dishonest behavior will be punished, there will be high levels of trust within society and each person will enjoy the benefits of cooperation. However, in many circumstances, it is often difficult to satisfy these two requirements at the same time. If dishonest behavior is not punished, people will not expect others to be honest, so no one will enjoy the benefits of cooperation.

Without a doubt, resolving the basic issues of coordination and cooperation relies on technology. For example, the clock is an important tool for coordinating our actions. We can imagine that if we set the start of class time as "late morning", not only would students come at different times, even the teacher would be late. Modern modes of communication like telephones, cell phones, and email are effective methods to coordinate behavior and promote cooperation. We can use them to immediately transmit information for improved decisions, thus achieving coordination and cooperation.

However, to resolve the two basic issues of coordination and cooperation, humanity has mainly relied on institutional means (such as culture and customs). For social activity, humanity has established various types of institutions. These institutions can be separated into formal institutions and informal institutions. These can also be called explicit rules and unwritten rules. Overall, the former refers to laws and regulations. The latter refers to unwritten behavioral rules, such as local custom and social norms. Almost every organization has its own formal and informal institutions. Corruption in officialdom can also be understood as an informal institution.[17] Culture can be understood as a combination of related formal and informal institutions. Generally speaking, the implementation of formal institutions relies on the authority of a third party. The executive branch and the judicial branch exist to enforce laws and resolve conflicts. As we discussed above, because of factors such as the collection of relevant information, relying on the authority of a third party for implementation comes at a relatively high cost. Therefore, we often utilize informal institutions as a complement. If two vehicles meet at a narrow bridge, who crosses first? Formal traffic regulations do not offer guidance, but people will coordinate their behavior according to customs, such as allowing the smaller car to cross first. Informal institutions like social norms often also require third-party enforcement, but the third party is made up of members of society, not a concentrated power structure. Compared to formal institutions like laws, the cost of enforcing informal institutions is relatively low.

Regardless if an institution is formal or informal, the reason it can aid in resolving the two basic issues of coordination and cooperation is because it constrains people's behavior, helps them formulate expectations, and even influence their preferences. Constraints change the reward that the choice of each behavior will bring about. Obviously, this is important for resolving the cooperation problem because we use the reward for cooperation to incentivize people to cooperate. In many circumstances, institutions (including informal institutions) will play a role in forming and changing people's expectations. For example, Heathrow Airport in the United Kingdom is huge, so it is easy for travelers to get lost. Finding a separated companion is a classic example of a coordination problem because it is difficult to anticipate the location the companion will wait at. To resolve this coordination problem, the airport authorities established "meeting points". Any lost travelers will think to wait for their companions at that location. Designing these "meeting points" was an informal institution used to resolve the coordination problem.

Economists differentiate between the price system and the non-price system. This differentiation is similar to that between formal institutions and informal institutions, but not identical. What is the price system? Simply put, it refers to market transactions for goods and services using monetary prices. Many reciprocal exchanges are not done in monetary terms. For example, we rarely see husbands pay their wives to do the cooking. This type of reciprocal behavior that does not include the exchange of money can be seen as a non-price system. Traditionally, economists have researched monetary transactions, but did not pay enough attention to non-monetary exchanges. Both the price system and non-price system are tools for people to coordinate expectations and promote cooperation in the market economy. Traditionally, people understand the price system as the market mechanism, but exclude the non-price system from the market mechanism. This is a misunderstanding. This misunderstanding leads to misunderstandings about the market economy itself. In the market economy, prices are only one form of market operations, but the majority of non-price systems (such as the reputation mechanism) are indispensable components of the market. The essence of the market is free choice and freedom of contract, not prices. Conversely, under the planned economy, prices were only a means of government control over the economy, not a true market mechanism, because prices were not freely formed.

Formal institutions, informal institutions, price systems, and non-price systems are all society's rules of the game. The ways in which they coordinate expectations and promote cooperation will be discussed further in later chapters in this book.[18] It is necessary to point out that regardless of the type of system, whether it is formal, informal, price, or non-price, they are all made and enforced by people, of which "entrepreneurs" are the most important non-government force for the creation and enforcement of systems.[19]

Section two: individual rational behavior

2.1 The methodology of Game Theory

In the section above, we analyzed the two basic issues of society and found that regardless if we are resolving the coordination problem or the cooperation problem, both of them require a deep understanding of individual behavior. All social sciences can be seen as sciences related to human behavior. Their aim is to uncover the rules, characteristics, and influence of human behavior. Of course, there may be considerable differences between the assumptions made above and the perspectives and methodologies of each science. Of the social sciences, there are three main ones with distinct methodologies: Economics, sociology, and psychology. Generally, economics explains social phenomena from individual behavior as the starting point (from micro to macro). The traditional method of sociology is to explain individual behavior from the perspective of society (from macro to micro).[20] Economics believes that any specific behavior of an individual is out of pursuit for individual interest. Sociology believes that individual behavior is the result of social norms. Jon Elster, a professor of political science and philosophy at the University of Chicago, came to the following conclusion in his article *Social Norms and Economic Theory*:

> One of the most persistent cleavages in social sciences is the opposition between homo economicus and homo sociologicus. The former is supposed

to be guided by instrumental rationality, while the behavior of the latter is dictated by social norms. The former is pulled by the prospect of future rewards, whereas the latter is pushed from behind by quasi-inertial forces. The former adapts to changing circumstances, always on the lookout for improvements. The latter is insensitive, sticking to the prescribed behaviour, even if new and apparently better options become available. The former is easily caricaturized as a self-contained, asocial atom, and the latter as the mindless plaything of social forces or the passive executor of inherited standards.[21]

Although there are considerable differences between the methodology of economics and sociology, there are also similarities. Both of them often utilize logical deduction to explain individual behavior. That is the process of starting from certain assumptions, inferring certain cause and effect relationships, and coming to corresponding conclusions. This point makes them quite different from psychology, which is considered the foundation of behavioral science. Psychology studies people's actual behavior and potential psychological mechanisms through experimental and observational methods. Expanding this type of experimental methodology to other fields becomes behavioral science, such as behavioral finance, behavioral economics, behavioral law and economics, organizational behavior, etc. These sciences are encompassed by behavioral studies.

Human behavior is also this book's object of study. The difference is that we will utilize the methodology of Game Theory to study human behavior from the perspective of interpersonal interaction. From the text above we know that the two basic issues of society – coordination and cooperation are actually issues of how people interact with each other. When Game Theory is mentioned, perhaps people will think of the movie *A Beautiful Mind*, which told the story of John Nash, a Nobel Laureate in Economics. Nash was a mathematics genius. In his twenties, he developed a concept called the Nash equilibrium. This concept is extremely influential and has become the core of Game Theory. Roger Myerson (1999), a well-known Game Theorist and Nobel Laureate in Economics, believed that the significance of discovering the Nash equilibrium is comparable to the discovery of the DNA double helix for biology. Because this concept propelled the development of Game Theory and its application in other social sciences, especially advancing the development of economics, Professor Nash received the Nobel Prize in Economics in 1994.

Perhaps the broad application of Game Theory in economics is the reason many people mistake Game Theory as the paradigm of economics. Really, Game Theory is only an analytical tool for research on human behavior. If we were to consider it a science, a more fitting name would be interactive behavior studies. Robert J. Aumann and Sergiu Hart, both influential Game Theorists and co-editors of the book *Handbook of Game Theory with Economic Applications*, introduced Game Theory in this way in the Preface to Volume I:

> Game Theory studies the behavior of decision makers ("players") whose decisions affect each other. As in one-person decision theory, the analysis is from a rational, rather than a psychological or sociological viewpoint.

The term "game" stems from the formal resemblance of these interactive decision problems to parlour games such as Chess, Bridge, Poker, Monopoly, Diplomacy, or Battleship. To date, the largest single area of application has been economics; other important connections are with political science (on both the national and international levels), evolutionary biology, computer science, the foundations of mathematics, statistics, accounting, law, social psychology, and branches of philosophy such as epistemology and ethics. . . .

Game Theory may be viewed as a sort of umbrella or "unified field" theory for the rational side of social science, where "social" is interpreted broadly, to include human individuals as well as other kinds of players (collectives such as corporations and nations, animals and plants, computers, etc.). Unlike other approaches to disciplines like economics or political science, Game Theory does not use different, ad-hoc constructs to deal with various specific issues, such as perfect competition, monopoly, oligopoly, international trade, taxation, voting, deterrence, animal behavior, and so on. Rather, it develops methodologies that apply in principle to all interactive situations, then sees where these methodologies lead in each specific application.

(Aumann and Hart, 1992)

In Game Theory, every interactive circumstance, from drinking games to wars, is a type of game and each participant, whether they are individuals or organizations, is called a "player". Their decisions are analyzed and the results are predicted. A unified methodology for dealing with all interactive circumstances is what makes Game Theory different from all other analytical frameworks. This is the reason that Game Theory is referred to as a "unified field theory".

Because Game Theory can provide a unified analytical framework for all interactive circumstances, it has slowly become a type of basic methodology for social science research. Frankly speaking, without an understanding of Game Theory, it is difficult to undertake frontier research in economics, legal studies, social studies, politics, or any other field. At the same time, Game Theory provided us with a way to consider issues, so it is very important for any matter that involves human interaction. Business schools, law schools, policy schools and other institutes that provide practical training have begun to establish courses on Game Theory.

As a method for studying interactive behavior, Game Theory has some distinctive assumptions. There are three main assumptions: (1) Each game player is instrumentally rational; (2) the instrumental rationality of each player is common knowledge; and (3) all participants understand the rules of the game.

Assumption Three is easy to understand and a reasonable requirement. For example, a person that does not know the rules of chess will not play chess. However, in many interactive circumstances, participants may not know all of the relevant rules. For example, a person could break the law and be sentenced without knowing that they broke the law. If everyone knew all of the relevant rules, industries like accounting and law would not have much to do.

Assumption Two assumes common knowledge. This assumption will be discussed in the next chapter, but will be described briefly here. What is the meaning of common knowledge? If this assumption is satisfied, it is difficult for one party to win over the other party. For example, in a game of chess, winning means the winner saw at least one step further than the opponent. However, the common knowledge assumption states that both parties' unlimited deductive abilities and foresight are equal. In this way, no party can rely on stronger deductive ability to beat the other party. Chinese has the idiom "*Jiāngjìjiùjì*", which means to beat someone at his own game. Assume that A plots to cheat B, but B knows of the plot, so B uses the plot to cheat A. This means that B knows that A is smart, but A does not know that B knows that A is smart. If A knows that B knows A's trick, the plot is worthless.

At this point, the reader probably doubts the fact that a theory based on an assumption as unrealistic as the common knowledge assumption can be at all persuasive. However, in Chapter 2 we will see that this is a relatively useful assumption for theoretical analysis and can provide rich insights.

2.2 The instrumental rationality assumption

Here, we will focus on Assumption One, the instrumental rationality assumption. What does the concept of a rational person mean? Simply put, we first say that a rational person has a well-defined preference. Then, under given restraints, that person will seek maximum satisfaction of his (or her) preference. This is our simplest definition of a rational person, which sometimes we refer to as the maximization issue. This assumes that in each activity people will seek to maximize the satisfaction of their preferences. It must be stated that in economics, "preferences" is a broad concept. We can explain any behavior as seeking the maximization of personal preferences. Suicide is an example. A person commits suicide because they believe that death is better than living. Similarly, always helping others can also be explained as behavior seeking the maximization of personal preferences. Therefore, a rational person is not necessarily selfish and self-interested. From this perspective, the rational person assumption is a thin-to-thick assumption.[22]

It was previously stated that preferences are given. However, an important issue is the way preferences are formed. Some preferences are related to a person's habits since childhood, such as the northern Chinese preference for eating noodles and the southern Chinese preference for eating rice. For other preferences, perhaps in the beginning they were not preferences, but instead were restraint conditions. After a period of time, they transformed from constraints into preferences. Some social norms can internalize as individual preferences, which is an important point for understanding human behavior. Social distaste for eating endangered animals is an example of this. Perhaps in the beginning, a person liked the taste of these animals, but felt guilty, so after a period of time it turned into a personal objection. People's religious behavior can be explained from this perspective. The formation of preferences is a complex process.

It was also previously stated that preferences are "well-defined". There are two basic characteristics for a "well-defined" preference. The first is the completeness assumption, meaning that an actor's preference between any two options can be compared. If given the choice between an apple and a pear, a person will know which one he or she prefers. The second is the transitivity assumption, meaning that if A is better than B, and B is better than C, then A is also better than C. This requires a person's preferences to be consistent.[23]

If a person's preferences satisfy the assumptions we discussed above, we say that person has well-defined preferences, and thus can consider that person to be rational. To use mathematical tools to study the behavior of rational people, economists made some additional assumptions about the preferences of rational people. The most important of those is the assumption about the continuity of preferences. It assumes that the degree of satisfaction toward the consumption of a material good will not fluctuate significantly. If this assumption is true, then we can use a function to depict the relationship between the degrees of satisfaction that two options provide a person. This is called the utility function.

We know that certain preferences do not satisfy the continuity assumption. There is one type of preference that economists call the "lexicographic preference". A lexicographic preference refers to a person's preference for different things being ranked like words in the English dictionary, meaning one thing comes after the next.[24] Imagine two products, alcohol and bread, are offered together in different ways. If a person has lexicographic preference for alcohol and bread, then if, regardless of bread, one combination has the most alcohol, it will be chosen. If two combinations have the same amount of alcohol, then the one with the most bread will be chosen. Because lexicographic preferences do not satisfy the continuity assumption, we have no way to depict it using the utility function.

For preferences with a utility function, we can represent it with an indifference curve. Indifference means that different combinations of products will bring about the same degree of satisfaction to the consumer. The indifference curve represents an arrangement of all of these product combinations. As Figure 1.4 shows, X represents pears and Y represents peaches. Each point represents different

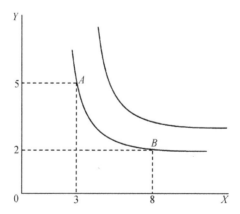

Figure 1.4 Indifference Curve

combinations of pears and peaches, and each point on the curve brings about equivalent levels of utility. For example, Point A represents three pears and five peaches and Point B represents eight pears and two peaches. Being on the same curve indicates they bring the same level of utility to the consumer. A higher position on the indifference curve represents a higher level of utility.

When studying human behavior, not only do we need to know a person's preferences, we also need to know the constraints he faces. Generally speaking, in addition to the wealth constraint, there are other constraints. The first of which is technical constraints. For example, our daily work or study time cannot exceed 24 hours. The next constraints are institutional. For example, the property rights system requires each person to purchase, instead of steal, the things they consume. Lastly, information constraints are an extremely important type of constraint. An example of this would be being faced with multiple choices of products without knowing quality.

Individual optimal choices are co-determined by preferences and constraints. In reality, people have different choices because preferences and constraints are different. In my view, the difference in people's preferences is smaller than the difference in the constraints people face. People's different choices are often caused by different constraints. For example, some people buy big houses and drive luxury cars, whereas other people buy small houses and drive economy cars. The main reason is not because their preferences are different, but because they have different incomes. Other times, it is because of different preferences, such as wanting to protect the environment, but not because of income.

Rules of the game, like laws and social norms, influence individual choices. They can play a role as both constraints and preferences, depending on the situation. If a person respects the law out of fear of the consequences, the law is only a constraint. If a person was raised a certain way so that doing illegal behavior causes them to feel guilty, then we could consider this a preference.[25]

If a person's preferences can be represented using a utility function and constraints are defined, then individual optimal choice becomes an issue of maximizing personal preference while satisfying constraints, so we can use mathematical optimization to calculate a person's optimal behavior.[26] The optimal choice is determined by the point where marginal utility equals marginal cost. In economics, if the volume of product is the independent variable and the level of utility is the dependent variable, then marginal utility refers to the increase in the level of utility as the volume of product consumed increases. Marginal cost refers to the increase in cost as the volume of product consumed increases (such as sacrificed utility from the reduction of other consumer products). The marginal concept in economics is the same as the differential concept in mathematics. From our knowledge of calculus, we know that the optimal volume of consumed products will cause marginal utility to equal marginal cost.

The examples above all deal with individual choices under conditions of certainty. The vast majority of our choices are made under uncertain conditions, and there is not a precise relationship between choices and results. When a person invests in equities, the future earnings are unknown. Economists use an analytical tool called expected utility theory for choices under uncertain conditions.[27] Expected utility refers to the weighted utility level of one choice under different circumstances. The weighting is derived from the probability of occurrence. An example of this would be deciding to take an umbrella with a 50% chance of rain. If you take an umbrella and it rains, your utility is u_1; if you take an umbrella and it does not rain, your utility is u_2; if you do not take an umbrella and it rains, your utility is u_3; if you do not take an umbrella and it does not rain, your utility is u_4. The expected utility theory states that in this situation, your decision to take an umbrella or not is decided by the relative expected utility between two choices. The expected utility of taking an umbrella is $(0.5 \times u_1) + (0.5 \times u_2)$ and the expected utility of not taking an umbrella is $(0.5 \times u_3) + (0.5 \times u_4)$. If $(0.5 \times u_1) + (0.5 \times u_2)$ is greater than $(0.5 \times u_3) + (0.5 \times u_4)$, then an umbrella should be taken; otherwise, an umbrella should not be taken.

Choices under uncertain circumstances touch upon people's attitude toward risk. For some levels of uncertainty, there are people that like to take risks and are willing to accept the challenges of uncertainty. Others are more conservative and are not willing to accept risk. Most people are somewhere in between. Imagine you have two choices: (1) Receive ¥100 without any risk; or, (2) based on a coin toss, receive ¥200 or ¥0. Income from flipping a coin is a type of uncertain income, but the expected income is also ¥100. People that enjoy risk will choose to flip a coin. Economists call these people risk lovers. More conservative people will choose the risk-free ¥100. These people are called risk averse. People that are indifferent to the two choices are called risk neutral.[28]

2.3 Limited rationality

The definition and description of rationality in economics described above is known as the perfect rationality assumption. The perfect rationality assumption is an extremely idealized assumption. It has very high requirements for people's cognitive and decision abilities, but in reality people's behavior is not perfectly rational. Therefore, the rational person assumption is naturally criticized. These criticisms can be summed up in three ways.[29]

The first is bounded rationality. Herbert Simon, a Nobel Laureate in Economics, developed the concept of bounded rationality to describe people's behavior. He believed that people's ability to process and remember is limited, so people cannot possibly exhibit perfect rationality, only bounded rationality. This is why we often see people impersonating others, leading to blind followership and superstition.

The second is bounded willpower. Perfect rationality means that people can precisely calculate the differences between short-term and long-term interests, but in reality people do things out of a lack of willpower or the inability to resist immediate temptation. Many people are unsuccessful when trying to quit smoking or lose weight because they lack willpower. Drug users know that using drugs harms their bodies, but are unable to withstand short-term temptation. For a perfectly rational person, spending money using a credit card and spending money using cash should be the same, but in reality, using a credit card often makes people more willing to accept higher prices and consume more.[30]

If the issues caused by bounded willpower are serious enough, it provides a reason for government intervention. In the United Kingdom, people on the dole receive their weekly benefits on Monday, but spend it all by Thursday. Children are the same. If a parent plans to give them ¥2,400 per year in allowance, the child would probably spend it all in two months, so it should only be given on a monthly basis. For children without self-control, allowance may need to be given on a daily basis.

People will rely on certain measures to reduce the number of problems caused by a lack of willpower. For example, to stop themselves from spending too much, people will carry cash to limit their use of credit cards. Smokers will limit the number of cigarettes they take with them each morning. In the North Korean film titled *The Undying Soldier* broadcast in China during the "Cultural Revolution", after a revolutionary was captured by the enemy, he bit his own tongue off. Why? He worried that he did not have the willpower to control himself from turning in his colleagues during the worst of the enemy's torture. If he bites his own tongue off, he has no way to talk, so no matter how bad the torture is, he will not plead guilty. This behavior is a type of commitment, which is an important concept in Game Theory and will be discussed later.

The third is bounded self-interest. There are a lot of definitions of bounded self-interest, such as altruism or emotional behavior. Many people exhibit emotional behavior. An example of this would be if a student claims a seat in a classroom by placing a book on it, but another student picks up the book and moves it, then sits down. If the other student came back and they got into an argument that led to a fight, the cost of medical treatment would not be minor. Is it worth it? Many people's behavior is not perfectly rational. The existence of emotional behavior is also a criticism of the rational person assumption. We will see that in repetitive games, emotional behavior is sometimes rational, and it sustains some social norms.

2.4 The significance of the rationality assumption

Although there are some extremes in the rational person assumption, choice theories built upon the rational person assumption still provide us with a good analytical tool to predict human behavior and evaluate institutions. Economists are not naïve enough to believe that people are as perfectly rational as their assumptions, but they still maintain their assumptions. Why? Myerson (1999), a Nobel Laureate in Economics and professor at the University of Chicago, provided three justifications.

The first is that without a better theory to choose from, accepting the rational person assumption is the best alternative. Even though we know that people are not perfectly rational, and sometimes do stupid things, at the current time no trustworthy or correct research framework has been developed on the basis of the assumption of irrationality. Although bounded rationality is more aligned with reality, efforts to structure a theory around this have not been successful. The irrational assumption could explain many phenomena, but could not possibly create a theoretical system with analytical ability. In the market for ideas, among the assumptions available, the rational person assumption is still the assumption with the most competitive advantage. This is the basic cause of the appearance of "Economics Imperialism".

The second is that from the perspective of social evolution, even if people are not rational at all times, if a person is irrational over the long-term, he (or she) will have difficulty surviving. Imagine a person whose preferences do not satisfy the transitive assumption, and he is given the choice between apples, pears, and peaches. When asked if he likes pears or apples, he will say pears. When asked if he likes apples or peaches, he will say apples. When asked if he likes peaches or pears, according to transitive preferences, his rational answer should be pears. Now imagine that this person is not rational, meaning he likes peaches and not pears. What would the result be? He will not be successful in market transactions. Imagine in the beginning he has an apple and another person has a pear and a peach. The other person wants to trade the pear for an apple plus one penny. Because according to the above assumption he prefers pears over apples, he will be happy to trade. Now, he has a pear and the other person has an apple and a peach. The other person wants to trade a peach for a pear. Because he prefers pears to peaches, he is willing to trade and pay an additional penny. Now, he has a peach and the other person has a pear and an apple. The other person wants to trade an apple for a peach. Because he prefers apples, he makes the trade and pays one additional penny. After three transactions, they are back to the original condition. He has one apple and the other person has a pear and a peach. The difference is that he has three fewer pennies and the other person has three more. After a while, he would have difficulty surviving in a competitive market. Therefore, even if a person is not rational at every point in time, over the long-term, people learn rationality.

The third is that the objective of social sciences is not only to predict individual behavior, but also analyze the benefits and defects of social institutions and evaluate policies. For this, we must have a prerequisite assumption and judgment of human nature. If we assume that all people are irrational, any social ills can be generalized as people problems, but institutions cannot be designed, so humanity could not progress. If we compare China to the United States, not only is resource efficiency lower, but the level of morality is also lower. We can only say that there is a problem with the Chinese awareness of ideas, or even a problem with the Chinese race, so the only way to resolve this issue is to implement ideological reformation as was done during the "Cultural Revolution". Some people advocate ethnic reformation. This obviously is not persuasive. If we assume that people are rational, our backwards economy and low moral level show that there is a problem with our institutions, incentive mechanisms, and policies. Of course, perhaps there is a problem with our culture. The way to resolve these problems is to transform our systems and institutions, change our policies, and remold our culture. Therefore, with the rationality assumption, we will focus on the role of institutions and policy so that the social sciences can better enrich humanity.

Based on the justifications listed above, even if we must recognize the rational person assumption is not without flaws, we still must accept it. In each proceeding chapter, unless stated otherwise, we will assume that people are rational.

Scholars from certain other fields and social activists blame win-lose behavior and moral failings on economists' rational person assumption. These critics are incorrect. As was described above, a rational person is not always selfish and self-interested. Taking one step back, even if economists assume that rational people are selfish and self-interested, win-lose behavior is not the end result of this assumption. If the assumptions of theorists can change human nature, why is it that moral guardians' profession of altruism over the centuries has not made human nature any more virtuous, but one assumption made by economists can make human nature wicked? A correct judgment of human nature can establish a foundation for social progress based on institutions that benefit interpersonal cooperation over the long-term. It is similar to a doctor diagnosing a patient's illness in order to save the patient's life. Would we blame a doctor's diagnosis for the patient's death? On the contrary, telling a patient he is not ill will lead to his death. Economists' rational person assumption promoted humanity's cooperative spirit and increased moral standards, not the other way around. More than 200 years ago, Adam Smith proved that the market is the most efficient means of interpersonal cooperation, based on a foundation of the rational person assumption. Today, we see that in countries that have implemented a true market economy, the cooperative spirit and moral standards of the people are much higher than in non-market economies. Similarly, if we say that a religion like Christianity helps improve the morality of followers, the reason is not because it assumes human nature is virtuous, but because it assumes people are born in sin. The planned economy is built on the assumption of "altruism", but brought about disaster for hundreds of millions of people. The state-owned economy and government intervention are built upon the assumption that bureaucrats are impartial, but the result is serious corruption and unfair income distribution. Understanding this point is important for understanding contemporary Chinese society's moral crisis.

Section three: the social optimum and the Pareto criterion

In this section, we will evaluate human behavior from the perspective of society. What criteria should society utilize to evaluate individual behavior? Specifically speaking, from the perspective of society, what behavior is proper, and what behavior is improper? Or, what behavior should be encouraged, and what behavior should be suppressed?

3.1 The Pareto efficiency criterion

If we acknowledge that each person is born equal and the best judge of one's own happiness, then the only restriction society can place on each individual is that when exercising one's own liberty, the liberty of others may not be harmed. Only behavior that involves others must be conscientious of society.[31] Extended to economics, this point refers to the Pareto efficiency criterion to measure whether a person's behavior should be encouraged or suppressed.

The Pareto efficiency, also known as the Pareto optimum, was proposed by Italian economist Vilfredo Pareto over 100 years ago. Stated simply, a Pareto efficiency refers to a social state (distribution of resources, social institutions, etc.) in which no other available state can improve one person's lot without degrading another person's lot. Correspondingly, changing one type of state so that no one's lot is made worse, but at least one person's lot is improved, is called a Pareto improvement. Obviously, if a society is already in a Pareto optimal state, then no Pareto improvements can exist (thus any change must harm some group of people). Alternatively, if the current state is not a Pareto optimum, then space for Pareto improvements exists.

For ease of understanding, we can use a society consisting of two people as an example to explain this concept. In Figure 1.5, assume that society is made up of two people, A and B. The straight line sloping downward to the right is the feasible distribution line. All points on the line represent feasible distributions of income. All income could go to A, or all of it could go to B, or each person could get one part. The intersection of the straight line and the horizontal coordinate represents all of society's income going to A and B receiving nothing. The intersection of the straight line and the vertical coordinate represents B receiving all of society's resources.

The Points F, X, and Y are all on the straight line, so according to the standards described above, they are all Pareto efficiencies. Point Z is within the straight line, so the distribution it represents is not a Pareto efficiency. As was described previously, if society does not exist in a state of Pareto efficiency, then Pareto improvements are possible. Any move to the northeast of Point Z in the graph is a Pareto improvement. Moving from Point Z to Point X, Person A's income does not change, but Person B's income increases, so it is a Pareto improvement.

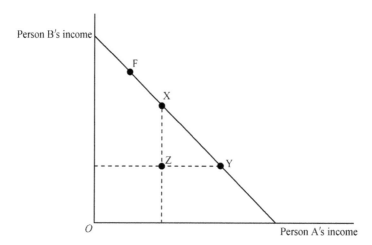

Figure 1.5 Pareto Improvement

Similarly, moving from Point Z to any point within the XYZ triangle is a Pareto improvement. Moving from Point Z to Point F is not a Pareto improvement, because although Person B's income increases, Person A's income has decreased.

This also means that moving from a non-Pareto optimum point to a Pareto optimum point is not necessarily a Pareto improvement. It must be noted that the standard for a Pareto efficiency does not take into consideration the fairness of the distribution. Both Pareto efficiencies and Pareto improvements can bring about very unfair distributions of income. On the extreme side, all social income concentrated in the hands of one person can also be a Pareto optimum. Different points of Pareto optimum cannot be compared. Without some other type of standard (such as social justice), we have no way to choose between two Pareto optimums. In my view, even if some Pareto optimal distribution is unequal, it is still worth pursuing Pareto improvements that benefit everyone (even if everyone's benefits are different). That is to say, even if we do not agree with the standards for a Pareto efficiency, there is no reason to oppose Pareto improvements. Of course, there is a bigger problem if one person's utility not only depends on his absolute income, but also his relative income compared to others – what Chinese refer to as "red eye sickness" – then the space for a Pareto improvement reduces drastically or even does not exist.

For individual behavior, the standard for Pareto efficiencies is when a person's behavior does not harm the interests of others, it is proper; otherwise, it is improper. Simply put, self-benefit that does not harm others and self-benefit that also benefits others is proper, but self-benefit that harms others is improper. In the cooperation problem discussed in the first section, both parties cooperating was a Pareto optimum, but not cooperating is not a Pareto optimum. Compared to not cooperating, both parties cooperating is self-beneficial while also benefiting others.

3.2 The Kaldor-Hicks criterion for efficiency

Three children go over to a neighbor's house. The host's television can be used to play video games or watch a soccer game. The three neighbor children want to play video games, but the host boy wants to watch soccer, leading to a dispute. The mother steps in and reprimands her own child for being selfish, but the child asks: "Mom, why is the selfishness of three people better than the selfishness of one person?"

Although this is just a story, the question raised by the host child is of philosophical significance. It is the same reason for the minority submitting to the majority in real life. Why should the minority submit to the majority? According to the Pareto efficiency criterion, violating the interests of the minority in the name of the majority is also improper. Similarly, no matter how large the benefit is that others will derive from change, as long as one person's interests are harmed, this change does not satisfy the Pareto improvement criterion. Imagine a two-person society where each person has ¥100. In an alternative state, the first person could have ¥1,000, but the second person has ¥99. Should this change be implemented?

It should be noted that even though this is not a Pareto improvement, it increases the overall wealth of society. According to the Pareto improvement criterion, it should not be implemented.

There are numerous examples of this, and it is very difficult for changes in real life to satisfy the Pareto criterion, so a new criterion must be used to measure social efficiency. One option is the Kaldor-Hicks criterion.[32] If during a transformation, gains made by the winners can be more than loses of the losers, then the transformation is a Kaldor-Hicks improvement. In the example of a two-person society used above, the transformation should not be implemented according to the Pareto criterion, but according to the Kaldor-Hicks criterion, it can be implemented because the gains (¥900) is much larger than the loses (¥1). The Kaldor-Hicks criterion is really a total maximization criterion, because any transformation that increases total wealth satisfies this criterion.

Why should this criterion be used? Because if we use the Pareto efficiency criterion, almost any transition could not take place. Vested interests exist under any institutional arrangement, so changing the *status quo* will necessarily harm vested interests. However, according to the Kaldor-Hicks criterion, reform can be implemented, as long as the gains of the winners exceed the losses of the losers. In this way, according to the Kaldor-Hicks criterion, anything that harms oneself but benefits all others should be done.

Further, the reason a Kaldor-Hicks improvement is worth consideration is the fact that it can perhaps transform into a Pareto improvement. If two people can negotiate so that the first person will compensate the second person more than one yuan, then a Pareto improvement is obtained. Therefore, we say that a Kaldor-Hicks improvement is a potential Pareto improvement. An example of this would be laying off employees so that a business can be more efficient and competitive. For the workers that are laid off, their interests will be harmed by no longer having a job. A layoff is not a Pareto improvement, but if the increase in gains achieved by the business can compensate the losses of the employees, then it is a Kaldor-Hicks improvement. If the real compensation for the unemployed workers is high enough so that their utility does not decrease, then it is a Pareto improvement.

Many social transformations are Kaldor-Hicks improvements, but in order to turn them into Pareto improvements the compensation issue must be resolved. According to the Coase Theorem,[33] if transaction costs were low, then negotiations between individuals could guarantee that Kaldor-Hicks improvements would appear as Pareto improvements. Efficiency and income distribution would not conflict. In reality, if transformations do impact small group of people, then the compensation issue can be resolved via negotiations between those involved. Market transactions mostly involved this type of negotiation. For big transformations that impact all of society and have large numbers of winners and losers, negotiation is not easy. Additionally, as was described above, because of people's focus on relative income levels and relative status, many potential Kaldor-Hicks improvements cannot be implemented. In our original example of both people having ¥100, imagine now that the first person has ¥1,000 and the second person still has ¥100. According to the above criteria, this is a Pareto improvement.

However, if fairness is calculated as part of people's utility function, this improvement will not be viewed as a Pareto improvement. The first person's income is much higher than before, so he is happy, but at the same time, the second person will see that his income discrepancy has increased, so he will be displeased. Therefore, this is no longer a Pareto improvement. Considering the psychological cost, it is difficult to have objective criteria for determining compensation to make the second person feel better. This is the reason that transformation is so difficult in societies with a strong sense of egalitarianism. Fortunately, society and culture influence the thoughts of the beneficiaries. Generally speaking, a person wants to live better than others, but also does not want the difference to be too great. If a rich person is surrounded by destitute people, he will not feel safe, so his own welfare will decrease. Therefore, most people do not want the polarization of society to be overly serious.

Furthermore, there may be a case where *ex-post* compensation will not happen, so unanimous consent for a transformation is not possible. If before institutional arrangements are made each person has equal chance at becoming a winner, then from the *ex-ante* perspective, a Kaldor-Hicks improvement is also a Pareto improvement. In the example above, if each person has a 50% chance of becoming the person that has ¥1,000, then after the transformation each person's expected return is $0.5 \times 1,000 + 0.5 \times 99 = 549.5$. That is larger than ¥100, so from the *ex-ante* perspective, no one loses in this transformation. Therefore, the change is a Pareto improvement, even if the result is not a Pareto improvement. According to John Rawls's Theory of Justice,[34] expected utility maximization means members of society will consent to institutional arrangements that maximize wealth. This point is also suitable for the Pareto criterion. If opportunities are equal for each person in society, even if the *ex-post* distribution is unequal, from the perspective of expected utility, the income distribution is fair.

It is precisely because of the significance of this do we use "Pareto efficiency" as a standard of social optimum and collective rationality. We will use "Pareto optimum", "social optimum", and "collective rationality" interchangeably. As Richard Posner (1980, 1992) pointed out, if a type of system involves systemic prejudice against certain members of society, then perhaps wealth maximization is not a rational standard. Using the traffic rule as an example, if the law dictates that only a privileged group of people can drive, and the process of obtaining this privilege is not open to all, then traffic rules that maximize wealth may not be just. From this we can see that the most important aspect of social justice is equality of opportunity.

3.3 The application of the efficiency criterion in law

The efficiency criterion that was discussed above was proposed by economists, but it is very important for our understanding of many social institutional arrangements.

Imagine two adjacent stores competing with each other. There are two circumstances possible. The first is that Store A hires thugs to destroy Store B so that it cannot operate, thus Store A benefits from the monopoly. The second is that

Store A relies on lower prices and better service to undercut Store B. The result of either circumstance is the same for Store B. Why do so many people view the first method is improper, but the second method is proper? From a legal perspective, the first method is illegal, but the second method is legal. Why? Because the second method satisfies the efficiency criterion.

Another example comes from tort law. Take a real story. A wall separating a factory and a residential area. To avoid having to go around the wall, the residents create a hole in it. One day, three children that live next door make their way into the factory. They discover a bottle containing a white liquid (methyl chloroform). Curious, they dump out the contents. Then, they play with matches and light the contents on fire. After pouring the contents of the bottle all onto the fire, the intensity of the fire becomes greater and greater. One of the children suffers serious burns. The grandparents of the child take the factory to court, and the court rules that the factory must pay compensation.[35]

There are numerous other examples like this. For example, if a child is playing with a toy that has an exposed chain that cuts off a finger, should the toy manufacturer be held responsible? If a child chokes on pudding, should the pudding manufacturer be held responsible? If a thief is killed by an electric fence, should the resident be held responsible?

There are similarities between all of the above examples. In law, there is something called the Hand Rule.[36] Using our example above, if the factory closed up the hole in the wall, the cost of doing so is C. If it does not close up the hole, the probability of an incident is P. If an incident happens, the loss is L. Therefore, if the hole is not closed up, the expected loss is $P \times L$. The Hand Rule states that if C is greater than $P \times L$, the factory does not have to take responsibility for the incidents caused by the hole, but if C is less than $P \times L$, the factory must take responsibility. The reason the judge ruled that the factory was responsible was because although closing the hole adversely affected the factory, the benefit to others of closing the hole vastly exceeds the cost to the factory, so the factory has a responsibility to close the hole. Tort law often uses this rule, which is precisely the maximization of wealth. In the example of the exposed chain, the manufacturer argued that the toys it made were in accordance with China's technical standards (which allow tire chains to be half exposed), but the court decided that satisfying national standards did not necessarily mean satisfying social responsibility, so it ruled that it was liable. From that point on, toy chains were completely covered. In reality, it is difficult to make a correct evaluation of costs, so similar cases often result in different judgments based on the judge.

We now return to our example of the competing stores. Most people believe that the second activity is proper, but the first activity is improper. Why is the first activity improper? If A wrecks B's store, B is harmed, but A may not be able to create more value. It may even be that the goods and services provided by A are not as good as those provided by B, so it also harms the interests of customers. In the second alternative, A relies on lower prices and higher quality to compete with B, so customers are more willing to patronize A. This means that resources in the hands of A are more efficient. From the overall perspective of society, it leads to the maximization of wealth.

Further, why should the law protect free exchange?[37] Generally speaking, if each person is rational, then free exchange is a Pareto improvement, or otherwise rational people would not make the exchange. If A values something at ¥50, but B values it at ¥100, then if free exchange takes place, then the price would fall somewhere between ¥50 and ¥100. As for the level, the price is set is determined by each party's ability to bargain. Why can we not force exchange? Imagine A owns an item that he values at ¥100, but B only values it at ¥50. If B can force A to sell it, perhaps he will only offer ¥20 and A must accept it. This would lead to social loss. If the purchase price was ¥20, B made a net gain of ¥30 from buying an item he valued at ¥50 for only ¥20, but A sold an item he valued at ¥100 for ¥20, so he suffered a loss of ¥80. Net social loss was ¥50. With free exchange, this situation would not happen. From this example, we can see the importance of liberty. Free exchange is a necessary condition for social efficiency.

Exchanges between people can be categorized into four types. The first is a difference in preferences. Imagine a school that gives T-shirts with three different colors to all 200 classmates. After they receive the shirts, there will certainly be some adjustments made. Exchange due to different preferences is a Pareto improvement. The second type of exchange is due to different specialization or production costs. The costs of a professor of economics producing a bottle of water is relatively high, but the cost of teaching a class is relatively low. This is precisely the opposite for a worker at a bottling plant, so the two can exchange. The product can be sold by the lower-cost producer to the higher-cost producer. The third type of exchange is due to different information. Many stock exchange transactions happen because two parties have different information. The buyer believes that each share is worth three yuan, but the more-informed seller believes that each share is only worth two yuan, so the transaction happens. The fourth type of transaction is due to different attitudes towards risk. Insurance is a type of difference in attitudes towards risk. Policy holders fear risk, but insurance companies reduce risk by pooling, so policy holders are willing to pay for insurance. Many institutional arrangements are like this in that the person that assumes responsibility for others receives a benefit.

Why do organizations like enterprises exist in society? If two people cooperating means that $1 + 1 > 2$, then cooperating benefits both of them. Strategic alliances between modern enterprises are also a case of $1 + 1 > 2$. In other words, the appearance of organizations is a type of Pareto improvement.

The same logic applies to marriage. Free courtship is a Pareto improvement for both parties. Given a person's preferences, he (or she) can freely choose a partner or not marry. Being willing to get married is a Pareto improvement. Is divorce a Pareto improvement? Perhaps, but perhaps not. If both parties agree to a divorce, it is a Pareto improvement. But, perhaps divorce only benefits one party, but makes the other party worse off. This is the reason that divorce settlements involve compensation.

The marriage question is complicated because there are many stakeholders. If an affectionless couple without children decides to split up, it is a Pareto improvement. With children, divorce may not be a Pareto improvement for the whole family. This gives way to what economics calls "externalities". Externalities refer to the influence a type of transaction has on the parties not directly involved. Because externalities exist, some behavior might benefit one person, but put a burden on someone else. This means that an optimal choice for one person may not be optimal for all of society. Some people enjoy singing at night, but no matter how much they revel in it, it may bother their neighbors. Many social institutions internalize externalities as individual cost or benefit. This realizes social Pareto improvements via individual choices. Of course, human compassion is an important force for the internalization of externalities. This is the reason that we see households with children being more stable than households without children, because the husband and wife will both consider the welfare of the child.

Notes

1 In economics, this characteristic is called the Law of Diminishing Marginal Productivity, the Law of Diminishing Marginal return, or the Law of Diminishing Marginal Utility.
2 Almost every introductory economics textbook introduces the equi-marginal principle. I recommend Mankiw's *Principles of Economics*.
3 For some selection activities, we can view a group as a decision unit. For consumption activities, we can view households as decision units. For production activities, we can view firms as decision units. We often refer to these units as individuals.
4 Edward O. Wilson, *Sociobiology: The New Synthesis*. Cambridge, MA: Harvard University Press, 1975.
5 This conclusion was inspired to a large degree by the well-known social theorist Jon Elster (1989a). In the book *The Cement of Society*, he defined the two basic issues of social order as behavioral predictability and cooperation. Correspondingly, he differentiated between two types of social chaos: Chaos caused by the failure of prediction, and chaos caused by lack of cooperation. However, the failure of predictability that he spoke of often was related to conflicts of interest. I use "coordination" to replace "prediction" in order to differentiate between coordination problems without conflicts of interest and cooperation problems with conflicts of interest.
6 Higher-order knowledge is a concept in Game Theory. It describes people's judgment and knowledge of other people's grasp of information.
7 Refer to Elster (1989a, pp. 2–4) for more on the lack of knowledge, excessive knowledge, and ineffective use of knowledge.
8 We have not considered the fact that some people purposefully conceal information or inhibit information. In economic literature, concealing information in the process of communication is called strategic information transmission. Crawford and Sobel (1982) made initial contributions to this field.
9 Depending on the situation, cooperating and not cooperating will have different meanings. In some cases, so-called "cooperation" is actually "conspiracy". If A and B are both criminal suspects, cooperation could refer to not exposing the other, whereas not cooperating could refer to exposing the other. In economic activity, A and B could be competitors, in which case cooperating could refer to maintaining high prices, whereas not cooperating could refer to lowering prices.
10 See Thomas Hobbes's (1996) *Leviathan*.

11 Collective rationality refers to the choice that maximizes total benefit or is best for all members. Whether or not interpersonal interests can be added together is an issue that awaits further discussion. In reality, because it is difficult to compare preferences between individuals, it is difficult to judge if one person's happiness can compensate for another person's suffering. In this situation, we can only utilize the weakest collective rationality standard, which is discussed in Chapter 3.

12 Using Hobbes's terminology, how do we avoid descending into a war of all against all?

13 This issue will be discussed in Chapter 14.

14 Humanity's thinkers recognized this early on. According to Maslow's Hierarchy of Needs, after satisfying the basics of survival and security, people will pursue a sense of belonging and self-fulfillment. This appears in real life as people's pursuit of fame and social status. It should be pointed out that Maslow's Hierarchy of Needs is overly simplistic. Even people that do not have adequate food and clothing seek honor. See Maslow (1943, 1954).

15 This is called a "self-fulfilling prophecy". It refers to incorrect expectations that impact people's behaviors in a way that incorrect assumptions become correct. See Jussim (1986).

16 Precisely upon realizing this point, Adam Smith theorized in *The Wealth of Nations* that the division of labor could increase the wealth of a nation, but also in *The Theory of Moral Sentiments* emphasized the importance of morality in promoting interpersonal cooperation.

17 Formal and informal institutions are a very mainstream classification. On the overall social level, it refers to laws and social norms. On the organizational level, it refers to explicit terms in regulations and organizational culture. Strictly speaking, this kind of separation leads to misunderstandings because implicit rules are not informal institutions. In this book, we will not strictly define these two concepts. The reader can rely on the text to understand our meaning when using these technical terms. There is a certain negative connotation about the idea of "unwritten rules", but we use it in the neutral sense. Loyalty is an unwritten rule in criminal organizations, and those who disobey are often punished by the boss. In the book *Yinbi de Zhixu* (*Hidden Order*), Mr. Si Wu gives a meticulous portrayal and detailed analysis of various "unwritten rules" in Ming Dynasty officialdom.

18 Each chapter of this book will discuss institutional issues. Chapter 13 will discuss the functions and mutuality of laws (formal institutions) and social norms (informal institutions).

19 We will differentiate between business entrepreneurs and norm entrepreneurs. The former refers to entrepreneurs engaged in commercial activities. The latter refers to creators and promoters of behavioral norms. Their commonality is innovation. Commercial entrepreneurs are the most common type of entrepreneur, and unless specified, this book refers to them as such. Norm entrepreneurs will be discussed in Chapter 14.

20 See James Coleman (1994), Chapter 1.

21 Elster (1989b), p. 99.

22 Precisely because it is so broad, it can explain anything, but at the same time lack the ability to predict. This is an issue that the rational assumption faces.

23 It must be explained that these assumptions on preferences all apply to individual preferences, but for collectives, the above assumptions may not apply, such as the transitivity assumption. Within a society, if the choice is between A and B, the majority of people may choose A; if the choice is between B and C, the majority of people may choose B; but, if the choice is between A and C, the majority of people may choose C. See Arrow (1963).

24 All English words can be put into sequence, but Chinese words cannot, so the "lexico" in lexicographic refers to the English dictionary.

25 Kaushik Basu (1998, 2000) differentiated between three types of social norms: Rationality-limiting norm, preference-changing norm, and equilibrium-selection norm.

This differentiation can also be applied to the law: Rationality-limiting law, preference-changing law, and equilibrium-selection law. We will discuss this issue in Chapter 13.

26 Basic knowledge about optimization can be learned in calculus, whereas the more complex issues touch upon dynamic control.

27 The creators of expected utility theory were von Neumann and Morgenstern (1947). Any intermediary micro-economics textbook will have a basic introduction to expected utility theory.

28 It must be pointed out that even though Expected Utility Theory is the standard theory in economic and Game Theory analysis of decisions under conditions of uncertainty, a large amount of studies have shown that this theory does not always provide correct predictions. Beginning in the 1970s, Kahneman, Tversky, and other psychologists developed Prospect Theory to challenge traditional Expected Utility Theory (Kahneman and Tversky, 1979). Daniel Kahneman received the Nobel Prize in Economics in 2002 (but Tversky passed away in 1996). For the classic literature about this theory, see the collection of essays edited by Kahneman and Tversky called *Choices, Values, and Frames* (2000).

29 The three points of criticism are summarized from Jolls, Sunstein, and Thaler (1998).

30 Drazen Prelec and Duncan Simester (2001), two professors from the Massachusetts Institute of Technology, conducted an experiment in 2000 related to auctions. The person that paid the highest price would receive tickets to sporting events. They randomly separated the participating students into two groups. They required one group to pay with cash and the other group to pay with a credit card. The result was that the group using a credit card offered a price that was on average double that of the group using cash!

31 See John Mill's (2002) *On Liberty*.

32 Nicholas Kaldor and John Hicks were British economists. Hicks received the Nobel Prize in Economics in 1972.

33 The Coase Theorem was proposed by Ronald Coase in *The Problem of Social Cost* (1960). The basic meaning of the theorem is that if property rights were clearly defined and transaction costs were zero, no matter how property rights were arranged in the beginning, market dealings could eventually realize a Pareto optimum. See Cooter (1991).

34 See Rawls (1971).

35 This example comes from Cheng Wang's, *Economic Analysis of Tortious Damages* [*Qīnquán Sǔnhài Péichǎng de Jīngjì Fēnxī*], Beijing: Renmin University Press, 2002, p. 122.

36 Learned Hand was a great American judge in the twentieth century.

37 Not all free exchanges are protected by law, such as drug dealing.

2 The Prisoner's Dilemma and the Nash equilibrium

The basic concepts of Game Theory include players, actions, information, strategies, payoffs, equilibriums, and outcomes. The goal of each player is to maximize his own payoffs (interests), but his payoffs are not determined by his own choices alone, but also depend on the choices of all other players. The optimal choices of all players constitute an equilibrium. The goal of game analysis is to predict players' actions and the equilibrium outcome.

Generally speaking, one person's optimal strategy depends on which strategy he believes other players will choose. However, in a game such as the Prisoner's Dilemma, the individual optimal choice does not depend on the choices of others. This type of optimal strategy is called the "dominant strategy". If every player in the game has a dominant strategy, then the dominant strategy of every player constitutes a dominant strategy equilibrium. Under this condition, as long as each person is rational, then we know the game's equilibrium outcome.

In the Prisoner's Dilemma game, "do not cooperate" is each person's dominant strategy. The Prisoner's Dilemma means individual rationality does not satisfy collective rationality. The reason for this is that individuals do not consider the externalities of their behaviors when making a decision. Negating individual rationality will not resolve the Prisoner's Dilemma. Instead, alignment between individual rationality and collective rationality can be achieved through the design of various institutions and thus realizing social cooperation.

If a game does not have a dominant strategy equilibrium, solely assuming that players are rational is insufficient to predict the actions of players. The way a rational player acts depends on whether or not he knows that other players are also rational. He might even want to know whether or not other players know he is also rational. Game Theory uses "common knowledge of rationality" to generalize this high-level rationality assumption. It is very difficult to satisfy complete common knowledge in reality, but it is a very useful assumption.

The Nash equilibrium is Game Theory's most important, most generalized equilibrium concept. It means given the strategies of other players, no one has an incentive to change their own strategy. In other words, strategies that constitute a Nash equilibrium are optimal for each player. The Nash equilibrium means that a choice based on beliefs are rational while at the same time the belief that supports this choice is also correct. Therefore, Nash equilibriums have self-fulfilling predictions. If everyone believes an equilibrium will appear, it will certainly appear.

From another perspective, assume that all players come to an agreement before the fact to stipulate each person's strategy. If given that other people will all respect this agreement, no one will violate this agreement, then this agreement is a Nash equilibrium. Otherwise, if any person has an incentive to unilaterally deviate from the agreement, then this agreement is not a Nash equilibrium. The Nash equilibrium is extremely important for our understanding of social systems (including law, policy, and social norms). As long as any system constitutes a Nash equilibrium, it will be consciously respected. A Nash equilibrium is not certainly Pareto optimal, but an effective Pareto optimal can only be realized through a Nash equilibrium. Effective system design is the realization of a Pareto optimum through a Nash equilibrium.

A pure Nash equilibrium does not exist in some games, but mixed strategy Nash equilibriums do exist. A mixed strategy refers to players randomly choosing actions. In this book, unless specifically stated, all of the Nash equilibriums we speak of refer to pure strategy Nash equilibriums.

Section one: the basic concepts of Game Theory

As we have already pointed out, Game Theory is a theoretical tool for the analysis of decision-making by rational people in a state of interdependence. In this chapter, we will formally introduce some basic concepts of Game Theory: players, action, information, strategy, payoff, equilibrium, and outcome. We will introduce each one.[1]

The first major concept is players. A player is the decision-making subject in a game. In the game, he has certain actions to choose from in order to maximize his utility and gains (payoff).[2] Players can be living, natural persons, but can also be enterprises or organizations, as well as countries or international organizations (such as the North Atlantic Treaty Organization or the European Union). In a game, as long as a subject's decisions have an important impact, we consider it a player.

According to our assumption in the first chapter, all players are rational in that they pursue the maximization of their self-interests. Applied to individuals, this assumption is easily accepted. Perhaps the reader has the following question: Even if individuals are rational, are organizations formed by individuals also rational? This question touches upon the "preference aggregation" problem in economics.[3] When we view an organization as a decision-making subject, we generally assume that it has a well-defined objective function. That way, we can expect it to be a rational subject. Of course, in reality, many organizations have not embodied proper collective rationality. But for any organization, if for key decisions, it cannot attach the most importance to the objectives of the organization, but instead focuses more on the interests of an individual or a small group, the ability for that organization to survive is limited.

In addition to the meaning of player in the general sense, when a game involves a random factor, we often introduce a pseudo-player called "nature". For example, for investment decisions, whether or not an investment will profit is not only determined by the choices of the investor, but is also determined by random factors out of the investor's control. The difference between the pseudo-player "nature" and a general player is the fact that the former does not have its own payoff or objective function, so it does not act purposefully.

The second concept is action. Action is the decision variable at some point in time for the player in a game. Each player has multiple possible actions to choose from during his turn. In a game of cards, the player can choose between putting up a spade or a diamond during his turn. The combination of all players' chosen action is called an action profile. Different action profiles lead to different results of the game. Therefore, in a game, in order to know the results of a game, a player must not only know his own actions, but also the actions of opponents.

Another important issue related to action is the order of action, meaning who goes first and who goes next. Generally speaking, as the order of action for each player is different, the results are often also different. For example, during a game of go (*weiqi*), most people prefer to act first because it often brings an advantage, so during formal competitions, players often draw lots in order to determine a fair order of action. The order of action for many games in reality is determined by technique, systems, history, and other external factors.

The third concept is information. Information is what each player in the game knows. This information includes understanding the characteristics of oneself and the opponent. An example of this is an opponent that is willing to compromise or is bellicose. Similarly, information also includes knowledge of certain actions of the opponent taken before the player's own turn.

In Game Theory, we rely on information sets to describe the amount of information a player has grasped. We will introduce the concept of an information set in Chapter 3.

If each player in a game has a full grasp of information about the actions taken by others, we call this a perfect information game. In the above example using weiqi, during the player's turn, he can observe the actions the opponent has made previously, so we call go a perfect information game. If nature participates in a perfect information game, then the initial action of nature will be correctly predicted by each player, so uncertainty does not exist.

In a game, if a player has a full grasp of other players' characteristics, we call this a "complete information" game. During a game of weiqi, your opponent could be a heavyweight or a lightweight. If you know this person and his level of skill, this is a complete information game; otherwise, it is an incomplete information game. Oftentimes, incomplete information games can be viewed as imperfect information games with nature participating in actions. Even if nature determines the type of opponent, the options that nature can take are not observable by all players. In a game of weiqi, the opponent's skill level can be seen as determined by "nature", but the opponent knows the decision of "nature", whereas the other player does not.

The difference between static games and dynamic games is related to the concept of information. So-called static games mean that all players act at the same time, and they can only act once. The "same time" action in a static game does not necessarily refer to time in the calendar sense. Instead, it refers to an information sense, meaning even two parties may not act at the same time, but when one player acts, he does not know what action the other party has taken. This is the reason we consider the static state to be an information concept. A classic example of a static game is the rock-paper-scissors game. So-called dynamic games refer to games in which one person acts and then the other person acts while knowing which choice the first person made. Chess is an example of a dynamic game. Because players take turns in dynamic games, these games are also called sequential games. In a dynamic game, if each player knows the moves that each other player (including nature) has taken, as well as the type of player each one is, then this is called a complete information dynamic game. If they only know the actions of each other player, but not the type of player each one is, then this is called an incomplete information dynamic game. In a game of poker, each player knows which actions the others have taken, but does not know which cards the other players have. This is an example of an incomplete information game. In China, we have the saying "to know the person, know the face, but not know the heart". This indicates that the process of interacting with others is also a type of incomplete information game.

The fourth concept is strategy. Strategy can be understood as players' contingent action plan. It determines the way in which players should act under certain circumstances. The contingency of strategy in reality provides rules for players to take actions. During the 1960s, Sino-Soviet relations were strained. Chairman Mao Zedong proposed a strategy of "We will not attack unless we are attacked; if we are attacked, we will certainly counterattack". This involves two actions: "We will not attack" and "we will certainly counterattack." It determined the specific conditions for utilizing these two types of actions: "Unless we are attacked" and "if we are attacked". If the condition is defined differently, but the action is the same, then the strategy is different. For example, "If others do not attack us, we will attack; if others attack, we will not counterattack", is a strategy. "Regardless if others attack us or not, we will attack" is a strategy, as well as "regardless if others attack us or not, we will not attack". Therefore, strategies are rules for action that set conditions for action.

Strategies must be complete so that they cover all possible conditions, to determine relevant action plans. For example, "If others do not attack us, we will not attack others" is not a complete strategy because it only determines what should be done when others do not attack us. It does not determine what should be done if others attack us. In reality, setting all possible strategies and plans is obviously very difficult. The reason is that many circumstances that happen in real life are very difficult to predict. However, it is still very important to pursue the completeness of strategy.

The fifth concept is payoff. It refers to the compensation that each player receives under given strategy sets. In a game, the payoff received by each player not only relies on each person's own choice of strategy, but it also relies on the strategies chosen by others. We refer to the strategy sets chosen by each player in the game as a strategy profile. Under different strategy profiles, the payoff received by players is generally different. Players in a game really only care about payoff from participating in the game. Payoff in each specific game perhaps has different significance. For example, perhaps an individual cares about his material compensation, or his social status. However, perhaps an enterprise cares about profit, market share, or continued competitiveness. The government is the same. Perhaps it cares about national income, gross domestic product, or the country's status in the world. A misunderstanding of players' payoff will perhaps cause mistaken predictions of the results of the game. This point is extremely important for the establishment of game models. For example, in the game involving competition between state-owned enterprises, the manager may only care about his power, so his payoff would be the size of his power. If we create a game model, and we assume that his payoff is the profit of the enterprise, then our predictions will be incorrect. The behavior that pursues maximization of profit and the behavior that pursues maximization of power are different.

The sixth concept is equilibrium. We can understand equilibrium in a game as a type of stable state. In this state, no player is willing to unilaterally change his own strategy. In other words, given the opponent's strategy, each player has already chosen the optimal strategy. Therefore, the stable state is formed by the optimal strategies of all players. We thus define the optimal strategy profile as equilibrium.

Generally speaking, in a game, players have multiple strategies, but the optimal strategy is the strategy that, given the strategies of other players, will bring about the largest payoff. A good example is the one involving China and the Soviet Union. Each player had four strategies as described earlier. If it is optimal for one player to implement the strategy "We will not attack unless we are attacked, if we are attacked, we will certainly counterattack", then it is also optimal for the other play to implement this strategy. At that point, neither player is willing to change his own choice, thus forming equilibrium.

It must be pointed out that the concept of equilibrium in Game Theory is different from equilibrium concepts in economics, such as "general equilibrium" or "partial equilibrium". Equilibrium in Game Theory means that no player is willing to change his own strategy, so the strategy profile is in a stable state. General equilibrium or partial equilibrium refers to a set of market clearing prices that cause supply and demand on the market to be equal so that the market is in a stable state.

The last concept is outcome. It refers to the things that occur as a result of game equilibrium, such as the strategies and actions chosen by players, or the related payoff profiles. The specific significance of the outcome is determined by context. For example, sometimes we refer to the strategies or actions of each player at the time of equilibrium, or sometimes we refer to the payoff of each player at the time of equilibrium. Attention must be given to the fact that when we speak of "outcomes", we are referring to things derived from our theoretical model, not necessarily the things that actually happen in real life. Actually, the objective of game analysis is to predict the outcome of games using theoretical models, but the outcome of utilizing different equilibrium concepts will also be different.

Section two: the Prisoner's Dilemma game

2.1 The Prisoner's Dilemma: a contradiction between individual rationality and collective rationality

Going forward, we will use these concepts to analyze a very simple, yet very important game: The Prisoner's Dilemma.[4] Imagine there are two suspects to a crime. After the police arrest them, they are detained separately. They are told that they can confess or not. If one person confesses, but the other does not, then the one that confesses will be released immediately, and the other one will be imprisoned for ten years. If both of them confess, each will be imprisoned for eight years. If both of them do not confess, due to lack of evidence, they both will be released after one year. How should the two suspects decide?

This game has two players: Suspect A and Suspect B.[5] Each player has two actions: Confess or not. Each player is investigated separately, so neither can observe if the other has confessed or not, so it is an imperfect information static game. Because the other's actions cannot be observed, there is no way for one of them to base his choice on the actions of the other, therefore, strategy and action is one and the same thing. (In static games, action and strategy can be used interchangeably.) The payoff structure of this game is displayed in Figure 2.1. The rows represent Suspect A and the columns represent Suspect B. Within the matrix, there are two numbers in each box. The first number represents the payoff for Suspect A and the second number represents the payoff of Suspect B.[6] This method of describing a game is called the normal form or strategic form.

Here we will see how Suspect A and Suspect B will decide. We will assume that each player is rational. They do not want to be in prison, even for one more day. Therefore, their objective is to do as little jail time as possible. We will also assume that each person only cares about himself, and not the other. (If the suspects were father and son or brothers, perhaps their actions would be different than in our situation.) We will first consider Suspect A's choices. If Suspect B confesses, then confessing himself would mean eight years in prison, whereas not confessing means ten years in prison, so confessing is better than not. If Suspect B does not confess, then by confessing A will be released immediately, whereas not confessing means one year in prison, so confessing is better than not. Therefore,

	Suspect B	
	Confess	Does not confess
Suspect A Confess	−8, −8	0, −10
Suspect A Does not confess	−10, 0	−1, −1

Figure 2.1 The Prisoner's Dilemma

from Suspect A's perspective, regardless if Suspect B confesses or not, his own optimal choice is to confess. Similarly, this is the case for Suspect B. Therefore, each person's optimal choice is to confess.

Generally speaking, in a game, each player's optimal choice depends on the choices of others. However, in the Prisoner's Dilemma game described above, each person's optimal choice is unrelated to the choices of others. This type of optimal strategy that is independent of the choices of others is called the dominant strategy of that player. The so-called "dominant strategy" refers to a strategy in which regardless of the other person's strategy, utilizing this strategy will bring about the maximum payoff for that player. Alternatively, this one strategy of the player is better than any other strategy under any circumstances. If each player has a dominant strategy, then obviously they will all choose this one strategy. A strategy profile composed of dominant strategies will form the game's dominant equilibrium.

In the Prisoner's Dilemma game, confessing is each player's dominant strategy. Both people choosing to confess becomes the game's dominant equilibrium. The result is that both people will confess, so they will both be imprisoned for eight years.

However, for these two prisoners, this game's Pareto optimal is to not confess so that they both only serve one year in prison, each. This is what we refer to when we speak of a contradiction between individual rationality and collective rationality. Even though for both people the best option is to not confess, each person will choose the optimal action on an individual basis, which is to confess. The result is not beneficial to either party. This takes us back to our previous discussion that individual rationality does not necessarily achieve a Pareto optimum.

We can use the concept of "externalities" discussed in the previous chapter to explain this. Externalities can simply be explained as the influence the actions of one person has on others. Given that Suspect A confesses, then Suspect B deciding to confess (eight-year sentence) rather than not (ten-year sentence) will reduce his sentence by two years. At the same time, this will increase Suspect A's sentence from zero years to eight years. In this way, not only do Suspect B's actions benefit himself, they harm Suspect A. Thus, Suspect B's actions have externalities for Suspect A. They are bad externalities, which are referred to as negative externalities in economics. The actions of Suspect A will also create negative externalities for Suspect B. We previously assumed that people are rational, meaning the objective is to maximize individual interests, not the maximization of collective interests. Based on this, under circumstances where negative externalities exist, a person's actions that are chose for the sake of pursuing the maximization of his own interests cannot possibly satisfy the maximization of collective interests. This causes a contradiction between individual choices and collective rationality.

The Prisoner's Dilemma is also known as "the Cooperative Paradox" or "the Collective Action Paradox". Even if cooperating will benefit both parties, neither parties will cooperate. The individual rational option is to not cooperate, but the collective rational option is to cooperate.

2.2 Examples of the Prisoner's Dilemma

There are numerous examples of conflicts between individual rationality and collective rationality in real life. An example would be the issue of Chinese school students concerning study time. In addition to normal class from Monday to Friday, on the weekends they also have to study math and English, among other topics. This is also a Prisoner's Dilemma. We can imagine that if all students take break on the weekends, then only the smartest children would test into prestigious secondary schools and universities. The problem is that if one student rests on the weekend, but others study more, even though the first student is smarter, he may not pass the test. The optimal choice is to study on the weekend. The result is that all students study seven days a week, so in the end, it is still only the smartest children that test into prestigious secondary schools and universities.

Competition brings about an irrational result in which everyone is busy, but in the end not everyone is better off. China's students today study intently, but from a social perspective this cannot be optimal.

Competition between businesses is also a Prisoner's Dilemma. On June 9, 2000, nine Chinese color television companies held a conference in Shenzhen. They formed a price cartel and set the minimum price on some models of color televisions. Three days later, certain companies already began to lower prices in Nanjing and other markets. The price alliance existed in name only.[7] Generally speaking, this type of alliance is very difficult to maintain. Given that one enterprise does not lower prices, but another one does, the second enterprise can increase sales and hold more market share.

Similarly, advertising is a kind of Prisoner's Dilemma.[8] The cost of advertising is very high and may not be profitable. Why is it that most businesses advertise? Imagine two enterprises that exist in some industry. If neither enterprise advertises, both receive ten units of profit. If each one advertises, both receive four units of profit. If one enterprise advertises, but the other does not, then the enterprise that advertises receives 12 units of profit and the other one receives two units of profit. This game's dominant equilibrium is that both enterprises advertise. Regardless if other enterprises advertise or not, an enterprise's optimal choice is to advertise. In the end, both enterprises have lower profits. Even if both enterprises agree to not advertise, this agreement will not be respected.

Arms races between nations are similar. If it is decided that no country will develop weapons, instead using those resources for civilian products, the people of each country will be better off. However, given that if another country does not produce weapons, but our country does, it will gain a military advantage. Otherwise, if other countries develop weapons and ours does not, we will be threatened. Therefore, every country will engage in an arms race.

A Prisoner's Dilemma also exists in the provision of public goods. So-called public goods refer to goods and services that are consumed without excluding others, such as national defense, roads, and bridges. The concept contrary to public goods is private goods, which are goods and services that are consumed by excluding others, such as food, clothes, and automobiles. If I eat an apple, no one else can. Public goods like national defense, roads, and bridges can be enjoyed simultaneously by myself and others, so they are not exclusive. Precisely because this type of consumption is non-exclusive are people therefore not motivated to provide these goods. Everyone hopes that others will provide them so that they can be free-riders. This means that if public goods are left to be provided by private individuals, insufficiencies will arise, thus reduce the utility of the whole society. For a society, the way in which public goods are efficiently provided is a core issue of public governance.[9]

Considering the importance of public goods, below we will use the example of paving a road to analyze the issue of providing public goods. Imagine a society composed of Player A and Player B with the need to pave a road. Both of them could choose to put in the effort, or not. If both of them put in the effort, the road could be paved, so each person receives a payment of four units. If neither of them put in the effort, the road will not be paved, so the payoff is zero. If one person puts in the effort, but the other does not, then the loss outweighed the gain for that one person, which we will denote as a payoff of −1 unit. The other person's payoff is five units. We can illustrate the public goods game using Figure 2.2.

In this game, the dominant equilibrium is for everyone to not provide the good. Thus, regardless if other people provide it or not, each one will choose not to. From this, we can predict that based on individual willingness, equilibrium means that no public goods are provided. Therefore, the provision of public goods generally requires the government to use forceful methods to make individuals provide relevant services or funds for public goods. In modern societies, each of us must pay taxes. In ancient times, members of society underwent forced labor or military service.

2.3 The general form of the Prisoner's Dilemma

A few specific examples were given above. Below, we will discuss the general form of the Prisoner's Dilemma. Figure 2.3 is the payoff structure of a two-person game.

Both parties in a game have two choices: Cooperate, or not. If both people choose to cooperate, the payoff for each is T. If one person chooses to cooperate and the other does not, the person that chose to cooperate receives payoff S,

		B	
		Provide	Does not provide
A	Provide	4, 4	−1, 5
	Does not provide	5, −1	0, 0

Figure 2.2 The Public Goods Game

Person B

	Cooperate	Does not cooperate
Cooperate	T, T	S, R
Does not cooperate	R, S	P, P

Person A (Cooperate / Does not cooperate rows)

Figure 2.3 The General Form of the Prisoner's Dilemma

Person B

	Cooperate	Does not cooperate
Cooperate	T, T	S, R−X
Does not cooperate	R−X, S	R−X, R−X

Person A (Cooperate / Does not cooperate rows)

Figure 2.4 Rewards and Punishments to Advance Cooperation

whereas the other person receives payoff R. If both people choose not to cooperate, then both receive payoff P.

To turn the above game into a Prisoner's Dilemma, the following condition must be met: $R > T > P > S$. Thus: For each person, the best result is when the other person chooses to cooperate, but he himself does not (R). The second best result is when both people cooperate (T). The third one is no one cooperate (P). The worst result is when the other person chooses not to cooperate, but he does (S). Additionally, we assume that $T + T > R + S$, so that the total gain from two people cooperating is greater than the gain from one person cooperating and the other not.[10] As long as these conditions are met, no matter what the specific numbers for the payoff are, the result will be that individual rationality does not satisfy collective rationality.

The Prisoner's Dilemma is the greatest difficulty faced by social cooperation. From ancient times to the present, all over the world, many institutional arrangements (including law and social norms) were designed in order to resolve the Prisoner's Dilemma. We previously discussed public finance as a way to resolve the Prisoner's Dilemma that exists in the provision of public goods. Later, we will also discuss the ways in which ownership rights also resolve the Prisoner's Dilemma. Now, we will consider the ways in which enforcement of the law assists in the resolution of Prisoner's Dilemmas in the course of exchange between two contracted parties. Imagine that Person A and Person B sign a contract before some activity. The contract states that the punishment for non-cooperation is X. Both parties believe that this contract will be enforced.

At this point, assume that Person B cooperates if Person A also cooperates, then both parties receive T. If Person A does not cooperate, then Person B receives pay-off S, but Person A receives payoff $R - X$. Obviously, as long as punishment X is large enough, causing $R - X < T$, then "cooperation" is each person's best choice. Both parties choosing to cooperate becomes an equilibrium, thus resolving the contradiction between individual rationality and collective rationality. This is the value of contracts. Of course, if the parties involved do not believe that the contract will be effectively enforced, or that the degree of punishment is not severe enough (meaning that $X < R - T$), we are back to a Prisoner's Dilemma, so cooperation will not happen.

In the example above, we could also resolve the Prisoner's Dilemma by means of rewards for the party that cooperates. In economics, punishments for the non-cooperative party are the same as rewards for the cooperative party. Both are part of the incentive mechanism. Yet, in psychology, the effects of rewards and punishments are not always the same. Households and enterprises have various internal rewards and punishment mechanisms, with the aim of resolving the Prisoner's Dilemma and advancing cooperation. Society generally implements punishments for uncooperative behavior in order to promote cooperation. It could be said that law is an important means of resolving the Prisoner's Dilemma and promoting social cooperation, although in Chapters 6 and 7, we will see that in repeated games, many instances of cooperation will appear without having to rely on law and other formal institutions.

Section three: rationalizable choices

3.1 Rational people do not choose bad strategies

In the previous section, we described dominant strategies with help from a Prisoner's Dilemma game. In the Prisoner's Dilemma, regardless which action one player chooses, each play has a unique optimal choice (i.e. dominant strategy). This is to say that when a rational player is making a decision, he does not have to assume that the other player is also rational. We can easily predict the result of this type of game. However, in certain types of games, it is possible for one player to have a dominant strategy, whereas the other does not. Thus, the latter's optimal action relies on his prediction of the choices the former will make. That player's optimal choices change as the other player chooses differently. At this point, what will the result of this game be? Below, we will use the Boxed Pig Game to analyze this problem.

Imagine there are two pigs, one large and one small, in a pig pen. On one side of the pen is a button, and on the other side is a trough. By pushing the button on one side, the trough on the other side will dispense 8 units of food. Regardless if the button is pressed by the big pig or small pig, the cost of pressing the button is 2 units of food. If both pigs push the button, both will pay 2 units of food in cost, then the big pig will be able to eat 6 units of food, and the small pig will be able to eat 2 units. Net of costs, the gain for each one is 4 units and zero, respectively. If the big pig presses the button, but the small pig does not, then the small pig can eat 3 units without paying any price. In this case, after pressing the button, the big pig could run back and eat 5 units, which net of costs would equal 3 units. Alternatively, if the small pig presses the button, but the big pig does not, then the big pig can eat 7 units without paying any price. That would only leave 1 unit left for the small pig, which net of costs would equal −1 unit. If neither pig presses the button, then no price is paid, but there is nothing to eat, so the net gain is zero. This is displayed in Figure 2.5.

Now, the question is: Who will press the button? First, we will consider the big pig's circumstances. If the small pig presses the button, the big pig's optimal choice is to wait (7 > 4). If the small pig waits, the big pig's optimal choice is to press the button (3 > 0). This is different than the Prisoner's Dilemma game discussed previously. In the Prisoner's Dilemma game, each player has a dominant strategy, e.g. regardless if the other player confesses, the optimal choice is to confess. However, in the Boxed Pig Game, the big pig does not have a dominant strategy. The big pig's optimal choice depends on the small pig's choices. Therefore, the big pig must predict the small pig's choice when making a decision.

How will the small pig choose? For the small pig, if the big pig presses the button, then its optimal choice is to not press the button (3 > 0); if the big pig does not press the button, its optimal choice is still to not press the button (0 > −1). This shows that the small pig choosing not to press the button is a dominant strategy.

What should the big pig do? We previously assumed that each player is rational, but we did not assume that one of them knew that the other one is also rational. Obviously, when the small pig is making a decision, it does not need to assume that the big pig is rational, because regardless if the big pig is rational or not, the small pig's optimal decision is to not press the button. However, the big pig's situation is different. Even if the small pig is rational, if the big pig does not know that the small pig is rational or not, then the big pig has no way to make a decision.

To predict the result of this game, we must make a further assumption about the big pig's degree of rationality. Assume that not only is the big pig himself rational, but also knows that the small pig is also rational. As a rational player, the small pig will not press the button. Because the big pig knows that the small pig

| | | The small pig | |
		Press	Does not press
The big pig	Press	4, 0	3, 3
	Does not press	7, −1	0, 0

Figure 2.5 The Boxed Pigs Game

is rational, it will also know that the small pig will not press the button, so the big pig's optimal choice can only be to press the button. The outcome of this game is: The big pig presses the button, the small pig does not, and each receives 3 units of net compensation.

From this example, we can further propose a concept called "dominated strategy". It refers to a strategy that one player will not choose regardless of the other player's choice. In the Boxed Pig Game, for the small pig, its dominated strategy is to press the button. Regardless if the big pig presses the button or not, for the small pig, pressing the button is not its best choice. Therefore, if the big pig knows that the small pig is rational, the strategy to press the button can be removed from the small pig's strategy profile. Now, the game faced by the big pig is displayed if Figure 2.6.

At this point, for the big pig, not pressing the button has also become a dominated strategy, because it will not use it. Therefore, we can remove this dominated strategy from the big pig's strategy profile. The result is displayed in Figure 2.7.

Through this, we determined that the only optimal strategy profile is: The big pig presses the button and the small pig does not. This is the Boxed Pig Game's strategic equilibrium. Finding this game's equilibrium was a process of successively disqualifying dominated strategies. Therefore, this equilibrium is called "iterated dominant strategy".

The Boxed Pig Game's equilibrium set has many applications in reality. For example, in joint-stock companies, stockholders assume a supervisory function

		The small pig	
		Press	Does not press
The big pig	Press		3, 3
	Does not press		0, 0

Figure 2.6 The Boxed Pigs Game After Eliminating the Small Pig's Dominated Strategy

		The small pig	
		Press	Does not press
The big pig	Press		3, 3
	Does not press		

Figure 2.7 The Boxed Pigs Game After Eliminating the Big Pig's Dominated Strategy

over management. However, there are both large and small shareholders, and the benefits they receive from that supervision are different. Supervising managers requires collecting information, which takes time. Under conditions of equal supervisory cost, the large shareholder obviously gains more benefit from supervision than the small shareholder. Here, the large shareholder is similar to the big pig, and the small shareholder is similar to the small pig. The equilibrium result is that the large shareholder takes on the responsibility to collect information and supervise managers, but the small shareholder is a free-rider. Stock market speculation is the same. In the stock market, there are institutional and small individual investors. Institutions are like the big pig, and individuals are like the small pig. Following the moves of institutions is the optimal choice of individual investors, meaning that institutions must collect information and do the analysis.

A similar issue exists between large and small enterprises in a market. It may be worthwhile for a large enterprise to undertake research and development or advertising, but not so for small enterprises. Therefore, large enterprises often are responsible for innovation, whereas small enterprises focus their energy on imitation.[11]

Counter-terrorist activities on a global scale are similar to the Boxed Pig Game. In the era of globalization, terrorism has already become an international phenomenon that harms all countries. However, the cost of counter-terrorism is high. Even if small countries do not like terrorists, they do not have an incentive to undertake counter-terrorism activities. Therefore, for international counter-terrorism initiatives, large countries take on more responsibility (manpower and materials), but small countries are free-riders. Thus, large countries play the role of the big pig, and small countries play the role of the small pig. With the rise of China, the international community has called on China to take on more responsibilities, for the same reasons.

International counter-terrorism can be understood as a public good on an international scale. We previously mentioned that the production of public goods is a Prisoner's Dilemma. Actually, the production of certain public goods is similar to the Boxed Pig Game. The beneficiaries are asymmetric, meaning some benefit more than others. Under these circumstances, the larger beneficiaries perhaps have an incentive to privately produce public goods. For example, in some rural areas of traditional China, rich families paved the roads and provided other public goods. This is to say that not all public goods must be provided by government.[12]

Similar circumstances occur in social transformation. The same reform will benefit one group of people more than another group. At that point, the former group has more incentive to reform than the latter group. Reforms are often pushed forward by these "big pigs". If reform can create more "big pigs", the speed of reform will quicken.

3.2 Rationality as common knowledge

Analyzing the Boxed Pig Game is a process of iterated eliminating dominated strategy. Specifically, we first find one player's dominated strategy, then reject it.

Then, from the remaining games, we find the next dominated strategy and reject it. We repeat this until we are left with only one strategy profile. That strategy profile is an iterated dominant equilibrium. Under this condition, we say that this game is an iterated-dominant-solvable game.

We have already seen that in order to predict the choices of each player in this type of game, we must know more about each player's degree of rationality. Assuming that each player is rational will not tell us what the equilibrium result will be. For example, in the Boxed Pig Game, in addition to assuming that the big pig and small pig are both rational, we must also at least assume that the big pig knows that the small pig is rational. However, if the big pig does not know that the small pig is rational, then the big pig does not know how to decide.

With that being said, this game's required degree of rationality is very low. We do not even need to assume that the small pig knows that the big pig is rational, because regardless if the big pig is rational or not, the small pig knows that its own optimal choice is to not press the button. In many games, even if we assume that each player knows that other players are rational, it cannot tell us how players will choose.

Here, we must introduce a concept called common knowledge of rationality, then define zero-order, first-order, second-order, and unlimited-order common knowledge. Zero-order common knowledge of rationality means each person is rational, but does not know if others are rational or not. First-order common knowledge of rationality means not only is each person required to be rational, but also know that everyone else is rational. Second-order common knowledge of rationality means that, in addition to satisfying the first-order, each player knows that other players know they are rational. This continues to the *nth*-order or even infinite-order common knowledge of rationality.[13]

Common knowledge of rationality usually refers to infinite-order common knowledge of rationality. It is like a person standing between two mirrors causing an endless amount of reflections. This is a basic assumption of Game Theory but is rarely seen in reality. This is an important reason that the predicted result of a game is divergent from reality. The reason we have stratagems is because players do not satisfy the requirement of common knowledge of rationality. Otherwise, the result of the game could be predicted by anyone, so no stratagem could prevail. For example, Player A is very smart, Player B knows that Player A is smart, but Player A does not know that Player B knows that Player A is very smart. In this situation, if Player A tries to cheat Player B, Player B could beat Player A at his own game, so in the end the winner is Player B. If Player A knows that Player B knows he is smart, then Player A knows that Player B will see through any strategy. During the Warring States period of ancient China, a military general challenged King Wei of Qi to a horse race.[14] Ranked in order, the general knew that none of his horses could beat the king's horses if matched equally. Instead, he raced his worst horse against the king's best horse, his best horse against the king's average horse, and his average horse against the king's worst horse. He won two of the three. The king lost because he did not know that the general was that smart. If the king had required the general to choose which horse will race first, the king could have won three out of three. Even if there are very few people that can achieve infinite-order common knowledge of rationality, there are also a limited number of people as "stupid" as the king.

To explain the importance of common knowledge of rationality in the process of iteration, consider the game in Figure 2.8. In this game, each person has three choices. Player R's choices are R_1, R_2 and R_3. Player C's choices are C_1, C_2, and C_3. (Going forward, R will represent rows, and C will represent columns.)

Visually, we can see that the most alluring result is (R_3, C_3). However, if both people are rational, then (R_3, C_3) will not appear as the equilibrium result. From here, we can analyze the optimal choice for both parties.

First, we will consider Player R's choices. If Player C chooses C_1, then Player R's optimal choice is R_1 ($10 > 9 > 1$). If Player C chooses C_2, then Player R's optimal choice is still R_1 ($1 > 0$). If Player C chooses C_3, then Player R's optimal choice is R_3 ($100 > 99 > 98$). This is to say that regardless of Player C's choice, Player R will not choose R_2. R_2 is Player R's dominated strategy.

Next, we will examine Player C's choices. If Player R chooses R_1, then Player C's optimal response is to choose C_2 ($5 > 4$). If Player R chooses R_2, then Player C will choose C_1 ($9 > 8 > 3$). If Player R chooses R_3, then Player C will choose C_2 ($100 > 98$). Therefore, regardless of Player R's choice, a rational Player C will not choose C_3. C_3 is Player C's dominated strategy, so it will also be eliminated.

In this way, as long as each player is rational (zero-order common knowledge of rationality), R_2 and C_3 will not be chosen. Further, if Player R knows that Player C is rational, then he knows that rational Player C will not choose C_3. Player R will also not choose R_3 because the only reason that Player R would choose R_3 is if Player C chose C_3. Similarly, if Player C knows that Player R is rational, then he knows that Player R will not choose R_2. Player C will also not choose C_1 because the only reason that Player C would choose C_1 is if Player R chose R_2. As long as each participant satisfies first-order common knowledge of rationality, then Player R's optimal choice is R_1 and Player C's optimal choice is C_2, with a payoff of 1 and 5, respectively. Obviously, strategy

		Player C	
	C_1	C_2	C_3
R_1	10, 4	1, 5	98, 4
Player R R_2	9, 9	0, 3	98, 8
R_3	1, 98	0, 100	100, 98

Figure 2.8 High-Order Common Knowledge of Rationality and Repeated Elimination of Dominant Strategy

profile (R_3, C_3) is Pareto optimal to (R_1, C_2), meaning that each person is better off. However, if each player satisfies the requirements of first-order common knowledge of rationality, then (R_3, C_3) will not appear as the equilibrium result.

First-order rationality only requires each player to know that the others are rational. This requirement does not appear to be unrealistic. After all, we generally do not assume that others are more stupid than ourselves. However, perhaps precisely because neither of us is stupid and we know that others are not stupid, do we make stupid decisions (from the perspective of results).

In the game described above, as long as the players satisfy first-order common knowledge of rationality, then we know what the equilibrium result of the game will be. However, in certain games, satisfying first-order common knowledge of rationality cannot tell us how the players will choose. In the example in Figure 2.9, each player has four choices,[15] and we still assume that rationality is common knowledge.

We will first examine Player R's choices. If Player C chooses C_1, then Player R should choose R_1.[16] If Player C chooses C_2, then Player R should choose R_2. Similarly, the optimal response to C_3 and C_4 is R_3 and R_4, respectively. Obviously, any choice by Player R is rational specifically depending on his judgment of Player C's choice.

Next, we will examine Player C's choices. If Player R chooses R_1, then Player C will choose C_3. If Player R chooses R_2, Player C will choose C_2. The optimal response to R_3 and R_4 is C_2 and C_1, respectively.

Generally speaking, the more choices players in a game have, the higher the requirement is for common knowledge of rationality. Actually, resolving the equilibrium of the above game requires fifth-order common knowledge of rationality.

Zero-Order Common Knowledge of Rationality: Player C is rational, meaning he will not choose C_4;

First-Order Common Knowledge of Rationality: Player R knows that Player C is rational, meaning he knows that Player C will not choose C_4, so he also will not choose R_4;

| | | Player C | | | |
		C_1	C_2	C_3	C_4
	R_1	5, 10	0, 11	1, 20	10, 10
	R_2	4, 0	1, 1	2, 0	20, 0
Player R	R_3	3, 2	0, 4	4, 3	50, 1
	R_4	2, 93	0, 92	0, 91	100, 90

Figure 2.9 Multiorder Common Knowledge of Rationality

Second-Order Common Knowledge of Rationality: Player C knows that Player R knows that Player C is rational, meaning Player C knows that Player R will not choose R_4, so he also will not choose C_1;

Third-Order Common Knowledge of Rationality: Player R knows that Player C knows that Player R knows that Player C is rational, meaning Player R knows Player C will not choose C_1, so he also should not choose R_1;

Fourth-Order Common Knowledge of Rationality: Player C knows that Player R knows that Player C knows that Player R knows that Player C is rational, meaning Player C now knows that Player R will not choose R_1, so he also should not choose C_3;

Fifth-Order Common Knowledge of Rationality: Player R knows that Player C knows that Player R knows that Player C knows that Player R knows that Player C is rational, meaning Player R knows that Player C will not choose C_3, so he should not choose R_3.

After the above inference, the final result is that Player R will choose R_2 and Player C will choose C_2.

This process of inference may have caused the reader to become dizzy. This shows that to solve and predict a game the requirements on common knowledge of rationality are very high. In reality, it is very difficult for participants in a game to meet this requirement. As we previously mentioned, this is a main reason that there are differences between the theoretically predicted result of Game Theory and the actual result.

Section four: the Nash equilibrium and aligned expectations

4.1 The Nash equilibrium

In certain games, even if player's common knowledge of rationality is higher, we still cannot use the iterated eliminating dominated strategy method to solve it. Consider the game shown in Figure 2.10.

First, we will consider Player R's choices. If Player C chooses C_1, then Player R's optimal choice is R_2. If Player C chooses C_2, then Player R's optimal choice is R_1. If Player C chooses C_3, then Player R's optimal choice is R_3.

		Player C	
	C_1	C_2	C_3
R_1	0, 4	4, 0	5, 3
Player R R_2	4, 0	0, 4	5, 3
R_3	3, 5	3, 5	6, 6

Figure 2.10 Rationalizable Strategies

Next, we will consider Player C's choices. If Player R chooses R_1, then Player C will choose C_1. If Player R chooses R_2, then Player C will choose C_2. If Player R chooses R_3, then Player C will choose C_3.

This means that in this game, each player could choose any one of three strategies, depending on his judgment of the other player's choice, so there is no absolute dominated strategy. Therefore, this game cannot be solved using the iterated eliminating dominated strategy method.

In this game, any strategy can be rationalized. This means that any strategy chosen by a player satisfies common knowledge of rationality. For example, Player R choosing R_1 satisfies common knowledge of rationality because if Player R believes that Player C will choose C_2, then Player R's choice of R_1 is rational. The question is: Why does Player R believe Player C will choose C_2? Obviously, if Player R believes that Player C believes that Player R will choose R_2, then Player C's choice of C_2 is rational. Further, why would Player C believe that Player R will choose R_2? If Player R believes that Player C believes that Player R believes that Player C will choose C_1, then of course Player R will choose R_2. Why does Player C believe that Player R will believe that Player C will choose C_1? Because Player R believes that Player C believes that Player R believes that Player C believes that Player R will choose R_1. After this round of first-, second-, third-, and fourth-order common knowledge of rationality, we can prove that Player R's choice of R_1 is rational.

We can see that in this game, each player's choice of any strategy could be rational. However, the process of reasoning that was described above involved inconsistent beliefs, or misunderstandings. The reason Player R will choose R_1 is because he expects Player C will choose C_2. The reason he believes Player C will choose C_2 is because he believes that Player C mistakenly believes that he will choose R_2, but he will actually choose R_1. If Player C knows that Player R expects him to choose C_2, then of course Player C will not choose C_2. If Player R knows that Player C knows that Player R expects Player C to choose C_2, then Player R has no reason to choose R_1. These are inconsistent beliefs (expectations).

In the game described above, there were nine possible strategy profiles. Only (R_3, C_3) satisfies consistent expectations. If Player R expects Player C will choose C_3, then Player R's optimal choice is R_3. If Player C knows that Player R expects him to choose C_3, then Player C will actually choose C_3. If Player R knows that Player C knows that Player R expects Player C will choose C_3, then Player R should actually choose R_3. Here, each person's expectation of the other's behavior is correct.[17]

From this point we will draw on an extremely important concept: The Nash equilibrium.

The so-called Nash equilibrium is when among each player's optimal strategy profiles, given the choices of other players, no player has an incentive to change his own choice. For example, strategy profile (R_3, C_3) is a Nash equilibrium. In this profile, given that Player C will choose C_3, then Player R's optimal choice is R_3. Similarly, given Player R's choice of R_3, then C_3 is also Player

C's optimal choice. They are mutually consistent and both optimal, thus they are a Nash equilibrium.[18]

An important characteristic of the Nash equilibrium is the consistency between beliefs and choices. This means that choices based on beliefs are rational and at the same time the belief that supports this choice is correct. The Nash equilibrium can also be considered self-enforcing, which means that if everyone believes there will be a certain result, then this result will really happen. (Every profile in a game can be examined to see that only the Nash equilibrium can satisfy the condition of self-enforcement.)

Now we will examine the Nash equilibrium from another perspective. Imagine that before the game, all players came to an agreement. Without external enforcement, would each person have an incentive to consciously respect this agreement? If each person has an incentive to respect this agreement, then this agreement constitutes a Nash equilibrium. In other words, given this agreement and that others will respect it, if no one has incentive to act contrary to the agreement, then this agreement is a Nash equilibrium.

An example is shown in Figure 2.11. Imagine that Player R and Player C want to sign a contract and each strategy profile can be seen as a potential contract. For example, (R_1, C_1) is a contractual requirement that Player R choose R_1 and Player C choose C_1. Similarly, (R_1, C_2) is a contractual requirement that Player R choose R_1 and Player C choose C_2. In total, there are nine possible contracts. Among these nine contracts, which one(s) will be consciously observed?

Only contract (R_2, C_2) will be consciously observed because it is a Nash equilibrium. In other cases, at least one person will not observe the contract. In contract (R_2, C_3), even if the one party observes it, the other will not. In contract (R_3, C_1), given that Party R observes the contract, then Party C would observe it; however, even if Party C observes the contract, Party R will not. In that case, R_1 (not observing) has a higher compensation than R_3 (observing). Neither of these profiles are Nash equilibrium. Similarly, it is easy to prove that except for (R_2, C_2), the other six profiles are not Nash equilibrium. This is the philosophical significance of the Nash equilibrium. If a contract (including a system) is not a Nash equilibrium, it may not be consciously observed by all.

| | | Player C | | |
		C_1	C_2	C_3
	R_1	<u>100</u>, <u>100</u>	0, 0	50, <u>101</u>
Player R	R_2	50, 0	<u>1</u>, <u>1</u>	60, 0
	R_3	0, <u>300</u>	0, 0	<u>200</u>, <u>200</u>

Figure 2.11 Contract Self-Enforcement

The Nash equilibrium can unify the previously discussed concepts of dominant equilibrium and iterated dominant equilibrium. Dominant equilibrium and iterated dominant equilibrium are both Nash equilibrium, but the opposite does not stand. In the Prisoner's Dilemma game, both parties choosing to not cooperate is a Nash equilibrium. In the Boxed Pig Game, the big pig pressing the button and the small pig not pressing the button is also a Nash equilibrium. However, in the example above, (R_2, C_2) is not a dominant equilibrium, nor is it an iterated dominant equilibrium. Because a dominant equilibrium only requires the player himself to be rational, but not to know if the other player is also rational, and an iterated dominant equilibrium only requires limited-order common knowledge of rationality, they are more easily seen in real life than a non-dominant Nash equilibrium.

4.2 Application examples: rent seeking and the property rights system

The Nash equilibrium is the most important concept for game analysis. It is extremely important for our study and understanding of institutions and many socio-economic phenomena. An institution may be bad for everyone involved, but if it is a Nash equilibrium, it will continue to exist. On the contrary, an institution may sound good, but if it is not a Nash equilibrium, it will not be consciously observed by all. If we want our society to escape the Prisoner's Dilemma, we must have a way to make each person choosing to cooperate a Nash equilibrium. This is the reason Nobel Prize in Economics laureate Myerson (1999) believed that the significance of discovering the Nash equilibrium was comparable to discovering the DNA double helix in the biological sciences.

The Nash equilibrium is an analytical tool that involves no value judgments. In later chapters and sections, we will often use this concept to analyze various rules, regulations, and policies. Here, we will first give some examples to show the power of this analytical tool.

In the 1990s Chinese stock market, many enterprises continuously sought rent through stock allotments. This could be understood as a Prisoner's Dilemma game designed by managers for shareholders. Imagine that an enterprise is currently worth ¥100 with 100 shares outstanding, so the price of each share is ¥1 (assume that the stock price accurately reflects the true value of the enterprise). Now assume that the manager wants to raise ¥100, but after the investment it is only worth ¥50. From the perspective of the shareholder's interests, this ¥100 should not be raised, but the manager has an incentive to do this based on control rights or other personal goals. If the shareholders are dispersed, such as 100 shareholders owning one share each, then they lack constraints over the manager. Now the manager decides to allot four new shares for each one, so the allotment stock price is ¥0.25 per share. If the allotment is completed, then ¥100 will be raised. The question is: Will shareholders accept the allotment? If a shareholder does not accept the allocation, the one share worth ¥1 that he originally owned will now only be worth ¥0.3. (The total value of the company is now ¥150, which is the original ¥100 plus ¥50, but divided by 500 shares after the allocation.) If the shareholder accepts the allocation, he now owns five shares, but those shares are still worth 1% of the total. The value of his shares is 1% of ¥150, or ¥1.50. He pays 4 × ¥0.25 = ¥1 in order to receive ¥1.20 (= ¥1.50 − ¥0.30) in gross value, so obviously, all shareholders accepting the allocation is a Nash equilibrium. The manager gets what he wants, but the shareholders collectively lose ¥50. The reason injury can be caused to all shareholders is because the design of the manager's allocation proposal caused the shareholders to be trapped in a Prisoner's Dilemma. If the allocation proposal was 1:1 and each new share was priced ¥1, then the shareholders would not accept the allocation. The loss from not accepting the allocation would at most be ¥0.25 (after the allocation the value of each share becomes ¥0.75), but the loss from accepting the allocation would be ¥0.50. This example also proves that the lower the allocation prices is in relation to the market price, the more likely the allocation is rent-seeking behavior of the manager instead of being in the interests of the shareholders. Even if we assume the manager is a major shareholder, as long as his control rights interests are greater than his ownership rights interests, this conclusion will not change.

This is also the case for many other systems in society. Social insurance is an example. Assume that a worker's gross wages are ¥10,000, but the government deducts ¥1,000 for social insurance, so the worker receives ¥9,000. Then, if the worker participates in social insurance, he pays an additional ¥1,000, and the government matches an additional ¥1,000. These added together constitutes the worker's social insurance account, which totals ¥2,000. However, because the social insurance fund is not managed well, when it comes to withdrawing the funds for retirement, only ¥1,500 is available. Obviously, if the whole ¥10,000 could go to the worker, the worker's best choice would be to not participate in the program and instead manage his own money. However, because the government now deducts ¥1,000, if the worker does not participate in the program, all of this money is lost. If he participates, he pays an additional ¥1,000 to receive ¥1,500, so participating in the program is better than not. This is a Prisoner's Dilemma game designed by the government for the citizenry causing every worker to have no choice but to "voluntarily" participate in social insurance. Of course, in reality, when the insurance funds managed by the government cannot make the necessary payments, governments often rely on inflation or increased taxes to make up for losses, instead of reducing retirement payments. However, printing money or increasing taxes for this reason is also a Prisoner's Dilemma game designed by the government.

The previous two examples were Prisoner's Dilemma games created for shareholders and the citizenry, respectively, by enterprise managers and government via systemic design, both of which are unfortunate. Luckily, society can also escape the Prisoner's Dilemma by means of ownership allocation and hierarchical organization design. Consider the Prisoner's Dilemma problem of team production shown in Figure 2.12.

In this example, if Player A and Player B both choose to work hard, each would receive a payoff of 6, which is the Pareto optimum. However, because of the

Player B

	Work hard	Shirk
Work hard	6, 6	0, 8
Shirk	8, 0	2, 2

Player A

Figure 2.12 The Prisoner's Dilemma Problem in Team Production

Employee

	Work hard	Shirk
Work hard	6, 6	4, 4
Shirk	2, 6	2, 2

Owner

Figure 2.13 Ownership Resolving the Prisoner's Dilemma

Prisoner's Dilemma problem, each person's dominant strategy is to shirk, so this game's Nash equilibrium is both people shirk. The outcome is each person only receives 2. How can the laziness problem in team production be solved? In 1972, two American economists, Armen A. Alchian and Harold Demsetz, published *Production, Information Costs, and Economic Organization* in *American Economic Review*. Their proposed resolution was to make one person an owner and the other person an employee, then have the former supervise the latter. Originally, the participants in this organization, Player A and Player B, were equal members, so both shirked. Now ownership rights entitle Player A to monitor Player B and such reward Player B according to his performance. If Player B does not shirk, he will receive a utility of 6, but if he shirks, he can only receive a utility of 4. In this way, Player B will have an incentive to work hard. At this point, another issue that arises is why would Player A have an incentive to supervise Player B? In other words, who monitors the monitor? We simply make Player A owner of the enterprise so that surplus value created by Player B belongs to Player A. This way, if Player A and Player B both work hard, each person will receive 6. If Player B works hard and Player A shirks, then Player A only receives 2. If Player B shirks and Player A's supervision is negligent, then Player A can only receive 2 (as shown in Figure 2.13). In this way, Player A and Player B both have an incentive to work hard. The significance of this is that ownership rights resolved the Prisoner's Dilemma issue in team production.

4.3 The Nash equilibrium in mixed strategies

In the previous examples, each player's optimal action is certain. However, in some games, players' optimal choice is not a certain action or strategy. In the Finger Guessing Game shown in Figure 2.14, each person has four choices (tiger, chicken, bug, and pole). If a person always chooses the same subterfuge (such as tiger), he will lose.

There is no the above-defined Nash equilibrium in this game. For example, if you know the opponent will play tiger, your best option is to play pole. However, if the opponent knows you will play pole, his best option is to play bug. If you know the opponent will play bug, your best option is to play chicken. If the opponent knows you will play chicken, his best option is to play tiger. This cycle continues on, so there is no previously discussed Nash equilibrium outcome.[19]

Now we will introduce another concept: The mixed strategy Nash equilibrium. In the previously discussed Nash equilibrium referred to a pure strategy Nash equilibrium, meaning a certain choice for a specific strategy. If two strategies are both optimal, it is a (pure strategy) Nash equilibrium. Obviously, there is no pure strategy Nash equilibrium in the Figure 2.14 example. In contrast with pure strategy, mixed strategy refers to players choosing an action based on probability. In the Finger Guessing Game, each player's optimal choice is to choose at random so that the opponent has no way of predicting the play. It is easy to see that in this example, each person's optimal choice is to select tiger, chicken, bug, or pole with a one-fourth probability. This constitutes a mixed strategy Nash equilibrium with an average payoff of zero.

Now, we will examine the application of the mixed strategy Nash equilibrium: The Supervision Game in which the worker chooses to shirk or not and the boss chooses to supervise or not. This is shown in Figure 2.15. If the worker shirks and the boss supervises, the boss receives 1 and the worker loses 1. If the worker shirks and the boss does not supervise, the worker earns 3 and the boss loses 2. If the worker does not shirk, and the boss supervises, then when the boss discovers that the worker has not shirked, he must give a reward, so the boss loses 1 and the worker earns 2. If the worker does not shirk and the boss also does not supervise, then both receive 2.[20]

		Player B			
		Tiger	Chicken	Bug	Pole
	Tiger	0, 0	1, −1	0, 0	−1, 1
	Chicken	−1, 1	0, 0	1, −1	0, 0
Player A	Bug	0, 0	−1, 1	0, 0	1, −1
	Pole	1, −1	0, 0	−1, 1	0, 0

Figure 2.14 The Finger Guessing Game

		Worker	
		Shirk	Does not shirk
Boss	Supervise	1, −1	−1, 2
	Does not supervise	−2, 3	2, 2

Figure 2.15 The Supervision Game

In this example, the employee not shirking and the boss not supervising is best (because the total gain is highest), but this is not a Nash equilibrium. We can see that if the employee does not shirk, the boss should not supervise. However, if the employee knows the boss will not supervise, the employee's optimal choice should be to shirk. If the boss knows that the employee will shirk, he should supervise. If the employee knows the boss will supervise, he certainly will not shirk. If the boss knows the employee will not shirk, then it is again best for him to not supervise. This creates a cycle, so there is no pure strategy Nash equilibrium.

The optimal strategy for players in this game is to randomly select various strategies. Assume that the boss believes the employee will shirk at a rate of P, so the probability of not shirking is $1 - P$. From the bosses' perspective, the expected gain from supervision is:

$$1 \times P + (-1) \times (1 - P) = 2P - 1;$$

If he does not supervise, his expected gain is:

$$(-2) \times P + 2 \times (1 - P) = 2 - 4P$$

From the employee's perspective, the employee hopes the boss will not predict if he chooses to shirk or not, meaning there must be no difference between supervising or not:

$$2P - 1 = 2 - 4P$$

Thus, $P = 1/2$. At that point, the employee chooses to shirk or not at a 0.5 probability, so the boss supervising or not is the same.

Assume that the boss chooses to supervise with probability Q and chooses to not supervise with probability $1 - Q$. At this point, from the employee's perspective, the expected gain from shirking is:

$$(-1) \times Q + 3 \times (1 - Q) = 3 - 4Q$$

The expected gain from not shirking is:

$$2 \times Q + 2 \times (1 - Q) = 2$$

To make there be no difference between these two choices, they must be equal, thus:

$$3 - 4Q = 2$$

This means that the probability of the boss supervising is 0.25 and of the boss not supervising is 0.75.

Therefore, the mixed strategy Nash equilibrium is: The employee shirks at a 0.50 probability and does not shirk at a 0.50 probability; the boss supervises at a 0.25 probability and does not supervise at a 0.75 probability.

If the probability of the employee shirking is less than 0.50, then the expected gain from the boss not supervising is greater than supervising, so the optimal choice should be to not supervise. If the probability of the employee shirking is greater than 0.50, then the boss should supervise. Similarly, for the employee, if the probability of the boss supervising is less than 0.25, he should choose to shirk, but if the probability of the boss supervising is greater than 0.25, then he will choose to not shirk.

Tax evasion is very common in today's society. Is the probability of high-profit enterprises evading taxes higher than low-profit enterprises? You may believe that tax evasion is more probable for higher profits because there is greater benefit. However, this judgment is incorrect because you overlooked the response of the tax authority. Because higher penalties can be charged on high-profit enterprises that evade taxes, the tax authority's response is to supervise high-profit enterprises to a greater degree. The equilibrium outcome is that large enterprises do not dare to evade taxes, only small enterprises do.

After introducing the mixed strategy, the pure strategy Nash equilibrium could also be called the (degenerated) mixed strategy Nash equilibrium.[21] With thus defined concept, Nash (1951) proved that in every finite game, at least one Nash equilibrium exists, whether it is pure strategy or mixed strategy. Generally speaking, Nash equilibriums are odd numbers. If two pure strategy Nash equilibriums exist in a game, then a third mixed strategy Nash equilibrium certainly exists. We will now turn to multiple Nash equilibria, which have very important implications for us to understand institutions and culture.

Notes

1 For a more precise and technical definition of the basic concepts of Game Theory, see Weiying Zhang's, *Bóyìlùn yǔ Xìnxī Jīngjìxué* [*Game Theory and Information Economics*]. Shanghai: Shanghai People's Publishing House, 1996.

2 For convenience, we generally use "he" to refer to all players, but there is no gender significance.

3 As we mentioned in Chapter 1, economist Kenneth Arrow made the initial contributions to this issue. In his 1951 book *Social Choice and Individual Value*, he proposed the "Impossibility Theorem". It states that under circumstances in which each person has certain preferences for the possible choices, it is impossible to find a choice that

aligns with everyone's preferences by means of a vote. This conclusion has had a deep impact on welfare economics and political economy.

4 The "Prisoner's Dilemma" is a basic issue faced by social cooperation. Almost all of Game Theory developed from this. It could be said that we must continuously touch upon it. The cooperation problem in the previous chapter was a Prisoner's Dilemma. Most Prisoner's Dilemmas in reality are multi-person games, but for simplicity, we will use two-person games as examples. Our conclusion is suitable for multi-person games.

5 In a bigger game, we must consider the police's choice, but in this small game, we will not consider the police, instead we will see them as the people that make or enforce the rules.

6 Directly representing prison time as the "payoff" is, of course, a simplification. In reality, there is not a linear relationship between prison time and utility. For example, the pain of two years in prison is not twice the pain of one year in prison. However, this point does not impact our conclusion.

7 For the sequence of events and related analysis, see *Liaowang Magazine*, 2000, Volume 27.

8 As we will see in Chapter 9, advertisements can transmit product quality signals. Our discussion here excludes this type of situation.

9 The so-called "the Tragedy of the commons" is a classic example of the public goods (Hardin, 1968). Public economics, a branch of economics, systematically researches this issue. In 2009, Indiana University Professor Elinor Ostrom received the Nobel Prize in Economic Sciences for her analysis on issues of public goods. Here key viewpoints can be seen in her representative work *Governance of the Commons* (1990).

10 This condition means that both people choosing to cooperate is a Kaldor-Hicks optimum, thus it maximizes social wealth. Reference Chapter 1, Section 3.

11 Of course, significant technological improvement comes from small enterprises. This phenomenon stands out in "creative destruction" because the "lock-in effect" exists for big enterprises that are not willing to change.

12 The are many classic examples of the private production of public goods, such as Coase's (1974) work on lighthouses and Klein's (1990) research on early American toll roads.

13 See Heap and Varoufakis (1995), page 44.

14 This famous story is from *Records of the Grand Historian* (*Shiji* in Chinese), Volume 65, written around 94 BC by the Han dynasty official Sima Qian. For its English translation, see Watson (1961).

15 Note that not everyone in a game has the same number of choices. Sometimes one player may have three types and another has four types, but in this example both players have four choices.

16 Given the other player's choice, each player's optimal response is underlined. This is the same for each game below.

17 This is a type of consistently aligned beliefs (abbreviated as CAB). We must differentiate between a game's two types of beliefs: Consistently aligned beliefs and internally consistent beliefs. The former requires that each player's expectations of the other player's actions are correct. In the latter, players have a rational reason to belief the other player will make a certain decision. According to consistently aligned beliefs, if two rational people have the same information, they will come to the same conclusions. This is the significance of 2005 Nobel Prize in Economics laureate Robert Aumann's statement that "rational agents cannot agree to disagree". See Aumann (1976a) or Heap and Varoufakis (1995, Chapter 2, Section 2.4).

18 The Nash equilibrium is an equilibrium concept proposed by John Nash in 1951.

19 There are multiple games like this. One example is ping pong, which emphasizes changes in placement. Players want to avoid letting their opponent know the next placement.

20 The Supervision Game can also describe the game between the tax authority and the tax payers, because taxpayers can either evade taxes or not, and the tax authority can either audit or not.

21 For example, when the probability of choosing to shirk $P = 1$ and the probability of choosing to not shirk $P = 0$, we generalize it.

3 Multiple equilibriums, institutions, and cultures

The reason it is difficult to predict other's actions is not because of a lack of a Nash equilibrium in a game, but instead is because there are too many Nash equilibriums. If a game has multiple Nash equilibriums, by only assuming that players are rational and rationality is the common knowledge of all players, we still cannot predict which Nash equilibrium will appear. We might not even be able to predict whether or not a Nash equilibrium will appear. If different players predict different Nash equilibriums will appear, then no Nash equilibrium will actually appear.

When multiple equilibriums exist, whether or not players can coordinate aligned expectations is key to the appearance of a Nash equilibrium. In reality, players will predict other's behavior according to commonly behavioral practices, and from this make their own choices. Common backgrounds, culture, behavioral norms, and even nature endow people with certain natural characteristics that assist people achieved aligned expectations. For this reason, under many circumstances, some specific Nash equilibrium will appear as a "focal point equilibrium".

If a Pareto efficiency disparity exists between different Nash equilibriums, then the Pareto equilibrium that benefits everyone might appear through no-cost or low-cost communications.

Laws and social norms coordinate expectations and thus are important tools for the realization of Nash equilibriums. Even if laws and social norms do not change the room for choice or payoff matrix for people in a game, a specific Nash equilibrium could be coordinated through changing people's expectations. Actually, this type of law and social norm itself is a Nash equilibrium, so it is consciously respected.

Culture is the outcome of long-term games. Conflicts between different cultures are actually conflicts between different rules of the game. There are three ways to resolve these conflicts: First, one rule can replace other rules. Second, a new rule can be established. Third, a rule for coordinating rules can be established.

The "lock-in effect" and "path dependency" exist in technological evolution and social development. Even if a certain technology or systematic arrangement is not Pareto optimal but is a Nash equilibrium, it is very difficult to change it. The "lock-in effect" and "path dependency" are often used to prove "market failure", but empirical studies and observations have shown that the seriousness of the problem has been exaggerated. In the short term, the "lock-in effect" exists. However, over the long term, with a sufficient degree of competition, the Pareto optimal equilibrium is more likely to appear. The failure of the planned economy system is an example.

Section one: the multiple equilibriums problem

Once, I conducted an experiment in my class. I randomly choose one male and one female student to participate in a number selection game. They each chose five numbers between 1 and 10. If they both chose different numbers, then their payoff is ¥50 each. But, if they chose any of the same numbers, then they both get nothing. They chose at the same time, and could not communicate. This experiment was repeated three times, but the students never collected ¥100 from me. The results of the experiment are below (Figure 3.1).

It is easy to see that the reason they never won ¥100 from me is that their three choices never formed a Nash equilibrium. However, they failed not for lack of a Nash equilibrium in this game. On the contrary, the main reason was that this game had too many Nash equilibriums. Given that the female student chooses 1, 2, 3, 4, and 5, then the male student choosing 6, 7, 8, 9, and 10 will form a Nash equilibrium. For the same reason, when the female student chooses 6, 7, 8, 9, and 10 and the male student chooses 1, 2, 3, 4, and 5 or the female student chooses 1, 3, 5, 7, and 9 and the male student chooses 2, 4, 6, 8, and 10 all of these choices are Nash equilibrium. Similarly, there are many other Nash equilibriums in this game.[1]

In real life, we frequently come across these situations. It is hard for us to predict which Nash equilibrium will manifest when there are so many possible equilibriums. This is the multiple equilibrium problem in Game Theory.[2] Next, we will discuss five classic types of multiple equilibrium games: product standardization, traffic, dating, resource disputes, and pie-sharing. Based on the analysis of these five games, we can learn how to coordinate expectations within a system and culture in order to resolve the multiple equilibrium problem.

1.1 Product standardization

Many products have compatibility issues and need to comply with certain product standards. If there are many different standards, usability will be limited, or the product may even be unusable. For example, the electrical outlets in China are

	The female student's selection	The male student's selection
First time	1, 3, 5, 7, 9	6, 7, 8, 9, 10
Second time	1, 2, 3, 4, 5	2, 4, 6, 8, 10
Third time	1, 2, 3, 4, 5	2, 4, 6, 8, 10

Figure 3.1 The Outcomes of Student Selections

Firm B

		3.5 inch	5.25 inch
	3.5 inch	8, 8	3, 2
Firm A			
	5.25 inch	2, 3	6, 6

Figure 3.2 The Product Standards Game

different from those in Europe, so when people travel, they must take converters with them. Similarly, if you buy an electronic device in Japan, the product may be fried when it is plugged into a Chinese outlet. The standard voltage in Japan is 110 volts, but 220 volts in China. This is a product standardization problem.

Floppy disks were once an important part of a computer's external hardware used for mobile storage of small files. There used to be two types of floppy disks: A 5.25 inch floppy disk with less storage space and a 3.5 inch floppy disk with more storage space.[3] Imagine there are two firms that produce computers. Each firm could choose to install different floppy disk drives in the computers they produce. The possible outcome of their choices is shown in Figure 3.2.

If both firms produce computers with 5.25-inch floppy disk drives, then they both earn a profit of 6 units. If both firms choose 3.5-inch floppy disk drives, then they both earn 8 units of profit. If they chose different floppy disk drives, then the firm that chose the 3.25-inch floppy disk drive will have a profit of 3 units and the one that chose the 5.25-inch floppy disk drive will have a profit of 2 units. Both companies want to produce computers with the same floppy disk, because there will not be any compatibility issues if all the computers accept the same floppy disks. This will be more convenient for the customers, and they will be more willing to buy new computers, therefore increasing the profits of both companies.

Two Nash equilibriums exist in this game. The first is both firms producing with 5.25-inch floppy disk drives, and the second is both firms producing with 3.5-inch floppy disk drives.[4] However, only one of these two Nash equilibriums is a Pareto optimum. The Pareto optimum one is both firms produce computers with 3.5-inch floppy disk drives. The reason is that when both firms transition from producing computers with 5.25-inch floppy disk drives to producing computers with 3.5 inch floppy disk drives, profits increase by 2 units. This equilibrium is beneficial to everyone, so players can coordinate expectations relatively easily.

1.2 Traffic games

Traffic issues are issues people face daily. We discussed this previously in Chapter 1, but for convenience, we will describe it once more. Two pedestrians or vehicles are traveling towards each other. They have two options: Keep left or keep right. The possible outcomes of their choices are displayed in Figure 3.3.

If Player A and Player B both keep to the left, they can both pass and gain one unit of utility, and the same happens if they both keep to the right. If they choose different sides, they will run into each other and both lose one unit of utility. Two Nash equilibriums exist in this game: Both keep left or both keep right. However, the payoff for each player is the same in both Nash equilibriums, so neither player has a serious preference for either one. Therefore, even though the multiple equilibrium problem exists in this game, a conflict of interest does not exist between players. Coordination between players is relatively easy.

1.3 Dating games

A couple goes on a weekend date with the option to watch a ballet performance or a soccer match. The possible outcome of their choices is shown in Figure 3.4.

If both choose to go to the ballet, then the boyfriend will gain one unit of utility and the girlfriend with gain two units of utility. If they both go to the soccer match, then the boyfriend will gain two units of utility and the girlfriend will gain one unit of utility. If they choose to go to different events, then they will both gain zero utility. In this game, both people want to be together, so they have common interests, but there is also a certain conflict because the man prefers watching soccer and the woman prefers watching ballet. This game also has two Nash equilibriums: Both watch soccer or both watch ballet. However, both parties have a preference for different Nash equilibriums, so coordination is not as easy as in the traffic Game.

	Player B	
	Keep left	Keep right
Player A — Keep left	1, 1	−1, −1
Player A — Keep right	−1, −1	1, 1

Figure 3.3 The Transportation Game

	Girlfriend	
	A ballet	A soccer match
Boyfriend — A ballet	1, 2	0, 0
Boyfriend — A soccer match	0, 0	2, 1

Figure 3.4 The Dating Game

| | Player B | |
	Hawk	Dove
Player A Hawk	−1, −1	<u>10</u>, <u>0</u>
Dove	<u>0</u>, <u>10</u>	5, 5

Figure 3.5 The Resource Dispute Game

1.4 Resource dispute games

The resource dispute game is two people competing for the same limited resource. This resource could be territory, property, markets, or leadership in international relationships. Each person has two choices: Be a "hawk", meaning aggressive and uncompromising, or a "dove", meaning gentle and compromising. The basic structure of this game is shown in Figure 3.5.

If one party chooses to be aggressive and the other party chooses to compromise, the aggressive party's payoff will be 10 and the compromiser's payoff will be zero. If both parties choose to be aggressive, the payoff for both will be −1. If both parties compromise, the payoff for both will be 5.

This game has two Nash equilibriums: One party chooses to be aggressive and the other party chooses to compromise. In other words, if the other party is expected to choose the hawk strategy, your own optimal choice is the dove strategy. If the other party is expected to choose the dove strategy, your own optimal choice is the hawk strategy. Obviously, a serious conflict of interest exists because different Nash equilibriums represent different lose-win situations. Each party hopes to be the winner. For this reason, the outcome is often that both sides lose (meaning both choose to be "hawks"), instead of the Nash equilibrium (meaning once party chooses to be a "hawk" and the other party chooses to be a "dove").

1.5 The pie-splitting problem

Imagine two people splitting one unit of pie by each stating the share they want. If the sum of their requirements is equal to or less than one, each person receives the portion they requested. If the sum of their requirements is greater than one, both of them receive nothing. In this game, as long is the sum of their requirements equal one, it must be a Nash equilibrium. For example, given that the other party requests a share of 0.9, then your own optimal choice is 0.1. Given the other party requests 0.1, your own optimal choice is 0.9. In Figure 3.6, $x[1]$ represents the share requested by the first person and $x[2]$ represents the share requested by the second person. All points on the line where $x[1] + x[2] = 1$ are a Nash equilibrium. However, all points above or below this line are not Nash equilibriums.

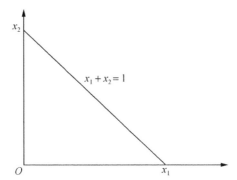

Figure 3.6 The Pie-Sharing Game

For example, both people requesting 0.4 is not a Nash equilibrium because when the first person requests 0.4, the second person's optimal choice is 0.6, not 0.4.

In other words, an infinite number of Nash equilibriums exist in this game. Each different Nash equilibrium represents a different allocation of interests, and players' interests are completely opposed. When one person's share of the pie increases, the other person's share must decrease by an equal amount to the other person's increase in share. Despite this, compared to the resource dispute game, this game includes certain relatively fair Nash equilibriums, such as both people choosing 0.5 or one person choosing 0.45 and the other person choosing 0.55. For this reason, in reality, this type of relatively fair Nash equilibrium is more likely to appear.

Section two: the focal point equilibrium and equilibrium selection

If multiple Nash equilibriums exist in a game, people's behavior cannot be predicted by solely relying on rationality. At this point, the ways in which people coordinate their own expectations to form expectation alignment are the key to predicting people's behavior in a game.

Coordinating people's expectations must rely on certain specific factors, such as social norms and laws. Even though game theorists and economists have had great success using abstract numbers and models to simulate people's interactive behavior, there are certain things that cannot be quantified, such as culture, education, and experience. These things may be the key factor in coordinating people's expectations. Therefore, when we predict people's behavior, we must incorporate certain unquantifiable factors into the abstract model.

I have deep personal experiences related to this. Three years ago, during a class on Game Theory, I did an experiment similar to pie-sharing. I pulled out ¥100 and had two classmates each write the amount they wanted. If the sum of both requirements were less than or equal to ¥100, then they would each receive the requested amount. If it was greater than ¥100, then neither would get anything.

One classmate wrote ¥90 and the other wrote ¥50, so neither of them got anything. The first impression was that the first classmate was too greedy. However, the opposite was actually true, because he did not want an instructor like me to have to pay out ¥100, so he purposely requested a high amount in order for a Nash equilibrium to not appear. However, he misunderstood me. My goal for teaching was not to save ¥100, instead it was to use a specific example to allow everybody to better understand the theory. From this simple example, we can see that people's actual behavior is extremely complex. Without considering specific examples, we will often not be able to correctly predict people's behavior. This example also proves that sometimes it is unclear which people are included as players in the game. I did this experiment imagining the game was between the two classmates, but the first classmate included me, the instructor, as a player when making a decision.

2.1 Focal point equilibriums

Introducing specific factors to predict the outcome of multiple equilibrium games was a breakthrough made by Thomas Schelling, the 2005 Nobel Memorial Prize in Economic Sciences Laureate. His 1960 book titled *The Strategy of Conflict* proposed the important concept of focal points.[5] The focal point equilibrium refers to the equilibrium that people expect to be the most likely to occur among multiple Nash equilibriums. The reason it will occur most easily is because it aligns with the behavior that the average person is accustomed to and is thus the easiest to predict. Schelling believed that when game theorists utilize game models to study social issues and people's behavior, they often neglect certain important factors, such as culture and environment. These factors often play a major role in people's actual decisions. Therefore, when multiple equilibriums exist in a game, we must reconsider the factors that coordinate people's expectations. From this, we can more accurately predict people's behavior.

In Section 3.1's numbers game, the two classmates actually had many choices. However, in the experiment, both classmates' choices in the three rounds were (1, 2, 3, 4, 5) and (6, 7, 8, 9, 10) or (1, 3, 5, 7, 9) and (2, 4, 6, 8, 10). Neither of them chose an irregular order of numbers like (1, 2, 8, 9, 10). The reason is that in this game, each party hopes the other will correctly guess their own choice, and most people when choosing numbers are accustomed to choosing odd numbers, even numbers, or numbers in order. When you are making your own choice, you will predict that the other party will most likely choose (1, 2, 3, 4, 5), (6, 7, 8, 9, 10), (1, 3, 5, 7, 9), or (2, 4, 6, 8, 10) because you know the other party will also expect you to make a similar choice. The reason the other party expects you to make this kind of choice is because he knows you will predict he will make the same choice. Therefore, even though a Nash equilibrium did not appear in our experiment, the choices they made were still the choices to most likely occur in the Nash equilibrium. If a person's thought process is relatively odd and chooses a number sequence like (1, 3, 7, 8, 9), then it would be more difficult for the other party to predict his behavior, so it would be very hard to form a Nash equilibrium. Further, we can expect that if we allow the experiment to continue, a Nash equilibrium would eventually appear. Additionally, as soon as the Nash equilibrium appears at some point, then both parties would repeat that Nash equilibrium choice when the experiment continued. They would not make the same mistake again. This is actually the process that human behaviors form customs.

In the classroom experiments of the number game, a Nash equilibrium occurred by the third round in most cases. Occasionally it appeared in the second round, and even rarely, it appeared in the first round. In one interesting case, one student in the first round chose all random numbers while the other student chose a clear pattern. In the second round, the first student matched the second student's initial pattern and a Nash equilibrium appeared. When I asked the first student about his change from random numbers to a number pattern, he said that he chose randomly at first so that he could see the other student's pattern, then match that pattern in the second round. This may have been an intelligent method, but if the other player had the same thought process, he would also choose random numbers in the first round. It would be even harder for a Nash equilibrium to appear. Therefore, generally speaking, choosing a number pattern is the choice most likely to lead to a Nash equilibrium.

Another example would be the City Game. Imagine two players are to list five cities. If neither list has the same city on it, both players win. If the same city appears on both lists, both players lose. Further, the rules state Player A's list must include Beijing and Player B's list must include Shanghai. We can imagine that Tianjin, Harbin, Dalian, and Shijiazhuang are more likely to appear on Player A's list and Hangzhou, Nanjing, Suzhou, and Ningbo are more likely to appear on Player B's list. This actually is a focal point equilibrium.

2.2 The Pareto criterion

Let us return to the product standardization issue. Two Nash equilibriums exist in this game. If the two firms have the opportunity to communicate, obviously they will choose to produce computers with 3.5-inch floppy disk drives. Because this benefits both parties, this equilibrium is a Pareto optimum. Generally speaking, when only one Nash equilibrium is a Pareto optimum among multiple Nash equilibriums, coordination is relatively easy.

At this point, players' communication is the so-called "cheap talk".[6] Cheap talk refers to neither party lying to the other while communicating. In our example using number selection, if we allowed the two classmates to communicate, then the Nash equilibrium would naturally be achieved. In other words, no-cost communication between players is an important means for the coordination of expectations to achieve the Nash equilibrium.

However, no-cost communication is only effective when serious conflicts of interest do not exist between players. When there are serious conflicts of interest between players, both parties are driven to implement dishonest strategic communication, or they cannot reach alignment on some Nash equilibrium. In the Resource Dispute Game, both Nash equilibriums are Pareto optimal, and neither one is more Pareto optimal than the other. Even if both parties could communicate beforehand, neither party would accept the unfavorable Nash equilibrium from their perspective. You may believe that negotiations could lead to both parties choosing "dove" so that each party receives a payoff of 5 units. However, this good agreement is not a Nash equilibrium, so no one will consciously respect it. In other words, communicating information between players cannot coordinate a specific Nash equilibrium.

We will analyze a game similar to product standardization. The payoff structure is shown in Figure 3.7.

In this game, there are two Nash equilibriums. The first is Player R chooses R_1 and Player C chooses C_1. The second is Player R chooses R_2 and Player C chooses C_2. Equilibrium (R_1, C_1) is the Pareto optimum because each person receives 9, which is better than the 7 each person receives under equilibrium (R_2, C_2). However, if now Player C tells Player R he will choose C_1, will Player R trust Player C and then choose R_1?

Player R may not trust Player C will choose R_1. The reason is that regardless if Player C chooses C_1 or C_2, he has an incentive to tell Player R he will choose C_1 to mislead Player R into choosing R_1. If Player R chooses R_1, then Player C will have a payoff of 9 for choosing C_1 and a payoff of 8 for choosing C_2. There is not much of a difference. However, when Player C chooses C_1, Player R's payoff is 9, but when Player C chooses C_2, then Player R's payoff is 0. Therefore, if Player R believes Player C will choose C_1 and then chooses R_1, he has a big risk of loss. Even if Player C has an incentive to choose C_1, but there is a certain possibility of Player C making a mistake and choosing C_2 or is a bit envious, then Player R should not trust Player C and choose R_2 to be safer. From this, we can see that although a Nash equilibrium exists that is beneficial to both parties in the game above, because of the existence of risk, even with free communication, people may not choose the Pareto optimal equilibrium.

In summary, when a game has multiple equilibriums, the Pareto criterion may aid in the coordination of people's expectations, but the role of the Pareto criterion is related to communication and risk factors. If players can communicate at no cost and the risk of choices is small, the Pareto criterion can effectively coordinate people's expectations. Otherwise, it is difficult for the Pareto criterion to play the role of the focal point.

| | | C | |
		C_1	C_2
R	R_1	9, 9	0, 8
	R_2	8, 0	7, 7

Figure 3.7 Risk-Dominated Coordination

Section three: the coordination function of laws and social norms

Multiple Nash equilibriums often exist in social games. In many circumstances, there are no advantages or disadvantages between the multiple Nash equilibriums. Even if there were, it is difficult to communicate at no cost to choose a specific Nash equilibrium. This created the need for institutions and cultures. An important function of social systems and social norms (such as culture and customs) is to coordinate people's expectations to form a certain Nash equilibrium.[7]

Social norms and laws, which are both norms, are manifestations of a system that in essence is rules to coordinate people's behavior. It facilitates a specific social order and social common sense to maintain the mainstream concept of values. Social norms were gradually formed through people's long-term interactions and are commonly accepted standards of behavior. Laws are behavioral rules established by a legislative body. Of course, many laws evolved from customs, not the intentions of legislators. However, regardless if something is a law or a social norm, one of the main functions is to coordinate expectations so that people can select a specific Nash equilibrium among multiple equilibriums.

3.1 The evolution of traffic rules

Two Nash equilibriums existed in the Traffic Game in Section 1.2. They were to either keep to the left or keep to the right. In reality, whether people keep to the right or keep to the left must be coordinated, and coordination is finalized through traffic rules. In the Traffic Game example, there is no difference between the two Nash equilibriums, so the role of traffic rules is primarily to coordinate expectations and prevent an accident.

Historically, many traffic rules did not start as laws, but instead evolved over the long term.[8] In early continental Europe, norms of the road were extremely localized. Some localities kept to the left and others kept to the right. Only with the increase in roads and inter-regional interaction, local customs gradually evolved into territorial norms. Later, they became national norms and even global norms.

Until the nineteenth century, rules of the road were respected because they were norms, not because they were traffic laws. Continental Europe's rules on keeping to the right started in France, and this was caused by chance. Before the French Revolution, the nobility's carriages kept to the left. When the poor saw their carriages, they stood on the right side of the road. Therefore, at the time of the revolution, keeping to the left was associated with "privileged classes", whereas keeping to the right was considered to represent "democracy". As a symbol of the revolution, all carriages keeping to the right became a legal requirement. With Napoleon's conquest of Continental Europe, he brought French rules to other countries, including keeping to the right. Of course, geographically this transformation gradually occurred from west to east. For example, Portugal, which shares a border with right-hand-driving Spain, did not transition until after World War I. Austria transitioned one province at a time from west to east. Hungary, Czechoslovakia, and Germany did not transition until after World War II. Sweden did not transition until a legal declaration in 1967.[9]

Why did Sweden change the rules so late? Why did they not maintain the tradition? Why did the law replace the social norm? This was caused by Continental European integration. As the European Community expanded, different national laws began to cause conflict and thus had to give way to common rules. Economic globalization is causing a convergence of rules. Laws cause rules to change faster. These same circumstances may happen to Great Britain. Even today, Great Britain still drives on the left. When Great Britain and Continental Europe were separated by the sea, British vehicles could not directly drive to Continental Europe, so there were no issues using different rules (or equilibriums). This would not lead to accidents. However, with the opening of the Chunnel, people can drive to the continent, which has caused a coordination problem for traffic rules. In other words, a game that originally would not have occurred has now occurred. Naturally, there will be expectation coordination and rule selection problems.

Another interesting example is the evolution of units of weight and measure. The current international standard unit of measure is the metric system (a system of units in increments of ten). This system also started in the early period of the French Revolution. Before the French Revolution, each European country had its own system of measurement. Even though some countries (such as Russia and Spain) had already recognized the advantages of unified weights and measures between trade partners, it was opposed by the vested interests that benefited from diverse units of weight and measure. This was especially prominent in France. In the early period of the revolution, the leaders of the National Constituent Assembly decided to introduce a completely new system of measurement based on logic and natural phenomenon, instead of standardizing the units of measure that currently existed. In the beginning, France attempted to implement this new system of common units of measure with other countries, but there was little interest. In 1790, Thomas Jefferson, the primary drafter of the American Declaration of Independence, submitted a plan on implementation of the metric system in the United States to the Congress, but it was not implemented. France formally transitioned to the metric system in 1799 (starting with Paris and then other provinces). European countries conquered during the Napoleon Era also accepted the metric system. After the Vienna Congress in 1815, France lost previously conquered territories. Some countries resurrected their original systems of measurement, while others (such as Baden) revised the metric system, but France maintained her metric system. In 1817, Holland re-introduced the metric system, but used the pre-revolutionary name. Certain Germanic countries also implemented a similar system. In 1852, the German Customs Union decided to implement a variant of the metric system for interstate trade. In 1872, the newly established German Empire made the metric system the official system of weight and measure. The unified Italian Kingdom also implemented the metric system. By the end of 1872, the only European countries that had not implemented the metric system were Russia and Great Britain. By 1875, two-thirds of Europe's population and close to half of the world's population used the metric system. In 1864, Great Britain allowed the metric system to be used in trade activities, and it later gradually expanded to other areas. Today, America is the only industrialized country to not use the metric system. However, in 1866, the U.S. Congress authorized the use of the metric system. In the later part of the 1920s, many American social groups lobbied the U.S. Congress to implement the metric system in America, but the tradition of using the imperial system in American society is very strong. Even today, the metric system is only used in scientific, military, and some industrial applications. Americans still use imperial units of measurement in everyday life.[10]

3.2 Conflicts and coordination between rules

Let us imagine the border between Hong Kong (driving on the left) and Shenzhen (driving on the right) is eliminated. A Hong Konger gets lost while driving and becomes unclear if he is in Hong Kong or Guangdong. Assume a Guangdong vehicle appears in front of the Hong Konger. Should he keep to the left or right? He may think that Mainland vehicles keep to the right, so he should also keep to the right. However, the Guangdongese may think that Hong Kong vehicles keep to the left, so he should also keep to the left. Alternatively, the Hong Konger may think he should keep to the left and the Guangdongese may think he should keep to the right. Regardless of the circumstances, as long as expectations are not aligned, there will be a collision.

Cultural conflicts, regardless if they are between organizations or nations, are for the most part nothing but conflicts on rules of the game, meaning different social norms and laws. In Game Theory terminology, it is an equilibrium-selection problem. Ten years ago, the merger of Peking University and Beijing Medical University caused multiple conflicts. Many things that were considered normal at Peking University were considered abnormal at Beijing Medical University, and vice versa. It was similar to the Traffic Game in that people from Peking University were accustomed to driving on the left and people from Beijing Medical University were accustomed to driving on the right, so it was difficult for their merger to not cause an "accident". Similar issues occur in international trade. When Americans and Japanese negotiate, Japanese often say, "Hai". When Americans hear this, they mistakenly believe the Japanese person agrees, whereas Japanese say this only to represent understanding, not agreement. Therefore, Americans often believe Japanese to be backtrackers.

More generally, when people from societies with different laws and social norms interact, if each person acts according to their own rules, then conflicts are unavoidable. At this point, there are three methods to resolve the conflict. One method is to use one rule to replace another rule so that one group of people changes their behavioral norms to adapt to the other group, which is so-called "integration". The previously discussed evolution of Continental European traffic rules is an example. Another means is to establish a completely new rule. Chinese and Germans communicate using English, not Chinese or German.[11] The third method is to establish rules for coordinating rules.

In reality, which method should be used to resolve conflicts depend on specific conditions, especially the characteristics of the behavior governed by the rules. For example, for traffic rules, there is no third option in addition to driving on the left or driving on the right, so one group of people can only accept the rules of another group. A completely new rule cannot be established. In addition, the "network effects" of a rule (meaning that the more people follow a rule, the more valuable the rule is to each person) leads to the minority adopting the majority's rules when rules change. Occasionally, a chance matter may determine the selection of rules, such as the impact of the French Revolution on traffic rules.

Our concept of "enter the village and follow the customs" is actually a social norm that coordinates rules. Because different "villages" have different "customs", if people acted according to their own "customs", then aligned expectations would be unattainable, leading to many misunderstandings and conflicts. "Enter the village and follow the customs" means acting according to the rules of the place you are at. The English idiom "When in Rome, do as the Romans do" has the same meaning. When Hong Kongers drive in the Mainland, they should drive on the right according to the Mainland's rules. When Guangdongese drive in Hong Kong, they should drive on the left.

In law, this type of rule used to coordinate conflicts between rules is called "laws of conflict". Many rules in international private law are used to resolve this kind of equilibrium selection between different rules. For example, when a Chinese person is hit by a car in Great Britain, should the judgment be made according to British law or Chinese law? This is a similar circumstance. The reason it is called international private law is because which country's laws are utilized in civil affairs is similar to the "keeping to the left or right" problem in the Traffic Game. In the field of public law, it is not this simple. Which country's rules are utilized often involves different interests.

When choosing different rules will bring about different distributions of interests, laws and social norms will still play a big role in coordinating expectations. However, at this point, the payoff structure of the game changes. In the Traffic Game, regardless if they kept to the left or kept to the right, the interests of both parties were the same. However, as soon as different social groups with different rules interact, in many cases, regardless of which social group's rules determine behavior, the distribution of interests is no longer symmetric. At this point, even if each person hopes for unified rules, there will be a conflict of interest on the issue of which rules to unify. Each person will prefer his own rules. For example, the 3G (third-generation wireless telecommunications) issue is a case of each country hoping for a unified international standard, but each country hopes that the standards produced by its own enterprises become the international standard.

This type of circumstance is similar to the "Door Entry Game" in Figure 3.8. Two people want to enter a door, but only one person can go at a time. Each person can choose to go first or go second. If both choose to go first, neither can pass, so each person's payoff is −1. If both wait, time will be wasted and again, each person's payoff is −1. If one person chooses to go first and the other chooses to go second, both can enter. In this game, two pure strategy Nash equilibriums exist at

Player B

		Go first	Go second
	Go first	−1, −1	2, 1
Player A			
	Go second	1, 2	−1, −1

Figure 3.8 The Door Entry Game

the same time: Either Player A can go first and Player B can go second, or Player A can go second and Player B can go first. However, under the different Nash equilibriums, each person's interests are different. The payoff for the person that enters first is 2, and the payoff for the person that enters second is 1.

These two equilibriums similarly face the coordination of expectations problem. If Player A knows that Player B will go first, and Player B knows that Player A believes Player B will go first, and Player A also knows that Player B knows that Player A believes Player B will go first, then Player A's best choice is to go second. Alternatively, if Player A believes that Player B will go second, Player B knows that Player A believes Player B will go second, and Player A also knows that Player B knows Player A believes Player B will go second, Player A's best choice is to go first.

In this situation, even if there is a payoff disparity, each person desires a rule to coordinate their expectations; otherwise, neither party benefits. Certain social norms and legal rules are established to resolve this type of coordination of expectations. For instance, when a young person and an old person or a small child meet at a door, it is often the old person or small child that goes first and the young person that goes second. This is the significance of the "respect the old and cherish the child" social norm. Similarly, when a teacher and a student meet, it is often the student that gives way to the teacher. This is the significance of the "respect the teacher and promote education" social norm. If a male and female meet at a door, who should go first? The Western social norm is for women go first, but men go first traditionally in China. This is not to say that the West's rules are more outstanding or civilized than China's rules. For most rules, there is not an issue of one being better than another, because the overall payoff does not change. The total utility for the two people cooperating is still 3. In this circumstance, social norms are for nothing more than resolving the coordination of expectations issue, not changing the total payoff. Of course, with globalization, China has also begun to imitate the West's "ladies first" rule. Perhaps the reason is the West is more economically advanced than China. People in developing countries easily view all rules in developed countries as more "civilized" rules.

Similar considerations exist for many social norms. For example, when Chinese eat, they often utilize the "official standard" to determine seating arrangements based on rank. When an instructor eats with students, the instructor sits at the head of the table. When people of different generations eat together, the elder sits at the head of the table as a sign of respect. When a dinner party is hosted, the rules are different from when different generations eat together. When hosting a dinner party, it is now common for the most important guest to sit to the right of the host, the second most important guest to the left of the host, and so on. Even though these are purely social norms, not laws, they are also important, because otherwise there would be issues. With rules, everybody forms expectations for their place without contradictions.

3.3 *Information in coordination*

The actual function of many social norms in everyday life is to coordinate expectations. However, even with norms, information problems will still occur during implementation. For example, when the instructor and the student in the Door Entry Game meet, assuming the instructor knows the student is a student, but the student does not know the instructor is an instructor, the student may rush to enter the door. The two will bump into each other, and the instructor may be angered by the student's lack of manners.

This means that the coordination of expectations not only requires rules, but also information. At this point, society will develop another norm in order to transmit necessary information, such as different-status people wearing different clothing. Clothing can be a type of identity, telling other people your status, and thus help people coordinate expectations. Twenty years ago in China, everyone in university had to wear a university badge. Instructor's badges were red, and student's badges were white. One look would tell you who was an instructor and who was a student. Military ranks play the same role. Without military ranks, it would be difficult to coordinate actions. The types of clothes worn, the types of houses occupied, the types of carriages, and even the number of bearers was different for ancient bureaucrats for the same reason. This is the reason that clothing is more important among strangers than among acquaintances.

The objective of rules is to coordinate expectations between people so that one specific Nash equilibrium can be selected among multiple equilibriums. In order for rules to coordinate expectations, they must be stable. If rules changed frequently, and people changed behavior according to constantly changing rules, then it would be difficult to form aligned expectations.

We can explain the importance of rule stability using the previously mentioned "meeting points" at Heathrow Airport. Heathrow Airport is one of the largest airports in the world, with many international transfer flights. If you go to the airport to meet a friend and have not pre-determined a location, which part of the airport should you meet him? You could meet him at the bookstore if you believe he will go to the bookstore and he also believes you believe he will go to the bookstore. You could also meet him at the coffee shop if you believe he will go to the coffee shop and he also believes you believe he will go to the coffee shop. Overall, waiting at any location in the airport is a Nash equilibrium. Therefore, it is extremely difficult to coordinate expectations between people. For this reason, Heathrow Airport created "meeting points" to help people coordinate expectations. Now, you believe your friend will most likely go to the "meeting point", and your friend also knows that you believe he will most likely go to the "meeting point". The problem is resolved when everyone goes to the "meeting point". If Heathrow Airport frequently changed the "meeting point", then people would not know the location of the new meeting point, so the "meeting point" will no longer function to coordinate expectations. Therefore, the stability of policy is extremely important. China's policies change frequently. This has a tremendous detriment on people's expectations as it causes everyone to be at a loss.

3.4 The justness of rules

In Section 1.3's Resource Dispute Game, two Nash equilibriums existed: One party chooses to be uncompromising, and the other party chooses to be compromising. Both parties hope to achieve a Nash equilibrium, and both parties hope to be the uncompromising party at equilibrium, so a conflict exists. How can the conflict be resolved?

One simple and workable method is drawing lots. The person that draws the lucky lot chooses to be uncompromising and the other person chooses to compromise.[12] From ancient times to the present, in small family disputes and matters of national importance, drawing lots has played an important role in resolving conflicts between coordinated expectations. During the Ming Dynasty, the prime minister Sun Yangpi's use of drawing lots to resolve conflicts is a classic example. He invented a type of selection mechanism for officials. As soon as a position needed to be filled, drawing lots would choose applicants. Obviously, selecting officials via drawn lots will allow some incapable people to serve high positions and would be less effective than selecting officials based on merit. However, why did Sun Yangpi select officials by drawing lots instead of based on merit? Sun Yangpi himself was very honest and also hoped to select officials based on merit. However, during the Ming Dynasty, eunuchs were extremely powerful and bestowed special favors. Sun Yangpi dared to offend anyone but eunuchs, because at best, the eunuchs would not allow him to see the emperor, and at worst, he would lose his position. Therefore, in order to select able people and not offend the eunuchs, Sun Yangpi utilized the drawing lots method to determine who became an official.[13]

Why is drawing lots an important method for resolving conflicts? The core reason is because a system like drawing lots is just. According to Rawls's (1971) theory, a so-called just system is a system determined under the veil of ignorance. Specifically speaking, when determining rules, as long as people do not know which future position they will be in can the rules be just. When people draw lots to resolve a dispute, each person has the same opportunity to draw the lucky lot. Therefore, because in drawing lots ignorance is default, it is just. Actually, justness is not only the important reason rules play a coordinating role, it is also an important reason rules are respected. If a rule always favors a specific group of people, then the people prejudiced against the rule will violate the rule. Because

the rule is unfair, violators of the rule will not be appropriately punished. Therefore, over time, no one will respect the rule.

Section four: the perplexity of path dependency

In the previously described computer product standardization issue, there were
two Nash equilibriums: Both firms produce computers with 5.25-inch floppy
disk drives, and both firms produce computers with 3.5-inch floppy disk drives.
Assume that in the beginning, firms can only produce computers with 5.25-inch
floppy disk drives, but the technology for computers with 3.5-inch floppy disk
drives will appear later. Would the firms use the new technology? If there were
only two firms, and both firms could communicate directly, it would be easy to
come to an agreement that both of them would use the new technology. Using
the new technology is beneficial to both parties. If there are multiple firms that
produce computers, then the cost of inter-firm negotiation and coordination is
very high, so it would be difficult to come to an agreement to use the new technology. At this point, even if each firm hopes to use the new technology, because
behavior cannot be coordinated via an agreement, a very likely outcome is all
firms still use the old technology. Each firm will worry other firms will not use
the new technology, although that is disadvantageous for all firms. This is the
so-called lock-in effect. A concept related to the "lock-in effect" is "path dependency", meaning choices at the start determine future choices. For example, if
bizarre houses are built in a new neighborhood, then all future houses must be
bizarre in order to be aligned with the original houses. This is a classic example
of "path dependency".

Because the "lock-in effect" and "path dependency" exist, all of society may
be in certain Pareto inefficient states. This is especially prominent for "network
products". So-called "network products" are products whose utility for each user
increases as the number of users increases. Telephones are a classic "network
product". If you are the only person with a telephone, your telephone is worthless. Only when your relatives and friends install telephones does your telephone
have value. The value of your telephone increases as the number of relatives and
friends using telephones increases. Because network externalities exist for "network products", the market may be locked into a Nash equilibrium that is disadvantageous to everyone.

The "lock-in effect" and "path dependency" are often used to prove "market
failure".[14] Yet, in the long term, it is doubtful the market will really be "locked in"
an inefficient state. My view is perhaps the lock-in effect exists in the short term,
but over the long term the Pareto optimal equilibrium is more likely to appear.
This is the case for both technological aspects and institutional aspects. Of course,
the amount of time that determines short-term and long-term is different for each
field. This can explain why even though Microsoft's standard has dominated the
software market for a long time, with the development of technology, Apple's OS
X and Google's Android have begun to challenge Microsoft's Windows system.

This can also explain why the planned economy could exist in Eastern European countries formerly part of the Soviet Union and China for many years, but in the end these countries had to move towards market reforms. The reason is that compared to the planned economy, the market economy is the Pareto optimal equilibrium.

4.1 The Keyboard Fable

A classic example is the "Keyboard Fable" (David, 1985). The computer keyboard we use today is a continuation of the QWERTY typewriter keyboard invented by Christopher Sholes in 1868. It is considered a low-efficiency keyboard. In 1936, an American named August Dvorak invented a simplified keyboard called DSK. According to the discussions at the time, people believed that by balancing the workload between hands and stronger fingers, the DSK would greatly increase typing speed while reducing fatigue and making it easier to learn. Why have people not used the DSK keyboard? The mainstream explanation is that because no office uses DSK keyboards, typists are not willing to learn to use DSK; furthermore, because no one can use DSK, offices are not willing to purchase DSK keyboards. In other words, because of the coordination problem, people still use low-efficiency keyboards, causing a "lock-in effect" phenomenon.

However, recent research shows that this is not the case. It has been found that:[15]

(1) There is insufficient proof of the superiority of the DSK keyboard, with most viewpoints being a guess;
(2) Ergonomic studies have found that DSK does not have reliable major advantages over QWERTY;
(3) Actually, at the time, the typewriter market was extremely competitive, and numerous types of keyboards were available;
(4) Certain recorded competitions show that many keyboards existed at the time that were superior to DSK.

Therefore, we cannot conclude that QWERTY's victory is because of the "lock-in effect".

4.2 The VHS secret

Before the invention of the DVD, the popular household recorders all used VHS, but Beta was considered higher quality, clearer, and smaller. Overall, Beta was thought superior to VHS. Some scholars, such as Arthur (1990), believe VHS's victory may be another outcome of the "lock-in effect".

However, this is not the case. Stan J. Liebowitz and Stephen E. Margolis (1999) did a detailed investigation into this period of history. In 1975, Sony Corporation began to produce Beta cassettes and provided the technology to Panasonic and JVC. In April 1976, the three companies agreed to compare the functionality of Beta, VHS, and VX. Because of JVC's persistence, the discussions ended on bad terms. In the end, Sony chose to produce Beta in an alliance with Toshiba and Sanyo. Panasonic began to produce VHS cassettes with Hitachi, Sharp, and Mitsubishi. The two camps began an intense rivalry where an improvement in one format was immediately followed by an improvement in the other format. Both formats were shown to be almost the same in every aspect but one: Screening time. VHS had a longer screening time than Beta. When Beta could screen for two hours, VHS could screen for four hours. When Beta could screen for five hours, VHS could screen for eight hours. The outcome of market competition showed that screening time was the determining factor. When the competition began, Beta dominated the market, but by 1984 Panasonic almost completely dominated the market. Only Sony produced Beta recorders.

4.3 The Microsoft legend

Many people believe that Microsoft's success is inseparable from IBM's support from the beginning.[16] It is said that at the time, Macintosh's operating system was better in function and performance than others. However, because Microsoft and IBM were partners and IBM was the primary supplier of computers, people believed that Microsoft would succeed. This led them to using DOS, so Microsoft succeeded. However, this is not the case. Liebowitz and Margolis (1999) investigated and found that the main reasons for Microsoft's success primarily were:

(1) Cost Advantage: Using the Macintosh operating system required more computing capacity and a high-cost Postscript printer.
(2) Speed Advantage: DOS was faster than Macintoshi's operating system.
(3) Functional Advantage: Although DOS was relatively difficult to learn, more technical operations were possible after learning it.
(4) Accessory Advantage: It was easier to write applications on DOS than on Macintosh.

Therefore, the success of Microsoft was not due to people's belief that it would succeed; instead, it was the outcome of technological advantage and market competition.

4.4 The university reform fable

In 2003, Peking University implemented the Faculty Restructuring Project. An important part of it was the end of "inbreeding system". So-called "inbreeding system" was the practice of hiring faculty from its own graduates of the same program. This system had been practiced in Chinese universities since 1950s and led to a very seniority-based ranking and academic nepotism. The core component of the reform of Peking University was the complete elimination of this phenomenon by hiring new faculty exclusively from outside. Graduates of the university could only return after working somewhere else for a few years. One opposition viewpoint at the time was that if Peking University was the only university to other universities

	Internal hiring	External hiring
Internal hiring	<u>2</u>, <u>2</u>	2, 0
External hiring	0, 2	<u>10</u>, <u>10</u>

Peking University (row label, left of table)

Figure 3.9 University Instructor Recruiting Reform

implement the reform, then it might lose good talent from its own program in exchange for second class graduates from other universities. It was claimed that the faculty system reform also faced the "lock-in effect". The reform could only succeed through unified coordination by the Ministry of Education. The argument can be modeled as the game shown in Figure 3.9.

In the game above, there are two Nash equilibriums: Hiring faculty only from its own graduates, with a payoff of 2 for each school, or hiring faculty from graduates of other universities, with a payoff of 10 for each school. In other words, all universities openly hiring faculty from outside is the Pareto optimal equilibrium. However, assume that only Peking University implemented the reform and other universities continue with the inbreeding system, then its payoff is 0, which is even worse than not reforming.

However, this may not be the case. China presently has more than 100 key universities. As long as a few of them implement the reform, then talent can rotate between them, and the payoff for these universities would certainly be higher than 2. Even if no other Chinese university reforms, Peking University can still choose hiring faculty from outstanding programs overseas. As long as Peking University starts the reform, other universities will observe the benefits of reform, and there will certainly be some universities that follow. As talent can rotate to a greater extent, the benefit of reform increases. Naturally, there will be more universities that implement reform until gradually all universities will implement the reform. The whole higher education will transition from a bad equilibrium to a good equilibrium. Indeed, since Peking University reformed, more and more universities have implemented the similar reform. It proves that the "lock-in effect" was not as serious as the opponents originally claimed.[17]

Notes

1 Using our knowledge of permutations and computations to make a simple calculation, we know the number of Nash equilibriums that exist in this experiment is C_{10}^5.

2 Elster believed there are three situations that predictions fail: (1) There are no equilibrium; (2) there are too many equilibriums; and (3) equilibriums are unstable. See Elster (1989a), page 8–11.

3 There were also rarely seen 8-inch floppy disks on the market. The reading and writing of floppy disks were done through a floppy disk drive. Floppy disk drives were designed to accept mobile floppy disks. The technological progress of the computer industry has been so fast that thumb drives and mobile hard drives have already replaced floppy disks.

4 According to the conclusions of Nash (1951), if two pure strategy Nash equilibriums exist in a game, then there must be a mixed strategy Nash equilibrium. In this book, we generally will not discuss mixed equilibriums.

5 Schelling proposed another important concept in this book: Commitment. We will discuss this concept in the next chapter. The book is considered to be one of the top 100 most influential books in the Western World to appear since the end of World War II. Also see Schelling (2006) for his other related papers.

6 Crawford and Sobel (1982) analyzed cheap talk games. In these types of games, the scope of information communication is determined by the alignment of players' interests.

7 Strictly speaking, customs and social norms are not completely the same. Customs are behaviors that people consider normal, but do not include value judgments. Social norms are socially accepted behaviors that include value judgments. Customs can be individualized, but norms are certainly socialized. When a type of custom is commonly considered to be something worth respecting, it becomes a social norm. We will more systematically discuss the formation of social norms in Chapter 12 and Chapter 13.

8 For a detailed discussion on the evolution of the rules of the road, see Young (1996).

9 This point shows that chance historical events may have an important impact on the formation of rules. See Young (1996).

10 See the Wikipedia entry on the Metric System.

11 Language in essence is also a social norm for the coordination of expectations. Without this type of norm, interaction would be extremely difficult. In China, there are significant pronunciation differences in each locality. If everyone spoke their own dialect, then interaction between people of different regions would be difficult. This created the need for "Standard Chinese". It could be said that Standard Chinese is a completely new language norm.

12 In Chapter 12, we will discuss how customs on property rights rules are formed through individual "labeling".

13 See Wu Si's, *Yinbi de Zhixu*. Haikou: Hainan Press, 2004.

14 Path Dependency Theory was originally developed by economists to explain the process of technological acceptance and the history of industrial evolution (Nelson and Winter (1982); Paul David (1985); and Arthur (1994)). North used path dependency to explain the evolution of institutions. This concept is also used in comparative politics and social studies research.

15 For further related analysis, see Stan J. Liebowitz and Stephen E. Margolis' article "The Fable of the Keys" (1990).

16 For an analysis of the Microsoft legend, see Chapter 5 of Daniel Spulber's, *Famous Fables of Economics*. Oxford: Wiley-Blackwell, 2001.

17 For a detailed discussion on Peking University reforms, see Weiying Zhang's *Daxue de Luoji* (The Logic of the University) (2004, 2005, 2012). Yi Shen's *Yanyuan Bianfa* (2003) contains many essays with differing viewpoints.

4   Threats and commitments

In dynamic games, players' decisions are made at different points in time. Thus, a strategy is not necessarily a singular action, but instead is a complete plan of action that stipulates an action for the player at each point in time. The person that moves later has an opportunity to adjust his own choices according to the actions of the person that moves first. Therefore, the first-mover must predict the late-mover's reaction to his action, then determine which action he should implement.

The Nash equilibrium strategy in a dynamic game might include non-credible threats (or promises). Non-credible threats appear to be optimal ex ante, but are not optimal ex post. Therefore, they are non-credible. Rational people will not believe non-credible threats. Perfect Nash equilibriums eliminate non-credible threats to guarantee the actions stipulated by the equilibrium strategy are optimal under each type of condition.

Backward induction is a basic methodology for eliminating non-credible threats to resolve the perfect Nash equilibrium. Whether or not this method is suitable is determined by the satisfaction of the common knowledge of rationality assumption. Only when every person is rational, every person knows other people are rational, and every person knows others know other people are rational and so on, will the prediction provided by backward induction be convincing.

Whether or not a threat is credible is determined by what other choices the player involved have. Actions that turn non-credible threats into credible threats are called "commitments". Commitments mean that less choices can cause threats to become credible, thus are beneficial to the player involved. Commitments can change the game equilibrium. Under certain situations, they can turn inefficient equilibriums into Pareto optimal equilibriums, and thus realize win-win. The value of commitments is determined by the cost of commitments. The greater the cost of a commitment is, the greater its value is.

The value of many systems derives from their role in commitments. Without these systems, the opportunistic behavior of the people involved will lead to the Prisoner's Dilemma problem. The greatest game in human society is the game between the people and government. Constitutional government and democracy can be understood as a commitment by the government to the people. Under this system, the government must accept the people's supervision and truly serve the people. The outcome is the government obtaining the people's trust. The totalitarian government appears to be strong but actually is very weak because it does not obtain the people's trust.

Section one: the credibility of threats

1.1 The description of dynamic games

In the analysis of games in the previous two chapters, all players acted at the same time or without knowledge of others' actions. This type of game is called a static game. In this chapter, we will focus on dynamic games. Different from static games, players in dynamic games act in sequence. After one player makes a decision, the next player adjusts his own actions. Most games in real life are dynamic games. When playing chess, one player moves after the other. When bargaining, one party offers a price and then the other party accepts or makes a counteroffer. During courtship, one party proposes and the other decides to accept or not. Price wars between firms are often dynamic because one firm reduces prices and another firm then adjusts its own prices.

Because actions in dynamic games are sequential, when describing a dynamic game, players' sequence of action must be depicted. Therefore, in Game Theory, a game tree is often used to describe dynamic games, such as is shown in Figure 4.1.

This game could be understood as a market entry game. (Imagine that the market scale is not very large, so only one firm can survive.) The hollow node represents the starting point and the solid nodes represent decision points. The straight lines are called paths and represent the player's actions at a specific time. Player (Firm) A first decides to "enter" or "not enter". After Player A chooses, Player B makes a decision. Assume that Player A decides to enter. If Player B similarly decides to enter, then both earn -1. If Player B chooses to not enter, then Player A receives 1 and Player B receives 0. Assume that A chooses to not enter. If Player B chooses to enter, then Player A will receive 0 and Player B will receive 1. If Player B also chooses to not enter, then both receive 0. Customarily, in the payoff structure at the end of the game tree, the first number represents the payoff of the

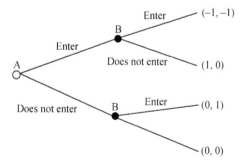

Figure 4.1 Game Tree

player that acts first, and the second number represents the payoff of the player that acts second. (This continues for games with three or more players.)

Using a game tree to describe a dynamic game can directly display the order of action, information, and payoffs. Its deficiency is that a game tree cannot directly indicate the strategy of players. This must be determined according to conditions like actions and information.

1.2 Strategy as an action plan

In static games, strategies and actions are the same. However, in dynamic games, a player's decisions are made at different points in time, so a strategy may not be a singly action, but instead is a complete plan of action to determine an action at each point in time. In the game described above, Player A must first act, his decision cannot be based on Player B's action, so his strategy must be to enter or not enter. However, Player B is different because Player B moves afterwards, so he can set his plan of action according to Player A's choice. Because Player A has two different choices, and Player B has two different choices for each of Player A's choices, Player B has a total of four strategies.

> Strategy #1: Regardless of Player A's choice, Player B will enter.
> Strategy #2: If Player A chooses to enter, then Player B will not enter; but, if Player A chooses to not enter, then Player B will enter.
> Strategy #3: If Player A chooses to enter, then Player B will enter; but, if Player A chooses to not enter, then Player B will not enter.
> Strategy #4: Regardless of Player A's choice, Player B will not enter.

For Player B, the four strategies described above are four plans of action. Before the game, he must determine a plan of action for himself. Assume that Player B announces that he will choose Strategy #1 in which he will enter regardless of Player A's choice. At that point, what choice should Player A make?

If Player A believes that Player B will really choose this strategy, then by choosing to enter Player A's payoff is −1, whereas by choosing to not enter the payoff is 0, so the optimal choice is to not enter. Actually, Player A choosing to not enter and Player B choosing Strategy #1 forms a Nash equilibrium because given that Player A does not enter, then Player B's strategy is optimal; and given Player B's strategy, then Player A not entering is optimal. However, the issue is whether or not Player B entering is credible.

In static games, as soon as a player selects a strategy (or action), it will not change. However, in dynamic games, the strategy (or action plan) chosen by a player before the start of the game may undergo adjustments after the start of the game. In other words, the *ex-ante* optimal strategy may not be the *ex-interim* or *ex-post* optimum. In this example, Player B declares before the game that his strategy will be to enter regardless of Player A's choice. However, as soon as Player A ignores this declaration and chooses to enter, then at this point, Player B will discover that the original strategy is no longer optimal. If at this point, he instead chooses to not enter, his payoff will be 0, whereas sustaining the original strategy will have a payoff of −1. This proves that Player B's declaration that he will choose Strategy #1 is not credible.

In real life, this type of declaration may be a "threat" by saying, "if you do not promise to do something, I will do something", or it may be a "promise" by saying, "if you do something, I will do something". Actually, a "threat" declaration can also become a "promise" declaration. For example, "if you do not promise to do something, I will do something" can become "if you promise to not do something, I will do something". A parent could threaten a child by saying, "if you do not stop playing games, I will take away your allowance", or make a promise by saying, "if you stop playing games, I will not take away your allowance". Similarly, a promissory declaration can also become a threatening declaration. In this way, from the analytical perspective, there is no need to separate declarations of promises and declarations of threats. Both of them are aimed at influencing the actions of others. Therefore, in the following text, we will refer to these declarations as "threats".

1.3 The credibility of threats

"Threats" are common in everyday life. For example, an employee may threaten his boss for a raise, a girl in love may threaten her boyfriend that she would not go on living if they broke up, or a country may threaten to go to war over a territorial dispute.[1]

After a player in a game declares a threat, the threatened party must judge the credibility of this threat. In the analysis described above, the source of the credibility issue of this threat was the game's non-aligned *ex-ante* and *ex-post* optimal. The Nash equilibrium, which is a suitable concept for static games, does not take this kind of inconsistency into consideration. Therefore, when we use the Nash equilibrium concept to resolve dynamic games, Nash equilibriums that include non-credible threats may appear.

Below, we will analyze the Teacher-Student Game to explain this issue. Schools design curriculum to pass on knowledge to students and test scores are used to motivate students to study. Considering professional ethics and reputation, teachers generally will give a fair score based on the student's performance at examination. However, regardless of the actual performance, students hope for a good score from the teacher, or at least a passing mark. This is because test scores impact the interests of the students, including graduating on time or finding a suitable job. Now imagine a student that does not study well, so he receives less than passing points on his final exam. He goes to the teacher hoping for a passing grade. This leads to the Teacher-Student Game shown below.

The teacher moves first. His strategy is to give a passing score or not when grading. The student moves next. His strategy is to accept or retaliate based on the score given by the teacher. So-called acceptance means to acknowledge the score given by the teacher and retaliation means acting in a way that harms the teacher physically or the teacher's reputation.

Specifically speaking, the student has four strategies to choose from.

Strategy #1: A passing grade will be accepted, but a failing grade will lead to retaliation.
Strategy #2: A passing grade will lead to retaliation, but a failing grade will be accepted.
Strategy #3: Regardless of the grade, it will be accepted.
Strategy #4: Regardless of the grade, there will be retaliation.

The payoff for both is as follows. If the teacher resentfully passes the student and is not retaliated against, his payoff is −1 and the student's payoff is 1. If he resentfully passes the student, but the student still retaliates, then his payoff is −10 and the student's payoff is −10 after being punished by the school. If the teacher faithfully fails the student, and the student retaliates, then the teacher's payoff is −10 and the student's payoff is −10. If the teacher faithfully fails the student and the student accepts it, the teacher's payoff is 1 and the student's payoff is −1. We can use Figure 4.2 to display this game's game tree.

We can notate the student's four types of strategies as (accept, retaliate), (retaliate, accept), (accept, accept), and (retaliate, retaliate). Here, (accept, retaliate) should be read as "if the teacher gives a passing grade, accept it; if the teacher gives a failing grade, retaliate". Similarly, (retaliate, accept), (accept, accept), and (retaliate, retaliate) can be understood in the same way. In this way, we can display the game described above in its normal form in Figure 4.3.

By the process of underlining, we will discover three Nash equilibriums.

The first Nash equilibrium is "the teacher chooses to pass the student, and the student chooses (accept, retaliate)". The equilibrium result is that the teacher chooses to pass the student, and the student does not retaliate. The teacher's payoff is −1, and the student's payoff is 1. This means that the student went to the

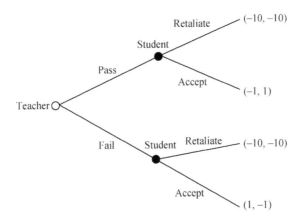

Figure 4.2 The Game Tree for the Test Game

		Student			
		(Accept, retaliate)	(Retaliate, accept)	(Accept, accept)	(Retaliate, retaliate)
Teacher	Pass	<u>−1</u>, <u>1</u>	−10, −10	−1, 1	−10, −10
	Fail	−10, −10	<u>1</u>, <u>−1</u>	<u>1</u>, <u>−1</u>	−10, −10

Figure 4.3 The Strategy Expression of the Test Game

teacher and declared that he will choose (accept, retaliate). Because the teacher fears retaliation, he resentfully passed the student and his payoff was −1. For the student, because he originally was not going to pass, but now will, his payoff is 1. This implies that the teacher submitted to the student's threat. However, if the student really retaliates, then the school will deal out a much more serious punishment, so his payoff will be −10. Therefore, if the student is rational, he should not select retaliation. Further, if the teacher knows that the student is rational, he should not believe the threat. Therefore, even though this Nash equilibrium is mutually optimal, it involves a non-credible threat.

The second Nash equilibrium is "the teacher chooses to fail the student, and the student chooses (retaliate, accept)". The equilibrium result is that the teacher chooses to fail the student, and the student does not retaliate. The teacher's payoff is 1, and the student's payoff is −1. This means that the student declared that if the teacher gives a passing grade, he will retaliate, but will accept a failing grade. The teacher gave the grade that was earned. Because the teacher was fair, his payoff was 1, and the student's payoff was −1. However, in this Nash equilibrium, the student's strategy (retaliate, accept) requires the student to retaliate when the teacher gives a passing grade, but doing so will cause the payoff to be −10. Therefore, this actually is a non-credible threat.

The third Nash equilibrium is "the teacher chooses to fail the student, and the student chooses (accept, accept)". The equilibrium result is that the teacher chooses to fail the student and the student accepts. The payoff for the teacher is 1 and the payoff for the student is −1. This means that the student had a correct attitude and would accept either grade. The teacher gave the grade that was earned. Because the teacher was fair, his payoff was 1, and the student choose to accept the failing grade, so his payoff was −1. This Nash equilibrium is relatively rational because it does not include a non-credible threat.

Two of the three Nash equilibriums described above included a non-credible threat. Why would these two Nash equilibriums include a non-credible threat or, in other words, have irrational strategies? The reason is dynamic discordance will occur in dynamic games, meaning the *ex-ante* optimal strategy is different from the *ex-post* optimal strategy. The student's declared strategy at the start of the game (such as "accepting a passing grade, but retaliating for a failing grade") may not be optimal when viewed at the end of the game. This is because if the teacher really decides to fail (or pass), the student's optimal choice is to accept. In this way, the threat is non-credible. This means that we cannot simply apply the Nash equilibrium to dynamic games. Dynamic games require equilibrium concepts that reflect dynamic consistency and eliminate non-credible threats. Therefore, we must improve the original concept of the Nash equilibrium.

Section two: sequential rationality

2.1 Rationality requirements in dynamic games

According to German economist Professor Reinhard Selten, the 1994 Nobel Prize in Economic Sciences Laureate,[2] in dynamic games, if players are rational, they should be forward-looking. Regardless of the original plan, the player should choose the optimal action based on current circumstances at each new point in time. We can refer to this type of rational behavior in dynamic games as sequential rationality. It requires players to choose the optimal action at one node after another.[3] Compared with the one-time selection of optimal actions before a static game, the requirement is much higher.

Because it is difficult to think of all possible circumstances beforehand, it is extremely difficult to create an optimal plan of action. At this point, adaptation becomes extremely important.

Further, if a player is always sequentially rational, then the strategy he uses is composed of his optimal action at each point in time. In other words, not only is this strategy *ex-ante* optimal, but it is also *ex-post* optimal, thus satisfying the requirement of dynamic consistency. This means that it does not contain non-credible threats.

We refer to all Nash equilibriums composed of strategy profiles that do not contain non-credible actions as a perfect Nash equilibrium. This means that perfect Nash equilibriums require players to be sequentially rational. This is the reason that perfect Nash equilibriums are also called sequential equilibrium.[4]

2.2 Subgames

A perfect Nash equilibrium must first be a Nash equilibrium. Among all Nash equilibriums, however, only those Nash equilibriums with strategies that do not include non-credible threats are perfect Nash equilibriums. The issue is: How can the perfect Nash equilibrium be found among all Nash equilibriums?

Perfect Nash equilibriums require players to be sequentially rational and choose the optimal action at each decision node. To determine whether an action is rational or not, the final payoff for this action must be compared with the payoff for other actions. These payoffs are not only determined by your own choice of actions, but also other player's reaction to your decision. This means that the circumstances for a decision starting from any node are like a "new game" based on the original game. If we can determine the optimal actions for each of these "new games", then the strategies which propose the optimal actions of all of these "new games" constitute the perfect Nash equilibrium of the original game.

In order to correctly depict "new games" based on the original game, Selten (1965) introduced a concept called the subgame.[5] Subgames are the portions starting with each decision node that constitute the game. It can be seen as an independent game that represents the circumstances of a decision at each node faced by players in the process of a game. Subgames appear in game trees, but start from a decision node within the game tree while still maintaining the original structure of the game tree. The original game can be seen as a subgame that starts at the beginning. If a subgame does not start at the beginning, we call it the original game's proper subgame.

A specific example is shown in Figure 4.4.

In Figure 4.4, the left-most game depicts the original game, starting at Node #1. If Player 1 decides to take the top path, the game will reach Node #2. If the bottom path is chosen, the game will reach Node #3. Both of the games starting from Nodes #2 and #3 are subgames of the original game.[6] Including the original game, this game has three subgames.

We can see that each subgame represents a decision point faced by the player. According to the definition of sequential rationality, as long as a player in the game chooses the optimal action at each subgame, then that player is sequentially rational. At the same time, since a subgame is also an independent game, it has its own Nash equilibrium. The Nash equilibrium of a subgame is formed by the optimal actions of all players in a subgame. This means that if players are sequentially rational, the optimal actions chosen in that subgame forms the Nash equilibrium of that subgame. If a game has multiple subgames, then the optimal actions chosen by players in each subgame forms the Nash equilibrium for the corresponding subgames. Obviously, the strategy profile formed by each subgame's Nash equilibrium strategy also constitutes the perfect Nash equilibrium of the original game. This way, we can individually determine each subgame's Nash equilibrium to arrive at the original game's perfect Nash equilibrium. Precisely for this reason is the perfect Nash equilibrium also called the subgame perfect Nash equilibrium.

We will revisit the Teacher-Student Game in the previous text. This game includes three subgames, inclusive of the original game, as shown in Figure 4.5.

In Figure 4.5's original game, according to our previous analysis, there are a total of three Nash equilibriums: (1) The teacher gives a passing grade, and the student

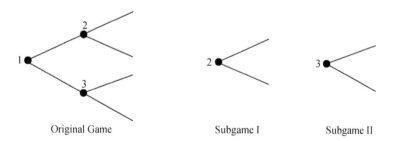

Original Game   Subgame I   Subgame II

Figure 4.4 Subgame

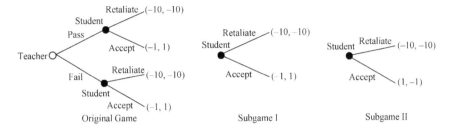

Figure 4.5 The Subgames in the Teacher-Student Game

selects (accept, retaliate); (2) the teacher gives a failing grade, and the student selects (retaliate, accept); and (3) the teacher gives a failing grade, and the student's strategy is (accept, accept). As was discussed previously, the first and second Nash equilibriums include non-credible treats, whereas the third does not. Now, we will test whether or not the three of them constitute the subgame perfect Nash equilibrium.

According to the definition of the subgame perfect Nash equilibrium, a player's strategy must determine the optimal action for the player in each subgame. In the first Nash equilibrium where the teacher gives a passing grade and the student chooses (accept, retaliate), the teacher's strategy in the corresponding subgame (which is actually the original game) requires the optimal action to be to give a passing grade. The student's strategy to (accept, retaliate) corresponds to two subgames and requires that accept be chosen in Subgame I and retaliate be chosen in Subgame II. In Subgame II, however, the payoff for choosing to accept is −1, whereas the payoff for choosing to retaliate is −10, therefore retaliation is not the optimal action in Subgame II. In other words, the student's strategy to (accept, retaliate) does not propose the optimal action in all subgames, so it does not satisfy sequential rationality. For this reason, the Nash equilibrium where the teacher gives a passing grade and the student chooses to (accept, retaliate) is not a subgame perfect Nash equilibrium.

In the second Nash equilibrium where the teacher gives a failing grade and the student chooses (retaliate, accept), the student's strategy to (retaliate, accept) requires the student to face Subgame I by choosing to retaliate. This is obviously not optimal and does not satisfy the sequential rationality requirement. Therefore, this Nash equilibrium is also not a subgame perfect Nash equilibrium.

In the third Nash equilibrium, the teacher's strategy is to give a failing grade and the student's strategy is to (accept, accept). The student's strategy requires him to accept in both Subgame I and Subgame II. If the teacher decides to give a passing grade, the student's payoff for accepting is 1, which is the optimal choice. If the teacher decides to give a failing grade, the student's payoff for accepting is −1, but it is also the optimal choice. This proves that the actions of the student's strategy to (accept, accept) are optimal in all subgames. Given that the student will always accept, the teacher's optimal choice is to give a failing grade. For this reason, this Nash equilibrium is a subgame perfect Nash equilibrium.

2.3 Backward induction and common knowledge of rationality

In the process of rejecting non-credible threats described above, we first confirmed the original game's Nash equilibrium, then tested whether or not the Nash equilibrium strategy constituted a Nash equilibrium in each subgame. From this we determined which of the original game's Nash equilibriums would constitute a perfect Nash equilibrium. This process is actually a type of forward induction. We first confirm the optimal choice in the starting-point subgame (which also confirms the original game's Nash equilibrium), then confirms the optimal choice in the second and third subgames in the direction the game develops. However, if there are numerous stages of a dynamic game, this process will be relatively complicated, and may even become very difficult to handle.[7] Therefore, we hope to find a relatively smooth method to determine the subgame perfect Nash equilibrium.

According to sequential rationality, players in a game will implement the best option at each subgame. So, the best option will be chosen at the last subgame and the second-to-last subgame. When it becomes difficult to determine the optimal choice moving in the direction that the game develops, we can implement backward induction to find the optimal choice for each subgame all the way back to the starting decision point. The action profiles discovered in this way forms a Nash equilibrium for each subgame, and thus is the subgame perfect Nash equilibrium for the entire game.

The Teacher-Student Game described previously will be used as an example. Look back on the three subgames in Figure 4.5. Starting backwards from Subgame II, the student's optimal response is to accept. Then, in Subgame I, the student's optimal response is also to choose to accept. This means that no matter what the teacher chooses, the student will always accept. After expecting this point, we will go back to the starting decision point of the original game. If the teacher decides to give a passing grade, the student will accept. At this point, the teacher's payoff will be −1. Otherwise, if the teacher gives a failing grade, the student will also accept, so the teacher's payoff will be 1. Obviously, the teacher should choose to give a failing grade. In this way, starting with backward induction from the last point, we determined the original game's perfect Nash equilibrium. This is much faster than the other method.

Next, we will examine the game shown in Figure 4.6.

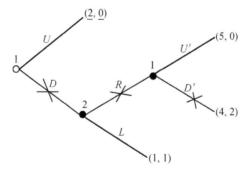

Figure 4.6 Backward Induction Example

Player 1 first chooses U or D (up or down). If U is selected, the game ends. The payoff for both players is 2 and 0, respectively. If D is selected, then Player 2 chooses R or L (right or left) next. If Player 2 chooses L, the game ends. The payoff for both players is 1. If R is selected, then Player 1 again selects U' or D'. If Player 1 chooses U', then the payoff for both players is 5 and 0, respectively. If D' is selected, then the payoff for both players is 4 and 2, respectively.

We can use backward induction to solve for this game's subgame perfect Nash equilibrium. Assume that the game has progressed to the last subgame, starting with Player 1's second decision node. At this point, Player 1 decides between choosing U' for a payoff of 5 and D' for a payoff of 4, so his optimal choice is U'. In this subgame, because there is only one party making a choice, its optimal choice is also the Nash equilibrium strategy. Next we will examine the second-to-last subgame, starting with Player 2's decision node. This is the point where Player 2 first acts to decide between R and L, then Player 1 acts to decide between U' and D'. How should Player 2 decide? Because in the next step Player 1 will choose U', if Player 2 now chooses R, in the end his payoff will be 0, but if he chooses L, his payoff will be 1. Obviously, Player 2 should choose L, so the second subgame's Nash equilibrium strategy profile is (L, U'). Next, we will go back to the first subgame (which is also the original game), and start from Player 1's first decision node. The payoff from choosing U is 2, but because Player 2 will later choose L, the payoff from choosing L is 1. Therefore, his optimal choice is U. In the first subgame, Player 1's optimal strategy is (U, U'), and Player 2's optimal strategy is L. Therefore, the strategy profile $[(U, U'), L]$ forms the entire game's subgame perfect Nash equilibrium. (Understand this as: Player 1 first chooses U, then if there is a second opportunity, choose U', and if Player 2 has the opportunity, choose L.) The equilibrium outcome is that from the beginning Player 1 chooses U and Player 2 does not have the opportunity to choose.

The rationale for backward induction is our assumption that players satisfy the common knowledge of rationality requirement discussed in Chapter 2. In this example, the reason Player 1 chooses U in the beginning is because he knows that the second person is rational. If he chooses D, then Player 2 will have the opportunity to make a move, and Player 2 will choose L. Why does he believe that Player 2 will choose L? Because he knows that Player 2 knows that if another opportunity is given to Player 1, then Player 1 will certainly choose U'. If Player 1 is rational, Player 2 is also rational, and Player 2 knows that Player 1 is rational, then Player 2 will choose L. If Player 1 knows that Player 2 knows he is rational, then Player 1 from the start will choose U. Thus, the rationality of Player 1 choosing U from the beginning is to a large degree determined by whether or not the common knowledge of rationality assumption stands. This proves that in the process of backward induction, it is required to assume that players have common knowledge of rationality, meaning each person is rational, and each person knows that others are rational.

In real life, if players do not satisfy the common knowledge of rationality requirement, conclusions from backward induction may not match players' actual choices. For example, if Player 1 does not know that Player 2 knows he is rational, Player 1 may choose D, expecting Player 2 to choose R, and then at the end choose

U' for a payoff of 5 units. Of course, if Player 2 actually knows that Player 1 is rational, then Player 1 will only receive a payoff of 1 from choosing *D*.

All of the decision nodes and optimal choices that the perfect Nash equilibrium passes through in a game tree forms a path, called an equilibrium path. Similarly, the decision nodes and choices the perfect Nash equilibrium does not pass through forms the non-equilibrium path. In the above example, only Node #1 and *U* form an equilibrium path. All other paths are non-equilibrium paths.

It must be noted that the formation of equilibrium paths depends on players' choices on non-equilibrium paths. For instance, the reason Player 1's choice of *U* will form an equilibrium path is because Player 2 will choose *L* on the non-equilibrium path. In the Teacher-Student Game, the equilibrium path is the teacher giving a failing grade and the student accepting it so the teacher's payoff is 1 and the student's payoff is −1. All other choices are non-equilibrium paths. The reason this equilibrium will appear is because on the non-equilibrium path, even if the teacher gives a passing grade, the student will also accept it. This proves that behavior on the non-equilibrium path determines the formation of the equilibrium path. As a common comparison, the reason one country will choose to not attack another country (the equilibrium path) is because it predicts that as soon as the war starts (the non-equilibrium path), the other country will strike back and the loss will be greater.

2.4 The counterfactual problem

Not only is the perfect Nash equilibrium strategy optimal on the equilibrium path, but also on the non-equilibrium path. In other words, when the impossible could occur, players should also select the optimal action according to rational principles. A paradox arises because the optimal strategy is based on the assumption of rationality, but to satisfy the assumption of rationality impossible events cannot occur. If impossible events occur, then the assumption of rationality does not stand. When determining the next action, why should we assume the other player is rational?

In the example in Figure 4.6, if Player 1 chooses *D*, then Player 2 should choose *L*, because he expects that the payoff from choosing *R* will only be 0. However, if Player 1 is really rational, knows that Player 2 is rational, and also knows that Player 2 knows he is rational, then he would not choose *D*. Now, if he really chooses *D*, then why should Player 2 believe that Player 1 is rational and also be aware of Player 2's rationality? Player 2 may think one possibility is that Player 1 is rational, but does not know that Player 2 is rational, or does not know that Player 2 knows that Player 1 is rational. At this point, Player 2 choosing *L* is still optimal. However, another possibility is that Player 1 is not rational. At this point, Player 2 choosing *L* is not optimal, because non-rational Player 1 may in the last round choose *D'*. However, this brings about another issue: Even if Player 1 is rational, he may choose *D* to mislead Player 2 into believing he is irrational. This gives him the opportunity to choose *U'* in the last round for a payoff of 5. However, how would rational Player 2 not think of Player 1 pretending to be irrational? After seeing through Player 1's trick, Player 2's optimal choice is still *L*. In this way, why would Player 1 still pretend to be irrational? In other words, if you believe something is impossible, it is possible, but if you believe something is possible, it is impossible.

This is called the counter-factual problem. To this day, Game Theory has not yet resolved this problem. Selton's "Trembling Hand" Theory explains the appearance of impossible events as mistakes made by players (Selten, 1975) as an attempt to resolve this issue, but it is not completely satisfactory.[8]

Section three: commitment

3.1 The role of commitments

In the previous section, we discussed ways in which to eliminate non-credible threats or promises while solving a game, thus making a rational prediction of players' behaviors. As was described above, an implied pre-requisite is that players have common knowledge of rationality. There are high requirements for common knowledge of rationality to be a condition, so in real life it is difficult to obtain. This also causes non-credible threats or promises to often appear in real life.

Even so, this theory still has a strong ability to explain reality. For instance, financial crises to a large degree are caused by non-credible threats. If poorly run firms must close and non-payment of debt led to prison, there would be much caution during financing activities. Financial crises may be avoided, or at least would not be that serious. However, in reality, because of the fear that the failure of large firms, especially large financial organizations, would bring about a series of social issues, once a large enterprise experiences a debt crisis, the government steps in. This phenomenon is called "too big to fail". Expecting this to happen, firms prefer risk when raising funds because the gains are theirs to keep, but the cost of losses are paid by society. The outcome is a financial crisis.[9]

Because non-credible threats or promises exist, some effective cooperation cannot happen, and thus the Pareto optimum cannot happen.

The game previously described in Figure 4.6 is an example. According to our earlier analysis, we know that the outcome of this game is the game ends after Player 1 chooses *U* and Player 1 and Player 2's payoffs are 2 and 0, respectively. However, this Nash equilibrium is not a Pareto optimal. Now, imagine that Player 1 commits to Player 2 that after choosing *D*, as long as Player 2 promises to choose *R*, then Player 1 will select *D'*. If Player 2 believes Player 2's promise and chooses *R*, and Player 1 also keeps his promise to choose *D'*, then at this point Player 1's payoff is 4 and Player 2's payoff is 2. Compared with the original outcome, this outcome causes both people's payoff to increase, so it could be called a Pareto improvement.

Notice first that Player 2 has an incentive to promise Player 1 he will choose *R*, even if he does not have an incentive to do so. But the problem is after Player 2 chooses *R*, Player 1 will go back on his promise to choose *U'*. At that point, Player 1's payoff is 5, but Player 2's payoff is 0. Player 2 will predict this situation; thus he will not choose *R* and instead choose *L* to guarantee his payoff is 1. And so on, Player 1 will know that Player 2's promise is empty, so from the beginning will not choose *D*, but instead choose *U* to guarantee a payoff of 2. In other words, each person has an incentive to promise, but no one has an incentive to follow through because the other's promise is not credible. Thus, a Pareto improvement cannot occur.

The relationship between the government and the market is similar. If the government cannot convince the market that it will not change policy at whim, then short-term behavior will occur on the market. For example, the chaotic situation in China's housing market is mainly the result of policy. In order to adjust the structure of the economy, the government puts pressure on real estate. However, the market suspects that as soon as the speed of economic growth slows down, the government will put more priority on growth and loosen restrictions on real estate, thus housing prices continue to rally. Therefore, if the government desires real estate policy adjustments to be effective, the key is to make its threats or promises credible.

Under this type of circumstance, whether or not promises or threats can become credible becomes the key to a Pareto optimum appearing through a Nash equilibrium. In the previously described example, if Player 1 can implement some type of action to make his promise to choose *D'* credible, then Player 2 will choose *R*, so cooperation can happen. For example, before the start of the game Player 1 could provide a collateral worth 2 to an independent third party and declare that if in the third stage of the game he does not choose *D'*, then the third party can confiscate the collateral. In this way, at the third stage of the game, if Player 1 chooses *U'*, then the payoff is only 3, which is less than the payoff of 4 from *D'*. Therefore, at this point Player 1's promise to Player 2 that if *R* is selected then *D'* will be selected becomes credible.

As was discussed previously, the source of non-credible threats is the misalignment between the *ex-ante* and *ex-post* optimal. For example, in the Teacher-Student Game, retaliation for a failing grade appears to be optimal before the fact, but after the fact it is not. In the Debt Game, punishment may be *ex-ante* optimal, but the *ex-post* optimal is assistance. In the game between the government and the property market, the *ex-ante* optimal is "structural adjustments", but after the fact the government may need to "protect growth".

In game theory, if a player implements an action that causes an *ex-post* non-credible threat to become an *ex-post* credible threat, which means the *ex-ante* and *ex-post* optimums are aligned, this type of action is called a commitment.[10] Note that "commitment" and the previously mentioned "promise" are different. "Promises" and "threats" can be seen as a type of expression, whereas "commitments" refer to actions that are true to one's word. This demonstrates that commitments are more important than promises. Only commitments can cause a Pareto optimal that would originally not appear to become the equilibrium outcome.

3.2 The cost of commitments

The key to commitments playing a role is their cost. In the example above, the collateral worth 2 that Player 1 provided was actually the cost of Player 1's commitment. Obviously, the greater the cost of a commitment, the more credible a promise is; thus the more likely cooperation will happen. In the above example, if Player 1 provided a collateral worth less than 1, his promise would still not be credible.

In ancient China, a married man could declare a divorce at any time, so even if he pledged his unending love, the woman still worried that the man would not respect the promise. Under these circumstances, the man could give expensive betrothal gifts or hold costly wedding as a commitment of his behavior during marriage. If the man declares a divorce after the wedding, the betrothal gifts would be kept by the wife. Obviously, the more expensive the betrothal gift and the higher the cost of the wedding is, the stronger the role of the commitment is. The people who spend their entire family fortune on a wedding are not likely to divorce.

In venture investing, the amount the founder invests can also play a commitment role. The more money the founder puts in, the more investors may be willing to invest. The reason is that as soon as the founder does not perform well, he suffers a big loss. More generally, a person's ownership of an asset can play a commitment role to society.[11] People with a substantial amount of assets hope for social stability, because in a turmoil their losses will be great. From this perspective, the middle class is an important factor of social stability.

The essence of commitment actions is limiting the scope of your own choices. By limiting your own choices, you can make your promises and threats credible. Similarly, increasing your opponent's choices can make your opponent's promises and threats non-credible. This could be called an "anti-commitment" policy. In Chapter 7 of the *Art of War*, it is said "when you surround an army, leave an outlet free. Do not press a desperate foe too hard". The first sentence means that when surrounding an enemy, not all four sides should be enclosed, only three. This allows the enemy army to escape from the side not enclosed. If all exits are denied to the defending army, then their only option is to fight to the end, increasing the harm to both parties. The second sentence means an enemy without the ability to fight should not be pushed too hard, otherwise he may become too desperate. The common meaning of these two sentences is that the opponent's willingness to resist can be reduced by giving the opponent more choices, thus denying the opponent the ability to commit to a bloody war to the end.

Commitment is a common strategy used by firms in market competition. In the 1972 paper *Durability and Monopoly*, Ronald Coase recognized that monopoly firms that produce durable goods must make commitments to consumers. Even though they do not have competitors, they often face competition between the present and the future (Coase, 1972). Imagine a firm has a production cost of zero, and it can produce between one and four units of a durable good. Also assume that consumers value good differently and each consumer demands one unit. If one unit is produced, then the first consumer will be willing to pay a maximum price of ¥100, so the firm's profit will also be ¥100. If two units are produced, then the second consumer is willing to pay a maximum price of ¥80, so the firm's profit is ¥160. If three units are produced, then the third consumer is willing to pay a maximum price of ¥50, so the firm's profit is ¥150. If four units are produced, then the fourth consumer is willing to pay a maximum price of ¥30, so the firm's profit is ¥120. From the perspective of profit maximization, the firm should produce two units for a profit of ¥160. However, further consideration will find that the best method is to produce the first unit and sell it to the consumer that is willing to pay ¥100, then produce the second unit and sell it to the consumer that is willing to pay ¥80, then produce the third unit and sell it to the consumer willing to pay¥ 50, and then finally produce the fourth unit and sell it to the consumer willing to pay ¥30. In this way, a total of ¥260 can be earned. We can say this is the maximum profit.

The problem is that the first consumer will expect the firm to reduce the price after his purchase, so he will choose to wait. For the same reason, the second person will also wait, because he expects the price to continue to decline to ¥50. The third person will expect the price to decline to ¥30, so he will also wait. In the end, the price is ¥30 and the total profit is 120. This is the famous Coase conjecture. These circumstances obviously do not benefit the firm. To change the circumstances, the firm may tell the first customer that only two units will be produced, but if the consumer is rational, he obviously will not believe it. The manufacturer needs to make a commitment such as price guarantee policy. The firm could set the price at ¥80, and then propose a sales condition that if within one year the price drops, then it will refund the price difference to anyone that has already bought the product at higher price. If this condition is legally enforceable or the manufacturer highly values its reputation, then it will not lower prices because one additional unit could be sold for ¥50, but a total of ¥60 must be paid in refunds to the first two buyers. Through this commitment, the maximum profit of ¥160 can be made.

The characteristics of an artist and the previously described producer of durable goods are similar. Paintings are durable goods, and as time goes on they may become more valuable. When an artist is about to sell a painting, because the cost of reproducing a painting is very low, an artist also faces the Coarse conjecture. In order to sell the painting for a good price, he must commit to not paint too many of them. It is very difficult for artists to make the market believe they will not produce more. The extreme circumstance is the death of an artist as a commitment to not produce more paintings. This is the reason we often see the phenomenon of artists' works becoming more valuable after their deaths. For similar reasons, when the post office issues commemorative stamps, they often destroy the original imprint as a commitment to increase the value.

We can also use this theory to explain university reform. One very important aspect of Peking University's reform in 2003 was the implementation of the "up or out" system,[12] meaning that those lecturers and associate professors who cannot be further promoted within a certain of years must leave. Some people criticized the reform because they were worried that the new system would make unfairly treated faculty members worse. Actually, "up or out" can be understood as a commitment to the fair treatment of faculty members. Under the old iron rice bowl system, all faculty members were guaranteed a tenured career. Just because of this, the university had no good incentive to promote high-quality faculty members. After all, regardless of being promoted or not, high-quality faculty members would still serve the university with their talents. Under the "up-or-out" system, however, it is no longer possible for the university to exploit the outstanding talent. This mechanism can be explained using the game shown in Figure 4.7.

In this game, lecturers can choose to work hard or not, and the school can choose to promote or not.[13] Assume that a hard-working lecturer can create a total value of 8. Under the old system, if the school promotes the lecturer, the payoff for the lecturer and the school is 4 each, but if the school does not promote, then the lecturer's payoff is 1 and the school's payoff is 7. If the lecturer is not hard-working, the school similarly must decide to promote or not. If a promotion is offered, the lecturer and school each receive a payoff of 3, for a total of 6. If a promotion is not given, the school's payoff is 4 and the instructor's payoff is 2. The game's equilibrium is that the lecturer is not hard-working and the school does not promote (meaning that there is no relationship between promotions and performance).

"Up or out" can change this game's equilibrium. Under the new system, anyone who is not promoted to a higher rank must leave, regardless if he works hard or not. Assume that the payoff structure when promoted will be the same for both the lecturer and the school as under the older system. However, the payoff structure when not promoted will be different from the old system. Assume that if the lecturer is hardworking but is not promoted, the school's payoff is 0 by losing him and the lecturer's payoff from somewhere else is x (which depends on his market value but less than 4). If the lecturer is not hard-working and not promoted, he will leave for a payoff of y (which depends on his market value but less than 3) and the school's payoff will be 0. What is the game's equilibrium under the new system? It is easy to say that if the lecturer is hard-working, the school's best choice is to promote him to get payoff of 4 instead of 0 by losing him; and given this expectation, the lecturer's best choice is to work hard. Thus, the perfect Nash equilibrium is that the instructor works hard and the school promotes him, and each receives payoff of 4.[14]

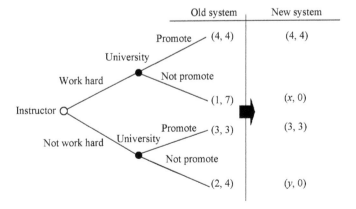

Figure 4.7 The Up or Out Promotion Game

Section four: constitutional government and democracy

4.1 Limited government as a commitment

Dynamic game theory is important for our understanding of democracy and the rule of law.

Since humanity has entered the civilized era, government has become an important player in social games. For any society to effectively operate, it must grant the government certain discretions. However, if the government has too much discretion, not only are the rights of the people not guaranteed, the government itself is also harmed. The reason is that the relationship between the government and the common people is a type of game. Under despotic systems, the common people also have certain choices (even slaves have ways to be lazy). If the common people do not trust the government, it is difficult for policy to attain its goals.

We will use sovereign debt game as an example to explain this point.[15]

Government expenditures come from two sources of income: Taxes and public debt. Taxes are compulsory, but ruthless taxes will reduce the productive activities of the people. This causes actual tax incomes to decline or in serious cases leads to the government being overthrown. Different from taxes, public debt is voluntary (and forceful public debt is the same as a tax). The ability of the government to issue debt depends on the people's willingness to subscribe.

The basic structure of the Sovereign Debt Game is as follows. The government first decides whether or not to issue public debt and how much, and then the people decide to buy it or not. When the debt comes due, the government decides to repay the debt according to the original contract or to default. If the government defaults, the people (as creditors) decide how to punish the government. Generally speaking, only when the government's expected punishment from defaulting is higher than the expense of repaying the debt will the government choose to repay. Only when the creditors expect a high enough probability of repayment are they willing to subscribe to the debt.

What is the maximum amount of debt the government can issue? If we use D to represent maximum debt, r represents the interest on debt and P represents the punishment for government default, then the conditions for repayment are: $D(1 + r) \leq P$. If this condition is not satisfied, the government may choose to default. If the government is expected to default, then the creditors will choose to not subscribe. Therefore, the maximum amount of debt the government can issue is $D \leq P/(1 + r)$.

This means that the greater P the punishment that the government faces for default is, the more public debt can be issued. The size of P is determined by multiple variables, but the most important is the people's ability to restrict the government. If the power of government is not limited, creditors have no means available when the government defaults, so the government's ability to issue debt is very small. On the contrary, if the government is limited and can only operate within the scope of the rule of law, then its ability to issue public debt is significant. This is an important reason that democratic governments have a much greater ability to raise money than despotic governments.

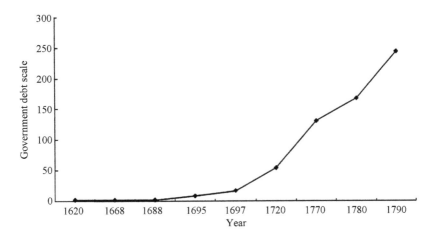

Figure 4.8 The Change in British Government Debt Between 1620 and 1790

Figure 4.8 displays the change in British government debt between 1620 and 1790. Before 1688, British government debt fluctuated around £2 million, but after 1688 it grew rapidly. By 1697, it had reached £16.7 million, in 1720, it had reached £5.4 million, and by 1790, it had reached £24.4 million. Over the span of 100 years, it had increased 120 times. The growth of government debt increased the government's fiscal capabilities and played a role in Britain's victory during multiple European wars, because war capabilities are determined to a large degree by fiscal capabilities.

Why did Britain's debt increase rapidly after 1688? The key factor was the Glorious Revolution's transformation of the political system from an absolute monarchy to a constitutional monarchy, or from an unlimited government to a limited government, and thus greatly increased the punishment the king faced for default (North and Weingast, 1989). Under the absolute monarch before the Glorious Revolution, even if the England king's behavior was restricted to a certain degree by Parliament, the king could unilaterally change lending terms, refuse to pay, or use foreign merchants to break up alliances among creditors, so creditors were not willing to lend money to the government. The Glorious Revolution caused the British political and economic system to undergo important changes. Private property was more effectively protected. The power to determine public debt was transferred to Parliament, which was composed mainly of potential creditors that could depose the king. Debt activities were coordinated by the Bank of England and seniority of debt payment reduced the probability that the government would "alienate" creditors. Because the punishment for default increased, the government's ability to raise debt increased.

More generally speaking, constitutional government and the rule of law could be understood as the government's commitment to the people. The government acts according to the law and accepts the people's supervision to not only protect basic individual rights, but also respect these rights as a restriction on government behavior. Under the system of constitutional government, government is more trusted by the people, so the government's strength is more powerful. Rule-of-man governments may appear to be strong, but are actually weak, at least over the long term because they are not truly trusted by the people. This point appears more obvious in today's competition between nations.

The law is separated into civil law and criminal law. Civil law deals with compensation between parties, whereas criminal law deals with punishment of criminal behavior by state organs. Why are some matters suitable for civil law and others for criminal law? An important reason is the value of commitments (Zhang, 2003). Behavior like murder and arson should be punished severely, but if these were decided by negotiations among relevant parties, criminals may not undergo the proper punishment. For example, wealthy criminals may be more willing to negotiate, and poor victims may be more willing to accept compensation. Or, in situations where the victim has already been murdered, then no plaintiff will exist. Criminal law is a type of commitment to deter potential crime.

4.2 Democracy as a commitment

Similar to constitutional government, democracy can also be understood as a type of commitment. There are multiple dimensions to a democratic system. Here, we will concentrate on the most core aspect of the democratic system: Elections. We will define the democratic system as a type of systemic arrangement with elections at certain intervals involving the whole people.[16] Under non-democratic systems, political power is held by a minority of people in the privileged class. Their means of obtaining political power was either through inheritance or violent conquest. Under the democratic system, political power is granted by majority vote and severely restricted by the law. This law is itself acknowledged by the government. For this reason, the democratic system has a tendency to look after the interests of the masses, whereas non-democratic systems have a tendency to maintain the interests of the privileged class. Naturally, the masses are more willing than the privileged elites to choose the democratic system. Of course, we must acknowledge that non-democratic governments sometimes also care about the interests of the common people. In any society, the common people care most about their own livelihoods, safety, and liberty. Historically, some enlightened despots have done more to advance the happiness of their people than the democratic system has. Regardless, under non-democratic systems, "serve the people" is a non-credible promise. Only under democratic systems can "serve the people" be a credible promise.

All of the world's democratic countries today have evolved out of non-democratic countries. How did this type of evolution occur? Why were the majority of people not satisfied with the enlightened despots that ruled them and choose the democratic system? Why would the ruling classes accept democracy? Below, we will give a brief account of the democratization theories of Acemoglu and Robinson (2006). Imagine that we live in a non-democratic society composed of a dominant minority and a dominated majority. The former has privileges and is relatively wealthy, whereas the latter lacks basic political power and is relatively poor. These two types of people not only care about today, but also tomorrow. Assume that for some reason, the dominated now have a certain amount of *de facto* political power. This type of *de facto* political power causes the dominant to concede to setting certain economic policies that improve the standard of living by increasing liberty and safeguards, thus increasing their happiness index. The reason this circumstance appears in non-democratic societies is because the dominated are the majority, so they can complain, protest, or even revolt to threaten social stability and the interests of the dominant. This is something the dominant cannot overlook. However, this type of political power held by the dominated is temporary, because it is *de facto* but not *de jure*. The welfare and liberties they obtain today are only "bestowed" upon them by the dominant. What is given can be taken away, and there is no systemic power that can inhibit the dominant from implementing the opposite policy, and therefore putting them in a worse situation. In reality, this situation often happened in the history. Acknowledging this point, they will require that *de facto* political power be transformed into systematized political power, turning temporary power into permanent rights. They not only hope to have bread, cloths, housing, and liberty today, they also hope to have these tomorrow. This goal can only be attained when they have the right to elect political leaders. This created a demand for democracy.

Of course, changes in the political system will not naturally occur just because the common people demand it. A transition to democracy means an expansion of political power to the majority. This also means an end to the ruling elite's special privileges, which is something the dominant will work to inhibit. When faced with strong political pressure from the dominated, the dominant often give the dominated the things they want today to alleviate their grievances. If the common people are still not satisfied, then the dominant may further declare continuations of these policies tomorrow. However, this type of promise is not credible, because as soon as the political pressure ends, the dominant will be back to their old tricks. When the common people are not convinced by these empty promises, they may revolt. This is of course not something the dominant want to see. To stop a revolution from occurring, the dominant must make a credible promise. To do this, they must change the structure of political power by putting political power in the hands of the common people. This establishes a democratic system. In this way, democracy became a type of commitment to protect the long-term interests of the citizens.

Even though this model is simple, overall it can explain many countries' process of democratization, including England.[17] England's democratization began with the establishment of Parliament in the fourteenth century. In the beginning, Parliament was only a forum for the nobility and the king to negotiate taxes and discuss public policy. Only after the Glorious Revolution in 1688 did Parliament meet regularly. However, the rights of citizens were severely limited. The Upper House composed of the nobility and archbishops played a leading role over the Lower House composed of representatives of the commoners. In principle, parliamentarians were elected, but before the mid-nineteenth century, elections were a formality because the candidates nominated by the archbishops and nobility were rarely challenged. Voting was open, and the majority of voters did not dare go against the wishes of the nominators. England's first major step towards democracy was the passage of the First Reform Act in 1832. It abolished many of the unfair rules in the old election system and implemented a voting rights system based on a unified standard for property and income. It increased the electorate from no more than 500,000 people to more than 800,000 people (or 14.5% of the adult male population). This reform act was passed precisely as the masses' dissatisfaction with the existing political system increased day by day. Before 1832, England experienced sustained riots and mass disturbances (such as the famous Luddite Movement). Historians are aligned in the belief that avoiding social unrest was a major driver of the 1832 reform act.

Precisely for this reason was this reform act only a strategic concession by the government. Mass democracy was not established. After the reform, the vast majority of Englishmen still did not have the right to vote, the nobility and archbishops could still manipulate elections, and corruption and intimidation during elections were still very serious.

The 1832 reform obviously could not satisfy the masses' demand for democracy. In 1838, the working masses launched the "Chartist Movement" proposing universal male suffrage, abolishment of the property requirement for the right to vote, implementation of parliamentarian salaries, and other demands. The Chartist Movement continued until 1848. Although it did not succeed, it had an important impact on later reform.

As the pressure for reform increased, in 1867, Parliament finally passed the Second Reform Act, which expanded the electorate from 1,360,000 to 2,480,000 and thus caused the working masses to become the majority in urban electoral districts. Multiple factors played a role in the outcome of this reform act. The most important was the increased threat of riots from the serious economic depression. In addition, the formations of the National Reform Union in 1864 and the Reform League in 1865 made the government acknowledge that reform was unavoidable. The Third Reform Act in 1884 applied the voting rules used in the urban electoral districts to rural electoral districts. This doubled the size of the electorate. After that, about 60% of adult males had the right to vote. The factor that led to this act's passage was still the threat of social disturbances.

At the end of World War I, the British government passed the Representation of the People Act in 1918. This expanded the right to vote to all men over 21 and women over 30 (that paid taxes or were married to a taxpayer). This act was discussed during the war and to a certain degree reflected the government's need to change worker's incentives for participating in the war and production, but may have been influenced by the October Revolution in Russia. In 1928, women obtained equal voting rights as men.

In the history of England's democratization, even if there were certain other factors playing a role, the threat of social disturbances was the main driving force behind the establishment of England's democratic system. This is also the reason that England's democratization was a gradual process. Each concession only satisfied the demands of the current "menace". For example, in 1832, "buying off" the middle class was enough to obtain peace, so the right to vote was only extended to the middle class. As the next threat appeared, the next concession was given until universal suffrage was realized.

Of course, not all governments of undemocratic societies can acknowledge the current state of affairs and react to the times like the British government did. Certain governments of undemocratic societies are accustomed to using violent means to suppress the democratization demands of the common people, or the wait until it is too late (such as the Qing Dynasty Government), so the only alternative is revolution.

Notes

1 The 2005 Nobel Prize in Economics laureate Thomas Schelling became famous for his analysis of "threats" in international relations. See Schelling (1960, 2006).

2 In 1965, Professor Selten published *An Oligopoly Model with Demand Inertia*, in which he proposed the concept of the subgame perfect Nash equilibrium as an improvement to the Nash equilibrium concept.

3 See Gibbons (1992), page 177 for discussions on sequential rationality.

4 See Kreps and Wilson (1982) and Kreps (1990), Chapters 12 and 14.

5 This chapter is a non-technical discussion of subgames focused more on introducing its significance. For a technical discussion, see Chapter 2 of *Boyi Lun he Xinxi Jingxixue [Game Theory and Information Economics]* by Weiying Zhang.

6 Actually, as long as someone is making a decision, it could be considered a game.

7 Chess is an example. Because there are multiple rounds, there is an extremely complicated process to determine the Nash equilibrium of the first subgame, which is the first step in determining the perfect Nash equilibrium. Further testing subsequent subgames is even more complicated.

8 There is much discussion on the counter-factual problem in the literature. See Elster (1978); Binmore (1987a); and Mahoney and Sanchirico (2003).

9 Andrew Ross Sorkin's book *Too Big to Fail* (2009) is a brilliant description of the 2008 Global Financial Crisis.

10 Thomas Schelling is recognized as the earliest person to define the concept of "commitment". (Schelling, 1960, Chapter 2) However, he said this concept was first proposed 2,400 years ago by Xenophon, a soldier, historian, and author in ancient Athens. (Schelling, 1960, Chapter 1) Of course, we could also say that a similar concept is found in *The Art of War*.

11 See Weiying Zhang, *Chǎnquán, Jīlì yǔ Gōngsī Zhìlǐ [Property Rights, Incentives, and Corporate Governance]*. Beijing: Jingji Kexue Chubanshe [Economic Science Press], 2005, Chapter 2.

12 Many firms actually implement the "up or out" system, such as McKinsey Consulting. If employees are not promoted from any rank, they must leave McKinsey.

13 Here, we only consider the issue of effort. Another factor that determines the value of a faculty member is ability. The reasoning for ability is similar. Because under the "up or out" system, people of high ability must leave if they are not promoted, and therefore the university has to treat them fairly. See *Daxue de Luoji [The Logic of Universities]* by Weiying Zhang (2004).

14 For theoretical models to describe the "up or out" system from this perspective, see Kahn and Huberman (1988).

15 For a complete model and the detailed story, see North and Weingast (1989).

16 This definition was provided by Joseph Schumpeter in *Capitalism, Socialism, and Democracy*. For the various theoretical models on democratic systems, see David Held (2006).

17 See Acemoglu and Robinson (2006), Chapter 1.

5 Bargaining and patience

Any transaction could be seen as a bargaining game. Reaching an agreement is the common interest of both parties; thus, it is Pareto improvement. However, different agreements mean different allocations of interest, so conflicts of interest exist.

There are two approaches for analyzing the bargaining issue: The cooperative game approach and the non-cooperative game approach. Collective rationality is the starting point of the cooperative game approach and individual rationality is the starting point of the non-cooperative game approach.

According to the cooperative game approach, the bargaining solution is determined by the bargaining power and bargaining strength (marginal contribution to the value creation) of parties involved. If the parties are symmetric, then the Nash bargaining solution means they will evenly distribute the surplus value brought about by the transaction. This conclusion provides a source of fairness.

According to the non-cooperative game approach, the bargaining equilibrium outcome is determined by the bargaining sequence (who bids first), the number of times bargaining takes place, the patience of the people involved, the cost of bargaining, etc. The more patient a person is, and the lower his cost of bargaining is, the more advantage he will have during the negotiation. If both parties are symmetric and allowed to bargain an unlimited number of times, then the perfect Nash equilibrium allocation is almost evenly split.

In reality, negotiation often take many rounds, and an agreement might not even be reached. This is primarily because information about the value of the transaction, bargaining power, and patience is incomplete. The process of negotiation is actually a process of both parties mutually obtaining information about the other.

People's behavior during negotiations is restricted by social norms. These social norms include procedural norms and substantial norms. Violating these social norms will lead to a breakdown in negotiations. Experiments with "The Ultimatum Game" show that the fairness concept held by most people, and has an important impact on the outcome of negotiations. However, this does not prove that people are irrational. Misalignment between theoretical projections and reality are primarily because theorists have too little information.

Section one: the bargaining problem

1.1 Cooperation and conflict

Bargaining (or negotiation) is a common occurrence in everyday life. For instance, when signing labor contracts, the employee and employer must negotiate working hours, working conditions, wages, the duration of the contract, and so on. Business partners must negotiate an agreement on investment of funds, stock rights, and profit allocation. When a company goes bankrupt or is reorganized, the stakeholders must negotiate on debt repayment, settlements for the staff, and other related issues. A husband and wife might negotiate to divide obligations such as housework or taking care of children. During a divorce, negotiations become much more complex when considering issues of property division and custody. In the political world, politicians must use negotiations when dealing with the arrangement of personnel and allocation of authority. Central and local governments must negotiate tax source allocation, transfer payment amounts, and funding allocation. Internationally, trade friction between China and the United States, the Diaoyu Islands conflict between China and Japan, and the Six-Party Talks on the Korean peninsula nuclear issue are all a process of negotiation. If no resolution is found, there might be an outbreak of war.

The nature of the bargaining problem lies in the fact that the parties involved have interests in common as well as conflicting ones. Generally speaking, reaching an agreement benefits all parties involved. However, different kinds of agreements can be reached through bargaining, thus creating different allocations of interest, resulting in different benefits for each party. This makes the bargaining problem very similar to the multiple equilibrium problem discussed in Chapter 3. Namely, if there are too many potential equilibriums in a game, they might prevent any one equilibrium from appearing. Unsuccessful bargaining is often the result of too many potential agreements. Every party hopes to reach the agreement where they are receiving the most possible benefit, resulting in the inability to achieve any sort of agreement at all.

But the multiple equilibrium problem in bargaining is different from the previously discussed multiple equilibrium problem which can be measured by different types of criteria. For instance, according to the Pareto criterion, if there are two Nash equilibriums present in a game and one of them is the Pareto equilibriums superior to the other, then all of the players will choose the first equilibrium. Another example is the aforementioned problem with traffic rules. In order to avoid accidents, all people must choose to stay on the right side of the road or the left side of the road. In this particular example, there is no benefit to diverging from these rules for any of the players. In the bargaining problem, there is a conflict of interest between the players. However, this type of conflict of interest is different than the zero-sum game, in which case one party gains the entirety of the other party's losses. If bargaining cannot result in an agreement, then all parties will be at a loss. If an agreement can be reached, each party will benefit and will make a profit greater than zero. In this sense, the bargaining problem is essentially a type of positive-sum game where a conflict of interest is present.

1.2 Cooperative game approach and non-cooperative game approach

Research on the bargaining issue generally follows two approaches. One is called the cooperative game approach and the other is the non-cooperative game approach. The cooperative game approach assumes that bargaining participants unite to make a strategic decision and emphasizes collective reasoning. When the goal of the agreement is to maximize mutual benefit, both parties will voluntarily comply with the strategic decision or agreement. In contrast, the basis of the non-cooperative game approach theory assumes that each of the bargaining players independently make strategic decisions. It emphasizes individual rationality and pursuit of individual interest maximization. This means if an agreement is not a Nash equilibrium, even an agreement which brings maximized collective benefits to each party is unlikely to be carried out. For instance, in the Prisoner's Dilemma, two prisoners can agree to "mutually disavow", meaning neither one of them will confess if caught. However, when they are actually arrested, each prisoner will make the strategic decision that maximizes his individual benefits and they will both choose to confess. It is important to note that the difference between cooperative game theory and non-cooperative game theory is not that the former studies cooperation and the latter studies non-cooperation. Instead, the basis is whether the process of making a decision is based on individual rationality or collective rationality. As we will see in later sections, non-cooperative game theory is the most appropriate theory for the study of how to achieve cooperation.[1]

Below, we will first discuss the bargaining problem from the cooperative game theory viewpoint, and then we will consider the bargaining problem from the non-cooperative theory viewpoint.[2]

Section two: bargaining power and the Nash bargaining solution

2.1 The size and distribution of the pie

An extremely important concept of the cooperative game is the Nash bargaining solution. John Nash presented this concept in his 1950 publication entitled *The Bargaining Problem*. Below, we will use a simple example of selling a painting to explain this concept.

Imagine there is a painter preparing to sell one of his paintings. He can go directly to the market to sell the painting himself, or he can give the painting to a gallery to be sold. If he sells the painting himself, he can sell it for ¥1,000; if he gives it to the gallery to sell for him, the price of the painting will be ¥3,000. Assume that if the gallery does not sell this painter's work, but instead sell another work, they will gain ¥500. Thus, if the painter does commission the sale to the gallery, the total gain will be ¥3,000. If the painter sells the painting himself and the gallery sells another work, the total gain for all parties is ¥1,500. In terms of the overall gain, clearly the collaboration between the painter and the gallery is the most efficient. The problem now is as follows: How will the ¥3,000 be divided between the two parties after the sale? How much should the painter and the gallery each get?

Now, we will generalize this problem. Suppose that now there are two players: Player A represents the painter and Player B represents the gallery. The total value V is to be distributed between them. If they are able to reach an agreement, it will be distributed based on the agreement. If they are unable to reach an agreement, the first person receives a minimum payoff a and the second receives b. Corresponding with the above example, $V = 3,000$, $a = 1,000$, and $b = 500$. Here, the value of a and b is called the "threat point", meaning the gain each party can obtain if the negotiation breaks down. Break-down means no cooperation, and so threat points are also called "bargaining power". The painter's power $a = 1,000$ and the gallery's power $b = 500$. It must be noted that in most situations, $a + b$ must be less than V. If their sum is greater than V, then a Pareto improvement cannot exist, so there is no point in bargaining. Precisely because $a + b < V$ can there be Pareto improvement and the cooperation have value. This also shows that the result of $V - a - b$ must be a positive number, meaning cooperation will bring about surplus.

Generally, if we use x to represent the value Player A receives and y to represent the value Player B receives from an agreement, then it should be that $x + y = V$, meaning both players will distribute the value entirely.[3] If we use h and k to represent the two players' respective share of the total surplus, then $h + k = 1$. It is easy to conclude that $x = a + h(V - a - b)$; $y = b + k(V - a - b)$. This is shown in Figure 5.1.

In Figure 5.1, the horizontal axis represents the amount x received by Player A, and the vertical axis represents the amount y received by Player B. The total value V could entirely go to Player A or entirely go to Player B. Line V-V is the boundary of feasible allocations. It is impossible for any of these allocation schemes to exceed this line. Point P represents the threat point discussed earlier, with coordinate values (1,000, 500). It shows that if an agreement cannot be reached, the

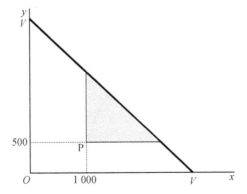

Figure 5.1 The Nash Bargaining Solution

painter stands to gain ¥1,000 by selling the painting himself and the gallery will gain ¥500 from the sale of another painting. Individual rationality implies that a feasible agreement must be in the shaded triangle area. That is, any type of allocation cannot be situated to the left or below Point P. If the bargained state is worse than the original state, why would any rational player agree to it?

In the previously discussed example, the total allocatable value V from bargaining was fixed. However, in real life, the value of V can be unfixed. For example, if the allocation proportions are not appropriate, the gallery will not have a good incentive to sell at best price; or, if the agreement is signed before the painting is completed, the painter might not have a good incentive to create a perfect painting. Either of these could cause the final price to be less than ¥3,000. Therefore, Line V-V shown in Figure 5.1 is not always a straight line. More likely, it is a curved boundary like the one shown in Figure 5.2.[4]

This situation is the most prominent type of social distribution issue. Imagine a society comprised of two people. Society's production requires cooperation between the two individuals. First, assume the two individuals are identical in capability and other relevant aspects. Then, if each person is allocated one half, then they can have the maximum gain. If one person gains more than the other, the one who gains less will not have an incentive to work. At the same time, because of complementarity of efforts, there is no point in the other person having more incentive to work. So, the total pie would be small. However, if the individual's abilities are unequal and their contribution to society is also not the same, equal distribution would not provide a right overall incentive to work. On the contrary, unequal distribution to some limit would provide right incentives to work. Of course, if distribution is too unequal, then once again no one will work hard. This shows the distribution problem (the pie-sharing problem) and the production problem (making the pie) cannot be completely separated. Depending on the distribution plans, the size of a pie produced by the society will be very different. If we assume all pies are fixed, then an egalitarian distribution has no side effect. If the size of the pie is not fixed, the egalitarian distribution is very

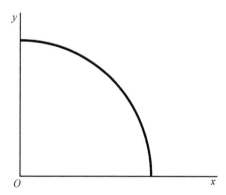

Figure 5.2 The Allocation Curve Boundary

unlikely to be a good solution. This is an issue we should consider when discussing distribution policies.

2.2 The Nash bargaining solution

Next, we will analyze the Nash bargaining solution. The Nash bargaining solution is built upon the following three axiomatic conditions: (1) Pareto efficiency; (2) invariance of linear transformation; and (3) independence of irrelevant alternatives.[5]

Condition (1) is an efficiency criterion for bargaining. It makes clear that the final agreement should be Pareto optimal. Graphically, it means that the allocation proposal is on the allocatable wealth boundary, but not below that line. If a solution is within the boundary, at least one person can obtain more without harming the interests of the other person; thus, it is not a Pareto optimal solution. Consequently, Condition (1) means that the allocation proposal must allocate the surplus entirely. In our previous example involving the ¥3,000, none of that money should be left over.

Condition (2) means that the utility function's linear transformation does not affect the result of bargaining, similar to that the conversion of Celsius to Fahrenheit does not change the actual value of the temperature itself. This is a basic assumption of the expected utility theory in economics. Each player's expected level of utility does is not influenced by the scalar quantity of the measurement.

With this assumption, we can reduce multidimensional bargaining issues into one-dimensional bargaining issues. One-dimensional bargaining refers to both parties bargaining on only one aspect. For instance, in the painting sale scenario, both parties only bargain on the price. Actually, bargaining in real life is often multidimensional. Both parties not only discuss the price, they also want to discuss the method of payment, the transaction deadline, whether or not they can return the product, and so on. Wins and losses in each dimension will have a certain impact on the utility of those involved. After we sum up the utility brought about by the different dimensions, then we can view the bargaining issue in one dimension, and thus simplifying the bargaining model.

Condition (3) put simply, means if choices that were originally feasible were not chosen, then getting rid of these choices will not influence the outcome of bargaining. For instance, in the previous painting example, it is feasible that the painter would receive 1,200 and the gallery would receive 1,800. If the agreement does not contain this choice, then even if the choice is eliminated in the restrictions, the agreement will not change. This is the meaning of independence of irrelevant alternatives.

Nash proved that if all players acknowledge the aforementioned three axiomatic assumptions and know that the other party also acknowledges these three assumptions, meaning they become "common knowledge", then the dual-party bargaining will equivalent to maximizing (two-person) social welfare function as shown below subject to the feasible allocation restriction $x + y \leq V(x, y)$:

$$W(x, y) = (x - a)^h (y - b)^k$$

This social welfare function can be understood as the weighted average of everyone's net gain (or utility) logarithm. The weights are each person's proportion of the surplus value.

To solve this optimization problem, we can obtain the following equation:

$$(y - b)/(x - a) = k/h$$

This is actually the surplus' allocation proportion between parties. As can be seen in Figure 5.3, it is the slope of the line between Point N and Point P.

In the above graph, Point N represents the contact point of the indifference curve W_1 and the feasible allocation line, which is the point where the social welfare is maximized. It is easy to say that any other feasible allocation point would lower the welfare level; any other point which gives higher welfare level would be infeasible. Point P is the threat point of both parties, also known as the reserved price point.

2.3 Marginal contribution and bargaining strength

The variables h and k can be understood as each party's bargaining Strength, or both parties' marginal contribution rate. A player's marginal contribution refers to the difference in surplus created by cooperating or not. A player's marginal contribution rate refers to his proportion of the total contribution margin. In the previously discussed painting example, the marginal contribution of the painter and the gallery are the same. Both are $V - a - b$. Without the cooperation of any one party, the painter will receive ¥1,000 and the gallery will receive ¥500, and the total value will decrease ¥1,500, so each party's marginal contribution is ¥1,500. In other words, without either one of them, this ¥1,500 added value will not appear. This way, both parties' total marginal contribution is ¥3000, so $h = k = 1,500/3,000 = 1/2$. This indicates that both parties' bargaining strength is completely equal.

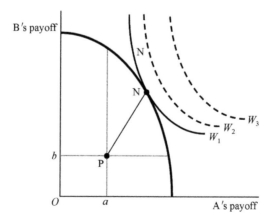

Figure 5.3 A Nash Bargaining Solution Example

Specifically for the painting example, the issue now becomes:

$$MaxW(x, y) = (x - 1{,}000)^{0.5}(y - 500)^{0.5}, \text{ subject } to \ x + y \leq 300$$

Solving the optimization problem above, we can obtain the following equation:

$$(y - 500)/(x - 1{,}000) = 1$$

Finally, we arrive at $x = 1{,}750$, $y = 1{,}250$. Thus, at the total selling price of ¥3,000, the painter receives ¥1,750 and the gallery ¥1,250. Compared with the non-cooperative state, each party receives an added value of ¥750, meaning the added value is allocated evenly.

This is a general conclusion that when two people's marginal contribution (bargaining strength) is equal, the surplus brought on by cooperation should be equally distributed. For instance, imagine a type of product that is only produced by one factory with a production cost of ¥50. Additionally, assume that there is only one buyer, to which the value is ¥100. Thus, the surplus brought about by the transaction is worth ¥50. The Nash bargaining solution price is ¥75, so each party receives ¥25 of the surplus.

The above was a Nash bargaining solution under symmetric conditions.[6] If h and k are unequal, then each party's marginal contribution rates are not the same. For example, cooperation between Player A and Player B can obtain V, but cooperation between Player A and Player C can also obtain V. In this way, Player A and Player B cooperation and Player A and Player C cooperation can bring about the same total value. From Player A's perspective, Player B and Player C are completely interchangeable. This way, both Player B's and Player C's marginal contributions become 0. If either one of them is removed, Player A can still obtain value from cooperation. At this point, Player B and Player C lose their bargaining strength. Returning to the painting example, imagine there is only one painter, but there are two galleries. If one gallery does not sell the painting for the painter, the painter can still choose the other gallery to sell his painting. The two galleries can be interchanged, so their bargaining strength is 0. In that case, the surplus value allocated to them from bargaining is 0. The painter takes all benefits of the cooperation. The gallery can only gain a ¥500 "reserved price" (which is the income level when an agreement cannot be reached).

Further, we can also assume that the marginal contributions Gallery B and Gallery C bring about for the painting are not the same. For instance, if Painter A and Gallery B cooperate, they create a total value of $V = 3{,}000$; if Painter A and Gallery C cooperate, they create a total value of $2V = 6{,}000$. Suppose that without Painter A, Gallery C could earn ¥1,000. Therefore, in the cooperation between Painter A and Gallery C, Gallery C's marginal contribution is $6{,}000 - 1{,}000 - 3{,}000 = 2{,}000$. The reason is because without Gallery C, Painter A can still let Gallery B earn ¥3,000 from selling the painting. Painter A's marginal contribution is $6{,}000 - 1{,}000 - 1{,}000 = 4{,}000$. Together, the marginal contribution of Painter A and Gallery C is ¥6,000, so Painter A's proportion should be two-thirds of the surplus value and Gallery C's proportion should be one-third. That is, out of the total ¥6,000 sales price, Painter A receives ¥3,667 (equal to two-thirds of the ¥4,000 plus an additional reserved price of ¥1,000), and Gallery C receives ¥2,333. Note that even though Gallery C's participation causes Gallery B to exit Painter A's market, it is precisely the existence of Gallery B that causes Painter A's bargaining ability to increase. If Gallery B did not exist, Painter A can only gain a share of ¥3,000 from the total price ¥6,000.

We can see that the amount of surplus a party in the bargaining process can obtain is determined by his marginal contribution, not the total contribution. This point is actually easily understandable. In simple terms, marginal contribution is "the difference between your presence and your absence". A person's bargaining strength is inversely proportional to his substitutability. The more substitutable a person is, the less bargaining strength he has; the less substitutable a person is, the more bargaining strength he has. For example, in the movie industry, big stars' high fee is because they have a high marginal contribution. With them, the box office and the advertisement profits are also higher, so their ability to negotiate is very strong. Yet, normal actors can easily be replaced by each other, so they do not have high bargaining strength.

Precisely because of this, the people that want to increase their bargaining strength must consider how they can increase their marginal contribution. One method is an alliance. If both Gallery B and Gallery C join up to negotiate with the painter, then the outcome is different (at this point, the painter can only gain half of the sales price). This is the reason that chain stores have more bargaining strength than individual stores in real life. In respect to the labor market, labor unions' main purpose also lies in the fact that collective bargaining can strengthen workers' ability to negotiate wages. A single individual can always be replaced, but an entire team of workers cannot be replaced.

2.4 Changing bargaining power

Another way to increase the ability to negotiate price is to strengthen bargaining power (the threat point or the reservation price), namely a and b in the aforementioned formula. According to the formula $(y - b)/(x - a) = k/h$ deduced above, given both parties' marginal contribution rate ratio k/h, we can see that changes in bargaining power a and b can change the allocation of the total value between both parties (x, y). Therefore, both parties will find ways to improve their own bargaining power or reduce the other party's bargaining power. In this way, we can model bargaining as a two-stage game. The first stage is a non-cooperative game where each player chooses their own bargaining power a and b. The second stage is a cooperative game where the bargaining proceeds according to a and b. Of course, this is only worthwhile when the cost of increasing bargaining power is less than the bargaining power's added value.

For example, as shown in Figure 5.4, the bargaining power (threat point) of both parties starts at Point P, and the Nash solution outcome is shown by Point E. However, if Player A can successfully lower Player B's bargaining power but maintain his own bargaining power, then both parties' threat point decreases from

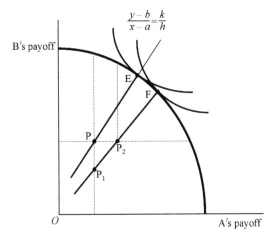

$$\frac{y-b}{x-a}=\frac{k}{h}$$

B's payoff

E

F

P

P_2

P_1

O A's payoff

Figure 5.4 The Influence of Changing Leverage on Negotiation

Point P to Point P_1 and the Nash solution outcome will change to Point F. In contrast with Point E, Player A's proportion of the total income has increased and Player B's proportion has decreased.

Obviously, if both parties try to increase their own bargaining power, it might constitute a "Prisoner's Dilemma." As shown in Figure 5.4, assume that at the start both parties' bargaining power is at Point P_1 and the Nash solution is at Point F. Then, each person spends a lot of energy increasing his own bargaining power, causing both parties' bargaining power to move to Point P_2. However, at this point because the relative proportion b/a did not change, the Nash solution is the same as before, which is still Point F. In order to increase bargaining power, both parties increased costs.[7] This shows that bargaining advantage is relative and determined by the relative value of b/a.

From this perspective, we can understand why in war there is often the "promote peace through war" phenomenon. Two parties at war are negotiating and fighting at the same time. The goal of fighting is actually to change your own leverage in the negotiation. The better the war is fought, the more bargaining power you have.[8] Negotiations between labor and capital are the same. Airline company strikes are concentrated before Christmas because business is best before Christmas, so it creates the most harm for the airline company.

Additionally, the distribution of formal authority (or ownership) also influences bargaining power. For instance, if a boss has the authority to choose whether or not an employee must work overtime, he will not necessarily pay overtime wages. If the worker is free to choose whether or not he works overtime, then if the boss wants him to work overtime, then he must pay overtime wages. This is the importance of legal power for bargaining power. From this we can see that while rules on legal power do not inhibit bargaining, they change bargaining power, and thus change the outcome of bargaining.[9]

Section three: alternating bargaining and patience

The premise of the bargaining model in the previously described cooperative game was collective rationality. When the three Nash assumptions are satisfied, the bargaining issue is the same as resolving the collective welfare maximization issue. Although it provides a possible rational and efficient allocation proposal, we do not see the actual bargaining process.

In reality, the bargaining is a process of offer and counteroffer between players. Each player seeks the maximization of individual utility, not the maximization of collective utility. Therefore, bargaining is more like a non-cooperative game. Below, we will discuss how to understand bargaining from the non-cooperative game perspective.

3.1 Limited-round bargaining and the last-mover advantage

The basic model of non-cooperative game bargaining is as follows. Player A and Player B share one piece of pie. Player A first proposes an offer; and Player B can either accept or decline it. If the offer is accepted, the pie will be allocated according to Player A's proposal, and the game ends. If the offer is rejected, then Player B proposes his own proposal, and Player A decides to accept or decline. If B's proposal is accepted, the game ends, and the pie is shared accordingly. If B's proposal is rejected, Player A again makes a proposal for Player B to choose from. Then, Player B again makes a decision to accept this proposal or not. This process continues until an agreement is reached.[10]

First, we must note that this kind of dynamic game has an infinite number of Nash equilibriums. For example, Player A could demand 0.9 each time and not accept any allocation proposal which gives him less than 0.9. If Player B is rational, his optimal response is to accept 0.1, because any share of more than 0.1 would be rejected. Actually, any proportion between [0, 1] that Player A demands and Player B agrees to can all form a Nash equilibrium.

However, a singular perfect Nash equilibrium exists in this game. The specific outcome of this perfect Nash equilibrium depends on factors such as the bidding sequence, the number of occurrences, both parties' degree of patience, and the cost of bargaining. Specifically speaking, when Player A receives proportion x, Player B receives proportion y, and $x + y = 1$. To display the degree of patience, we assume that Player A's discount factor is δ_A and Player B's discount factor is δ_B. Both δ_A and δ_B are decimals greater than 0 and less than 1.[11] For simplicity, we will first not consider fixed costs.

First, we will consider the simplest situation in which the bargaining only lasts two rounds at most. At this point, Player A makes a proposal in the first round, and if Player B accepts it, then the negotiation ends. If Player B does not accept, then Player B makes a proposal in the second round that Player A can either accept or reject. If Player A accepts, then the pie will be allocated according to the agreement, otherwise the negotiation will end with neither party getting any pie.

To find the perfect Nash equilibrium, we can use backward induction method by first considering the second round. At that point, Player B's optimal proposal is

(0, 1), meaning Player A receives 0 and Player B receives the whole pie. The reason is that from Player A's perspective, if he does not accept, the negotiation will end, and he will also receive 0. So, we assume that he accepts any share. Knowing this, Player B needs to offer Player A nothing. Given that Player B will propose (0, 1) in the second round, in the first round, Player A's optimal proposal is $(1 - \delta_B, \delta_B)$. Because Player B's discount factor is δ_B, the whole pie in the second round is worth proportion δ_B in the first round. Thus, Player B would accept offer not less than δ_B and reject any offer less than δ_B in the first round. Player A does not need to offer Player B anything more than δ_B. Therefore, the bargaining will end in the first round when Player A receives $x = 1 - \delta_B$ and Player B receives $y = \delta_B$. This is the perfect Nash equilibrium for two-round bargaining. For example, if $\delta_B = 0.9$, then Player A will receive 0.1 and Player B will receive 0.9.

If the negotiation is allowed to continue for a third round, then this proposal is not optimal for Player A. We can still use the logic of backwards induction to start from the third round. At that point, it would be Player A's turn to make a proposal. If Player A proposes (1, 0), meaning he gets the whole pie and Player B receives nothing, then Player B will also agree to this, because the negotiations will not continue for another round. Then, we will consider the second round, where Player B makes a proposal. Because Player A's discount factor is δ_A, the whole pie in the third round discounted to the second round becomes proportion δ_A. Therefore, Player B's optimal proposal in the second round is $(\delta_A, 1 - \delta_A)$, i.e., giving A δ_A and keeping $1 - \delta_A$ for himself. We will next work backwards to the first round, where Player A makes a proposal. Because Player B can receive $1 - \delta_A$ in the next round, the value of that discounted to the first round is $\delta_B (1 - \delta_A)$. Thus, if in the first round, Player A offers Player B proportion $\delta_B (1 - \delta_A)$, then Player B will accept. Therefore, Player A's optimal proposal in the first round is $(1 - \delta_B (1 - \delta_A), \delta_B (1 - \delta_A))$, meaning he gets $x = 1 - \delta_B (1 - \delta_A)$ and leaves $y = 1 - \delta_B (1 - \delta_A)$ for Player B. This is the perfect Nash equilibrium for three-round bargaining. If we assume that $\delta_A = \delta_B = 0.9$, then Player A would receive 0.91 and Player B would receive 0.09.

Similarly, we could extend this to the n-round bargaining. We will come to two general conclusions.

(1) If both people are patient enough, the negotiation will have a "last-mover advantage", meaning the person who has chance to bid at last round has an advantage. In the example described above, if the negotiation can only last two rounds, then Player B is the bidder in the last round, so he could receive 90% of the pie, but Player A can only receive 10%. However, if the negotiation is allowed to last three rounds, then Player A is the bidder in both the first and the last rounds, so Player A can receive 91%, but Player B can only receive 9%.

(2) The more patient a person is, the bigger an advantage he can have in the negotiation. The less patience a person has, the less he can receive from the negotiation. The reason is the patience (discount factor) determines one's present value of the future share and thus determines minimum share he is willing to accept when the opponent makes offer. In the previous two-round

negotiation example, if Player B's patience $\delta_B = 0.9$, then in the beginning Player A will give him 0.9. However, if $\delta_B = 0.6$, then Player A will only give him 0.6. In the three-round negotiation, if $\delta_B = 0.9$ (and we assume that Player A's patience $\delta_A = 0.9$), then Player B could receive 0.09. If $\delta_B = 0.6$, then Player B can only receive 0.06.

3.2 Unlimited-round bargaining and patience

If the bargaining does not have a final round, meaning as long as an agreement is not reached, the negotiations will continue until an agreement is reached, what will happen?

Because there is no final round, we cannot start from the last round and work backwards to the first round. However, we can still find the perfect Nash equilibrium by using similar logic.

Assume that Player A and Player B undertake an unlimited-round bargaining. Player A makes a bid in the first round. For any odd number $T > 3$, if the negotiations start from stage T, it is Player A's turn to make a bid. Assume that the best payoff he could obtain at round T is x. Returning to round $T - 1$, it is Player B's turn to make a bid. From Player A's perspective, the value of x in round T is equal to x times his discount factor in round $T - 1$, thus $x\delta_A$. In other words, if Player B in $T - 1$ offers Player A proportion $x\delta_A$, Player A will accept. Therefore, in round $T - 1$, Player B could obtain $1 - x\delta_A$. Backwards to round $T - 2$, it is again Payer A's turn. If Player A offers Player B proportion $\delta_B (1 - x\delta_A)$, which is equal to Player B's payoff $1 - x\delta_A$ in round $T - 1$, then Player B will accept. Therefore, Player A can receive $1 - \delta_B (1 - x\delta_A)$. Because this is an unlimited-round negotiation, starting from any round t where Player A makes an offer, the equilibrium payoff for Player A is the same. At the equilibrium, the payoff x in round T and is the payoff $\delta_B (1 - x\delta_A)$ in round $T - 2$. Solving $1 - \delta_B (1 - x \delta_A) = x$, we the perfect Nash equilibrium payoffs as follows:

$$x = \frac{1-\delta_B}{1-\delta_A\delta_B}; \; y = \frac{\delta_B(1-\delta_A)}{1-\delta_A\delta_B}$$

To repeat, here, x and y are the respective shares of Players A and B. In other words, although the bargaining is allowed to last infinitely, the agreement would be reached in the first round if Player A offers the above proposal, which is the perfect Nash equilibrium.

From this formula, the conclusion we come to is that there are two factors that influence a bargaining's final allocation outcome: The bidding order and players' patience.

If the degree of patience is the same, meaning $\delta_A = \delta_B = \delta$, then the equilibrium solution is:

$$x = \frac{1}{1+\delta}; \; y = \frac{\delta}{1+\delta}$$

Because δ is always less than 1, Player A's payoff is greater than 1/2 and Player B's payoff is less than 1/2. This shows that when the degree of patience is the same for both parties, an unlimited-round bargaining has a first-mover advantage. Thus, when a final round does not exist, the first bidding person will receive a little bit more. This is different from the last-mover advantage in the limited-round bargaining game.

Similar to limited-round negotiations, the more patience a player has, the greater advantage he has in the negotiation. Assume that Player B is completely impatience. This means that y = 0. Even if he can continue to negotiate, tomorrow's pie is worthless. Under these circumstances, the first person will receive the full 1. Alternatively, if the second person is absolutely patient and the first person is impatient, then $x = 0$ and $y = 1$.

Patience can be understood as the value of time. It is one of the most important concepts in economics. Life proceeds through time. A basic characteristic of human nature is that the present is more important than the future. Not only is the future uncertain (a person can die at any time), but also the present is the premise of the future. If we want a person to give up today's consumption for tomorrow's consumption, there must be compensation. This is the source of interest. Of course, there are differences between people. The less patient a person is, the more compensation they require. This is the reason the rate of discount (interest) or the discount factor is used to display patience in economics.

Our previous conclusion is aligned with real life observations. Imagine you are in a collision while driving (and you are completely at fault). Should you handle it privately or get the police involved? If you handle it privately, how much should you compensate the other driver? The answer to a large degree depends on your and the other party's relative degree of patience. If time is not important to the two of you, you may be more willing to wait for the police to handle it. If time is precious for at least one person, the issue might be handled privately. When it is handled privately, if you are in a rush but the other party is not, you may have to offer more compensation. If the other party is in a rush but you are not, then comparatively less compensation can resolve the issue.

3.3 Patience and fairness

In the cooperative game model in Section Two, we explained both parties' bargaining strengths h and k as the marginal contribution rate to cooperating. Now, we can explain bargaining strengths in a new way.[12]

Stated simply, bargaining strengths h and k possibly is determined by their discount factors in non-cooperative games. The greater the discount factor is, the more patience a person has, so the greater the bargaining strength. In unlimited-round bargaining, if both parties are equally patient and great enough, then each person can obtain about half. This is strictly defined below.

Defining Party A's discount rate $r_A = (1 - \delta_A) / \delta_A$ (i.e., $\delta_A = 1 / (1 + r_A)$) and Player B's discount rate $r_B = (1 - \delta_B) / \delta_B$ (i.e., $\delta_B = 1 / (1 + r_B)$). Then, in an unlimited-round bargaining where Player A bids first, the proportional ratio that both parties receive is $x/y = h/k \cong r_B/r_A$. Player A's bargaining strength $h = r_B /$

$(r_A + r_B)$, and Player B's bargaining power $k = r_A / (r_A + r_B)$. For example, if Player A's discount rate $r_A = 0.1$ and Player B's discount rate $r_B = 0.05$, meaning Player B is more patient than Player A, then Player A's bargaining strength $h = 1/3$ and Player B's bargaining strength $h = 2/3$. Obviously, when $r_A = r_B = r$, the perfect Nash equilibrium outcome will be close to each person receiving about half. At this point, according to the previous cooperative game analysis, the Nash bargaining problem becomes: $\max(x - a)(y - b)$. If the opportunity cost for both people is equivalent, meaning $a = b$, then in the end they will implement an equal allocation.

This shows that, if the patience, opportunity cost, and productivity of both people are the same, equal allocation is an equilibrium. Perhaps this is the source of the fair social norm that similar people should obtain similar proportions. Humanity's concepts about allocation justness were formed through bargaining over the long term. With this concept, similar people do not need to repeat the same bargaining process every time there is a bargaining problem, because final outcome of bargaining might be the same.

3.4 Negotiation costs

Now, we will consider the impact of fixed costs during bargaining. Fixed costs refer to both parties spending a certain amount of money, energy, time, and other direct costs as well as other opportunity costs during the process of negotiation. For example, if the firm and trade union cannot come to an agreement during the strike, the firm must pay damages for late deliveries and the trade union must pay wages to its members. When fixed costs in negotiations are substantial, each additional round of negotiation leads to both parties receiving less of the total payoff from the agreement. It is like a pie that needs to be allocated shrinking by one fixed piece each turn of the negotiation.

For descriptive convenience, we will assume that all players' discount factor equals 1.

We will still consider the model where Player A and Player B take turns bidding. Imagine a pie that shrinks by one quarter each round. By the fifth round, there is nothing left, in the fourth round there is 0.25 left, in the third round there is 0.50 left, in the second round there is 0.75 left, and in the first round there is 1.0 left. In the fourth round, Player B makes a bid. He will leave the entire pie to himself (worth 0.25). In the third round, Player A makes a bid. He can receive half of the pie (worth 0.25). In the second round, Player B makes a bid. He can receive two-thirds of the pie (worth 0.50). In the first round, Player A makes a bid. He can receive half of the pie (worth 0.50). Therefore, the perfect Nash equilibrium is each person receives half the pie.

Now, we will consider general circumstances. Assume the total allocation amount is 1, and after N rounds it will reduce to 0. Further, we will define the amount reduced in round i as X_i, therefore $\sum_{i=1}^{N} X_i = 1$. The last person to make an offer in round N can take the final remaining amount X_N. The reason is that if the other party does not agree to this allocation, in round $N + 1$ neither party will receive anything. From this, we can deduce that in round $N - 1$, by taking into account that the other party must receive X_N, so the bidder will in the current round can receive X_{N-1} (remember that the total amount in round N-1 is $X_N + X_{N-1}$). In round N-2, the bidding player will receive the amount of $X_{N-2} + X_N$. And so forth, in the first round, Player A as the first bidder will bid according to the principle that the bidder can receive the portion that will be disappear in all his turns. The specific description is below:

> If N is an odd number, notated as $N = 2y + 1$, then the perfect Nash equilibrium will be that Player A in the first round will bid and receive $\sum_{i=0}^{y} X_{2i+1}$ and Player B will receive $\sum_{i=1}^{y} X_{2i}$.
> If N is an even number, notated as $N = 2y$, then the perfect Nash equilibrium is that Player A in the first round will bid and receive $\sum_{i=1}^{y} X_{2i,-1}$ and Player B will receive $\sum_{i=1}^{y} X_{2i}$.

For example, if the pie becomes bad when the negotiations do not succeed the first time, (i.e., $X_1 = 1$), then Party A can receive the whole pie. If the pie becomes bad after two failed rounds (i.e. $X_1 = X_2 = 0.5$), then both Party A and Party B will receive half in the first round. It is easy to prove that this type of bidding strategy profile forms a perfect Nash equilibrium.

What will the circumstances be if the two people have different bargaining costs? Generally speaking, the party with the higher bargaining cost will be at a disadvantage. This is similar to patience.[13]

A special form of fixed costs is external opportunity loss. So-called external opportunity cost refers to the loss of external opportunities during the bargaining period. At this point, the greater the external opportunity loss one has, the more disadvantaged he will be in the negotiation. Let us consider divorce negotiations. If the husband has another lover waiting to get married, but the wife does not, the husband has a higher opportunity cost than the wife. Thus, the husband is at a disadvantage because the woman can afford to delay, but he cannot. At this point, the husband is often willing to give the wife higher compensation in order to end their marriage earlier. The opposite is also true. Similar situations also appear in business negotiations.

3.5 Bargaining and information

In the previous discussions, even although the negotiations could last multiple rounds, the equilibrium agreement is reached at the beginning, and thus the latter negotiation paths are non-equilibrium paths. In other words, as soon as the game starts, the negotiation ends. In reality, this is not the case. Often, both parties must undertake multiple rounds of negotiation before reaching an agreement. In some cases, even after multiple rounds, the negotiation may still fall apart. For example, it took decades for China to negotiate with USA and others to join the World Trade Organization. The negotiations with the United States were the most difficult and long process.

Why are negotiations in real life different from the theory we previously discussed? The reason is that previously we assumed the people involved had complete information. They knew value V, each person's opportunity cost or bargaining power, each person's patience, time limits, etc. Additionally, each person knew that each person knew, and each person knew that each person knew that each person knew, and so on.

However, in reality, the greatest problem faced in the negotiation is that the above information is very limited and incomplete. For example, the seller is not completely clear how much value (V) a product will bring about to the buyer. The buyer is not clear how much the firm's production costs are. Neither party is clear on each party's bargaining power (a, b), patience, or opportunity costs. Sometimes, we are not completely clear on the value of these for ourselves. Under these types of incomplete information conditions, the equilibrium outcome cannot be known before the fact, so of course an agreement cannot be reached at the start of the negotiation.

Real-life negotiations are a process of revealing and detecting information. Each party wants to use negotiations to understand the cards the other player has been dealt. Each player wants to display beneficial information while hiding non-beneficial information as much as possible. Because information advantage determines status in the negotiation, so each party will try as hard as possible to obtain information. This led to the development of detectives and spies. When information is sufficiently obtained, the negotiation comes to an end, but in the theoretical bargaining model discussed earlier, this is the beginning point of the negotiation.

Under conditions of complete information, the outcome of negotiations is certainly a Pareto optimal. However, because information is incomplete, the outcome of negotiations is not always Pareto optimal. Actually, many win-win opportunities are not realized. An example would be a consumer that is willing to buy a piece of clothing for a price higher than the retailer's true reservation price. Obviously, undertaking a transaction is Pareto efficient for both parties when the seller's reservation price is lower than the buyer's value. However, because both parties want to contest the price in order to benefit themselves, when their information is private, they will to the greatest extent display a limited willingness to transact. In the end, no transaction will take place.

Section four: social norms in bargaining

4.1 The ultimatum game

Consider a one-shot bargaining game involving Party A, Party B, and ¥100 to be shared. Player A will make a proposal of how to share it between them. If it is accepted by Player B, the ¥100 will be allocated according to the proposal. If it is rejected by Player B, the ¥100 will be withdrawn and neither party will receive anything. This is called "the ultimatum game".[14]

How much should Player A offer to Player B? Because there is no second round of negotiation, if Player B rejects Player A's proposal, he will only receive zero, so following the dynamic game thought process we discussed previously, Player A's optimal choice is to offer nothing to Player B and keep the full ¥100 to himself. This is a perfect Nash equilibrium. However, numerous experiments have shown that Player A will not actually do so. He will offer considerable amount to Player B, sometimes even close to ¥50. In addition, proposals that offer less than 20% to Party B are often rejected.[15]

I did the following experiment in a class of almost 300 students. I had one group of students play the role of Player A, who determined the allocation proposal (how much they were willing to give the other party), and the other group of students played the role of Player B, who determined the minimum they were willing to accept (anything lower would be rejected). I also gave them three scenarios: (1) The other party is a classmate; (2) the other party is a Peking University student, but not in the same class; or (3) the other party is a stranger. There were also four amounts of money to be allocated: ¥10, ¥100, ¥1,000, and ¥10,000.

Table 5.1, Table 5.2, and Table 5.3 show the results of the experiment (using average values).

Table 5.1 The Players Are Classmates

total amount (Yuan)	the amount A gives to B (Yuan)	the minimum amount B accepts (Yuan)
10	4.9	3.39
100	48.17	35.64
1,000	463.0	363.45
10,000	4,537.43	3,595.13

Table 5.2 The Players Are Alumni, Not Classmates

total amount (Yuan)	the amount A gives to B (Yuan)	the minimum amount B accepts (Yuan)
10	4.57	3.74
100	43.26	37.72
1,000	409.26	370.17
10,000	3,880.78	3,539.68

Table 5.3 The Players Are Strangers

total amount (Yuan)	the amount A gives to B (Yuan)	the minimum amount B accepts (Yuan)
10	4.09	4.05
100	35.41	35.04
1,000	343.11	342.67
10,000	3,134.37	3,126.78

The outcome of the above experiment shows that regardless if the other party is a classmate, colleague, or stranger or the amount to be allocated is ¥10, ¥100, ¥1,000, or ¥10,000, the proposer is on average not willing to offer less than 30% and the other party is also not willing to accept a minimum average value less than 30%. However, there are two interesting phenomena. First, the average amount offered to the other party is highest for classmates, then colleagues, and lowest for strangers. Second, regardless which type of relationship the other party is, the average value offered to the other party decreases as the amount to be allocated increases. For example, when the other party is a stranger, the proportion given in sequence is 40.9%, 35.4%, 34.3%, and 31.3%. The first phenomenon perhaps is related to the probability of repeated games, which we will discuss in the next chapter. In long-term relationships, people focus more on reputation. Classmates are most likely to be a long-term relationship, followed by colleagues, but repeated games between strangers have a very low probability. The reason for the second phenomena perhaps is because when the relative amount is relatively large, even if the proportion is lower, the other party will not likely reject. For example, if someone allocates ¥1 out of ¥10 to me, I may angrily reject. However, if someone allocates 10% of ¥1 million to me, I am more likely accept it, even unhappily.

Circumstances in classroom experiments are imagined and of course cannot equate to reality. However, we do find similarities in society. For example, more people are accustomed to leaving a tip at restaurants and hotels after services are provided. Given that the services have already been provided, why would a tip still be given? In addition, tips that are too stingy are often rejected. Why would a server not accept a one penny tip? Why must additional thanks be given after the fact?

These issues show that the dynamic game theories we discussed previously overlook certain important factors that influence people's behavior in real life. One of the most important factors is the social norms that have been formed over a long period of history.

4.2 Social norms

The model discussed in Section Three is called norm-free bargaining theory. Each type of circumstance is built on an assumption of pure rationality, meaning each person seeks the maximization of individual payoffs. Actually, people's behavior in bargaining is norm-constrained.[16] This does not mean that respecting social norms is irrational. On the contrary, in most circumstances, respecting social norms is the best choice of rational people. As we discussed in Chapter 3, social norms are the outcome of long-term interactions between rational people and are a Nash equilibrium. Throughout life, a person will participate in an innumerable number of games, with decisions in each game possibly concerning his whole life. However, for the convenience of analysis, when theorists isolate a game to analyze it, they have no choice but to overlook many factors. Nevertheless, this does not mean that people in a real-life game do not considering these factors. We must take note of this point.

Many social norms restrict the behavior of participants in games. Social norms in bargaining can be classified into two types. The first type is called procedure norms, and the second type is called substantial norms. Procedure norms include which person should bid first, under which circumstances an agreement is considered to be reached, which means can or cannot be used in negotiations, etc. Substantial norms refer to what is just, what is cooperative behavior, etc.

First, we will examine procedure norms. For example, in courtship, who "makes a bid" first, male or female? In China's traditional society, the man proposes marriage, not the woman. This is a social norm. If the woman takes the initiative to propose, it would be contrary to social norms and reduce the woman's status in marriage relation. This norm also exists today, so we find that even if a girl loves a boy, she will think of a way to have the boy propose first, instead of taking the initiative herself. Procedural social norms also exist in transactions. For example, in the past when a house was for sale, people would first ask their neighbors. Only when the neighbors did not have interest, could that house be sold to someone else.

Another example is when we go to the store to buy something. Generally, the seller bids first, with the price often listed on the product. Now, most stores do not allow bargaining. The buyer can only choose to accept the price or not buy the product. In this type of store, if you negotiate the price, you will violate a procedure norm. Certain transactions allow for bargaining. At this point, the buyer can propose a counter-offer. In the end, both parties may come to an agreement. In circumstances where bargaining is allowed, as soon as one party accepts the other party's offer, the other party cannot go back on one's word. Without this type of norm, the agreement reached during negotiations would not be guaranteed, so neither party will trust the other. Certain other procedure norms are also very important. For example, when negotiations are underway between two parties, a third party cannot come in and increase the price. Certain transactions can be a public bid, but others require secret negotiations (such as negotiations between countries), and the process of negotiation cannot be leaked to a third party, and so on. Violations of procedure norms often cause negotiations to break down.

In substantial norms, the most important issue is the fairness and justice of distribution of interest.[17] In negotiations, if there is a commonly acknowledged standard of justness, it is easy to reach an agreement. Two frequently used standards are the norm of equality and the norm of equity. The norm of equality refers to the benefit received by each person being the same. For example, if the cost of a product is ¥5 and its value to the buyer is ¥10, a fair price is ¥7.5, thus each person receives a ¥2.5 surplus. Otherwise, it would be unfair. In the previously discussed ultimatum game, the reason Player A gives Player B a certain proportion is respect for the norm of equality. The norm of equity refers to rules such as equal pay of the equal work, to each according to his contribution, or to each according to his need, etc. In corporate governance, the person of the largest shareholder will often serve as the chairman. This is a commonly accepted norm of equity.

Sometimes, the norm of equality and the norm of equity contradict each other. For example, the founder of Baidu became a billionaire. This agrees with the norm of equity, but not the norm of equality. Certain societies put more weight on equality, whereas others put more weight on equity. The relative importance of equality and equity change over time. Also, different institutions have different underlying norms. For example, the planned economy was primarily based on the norm of equality, whereas the market economy is based on the norm of equity.

In different environments, equity may have different meanings. For example, in exchanges between acquaintances, if the seller is rich and the buyer is poor, then the price should be relatively low. Alternatively, if the seller is poor and the buyer is rich, the price should be relatively high. Otherwise, it will be considered inequitable. However, transactions between strangers do not need to follow this rule, in which case the market price is the most equitable. Another example would be a product that many people want to buy. The product going to the highest bidder is often considered to be equitable. However, if there is a shortage of seats on a train, even if there are people willing to pay the price to occupy two seats, it would be considered inequitable.

Bargaining is actually an interest allocation issue. However, as we have already pointed out, this allocation is not a zero-sum game, instead it is a positive-sum game. If an agreement is not reached, neither party has any benefit. We can see that bargaining is the dual process of cooperation and competition between the parties involved. This characteristic of bargaining determined that in real-life negotiations, we can neither always implement overbearing "hard negotiations" nor excessively compromising "soft negotiations". The "principled negotiations" summarized by Harvard scholars fully reflects this point.[18]

Notes

1 The cooperative game approach and the non-cooperative game approach correspond to the "axiomatic approach" and the "strategic approach" that Nash (1953) differentiated. The former derives the optimal outcome from commonly accepted axioms and the latter analyzes what kind of equilibrium would be achieved through each player making his own optimal choice. See Roth (1979, 1985).

2 Game Theory generally refers to non-cooperative game theory, and most Game Theory textbooks rarely discuss cooperative games. James Friedman's *Game Theory With Applications to Economics* (1991) is a rare exception. The book has a relatively systematic approach to cooperative games.

3 Here, we are assuming that the object is infinitely divisible. In reality, some things cannot be divided. In these cases, monetary transfer payments will often be used to equalize the distribution of interests. However, monetary transfer payments cannot always resolve the issue. See Elster (1989b), Chapter 2.

4 If we use the utility level to display allocation, because marginal utility decreases, even if total wealth is fixed, the feasible allocation curve would be an outward-protruding curve like the one shown in Figure 5.2.

5 Our discussions of these three conditions will be extremely simplified. For a more detailed discussion, see Chapter 6 of Friedman (1991) or Chapter 2 of Elster (1989b).

6 Generally, if we add the "symmetry" assumption to the foundation of the three previously discussed axioms, then the Nash bargaining solution is the equal distribution of added value between two people. Here, the symmetry assumption refers to that if both parties' bargaining strengths are equal, then the bargained outcome should in some way reflect this equality.

7 For simplicity, the figure did not show the cost of changing bargaining power. However, in reality, this cost often exists.

8 However, a "Prisoner's Dilemma" means that the final outcome might be the same as the original state. This is a situation often faced by the warring parties, such as was the case in the Korean War.

9 Grossman and Hart (1986) discussed the effect of ownership arrangement on bargaining power and the incentive to invest in human capital. Their paper has become a classic in the firm ownership theory literature.

10 Rubinstein (1982) used non-cooperative game theory to study bargaining. Shapiro, Shaked, and Sutton (1984) used a relatively simple model to prove Rubinstein's conclusion and expanded the model to apply it to the analysis of negotiations between labor and capital.

11 The discount factor measures the value of future earnings discounted to the present. The closer a person's discount factor is to 1, the greater the value of future earnings in the present. In other words, a person puts more weight on the future and is thus more patient. In the next chapter, we will discuss the discount factor further.

12 Research that connects the cooperative game Nash bargaining solution with the non-cooperative game Nash equilibrium is called "the Nash program". Its goal is to provide a non-cooperative game equilibrium foundation for Nash bargaining solutions deduced through axiomatic means. See Nash (1953); Binmore (1987b, 1997); and Houba and Bolt (2002).

13 A discount factor less than 1 means the pie shrinks by a certain proportion as time passes.

14 The ultimatum game was first formally proposed by Güth, Schmittberger, and Schwarze (1982). It has become one of the most popular experimental research fields.

15 See Thaler (1988); Tompkinson and Bethwaite (1995); and Oosterbeek, Sloof, and van de Kuilen (2004).

16 Chapter 6 of Elster (1989a) is a detailed discussion of norm constraints in bargaining.

17 The basic axioms related to cooperative games in Nash (1953) reflected concepts of fairness and justice.

18 See Fisher, Ury, and Patton (1991).

6   Repeated games and cooperative behavior

Repeated games increase the strategy space of game players, thus leading to a Nash equilibrium differently from one-shot games.

Particularly, repeated games can help us escape the Prisoner's Dilemma. This is one of the most important successes of Game Theory. In the one-time Prisoner's Dilemma game, the only Nash equilibrium is both parties do not cooperate. However, in repeated games, if players are sufficiently patient, then cooperation can appear as the perfect Nash equilibrium outcome. The key here is that patient people care more about long-term interests, so they are willing to let go of short-term opportunistic behavior for long-term interests.

In addition to patience, whether or not cooperation appears is influenced by the probability a game repeats, the observability of behavior, the credibility of punishment for violations, and other factors. The greater the probability a game repeats, the easier behavior is to observe, and the more credible punishments are, the greater the probability of cooperation. Monopolies cause punishments to be non-credible, so they are disadvantageous for cooperation.

People are willing to choose cooperation in repeated games because non-cooperative behavior will be punished. Without uncertainty, the more serious punishments are, the more they help cooperation. However, with uncertainty, punishments that are too serious still will not benefit cooperation. At this point, the best punishment requires some kind of forgiveness. Multiple relationships are also beneficial for the appearance of cooperation. This is the value of social relationships. However, multiple relationships might also lead to non-credible punishments, such as the situation we see in family firms.

A simple repeated game model is the game between fixed partners. However, repeated games in society are often not repeated between the same pair of people, but instead are undertaken between different people. At this point, in order to make people have an incentive to cooperate, a third party is needed to implement punishments for violations. This brings about the "second-order Prisoner's Dilemma" problem. Why do non-victims have an incentive to punish? "Boycotts" as a type of social norm can constitute a perfect Nash equilibrium and thus resolve the second-order Prisoner's Dilemma problem. Joint responsibility also aids in supervising behavior and thus promoting social cooperation.

Firms and other forms of social organizations as a type of joint responsibility mechanism are important for social cooperation. Government monopolization of social organizations is disadvantageous to social cooperation. Only with true freedom of association, can a great society possibly establish true social trust.

Section one: escaping the Prisoner's Dilemma

1.1 Repeated games

In the second chapter's Prisoner's Dilemma Games, even though cooperation was a Pareto optimal choice, each player's individual rationality determined they would choose to not cooperate. This caused the Pareto optimal to not appear and both parties to lose out.

This outcome sounds depressing. However, in real life, a large amount of cooperative behaviors happen, and we could even say that the entirety of human civilization is the outcome of cooperation. Progress in human society is obtained through a process of continual cooperation. Not only is there cooperation between individuals, families, and firms, there is also a large amount of cooperation between peoples and nations. There are numerous types of human cooperation and they are continuously evolving. From simple barter to today's complex monetary economy, from families to firms, and from tribes to international alliances are all means of human cooperation. Without cooperation, humanity may still be living in its primitive state. Through international and regional comparisons, we will discover that the higher a society's degree of cooperation is, the more advanced this society is and the better the living standards of its people are.[1] Therefore, the theoretical answer to escaping the Prisoner's Dilemma and transforming various non-cooperative behaviors into cooperative behaviors is an important task of Game Theory research.

Is there anything wrong with our assumption that humanity is rational? No. Rational people may choose to not cooperate, or they may choose to cooperate. The majority of the cooperation that we observe is precisely the outcome of people's rational choices. Irrational people on the contrary may not choose to cooperate.

The key point in this issue is that in the previous discussion on the Prisoner's Dilemma, we assumed that the game was a one-time thing and each person only considered immediate interests. In real society, even though there are one-time, short-term games between people, there are also repeated games over the long term. Humanity also has the ability to turn one-time games into long-term games. Game Theory has proven that in repeated games, cooperation may be the best choice for each rational person. It is precisely repeated games that caused rational people to escape the Prisoner's Dilemma. There are means in a non-cooperative game to obtain a cooperative outcome. This is one of the great achievements of Game Theory.[2]

Repeated games are a special type of dynamic games. In the dynamic games discussed in Chapter 4, we assumed that a similarly structured game will only occur once. However, in repeated games, the same structure of a game will repeat multiple times. For example, in real life, we must repeatedly interact with relatives, friends, and neighbors. At work, we must interact with the same colleagues every day. Marketplaces sell products every day, not once. These are all similarly structured games that repeat multiple times. We call each subgame in a repeated game a stage game. Each stage game itself may be a dynamic game, and could appear repeatedly.

The three theoretical basic characteristics of repeated games will be further discussed below.

First, there is no physical link between stage games, meaning that the outcome from a previous game does not change the structure in a later game. For example, when two people play two games of Rock, Paper, Scissors, the players can choose rock, paper, or scissors and regardless of their choice in the first round, the same three actions are available in the second. The first choice will not influence the second choice. Of course, in reality this characteristic of repeated games cannot be strictly maintained. For example, repeated games exist between firms and customers, but the products produced by the firm and customer preferences will frequently change. Repeated games exist between China and the United States, but their internal structures and relative status in international relations are different at different times. However, "Tianji's Horse Race"[3] is not a repeated game, because the horses chosen by Tianji and the King of Qi in the first round could not be used in the second round, so the choices in the first stage will influence the choices in the next round. Of course, if Tianji and the King of Qi are willing, they could hold a second horse race, which would be a repeated game.

Second, each player can observe the game's history or the things that happened in the previous stage games. For example, each player's choice to cheat or be honest or cooperate or not cooperate in previous games is observable.[4]

Third, each player cares for the total payoff which is the discounted value of payoff flow over all stage games. The significance of this is that because the game repeats multiple times, players do not only care about the current stage's gains, but also gains in the future. This point causes them to have an incentive to choose differently than in one-time games.

Repeated games are separated into finitely repeated games and infinitely repeated games. So-called "finitely repeated games" refer to games that end after a certain time or number of occurrences, after which the related parties do not again engage in the same game. So-called "infinitely repeated games" refer to games that will continue forever. They do not have an ending point, or at least players do not know when they will end (similar to how every day there is a possibility of death, but we do not know when we will die).

In this chapter, we will concentrate on infinitely repeated games. In the next chapter, we will discuss finitely repeated games.

1.2 Strategy space

The reason repeated games will lead to cooperation is because they change players' strategic space. In the one-time Prisoner's Dilemma, players only have two types of choices: Cooperate or not. There is no way for the choices of each player to be based on the information of the other player's actions. However, in repeated games, because the historical actions of each player can be observed, each player can base today's choices on the action history of other players. For example, if in the past you cheated me, then this time I will choose to not cooperate with you or cheat you; whereas if in the past you cooperated with me and the outcome was pleasant, then this time I will also choose to cooperate with you. Because the history of actions is varied, the means to link current actions with history are also varied. This causes each person's strategy space to significantly expand. It is precisely this kind of possibility that causes cooperation to possibly appear as the equilibrium outcome.

For example, when a one-time Prisoner's Dilemma game is repeated multiple times, players can choose a strategy to always defect, regardless of what happened in the past (abbreviated as "All-D"). Alternatively, players can choose a strategy to always cooperate, meaning regardless of what happened in the past (abbreviated as "All-C"). Neither of the above two strategies depend on the history of actions. More complicated strategies could be: (1) Interchangeably cooperate or not, regardless of your choice; (2) if you cheat me once, I will forgive you once and continue to cooperate, but if you cheat me once more, I will never cooperate with you again; or (3) first cooperate three times, then do not cooperate twice, then cooperate three times, then do not cooperate twice. All possible strategies are too numerous to list.

In this way, in repeated Prisoner's Dilemma Games, the strategies that players can choose increased substantially. The appearance of new strategies allows players to punish or reward each other's past actions, thus allowing cooperation between both parties to become possible. However, whether or not the outcome of cooperation can appear depends on the type of strategy that players choose. For example, if both parties choose "never cooperate", then cooperation will not occur. You may believe that if both parties choose "always cooperate", then cooperation will appear. However, this kind of strategy is not a Nash equilibrium, because given that the other player will choose "always cooperate", your optimal choice is "always defect", and thus, you take advantage of the other, instead of "always cooperating".

Because mutual cooperating can benefit both parties, naturally, players may have an incentive to choose strategies that will cause cooperation to be the outcome. The question is what type of strategy both satisfies individual rationality and can guarantee cooperation is the outcome?

Real-life observations prove that two types of strategies are most commonly used. Theory and experiments have proven that these two types of strategies are most likely to lead to cooperative behavior.

The first type is a "tit-for-tat" strategy. Each action is based on the opponent's previous action. For example, in the beginning I will cooperate with you, but if you cheat me today, then tomorrow I will not cooperate with you. If tomorrow you do not cheat me again, then the day after tomorrow I will cooperate with you again. In other words: "An eye for an eye and a tooth for a tooth".

Another type is a "trigger strategy". In the beginning, I will cooperate with you, and as long as you do not cheat me, I will continue to cooperate with you. However, if you cheat me even once, I will never cooperate with you again. Alternatively, if you cheat me once, I will cheat you forever. This shows that in the trigger strategy as long as once person does not cooperate, all cooperation is ruined. This type of strategy is actually very ruthless, because even if the other party makes a mistake, it will cause the cooperative relationship to be broken. Precisely because of this, it can lead people to be more careful and serious when making a decision.

1.3 The value of cooperation and patience

In the repeated Prisoner's Dilemma Game, the reason cooperation can occur is because players not only care about immediate interests, but also long-term interests. Therefore, before specifically testing which kind of strategy may lead to cooperation being the outcome, we must first discuss how to calculate long-term interests. In other words, how much is maintaining long-term cooperative relationships worth?

In the second chapter, we relied on the general Prisoner's Dilemma Game described in Figure 6.1.

As is shown in the figure, in the one-time game, if Player A and B cooperate, each person will receive T. If neither player cooperates, each person will receive P. If one person cooperates and the other does not, then the person that cooperates receives S and the person that does not cooperate receives R. In this way, for any individual, the best outcome is for the other person to cooperate but you to not cooperate for R. The next best outcome is both people cooperate for T. The third best outcome after that is both people do not cooperate for P. The worst outcome is for you to cooperate but the other person to not cooperate for S. Therefore, we have $R > T > P > S$. At the same time, we assume that the total value of cooperation is greater than the total value of one party cooperating and the other party not cooperating, thus $(T + T) > (S + R)$.

Now, we will assume that Player A and Player B undertake an infinitely repeated Prisoner's Dilemma Game. Assume that both people never cooperate, so in the first round they receive P, in the second round also receive P, in the third round still receive P, and so on. In this scenario, the payoff from each round is

	Player B	
	Cooperate	Does not cooperate
Cooperate	T, T	S, R
Does not cooperate	R, S	P, P

Player A (label on left, between the two rows)

Figure 6.1 The Prisoner's Dilemma Game

the same as the payoff produced from the Nash equilibrium in the one-time game. Alternatively, if both parties cooperate from the start and never defect, each person's revenue flow is $T, T, T, T \ldots$

Imagine that both parties previously have always cooperated, but at a certain point in time t, what is the value of continuing mutual cooperation indefinitely to each party?

To calculate this value, we must introduce the individual discount factor, which is today's value of one yuan tomorrow. One yuan tomorrow is of course not equal to one yuan today. We will use $\delta < 1$ to represent the discount factor. As argued in the last chapter, it reflects a player's degree of patience. The larger δ is, the more a person weights the future. In this way, today's one yuan equals one yuan, tomorrow's one yuan equals today's δ, the next day's one yuan equals today's δ^2, and so on. The further away one yuan is, the less valuable it is today.

This way, the discounted value of maintaining a long-term mutual cooperative relationship is:

$$V = T + \delta T + \delta^2 T + \delta^3 T + \delta^4 T +$$

Mathematically, we know that this value equals $T/(1 - \delta)$.[5] Obviously, δ plays a key role here. The greater δ is, the greater the long-term value of cooperation, and the opposite is also true. This is the root of patient's importance to cooperative behavior.

We can also explain δ in another way. We can see it as the possibility of a game repeating. Assume that today there is a game, how large is the possibility that I will continue this game tomorrow? Even if tomorrow's one yuan equaled today's one yuan, but the possibility of gaining one yuan tomorrow is less than one, then players will also discount tomorrow's income. In this way, the payoff for both parties cooperating today is T and the payoff for continuing to cooperate tomorrow is still T, but if the probability of having a game tomorrow is only δ, then tomorrow's expected income is only δT. Given the circumstances of tomorrow's game, if the game on the next day also has an occurrence probability of δ, then from today's perspective, the probability of the game on the next day occurring is δ^2, so the next day's expected income is $\delta^2 T$. This process continues on and on. Of course, the longer the time horizon, the probability of continuing a game becomes lower, and thus the expected income is also smaller.

We could also consider the discount factor and the probability of a game repeating in combination. For example, if the discount factor is a, then tomorrow's one yuan is worth today's a yuan. However, the probability of earning one yuan tomorrow is only b, so the two of them multiplied together is $\delta = ab$.

The three types of explanations actually have a common meaning, which is to represent future earning's degree of importance to players. This is also why we broadly explain the discount factor δ as "patience".

In real life, the degree of importance of future interests is related to a person's character, age, health condition, family relation, and faith, as well as social environments. In China, there is something called "the 59 Years Old Phenomenon", which means government officials are likely to start corruption at 59 years old. Given the retiring age at 60, they may put more weight on immediate interests, so they misuse their power for private interests. A person that expects to die tomorrow and a person that expects to die in 20 years will behave differently. A person with a fulfilling marriage and happy family often puts more focus on the future. A religious person that accepts judgment in the afterlife will also put more focus on the future. From this perspective, religion can promote cooperation between members of society, which is also the important social function of religion.[6]

The weight of future interests is an important variable for determining players' behavior. According to the folk theorem in Game Theory,[7] in infinitely repeated games, if each player weights the future enough, meaning δ is large enough, then any degree of cooperation could appear as a perfect Nash equilibrium outcome. Here, "any degree of cooperation" refers to the frequency of cooperation appearing throughout the whole game. It could be 100% cooperation, which means no one is ever cheated, or it could be 0% cooperation, meaning someone is cheated each time.

Section two: cooperation and punishment

2.1 Tit for tat

From here, we will discuss which types of strategies may lead to cooperation and the factors that determine the specific degree of cooperation.

First, we will consider the tit-for-tat strategy. As was described previously, this strategy refers to starting with cooperating, but the action in the next round completely depends on the choices of the opponent in the previous round. If both players maintain this kind of strategy, no one will instigate non-cooperation, and they cooperate with each other every round. Thus, the payoff for each party in every round is T, so the discounted value of payoffs is $T/(1 - \delta)$. It is easy to prove that if δ is large enough, this strategy forms a Nash equilibrium.

Given that the other player uses a tit-for-tat strategy and chooses to cooperate in the first round, then if you choose to never cooperate (All-D), starting from the second round, the opponent will choose to never cooperate. So, in the first round, the opponent's payoff is S, your payoff is R, and starting from the second round, the payoff for each person is only P. After being discounted, we get a payoff of $R + P(\delta/(1 - \delta))$ for you. When comparing the total value of the two choices, it is easy to see that as long as δ is large enough to satisfy $\delta \geq (R - T)/(R - P)$, then given that the opponent will choose the tit-for-tat strategy, then you choose the strategy to always betray is certainly not optimal,[8] so you should also choose to cooperate.[9] Of course, if this condition is not satisfied, then cooperation is not optimal. Further, the minimum value of δ that is required to maintain cooperation depends on the relative values of R, T, and P. Obviously, the larger the benefit of cooperation (T) is and smaller the benefit of unilateral non-cooperation (R) or of both parties not cooperating is, then the smaller δ is to satisfy the condition for cooperation. Thus, the greater the likelihood of cooperation is.

Both parties using a tit-for-tat strategy form a Nash equilibrium, but it is not a perfect Nash equilibrium. Why? Imagine that in stage *t* Player A does not cooperate. This strategy means that Player B should choose to not cooperate with Player A in the stage *t* + 1. However, should Player B do this? If Player B believes that Player A has implemented the tit-for-tat strategy, then punishing Player A's non-cooperative behavior in stage *t* will lead to the following situation from stage *t* + 1:

> Player A's Behavior: Cooperate, do not cooperate, cooperate, do not cooperate,
> . . .
>
> Player B's Behavior: Do not cooperate, cooperate, do not cooperate, cooperate,
> . . .
>
> Player B's payoff flow alternates as follows forever:
>
> $$R, S, R, S, R, S, \ldots$$
>
> However, if Player B chooses to forgive Player A, then cooperation resumes from stage *t* + 1, so Player B's payoff flow is:
>
> $$T, T, T, T, T, T, \ldots$$

When these two income sequences are compared, the latter is greater than the former.[10] In other words, given that one party choose to not cooperate at some stage, as long as the one party believes that the other party has implemented the tit-for-tat strategy, then he has no incentive to implement punishment. Instead, he will choose to forgive the other party and continue cooperation. However, at this point, the other party will consider that as long as he is forgiven, then why not continue to cheat? Therefore, the tit-for-tat is not a perfect Nash equilibrium.

However, the "tit-for-tat" strategy is the most used strategy in real life, regardless if it is based on rational consideration or emotions. Actually, this kind of behavior has become a type of commonly accepted social norm. In most societies, a person that acts in this way is considered "courageous." On the contrary, a person that always forgives others is considered cowardly. In research on social cooperative games, Axelrod (1984) did a large amount of computer model experiments and found that among all of the submitted strategies, tit-for-tat had the highest rate of success. People that chose this strategy had the highest compensation on average. When we discuss evolutionary games later, we will discuss this point again.

2.2 Never forgive

Now we will discuss the trigger strategy. As was described previously, the trigger strategy means that if any party acts in bad faith once, neither party will ever cooperate again. This strategy means even if your partner makes a mistake, you will never forgive him. Because of this un-forgivingness, it is also called the grim strategy. Interestingly, under conditions of complete information, this strategy actually most easily leads to cooperation. This may be the reason that members of mafia organizations are the most unified and loyal.

It is easy to prove that if δ is large enough, the trigger strategy not only forms a Nash equilibrium, but it is also a perfect Nash equilibrium. Specifically, assume that both parties choose the trigger strategy and begin by cooperating and cooperate until one day it is discovered that the opponent did not cooperate, at which point cooperation never happens again. Imagine that both parties cooperate until the point in time t, at which point we will consider if one of the players should choose to cooperate or not.

At this point, given that your opponent utilizes the trigger strategy, if you cooperate, then your payoff is T in this round and every round after that, so the discounted value of your payoffs is $T/(1 - \delta)$. However, if you choose to defect, this one time your payoff is R, but starting from the next stage the opponent will choose to never cooperate with you. At that point, your best outcome is also to never cooperate, so your payoff for each later stage can only be P. The total discounted value is $R + P(\delta/(1 - \delta))$. If the value of δ satisfies $T/(1 - \delta) \geq R + P(\delta/(1 - \delta))$, then your optimal choice is to cooperate. In other words, as long as $\delta \geq (R - T)/(R - P)$, then both parties choosing a mutual trigger strategy (not choosing to defect first) is optimal. At the same time, because the outcome is the same starting from any point of time, it is also a perfect Nash equilibrium.

The above condition could be re-written as $\delta(T - P)/(1 - \delta) \geq R - T$. The right side of the equation $R - T$ represents the one-shot gain from not cooperating at some point and the left side of the equation $\delta(T - P)/(1 - \delta)$ represents the discounted value of future losses caused by non-cooperative behavior (of which $T - P$ is the loss in every period). Therefore, players cooperating or not is decided by whether or not long-term interests can overcome the appeal of immediate interests, as well as the degree of patience. Specifically speaking, given the degree of patience (the weight of future interests), the greater the appeal of not cooperating once is, meaning the immediate interests of not cooperating relative to the long-term interests of cooperating, the more likely players will choose to not cooperate. Alternatively, the lesser the appeal of one-time immediate interests from not cooperating relative to the long-term interests of cooperation is, the greater the likelihood of cooperation. Additionally, given the appeal of not cooperating and the long-term benefits of cooperating, the greater the weight on the future, the more likely cooperation is.

Let us use a specific example to explain this point. Assume that when the opponent cooperates and you do not, the payoff $R = 3$. When both parties cooperate the payoff $T = 2$. When neither party cooperates, the payoff $P = 1$. Only when $\delta \geq 0.5$ do both parties have an incentive to cooperate. However, if we increase R to 3.5, but do not change the other payoffs, then in order to incentivize both parties to cooperate, δ must be greater than or equal to 0.75. Assume that players' actual discount factor $\delta = 0.6$. Cooperation could appear in the first instance but not in the second.

This can explain the circumstances that we often see in real life where two people that ordinarily cooperate suddenly do not cooperate again once there is an opportunity for exorbitant gains, even among friends. The reason is that the discount factor of cooperation that supports the ordinary circumstances becomes insufficient when measured against exorbitant gains.

If we explain δ as the possibility (probability) that players expect the game to repeat, then the circumstances for cooperation described above means that the less likely a game is to repeat, the less likely cooperation will occur. This can explain why people in stable societies are more trustworthy than people in chaotic societies. It can also explain why people in rule of law societies have more of a cooperative spirit than people in rule of man societies. Compared with rule of law societies, rule of man societies are more uncertain.[11]

If we explain δ as the combination of the discount factor and probability, then they have a substitution relationship. If players' discount factor is relatively low, then for cooperation to appear as the equilibrium the game must have a relatively high probability of repeating. Alternatively, if the probability of the game repeating is relatively low, then players are required to have a higher discount factor. In the previous example ($R = 3$, $T = 2$, $P = 1$), if the probability of the game repeating is 1, then a discount factor greater than 0.5 can lead to cooperation. However, if the probability of the game repeating is only 0.7, then cooperation will only occur when the discount factor is greater than 0.715. If the probability of the game repeating is less than 0.5, then regardless of how high the discount factor is (the extreme is 1), cooperation cannot occur.

In Figure 6.2, we draw the cooperation area and non-cooperation area on a two-dimensional space. The horizontal axis represents the discount factor a, and the vertical line represents the probability b of the game repeating. The curve DD represents the set of all points (a, b) that satisfy $\delta = ab = (R - T)/(R - P)$. If a coordinate point of probability and discount factor is on the right side of the curve, then coordination could appear. If they are on the left side of the curve, cooperation cannot occur. If the gain R from a one-time betrayal increases, assuming that other conditions do not change, then the curve will move to the right. If the gain T from both parties cooperating increases or the gain P from neither party cooperating decreases, then the curve will move to the left.

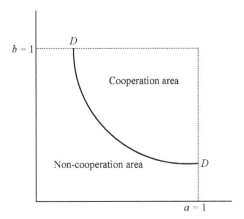

Figure 6.2 The Cooperation Area and the Non-Cooperation Area

2.3 Information and cooperation

In the previous analysis, we assumed that the behavior of each player could be immediately observed by the other player, meaning that if one player swindles, the other player can immediately punish it. However, assume that one player's means of deceit are hidden so that the other player does not know until multiple rounds later. What will the consequence be then?

Assume that deception will be discovered after two rounds and will then be punished. The deceptive player will choose to not cooperate, so in the first stage the payoff is R, in the next stage the payoff is still R, but starting from the third stage the other player will not cooperate, so the payoff becomes P. At that point, the expected payoff from not cooperating at any point should be:

$$R + \delta R + \delta^2 P + \delta^3 P + \ldots = (1+\delta)R + \frac{\delta^2}{1-\delta}P$$

The expected payoff from choosing to cooperate is still $T/(1-\delta)$. In this way, to guarantee that both parties cooperate, the value of δ must make the inequalities below hold:

$$\frac{T}{1-\delta} \geq (1+\delta)R + \frac{\delta^2}{1-\delta}P$$

That is

$$\delta \geq \sqrt{\frac{R-T}{R-T}} > \frac{R-T}{R-P}$$

Remember in the previous analysis that if a swindle will be observed at the first instance, then δ only needed to satisfy $\delta \geq (R - T)/(R - P)$. Here, we can see that compared to the conditions for cooperation previously, the requirement for δ is much higher. For example, if $R = 3$, $T = 2$, and $P = 1$, then when a swindle is discovered at the first instance, as long as $\delta \geq 0.5$ cooperation will occur. If a swindle will not be discovered until after two rounds, then δ must at least be equal to 0.71 for cooperation to occur. This means that cooperation is more difficult than before. Imagine that a person's $\delta = 0.6$. If his swindle will be discovered at the first instance, then he has an incentive to cooperate. However, if his swindle will not be discovered until after two rounds, then he will not choose to cooperate.

It is easy to prove that the longer the observation lags, the greater the requirement that cooperation puts on the discount factor. In other words, when swindling is not easy to observe, players must be more patient and put more weight on future interests in order to maintain cooperation. Alternatively, the more difficult it is to discover swindling, the more likely swindling is to occur, so the more difficult it is to cooperate. In the extreme case, if swindling will never be observed by the other party, then cooperation is an impossible outcome.

There is a significant relationship between the number of times a person can swindle others before being discovered and the speed of information transmission in a society. For example, in the countryside in the rural society, villagers knew each other. Gossips amongst villagers played a role in transmitting information, so once a person did something bad, everyone would know very quickly. This is the reason bad people went to other villages to do bad things. Now, the mobility of urban residents is high, so most people are strangers. It is easy for a person to do bad things but still not be discovered, so we must rely on public media platforms or specialized providers of information.[12] Therefore, in modern society, the development of public media is very important for the maintenance of social cooperation. Additionally, the appearance of new communication media, such as microblogs (Twitter and WeChat), social networks (Facebook and Renren), and ratings websites (Yelp and Dazhong Dianping), aid in the rapid transmission of information, which is also very important for maintaining cooperation in society. The transmission of information relies on many technological and institutional factors. Technological factors specifically refer to the various tools that allow for the faster transmission of information. Institutional factors, such as players' incentives for revealing information, will be further discussed later.[13]

2.4 The carrot and the stick

The reason that cooperation appears in repeated games is because people worry about the punishments for not cooperating. In the previous model, this type of punishment is the other party stopping cooperating with the cheater, or the discontinuation of profitable transactions. If punishments do not exist or the strength of punishments is not sufficient, then cooperation will not occur. Therefore, an important question related to punishments is: What kind of punishment encourages people to cooperate the most?

Abreu's (1986) paper pointed out that even if an infinite punishment strategy is not used, using a strongly credible punishment can also cause people in a game to choose to cooperate. The so-called "strongly credible punishment" refers to when the other party's non-cooperative behavior is discovered, the punishment is long enough and large enough, as well as being optimal for the person implementing it. For example, assume that when I know that you have swindled me, I will punish you three times for each time you swindle me. At that point, your total discounted gain from swindling me once is R plus the three times being punished, that is $R + \delta P + \delta^2 P + \delta^3 P$, whereas the payoff from always choosing to cooperate is $T + \delta T + \delta^2 T + \delta^3 T$. As long as the following inequality is true, you will choose to cooperate:

$$T + \delta T + \delta^2 T + \delta^3 T \geq R + \delta P + \delta^2 P + \delta^3 P$$

In other words, it is not necessary for punishments to be infinite; and they just have to be long enough.[14]

A special mention must be made of Abreu's so-called "carrot and stick" strategy. This strategy involves cooperating in the beginning, but if I discover that you have swindled me in round t, then I will not cooperate with you in round $t + 1$ (as stick). However, in $t + 1$, you must cooperate with me (representing your willingness to pay the penalty). If you do so, then starting from $t + 2$ I will resume cooperation (as a carrot). If the party that should have cooperated in $t + 1$ does not cooperate, or the party that should have been punished is not punished, then both parties should be punished at the following rounds as described for $t + 1$, until proposed punishments are implemented. In other words, if I cooperate with you in round t, but you do not cooperate with me in round t, then non-cooperation will continue until you admit your fault and cooperate with me. Punishments are not only to punish the first player who does not cooperate, but also to punish the player who should punish but does not. The general significance of this game is that after you honestly admit your fault and punish yourself, then I will forgive you and mutual cooperation can resume.

Specifically speaking, assume that each person chooses the carrot and stick strategy. There are two scenarios to discuss: cooperation scenario and punishment scenario. First, consider the cooperation scenario. If players choose to cooperate at this point, then the payoff in the first round is T, and will also be T in the next round. If at this stage I do not cooperate, my payoff will be R, but punishment will come in the next round and the payoff will be S if I accept the punishment by choosing cooperation at $t + 1$ (If punishment is not accepted in the next round, then the game will become a situation discussed in the next scenario). In order for cooperation to occur, the inequality $T + \delta T \geq R + \delta S$ must be satisfied, that is, $\delta \geq (R - T) / (T - S)$.

The punishment scenario is that I swindled you last time, and then you punish me this time. If I accept the punishment by choosing to cooperate while you punish me by not cooperating, my payoff is S; and then we return to cooperate starting from the next round and each person's payoff is T. The discounted payoff of two periods is $S + \delta T$. If I do not accept the punishment by not cooperating again, my payoff is P. But in the next period I will still need to be punished, so the discounted value of two periods is $P + \delta S$. If $S + \delta T \geq P \delta S$ is true, that is, $\delta \geq (P - S) / (T - S)$, then I am willing to accept the punishment.

These two scenarios show that if the discount factor δ is high enough, infinite punishments are not necessary. As long as punishments are strict enough, they can form deterrents that encourage players to cooperate.

Previously, we assumed that punishments were credible. Conditions for players to implement punishments are as follow. When your swindle is discovered, if a punishment is implemented, then my payoff in this period is R, and the next period's payoff is T. If no punishment is implemented, then my payoff for this period is T, and the next period's payoff is S. Obviously, the payoff from implementing a punishment is certainly larger than from not implementing a punishment, given $R > T > S$. Therefore, the condition for implementing punishments is satisfied.

2.5 Non-credibility of punishment

In some repeated games, however, punishments are not credible.

Consider the game between a monopoly (such as a telecommunications, gas, or water company) and its customer. Because the customer uses its service every day, it is a repeated game. The consumer is faced with two choices: Buy or not. If the consumer chooses to not buy, both receive a payoff of 0. If the consumer chooses to buy, the producer is faced with two choices: Honesty (high quality service) or dishonesty (low quality service). If the producer chooses honesty, then both parties receive a payoff of 5. If the producer chooses dishonesty, then the consumer receives a payoff of 1 and the producer receives a payoff of 7. This game is shown in Figure 6.3.

If this game only occurs once, then the perfect Nash equilibrium is the producer chooses dishonesty and the consumer chooses to buy. If the game has an infinite number of occurrences, will the producer become honest? Imagine the consumer declares this strategy: If the producer is honest, I will continue to buy, but as soon as I am cheated, I will not buy again. If the producer believes the consumer will actually behave in this way, then his best option is to be honest. However, the producer knows that this declaration is not credible. Once the consumer is cheated and does not buy, his payoff is 0, which is not his optimal choice. Therefore, the punishment is not credible, so the producer will never choose to be honest.

This is actually a one-sided Prisoner's Dilemma. In other words, only one player behaves opportunistically. In our example, the producer behaves opportunistically, but the consumer does not. Because the non-cooperative firm is a monopolist, the consumer has no means to punish it, so obviously the firm will not improve its service.

This can explain the poor quality of state-owned enterprise services. Introducing competition will resolve this issue. If another firm can provide similar products or services, then consumer's punishments become credible, so each firm has no choice but to choose honesty.

Actually, government's rule over people is the same. Dictatorial governments must have strict border controls. With free movement across borders, there is competition between governments. When people have the possibility to "vote with their feet", then governments must focus on their people. This is an important reason that entering the World Trade Organization can change government behavior.

2.6 Going too far is as bad as not going far enough

In the previous model, we proved that the stricter the punishment for non-cooperative behavior is, the higher the degree of cooperation is. It is precisely the

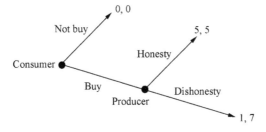

Figure 6.3 Punishments Are Not Credible

fear of punishments that make people not dare to swindle. However, this conclusion only stands in circumstances without uncertainty. In a certain world, any wrongdoing is objectively observable by the people involved. At that point, punishments are only a type of threat, but the actual equilibrium circumstance is that they will not happen. Therefore, this type of punishment does not have a cost.

However, the real world is not certain and has multiple factors influencing people's behavior that are not controllable by the people involved. Much of the non-cooperative behavior that we observe may not be the intention of the people involved, but result of other factors such as outside pressure, a misjudgment, or an accident. People are also not always rational, and may do things out of emotion that they otherwise would not want to do. At this point, if the punishment is too severe, such as the trigger strategy, then a mistake may lead to unending punishment. This is not beneficial to long-term cooperation.

For example, imagine that for uncontrollable reasons a buyer cannot pay bill on time. If because of this the seller will never provide goods again, then cooperation that could have happened is cut off. The buyer may not even be willing to sign a contract with this provider because cutting off supplies may lead to huge losses.

Therefore, infinite punishments may not bring about cooperation. However, no punishments at all will also not bring about cooperation. The reason is that if any error can be blamed on external factors, why not take advantage of the other party? This leads to the optimum punishment question. For instance, when the other party's breach is discovered, it may be optimal to at first punish a few times, and then resume the relationship (Green and Porter, 1984). In this regard, we say that the tit-for-tat strategy may be more rational.

In reality people will not mechanically enforce given orders of punishments. When they come across the other party's breach, people will attempt to obtain certain relevant information, then judge to what degree this behavior was intentional or created by objective circumstances in order to determine whether or not to punish and to what degree. A person with a good reputation that occasionally makes mistakes will often be forgiven, but a person with a poor reputation that makes a mistake once may lead to cooperation ending permanently.

In criminal law, the sentence must be appropriate. The social order must temper justice with mercy. Management must use the carrot and the stick. These are all based on the same reason.

Section three: cooperation in large societies

In our previous discussion, the repeated game was a long-term game in a two-person world. It was a one-on-one transaction taking place in a fixed relationship. Also, their relationship was one dimensional involving one type of special commodity and nothing else. In this type of two-person world, punishments to maintain cooperation are implemented by the injured party. The so-called punishment is cutting off cooperation in this relationship (and thus returning to a one-time Prisoner's Dilemma Nash equilibrium).

The real world is a large society formed by many people. In this type of society, cooperation partners are not fixed even in long-term games. In addition, there are often multiple types of interpersonal relationships. There are differences between the mechanisms need to maintain cooperation in a multi-person society with multiple relationships and in a two-person society with a singular relationship. In this section, we will discuss the multi-person, multi-relationship cooperation issue.

3.1 Multi-relationship cooperation

In life, interpersonal interactions are multi-dimensional. For example, two business partners may be university alumni; your boss may be your father's old friend; your raw materials supplier may also be your customer; your comrade-in-arms may also be your fellow-villager; your competitor in the color television market may also be your competitor in the refrigerator market, and you may all be members of the same club. These are multi-transactional relationships between people. These types of multi-transactional relationships have an important influence on people's behavior in games, allowing them to cooperate more easily. Even if some specific transaction is a one-time game, in another aspect it may be a repeated game, so the latter relationship will influence the behavior in the former game. It is easy to imagine that even a truly one-time game, if the players in the Prisoner's Dilemma are brothers, they may not betray each other, because it would cause family issues.

Specifically, we will consider the two types of relationships shown in Figure 6.4.

These are two types of Prisoner's Dilemma games.[15] If it is a one-shot game, both parties will choose to not cooperate. Assume the two transactional relationships above are undertaken by two different pairs of people. For instance, Player

	Transactional Relationship I	
	Cooperate	Does not cooperate
Cooperate	3, 3	−1, 4
Does not cooperate	4, −1	0, 0

	Transactional Relationship II	
	Cooperate	Does not cooperate
Cooperate	5, 5	0, 9
Does not cooperate	9, 0	4, 4

Figure 6.4 Multi-Transactional Relationships and Cooperation

A and Player B undertake Transactional Relationship I and Player A and Player C undertake Transactional Relationship II. In an infinitely repeated game, in order to maintain cooperation in the first relationship, $\delta \geq 0.25$, and to maintain cooperation in the second relationship, δ must not be less than 0.8 (assuming that both parties implement the trigger strategy). Obviously, the degree of difficulty maintaining the second transaction is much higher.

Now, if we put the two transactions together and they are done by the same pair of two people, what would the outcome be?

Assume the players implement this kind of strategy: If one party cheats the other party in either transaction, the other party will not cooperate in both markets as punishment. In this situation, maintaining cooperation in both markets requires $\delta \geq (4 + 9 - 3 - 5)/(4 + 9 - 0 - 4) \cong 0.56$. In other words, if we combine the two transactions, then $\delta > 0.56$ can cause cooperation. Imagine that $\delta = 0.6$, then when the two types of transactions happen between different pair of people, then cooperation will only occur in the first transaction, but not the second. If both transactions happen between the same two people, then cooperation will occur in both markets. From this we can see that under certain conditions multiple-transaction relationships can promote the occurrence of cooperation.[16]

Actually, it is easy to prove that even if Transactional Relationship II only occurs once, as long as Transactional Relationship I is a repeating game, then $\delta \geq 0.56$ can also maintain cooperation on both markets. If the two transactions are undertaken by different pair of people, regardless of how large δ is, neither party in Relationship II can possibly choose cooperation.

This is the reason that in life we always hope to establish more relationships to maintain cooperation or add new transactions to existing relationships. For instance, there is a work relationship between employees, and many firms encourage other types of relationships (such as inviting family to participating in group travel) to further promote the cooperative spirit within the firm. These relationships are called social relationships. Social relationships facilitate cooperative behavior in economic relationships. This is one reason that people are willing to develop these kinds of social relationships. Generally speaking, all economic relationships are embedded in various complex social relationships.

Let us consider a numerical example of social relationship. Imagine that the present value of this relationship for each party is V. If you cheat me once, I will not be your friend again, so you will lose V. When V is large enough (such as $V \geq 4$ in this case), even if the Prisoner's Dilemma game as described in the transaction II of Figure 6.4 is one-shot, neither will have incentive to betray the other. At this point, cooperation could even occur in one-time transactions. For this reason, we can understand the greater degree of trust between friends. If cheating a friend in a one-time transaction ends the friendship, and thus causes a loss of V, it may not be worth it.[17]

Similarly, this is the case for colleague and hometown relationships. For example, many Chinese urban families prefer to find nannies from their hometowns. The reason is that in addition to an employment relationship, there is an additional relationship, such as being your niece. With this additional relationship, if she

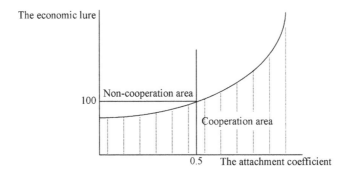

Figure 6.5 Interpersonal Relationships and Cooperation

steals something or leaves without notice, her family can take care of it and you have no worry.

However, social relation has limit in supporting economic transaction. We can rely on Figure 6.5 for a simple representation of this meaning (Zhang, 2003).

In Figure 6.5, the horizontal axis represents the depth of interpersonal relationships, which we can call the attachment coefficient. The vertical axis represents the temptation of a one-time economic transaction. The curve represents the relationship between the attachment coefficient and the maximum economic temptation. The greater the attachment, the greater the ability to suppress the temptation of a one-time cheat is. Cooperation can occur in the area below the curve, but not above. For instance, when both people's attachment index is 0.5, as long as the temptation for a one-time cheat is less than 100, then both parties can rely on each other to cooperate.

This also explains other issues. Not all friends' mutual reliance can be unlimited. Many friendships are ended after one big business deal. If the temptation of a one-time cheat exceeds the maximum from both party's attachment, neither will follow the rules. For example, Person A lends ¥100,000 to Person B who speculates on the stock market, but the arrangement is not documented. When Person B's speculation earns ¥1 million, Person A may claim that he did not lend money to Person B, instead he entrusted Person B for investment. The dispute may need to be solved in the court. This example shows that as soon as economic temptation becomes great enough, it may be difficult for friendship to continue. In real life, small transactions do not need a written contract, but land and real estate transactions certainly require a written contract, because the temptation of opportunism is too great.

Multi-dimensional transactional relationships may cause punishments to be non-credible. If a stranger cheats you, you can take him to court. However, if a family member cheats you, would you take him to court? Usually the answer is no. The reason punishments become non-credible is because punishments not only punish the punished, but also punish the punisher.[18] Non-credible punishments brought about the governance issue of family enterprises. It causes implementing standard modernized management in family enterprises to be extremely difficult. Certain people specialize in cheating friends, which is also related to non-credible punishments.[19] This is not a new phenomenon; instead it has existed since ancient times. In feudal society, revolts were often led by the emperor's relatives, such as the Rebellion of the Seven States during the Emperor Jing of Han's reign. The difficulty of managing a family enterprise is similar to the difficulty ruling a feudal kingdom.[20]

3.2 Long-term players

The games we have discussed so far are games between two fixed players. In such a fixed pair relation, cooperation can be achieved in a repeated contact if, when one player cheats, the other as victim can punish him by switching to one-shot Prisoner's Dilemma Nash equilibrium action. This type of punishment mechanism is called a "second party enforcement", or "personal enforcement". Of course, if players rely on their own morality for an incentive to enforce a cooperative agreement, we call this punishment mechanism self-restraint.

Transaction participants in real life are often not fixed. For example, a store may be relatively fixed, but consumers are not. Automobiles and other durable goods are even more so. Very few people buy a new car every year. How can cooperation be guaranteed in this type of situation? Obviously, in this case, some kind of "third party enforcement" mechanisms are needed. By the third-party enforcement, we mean the punishment for deviating is implemented by someone else instead of the victim. For example, the law regulates certain contracts. Here, the "third party" that enforces the punishment is the government.

"Third parties" that are not legal enforcers in nature merit our study more. This type of "third party" will face the self-incentive problem. The third party that implements punishments will do so at a cost, possibly making a loss or losing out on future opportunities for cooperation. Implementing a punishment equates to the third party providing a public good. For instance, imagine that Player A cheats Player B, and Player B has no means to punish Player A, so Player C as the third party will no longer transact with Player A as a punishment for Player A's behavior. Player C faces a self-interest problem, because stopping transactions with Player A may forfeit a beneficial opportunity. This problem is called the "second-order Prisoner's dilemma" or the "second-order collective choice problem".[21] In other words, what is the incentive for the third party to implement punishments?

We will discuss the "second-order Prisoner's Dilemma" in different specific circumstances.

First, we will consider the simplest circumstance, which is the game between a store and numerous consumers. In this game, the store is called the long-term player and the consumer is often a one-time player, such as someone that will generally only buy one television in the short-term. The cooperative outcome of this game means the store does not sell inferior goods and the consumer does not stop the transaction. In this game, how can cooperation be the outcome? People may think that after consumers buy inferior goods they can go to a third party with authority, such as the Ministry of Commerce, to submit a complaint, then the Ministry of Commerce will punish the store. When the operation of public power is highly effective or consumer protection laws are complete, this arrangement can play a role. However, when government is very ineffective or the cost of utilizing legal channels is extremely high, who should the customer turn to? We can prove that under certain conditions, other consumers without public power can also effectively punish the store, thus causing the store to choose cooperation.

Specifically, we can use the game below to display this issue. Consumers can choose to purchase or not, and the store can choose to provide high-quality products or low-quality products. The payoff for both parties in one-shot game is shown in Figure 6.6.

If the game is only undertaken once, then the equilibrium is the consumer does not purchase and the store provides low-quality products, meaning both parties do not cooperate. We call this type of situation a one-sided Prisoner's Dilemma. The reason is that only the store has an incentive problem, whereas the consumer does not. The consumer can only choose to purchase or not, and there is no issue of swindling.

Now, assume there are an infinite number of consumers undertaking a game with the store. Only one customer comes each round, and each customer only purchases once. We can prove that if the store's discount factor δ is large enough, then the following strategy profile forms a perfect Nash equilibrium that causes the store to provide high-quality products.

The Store's Strategy: If from the beginning high-quality products are provided, then high quality products will continue to be provided, unless low-quality products have been provided before. If low-quality products are provided at any one time, then low-quality products will be provided forever.

The Consumers' Strategy: The first consumer will choose to purchase. The quality of the product bought by the first consumer will determine the actions of the second consumer. As long as the previous consumer is provided with a high-quality product, the next consumer will continue to purchase. As soon as any one consumer is cheated with a low-quality product, then no consumer will purchase again.

We will test the reasons this strategy profile can form a perfect Nash equilibrium.

| | | Vendor | |
		High-quality	Low-quality
Consumer	Purchase	1, 1	−1, 2
	Not	0, 0	0, 0

Figure 6.6 The Vendor and Consumer Game

First, we will examine the store's strategy. Given the consumers' strategy, and assuming that the store has never provided low-quality products before, then from any period if the store continues to provide high-quality products, consumers will continue to purchase. The store's payoff from the first consumer is 1, still 1 from the second consumer, and so on. Therefore, the total discounted payoff is $1 / (1 - \delta)$. On contrary, if the store provides low-quality products, his payoff from the first consumer is 2, but afterwards, no new consumers will purchase, so the store's payoff for every later period is 0.

Therefore, given the consumers' strategy, when $1 / (1 - \delta) \geq 2$, and thus $\delta \geq 0.5$, meaning the store's patience is enough to be greater than 1/2, then the store will provide high-quality products.

Now, we return to the consumers. For the first consumer, if the store's discount factor $\delta \geq 0.5$, then the store will not cheat him, so his decision to purchase is correct. For later consumers, if the vendor did not cheat the previous consumer, then this proves that $\delta \geq 0.5$, so he does not have an incentive to cheat the next person. Therefore, purchasing is the correct thing to do. Otherwise, if the store cheats the previous consumer, it proves he will cheat all future consumers. Then, the optimal choice for the consumers is to not buy.

From this we can see that if $\delta \geq 0.5$, then cooperation will appear as the perfect Nash equilibrium in which consumers purchase and the store produce high quality products.[22]

This conclusion aids our understanding of the value of chain stores. We know that generally prices are high and quality is low at restaurants in tourist destinations. Why? Because tourist destination restaurants and customers play a one-time game, so there is no incentive to provide high-quality products. Chain stores are different from single restaurants because their chaining turns the one-time game into a repeated game. McDonald's, for example, has tens of thousands of branches and millions of employees globally. In this way, low-quality products from any one branch will damage the reputation of all branches. Each branch has an incentive to maintain this reputation, so they all provide high-quality products. Therefore, when you come to a new place and do not know which restaurant you should eat at, the worry-free option is to go to a chain store restaurant.

3.3 Monks and temples

Actually, in the market economy, all firms are a long-term player. Each person's life is limited, but the longevity of organizations can be unlimited. Firms turn one-time games into infinitely repetitive games, and thus allow us to better escape the Prisoner's Dilemma to realize a greater scope of cooperation. Kreps (1986, 1990) used a simple model to prove this point.[23]

Imagine a person's life lasts for two stages. In the first stage, he is engaged in productive activities. In the second stage, he retires (or gives his assets to others). Assume that in the productive stage, if he is honest, he will receive a payoff of five, but if he cheats, his payoff will be 10. If his activities are attributable to him personally, then there is no point in being honest in the first stage. However, assume that he establishes a trademarked business. The activities of the trade-marked business do not end when he retires. His living expenses after retiring are covered by the income from selling the business. Obviously, the better the reputation of the trademark, the more valuable it is. As long as the discounted value of the payoff from selling the business is greater than 5, then he will put weight on the reputation of the business and operate honestly. Why are there people willing to buy businesses with good reputations? Because rational consumers are only willing to do deals with businesses that have good reputations. Newly established businesses do not have good records, so it is more difficult for them to be trusted by consumers. Therefore, for a new entrant, purchasing a business with a good reputation on the market might be better than establishing a new business, whereas starting a new business might be better than purchasing a business with a bad reputation.[24]

These "businesses" are called "firms" in economics. With firms, dishonest behavior is easier to observe (it might not be easy to know which McDonald's employee cheated you, but it is comparatively more easy to communicate dishonest behavior at McDonald's). "Businesses" in modern society plays the same role that "surnames" played in traditional society. In other words, modern society restricts the behavior of "monks" via the reputation of the "temple". It is easy for an individual to disappear, but not for a firm.[25] This is the value of firms.

3.4 The social norm of boycotts

Now, we will transition our discussion to the cooperation problem in the great society where transactions are repeated but partners are not fixed. In society, each of us undertakes various exchanges with others. Even if there are long-term organizations like firms, our exchange cooperation partner is often not fixed. In an interpersonal network as complex as this, how can we incentivize each person to cooperate? Because the probability of each of us continuing an exchange with another particular person is 1% or even 0.1%, the incentive for each party to cheat in any individual deal seems large. In this way, there is basically no way to cooperate in this society. However, we can still depend on certain special social norms to promote cooperation among members of society.

For example, in our previous discussion on the issue of third-party punishments, when Party A swindles Party B and Party C punishes Party A, then cooperation between members of society can appear. This type of incentive for Party C to punish Party A can be guaranteed through a social norm like a boycott. Each member of society should be honest and cooperate with other members. A boycott refers to the responsibility of each member to punish those that have swindled others. If a member does not punish someone that has swindled others, then others should also punish that member. In other words, as a member of society, there should be punishment for not advocating justness or tolerating swindling behavior.

Intuitively, if a social norm includes punishments for those that do not carry out their responsibility for punishments, then each person has an incentive to both cooperate and punish violators. This social norm is a perfect Nash equilibrium, so it can be self-enforcing. Mahoney and Sanchirico (2003) proved this point.

Imagine a society formed by multiple people. The game repeats an infinite number of times. Each time a one-shot game takes place between two random people. Each person can choose to cooperate or not. The behavior of each person can be observed by everyone. Consider the following social norms: (1) At the first occurrence, each person must cooperate; and (2) from the second round on, no one will cooperate with transgressors from previous rounds as a punishment, and any transgressor that accepts punishment will be forgiven and will be cooperated with next time. Here, "transgressor" includes: (a) The person that first chooses to not cooperate; (b) the person that does not punish the first person that chooses to not cooperate; and (c) the person that does not punish the person that should have been punished.

Note that this social norm is different from the simple "tit-for-tat" strategy because the tit-for-tat not only punishes the first person that chooses to not cooperate, but also punishes the punisher (meaning if Player A does not cooperate in the first round, then Player B will not cooperate in the second round as punishment for Player A, but in the third round Player A will also choose to not cooperate as punishment for Player B, and so on) but does not punish the non-punisher (meaning if Player B does not punish Player A in the second round, then Player A will continue to cooperate in the third round). Therefore, the tit-for-tat is not a perfect Nash equilibrium. The boycott social norm not only punishes the first person that does not cooperate, it also punishes the non-punisher (meaning that those who do not play the duty of punishment should be punished), but does not punish the punisher (meaning behavior that punishes swindlers does not get punished).[26]

Let us explain this with an example. Assume there is a society formed by ten people: A, B, C, D, E, F, G, H, I, and J. In the first stage, one game involves Player A and Player B, another game involves Player C and Player D, and so on. In the second stage, one game involves Player A and Player C, another game involves Player B and Player D, and so on. In the third stage, one game involves Player A and Player D, another game involves Player B and Player E. This sequence continues endlessly. Imagine that in the first stage everyone chooses to cooperate, but Player A swindled Player B. Then, according to the social norm, in the second stage Player C should punish Player A by choosing to not cooperate, but Player A should choose to cooperate to show his acceptance of punishment. Everyone else cooperates as normal. If Player A and Player C act according to this rule, then at the start of the third stage everyone will choose to cooperate. However, if in the second round Player C does not punish Player A (assuming that Player A choose to cooperate to show his acceptance of punishment), then in the third stage, Player F (for instance) should choose to not cooperate as punishment for Player C, and Player C must choose to cooperate. If Player F does this and Player C accepts the punishment, then cooperation would resume starting in the fourth stage. If Player F does not punish Player C, then in the fourth stage, Player J (for instance) should choose to not cooperate as punishment for Player F, and Player F must choose to cooperate. This pattern continues infinitely.

It is easy to prove that if everyone is patient enough, then this punishment rule can guarantee the appearance of cooperation. Same as before, assume that in any stage game, the payoff when both parties cooperate is T, the payoff when neither party cooperates is P, and the payoff when one party cooperates but this other does not is S for the former and R for the latter. The discount factor is δ. Then, in any stage game, given the other party will cooperate, if he does not cooperate, he will get more $(R - T)$, but in the next round he must accept punishment for less $(T - S)$. Therefore, as long as $R - T \leq \delta(T - S)$, and thus $\delta \geq (R - T)/(T - S)$, he has no incentive to choose to not cooperate.

Now we will consider whether or not players should choose to punish transgressors when they should be punished. Assuming the transgressor is willing to accept punishment (meaning choose to cooperate after one-time defect), if the due punisher chooses to punish (meaning not cooperating with the previous transgressor), this round he receives R, and in the next round he receives T from cooperating with others. If he chooses to not punish (meaning he cooperates with the previous transgressor), he will receive T in this round, but will be punished in the next round and only receive S. Given our assumption that $R > T > P > S$, regardless the value of δ, he has an incentive to punish the transgressor.[27]

Now we will consider whether or not the transgressor is willing to accept the punishment. Accepting the punishment means choosing to cooperate when the other party chooses to not cooperate. If he accepts the punishment, this round he receives S, but in the next round receives T. If he does not accept the punishment, then in this round he will receive P (meaning the Nash equilibrium outcome of a one-time game), but in the next round he still must accept the punishment and only receive S. In this way, if $S + \delta T \geq P + \delta S$, and thus $\delta \geq (P - S)/(T - S)$, it is optimal to accept punishment. Overall, as long as δ is greater than the larger of $(R - T)/(T - S)$ and $(P - S)/(T - S)$, then no one has an incentive to first choose to not cooperate, each person has in incentive to punish transgressors, and each transgressor is willing to accept punishment. Cooperation in the whole society will appear as a perfect Nash equilibrium.

3.5 Rules for friends and foes

The boycott rule not only includes punishment, but also forgiveness. It embodies the Confucian forgiveness spirit of "return good for good and return right for evil", and implementation is not complex. It is very similar to the "rules for friend and foe" in everyday life. The rule goes like this: In the beginning, each member of society is your friend, but whether or not any member of society is your friend in the next game is determined by his behavior in the previous game. If that member did not swindle anyone in the previous game and did not cooperate with any of your foes, then he continues to be your friend. Otherwise, if that member swindled any of your friends, or if he cooperated with your foe, then he will be a foe forever. This rule can be formed by the following specific rules: (1) "A friend of a friend is a friend". (2) "A foe of a friend is a foe". (3) "A friend of a foe is a foe".

Assume that Player A and Player B are friends and have a cooperative partner relationship. Player A has not swindled Player B, and Player B has also not swindled Player A. Player C and Player B are also friends and have a cooperative partner relationship. Player C has not swindled Player B, and Player B has also not swindled Player C. "A friend of a friend is a friend" means that Player A sees Player C as a friend and Player C also sees Player A as a friend, so they can mutually cooperate.

"A foe of a friend is a foe" means that if Player A and Player B are friends, but Player C swindles Player B, then Player C becomes Player A's foe, and Player A should not cooperate with Player C.

"A friend of a foe is a foe" means that, given Player C becomes a foe of both Player A and B after cheating B, if Player D chose to cooperate with Player C, then Player D becomes a foe of Player A and Player B.

Bendor and Swistak (2001) proved that if each person puts enough weight on the future, not only is the "friend-and-foe-rule" described above a Nash equilibrium strategy, it is an evolutionary stable strategy. This means that people that utilize this strategy are most able to survive social competition, so the evolved outcome is the whole society becomes a cooperative society.[28] Intuitively, given that everyone else respects this rule, if you swindle any one person, you become the foe of everyone.

However, is it possible that no one respects this rule? This touches upon the convictions of all members of society. If a member of society believes that enough people will respect this rule, then this member of society will respect this rule and the cooperation equilibrium might appear. As an example, in our society, we believe the proportion of thieves in society is very low, such as 1–2%. If everyone believes the proportion of thieves will not exceed 1–2%, then most people in society will respect the property rule, and society's cooperation equilibrium can be sustained. However, if the proportion of thieves in society exceeds 30%, the perhaps everyone in society will eventually become a thief.[29]

A large amount of opportunities for cooperation in real life rely on the boycott model to be realized and maintained. Examples of collective punishment maintaining cooperation range from the classroom to international alliances. Assume that Classmate A swindles someone in class. Other classmates will isolate A. If certain classmates still have a good relationship with A, all other classmates will also scorn those classmates. If all classmates, including A, will foresee this outcome, then A will not swindle others. In international alliances, boycotts are the alliance's collective action. For example, during the Iraq War, some of America's allies entered the war because of fear of the possible punishment from USA and other coalition members if they didn't participate.

Obviously, the "second-order Prisoner's Dilemma problem" may exist for single members of the alliance because they will lose out on opportunities to cooperate with the object of the boycott. If this type of opportunity's temptation is great enough, the alliance will not sustain. This is the greatest challenge faced by international trade boycotts.

Law merchants of the Mediterranean region in the Middle Ages were similar to a boycott mechanism. The basic operation of this system was: Before a merchant did business with a stranger, he would first consult the law merchant. The law merchant's records would show if this person had broken one's promise or obeyed the law merchant's punishment after doing so. Of course, this was a paid service. Business could be done with people that had a good record. If any party was swindled after doing business, then the victim could appeal to the law merchant who would make a judgment. If the transgressor did not implement the punishment, then the matter would be recorded. If you did business with a person that had a bad record, the law merchant was not responsible for a judgment. Or, if you did not consult the law merchant before doing business and being swindled, the law merchant was not responsible for a judgment. Milgrom, North, and Weingast (1990) proved that if the income from cooperation is great enough and each person is patient enough, then this mechanism could form a perfect Nash equilibrium. Each person would have an incentive to cooperate, each person would have an incentive to consult the information, victims have an incentive to appeal, transgressors have an incentive to implement the law merchant's judgment, and the law merchant has an incentive to provide true information. This system of law merchants evolved into today's international arbitration organizations.

An important function of law merchants was to use a concentrated means to transmit information on the credit of the people involved. This type of information was extremely important for the maintenance of cooperation. The law merchants only transmitting this information to the people that needed it significantly reduced the cost of information. Courts in today's society have a similar purpose.

3.6 Joint liability

Another mechanism that maintains cooperation between people in a large society is "joint liability". When one member of a group transgresses against a person outside of the group, then people outside of the group will implement joint punishment for every member of the group, such as not doing business with any of them.

Joint liability is partially formed by nature. For example, China has different provinces, so there are Henanese, Shanxiese, Zhejiangese, Guangdongese, etc. Each province has different regions, so among Shanxiese there are Shanbeiese, Guangzhongese, Shannanese, etc. In this way, people from the same region in reality have a certain joint liability for each other. If a Shanbeiese does something bad, it will impact the reputation of all Shanbeiese. All Chinese have joint liability for each other internationally, because the bad behavior of one Chinese will damage the reputation of all Chinese.

Of course, most joint liability comes from the systemic design of organizations. Even if joint liability is not considered when an organization is formed, as soon as it is established there is joint liability among members. As Weber observed 100 years ago, joining a social organization means gaining "a social seal of approval".[30] If some member does something bad, outsiders may have no way of pursuing that specific person, but it is easy for them to identify the group that person belongs to and implement "group punishment".[31] In this way, the inappropriate behavior of individual group members will damage the reputation of the whole group. Because this harms the individual interests of each group member, group members have an incentive to implement internal punishment. This may be the reason the faithful are more trustworthy than the non-religious and uniformed military personnel are more trustworthy than non-uniformed military personnel. The reputation capital of groups causes individuals to have an incentive to enter groups and work to maintain the reputation of the group.[32] Of course, there are two pre-requisites for the existence of group reputation capital. First, group members cannot have monopoly privilege. Second, they must be free to enter and leave. If group members enjoy monopoly privilege, then joining this group may become a type of rent-seeking behavior, instead of reputation-building behavior. There are certain organizations like this in Chinese society. If group members are not free to leave, it may be difficult to effectively punish transgressors, and individuals are more likely to engage in swindling.[33]

Perhaps modern society's most important joint liability comes from firms. The firm consists of many people, but consumers on the market pay prices based on an enterprise's overall performance (such as product and service quality). Therefore, there must be joint liability between members of a firm. Ownership of firms was created in order to make this kind of joint liability effectively play a role. A so-called "boss" is actually a person that takes on joint liability for all employees. With this type of joint liability, owners attained the incentive and authority to oversee employees, thus allowing orderly market exchanges. In reality, firms that produce final consumer goods must also be jointly liable for all suppliers. Without firms, or if firms did not have owners, the market economy could not operate efficiently and effectively.[34]

Notes

1 See Fukuyama (1996); Putnam (1993); Knack and Keefer (1997); and Weiying Zhang and Rongzhu Ke (2002b), etc.
2 Of course, repeated games are not the only way to escape the Prisoner's Dilemma. It must be pointed out, as was discussed earlier, we cannot think that non-cooperative games teach people to not cooperate. Non-cooperative games are only one type of methodology where each person makes an independent decision based on individual rationality. The outcome of that decision might be to not cooperate, or it might be to cooperate.
3 For the story of Tianji's horse race, see page 79.
4 Under certain circumstances, the outcome of stage games might not be immediately observable. This will have an impact on the outcome of the game.
5 The reason is that $1 + \delta[^1] + \delta[^2] + \delta[^3] \ldots = (1 - \delta)$. When we are calculating the value of any asset, we use this kind of discounting concept. For example, when buying an annuity, it earns the investor P every year, so its value is $P/(1 - \delta)$. If the price of the annuity is lower than this, it should be bought; otherwise, it is not worth investing in.
6 We will discuss religion's influence on people's behavior in Chapter 14.
7 Starting in the 1950s, every Game Theorist knew this conclusion, but no one could prove they were the first to propose it, so it was called the folk theorem (or "no-name" theory in Chinese). Friedman (1971) developed the folk theorem into the subgame perfect Nash equilibrium.

8 We can test that when $\delta \geq (R - T) / (R - P)$, then $T / (1 - \delta) \geq R + P (\delta / (1 - \delta))$. In that equation, $T > P$, so it satisfies the assumption that $\delta < 1$.

9 It is easy to see when δ is sufficient large, no other strategy is strictly better for you than the tit-for-tat, given the opponent chooses the tit-for-tact.

10 The reason is simple. As was described earlier, $T + T > R + S$, so when any two corresponding segments of the sequence are averaged, the sizes can be compared. When the discount factor is taken into account, a sufficient large δ is needed.

11 This point can partially explain the reason the degree of cooperation is relatively low in Chinese society.

12 See Shearmur and Klein (1997) and Klein (1997b) for articles related to the information transmission mechanisms for the maintenance of cooperation in agricultural and industrial societies.

13 Using multi-country data analysis, Fisman and Khanna (1999) discovered that information communication, especially two-way information communication, had an obvious impact on trust.

14 Here, being punished three times is enough. That means being punished three times can make the reduction in present value of the other party's payoff $(T - P) (\delta + \delta[^2] + \delta[^3])$ exceed the appeal of the one-time swindle $(R - T)$.

15 Bernheim and Whinston (1990) analyzed how multi-market contact influenced cooperation between firms in an oligopoly competition framework. The contents of this section was to a large degree inspired by them.

16 Of course, we can also discuss the opposite. Assume that δ does not equal 0.60, and instead is 0.5. What will be the outcome? If the two exchanges are put together, neither will attain cooperation. However, if they are separated, cooperation will at least appear in one market. We can see that multi-transaction relationships leading to cooperation depends on specific circumstances.

17 By understanding this point, we can explain many other truths. Family relationships are multidimensional relationships, and of course a more important part of family relationships are blood relationships. As pointed out by Richard Dawkins in his *Selfish Genes*, we all are laborers for genes. Competition for survival is actually gene competition, not human competition. Because you are made up of one half of each of your parent's genes, they will internalize your welfare. At this point, blood relationships become a type of internalized cooperation. The friend relationship we just mentioned actually play the similar role. In addition to general economic relationships, if we are also friends, with accumulated social capital, it is unlikely we will cheat each other.

18 The idiom "hesitate to pelt a rat for fear of smashing the dishes" means the same thing.

19 However, this phenomenon has one benefit in that it causes everyone to gradually transition towards standardized exchanges because friends cannot always be trusted.

20 In the past, the emperor of China could not keep all of his kin by his side. He must give them a fiefdom and command them to not leave the fiefdom.

21 The second-order Prisoner's Dilemma is an important challenge faced by the implementation of social norms. See Ellickson (1991), page 237; Ellickson (1999); and McAdams (1997), page 352.

22 The example described above is a simplification of the Klein and Leffler (1981) model. Simon (1951) and Kreps (1986, 1990) used a similar thought process to explain employment relationships. They believed that one of the values of firms existing is precisely that it creates a "long-term player". Because of future interest considerations, this long-term player will put more weight on trust. In the next section, we will outline Kreps's model.

23 The text from the next paragraph in this section comes from Weiying Zhang (2001).

24 This can explain the companies that for whatever reason have damaged reputations are more likely to change their names (Tadelis, 1999), and also shows that trademark protection is extremely important for social cooperation.

25 Kreps (1990) emphasized the role of firms as long-term players, but did not emphasize the information function of firms.

26 Mahoney and Sanchirico (2003) used def-for-dev to represent the tit-for-tat strategy, meaning defect for deviate.

27 Here, given that the transgressor is willing to accept punishment, the punisher's payoff in that round is greater than the payoff when not punishing, so this simplified model does not actually deal with the "second-order Prisoner's Dilemma" problem. Of course, under the condition that the transgressor is willing to accept punishment (as is proved later), the punisher's incentive is not a problem. The reader can construct a more complex model that proves even if the punisher's payoff during the punishment round is lower than otherwise, considering long-term interests, he has an incentive to implement the punishment.

28 In Chapter 12, we will discuss the "evolved stable strategy".

29 This is actually also related to the process of evolution we will discuss in Chapter 12. When enough people respect a rule, not respecting the rule is not an individual's best choice. However, when very few people respect a rule, respecting the rule might not be an individual's optimal choice.

30 In 1904, Weber met a banker that had been baptized. He came to understand that because the church's requirements for baptism were strict, only after this banker was baptized and joined the local church did the local residents trust him. This inspired him to believe that social groups can endorse an individual's trustworthiness. An individual joining a social group is similar to an organization stamping a "seal of approval". See Shearmur and Klein (1997); Weber's (2002) *The Protestant Ethic and the Spirit of Capitalism*.

31 Weiying Zhang and Feng Deng (2003) analyzed the *liánzuò* system in ancient China from the incentive mechanism perspective.

32 Putnam (1993) discovered that the degree of social trust was greater in northern Italy than in southern Italy. The reason is that there are more developed social organizations in the north.

33 This can explain why China's social organizations not only cannot become tools for maintaining reputations, but instead often become sanctuaries for fraud. See Weiying Zhang (2001). Knack and Keefer (1997) discovered that rent-seeking social groups harmed social trust.

34 See Weiying Zhang (2015).

7 Incomplete information and reputation

According to the logic of backward induction, cooperation will not appear in finitely repeated Prisoner's Dilemma games. However, in real life, we also see cooperation appear in limited-occurrence repeated games. This is called "the chain store paradox".

Introducing incomplete information can resolve this paradox. The reason is rational players have an incentive to establish a "cooperative-type" reputation when information is incomplete, and thus obtain the long-term gains brought about by cooperation. It is undeniable that certain people in society are innately more cooperative than others. Even if the proportion of this type of person is small, it can still promote the cooperative spirit throughout society.

The reputation mechanism is a major force in society escaping the Prisoner's Dilemma. It is because of the focus on reputation that people trust others and are willing to exchange. Within a society, the more weight is put on reputation, the higher degree of trust is. The market order to a large degree is maintained by the reputation mechanism. If firms and individuals do not care about their own reputations, no law could make the market operate efficiently.

The reputation mechanism has a strong ability to explain the social phenomena we observe in society. Many behaviors that appear to be irrational are actually rational. Even certain emotional behaviors are rational.

A government's reputation is extremely important for both internal governance and international competition or cooperation. Governments that put weight on reputation can earn the trust of the people and succeed internationally. Government disregard for reputation causes the greatest harm to society's cooperative spirit.

The establishment of reputation is a process of accumulation. Both good names and bad names are accumulated. People continuously revise their judgments according to observed behavior. Therefore, one should not make promises he cannot keep.

Section one: the chain store paradox

1.1 The chain store paradox

The repeated games discussed in the previous chapter were infinitely repeated games. However, in reality, repeated games are generally finite. Are the basic conclusions we obtain in infinitely repeated games still valid in finitely repeated games? In my person observations, the conclusions are confirmed. However, in theory a problem exists. According to backward induction, cooperative behavior would not appear in finitely repeated games. For example, assume the Prisoner's Dilemma game repeats 10,000 times. At the ten thousandth time, which is the last round, the players would not choose to cooperate. By further working backwards, we know that neither party would choose to cooperate at the 9,999th occurrence, because whatever doing in this round will not influence the choices in the final round. Similarly, in the 9,998th occurrence and every occurrence beforehand, neither party would choose to cooperate.

However, in reality, even if a repeated game is limited-occurrence, we can still see cooperation appear. For example, we are often willing to lend a helping hand to casual acquaintances. How can cooperative behavior in these types of finitely repeated games be explained?

Reinhard Selten, the 1994 Nobel Memorial Prize in Economic Sciences Laureate, was the first person to note the cooperation paradox in finitely repeated games. In Selten (1978), he used the "chain-store paradox" to describe this problem. Specifically speaking, imagine there are two firms that produce the same product. One firm is already in the market (called the "incumbent") and the other firm (called the "entrant") must choose between entering this market or not. If the entrant does not enter, the incumbent's profit is 100 and the entrant receives 0 profit. If the entrant enters, the incumbent must decide whether to acquiesce or start a price war (or "fight"). If the incumbent chooses to acquiesce, then the market will be split with the entrant, so both make a profit of 50 in that round. Assume the cost of entry is 10, so the entrant's net gain is 40. If the incumbent chooses to fight, both sides will suffer so that in the end the incumbent's profit is 0, and the entrant suffers a 10-unit loss. This game's development is shown in Figure 7.1.

In a one-time dynamic game, given that the entrant has already entered, the incumbent's optimal choice is "acquiesce", not "fight". Because the incumbent can be rationally expected to acquiesce, the entrant will choose to enter the market. Therefore, the game's perfect Nash equilibrium outcome is "the entrant chooses to enter, and the incumbent chooses to acquiesce". Of course, the incumbent might threaten the entrant beforehand that a price war will start. However, in the one-time

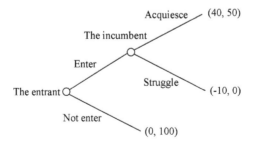

Figure 7.1 The Entry Game

game, this kind of threat from the incumbent is not credible. Therefore, the entrant will choose to enter.

Now imagine the incumbent is a chain store simultaneously operating in 20 markets. The potential entrant might enter 20 markets in succession (or there are 20 potential entrants that might enter each market in succession). When the entrant enters the first market, what should the incumbent do? Intuitively, if the incumbent tolerates the entrant in the first market, then the entrant will also enter in the other 19 markets. While it suffers a loss in the first market when the incumbent chooses to squeeze out the entrant, it is worthwhile if fighting could deter the entrant from entering in the remaining 19 markets. Therefore, from the beginning the incumbent should choose "fight".

However, this intuitive conclusion contradicts with backward induction. Imagine the entrant has already entered the previous 19 markets and now is deciding to enter the twentieth market or not. Because in the last market the incumbent's optimal choice is to tolerate, the entrant will choose to enter. Given that the incumbent will choose to tolerate, and the entrant will choose to enter in the twentieth round, then in the nineteenth round, the game's outcome will also be the incumbent chooses to tolerate and the entrant will choose to enter. Reasoning backwards, starting from the first market, the incumbent will choose to tolerate, and the entrant will enter all markets.

This is what we obtained through backward induction. It proves that a contradiction exists between backward induction logic and the intuition. Selten called this contradiction the "chain store paradox". Casual observation shows that the reality is more likely to be consistent with the intuition rather than the backward induction conclusion.

What created this type of contradiction between theory and reality? One possibility is a discrepancy between reality and our assumption of rationality when using backward induction. Another possibility is a discrepancy between reality and our assumption about information player have. In our previous analysis, we assumed that players were completely rational, this type of rational person had perfect computational ability, and knew each outcome like the back of his hand. In addition, rationality was the same for each person. In reality, people's rationality is not perfect. We have our own overall judgment of many outcomes, but we cannot calculate them precisely. Everyone has the possibility to make a mistake. Even if we know a person is rational, we cannot completely understand his preferences. Only for these reasons do our assumptions on complete information about payoff functions and strategic space not hold in reality. A person's "payoff" in certain circumstances might only be our subjective judgment, not his actual payoff. For example, a naturally good person might have "intention guarding against others' evil", but have no "intentions to harm others". Even if this type of person could gain ¥10 from swindling someone once, he still would not do so. This is not because he is not rational, but instead it is because the psychological cost of swindling someone is much higher than the ¥10 monetary gain. If we only predict his behavior based on monetary gain, we would make an incorrect judgment. Or, if because he does not choose the "payoff" maximization behavior we say he is not rational, this is also incorrect. In addition, as we saw previously, in a game, incomplete information has a major influence on people's behavior.

Another possibility is that in real life games, players have multiple tactics to effectively punish non-cooperative behavior or reward cooperative behavior, not just the one that we assumed previously. In the previous discussions on repeated games, we assumed that stage games only have one Nash equilibrium, and it is not Pareto optimal. Punishment for non-cooperative behavior was to return to the one-time game Nash equilibrium. In reality, as we saw in Chapter 3, many games have multiple Nash equilibriums. The existence of multiple equilibriums increases the credible punishment measures for non-cooperative behavior in repeated games. Even if a repeated game's repetitions are finite, cooperation can still appear.[1]

Below, we will loosen these assumptions to investigate the cooperation issue in finitely repeated games. We will first discuss the cooperation issue under multiple equilibriums, and then transition to the key point of this chapter: Incomplete information and reputation.

1.2 Rewards and cooperation

The simple one-shot Prisoner's Dilemma game has only one Nash equilibrium. When this game is repeated, the only credible punishment for cheating behavior is to switch to the one-shot game's Nash equilibrium. However, in other games which have multiple one-shot Nash equilibria, some other Nash equilibria can be used to punish the cheater or reward the cooperator when the games are repeatedly played.

In order to better display this point, we will construct a game like the one shown in Figure 7.2.

If this game only occurs once, there are two Nash equilibriums: (L, L) and (R, R). The payoffs they bring about are $(1, 1)$ and $(3, 3)$, respectively. This game is still a Prisoner's Dilemma in the sense that the Pareto optimum (M, M) is not a Nash equilibrium, and neither Nash equilibrium (L, L) nor (R, R) are Pareto optimal. Now assume that Player A and Player B will repeat this game twice. Note that in the second game, because the game ends at that point, neither party will

		Player B		
		L	M	R
Player A	L	1, 1	5, 0	0, 0
	M	0, 5	4, 4	0, 0
	R	0, 0	0, 0	3, 3

Figure 7.2 Rewards and Cooperation

cooperate, but they can "end on good terms" (meaning everybody chooses *R* for a payoff of 3 each) or "end on bad terms" (meaning everybody chooses *L* for a payoff of 1 each). Will both parties cooperate in the first round?

If each party uses a strategy like "tit-for-tat" that has both rewards and punishments in this game, then cooperation can happen for both parties in the first round. Specifically speaking, cooperation at the first round be obtained if each party implements the following strategy: I will choose *M* in the first game, and if the other party also chooses *M* in the first round (meaning the payoff for both is 4), then I will choose *R* in the second round; if the other party does not choose *M* in the first round, then I will choose *L* in the second round. The direct significance of this strategy is I first choose to cooperate, and if the other party also cooperates, then while in the second round neither party will choose to cooperate, I will choose to "end on good terms". If the other party does not cooperate in the first round, I will choose to "end on bad terms". In this way, we can simplify the payoffs of the two rounds into the one-time game shown in Figure 7.3. In addition to adding (3, 3) to the payoff for (*M*, *M*), everything else added (1, 1) compared to the payoffs of the one-time game. Obviously, now given that I will use this strategy, meaning I will choose M in the first game and R in the second game, the opponent's best response is the same strategy. Therefore, (*M'*, *M'*) shown in Figure 7.3 forms a Nash equilibrium. This Nash equilibrium involves both parties choosing to cooperate in the first round, and both parties have maximum gain of 7 each.

In the above game, players' ability to reward and punish primarily manifests in players' choice between Nash equilibriums with unequal payoffs in the second round. If the other party cooperates in the first round, then a high-payoff Nash equilibrium can be chosen to reward the other party. If the other party does not cooperate in the first round, then a low-payoff Nash equilibrium can be chosen to punish the other player.

However, a credibility problem exists when implementing rewards and punishments. Actually, considering the game shown in Figure 7.2, if Player A does not choose cooperative behavior *M*, and instead chooses *L*, but Player B chooses cooperative behavior *M*, then at this point, Player A's payoff is 5 and Player B's payoff is 0. Now, Player B is extremely angry and decides to choose *L* in the

		Player B		
		L'	*M'*	*R'*
	L'	2, 2	6, 1	1, 1
Player A	*M'*	1, 6	7, 7	1, 1
	R'	1, 1	1, 1	4, 4

Figure 7.3 The Combined Payoffs of Both Games

second game to punish Player A. However, before Player B takes action, Player A tells Player B:

> If you choose *R*, I will also choose *R*, so we can both receive 3. If you choose *L*, my only choice is to also choose *L*, so we will both only receive 1. At the same time that you are punishing me, you are also punishing yourself. Let the past be the past, let us both look towards the future and choose R!

Obviously, if Player B is rational, he will accept Player A's advice and abandon his choice of L to punish the other party. Then, if Player A knows that even if he does not cooperate in the first round, the other party will still not punish him, so he will persist in his choice to not cooperate. At this point, cooperation will not appear in the first round. The reason is that equilibrium (*R*, *R*) being Pareto optimal over (*L*, *L*) in the stage game will lead to re-negotiations that make punishments non-credible.

If the Pareto superiority issue does not exist between multiple Nash equilibriums in the stage game, then punishments can become credible. Below, we will analyze the game shown in Figure 7.4.

Obviously, in this game, there exist four Nash equilibriums: (*L*, *L*), (*R*, *R*), (*P*, *P*), and (*Q*, *Q*). Among them, equilibrium (*R*, *R*) is Pareto optimal over (*L*, *L*), but not over (*P*, *P*) and (*Q*, *Q*).

Now, assume Player A and Player B will repeat this game twice. What will the result be? If both players still implement a strategy with reward and punishment characteristics, cooperation will certainly appear as the outcome. Specifically speaking, assume both players pursue the follow strategy:

> If the first stage results in cooperative result (*M*, *M*), then both parties will choose (*R*, *R*) in the second stage;
>
> If the first stage results in (*M*, *X*) because Player B does not cooperate (here *X* represents Player B's choice that is not *M*), then Player A will choose *P* in the second stage;

		Player B				
		L	*M*	*R*	*P*	*Q*
	L	1, 1	5, 0	0, 0	0, 0	0, 0
	M	0, 0	4, 4	0, 0	0, 0	0, 0
Player A	*R*	0, 0	0, 0	3, 3	0, 0	0, 0
	P	0, 0	0, 0	0, 0	4, 1/2	0, 0
	Q	0, 0	0, 0	0, 0	0, 0	1/2, 4

Figure 7.4 Pareto Optimality and Credible Punishments

If the first stage results in (Y, M) because Player A does not cooperate (here Y represents Player A's choice that is not M), then Player B will choose Q in the second stage;

If the first stage results in (Y, X) because neither side chooses to cooperate, then both players will choose (R, R) in the second stage.

Given the above strategy, we will see that the equilibrium outcome is: Both parties choose (M, M) in the first stage and (R, R) in the second stage. This outcome includes the outcome of both parties choosing to cooperate in the first stage.

Comparing the games shown in Figure 7.2 and Figure 7.4, we will find that in the first game, because the equilibrium (L, L) that is used to punish players' non-cooperative behavior is Pareto inferior to (R, R), punishing the other party also means punishing yourself. This leads to ex-post renegotiations, making the punishment non-credible. In the second game, because there are three equilibriums on the Pareto boundary, (R, R) can reward cooperation and the other two equilibriums can punish the non-cooperative person with rewarding the punisher. In this way, as soon as punishments must be implemented in the second stage, the punisher will not hesitate, which will guarantee the credibility of the punishment.

The general conclusion of this example is that if there are enough credible punishment measures in a game, cooperative behavior might occur in repeated games that would not appear in one-time games, even if the repetitions of a repeated game are finite.

Section two: incomplete information and the reputation mechanism

Now we will discuss finitely repeated games under incomplete information circumstances. Incomplete information refers to one player's incomplete knowledge of the other player's preferences, payoff function, strategy, etc. For instance, a firm in the market does not completely understand competitors' production costs, technological capabilities, or management decision procedures. In real life, we are not clear if a person is "born virtuous" or "born evil". In international negotiations, one negotiator perhaps does not know the other negotiator's preference for compromise or assertiveness. Game Theorists use "type" to depict incomplete information, such as Type 1 representing "born virtuous" and Type 2 representing "born evil". When we do not know if a person is actually born virtuous or born evil, then our information about him is incomplete.[2]

How does incomplete information influence people's behavior in repeated games? For this issue, Kreps, Milgrom, Roberts, and Wilson proposed a formal model in 1982.[3] They proved that if players did not have complete information about the characteristics of other players, then even if games are finitely repeated, the players still have an incentive to establish a reputation for cooperation. Therefore, it is still possible for cooperation to appear.

2.1 *Single party incomplete information*

We will explain their thinking using the Prisoner's Dilemma shown in Figure 7.5 as an example. Under the complete information condition, Suspect A knows all of Suspect B's characteristics (type, strategy space, gain, etc.), and Player B knows all of Suspect A's characteristics. Both suspects are rational, and each has two types of choices each time: Cooperate or betray. If the game is undertaken a limited number of times under complete information, according to our previous analysis, each game will repeat according to the stage game, and the equilibrium for each round is (betray, betray).

If information is incomplete, the situation will change. First, we will consider the case of single party incomplete information. This means that one party well understands the other party, but the other party does have incomplete information about certain characteristics of the first party. Examples include not knowing if the other party is the assertive type or the compromising type, as well as whether or not the other party has hidden methods (strategy space). Specifically, assume all of Player B's characteristics are known by Player A, but Player B does not know Player A's characteristics. In Player B's eyes, Player A has two types: Possibly irrational and possibly rational. Assume that irrational Player A will only use the tit-for-tat strategy, meaning if the other party always cooperates, then cooperation will continue, but as soon as the other party betrays, cooperation will stop until the other party takes the initiative to resume cooperation. Rational Player A, on the other hand, will choose any strategy that benefits himself. Assume that Player B believes the probability of Player A being irrational is p and the probability of Player A being rational is $1 - p$.

It is important to remind the reader that the "irrationality" here is merely a brief summary of some possible characteristics of player A. It is different from the usual definition of irrationality in the practical sense. We can also use "crazy-type", "cooperative-type", "kindhearted-type", "loyal-type" and other words to describe this type of person. People with this characteristic are not calculating everything as "rational people", but instead are more like a pre-programmed computer program. In other circumstances, it might mean "assertive" (in negotiation games) or "low-cost" (in market entry games), etc.

		B	
		Cooperate	Betray
A	Cooperate	3, 3	−1, 4
	Betray	4, −1	0, 0

Figure 7.5 The Prisoner's Dilemma

	$t = 1$	$t = 2$
A ⟨ Irrational (p)	Cooperate	X
A ⟨ Rational ($1-p$)	Betray	Betray
B (Rational)	X	Betray

Figure 7.6 The Prisoner's Dilemma Game Repeated Twice With Incomplete Information

Now assume that under this type of single party incomplete information condition, both players will repeat the Prisoner's Dilemma game twice. We will use Figure 7.6 to represent this game.

As shown in Figure 7.6, when this game is played the second time ($t = 2$), then the Player B must choose to betray in order to maximize his own payoff. If Player A is also rational, then at this point he will also choose to betray. If Player A is irrational, then his choice in the second stage is determined by Player B's choice in the first stage. This choice could be cooperate or betray, so for simplicity we will notate it as X.

If Player A is rational, he will certainly choose to betray in the first stage, because his choice will not influence Player B's behavior in the second stage. If Player A is irrational, in the first stage he will instinctively choose to cooperate.

However, Player B are different. Even though he is rational, it might not be optimal to choose betrayal from the start, because it means he has probability p of losing the opportunity to take advantage of the second stage. Rational Player B must calculate whether or not this is worth it.

If in the first stage Player B chooses to betray, his expected payoff in this stage is $p \times 4 + (1 - p) \times 0 = 4p$. His expected payoff in the second stage is $p \times 0 + (1 - p) \times 0 = 0$. The total expected payoff from both stages is $4p$ (the discount factor is ignored).

If in the first stage Player B chooses to cooperate, his expected payoff in this stage is $p \times 3 + (1 - p) \times (-1) = 4p - 1$. His expected payoff in the second stage is $p \times 4 + (1 - p) \times 0 = 4p$. The total expected payoff from both stages is $8p - 1$.

Obviously, if $8p - 1 \geq 4p$, meaning $p \geq 0.25$, then Player B will choose to cooperate in the first stage. In other words, if Player B's judgment of the probability Player A being the irrational type is greater than or equal to 0.25, then he will choose to cooperate with Player A in the first stage and betray him in the second stage.

This is to say that because information is incomplete, even if there are only two stages in the game, rational Player B will choose to cooperate in the first stage. The possibility of Player A being irrational changed rational Player B's behavior, whereas if Player B definitely knew that Player A is rational, then B's cooperation would not appear. Of course, if Player B believes that the probability of Player A being irrational is less than 0.25, then Player B will not choose to cooperate in the first stage. Player B still weighs the between immediate and long-term interests. Is it worth losing future payoffs for the immediate payoff from betrayal?

Now we will see the situation where the game repeats three times (as shown in Figure 7.7).

First, we will look at Player A's choices. If Player A is irrational, then he will cooperate in the first stage, and his choices in the second and third stage will be determined by Player B's choices in the first and second round. If Player A is rational, then he will certainly choose to betray in the second and third round, same as in the previous two-round games. However, betrayal in the first round may not be rational Player A's best choice, because choosing betrayal will expose Player A's rational characteristic and Player B will choose betrayal in the second stage. Rational Player A must now weigh whether or not it is worth it to expose his identity.

Assume that Player B chooses to cooperate in the first stage. If rational Player A chooses to betray in the beginning, he will receive 4 in the first stage, but from the second stage Player B will know he is rational (because irrational Player A would not betray first), so in the second and third stage Player B will choose betrayal. Rational Player A's total expected gain is $4 + 0 + 0 = 4$. In contrast, if rational Player A chooses cooperation in the first stage, his rational characteristic is concealed. When Player B makes a decision in the second stage, it is like that the first stage never happened. Player B's judgment of Player A's type does not change; thus, Player B will continue to choose cooperation in the second stage. (The premise here is that $p \geq 0.25$.) According to the previous analysis, it is easy to understand that as long as Player B believes the probability of Player A being irrational is not less than 0.25, then Player B will choose cooperation. The total gain for Player A from choosing betrayal in the second and third stages is $3 + 4 + 0 = 7$. From rational Player A's perspective, as long as Player B does not choose betrayal at the start or in the second stage, then it is most optimal for Player A to choose cooperation in the first stage.

Now, we will look at Player B's strategy. Player B has four strategies to choose from: (cooperate, cooperate, betray), (cooperate, betray, betray), (betray, betray, betray), and (betray, cooperate, betray). For convenience, the games under the four different strategies are presented in figures.

As shown in Figure 7.8, given rational Player A's strategy (cooperate, betray, betray), if Player B chooses (cooperate, cooperate, betray), irrational Player A chooses cooperate in all three stages. Then Player B's total expected utility is $3 + [3p + (-1)(1 - p)] + [4p + 0] = 8p + 2$.

	$t=1$	$t=2$	$t=3$
A ⟨ Irrational (p)	Cooperate	X	X
Rational ($1-p$)	?	Betray	Betray
B (Rational)	X	X	Betray

Figure 7.7 The Situation After Repeating the Game Three Times

As shown in Figure 7.9, if Player B chooses (cooperate, betray, betray), irrational Player A chooses to cooperate in the first and two stages, but to betray in the third stage. Then Player B's total expected utility is $3 + [4p + 0(1 - p)] + 0 = 4p + 3$.

As shown in Figure 7.10, if Player B chooses (betray, betray, betray), irrational Player A cooperates in the first stage, but chooses to betray in the second and third stage. Thus, Player B's total expected utility is $4 + 0 + 0 = 4$.

	$t=1$	$t=2$	$t=3$
A ⟨ Irrational (p)	Cooperate	$X=$ Cooperate	$X=$ Cooperate
Rational ($1-p$)	Cooperate	Betray	Betray
B (Rational)	$X=$ Cooperate	$X=$ Cooperate	Betray
Player B's total expected payoff =	3	$+\ 3p+(-1)(1-p)\ +$	$4p+0\ =8p+2$

Figure 7.8 Player B Chooses (Cooperate, Cooperate, Betray)

	$t=1$	$t=2$	$t=3$
A ⟨ Irrational (p)	Cooperate	$X=$ Cooperate	$X=$ Betray
Rational ($1-p$)	Cooperate	Betray	Betray
B (Rational)	$X=$ Cooperate	$X=$ Betray	Betray
Player B's total expected payoff =	3	$+\ 4p+0(1-p)\ +$	$0\ =4p+3$

Figure 7.9 Player B Chooses (Cooperate, Betray, Betray)

	$t=1$	$t=2$	$t=3$
A ⟨ Irrational (p)	Cooperate	$X=$ Betray	$X=$ Betray
Rational ($1-p$)	Cooperate	Betray	Betray
B (Rational)	$X=$ Betray	$X=$ Betray	Betray
Player B's total expected payoff =	4 $+$	0 $+$	0 $=4$

Figure 7.10 Player B Chooses (Betray, Betray, Betray)

As shown in Figure 7.11, if Player B chooses (betray, cooperate, betray), irrational Player A cooperates in the first round, betrays in the second round, and cooperates in the third round. Then Player B's total expected utility is $4 + (-1) + [4p + 0 (1 - p)] = 4p + 3$.

Putting these four strategies on a graph, using the horizontal axis to represent Player A's probability of irrationality and the vertical axis to represent Player B's expected payoff from each strategy will become Figure 7.12.

Obviously, from Figure 7.12, we will learn that when $p \geq 0.25$, the payoff $8p + 2$ from choosing (cooperate, cooperate, betray) is the highest. As long as $p \geq 0.25$, the following strategy profile is a perfect Nash equilibrium: Rational-type Player A chooses to cooperate in the first stage, and then chooses to betray in the second and third stages; Player B chooses to cooperate in the first and second stages and then chooses to betray in the third stage.

This conclusion could be extended to any multi-occurrence repeated game. It is easy to prove that if the game repeats T times, as long as $p \geq 0.25$, then for any $T \geq 3$, the following strategy sets form a perfect Nash equilibrium: Rational-type Player A

		$t = 1$	$t = 2$	$t = 3$
A ⟨ Irrational		Cooperate	X = Betray	X = Cooperate
Rational		Cooperate	Betray	Betray
B (Rational)		X = Betray	X = Cooperate	Betray
Player B's total expected payoff	=	4 +	(−1) +	$4p + 0(1-p) = 4p + 3$

Figure 7.11 Player B Chooses (Betray, Cooperate, Betray)

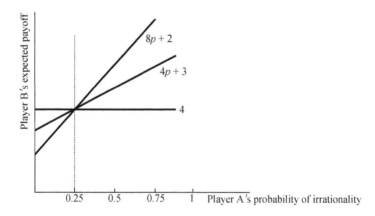

Figure 7.12 Player B's Gain Under Different Strategies

chooses to cooperate in $t = 1, \ldots, T - 2$ stages, but switches to betray in $T - 1$ and T stages; Player B chooses to cooperate in $t = 1, \ldots, T - 1$ stages, but switches to betray T stage. Non-cooperative behavior only appears in the final two stages. If the two players undertake a ten-thousand-occurrence game, they will both cooperate in the first 9,998 occurrences. In the 9,999th occurrence, rational Player A will choose to not cooperate, but Player B will still choose to cooperate. In the 10,000th occurrence, neither of rational players will cooperate (except for irrational Player A).

Why will there be this kind of game outcome?

The reason is that when information is incomplete, rational people have an incentive to establish a "cooperative type" reputation.

From Player A's perspective, if he is rational, under conditions of complete information, he will not choose to cooperate; however, under conditions of incomplete information, he cannot reveal his rational characteristic too early. He will first pretend to be a cooperative type person. In the final stage, there is no need to pretend, so there is also no need to pretend in the second-to-last stage. From Player B's perspective, he has incentives to behave cooperatively in the earlier stage until the last one, because if the other party is cooperative type, then B's cooperation in the earlier stages can be exchanged for more future opportunities for cooperation. In contrast, if Player B does not cooperate in the earlier stages, even if Player A is cooperative type, he will not cooperate with Player B in the stage following. After weighing long-term interests with immediate interests, Player B's optimal strategy is cooperation.

At what degree of incomplete information will people have the incentive to establish a reputation for cooperation? In the previous example, $p \geq 0.25$ was determined by our specific assumption about the numerical value of payoffs. It is easy to prove that the more payoff cooperation brings about in each game, the less this lower limit is. In other words, if cooperation brings about huge gains, even if there is a tiny possibility the other party is irrational (cooperative type), both parties have an incentive to cooperate in the earlier stages.

2.2 The reputation mechanism under two-sided incomplete information

Above, we discussed a single party having incomplete information. We assumed that player A knew Player B is rational, but Player B did not know whether or not Player A is rational. Under this condition, strictly speaking, only Player A chooses to cooperate in order to establish a good reputation. The issue of establishing a good reputation does not exist for Player B, because from beginning to end, Player A is very clear that Player B is an opportunist. Choosing to cooperate is completely based on rational calculations, the same as we discussed in the chapter above. At this point, as soon as Player A betrays once, Player B will know he is rational, and cooperation will break apart. However, in reality, very few people's judgments of others' characteristics can be 100% correct. People judge the characteristics of others based on their behavior. In this way, even if Player A initially believed that Player B is completely rational, if Player B chooses to cooperate in multiple times, Player A's view of Player B may change: Perhaps B is essentially a good person. If Player B can create the same impression on Player A, then Player B also has an incentive to maintain a reputation. At this point, the game becomes a two-sided incomplete information game.

If Player A and Player B both have incomplete information, such as neither party knowing the other party's type, it can be proved that no matter how small p is, as long as the game repeats enough times (but not necessarily infinitely), cooperation will appear. The reason is the same as for single-party incomplete information. If the game repeats enough times, neither party is willing to ruin their own reputation in the early stages. The difference is now the degree of uncertainty (the value of p) required to maintain cooperation is related to the number of game repetitions.

To prove this point, consider both parties in the game utilizing the grim strategy. Different from the tit-for-tat strategy, under the grim strategy, as soon as any player betrays once, cooperation will never resume again. If Player A betrays in the beginning and exposes himself as non-cooperative type, the other party will forever choose to not cooperate. In this way, the only equilibrium starting from the second stage is each person betrays. Player A's maximum expected payoff is $4 + 0 + 0 + \ldots = 4$.

Assume Player A implements the grim strategy. Assume the probability of the other party being cooperative type is p and the probability of the other party being non-cooperative type is $1 - p$. If the other party is cooperative type, then Player A's payoff in each stage will be 3. Assume there are a total of T stages, so the total payoff is 3T. If the other party is non-cooperative type, then under the worst circumstances, Player A's payoff in the first round is -1, and then 0 in every proceeding round. The total payoff is $-1 + 0 + 0 + \ldots = -1$. Therefore, Player A's minimum expected payoff from implementing the grim strategy is $p(3T) - (1 - p)$.[4]

If the minimum expected payoff for Player A implementing the grim strategy is not less than 4; thus, $T \geq (5 - p) / 3p$, then choosing to not cooperate from the beginning is not the optimal strategy. The same is for Player B.

Up to this point, we've loosely proved that if both parties have incomplete information, regardless how small p is, as long as the game repeats enough times, choosing to betray in the beginning is not optimal and players still have an incentive to establish a reputation for cooperation. For example, even if the probability of the other party being cooperative type is as small as 0.01, as long as the number of repetitions $T \geq (5 - p) / 3p = 164$, then cooperation can occur.

Generally speaking, we can arrive at the following KMRW Theory: Under conditions of incomplete information, as long as the game repeats enough times and each player is patient enough, then players have an incentive to establish a reputation of "cooperation" early on, and they will only choose to betray in the last part of the game. In addition, the number of the non-cooperative stage is only related to p, but is unrelated to the total number of game repetitions T.

The intuition of the KMRW Theorem is even though when each player chooses to cooperate they run the risk of being betrayed, if they choose to not cooperate, they will expose their own non-cooperative type, and thus lose the possibility for long-term gain from cooperation. If the game repeats long enough and players are patient enough, the loss of future gains will exceed the loss of short-term being betrayed. Therefore, at the start of the game, each player will establish a cooperative image (causing the other party to incorrectly believe you like to cooperate, even though you are non-cooperative type). Only when the game is about to end will players milk their past reputations and cooperation will stop.

Why is the number of non-cooperative stages only related to p, and not to the total number of game repetitions T? According to the conditions derived previously, for any given p, there exists a critical value T^* for the number of times the game repeats. When the number of games is lower than this critical value the expected gain from cooperation is insufficient to suppress immediate temptations, and thus players will choose to betray. This critical value is the number of non-cooperative stages and the previous stage games greater than this critical value are cooperative stages. In this way, rolling backward to T_0 by T^* rounds from the final round, every round from the beginning until rounds T_0 is a cooperation stage, but last $T - T_0 = T^*$ rounds are a non-cooperation stage. Each player from the start will establish and maintain a "cooperation" reputation until round T_0; and then they will no longer cooperate. This means that the more times a game repeats, the longer both parties will cooperate. For example, assume given p determines non-cooperative game stage $T^* = 3$, then if the game repeats 100 times, they will cooperate in the first 97 occurrences, but starting in the 98th occurrence, they will not. If the game repeats 1,000 times, they will cooperate in the first 997 occurrences, but not cooperate starting in the 998th occurrence.

Section three: applications of the reputation model

3.1 Unraveling the chain store paradox

Now, we can unravel the "chain store paradox" introduced in the first section of this chapter. In the first section, we assumed that the entrant had a clear understanding of the incumbent's production costs and profit from choosing to acquiesce or fight. Under these circumstances, as soon as the entrant enters, the incumbent had better choose to acquiesce, because fighting cannot deter future entering. So, "fight" threat is not credible.

However, imagine the incumbent has two possible types: High cost and low cost. If it is high cost, the game structure is the same as shown in Figure 7.1. However, if it is low cost, when the entrant does not enter, the incumbent's profit is 200. When the entrant does enter, if the incumbent chooses to acquiesce, both parties will share the market. The entrant will receive 90 and the incumbent will receive 100. If the incumbent chooses to fight, the entrant loses 10 and the incumbent receives 120 (as shown in Figure 7.13). Here we assume that because the incumbent's costs are low enough, even if he chooses to fight, his profit is still greater than when it acquiesces.

Obviously, when the incumbent is low cost, even if it is a one-time game, as soon as the entrant enters, the incumbent's optimal choice is to fight, not acquiesce.

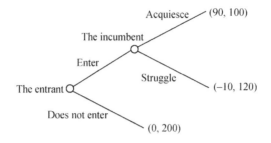

Figure 7.13 The Entry Game With a Low-Cost Incumbent

Therefore, fighting is a credible threat. If the entrant knows the incumbent is low-cost, the optimal choice is to not enter, because entry means a loss of 10 units.

Now we will assume that the potential entrant does not know if the incumbent is actually high cost or low cost. Should the entrant choose to enter or not? The answer depends on how great he believes the probability of the incumbent being low cost is. Assume he believes the probability is p, then if he enters he has p probability of losing 10 and $1 - p$ probability of gaining 40. His expected payoff is:

$$p \times (-10) + (1 - p) \times 40 = 40{-}50p$$

If he chooses to not enter, his certain payoff is 0. Therefore, only when $40 - 50p > 0$, thus $p < 0.8$, should the entrant choose to enter. Otherwise, if $p \geq 0.8$, he will choose to not enter.

Assume the incumbent is actually high cost. If he only sells product in one market, he of course will choose to acquiesce. However, if he is in 20 markets, when the first market is entered, what should he do? If he chooses to acquiesce, he immediately reveals that he is high cost, so the other 19 markets will be entered one after another. In each market, he can only receive a payoff of 50. However, if he chooses to fight, even if he will earn 50 less in the first market, as long as he can make the potential entrants believe he is more likely to be low cost, then he can protect the other 19 markets. Each other market can still earn 100. Obviously, even if the incumbent is high cost, he also has an incentive to establish a low-cost reputation by punishing entrants. Expecting this, perhaps from the beginning the entrants will not dare to enter.[5]

Of course, competition in real life is more complicated than in our theory. Market leaders like Microsoft and Tencent always think of ruthless means to inhibit entrants, but whether or not they will succeed depends on the capabilities of potential entrants and customer choices. If the entrant is strong enough (such as having a product that suits the market), the incumbent's block may not succeed. Therefore, on the market we still continuously see new entrants rivaling established business and even forcing them out of the market.[6]

Another related issue is that there is rarely only one incumbent in a market. For example, in the fast food market there are multiple operators like McDonald's,

KFC, and Pizza Hut. At this point, the incumbent is faces another issue. On the one hand, a repeated game occurs between incumbents, so they do not wish to enter a price war. Because of this, each incumbent hopes to establish a high-cost image (the higher costs are, the less likely prices will be reduced). On the other hand, they have a common interest in inhibiting new competitors from entering, so they hope to establish a low-cost image for potential entrants. This is a dilemma.

3.2 A man of great wisdom often seems slow-witted

The KMRW Reputation Model can explain many behaviors that appear to be irrational in real life as actually rational.

The old saying "a man of great wisdom often appears slow-witted (*dà zhì ruò yú*)" could be understood as a strategy to accumulate reputation. "*Zhì*" means wisdom. It also refers to people who play petty tricks, care about each penny, do not want to get the short end of the stick, are good at calculating, tough, etc. It is similar to the "rationality" that we mentioned before. "*Yú*" means clumsy, it refers to people who are generous, do not play petty tricks, are willing to suffer, are honest, are not aggressive, etc. It is similar to the "irrational" or "cooperative-type" that we mentioned before. People who love to play petty tricks or do not want to get the short end of the stick seem smart, however, they are actually stupid. The reason is that this type of person will have difficulty earning other's trust or find cooperative partners. On the contrary, honest people that are willing to get the short end of the stick are more likely to get someone else's trust and have more opportunities for cooperation with others. Therefore, if people in the game consider the balance between future gains and losses, given enough game occurrences, appearing slow witted is the best strategy for truly wise people. "Wise men" seem "slow-witted", but they only appear this way to establish a good cooperative appearance. If a person wants all the benefit in the beginning and appears crafty, in the end, they will achieve nothing.

Of course, in real life, the type of image a person should establish depends on his environment. For example, in a harsh society, establishing a "tough" or "unreasonable" image may be the best choice. In this type of society, if a person always appears weak, others will take advantage of him and in the end he will gain nothing. Therefore, even if a person is actually very weak, sometimes he must appear strong in order to build a reputation. This will make others think that person is not so easily taken advantage of. Something that appears to be unwise behavior may be wise over the long-term. Alternatively, in a just society where everyone follows the rules which are fair, it may be optimal to have a "weak" image. This might be the reason for differences between peoples of different regions.

3.3 The government's reputation

The reputation mechanism is extremely important for understanding the government's behavior.[7] A government that puts weight on its own reputation will respect the law more, be more likely to do what it says, less likely behave opportunistically, and respect private property and individual liberty more. From this, it more easily earns the people's trust. When it does the opposite, earning the people's trust is difficult.

A government will to a large degree put weight on its own reputation. This is influenced by multiple factors, and the most important are the political system and administrative structure. Generally speaking, in countries that have implemented constitutional government and democracy, the government puts more weight on its own reputation.[8] The reason is that constitutional government and democracy mean the people have bigger and more punishment measures and restraints on the government. Information is also more transparent. However, we also see democratically elected politicians playing one-time games because of term limits. They have serious opportunistic behavior and do not consider long-term interests. On the contrary, emperors and kings in ancient times ruled for uncertain lengths of time. It was like undertaking repeated games, so they must consider long-term interests. If they did well, the ruling power would pass from one generation to the next of the same blood lineage. If they did poorly, they could be overthrown at any time. This may be the reason governments that are neither democracies nor monarchies are the least trustworthy governments.

Government reputations are also extremely important in international relations. The best type of reputation a country establishes internationally is related to the issue that must be handled. For example, on the issue of territory and sovereignty, it may be beneficial to establish an "tough" reputation. In trade and disarmament negotiations, it might be better to establish a "cooperative type" reputation. Weakness on territorial issues might lead to a loss of sovereignty. Excessive assertiveness in trade negotiations might lead to a breakdown of negotiations. However, one point is certain. Regardless which issue a country is facing, establishing a "mean what one says" image is extremely important.[9]

Of course, establishing an assertive reputation comes at a huge price. Since the end of World War II, America has established an assertive image internationally. A common saying in Chinese society is: In the house, do not offend your wife; in society, do not offend the government; internationally, do not offend America. Throughout the Korean War, Cuban Missile Crisis, Vietnam War, Iraq War, and Afghan War, American has always been assertive. However, at least the Vietnam War and Iraq War were a huge price to pay for America. They seriously damaged the international reputation of America and are important factors leading to the decline of American power.[10]

3.4 "The penal statutes do not go up to great officers"

The reputation mechanism is an important mechanism for maintaining social cooperation. The market order is to a large degree maintained by the reputation mechanism. If firms and individuals do not care about their own reputations, even perfect laws could not make the market operate efficiently and orderly. In reality, the effectiveness of laws cannot be separated from the reputation mechanism, especially the weight judges put on their reputation (Zhang, 2003). If a judge does not care about his own reputation, fair judgments would be impossible, because under any law, judges have some discretion. Only when judges have an incentive to establish a reputation for fairness and justness will they not abuse their discretional powers.

The Confucian saying, "the rules of etiquette do not go down to the common people and the penal statutes do not go up to great officers" is often criticized as Confucian opposition to "equality before the law". This might be a misunderstanding. Confucius did not argue that senior officials should not be sanctioned for breaking the law. While serving the State of Lu, Confucius himself sentenced Shao Zhenmao, a senior official, to death. Perhaps the original meaning of this sentence was that senior officials were under the watchful eyes of the public, so they should pay close attention to their own reputation and not get to the point of committing a crime. However, members of the general public, who can be anonymous, might not care about their reputation and are more tempted to commit crimes. "The rules of etiquette do not go down to the common people and the penal statutes do not go up to great officers" can be understood as: The senior officials are governed by reputation and the common people are governed by regulation.

Regardless, when government officials do not care about their own reputations, that society cannot possibly have a good cooperative spirit and social order.

Section four: the accumulation of reputation

4.1 Bayes' Rule

In real life, a reputation is formed through a process of continuous accumulation, regardless if it is the reputation of an individual, firm, or nation. People always form judgments of a person's character through a large amount of observations and analysis. Generally speaking, when we meet a person for the first time, we have an *a priori* judgment of his character (possibly from other's information, or that person's resume), then we adjust our own judgment based on that person's behavior. Therefore, we can use Bayes' Rule to explain the accumulation of reputation.

Bayes' Rule in statistics is the use of observable information to revise *a priori* probability to determine *a posteriori* probability. For convenience, we will assume that there are two possible types of people: Good people and bad people. There are also two types of actions: Good actions and bad actions. For any person, at any time, we have a concept or judgment as to whether he is a good person or a bad person (called "a priori probability") and we know the probability that a good (or bad) person does good (or bad) actions (called conditional probability). Now, when we see he does a good (or bad) action, what is the probability he is a good (or bad) person (called "a posteriori probability")?

Assume Player A believes the a priori probability of "Player B being a good person" is $P(\theta^0)$ and the priori probability of "Player B being a bad person" is

$P(\theta^1)$ (here θ^0 represents a good person and θ^1 represents a bad person.) Also, the probability that good people do good actions is $Q(g/\theta^0)$ and the probability good people do bad actions is $Q(b/\theta^0)$. (g represents a good action and b represents a bad action.) The probability that a bad person does good things is $Q(g/\theta^1)$ and the probability that a bad person does bad things is $Q(b/\theta^1)$. Then, if Player A observes Player B has done a good action, according to Bayes' Rule, the *a posteriori* probability of "Player B being a good person" is:[11]

$$P\left(\theta^0/g\right) = \frac{Q\left(g/\theta^0\right)P\left(\theta^0\right)}{Q\left(g/\theta^0\right)P\left(\theta^0\right)+Q\left(g/\theta^1\right)P\left(\theta^1\right)}$$

For example, assume Player A believes the a priori probability of "Player B being a good person" is 0.5, the probability that good people do this good action is 1, and the probability bad people do this good action is 0.5. Then, after Player A observes Player B does this good action, he believes the probability of Player B being a good person changes from 0.5 originally to:

$$(1 \times 0.5)/((1 \times 0.5) + (0.5 \times 0.5)) \approx 0.7$$

In other words, Player A believes the probability of Player B being a bad person changes from 0.5 originally to 0.3.

If some day later, Player B does the same good action, then the *posteriori* probability of Player B being a good person changes from 0.7 to:

$$(1 \times 0.7)/((1 \times 0.7) + (0.5 \times 0.3)) \approx 0.8$$

Player A's opinion of Player B further changes favorably. If Player B continues to do the same good activity, in the end Player A will certainly believe Player B is absolutely a good person. This is the reputation accumulation issue.

Note that the reason Player A's opinion of Player B continuously improved is because Player A believed good people will certainly do this good action, but there is only a 50% possibility bad people will do it. If the probabilities that good people and bad people will do the same good thing is the same, then regardless how many times Player B does this good thing, Player A's opinion of B will not change. The reason is that Player B doing good actions does not add information. On the other hand, if there is one good action that only good people do (thus, $Q(g/\theta^0) > 0$) and bad people will absolutely not do (thus, $Q(g/\theta^1) = 0$), then if Player B does this good action, Player A will be certain Player B is a good person.

A person doing a good action does not certainly mean he is a good person, because bad people might also do the same good action. Bad people do good actions to pretend they are good people in order to establish a good reputation. (This in itself is not a bad thing.) Therefore, good actions do not necessarily transmit information. However, generally speaking, bad actions transmit information, because good people would not possibly do bad actions. If Player B does a bad action, he is certainly a bad person.

Of course, real life is much more complex. If uncertainty exists, because of ignorance, a good person that wants to do something good might end up doing something bad. There are numerous examples of this. Politicians easily make this mistake. Therefore, when a person with an outstanding reputation occasionally makes a mistake, other people often forgive him because it was not intentional.

4.2 The reputation of universities

The speed that reputations are accumulated or destroyed depends on different circumstances. Let us take university as an example to show this point.

Universities are organizations that have difficulty accumulating reputations, but are also slow to destroy them. The reason is that the reputation of the university to a large degree is determined by the quality of alumni, not merely the quality of faculty. The accumulation of alumni is a long-term process. According to Henry Hansmann (1999a), university education is a type of "associative good". People's demand for a particular university education is not primarily determined by fees, instead it is determined by the quality of students in the past, the current students, and expected future students. Even if your talent is not very high, but as long as other alumni's qualities of your university are high, then you will be judged as a high quality person, so you will have an advantage in job markets. Similarly, if the quality of other alumni is low, even if you are very talented, because of information asymmetry, you will be judged as low quality person. Therefore, when you go to study at a university, first consider which type of people also go to this university.

Precisely for this reason, establishing a new university is extremely difficult. It is easy to imagine that a new school with reasonable fees and high-quality faculty may not be able to attract high quality applicants, since no high-quality "customers" or alumni have been accumulated. Even if the new school has high quality program, its students might have difficulty finding work after graduation.

This is also an important reason the status of universities changes slowly. This is not the case for a business firm. If a firm does not produce high quality products for three years (even one year), customers will certainly go elsewhere and the firm will collapse. In real life, we can see this difference. Every year, so many enterprises start and close down, but how many universities start and closed down? Very few! This characteristic of universities has determined their inertia. Even if a university's level drops in the short term, it can still be raised back up. Assume that Peking University does not progress for 30 years, it would still be China's best, because the best students would still choose to come for its brand name.

However, slow accumulation does not mean accumulation cannot happen. When Harvard University was established, Oxford and Cambridge had already existed for hundred years. Even up to the Second World War, Harvard was still behind Oxford and Cambridge. However, today's Harvard is already above Oxford and Cambridge.

Similarly, slow depletion does not mean a reputation will never be depleted. If Peking University and Tsinghua University cannot inhibit their decline, outstanding students will look elsewhere. The recent choice by some outstanding students to choose Hong Kong universities over Peking University or Tsinghua University is an important signal.

Notes

1 See Fudenberg and Tirole (1991), page 112.
2 John Harsanyi (1973) did breakthrough research on incomplete information games. He won the 1994 Nobel Memorial Prize in Economic Sciences for his contributions.
3 Their model is nicknamed "the gang of four model". See Kreps, Milgrom, Roberts, and Wilson (1982).
4 This strategy is not sequentially optimal. There are some strategic actions which can give higher expected payoff. However, to prove our conclusion, the minimum expected payoff is enough. See the original article by Kreps, Milgrom, Roberts, and Wilson (1982).
5 This is actually the "pooling equilibrium" that we will discuss in Chapter 9, meaning a high-cost incumbent will act the same as a low-cost incumbent so that potential entrants do not know which type the incumbent actually is, and thus do not dare to enter. If the potential entrant believes the a priori probability that the incumbent is low-cost is low enough, then without new information he will choose to enter. A low-cost incumbent must think of some other signaling to differentiate himself from a high-cost incumbent. If a low-cost incumbent can accomplish this, then we say a "separating equilibrium" exists. Perhaps price is one such signal. The low-cost incumbent sets the price of his product low enough so that the high-cost incumbent firm cannot match him. When potential entrants observe this low price, they will know the incumbent is low-cost, and thus choose to not enter. Otherwise, they would enter. See Milgrom and Roberts (1982) (or Weiying Zhang (1996) for a simplified proof of their model).
6 A classic example is Qihoo 360 entering the search engine market to compete with Baidu which has been the dominant player of this business.
7 Research on the reputation of governments first appeared in the field of macroeconomics. Robert Baro (1986) and John Vickers (1986) proved that even if the term of office is limited, governments perhaps have an incentive to establish a reputation for not creating inflation. Fields that involve the reputation of governments include public policy, sovereign debt, territorial disputes, trade negotiations, counter-terrorism, environmental protection, corruption control, and the rule of law.
8 See Chapter 4, Section 4's discussions on constitutional government and democracy.
9 For theories on reputation in territorial disputes, see Walter (2003).
10 See Barnett (2009).
11 The posteriori probability of Player B being good after he was observed doing something bad can be similarly defined.

8 Adverse selection, brands, and regulation

Asymmetric information can be classified into *ex-ante* asymmetric information and *ex-post* asymmetric information. *Ex-ante* asymmetric information leads to adverse selection. *Ex-post* asymmetric information leads to moral hazard.

So-called adverse selection refers to the bad driving out the good because of asymmetric information. For example, bad cars cause good cars to not sell, high-risk policy holders cause low-risk policy holders to be uninsured, low-quality projects cause high-quality projects to be unfinanced, fake beggars cause real beggars to be neglected, high-quality scholars cannot complete with low-quality scholars, etc.

Adverse selection means a potential Pareto efficiency cannot appear. In essence, it is also a Prisoner's Dilemma issue.

Resolving adverse selection to realize a Pareto efficiency is a big issue faced by society. Methods to resolve adverse selection include both market mechanisms and non-market mechanisms.

Market mechanisms include: (1) The party without private information directly collects and investigate the information; (2) specialized providers of information collect and transmit information; (3) the party without private information indirectly obtains information through mechanism design; (4) the party with private information signals private information with some costs; and (5) the reputation mechanism.

The reputation mechanism primarily manifests as the party with private information establishing a brand. The value of brands depends on the degree of asymmetric information. The brand of products with more asymmetric information are worth more. The value of brands is also related to income levels and technological progress. The higher incomes are, and the more complex technology is, the more important brands are.

Government regulation is the primary non-market mechanism to resolve adverse selection. However, recent theoretical and empirical studies have shown that government regulation is not an effective means of resolving adverse selection. Asymmetric information more easily leads to government failure rather than market failure.

Perhaps the most serious consequence of government regulation is damage to the effectiveness of the reputation mechanism. There are three reasons: (1) Regulation causes unstable entrepreneurial expectations and short-term behavior; (2) regulation causes monopolies, which make market punishments non-credible; and (3) regulation leads to corruption and rent-seeking behavior because relying on government relationships is more profitable than establishing brands.

Section one: asymmetric information and its consequences

1.1 The asymmetric information issue

In the previous chapter, we considered the importance of the reputation mechanism under a condition of incomplete information. Starting with this chapter, we will spend the next four chapters discussing more general incomplete information games.

Actually, incomplete information is a basic characteristic of human life.

An example of this would be the beggars we encounter while walking on the street or waiting at a traffic light. Most of us are sympathetic, and are willing to offer help to those in need. One troublesome issue we face is that it is not easy to determine whether the beggars we encounter are really on hard times or are "professional" beggars. Because of the difficulty differentiating between the two, we perhaps are not willing to give.

In the buying and selling of products, the producer always has more information about the product than the buyer. The more complex the product is, the more of an information advantage the manufacturer has.

In employment relationships, an employer generally has no way of fully knowing an employee's ability or moral character. A boss will also not be completely clear on the things an employee does all day or how much effort he puts into his work.

In commercial lending, the bank has no way of fully knowing the debtor's degree of trustworthiness or the profitability of a project. The bank cannot fully grasp whether or not the borrowed funds are being used according to the contract.

In doctor-patient relationships, the doctor knows more about treatments and medications than the patient. The patient cannot easily judge whether a medicine is prescribed to treat an illness or to receive pharmaceutical company kickbacks.

In the process of finding a lover, a person's appearance can be observed, but his character cannot. Even husbands and wives that have lived together for a very long time are not aware of certain information about the other.

Government officials call themselves "public servants", but whether a government official makes a decision in the public's interest or his personal interest is known by himself but not the public.

These kinds of examples are endless.

We call information known by one party in a transaction, but not the other, asymmetric information. Asymmetric information can be separated into two types: ex-ante asymmetry and ex-post asymmetry. Ex-ante information asymmetry refers to information asymmetry that exists before the exchange, such as the previously mentioned quality issue. Ex-post information asymmetry refers to the behavior of one party after the exchange, such as an enterprise not knowing whether or not an employee is hard-working after hiring him.[1] Ex-ante information asymmetry causes adverse selection, whereas ex-post information asymmetry causes moral hazard. This chapter and the two chapters that follow discuss ex-ante information asymmetry. Ex-post asymmetry is the main topic of Chapter 11.

1.2 Adverse selection

When people partake in an exchange, if the relevant information is symmetric, then they will choose a suitable good or exchange partner, and negotiate conditions for the exchange that benefit both parties. A potential Pareto improvement can appear. However, if the relevant information is asymmetric during the transaction, such as the buyer not knowing the product quality information that the seller knows, then perhaps the product or partner that is chosen is not the one that each person hoped for. Because of the fear of being cheated, a good product may not be sold for a good price, or a good person may not be compensated well. We call this situation adverse selection. The existence of adverse selection causes many potentially beneficial exchanges to not happen, and, in some serious cases, causes the market to collapse.

The earliest to focus on adverse selection was George Akerlof, the 2001 Nobel Laureate in Economics. In 1970, Akerlof published the paper titled *The Market for Lemons: Quality Uncertainty and the Market Mechanism* (Akerlof, 1970). He discovered that in the exchange of second-hand cars, information asymmetry will inhibit a smooth market transaction.

In comparison with new cars, the quality of old cars on the second-hand market is uneven. For simplicity, we will assume that there are two types of second-hand cars: Good and bad. We will assume that the seller values a good car at ¥200,000, and the buyer values it at ¥220,000. The seller values a bad car at ¥100,000 and the buyer values it at ¥120,000. With complete information, the buyer can differentiate between a good and bad car, so the buyer and seller can easily come to an agreement after negotiations. If a good car is priced at ¥210,000 and a bad car is priced at ¥110,000, then both cars can be transacted.[2] However, if information asymmetry exists, then the seller knows whether a car is good or bad, but the buyer only knows that (for example) there is a 50% probability that it is a good car and a 50% probability that it is a bad car. Then, according to a simple weighted average, the car's expected value to the buyer is ¥170,000. How much is the buyer willing to pay for this car? It is easy to misunderstand that as long as the seller is willing to accept a price no higher than ¥170,000, then both parties will make a transaction. This perception is wrong. Imagine the seller is willing to accept a price of ¥150,000. Will the buyer buy the car? Certainly not. The buyer knows that if the seller is willing to sell the car for ¥150,000, then it must be a bad car, and thus is only worth ¥120,000 to the buyer. The reason is the seller of a good car would not accept anything less than ¥200,000. Therefore, the buyer cannot pay the average price, and the highest acceptable price is ¥120,000. Thus, only bad cars can be transacted, but not good cars. Because of information asymmetry, bad

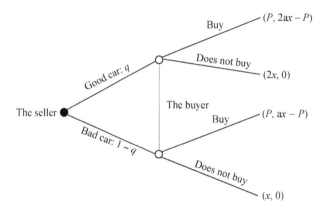

Figure 8.1 The Second-Hand Car Market Under Asymmetric Information

cars pushed good cars out of this market. This is adverse selection, similar to the concept of "bad money driving out good money".[3]

Generally, we display an asymmetric information game as shown is Figure 8.1.

Assume that the seller only sells two types of cars: Good and bad. There is a dotted line between the two nodes that correspond with the buyer's decisions. It represents the buyer does not know in which decision node he is. The buyer does not know the quality of the car, only that the probability it is a good car is q, and the probability it is a bad car is $1 - q$. Assume that, to the seller, the value of retaining the good and bad cars is $2x$ and x, respectively. The value to the buyer is assumed to be $2ax$ and ax. Here, we will assume that for both the seller and the buyer, the value of the good car is twice the value of the bad car. Also, the value of the car to the buyer is a times for the seller (and $a \geq 1$; otherwise the transaction is pointless). We use P to represent the transaction price. Because there is no way to differentiate good cars from bad, P is the transaction price of all used cars. If it is a good car, the added value to the buyer after the transaction is $2ax - P$. If it is a bad car, the buyer received $ax - P$. For the seller, regardless of whether a good car or bad car is sold, as long as the transaction happens, the payoff is P. If the transaction does not happen, the used car still belongs to the seller, so a good car is worth $2x$ and a bad car is worth x. The buyer's payoff is zero.

Assume that both the buyer and the seller are rational, so neither of them will engage in loss-making activities. The buyer will only buy the car if the expected net benefit of buying the car is greater than the net benefit of not buying the car. The transaction price cannot be lower than the seller's value of keeping the car. Thus, the selling price of a bad car cannot be lower than x, and the selling price of a good car cannot be lower than $2x$.

Specifically, for the buyer to buy a car, the following condition must hold:

$$q \times (2ax - P) + (1 - q) \times (ax - P) \geq 0$$

Simplified, this becomes:

$$(1 + q)ax \geq P$$

Thus, if asymmetric information exists, the highest price the buyer is willing to pay is $(1 + q)ax$. The lowest price a seller of a bad car is willing to accept is x. A transaction will take place for any price between x and $(1 + q)ax$. The lowest price a seller of a good car is willing to accept is $2x$. The price that both parties would accept must satisfy the condition that:

$$(1 + q)ax \geq P \geq 2x$$

This also means:

$$(1 + q)ax \geq 2x$$

As long as x does not equal zero, the next simplification is:

$$q \geq (2 / a) - 1$$

In other words, given the consumer's valuation of the car, good cars can only be exchanged if the proportion of good cars on the market is high enough. Or, the equivalent condition is:

$$a \geq 2 / (1 + q)$$

Thus, given the proportion of good cars, good cars can only be exchanged if the buyer's valuation of a used car is sufficiently higher than the seller's.

This condition, which was derived algebraically, actually required the gap between the buyer and seller's valuation of a commodity to be large enough. For example, given that $q = 1/2$, then a must be no smaller than 4/3. Under conditions of complete information, as long as a is greater than 1, a deal can be made. Obviously, if information is asymmetric, and a is between 1 and 4/3, a deal cannot be made. This shows that an otherwise win-win deal between the buyer and seller now cannot happen because of asymmetric information. In the previous example, when we assume that $a = 1.2$ (bad car) and $a = 1.1$ (good car), the good car cannot be exchanged. In fact, if we assume that the buyer's valuation is 20% higher than the seller's (thus $a = 1.2$), then a good car can only be exchanged if the proportion of good cars is not less than 0.67.

We can use Figure 8.2 to display the critical conditions for a deal to be made with incomplete information.

As the curve AB in Figure 8.2 shows, either the buyer's valuation of the car is high enough (a is large) or the proportion of good cars on the market is high enough (q is large); otherwise, the transaction would not happen. Triangle ABC represents the area where deals can be made under complete information, but will

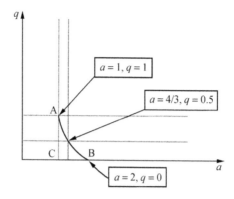

Figure 8.2 The Critical Condition for a Deal

not happen under incomplete information. This represents a loss of efficiency, and so is also called a market failure.

The same principle applies to trust among strangers in society. Interpersonal interactions are like a type of transaction. There are two main factors that determine whether or not strangers interact. The first is the proportion of "good people" among strangers. The second is the benefit of interacting with strangers. According to the derived conclusion above, if the proportion of good people in society is high, such as 90%, then cooperation will happen as long as *a* is not less than 20/19. Otherwise, if the proportion of good people is only 30% of the population, then cooperation will only happen if *a* is greater than 1.54. If the number of good people is high, even if the benefit of interacting with people is not very large, then people will still be willing to interact. If the proportion of good people is extremely low, people will only be willing to make a deal if returns are very high. Even a very low trustful person may be able to attract friends if the value of contact is large enough.[4]

1.3 Adverse selection in financial markets

Asymmetric information in financial markets is much more serious than in markets for other products. Here, we will analyze the information asymmetry problem in the insurance and bank lending markets.

First, we will examine the insurance market. People detest risk and hope to buy insurance to reduce losses due to risk. For sickness insurance, if information was symmetric and complete, insurance companies could set the standards according to each policyholder's likelihood of illness. For ¥1 million policies, if the likelihood of illness is 10%, then the premium would be ¥100,000. If the likelihood of illness is 5%, then the premium would be ¥50,000. Each person could buy insurance that suits them.

However, if the insurance company only knows the average likelihood of sickness for a group, but not the specific condition for each person, then it can only set a unified premium level based on the average likelihood of sickness, such as ¥80,000 for each person. At this point, people with a low likelihood of sickness will feel they are taking a loss, so they possibly will leave the market for insurance. With the exit of low-risk customers from the market, insurance companies face a higher likelihood of sickness among the remaining policy holders. Because they will certainly lose money using the original fee standards, insurance companies must increase fee standards. After the increase, the next group of people with the lowest likelihood of sickness will leave the market. Then, the average likelihood of sickness for policy holders will further increase, so the insurance companies will further raise prices. This will cause more "good customers" to leave, thus creating a vicious cycle. In the end, only people with the highest likelihood of sickness will be willing to buy insurance. This process is shown in Figure 8.3. (In the figure, the actual likelihood of sickness for each person is ranked from low to high, and the horizontal line represents the average likelihood. An increase in the premiums and "quality" customers leaving reinforce each other, causing the average likelihood of sickness for policy holders to increase continuously.) This is the insurance market's adverse selection problem (Rothchild and Stiglitz, 1976).

In reality, many types of insurance do not exist in the market because of adverse selection (and moral hazard which will be discussed in Chapter 11). Currently, insurance companies do not provide bicycle theft insurance. In the 1980s, The People's Insurance Company of China (PICC), which was the sole insurance provider, offered bicycle theft insurance. Initially, premiums were calculated based on the rate of bicycle theft without insurance, but PICC soon saw the rate of theft for covered bicycles increase significantly. The reason is that those of low probability of their bicycles being stolen (such as those who were residents of an army base or had someone look after their bicycle while at work) chose not to cover their bicycles. When PICC increased premiums accordingly, more low-risk people ended their policies. In the end, bicycle insurance was discontinued. (Another reason for increasing of bicycle theft rate was because of moral hazard, policy holders were less careful about preventing theft, or even committed insurance fraud.)

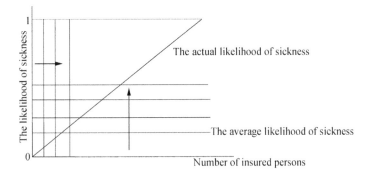

Figure 8.3 Adverse Selection in the Insurance Market

The bank lending market also faces the adverse selection problem. Imagine there are two projects, A and B, which both need ¥1 million in funding. Project A has a 90% chance of success, with success earning ¥1.3 million and failure earning zero. Project B has a 50% chance of success, with success earning ¥2.0 million and failure earning zero. Project B carries more risk than Project A, but success brings higher earnings. Project A is less risky than Project B, but success brings relatively lower earnings. If we compare expected earnings, Project A's expected earnings are ¥1.3 million × 0.9 = ¥1.17 million, whereas Project B's expected earnings are ¥2 million × 0.5 = ¥ 1.0 million. From this perspective, Project A is preferable to Project B.

If information is symmetric, so that the bank knows which project is high-risk (Project B) and which project is low-risk (Project A), they could set respective interest rates for each. Assume the bank requires the rate of expected return to be 10%. If Project A applies for a loan, to guarantee a 10% rate of expected return, given a 90% rate of success, the bank would require Project A to repay at a rate of 22% (110/0.9 = 122). Similarly, if Project B applies for a loan, the required interest rate should be 120% (110/0.5 = 220). At this point, Project A will be willing to borrow money because if it succeeds, it will bring in ¥1.3 million, which, after repaying the bank ¥1.22 million, leaves ¥80,000 in net earnings. If it fails, it will declare bankruptcy, so in the end, earnings will be zero. Project B would not be willing to borrow money because even investment succeeded, the ¥2.0 million it brings in is not enough to repay the bank ¥2.2 million. Here, the socially optimal decision is aligned with the individually optimal decision. Project A's expected rate of return is greater than the bank's cost of capital, so not only should it borrow money, it will actually receive funding. Because Project B's expected rate of return is zero, it is lower than the social cost, so it should not borrow money and will also not get funding even if it does apply for a loan. This is the ideal state with complete information.

If information is incomplete, then there is no way for the socially optimal allocation of capital to occur. Assume that the bank does not know whether a project is Project A or B, only that a project has a 0.5 probability of being A or B. To maintain an expected rate of return of 10%, the bank can only collect an average interest rate, meaning 22% × 0.5 + 120% × 0.5 = 71%. In order to borrow money, the borrower must pay a rate of 71% to the bank. That means an enterprise must repay ¥1.71 million if the project is successful. Therefore, only the high risk Project B will apply for lending, whereas the low risk Project A will not. The reason is that under the best circumstances, Project A can only earn ¥1.3 million, so borrowing money is not worthwhile. On the contrary, if Project B succeeds, it will earn ¥2 million, so after repaying the bank, it will still have ¥0.29 million in net profit. Of course, the bank is not stupid. It knows that the project which is willing to accept a 71% interest rate, must be the high risk one, so it is not worth lending to. In this way, because of the adverse selection problem, the good project does not receive funding.

This is actually the reasoning behind 2001 Nobel Prize in Economics Laureate Joseph Stiglitz's research on credit rationing. (Stiglitz and Weiss, 1981) We know that in general goods markets, as long as the buyer is willing to pay higher prices, the seller is always willing to sell, whereas the rationing system only occurs when prices are controlled in the planned economy. However, even without interest rate control, banks will still implement rationing for credit applications. The person willing to pay the most interest will not necessarily be lent to. The reason is that the bank's expected return is not only determined by the interest rate level, but also the probability of repayment. It is not the case that banks' returns increase monotonically with interest rates. In the previous example, when the interest rate was 22%, the "good" enterprise would borrow money, and the probability of repayment was 90%. If the interest rate increased to 71%, the "good" enterprise would withdraw, leaving only the "bad" enterprise willing to borrow, with a probability of repayment of 50%. Because of adverse selection, the higher the interest required by the bank, the lower the average quality of debtor applicants. When banks ask extremely high interest rates, only gambler-style enterprises are willing to apply for lending. Therefore, banks' expected rate of return and interest rate level form an inverted-U relationship, as shown in Figure 8.4.

In Figure 8.4, in the beginning, along with the increase in interest rates, expected returns also increase. After a certain point, each increase in interest rates will lead to lower expected returns. The higher interest rates are, the more likely it is that people who apply for lending are "gamblers". Banks generally will not be willing to provide credit to a person just because he is willing to pay more interest.

From this point of view, information asymmetry will cause good projects in the credit market to not necessarily be funded, and also greatly increase the operational risks of banks. To resolve this issue, there are relevant institutional guarantees in the financial system, of which credit rationing is one. The rationing system assists in overcoming inefficient resource allocation under conditions of asymmetric information, so from a social perspective, it is proper. If a store refuses to sell a product to a customer, the customer can complain or even sue, but if a bank refuses to lend money to a customer, the customer has no recourse to complain or sue.

In almost every country, small- and medium-sized enterprises have difficulty borrowing money. The reason for this is the existence of serious information asymmetry. For large enterprises, financial statements are public, so banks are

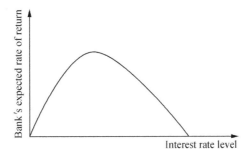

Figure 8.4 The Interest Rate Level and the Bank's Expected Return

more confident. For small enterprises, it is difficult for banks to differentiate between good and bad, so they are not willing to lend money. The result is the difficulty that small- and medium-sized enterprises have in borrowing money.

1.4 Some other adverse selection phenomena in real life

As was mentioned in the opening of this chapter, many people are not willing to give charity to beggars. The main reason is that they are unable to differentiate between real and fake beggars, as opposed to them being uncharitable. For example, one year, the Nanjing Municipal Police registered vagrants in a certain area for assistance. Among 1,733 vagrants, only 85 were willing to accept assistance. Of those, only 13 were willing to go to an aid station. This shows that many beggars are actually "professional beggars".[5]

Imagine that you come across a beggar. Should you give money or not? Consider the game shown in Figure 8.5. Here we assume that if money is given to a real beggar, the beggar receives 20 units of utility, and you receive 10 units. Without giving, you both receive zero. If money is given to a fake beggar, the beggar receives 10 units of utility, and you lose 20 units. The reasoning behind

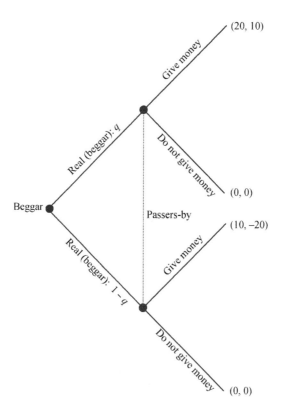

Figure 8.5 The Charity Game With Asymmetric Information

this assumption is that the real beggar needs this money much more than the fake beggar, so charity provides more utility to the real beggar. For you, helping people that truly need assistance brings about a sense of joy (so the assumed gain is 10), but being defrauded and helping those that do not need it causes you unease (so the assumed loss is −20).

Obviously, if you come across a real beggar, you will give money, but if you come across a fake beggar, you will not give money. From the social perspective, this is optimal, because if the real beggar gets money, total social utility is 30, whereas if the fake beggar gets money, the total utility is −10. The problem is: If you cannot differentiate between real and fake beggars, and you only know that the probability of real and fake is q and $1 - q$ respectively, what should you do? At this point, if you give money, your expected payoff is: $q \times 10 + (1 - q) \times (-20) = 30q - 20$. If you do not give money, your expected payoff is zero. Therefore, only when $30q - 20 > 0$, thus $q > 2/3$, will you choose to give money. This means that if you believe that half of the beggars you come across are real, then you will choose not to give money. The result is that cheats do not gain anything, but those that need help are also not helped.

This is adverse selection for begging. Just as bad cars drive good cars out of the used car market, fake beggars also harm real beggars. The reason that real beggars do not receive charity is not because people are uncompassionate, but instead because information is asymmetric.

Similar situations are numerous in real life. There is even a book titled *Who did Henanese Offend?*[6] It deals with the common belief that people from Henan Province are untrustworthy and sell mostly fake goods. In reality, Henanese are the same as people from other parts of China. There are good and bad people, so one assumption cannot apply to all of them. Henan, as part of the Central Plain, has inherited many outstanding cultural traditions of the Chinese people. The vast majority of Henanese are honest. Why is it that Henanese have such a negative image? Who did Henanese provoke?

Frankly, it was not all Henanese that caused the provocation, only some. After this group of Henanese provoked others, they created a negative image for all Henanese. Each province has con artists, so why does public opinion focus on Henan? One possible reason is that Henan has a large population, with many of them spread all over the country. The Henan dialect is relatively unique, so many people can distinguish it and remember it. Therefore, it is easier for people to differentiate people from Henan than people from other provinces. This characteristic has made Henanese a joke in movies and television. Frequent use of a joke will lead people to incorrectly believe it is based on fact, thus strengthening the poor image of Henanese. Another possibility is that the ratio of con artists in Henan is actually higher than in other provinces. Regardless of the reason, the inability to differentiate between good and bad people will lead to the problem of "one rotten apple spoiling the barrel". As soon as people are cheated by one Henanese, it will negatively impact the image of all Henanese, so honest Henanese will not be treated fairly. This is similar to good cars not fetching a good price. Because of asymmetric information, the untrustworthy behavior of some Henanese harms the interests of the vast majority of honest Henanese.

The adverse selection issue also exists in academic circles. In the case of innovation and plagiarism, if the academic "market" does not have good academic standards or objective evaluations, it is not easy to differentiate between innovation and plagiarism, so the problem of information asymmetry will exist. The innovator and plagiarist know their own qualities, but most reader on the market do not have the ability to differentiate. They will only know that the viewpoints of each are similar, but will not know who is the creator is and who is the plagiarist. The less fairly rigorous scholarship is evaluated, the more there will be plagiarism. In the end, no one is willing to innovate. This leads to a loss in social efficiency as more intellect and energy that would have been applied to academic research is instead wasted on useless plagiarism.

Additionally, there is the issue of article quality and quantity. Some people, such as previously mentioned George Akerlof, relied on one article to win the Nobel Prize. If China also had a good system to evaluate the quality of articles, then the quantity of articles would become unimportant. However, if most people do not understand the quality of articles, instead only focusing on the quantity of articles, the end result will be that people with the greatest quantity of articles will be praised and promoted. The truly exceptional scholars, if they are above just making the number, will lose interest in academic circles so that those staying in academic circles are not necessarily the most exceptional.

In today's institutes of higher education of China, a serious issue is that good academic standards and evaluation systems have not been established. Overall, the problem of adverse selection in the Chinese academic market is extremely serious.

Section two: asymmetric information and brand value

2.1 Market mechanisms that resolve asymmetric information

Asymmetric information will perhaps lead to Pareto improvements being unachievable and win-win transactions not being made. Therefore, in order for people to effectively cooperate, they must find ways to overcome the problem of asymmetric information.

Generally speaking, mechanisms that resolve the problem of asymmetric information can be classified into two groups: Market mechanisms and nonmarket mechanisms (such as government intervention).

Many economists believe that information asymmetry causes "market failure", thus necessitating government intervention. Stiglitz, a person that has made significant contributions to information economics, also holds this view.[7] This is regrettable. Actually, it is precisely because of information asymmetry that we even have the market and need the market.[8] For resolving the problem of information asymmetry, not only are market mechanisms more important than non-market mechanisms, they are also more effective. If information was symmetric and complete, the planned economy could solve problems. Just as F.A. Hayek pointed out, only competitive markets can produce the information needed for exchange.[9]

The simplest way the market overcomes asymmetric information is the collection and processing of information by the disadvantaged party. For example, in the insurance industry, insurance companies developed actuarial methods to directly gather information. The main function of actuaries is to deals with the measurement and management of risk and uncertainty based on analysis of statistics for policy holders. With this foundation, when setting insurance premiums, insurance companies can deal with different types of people differently. For instance, in medical insurance, a person's age will certainly influence a person's likelihood of illness, so older people pay more than younger people. The same applies to smoking, in that premiums are different for smokers and non-smokers.

The market has also developed a large number of specialized providers of information. In the car market, when buying a car, a person can read professional car magazines to obtain relevant information, find out information about the seller, or hire a mechanic to help. In university admissions, tests are a means to acquire information about a person's intelligence and ability, so the market has developed specialized testing organizations like TOEFL, IELTS, GMAT, etc. There are also numerous other notified bodies that serve as specialized producers of information. Consulting, accounting, and credit rating can all be seen as industries that help people obtain information. Without these types of markets, most of the information required for exchange would not exist.[10]

The reader should not mistakenly believe that only the disadvantaged party (such as the buyer) has an incentive to obtain information, whereas the advantaged party (such as the seller) always attempts to conceal information. In reality, in a competitive market, the seller also has a very strong incentive to reveal true information to the buyer, just as a good person hopes that others know he is a good person. The reason is that eliminating asymmetry helps to facilitate a win-win transaction. A large amount of information related to a product in the market is provided by the manufacturer, such as manufacturer-provided consultation services or demonstrations to show the functions of a product.[11]

In addition to directly obtained and provided information, information is also obtained and collected indirectly. The main means of indirectly providing information is called "signaling". It refers to the process by which the advantageous party with information transmits true information about himself via a costly method to the information-disadvantaged party. For example, a car seller providing free maintenance perhaps indirectly indicates the quality of the car. Mechanisms that indirectly obtain information are called "screening" or "mechanism design." They are a type of incentive designed by the information-disadvantaged party to make the information-advantaged party tell the truth. For example, insurance companies design different policies for policy holders to choose themselves, thus allowing the insurance company to know which type of risk profile a policyholder has. We will discuss signaling in Chapter 9 and mechanism design in Chapter 10.

Perhaps the most important market mechanism for the resolution of information asymmetry is the "reputation mechanism" discussed in the last chapter. The major form the reputation mechanism takes in playing a role in the market is the establishment of brands. The purpose of brands is to resolve information asymmetry. The more serious information asymmetry is, the more necessary brands are. With brands, if fraudulent activity occurs, the brand will lose value, so the producer will suffer losses. For individuals, reputation is also a type of brand.

2.2 Industries and the value of brands

This section examines the relationship between brands and information asymmetry.[12] It was stated in the previous section that the more information is asymmetric, the higher the brand value. This relationship is displayed in Figure 8.6.

From Figure 8.6, we can see that a product with the lowest degree of information asymmetry, such as potatoes, also has the least brand value. This is the reason that potatoes often do not have brands. In the home appliance industry, which includes televisions and refrigerators, information is a bit more important, so brand values are a bit higher. In the more complex pharmaceutical, service, and automotive industries, safety requirements are higher and information asymmetry is more serious, so brand values are even higher. Of the four types of industries, consulting has the highest degree of information asymmetry. The function of an accounting firm is to resolve the problem of asymmetric information by telling the investing public of the financial condition of a publicly listed company. The brand of this type of organization is extremely important. Similarly, brand values of consulting firms, credit rating agencies, investment banks, and insurance companies are very high. Universities are also an industry with very high brand values. For industries with very serious information asymmetry, brands are a core competitive strength in the market. Often, there are only a limited number of suppliers or service providers because it is not easy for new enterprises that have not established a brand to enter the market. For example, students will not apply to a newly formed university

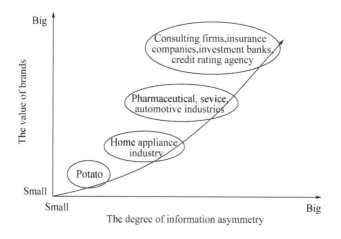

Figure 8.6 The Relationship Between Brands and Information Asymmetry

because they prefer to enroll in a well-known university, such as Peking University, Tsinghua University, Fudan University, Nankai University, etc.

In competitive markets, there are three main types of competitive advantage: Cost advantage, product advantage, and brand advantage. Cost advantage determines the lowest limit of price, thus influencing the product's appeal to customers. Product advantage refers to the differentiation in quality and function that a product has in comparison with its competitors. Price is not the only factor considered when consumers make a choice. Universities, for example, will have difficulty attracting students just by charging low tuition. Brand advantage refers to customers' trust, reducing the cost of the customer collecting information. Figure 8.7 displays these types of advantages together. The horizontal axis represents the value of brands (or degree of information asymmetry), and the vertical axis represents the relative importance of these types of advantages.

Because brand value and information asymmetry are counterparts, the relative importance of the three types of advantage differs from product to product. The more valuable brands are, the more important brand advantage is. The less valuable the brand is for a product, the more its cost advantage is important. The more valuable the brand is for a product, the less its cost advantage is important. As the value of the brands increase, so too does the product differentiation advantage gradually increase. However, as soon as brand values become extremely high, the product differentiation advantage will decrease. Therefore, Figure 8.6 can be updated to become Figure 8.8.

When enterprises are determining their competitive strategies, they must do so according to industry characteristics. If they sell potatoes or other commodities, making costs low is of the highest importance. If they sell home electronics, perhaps cost advantage, product advantage, and brand advantage are all relatively important. In the automobile and pharmaceutical industries, brand advantage is more important than in other industries. For the industries in the top-right hand corner of the figure, perhaps brands are the most important. For example, in the investment banking industry, because information asymmetry exists, investors have difficulty believing in an unknown company, so investment banks use their brand names to guarantee the quality of listed enterprises. Some large international

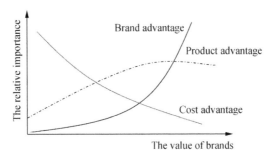

Figure 8.7 The Relative Importance of Brand Value and Competitive Advantage

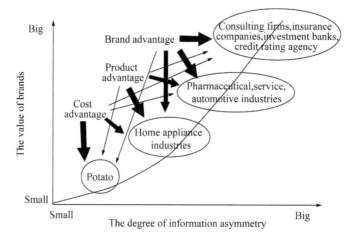

Figure 8.8 Information Asymmetry and Brand Value

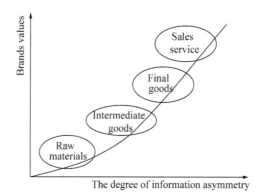

Figure 8.9 Brand Values and the Industry Chain

investment banks, such as Morgan Stanley, collect extremely high service fees. The reason is that their good reputation allows IPO firms to sell their shares at a higher price to raise more money than otherwise.[13] The consulting industry is also similar. A world-class consulting firm like McKinsey can collect surprisingly high fees but still have a huge market.

The same relationship exists between information asymmetry and brand values in the industry chain, as shown in Figure 8.9.

The industry chain is formed by links between raw materials, intermediate goods, and final goods. The further down something is on the industry chain, meaning closer to the final consumer, the higher the degree of information asymmetry, so the higher brands values are. The reason is that in the producer's products markets, the buyer is a manufacturer, and generally a "specialist", so the degree of information asymmetry between the buyer and the seller is relatively low. For example, an automaker's understanding of components is little lower than that of the component-maker. A steelmaker's understanding of iron ore is another example. However, the final consumer's knowledge of the product is very limited. Nike and Adidas could be seen as brand operating companies. They often do not manufacture, or manufacture very little. Instead, most of their products are made by contract manufacturers via OEM system, and they are only responsible for designing products and managing their brands. Actually, these branded companies control the sales link in the industry chain. Nike, for example, is only responsible for the design and marketing of shoes, whereas contract manufacturers produce the shoes according to Nike's design and quality specifications. Because its brand value is very high, it gets the largest piece of the pie.

2.3 *Technological progress and brands*

Technological progress has an important impact on brands. This is because as technology progresses, division of labor on the industry chain becomes more specialized. As the technological content of products increases, information asymmetry between producers and consumers becomes more serious. Therefore, technological progress will certainly increase the value of brands. This is especially the case when technological progress causes division of labor in the value chain to become international division of labor. When a small number of countries and regions supply the entire world with their final products, the distance between producers and consumers becomes vast, so trust becomes even more important. The result is that a small number of large branded multinational companies can lead the international market of whole industries.

Technological progress causes traditional products that originally did not have brands to now have a need for brands. As was mentioned before, potatoes do not need brands because potatoes are a product of nature that producers cannot counterfeit. However, with the application of genetic engineering to agriculture, this point no longer stands. With genetically modified products, consumers are more and more sensitive about food safety. They are only willing to buy the products produced and provided by trustworthy enterprises. There is a large price discrepancy between organic and nonorganic foods in the market, but regular consumers have difficulty differentiating between organic and non-organic foods. At this point, brands become a commitment by the enterprise to the consumer. Only organic foods sold by enterprises with good brands will be trusted by consumers. Even if a producer produces organic foods, without a brand, they will be hard to sell. Only with the help of large branded chain stores like Walmart, Carrefour, and Wumart can these products be sold. This will have an important impact on the organizational form of agricultural production.

Another example is construction materials. Traditionally, construction materials came from nature, and the difference in price was also determined by nature because the degree of information asymmetry was small. However, with technological progress, the technological content of construction materials increased, so the chemical component of products that appear similar was different and the difference in impact on human health became extreme. At that point, the manufacturer's brand became an important factor determining market competitiveness.

This is the major reason that construction material chain stores like Easyhome, Inc. appeared.

Because of information asymmetry, technological progress can also eliminate certain traditional industries. In the early 1990s, soft shell turtles, edible birds, and shark fins were in favor with Chinese consumers, causing prices to increase rapidly. However, people soon discovered that with the help of new technology, these types of foods were easily faked. Customers were paying high prices for potentially harmful products. Consumption of the product decreased because of this. It even got to the point where very few customers purchased about soft shell turtles because they were rumored to be grown using birth-control medicine. The only way to resolve the problem was to use brands. Today, we are already starting to see trademarks on crabs.

2.4 Income levels and brand values

Brand values are also related to income level of households. In Figure 8.10, the horizontal axis represents income level and the vertical axis represents brand value. In the three regions of low-, medium-, and high-income segments, as the income level rises, so too does brand value.

One reason for this is that brands are a type of status symbol. Wealthy people have higher purchasing power and are willing to pay higher premiums for brands. Here, brands are used to resolve a different type of information asymmetry, which is information asymmetry related to consumers. A person's wealth is not known to everyone they come across, so brands can tell strangers a person's status. Obviously, there is no need between associates to display status by wearing famous brands.

Perhaps more important reason is that wealthy people's time is more valuable than others'. Their opportunity cost of directly collecting information is higher, so they are willing to pay for trust. Therefore, wealthy people generally buy branded products, whereas poor people are willing to collect information by themselves. In the 1980s and early 1990s, Beijing had peddlers everywhere, as observed in many developing regions. Starting in the late 1990s, a large number of supermarkets

Figure 8.10 Brand Values and Income Levels

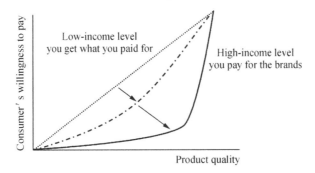

Figure 8.11 Product Quality and Consumer Willingness to Pay

and chain stores began to enter Beijing, so the number of peddlers gradually decreased. One of the reasons for this is that when people's incomes were low, the opportunity cost of time was relatively low. Even though the peddler's vegetables were of mixed quality, people could pick and choose the freshest vegetables. After income levels increased, people gradually became unwilling to pick through vegetables, so supermarkets did it for them. Gradually, peddlers were replaced by supermarkets. In the early days, when students bought computers, they relied on friends with know-how to put them together, whereas now they directly buy branded computers. The reasoning is the same.

We can view the relationship between income levels and brands from another perspective. In Figure 8.11, the horizontal axis represents product quality, and the vertical axis represents prices consumers are willing to pay. The dotted line at a 45° angle represents the notion that when people have low incomes, they accept "one piece of money for one piece of good." For example, if a bunch of chives that are all good quality is worth ¥10, then a bunch with 20% bad chives is worth ¥8. After people pick out the good quality chives, the rest can be sold at a lower price. In the end, the equilibrium result is one piece of money for one piece of good. As people's incomes increase, time becomes more precious, so the relationship between consumers' willingness to pay and quality becomes more curved, meaning they become disproportionally less willing to buy low quality goods. As income increases further, the relationship curves even further to the right. Something with quality of "10" can be sold for ¥10, but something with quality of "9" can only be sold for ¥ 5. People's willingness to pay more for brands increases with their income.

Section three: asymmetric information and government regulation

3.1 Non-market mechanisms that resolve asymmetric information

Of course, not all asymmetric information issues can be resolved by market methods. Even if the market could resolve them, the government and consumers may not like the way in which the market resolves them.

An alternative option is government regulation. Under conditions of asymmetric information, the government can aid the party without information in obtaining information. Market entry is an example. Because consumers can easily become victims of fraud in certain industries like finance, the government can impose requirements on market entry. Another example is government approvals. In the United States, a new type of medicine must be approved by the Food and Drug Administration; otherwise, it cannot be sold. China has a similar authority (the China Food and Drug Administration). Additionally, in many service industries, the government implements professional certifications, such as medical licenses and lawyer qualifications.[14]

Outside of the market and government, there are also nonprofit organizations that play an important role in resolving asymmetric information. A relatively classic example is the Association of Accounting Practitioners, which is a league that sets all professional accounting standards, financial information standards, accountant qualification standards, etc., and which standardizes the entire accounting industry. There are also legal associations, medical associations, teaching associations, etc. These types of non-governmental organization are actually important components of the market, although in China, they are more like quasigovernmental organizations.

3.2 Regulation vs. reputation

Many scholars, including economists, believe that incomplete and asymmetric information results in market failure, just as monopoly and externality do, which required the government to make up for market deficiencies. This viewpoint implies a few basic assumptions. The first is that government is all-knowing. The second is that bureaucrats only serve the interests of the public and consumers, not their own selfish interests. The third is that the government honors its word. In reality, these three assumptions are untenable.[15] There is also an ignorant side of government. Serious information asymmetry exists between the regulator and the regulated. For example, the Ministry of Industry and Information Technology (MIIT) regulates telecommunications companies, but MIIT does not know the true information related to telecommunications companies' costs or price-setting. Bureaucrats also do not necessarily have the public's best interests in mind; they, like the average person, have their own interests. In reality, many regulations are rent-seeking activities of bureaucrats, not protection against fraud by producers. The government's threats are often incredible, such as when large enterprises are unable to repay debt, and the government often intervenes to prevent them from going bankrupt. It is easy for the regulated to capture the regulators, causing regulator to serve the interests of enterprises, not the interests of consumers (Stigler, 1971). As these factors combine, they often lead to the regulation failure.

Government regulation and market reputation are the two basic mechanisms for resolving asymmetric information problems, but they are not simply added together. There is a certain amount of substitution, but also some supplementation.

In reality, the relationship between regulation and reputation is the result of mutual games between the government and the market.[16]

First, we will examine the government. To maintain normal market order, we can either rely on reputation or regulation. Assume that regulation is imposed by government with the goal of maintaining market order. From this perspective, if the reputation mechanism is operating effectively in the market, enterprises have an incentive to provide high-quality products, so not very much regulation is necessary. Alternatively, if the reputation mechanism cannot effectively play a role, more regulation is necessary. Therefore, the government regulation's response to market reputation can be shown as a downward sloping "government reaction curve". It shows that as reputation increases, regulation decreases, and vice versa.

Next, we will examine how the market reacts to regulation. Market reputation is based on market players' (including enterprises and individuals) actions. The more the market players value their reputation, the greater a role the reputation mechanism plays. As we know, in order to give enterprises and individuals an incentive to establish a good reputation, the following conditions must be met: (1) There must be effective protection of private property rights so that people have an incentive to engage in long-term games; (2) there must be relative stability in the operating environment, so that the potential for repetitive games is high enough; (3) information must be transparent enough and flowing quickly so that breach of contract can be observed on time; and (4) the law must be effectively enforced, so that breach of contract is punished.[17]

From this we can see that regulation and reputation are complementary when regulation helps to consolidate the above conditions. In a state of complete absence of government, people have no sense of security, fraudulent behavior goes unpunished, and market reputation is difficult to establish. With the appearance and enforcement of laws, people's incentive to establish a reputation increases. Foundational laws and regulations that aid people in considering long-term interests, increase informational transparency, and effectively punish fraudulent behavior will increase market reputation. For example, unified standards for units of weights and measures or legal protections of trademarks are both types of foundational laws and regulations.

However, after government regulation exceeds a certain degree, market reputation will decrease as regulation increases. The reasons are as follows. First, as government regulations become excessive, bureaucrats have greater discretion. With it, their behavior becomes more uncertain, so market players feel that the future is harder to predict, and they are more likely to pursue short-term interests. Second, the government's excessive regulation of market entry will perhaps create monopolies and monopoly rents. Enterprises that enjoy monopoly rents will no longer care about their own reputation. Further, because monopolies exist, the government and consumers' punishment to enterprises become incredible. Finally, regulation itself leads to corruption and collusion between the regulator and the regulated. Regulation entices enterprises to obtain quotas and privileges through bribery of government bureaucrats, instead of better servicing customers.

When currying favor with bureaucrats is more profitable than with consumers, enterprises will not value their own market reputation.

Therefore, as shown in Figure 8.12, market reputation's response to regulation can be shown as an upside-down U-shaped curve (which can also be called reputation's "supply curve"). The intersection of the two curves is the Nash equilibrium level of regulation and reputation.

If administration is inefficient and government bureaucrats' behavior is not effectively restricted, then the situation shown in Figure 8.13 will occur. At this point, the two curves will not interact, so there is no interior Nash equilibrium, leading regulation and reputation to enter a vicious cycle. With market reputation lacking, the government reacts with more regulation. With the increase in regulation, market reputations deteriorate further. The government further increases regulation so enterprises become less focused on reputation. This continues on, until there is only regulation and no reputation, so the market is in a state of regulated chaos. This vicious cycle is one issue that China currently faces.

The above was a theoretical analysis of the interaction between reputation and regulation.[18] We now consider some examples in real life.

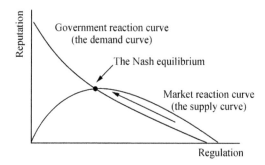

Figure 8.12 The Game Between the Government and the Market

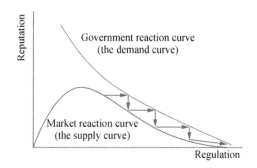

Figure 8.13 Regulation and Reputation Enter a Vicious Cycle

Higher education is no doubt a sector with serious information asymmetry. Faculty proficiency and school quality can either be differentiated by the reputation mechanism built on a foundation of market competition, or they can be evaluated by governmental supervisory departments. However, we can observe that relying on government to resolve information asymmetry on the higher education market has not been successful. The biggest difference of the higher education system between Continental Europe and the United States is that higher education in the United States relies on competition and the reputation mechanism, whereas Continental Europe relies on government regulation. An important reason for declining of universities in Continental Europe compared to US universities is the government's over-regulation.[19] The same issue exists with China's reliance on government supervision of universities. As soon as they are regulated by the government, universities do not need to focus on their reputation. In order for higher education to develop, it must rely on competition, not government regulation. With competition, truly good university brands will gradually be established, so the higher education industry will enter a virtuous cycle.

China experiences frequent coal mine accidents. One reason is because the government can eliminate the owner's mining rights at any time. Coal owners have unstable expectations, so they only focus on short-term interests. As result, the equipment they installed is generally extremely simple, and safety measures are not up to standard. The Chinese government's method of dealing with coal mine accidents is often to shut down surrounding coal pits or all small coal pits throughout the large area after one coal pit has an accident. This further causes investors in coal pits not to invest in reliable safety measures, thus forming a vicious cycle.

China's stock market is similar. Because government regulation is excessive (such as public listings requiring government approval), listed Chinese companies do not care about their own reputations. As long as they handle their relations with the government well, they can seek rent on the stock market. The entire stock market becomes a place for rent-seeking.[20] As soon as it is known that listed companies do not care about their own reputation, the government will think of more tough measures to supervise them, such as requiring a certain rate of return on equity for stock reissuance, which induces another round of false accounting.[21] False accounting will cause the government to further increase regulations. The more regulation there is, the more fraudulent methods enterprises employ to deal with it. This is the current situation of China's stock market. A properly operating market has not been established.

Research into the experience of multiple countries has shown that government regulation is not an effective method to resolve asymmetric information. In many situations, regulation makes matters worse. The World Bank commissioned Simeon Djankov, Rafael La Porta, Florencio Lopez-de-Silanes, and Andrei Shleifer to research market entry regulations in 85 countries (Djankov, La Porta, Lopez-De-Silanes, and Shleifer, 2002). Their research found that when comparing the degree to which enterprises adhered to international quality standards, the more regulation a country had and the more examination and approval procedures there were, the less enterprises from those countries adhered to international quality standards. They also found that as the number of examination and approval

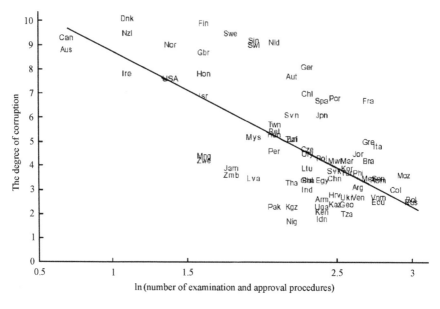

Figure 8.14 Regulation and Degree of Corruption

Source: Djankov, La Porta, Lopez-De-Silanes, and Shleifer (2002)

procedures increased, pollution did not decrease. In addition, the proportion of the underground economy and employment increased, but profits did not increase. According to the "Grabbing Hand" principles, regulated enterprises are dependent on the government, and because of barriers to entry, an enterprise's profits should be higher due to enjoying monopoly profits. However, this does not seem to be the case. Why? Because the degree of competition measured by the degree of industrial concentration does not decrease. Instead, rent-seeking leads to excessive entry, so the result can only be that countries with more regulation have experienced more serious corruption.[22] In Figure 8.14, the vertical axis represents a corruption index (a higher number indicates a cleaner government), and the horizontal axis represents the degree of regulation (the log of the number of examination and approval procedures required to establish a medium-scale company in different countries). The downward-sloping regression curve shows that as regulation becomes more serious, the degree of corruption increases.

Notes

1 Strictly speaking, ex-post information asymmetry also includes the information that one party obtains but is not known by the other party after signing a contract. An example would be an engineering project contract. The contractor knows the actual cost, whereas the client does not. For a detailed discussion on categories of information asymmetry, see Rasmusen (1994, Chapter 7, Section 1); Weiying Zhang (1996, Chapter 5, Section 1).
2 This price is a Nash bargaining solution price because each party receives half of the added value.

3 "Bad money driving out good money" is called "Gresham's Law" in monetary history, which is often used as an analogy for adverse selection caused by asymmetric information. However, this is a misrepresentation of this principle because bad money driving out good money is not caused by information asymmetry, but is instead the result of government's overvaluation of currency. When two types of currencies coexist on the market, with one overvalued (bad money) and one undervalued (good money), then people will hoard the latter until there is only one type of currency circulating on the market. If the government did not distort the currency, different types of currencies could co-circulate. There would be no differentiation between "bad money" and "good money". See Rothbard (2005).

4 For issues related to transaction's reliance on the potential earnings from transactions and the credibility of the parties in the transaction, see Coleman (1994, Chapter 5).

5 Tingting Shi, "The Big Social Issue of the Resurgence of Begging." *The Jiangnan Times*. December 29, 2004.

6 Shuo Ma, *Henanren Re Shei Le?* Hainan Chubanshe, 2002.

7 See Stiglitz (1994).

8 Division of labor and specialization are the precondition of market exchanges. Advantages of division of labor come exactly from specialization of knowledge.

9 See Hayek (1935, 1937, 1945) and Huerta De Soto (2010).

10 Dun & Bradstreet was the earliest credit rating agency, started in 1841. Newman (1956) described the history of Dun & Bradstreet's development, providing us with a classic example of a producer of specialized information.

11 Daniel Klein (1997a) believed that the three types of private provision of product quality information in the market was like the ways parking is provided: (1) Many people spending their own money to build a garage; (2) some entrepreneurs provide parking for a fee; and (3) some malls, hotels, and offices provide free parking for clients. Consumers collecting their own information is like the first way, specialized service providers are like the second way, and producers providing information themselves is like the third way.

12 The contents below are revised portions from Weiying Zhang's, *Competitiveness and the Development of Enterprises*. Beijing: Peking University Press, 2006.

13 DeLong (1991) provided an illustration of the impact an investment bank's reputation has on its clients' value. He finds that between 1910 and 1912, clients with a J. P. Morgan partner on the board of directors had a 30% increase in common stock market values.

14 Of course, these qualifications are not necessarily done by the government, in many cases market mechanisms are fully competent. This issue will be discussed later in this book.

15 For theories and empirical research in support of or opposed to the various forms of government regulation, see Armstrong, Cowan, and Vickers (1995); Shleifer and Vishny (1998); and Rothbard (1970).

16 The model below is a simplification of Weiying Zhang (2005, Chapter 6, Section 5).

17 See Weiying Zhang's, "The Reputational Foundation of Legal Systems." *Economic Research Journal*. 2001, Volume 1 (in Chinese).

18 Interested readers can further read Weiying Zhang's *Property Rights, Government, and Reputation* (in Chinese, 2001) and *Information, Trust, and Law* (in Chinese, 2003).

19 For a comparison of American and European systems of higher education, see Hansmann (1999b).

20 Weiying Zhang, "The Chinese Stock Market Is a 'Place of Rent-Seeking'." *Modern Economics*. 2007, Volume 8 (in Chinese).

21 See Shuli Hu's, "The Pumped Up Year of the Ox: Doubts on the Profits Reported by Listed Companies." *Caijing Magazine*. 1998, Volume 2.

22 Weiying Zhang (1998) proved that because of rent-seeking behavior, regulation may possibly lead to excessive entry. This is a characteristic of most manufacturing industries in China. Regulation only creates monopoly profits in resource industries (such as petroleum) and public utilities (such as telecommunications).

9 Signaling and social norms

When information is asymmetric, in order to realize the benefit of a transaction, the party with good information has an incentive to report it to the party without information. However, words are worthless, so there must be a way to make the other party believe it.

So-called signaling is using credible methods to reveal a person's type. The reason a signal is credible is because the same signal has different transmission costs for different type of people. The cost of transmitting a signal for a "good" type of person is lower than for a "bad" type of person, so the latter will not dare to imitate the former. Therefore, the party without private information can judge another person's type by observing signals.

Any costly, observable behavior can become a signal that transmits information. High-ability people can tell employers they are high-ability through education because the same education will be too difficult for low-ability people. The owner of a good car can tell the buyer he has a good car by providing a guarantee, because the cost of providing a guarantee for a bad car is too high. High-efficiency firms can tell the market they are high-efficiency by more leveraging, because low-efficiency firms do not dare to hold more debts. Advertisements tell consumers a product is high quality because advertisements are too costly for low quality products. In all of these cases, we get separating equilibrium. If the cost of sending the same signal is not sufficiently large, then the bad type will imitate the good type, which will result in a pooling equilibrium. Under a pooling equilibrium, signals do not transmit "good" information, but can conceal "bad" information.

The signaling function of a type of behavior might also come from the different value a cooperation has for different people. The reason gift giving and certain other social norms can transmit the signal a person is willing to cooperate with others is because patient people put more weight on future benefit. The signaling function of gifts means the value of the gift to the recipient is not important. Instead, the cost to the giver is important.

When the cost of a gift is paid for by "someone else", then the information content of a gift declines significantly. This leads to gift price inflation.

The behavioral correlation means that even in one-time games, people are still not willing to undertake opportunistic behavior. Opportunistic behavior will transmit disadvantageous information about the actor.

Asymmetric information might also lead to norm change. If some "bad" types of people are numerous, but only a small portion can be observed, then society will be more tolerant toward this type of person. This might be the major reason for quickly spreading of corruption in China.

Section one: signaling mechanisms

1.1 Academic degrees and ability

In the last chapter, we discussed the information asymmetry problem and certain methods to resolve information asymmetry. As part of this, we touched upon asymmetric information creating adverse selection, which is disadvantageous to the party with private information. Therefore, the party with private information will have incentives transmit information to the party that lacks information. The problem is that the party that lacks information may not believe the information transmitted. Then, how can the party with private information reveal his information credibly?

Michael Spence, the 2001 Nobel Memorial Prize in Economic Sciences Laureate, was the first to do in-depth research on this topic (Spence, 1973, 1974). By focusing on the labor market, he shows that employees can signal information about their ability to employers via schooling in order to resolve the information asymmetry problem.

Below, we will utilize a relatively simple model to discuss the ways in which education level can signal information about ability. For simplicity, we will assume that education itself is useless, meaning that going to university will not increase a student's ability. Of course, this is a radical assumption. Being that this is the case, we will still find that being educated can be useful as a signal of ability.

Consider a person that is looking for work. Perhaps he is high ability (represented by H) or low ability (represented by L). If he is high ability, his productivity is 200; but if he is low ability, his productivity is only 100. The employee knows his own ability, but a potential employer does not. Assume that the employer only knows that there is a 50% probability the person is high ability and 50% probability the person is low ability. In other words, the employer believes that the employee's expected productivity is 150. This way, if the employer has no other information, he is at most willing to pay a salary of 150. At this point, the high-ability person will feel at a loss, but the low-ability person has gained an advantage. The high-ability person will think of ways to prove that he is high-ability. One such means is to get an education.

Assume that the cost of an education for a high-ability person is 40, but for a low-ability person it is 120. The cost difference between two results from an underlying observation that the smarter the person, the less time and effort are needed to understand the lectures, do homework and pass the examination. The high-ability person can also be more respected, admired, and appreciated by fellow students and teachers during schooling. In contrast, for the low-ability person, schooling is miserable. Anyway, it is reasonable to assume the high-ability person's utility costs of education are lower than the low-ability person's.

Assume that the employer holds the following belief: those who received education are high ability and those who did not receive education are low ability. Accordingly, the employer implements the following education-based compensation policy: The employee with education is paid 200, and the employee without education is paid 100.

Given the employer's belief and compensation policy, if the high-ability person goes to college, his salary will increase to 200, which net of the cost of education is 160. This is much better than the 100 he would have received if he had not gone to college. Therefore, his optimal choice is to go to university. If the low-ability person wants to pretend to be high-ability, he can also go to college. However, if he does so, his payoff is only $200 - 120 = 80$, lower than payoff of 100 without going to college. Therefore, he is better off honestly admitting that he is low ability by not going to college.

In this way, employees with different categories of ability can be clearly differentiated. High-ability people go to college and receive high salary of 200, and low-ability people do not go to college and receive low salary of 100. This shows that the employer's belief is correct and his compensation policy is optimal. So, we got a Nash equilibrium in signaling.

Therefore, even if getting an education does not increase a person's ability, degrees can be a signal of innate ability.

It should be pointed out that the reason that degrees can signal ability is because the difference in the cost of education between different abilities is relatively large. If the difference in the cost of education were not large enough, then degrees would not be able to differentiate the two. For example, if we still assume that the cost of the high-ability person attending college is 40, but the low-ability person's cost is not as high as 120, instead only 80, then it would still be worthwhile for the low-ability person to go to college. By going to college, his net payoff would be $200 - 80 = 120$, which is still greater than 100. The employer would discover that his judgment of university graduates being high-ability is flawed. At this point, the employer would only be willing to pay a salary of 150, and no employee would be willing to go to university.

Under our assumption that the education has no impact on productivity, from a social perspective, going to college is completely a waste. Without information asymmetry, employers could directly judge which person is high-ability and which person is low-ability, so there is no need for degrees. However, because of asymmetric information, high-ability people must pay "signaling costs". Of course, if different jobs need people with different abilities, then signaling via education can make best allocation of human resources, so this signaling cost is valuable to society.

The above assumption is quite extreme. In reality, in most cases education does increase an employee's productivity. For example, if s is years of education, then a high-ability person's productivity will be $2s$ and a low-ability person productivity will be s. The analysis would be a bit more complex, but the conclusion would be completely the same.[1] Actually, the core of the issue is not whether or not education can increase people's productive ability. The key point is that the cost of different types of people getting educated is different so that the choice of education can signal ability.[2]

With the same reasoning, we will further examine why the better a university is, the more valuable its degrees are. Simply put, first, the better the university, the harder and costlier it is to attend. Second, the better the university, the greater the difference in the degree of difficulty faced by high-ability and low-ability people. We can use Figure 9.1 to analyze this issue.

In Figure 9.1, the horizontal axis represents university rank, with the worst university on the left and the best university on the right and the vertical axis represents the cost of an education. The two upward sloped lines represent the different cost curves of a high ability and a low-ability person getting an education. Both the cost curves start from the same point, meaning that for a very low quality school, the cost of education is the same for both types of people. However, as the quality of universities increases, the two cost curves will differentiate, with the low-ability person's education cost curve higher than the high-ability person's education cost curve. The reason is that as the quality of university increases, the low-ability person finds more difficult to follow the course and pass the exam than the high-ability person. In this way, the gap between the two costs increase as the quality of the university increases, so the higher the quality of the university, the greater the difference between the costs paid by these two types of people.

The two solid and flat lines represent two types of productivity. The productivity of the high-ability person is shown by the line on top, while the productivity of the low-ability person is shown by the line on bottom. The dotted line in the middle represents an employer's expected value of individual ability under the condition where signals are lacking. The productivity curves are both flat, meaning education does not increase employee's productivity.

To use education level as a way to distinguish the two, the benefit of a low-ability person passing off as a high-ability person (by pursuing the same level of

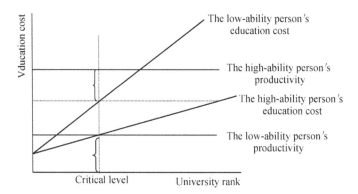

Figure 9.1 The Signal Function of University Level

education for the some pay) must be low enough, lower than honestly revealing his own ability (by not pursuing an education and earning a low-ability salary). The so-called critical condition is where the university's quality causes the difference between the high-ability person's productivity level and the low-ability person's cost of education to be precisely the same as the low-ability productivity level. Only after the university surpasses this critical level can attending university differentiate a high and low-ability person. If the university's actual level is lower than this critical vale, then the low-ability person will impersonate the high-ability person.

Of course, we know that it is unrealistic to simply differentiate a person's ability as high or low. Ability is a continuous variable, so we see different rankings of universities provide different classifications. The person with the lowest ability may from the beginning choose not to attend university at all. A slightly more able person may choose a decent university in order to differentiate himself from the person with the least ability. A more able person may choose to attend a better university in order to differentiate himself from the other less-able people. This trend continues on up to the most prestigious university. This is why it is said that the better a university is, the more valuable is its diploma, because attending a better university is more costly.[3]

1.2 A general model of signaling

Generally speaking, we can model signaling as an incomplete information dynamic game, such as is shown in Figure 9.2.

First, "nature" decides which type of person Player A with private information is. Assume that Player A can only be one of two types, and Player A knows whether he is Type I or Type II, but Player B only knows that the probability of Player A being Type I is p and the probability of Player A being Type II is $1 - p$. Player A also knows that Player B believes that the probability of Player A being Type I is p and being Type II is $1 - p$. At this point, Player A could send a signal about his type to

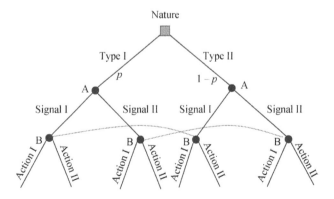

Figure 9.2 Signal Transmission Model

Player B. We will assume that there are only two types of different signals: Signal I and Signal II. Even though Player B cannot directly see what type Player A is, he can observe what signal Player A sent. Then, he uses Bayes' Rule to adjust his judgment on Player A's type based on the signal he observes. Then, he decides an action based on this revised judgment. Therefore, this game is not just a process of players choosing the best action, but is also a process of revising beliefs.

In reality, when one party has private information that another party does not have, people will attempt to infer the other person by observing their behavior. At this point, any action by the party with private information can become a type of signal to transmit his own private information. Thus, when the party with private information chooses an action, he must be extremely cautious. For example, you hope to choose an action that will transmit a beneficial signal, but the other party will also make a rational judgment based on this signal. In other words, actions and signals have a reciprocal function and adapt to each other.

Below, we will use the Market for Lemons example discussed in Chapter 8 to specifically explain these issues. We will display the exchange between the buyer and seller in the Market for Lemons by referencing the asymmetric information dynamic game shown in Figure 9.3.

First, nature determines if the car sold by Seller A is good or bad. The seller knows if the car being sold is good or bad, but the buyer does not. The buyers only know that there is a one-half chance that the car is either good or bad. We will assume that the used car is worth 20 to the seller and 30 to the buyers, regardless if it is a good or bad car. How can a good and bad car be differentiated? It is based on the probability of them breaking down. We will use Q to represent the probability of a good car having a problem and q to represent the probability of a bad car having a problem. Of course, we assume that $Q < q$. We will assume that the cost of repairing after a breakdown is the same, represented by C.

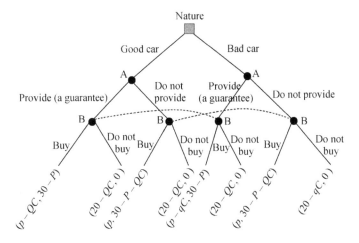

Figure 9.3 Signal Transmission Model of Second-Hand Car Transactions

Now we will consider if the seller will choose to provide a guarantee. If the seller provides a guarantee, there is a possibility of the buyer buying or not. If the buyer buys the car and the price he pays is P, then $30 - P$ is the payoff the exchange brought to the buyer. For the seller, if he provides a guarantee, he must assume the expected cost of repair QC, so his expected payoff is $P - QC$ (for a good car) or $P - qC$ (for a bad car). If the buyer does not buy the car, then it is still in the hands of the seller valued at 20. After accounting for the expected cost of fixing the car, the expected payoff is $20 - QC$ (for a good car) or $20 - qC$ (for a bad car). The buyer's payoff is zero.

If the seller does not provide the guarantee, the buyer also has the same choice to either buy the car or not. If the buyer buys the car, he pays price p (note that it is a lower case letter to differentiate from the uppercase letter that is the price when the guarantee is provided). Additionally, he must assume the expected cost of repairing because the seller did not provide a guarantee. So if he buys the car, his payoff is $30 - p - QC$ (for a good car) or $30 - p - qC$ (for a bad car). The seller receives p. If instead, the buyer does not buy the car, the car remains in the hands of the seller. His expected payoff is $20 - QC$ (for a good car) or $20 - qC$ (for a bad car). The buyer's payoff is zero. This is a complete description of this dynamic game.

First, we will see if a guarantee can send a signal about quality.

Without the guarantee, given the probability of it being a good car is 0.5 and the probability of it being a bad car is 0.5, if he buys the car, his expected payoff is $30 - p - 0.5qC - 0.5QC$. If he does not buy the car, his expected payoff is zero. If $30 - p - 0.5qC - 0.5QC < 0$, then the buyer will not buy the car. After simplifying the equation to $0.5(q + Q)C > 30 - p$, we could say if the expected cost of repairs is greater than the value of the car minus the price paid, then the buyer will not buy the car. This shows that without any types of signals, the highest price the buyer is willing to pay is $30 - 0.5(q + Q)C$.

For the seller, the payoff from selling a used car is p. The payoff from holding on to the car is $20 - QC$ (for a good car) and $20 - qC$ (for a bad car). This is the reservation price for the owners of good and bad cars. The used car will only be sold if it is above this price. A bad car owner's reservation price is lower than that of a good car owner, so bad cars sell more easily. Combining both the seller's willingness to sell and the buyer's willingness to buy, the condition in which a good car can be sold is $20 - QC \leq 30 - 0.5(q + Q)C$, so that when $(q - Q)C \leq 20$, a good car can be sold without a guarantee as a signal. This inequality holds when the cost of repairs is sufficiently small or the difference of probability of breakdown between a good car and bad car is sufficiently small. Therefore, not all incomplete information will cause a market to fail. However, as soon as $(q - Q)C > 20$, a good car will not be sold without a guarantee. The condition that must be met for a bad car to be sold is $20 - qC \leq 30 - 0.5(q + Q)C$, or simplified as $(Q - q)C \leq 20$, which always holds, given $Q < q$. In other words, a bad car can always be sold without a guarantee.

Let us assume that $(q - Q)C > 20$. At that point, the owner of a good car will perhaps be willing to provide a guarantee, thus transmitting a signal to the buyer to prove that his car is good. If this is indeed the case, the buyer will be willing to pay a higher price for a used car with a guarantee, such as P, whereas the price of a car without a guarantee is still p.

To the seller of a good car, if the guarantee is provided, the payoff of selling the car is $P - QC$. Without the guarantee, the payoff of selling the car is still p. The seller of the bad car choosing to provide a guarantee means that $P - QC > p$, thus $QC < P - p$, meaning the expected cost of repairs is smaller than the price difference. To the seller of the bad car, the payoff of providing a guarantee and selling the car is $P - qC$. Without the guarantee, the payoff is still p. The seller of the bad car choosing not to provide a guarantee means that $P - qC < p$, thus $qC > P - p$, meaning the expected cost of repairs is greater than the price difference.

In order for a measure like providing a guarantee to become a true signal, it must be able to differentiate between a good and a bad car. In this case, if it is a good car, the seller would be willing to provide a guarantee. If it is a bad car, the seller would not be willing to provide a guarantee. This means that the cost of a guarantee must satisfy the following condition:

$$QC \leq P - p < qC$$

Of which, $QC \leq P - p$ proves that a good car with a guarantee is worthwhile, whereas $P - p < qC$ proves that a bad car with a guarantee is not worthwhile. If both conditions are met, then we have attained a "separating equilibrium". The "separating" refers to differentiating "good" from "bad" by the guarantee: The buyer knows correctly that a car with a guarantee is good and is willing to pay a higher price P, but a car without guarantee is bad and is only willing to pay a lower price p.

The above reasoning process may appear tedious, but the basic conclusion can be summarized as follows: In order to make the guarantee a signal for transmitting the quality of the used car so that the exchange can succeed, the following conditions must be met:

(1) **The Incentive Compatibility Constraint:** There is an incentive to provide a guarantee for the good car because $QC \leq P - p$ and there is not an incentive to provide a guarantee for the bad car because $P - p < qC$.
(2) **The Rational Participation Constraint:** Regardless if the car is good or bad, the seller is willing to sell, thus $P - QC > 20$ (for a good car) and $p > 20$ (for a bad car). Also, the buyer is willing to buy, thus $P \leq 30$ (for a good car) and $p \leq 30 - qC$ (for a bad car).

Next we will examine some specific numerical examples. For example, $Q = 0.1$ (meaning the probability of a good car having a problem is 0.1), $q = 0.5$ (meaning the probability of a bad car having a problem is 0.5), and the cost of repairs $C = 10$. Then, the price difference $P - p$ can be neither less than 1 nor greater than 5. If it is less than 1, then there is no incentive to provide a guarantee for a good car. If it is greater than 5, a bad car could be passed off as a good car by providing a guarantee. A possible set of prices is $p = 20$ and $P = 24$. A good car is 4 units higher in price than a bad car, which is the payoff brought about by signals. The reason a signal can bring about this payoff is because the cost of transmitting this signal is different for each type of car. For a good car, the expected cost of repairs is only one unit, whereas a bad car requires 5 units.[4]

More generally speaking, the higher the quality of the product, the more willingly guarantees are provided. This applies to all products. For example, when a television has a five-year guarantee, it signals that the manufacture is very confident in its own product to not have problems over long period or have a very low probability of having problems.[5] If the quality of the television is very low, of course the manufacture would not be willing to provide a long-term guarantee, because the cost of repairs over that period of time might far exceed the net gain by selling at a higher price.

From the formula $QC \leq P - p < qC$, we will discover that in order to differentiate good and bad products on the market, there must first be a certain gap between P and p. In other words, the price difference between high-quality products and low-quality products must be great enough. Only when this price gap is large enough are people with good products willing to provide guarantees. If good and bad cars sell for the same price, the person with a good car would not be willing to provide this signal. This is just an issue of quality's premium, as good products must be expensive. On the other hand, they cannot be too expensive, because if the relative difference is too great, the condition on the right will be broken. At that point, bad products would also be passed off as good products. This is to say that if information asymmetry exists, in order for signals to be informative, there must be a suitable gap between different quality levels of products so that the premium is high enough, but not too high.

Of course, there is also another possibility:

$$QC \leq P - p;\, qC \leq P - p$$

Where both conditions can stand at the same time, meaning a seller of a bad car is also willing to provide a guarantee. This is a type of pooling equilibrium. When guarantees are provided for both cars and the selling price is the same, then guarantees do not signals quality because bad cars can imitate good cars, so buyers cannot use guarantee to differentiate between good and bad cars.

To review, a separating equilibrium means that guarantees are only provided for good cars. As long as the buyer observes that a guarantee is provided, he knows that the probability that car is a good car is 1.0, while at the same time knowing that the probability of a car without a guarantee being a good car is 0. The buyer can update his own judgment based on the signals he observes. Under pooling equilibrium, guarantees are provided for both good and bad cars, so after seeing that a car has a guarantee, the buyer's judgment of the probability of the car being good or bad is unchanged from his original judgment. This is to say that a pooling equilibrium does not provide new information, whereas separating equilibrium does provide new information.

We can see on the market that if a signal is to transmit information, it is certainly because the cost of transmitting information is different for different types of people.[6] Only when "good behavior" is too costly for bad people to do, can "good people" not be impersonated by "bad people" and differentiate themselves from the latter.

Section two: signaling in economic and social life

2.1 The role of advertising in transmitting signals

The market is full of large amount of commercial advertisements. What signals do these advertisements transmit?

In economics, products are separated into three categories according to the degree of product quality information asymmetry between the buyer and seller. The first category is a search good. Even if the buyer at first does not know the quality of a product, after paying a certain search cost, he probably could identify the product's quality. This applies to products like household furniture. The second category is an experience good. Only after these products are used does the buyer know if it is good or not. An example of this could be a car. Only after driving the car for a period of time does the driver know if it is good or bad. There is no way to pay search costs to understand this. The third category is a credence good. For these products, not only does the buyer not know the quality of the product before buying it, but also still does not know if the quality is good or bad after using it. Many healthcare products fall into this category.

In terms of these three categories of products, advertisements serve a different function for each. For the first category of products, advertisements provide hard information such as product materials, manufacturing, price, sales locations, etc. For the third category of products, it is difficult for advertisers to provide any reliable information. For the second category of product, although advertisements do not provide any specific hard information about the product, the most important information is that the business paid money to advertise.[7] Let us discuss this point.

Now we will assume that a type of product is possibly high or low quality. The firm knows which type it is, but the consumer only knows after the first use. If it is high quality, then after buying the first one, the consumer will buy a second one. If it is low quality, then after buying the first one, the customer will feel cheated and not by a second one. Assume that the cost of advertising is ¥5 million and the potential market is ¥4 million each period. Consumers initially believe that advertised products are high-quality products and unadvertised products are low-quality products and then adjust their judgments on actual results. Assume that the market lasts two periods. Which type of product will be advertised?

For high-quality products, after advertising, the product can be sold the first time for ¥4 million, then consumers will come back a second time to spend another ¥4 million. Added together, the firm can receive ¥8 million, which is higher than the advertising expense of ¥5 million. For low-quality products, after advertising, the product can be sole the first time for ¥4 million, but the consumer would not come back a second time. The enterprise would only earn ¥4 million, which is lower than the ¥5 million advertising cost. Obviously, advertising is worthwhile for the producer that produces high-quality products, but not for the producer that produces low-quality products. The consumers' initial belief is correct that advertised products are high quality and can be bought, but unadvertised products are low-quality and should not be bought. This is the signaling function of advertising.

Advertising is the cost that firms with high-quality products pay to transmit information to the market. Only when this type of cost is high enough will firms that produce low-quality products not dare to imitate high-quality product firms by advertising, thus advertising plays a role in transmitting signals. In the above example, if the cost of advertising was ¥3 million instead of ¥5 million, firms with low-quality products will mislead the consumer by also advertising. Therefore, advertising itself carries no information. From this, we can see that the massive advertising fees on the market are actually a competitive way for good firms to differentiate themselves from bad firms. Consumers will have a rational expectation that such a large amount of money spent on advertising a product signals that the product is high-quality. Therefore, it is worth buying. Not being willing to advertise signal the producer does not have confidence in its products, so the consumer will not buy it. This also means that for experience goods, advertisements do not need to include specific information about the product. Many of the advertisements we see in public media are imagery advertisements that have an abstract name and celebrity spokesperson to give a deep impression, but not detained information. This is the reason.

Based on the theory of signaling, we know that the more product information is asymmetric, the greater a role advertising plays. From this we can also evaluate certain government regulations and policies about advertising. A few years ago, the China State Administration of Taxation declared that advertising expenses could not exceed 2% of sales revenues. This obviously is illogical because it ignored the difference of each product. Just as in the example above, it is possible for the advertising expenses of an enterprise to exceed its sales revenue in the first year. When it believes its product is good, it believes that the consumers that buy its product in the first year will buy it in the second year. As information spreads, there will be even more people that buy this type of product in the third and fourth years. Government restrictions on advertising costs will damage the signaling function of advertising, which benefits enterprises that produce low-quality products. In the example above, if the government declared that advertising costs could not exceed ¥3 million, advertisements would be of no information.

Of course, if a product is a credence good, advertisements may not signal information. We often see many health care products with high advertising expenditures and good sales, but this does not prove that the products are of good quality. For this type of advertisement, does the government have to intervene? The answer is not certain, because if consumers have no way of differentiating if this product is good or bad, the government may not be able to, either. This type of product must be guaranteed by the firm's reputation accumulated over the long-term. For example, in China, people are more willing to purchase medicine produced by Tong Ren Tang, which is the oldest brand of pharmaceutics, rather than products from non-famous firms.

2.2 Signaling in the capital market

We previously discussed the signaling issue on the product market, but going forward we will examine the signaling issue in the capital market. For example, debts can serve as a signal to transmit a firm's profitability. Ross (1977) proved that under certain conditions, the higher a firm's debt-equity ratio was, the stronger its ability to make a profit was. The reason for this is that if a good and bad firm both has liabilities reaching (for example) 70% of assets, perhaps the probability of the good firm going bankrupt is 5%, whereas the probability of the bad firm going bankrupt may be as high as 50%. If liabilities were only 30% of assets, perhaps the probability of a good firm going bankrupt is only 1%, whereas the bad firm's probability is 5%. This means that in situation the outside world does not understand the firm's information, in order for a good firm to tell the market it is a good firm, it will increase its liabilities to 70% of assets. A bad firm would not dare to keep up, because a 70% liability rate means a 50% probability of going bankrupt, which is too great dangerous for management team. This shows that high-quality firms are willing to take on large amount of debt, whereas low-quality firms do not. Therefore, when we observe that a firm has a high level of liabilities, we can understand it as a signal of high quality.

Of course, the premise of this conclusion is that the enterprise is privately owned and the burden of bankruptcy falls on the managers and shareholders. For state-owned enterprises, even if the enterprise goes bankrupt, not only does the general manager not have to take on the burden of bankruptcy, instead he can take on another important role, so the liability ratio does not transmit information. Actually, the higher the liability ratio is for a state-owned enterprise, the more likely it is to be a bad firm, because the government makes the state-owned banks support the poorly performing state-owned enterprises with loans. Even for privately owned enterprises, if the general manager does not bear any of the burden of bankruptcy, then the leverage ratio signal is ineffective. If a firm's scale becomes large enough and has enough debt, then the government will not want to see the firm close because that would lead to considerable unpaid loans and unemployment. Under this condition, an enterprise's liability ratio also cannot transmit correct information about the firm' quality. Only when a firm solely takes on market risk and bankruptcy costs with autonomous decision rights does the level of liabilities transmit signals about the firm's profitability.

In corporate finance, there is a well-known "pecking order theory".[8] This theory states that when funding investments, firms will first use internal funds, but if these are insufficient, the firm will issue debt, and lastly issue equity. Why must financing be done in this order? The main reason is that under conditions of information asymmetry, different instruments of financing transmit different information. Specifically, some firm perhaps is a good firm worth ¥3 million, or perhaps a bad firm only worth ¥1 million. When there is not enough information to support the market's judgment of firm quality, then the market can only set stock prices according to the belief that there is a 50:50 chance of a firm being good or bad. This price would be between the fair value of a good and bad firm. The good firm would be undervalued and the bad firm would be overvalued. Assume that a firm has a new investment project that needs funding. If the firm issues equity to raise money, rational investors will believe this is bad news, because only overvalued companies are willing to issue shares, so the stock prick will go down. Debt is different, because the interest rate is set ahead of time, so at maturity a fixed amount of interest can be collected. As long as bankruptcy does not occur, at least principle can be recovered. In other words, compared to equity finance, debt finance is not as sensitive to the value of the firm. Naturally, the optimal pecking order of financing is: first, internal financing, then debt issuance can be considered, but if that is limited and more external financing is still required, then equity will be issued. Issuing equity is a last resort, the method when no other methods are available. This also means that firms will generally choose to issue new stock when there is the least amount of information asymmetry, such as after releasing an annual financial report or announcing a new product to the market.

2.3 Capital-hiring-labor

Below, we will discuss an important issue of classical capitalist firm: why does capital hire labor, instead of labor-hiring-capital.[9] The key point here is information asymmetry about entrepreneurial ability. A person's wealth is relatively easy to observe,[10] but a person's entrepreneurial ability is not easy to observe. Under this type of situation, wealth can become a signal to transmit entrepreneurial ability, so capital employing labor assists in ensuring the operational control of an enterprise remains in the hands of the most entrepreneurial person.

In a market economy, a person is free to choose to be an entrepreneur or a worker. What is the biggest difference between an entrepreneur and a worker? Workers receive contract wages and bear "negligence liability". Entrepreneurs receive residual income and bear "strict liability". To an entrepreneur, any mistake of others not discovered is his own fault and he must bear full responsibility. As long as a worker goes to and leaves the work field on time and does not make misconduct, when it is time to get paid, the employer has no option but to pay. An entrepreneur cannot say to the customer, "This year I did not make any mistakes, so you must let me make profit!" Therefore, an entrepreneur bears much more risk than a worker.

Specifically, assuming that a firm's revenue is Y. If a person chooses to become an employee, then he can receive market wage X. For the entrepreneur, he must pay wage X to the worker, so the remainder of $Y - X$ is his. This residual revenue is uncertain because it could be positive (profit) or negative (loss). The size of the specific amount is related to the entrepreneur's ability (as well as other factors outside of the entrepreneur's control). On average, the more able the entrepreneur is, the higher the expected residual revenue. When should a person be an entrepreneur and when should a person be a worker? Given a person's entrepreneurial ability, if the expected revenue of being an entrepreneur $E(Y - X)$ is greater than the worker's market wage X, then that person should choose to be an entrepreneur, otherwise he should choose to be a worker. If $E(Y - X) = X$, then there is no difference between being an entrepreneur or a worker. This equation determines "critical entrepreneurial ability". If a person's actual ability is greater than this critical ability, he should be an entrepreneur. Alternatively, if his actual ability is less than this critical ability, then he should choose to be a worker.[11]

Further, a person's "critical ability" to be an entrepreneur is related to his personal wealth. Why? If a person does business with his own money, then profit made is his to keep, but loss is also his burden. If a person invests someone else's money, then profit made is his to keep, but someone else holds the burden of losses. Obviously, the second person has more incentive to be an entrepreneur than that first. This means that the more a person invests, which also means the more wealth he has, then the higher are his critical entrepreneurial ability. Therefore, we could say that the more wealth a would-be person has, the higher his critical ability is for being an entrepreneur. The critical entrepreneurial ability curve is shown in Figure 9.4.

In Figure 9.4, the vertical axis represents an entrepreneur's level of ability and the horizontal axis an entrepreneurs' personal wealth. Critical entrepreneurial ability increases as personal wealth increases, so it is an upward sloping curve. For example, to a penniless person, critical ability is 0.2, whereas for a person with ¥1 million, critical ability is 0.8. As was described above, when a person's actual ability is greater than his critical ability, then he will choose to be an entrepreneur, otherwise he will choose to be a worker. Therefore, people above the curve are willing to be entrepreneurs and people below the curve are willing to be workers.

When a stranger can only observe information about a person's wealth, but not information about that person's ability, he will rationally infer that among all people that are willing to become entrepreneurs, those with the most wealth have higher average entrepreneurial ability. In this way, personal wealth becomes a signal to transmit entrepreneurial ability. The wealthier a would-be entrepreneur is, the more likely he is to be trusted by other investors and employees, and thus,

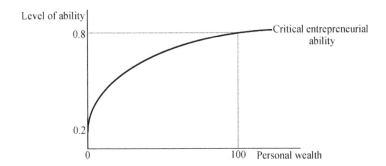

Figure 9.4 Personal Wealth and Critical Entrepreneurial Ability

he is more likely to actually become an entrepreneur. Alternatively, even if a penniless person wants to be an entrepreneur, it is difficult for him to gain investor's trust. This is our explanation of "capital-hiring-labor".

The reader must be reminded that when we say wealth is a signal of ability, we are not saying that a wealthy person is certainly high-ability. Instead, we are saying that a wealthy person is less willing to pretend to be high-ability. If his ability is not high enough, he will not choose to be an entrepreneur. In fact, it is assumed that wealth itself has no direct relationship with entrepreneurial ability.

The above argument also shows that if private property does not exist in a society, and so everyone is penniless, the selection of entrepreneurs becomes very difficult. All people are distributed along on the vertical axis, so there is no credible signal of the ability each one has. The result is that everyone declares he is capable and could manage a firm. This is the reason why the state-owned enterprises are too often managed by incompetent people.

Similar reasoning exists for venture capital. Venture capitalists choose start-up entrepreneurs. The biggest challenge they face is information asymmetry. When making investment decisions, venture capitalists will evaluate the entrepreneur's ability and performance, but the entrepreneur must also tell the venture capitalist how much he is personally investing in the proposed project. In order to obtain venture capital funds, the applicant must also put his own "wager" in. For example, if you have a $200,000 house that you use as collateral for a $100,000 loan from the bank, you are more likely to find a venture capital finance than without collateral. The act of using the house as collateral is a signal that you are willing to put your wager in because you have confidence in yourself. Only if you are confident in yourself will other people be confident in you.

2.4 Signaling in daily life

Based on signaling theory, we can re-interpret certain phenomena in everyday life. For example, when seeking employment, appearance is a signal. When hoping to work in a large corporation, wearing a suit is a necessity during the interview. Wearing a suit and tie might feel restrictive, but precisely because it is uncomfortable is it useful. The reason is that for different people, the degree of hardship is not the same. People who are more accustomed to disciplining themselves will experience a lower degree of difficulty; whereas those more accustomed to indulgence will experience a higher degree of difficulty, so the cost will be higher. Interviews are a type of test: If you cannot even bear the difficulty of wearing a tie, will you be able to abide by the discipline within the organization? Therefore, appearance becomes a useful signal.[12]

The previous examples were all used to show that under conditions of asymmetric information, the party with beneficial private information is willing to transmit this information via signals in order to be differentiated from others. To the contrary, there are also people with unbeneficial information that will attempt to conceal it. There is a saying: "The clumsy bird starts flying earlier". This means that to have the same result as others, one may have to first put in a painstaking effort. It must be noted that others cannot be allowed to see this effort. Some students will only study when others are not around, but stay idle when others are around. This is a smart way to conceal information about oneself.

Of course, the party without the private information is also smart, so information cannot always be concealed successfully. Sometimes, no news is good news, but other times no news is bad news. If other people undertake some type of action, but you do not, this will expose you as the person with bad information. For example, assume that a voluntary system for official assets reporting is implemented. Officials can choose to report or not, but choosing to not report signals a problem of possibility of owning illegal property.

Whether or not people are willing to reveal their private information is related to institutional design. Imagine we are to vote in an election. The authority first nominates a candidate for everyone to vote on. If you disagree with the nominee, you hope that authority and others do not know you voted in opposition. Assume now that in order to be "democratic", you are given the choice to fill out the ballot in public or in a voting booth. Who would go to the voting booth? Going to the voting booth is an obvious signal that you oppose the nominee. Once the ballots are counted, if the votes for the nominee come up short, you will be suspected of voting in opposition, so you revealed yourself.

What results will this type of institutional design create? It will be like the title of the book *Private Truths, Public Lies* (Kuran, 1997). This phenomenon is just like the story of the Emperor's New Clothes by Hans Christian Andersen. Everyone sees that the emperor is not wearing clothes, but everyone says that the emperor is wearing clothes, because everyone believes that if they say the emperor is not wearing clothes, they will reveal themselves as being stupid. Only the child that does not understand speaks the truth. The above examples also explain that in society, how we act or what we say does not entirely depend on our belief, but is also determined by what we think others will believe. If one day we suddenly discover that others do not believe something, then we also will not believe it. This type of sudden transition in collective belief will cause society to undergo massive changes, perhaps without warning. In contemporary society, this is something worth being vigilant of and paying attention to.

Section three: the signaling and social norms

3.1 Interpreting gift giving

Below, we will use signaling theory to explain certain social norms.

From previous theories, especially the repetitive game model, we can come to the conclusion that one of the major determinates of whether people are incentivized to cooperate is their patience, or discount rate. The lower a person's discount rate, or the higher his discount factor, the more patient this person is, and the greater is his incentive to cooperate. The problem is that discount rates or patience to a large degree are private information. Another person does not know your degree of patience. At this point, a person's degree of patience can be transmitted via respect for social norms.

In the book *Law and Social Norm*, published in 2000, Erik Posner specifically applied signaling theory to social norms. Simply put, his theory is that any costly and observable action can transmit a type of discount factor signal, thus promoting cooperation.

We will first examine a common social norm like gift giving. Assume that the value of future cooperation between two people is 10 for each. People are different in their discount rates. Some people have a discount rate of 10%, meaning ¥1 tomorrow is worth ¥0.90 today. The others have a discount rate of 30%, meaning ¥1 tomorrow is worth ¥0.70 today. The degree of patience between these two types of people is obviously different, so which is more willing to cooperate? Of course, it is the first type. However, if a potential partner does not know whether your discount rate is 10% or 30%, how will you tell him that your discount rate is 10% rather than 30%? One solution is to give gifts. If there is a gift priced at ¥8, only the person with a 10% discount rate would be willing to give this gift in exchange for future cooperation which would bring about payoff of ¥10, the person with the 30% discount rate would not. The reason is that you paid ¥8 for the gift, so the other person is willing to cooperate with you, thus you will gain ¥10 from future cooperation. If your discount rate is 10%, then that ¥10 discount to the present is worth ¥9, so you actually earned ¥1. If, however, your discount rate is 30%, ¥10 in the future is only worth ¥7 today, so you lost ¥1. From this example, we can see that only the person with a low discount rate is willing to give gifts, so giving gifts becomes a signal to transmit relevant information. You have an incentive to give gifts because you want to tell other people that you are a patient person that is willing to cooperate, whereas the impatient person will not make this choice.

From this example, we can also see the most important part of gift giving is not the value of the gift to the recipient, but the cost to the giver. Just as in education we discussed previously, from the perspective of signaling, important is the cost of you receiving an education, not the value of the education to the firm.

Of course, in real life, people have different objectives for giving gifts, and signaling is not the only explanation for this type of behavior. One possibility is that gift giving is done altruistically, in hopes of helping others. Another reason is that "one gives as good as one gets". However, the key point is that there are many phenomena that these reasons have difficulty explaining, such as when the value of a gift to the recipient is lower than the actual expense of the gift. For example, if I spend ¥1,000 treating you to a meal, my cost is ¥1,000, but you may have preferred to be given ¥100 then go home and have a bowl of noodles. Gift giving may not bring about any Pareto improvement. So why would I treat you to an expensive meal instead of giving you ¥100? As was stated earlier, from the perspective of signaling, the most important is the cost of the gift to the giver. If the cost is too low, it cannot indicate the giver's patience.

For different types of people, the personal cost of gift giving is different. In order to reach different objectives, different people will undertake different actions. In other words, the same action transmits different information for different people.

For example, there would be a significant difference between a poor person giving a gift and a wealthy person giving a gift. Poor people are short on money, and rich people are short on time. If a millionaire gives you ¥100, it may only be a type of charity, but it does not transmit a signal that indicates he is willing to cooperate with you in the future. Of course, he may also be altruistic. Similarly, if a poor person sits and chats with you, it also is not a signal, because he did not have anything to do, anyway. The signals transmitted by a ¥100 gift from a poor person and a ¥1,000 gift from a rich person cannot be evaluated by their actual price. The signal transmitted by the poor person's ¥100 gift may be stronger than the signal transmitted by the rich person's ¥1000 gift. Alternatively, if a poor person spends the whole day with you, but a wealth person only spends an hour with you, the signal may be the wealthy person is more willing to cooperate with you in the future and values your relationship more. Therefore, in order to understand different people, we must understand the personal cost of each type of gift, because there are big differences between similar actions of different people.

Of course, generally speaking, you hope that the recipient will like the gifts that you give. There is no contradiction between this and our previous discussion. The reason is that each person's interests are different, so in order to know what someone likes, you must spend time understanding that person, and then spend time finding the things that person likes. These costs may be significant, so unless you value the relationship, you will not spend the effort. Therefore, giving a gift the recipient likes is a signal that you care about him. This is the reason that people prefer to give gifts instead of directly giving money. Giving money is the simplest thing to do because you do not need to know what the recipient likes. If you do not care about him, you should give him money. Similarly, if you give the recipient a gift he himself would not buy, this will have a better effect because it means you value his relationship even more.

Of course, if the objective of your gift giving is to help someone instead of transmitting a signal, then it is best to give money. After giving that person money, he can spend it however he chooses, so it provides the most help. For example, when friend's children marry, perhaps giving money is most suitable. If your friend is rich and does not need your help, then giving money is not as good as finding a gift he likes.

Above, we discussed one-sided information asymmetry. Now we will examine a situation in which neither party knows if the other is willing to cooperate over the long term, which is to say that neither party knows the other's discount rate. At this point, both parties may need to exchange gifts. If I give a gift to you, it sends a signal that I am willing to cooperate with you. Similarly, if you give a gift to me, it also sends a signal that you are willing to work with me. Both of us hope to find a trustworthy, patient, and reputable person. Under this condition, if I give you ¥8 and you give me ¥8, the two cancel each other out and no signals are transmitted. Posner proposed an important viewpoint: That in the case of gifts as a reciprocal, gifts must destroy their intrinsic value in order to make a sense of signaling. The objective of so doing is to make your cost of gift giving greater than the value of the gift to the receiver. For example, I spend ¥8 on a gift that you only value at ¥2, and you also spend ¥8 on a gift that I only value at ¥2. By exchanging gifts, each of us get lower value. Something that was originally worth ¥8 is now only worth ¥2. However, from the individual's perspective, this is not a waste, but it makes a significant sense because it displayed each party's evaluation of the other. Only after some value is destroyed can it be shown I value the relation with you. This also explains why we cannot give each other cash but instead must give gifts.

In real life, many gifts are actually wasteful. A classic example is the moon cakes that Chinese give during the Mid-Autumn Festival. Very few people actually like eating moon cakes, and even if they enjoyed eating them, there is no reason they cannot buy moon cakes before the Mid-Autumn Festival. Actually, the people that buy and give moon cakes during Mid-Autumn Festival are not focused on moon cake's utility, instead of they want to show how much money they spent and that they were thinking of the recipient. Moon cakes are made more and more sophisticated. It no longer matters what is in the moon cake. Instead, the packaging is more important. The cost of the packaging is always many times higher than the ingredients in the moon cakes. Only because of this reason can moon cakes transmit a signal of sincerity. It says: "Look how much money I spent on a worthless item, proving how much I care about you". In the end, this situation evolved into everyone giving each other moon cakes and then throwing them away after receiving them.[13]

Similarly, from this perspective, we can also explain the high price of China's branded cigarettes and liquors. How many people buy branded cigarettes for their own consumption? Very few! Such expensive cigarettes and liquors are certainly not for self-consumption. However, buying cheap ones as a gift means nothing. They must be expensive. Similarly, we can examine dinner parties in China. The development of upscale restaurants has been much faster in China than other countries, and they are much more luxurious. In certain parts of China, spending more than ¥10,000 on a meal is very common. When treating others, it is not important that they eat what they want. If someone were to treat me to a meal, I may only want a bowl of noodles. However, the inviter could certainly not accept this, because it does not display the value of the relationship, so he will choose a more upscale location. This eventually formed into the idea that value of the relationship is judged by the cost of the meal and the location, not preference. This has led to more and more upscale restaurants in China.

You may say that if the goal is to transmit a signal, other countries should be the same as China. Why are other countries not as luxurious as China? An important reason is that in China dinner parties and gift giving is paid for using "public" money, not paid for by the private. If an individual pays, then one yuan is one yuan, but the private cost of spending ¥10 of public money may only be equivalent to spending ¥1 of his own money. In order to transmit the same signal, the public expenditure must be 10 times higher than on an individual basis. The signal that could have been transmitted using ¥100 of your own money now requires ¥1,000, so gifts and restaurants in China become more and more upscale. If you pull out your own pocketbook to spend ¥500 to treat a friend, your friend will know you care about him because that is one week's salary. However, if you pay with public money, that ¥500 would be an insult. Spending ¥5,000 to ¥10,000 would be more appropriate in that case. From this, we can see the importance of who the payer is.[14]

Currently, there is another interesting part of the gift-giving phenomena in China. Giving gifts is no longer signaling. Instead, not giving a gift has become signaling. When every subordinate is giving a gift to the superior, giving a gift no longer means anything. On the contrary, not giving a gift is a problem. When many people give a gift, a leader may not remember who gave a gift or what gift was given, but he is very clear on who did not give a gift, because people that did not give gifts are few. The result is that everyone gives a gift, but the information content of a common gift is minimal. In the end, only the cost of the gift can be compared.

It is necessary to point out that in China, in many cases gift-giving is not done in order to "cooperate", but instead to "co-conspire", which is often called "rent-seeking" (a type of corruption). Under this condition, the signal gift-giving transmits is that the gift giver or receiver is a "bad person" from the public perspective. Truly good people would not give or receive expensive gifts. This also means that from society's perspective, gift-giving as a type of social norm may not be a Pareto optimum.[15]

3.2 Marriage contracts

Below, we will examine marriages. We know that marriage contracts are much different from other transactional contracts. In other types of transactional contracts, the degree of freedom is much larger. When both parties sign a contract, it is a manifestation of their desire. The law protects their desires and guarantees the enforcement of the contract. This is called "the right of free contract". For example, whether or not I am willing to pay the price for something is my decision to make. However, marriage contracts have very serious legal restrictions, as well as many customary restrictions. For example, if the law dictates monogamous marriages, you cannot practice polygamy or polyandry. This is also to say that all of our laws and customs related to marriage cause the men and women involved to lose a lot of freedom. All contracts will cause the participants to lose partial freedom, but other contracts are relatively easy to discontinue, whereas this is more difficult for marriage contracts. Why? One reason that was previously mentioned is to prevent opportunism. Because marriage is relatively difficult, as soon as you agree to get married you have made a commitment. Otherwise, you may get married only for the benefits of marriage, but not be willing to take on any of the costs, such as raising children, doing chores, or taking care of each other during times of sickness. Perhaps the most important significance of all rules on marriage is to prevent your opportunistic behavior.

When finding a spouse, we all hope to find someone we love that also loves us. However, there is serious asymmetric information. Someone saying they love you cannot prove he or she really loves you, nor does it prove that he or she is willing to grow old with you, because there is no cost in saying so. We can understand people's respect for laws and social customs as a signal of being willing to commit. For example, obtaining a marriage certificate is a signal that both parties are willing to commit. Imagine you have been in a relationship with your boyfriend for many years. He has said he will love you and is also willing to live with you forever. But even after some pushing, he is not willing to get a marriage certificate. This means he is not willing to make a true commitment, and may leave you at any time. On the contrary, if he is willing to get a marriage certificate, it means he is willing to make a commitment. Some people say that marriage certificates are just a piece of paper that will not stop him from falling in love with someone else. However, this piece of paper is important because it causes the cost of divorce to increase substantially. Because divorce is costly, getting a marriage certificate has become a signal he loves you and is willing to live with you long term.

Actually, any behavior that causes the cost of divorce to be high enough can become signals of marriage commitment. Betrothal gifts are a signal because if I give all of my money away, I would not have any money to give to a second person, so it displays my willingness to be with you for the rest of my life. Similarly, holding an extremely expensive marriage ceremony is also a signal. Marriage ceremonies are generally extravagant and for most people account for years' worth of living expenses.[16] However, this is precisely the reason that marriage ceremonies can transmit a signal. When a person does not have money for a second marriage ceremony, then divorce does not come easy. Of course, if both parties have absolute trust, it is not necessary to spend that much money.

The cost of marriage is not just material, but also reputational, which is something more important. The value of a marriage ceremony is not just based on the money spent, but also based on the "publicity". If all family and friends know that you are married, the cost of transgression will be much higher, because doing so will damage your reputation. If a person is in a relationship and lives with you, but is not willing to let anyone else know, or even introduce the parents, then that person does not truly love you, or is not prepared to marry you.

Of course, the types of behaviors that transmit what type of signal is related to the viewpoints commonly accepted by society. For example, in the past, if a woman was willing to have a sex relation with a man, that meant she was determined to be married with him. Today, this behavior may not transmit any information, because, at least in urban areas, pre-marital sex has become a commonly accepted phenomenon.

3.3 Wasteful consumption

Below, we will again examine the issue of wasteful consumption. Much of our consumption is actually a type of waste, but sometimes it can also transmit a type of signal, such as your status or wealth.

According to our previous analysis, if a person focuses more on the future, he should be more willing to save. Savings are in reality determined by your patience, because a patient person is willing to delay consumption. From certain perspectives, wasteful consumption should not happen, but from others it should.

For example, if other people do not know your wealth, nor your status, then you could use wasteful consumption to send a signal. From this perspective, we can understand the value of branded clothing. Brands to a large degree transmit signals about the user's money and tastes. As we discussed in the previous chapter, if quality information is asymmetric, brands can transmit product quality signals for the producer. From another aspect, brands also transmit signals about the user. Some people are wealthy while others are poor, but they may not be differentiated among strangers, so wearing brands will display your wealth. At this point, product quality is not itself important. The same quality product with a different brand can be sold for completely different prices because the consumer wants to transmit a specific signal. From this we can see that among acquaintances, there is no need to wear expensive brands, so at home or at school we can wear whatever is comfortable.

Sometimes brands are used to transmit information that we belong to a specific group. If all people in a certain group wear a specific brand of clothing, then if you do not wear this brand of clothing you will expose yourself as not being a part of this group. In society, different groups of people wear clothing and hairstyles based on long-established customs. Riffraff that roam the streets have their own dress and hairstyles, so if you want to tell others that you are riffraff, you will wear the same clothes and hairstyles as them. On the contrary, if you do not want other people to mistake you for this type of person, then you cannot appear like them. If a person wants to display his uniqueness, his appearance must be different from others. Therefore, some people dress quite curiously, whereas some people cover themselves in brands. It all depends on the information you want to tell others.

3.4 The role of etiquettes and laws

Why do people want to respect certain etiquettes and laws? Etiquettes are intricate, and sometime laws are not just or rational. Etiquettes themselves have no value, but precisely because they are intricate and valueless do they display the involved parties' willingness to cooperate. Your willingness to take on the cost of respecting a rule explains that you are willing to become that type of person. For example, before you attend a formal ceremony, you will be notified of the dress code. The Nobel Prize Award Ceremony requires wearing a swallow-tailed coat. Swallow-tailed coats in Sweden are different from those in England, so the English must find a tailor on arrival. Only after accepting this restriction do you have the credentials to participate in this event. To participate in this activity, many people have no choice but to rent suitable attire that will only be worn for a few hours for a total cost of about US$200. If you buy as opposed to rent, the cost may be closer to US$2,000. Your willingness to spend money on this attire indicates that you attach importance to this affair and are willing to accept this social norm. Precisely because many norms do not have value are they able to transmit a signal.

Similarly, the law has the same function. Although the law may not be just, signing a contract or accepting a judgment transmits the signal of your willingness to cooperate. This is an important viewpoint proposed by Posner (1999) in another article. As long as there are not systemic deviations from the law, the rulings of judges must be obeyed. A judge might even draw lots[17] or not be entirely certain who is in the right. If beforehand you do not know which lot the judge will pull, nor do you know if you will win, are you willing to commit to accepting the judgment? At this point, transmitting signals is of most importance. If you are willing to sign a contract, it signals you will not choose opportunistic behavior because litigation is costly. For this reason, courts and legislators have proposed certain contract formalities, such as requiring parties to the contract to sign in person. If a person is not willing to respect this formality, it shows that he would try to avoid legal sanctions, so he is not trust worthy.

Here, I would like to propose a concept: The behavior correlation assumption.[18] People will behave differently in different circumstances. However, some things do not change about human nature, or come naturally after long use, so behavior in one situation may signal information relevant to another situation. For this reason, sometimes, even if you are in a short-term game, without any need to cooperate with others, you will still display willingness to cooperate.

Imagine there are two types of situations. In the first situation, you travel alone to a strange land that you will only visit once. In the second situation, you travel with three other colleagues. In which situation would you behave better? Of course, it would be in the second situation. If you do not conform to social norms, even if these actions do not harm your colleagues or benefit them, this type of behavior transmits a signal that if you were cooperative person, you would do the same thing in a different situation. Therefore, we call this behavior correlation. Precisely because behavior correlation exists do you pay attention to the information your behavior transmits in every situation.

This type of correlation exists between a person's respect for parents and loyalty towards others. Generally speaking, if a person does not respect his parents, others are often not willing to become friends with him. If a person does not respect his parents, how could he be loyal to his friends? Your attitude to your parents has a big impact on your relationship with other members of society. Similarly, your attitude towards friends is also a signal that can transmit your attitude towards strangers. This has led to many behavioral norms and social restrictions taking effect.

3.5 Information asymmetry and change of norms

Lastly, we will discuss norm change caused by information asymmetry. As was discussed previously, in a separating equilibrium, such as good people and bad people, high ability and low ability, or high risk and low risk that can be separated by some type of signal, each person would have a specific behavior unique to his type. The behavior of good people and bad people would be different. Signals of high risk and low risk would be different. The decisions of high ability and low ability would also be different. For example, high-ability people attend university and low-ability people only attend junior high. In a pooling equilibrium, everyone's behavior is the same, so their behavior does not transmit a new signal.

There is another type of situation where separating equilibrium and pooling equilibrium are combined. We call this "semi-separated equilibrium". At that point, some behaviors transmit signals whereas other signals do not. Sometimes doing a good thing does not transmit a type of signal. Good people do good things, but bad people will imitate good people by also doing good things. Doing bad things, however, will certainly transmit a signal. When we observe a person doing good things, we cannot be certain that he is a good person, but when we observe a person doing bad things, we can conclude he certainly is a bad person.

If we observe these together, we will discover that sometimes social changes will transform separating equilibrium into pooling equilibrium, or a semi-separated equilibrium. Then, social norms might change.

A classic example of this is our change in attitude towards pre-marital sex. In China's traditions – actually in every country's traditions – attitudes towards pre-marital sex and extra-marital sex were very strict. This strictness spanned thousands of years of history. This is a separating equilibrium, which means that good people would certainly respect these rules, whereas those unconventional people do not care about other's opinions and so take actions that violate social norms. In a relatively closed society, or within a certain scope, such as within a village, information is relatively transparent, so pre-marital and extra-marital sex are relatively easy to observe. If a woman is engaged but not formally married and does not return home at night to stay at her fiancé or another man's house, it will be gossiped by everybody. Because this signal is very clear, the condemnation and punishment of those observed will be relatively fair. In the city, because the population is highly mobile, some pre-marital sexual behavior is observable, while most is not. If the observed behavior is but a small part of this type of behavior, then condemning some people for this type of behavior is not very fair. This will result in norm transforming, so in this case people are more and more tolerant of pre-marital sex.

Similarly, people's attitude towards the treatment of the corruption problem has changed in China. Assume that all (or the vast majority) of corrupt officials can be detected. If this were the case, corrupt officials would be punished. The first punishment would come directly from the law, such as imprisonment or fines, while the second punishment would come from social opinion. In real life, if among ten corrupt people, only one is caught, then the second type of punishment will decrease significantly for the person caught. It is easy to understand why in most cases that a corrupt bureaucrat is caught everyone believes he has bad luck. Moral punishment of corruption decreases because most corrupt behavior cannot be observed. This is an important reason why as soon as corruption spreads, it quickens.

The above analysis shows that only a society with relatively transparent information can effectively remodel values and social norms.

Notes

1 See Spence's original work. Weiying Zhang (1996) provides a simplified model.
2 From this perspective, we can re-interpret China's ancient imperial examination system (*kejuzhi*) (for the details of this system, see He, 2011). The traditional viewpoint

was that the eight-part essay imperial examination encouraged candidates to study worthless subjects. Actually, from the perspective of signaling, which is learned is not important; instead, the important part is that the cost of participating in the Imperial Examination System was different for intelligent and stupid people. With the same cost, intelligent people have a higher rate of passing the test than stupid people. If a family has multiple sons, the father would certainly choose the relatively intelligent son to participate in the Imperial Examinations System and the relatively stupid son would stay to work on the land field, instead of the other way around. Thus, imperial examinations were still a type of relatively valuable talent selection mechanism.

3 It should be pointed out that above, we assumed that the cost of education is paid by the individual, and we also didn't make distinction between pecuniary cost and nonpecuniary cost. In reality, party of pecuniary costs are paid by the public fund or by scholarship, and individuals may also face wealth-constraints. Either of them would make education less signaling.

4 In this specific numerical example, even without a guarantee, the good car can be sold. The reason is that without signals, the highest price the buyer is willing to pay is 27, which is greater than the seller's reservation price of 19 (for a good car) and 15 (for a bad car). However, assuming that the negotiated price without a guarantee is 22, then the seller with a good car is still willing to provide a guarantee as long as the price is higher than 23 after providing a guarantee.

5 We assume here that all commitments are credible. Some people might be willing to provide a ten-year guarantee, but then close after three years.

6 This is called the Spence-Mirrlees separating condition.

7 See Nelson (1974); Schmalensee (1978); and Tirole (1988, pp. 118–119) for the ways in which advertisements transmit information on product quality.

8 See Myers and Majluf (1984) and Brealey and Myers (2000).

9 This is the core theme of Weiying Zhang's book The Origin of the Capitalist Firm: *An Entrepreneurial-Contractual Theory of the Firm.* The Chinese version of the book was published in 1995 and its English version is published in 2017 by Springer Press.

10 Of course, this is not absolute, because some very wealthy people dress very plainly and some poor people dress lavishly. However, it is still not easy for a person with no money to eat at a high-end restaurant or an extremely wealthy person to completely conceal this information.

11 For simplicity, we only considered monetary compensation. When people actually choose their own work, they do not only consider monetary return, but also more complex psychological and preference factors. Some things people will not do for money. For example, if I gave you the choice between a ¥500,000 annual salary where you had to do anything I told you to do or a ¥250,000 annual salary where I had to do anything you told me to do, which would you choose? It is more likely people that care about money will choose the first, but people that care about power will choose the second. This is a preferential difference towards control rights. Some people prioritize freedom, so even if supervised working means more money, they will not want to lose the freedom of being self-employed. However, after we add these factors in, we can still obtain a critical entrepreneurial ability value.

12 There are also many interesting phenomena within nature. For example, male peacocks have large, long tails to attract female peacocks. Why? Israeli biologist Amotz Zahavi (1975) proposed an interesting principle called the handicap principle to explain this phenomenon (also see Zahavi, 1997). This principle believes that a long tail is actually a signal that can transmit the male peacock's reproductive ability. Because a long tail is a handicap, the longer the tail, the greater the burden, so male peacocks can use it to tell female peacocks the state of their health. Only a peacock in a good physical state would be able to have a long tail and still be able to walk. At this point, the tail becomes a signal to transmit a peacock's private information.

13 Smith (1998) described China's contemporary Mid-Autumn Festival moon cake gift etiquette in a *Wall Street Journal* article. Posner (2000) cited this example in his book.

14 Since Xi Jinping's Anti-Corruption Campaign launched in 2013, the government and corporate funding of gifts and treats has been very restricted. As a result, prices and demands of branded cigarettes and liquors, and upscale restaurants and five-star hotels, all have dropped down dramatically. Sale of branded Swiss watches has also fallen significantly.

15 For more discussions on the relationship between social norms and efficiency, see Posner (2000).

16 Of course, in real life, some government officials use weddings as a means to collect money.

17 Of course, he cannot show that he used the drawing lots method, but he might psychologically be drawing lots when making a judgement.

18 This concept is related to the "behavioral consistency" concept in psychology. However, from the perspective of signaling, I want to emphasize the way behavioral methods in a situation transmit information about the participants' essential characteristics. If the observer is cognizant of this, then the behavior of the observed will be different from when others are not cognizant. In this way, for instance, if long-term cooperation partners are present, even if I am undertaking a one-time game with strangers, I would act the same as when I am undertaking a repeated game.

10 Mechanism design and income distribution

So-called mechanism design refers to the party without private information designing a mechanism (contract) to make the person with private information honestly reveal his type. It can be either the direct mechanism and the indirect mechanism. Under the direct mechanism, the person with private information reports his type. Under the indirect mechanism, the person with private information chooses the contract intended for his type.

The essence of mechanism design is making people tell the truth. For this purpose, a feasible mechanism must satisfy the incentive compatibility constraint of each type. The incentive compatibility constraint means for each type, telling the truth (or choosing the contract designed for his type) is better than telling a lie (or choosing a contract designed for another type). When telling a lie has a greater cost than telling the truth, then people will tell the truth.

Optimal mechanism design can make the designer obtain maximum possible profit, but resource allocation will not reach the Pareto optimal under asymmetric information. The design of insurance contracts and pricing systems of firms are classic examples of mechanism design. These mechanisms do not require the customer to directly report their type. However, by selecting a contract or price menu, customers indirectly reveal their true types.

Under the Vickrey auction mechanism, bidders have an incentive to report their true type, because in any situation, telling the truth is better than telling a lie.

In order to make a person tell the truth, the person with private (good) information must obtain information rent. This leads to a contradiction between inequality and efficiency in income distribution. The existence of information asymmetry means that in any situation, high-ability people are better off than low-ability people. Even if we are willing to lose efficiency, we still cannot realize complete equality, because high-ability people can pretend to be low-ability.

University faculty selection is an important mechanism design. A good mechanism must reach a separating equilibrium so that people who are truly able and passionate about scholarship will self-select to be professors, whereas low-ability people unsuitable for scholarship will self-select do not to be professors. Promotion standards must be demanding enough and compensation must be high enough. Low promotion standards necessarily lead to low-ability people passing themselves off as high ability people.

Providing right incentives to selectors is also an important issue. The tenure system and the bottom-out system aids in resolving this issue.

Section one: mechanism design theory

1.1 Making people tell the truth

In the previous chapter, the party with "good information" will take the initiative to transmit this information to the other party. However, generally speaking, the party with "bad information" does not have an incentive to reveal his information. For example, when a high-risk firm is borrowing money from a bank, it may not be willing to truthfully tell the bank the risk level of the project. Someone buying insurance will not be willing to reveal their bad health condition to the insurance company. A government official might exaggerate good information and conceal bad information. Also, in many instances, the party with "good information" has no means to signal. Under these cases, what should the uninformed party do?

At this point, we will often see the person without information design proposals (contracts) for the person with information to choose from. Private information will be revealed through the choices made. A classic example is the judgment of King Solomon in the Old Testament of Bible. Two women in the same house gave birth at about the same time. Shortly afterwards, one of the infants died, but both women claimed the living child as her own. They took their dispute to King Solomon. King Solomon did not know which woman was the mother of the child, but both women knew that one of them was actually the mother and the other was not. However, the actual mother had no way to tell she was the actual mother, and the fake mother did not have an incentive to tell everyone she was lying. Under this condition, King Solomon told them he could only cut the child in half to split it between them. Then, one woman cried out to say the child was not hers, while the other was completely indifferent. In this way, King Solomon knew which woman was actually the mother and which was not, so he gave the child to the former. King Solomon knew that the real mother would rather lose her child than to have the child die, whereas the other woman would be indifferent either way. There is a similar example in China's history. Two women disputing the same child took their case to the county official. The county official put the child in the middle of a ring on the ground and told the women that whoever could pull the child out of the ring would be declared the mother. However, the county official knew that the woman that pulled on the child hardest was certainly not the real mother.

The Chinese idiom "to call a deer a horse" is actually the story of Zhao Gao discovering disobedient ministers. According to the *Records of the Grand Historian*, in 207 B.C., Prime Minister Zhao Gao was plotting a rebellion, but feared his ministers would not obey him. He devised a way to discover who would not obey him. He presented a deer to the Second Emperor of Qin, but told him it was a horse. The Second Emperor of Qin laughed at his prime minister for confusing a deer with a horse, then asked his ministers. Some remained silent, but some said it was a deer. Afterwards, the ministers who declared a deer were all framed up by Zhao Gao. From that point on, all of the ministers feared Zhao Gao.

In Game Theory, we call this method mechanism design. Mechanism design theory studies the ways parties without private information make the party with private information to honestly reveal it.[1] There are two mechanisms: the direct mechanism and the indirect mechanism. Under the direct mechanism, the person with private information reports his type. Under the indirect mechanism, the party with private information chooses among contracts. According to the revelation principle, a corresponding direct revelation mechanism exists for any indirect mechanism such that under this direct mechanism, each person will truthfully report his own type, and the resource allocation outcome is the same for both types of mechanisms.[2] In this chapter, we primarily discuss the indirect mechanism (although Section Three discusses the direct mechanism).

The more general mechanism design issue can be displayed in the game below. Imagine there are two players: A and B. Player A can either be good-type or bad-type. Player A's type is private information known by Player A, but Player B does not know Player A's type, only that the probability Player A is good-type is p and bad-type is $1 - p$. Player B can design two contracts for Player A to choose one, regardless if Player A is a good type or a bad type. Through Player A's selection, Player B also can also know whether Player A is actually a good person or a bad person. We can use Figure 10.1 to intuitively describe this game.

Here, the purpose of the contract menu designed by Player B is to reveal Player A's type through his self-selection. To guarantee the realization of the self-selection process, the designed contract menu must satisfy the two constraints mentioned in the previous chapter. The first is the participation constraint: Player A is willing to accept at least one contract from the menu designed by Player B. The second is the incentive compatibility constraint: Player A has an incentive to accept the contract intended for his type and not the contract intended for other

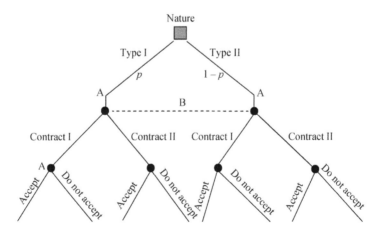

Figure 10.1 The Mechanism Design Game Tree

type. The participation constraint means that the people involved have an incentive to participate in the transaction, and the incentive compatibility constraint means the party with private information will "tell the truth". In this type of "tell-the-truth" mechanism, a good person's choice will reflect he is a good person and a bad person's choice will reflect he is a bad person. How can these two constraints be satisfied to guarantee the appearance of a "tell-the-truth" mechanism? Below, we will use the medical insurance market example to explain this issue.

1.2 The pooling equilibrium and the separating equilibrium

Consider a two-year medical insurance example. Assume there are two types of people in the insurance market: High-risk with a 50% probability of becoming ill and low-risk with a 30% probability of becoming ill.[3] Thus high-risk people have a 75% probability [$= 0.5 + (1 - 0.5) \times 0.5$] of becoming ill within two years and low-risk people have a 51% probability [$= 0.3 + (1 - 0.3) \times 0.3$]. Assume also that each type of person composes half of the total population. If both types of people want to purchase medical insurance that covers up to ¥100,000, what is a fair premium to charge them? Table 10.1 lists the details for both types.

First, we will consider the complete information situation. At this point, insurance companies know each person's type (low risk or high risk). Insurance companies will only provide insurance products when they expect to not lose money. Thus, to obtain ¥100,000 in coverage, high-risk people must pay a minimum premium of ¥75,000 and low-risk people must pay a minimum premium of ¥51,000. If there are 100 high-risk policy holders, total premium income is ¥75,000 × 100 = ¥7.5 million. Because 75 policy holders will become ill and 25 will not within two years, the insurance companies' total expenses are 75 × ¥100,000 + 25 × ¥0 = ¥7.5 million. Insurance companies break even. Similarly, the revenue and expenses for insurance companies to provide insurance for 100 low-risk policy holders is ¥5.1 million. If premiums are lower than the standards described above, then insurance companies will lose money, so providing insurance is not worth it.

Of course, the reason people are willing to purchase insurance is they are averse to risk (which is precisely the value of the insurance industry). In other words, high-risk people prefer the certain ¥25,000 after purchasing insurance as opposed to the uncertain 25% probability of having ¥100,000 and a 75% probability of having nothing (thus the average value is ¥25,000). Low-risk people prefer the certain

Table 10.1 Two Types of Risks and Insurance Contracts

	probability of becoming ill in the first year	*probability of becoming ill within two years*	*insurance coverage (ten thousand)*	*minimum premium (ten thousand)*
high-risk group	0.5	0.75	10	7.5
low-risk group	0.3	0.51	10	5.1
Average	0.4	0.63	10	6.3

¥49,000 after purchasing insurance as opposed to the uncertain 49% probability of having ¥100,000 and 51% probability of having nothing (thus the average value is ¥49,000). Thus, the insurance companies' premium policies described above also satisfy policy holders' participation constraint because policy holders are better off by purchasing insurance.

Further, because policy holders are risk-averse, they are willing to pay a premium in exchange for certain income. Therefore, even if the premiums charged by insurance companies are a little bit higher than the standard described above, policy holders are still willing to purchase insurance. Assuming that the risk premium for high-risk people is ¥5,000 and for low-risk people is ¥3,000 (note: Risk premiums are related to risk size), then the maximum premiums that satisfy policy holders' participation constraint is ¥80,000 (= ¥75,000 + ¥5,000) for high-risk people and ¥54,000 (= ¥51,000 + ¥3,000) for low-risk people. The actual premiums charged will be between the minimum premium and maximum premium. If it is lower than the minimum premium, then insurance companies will lose money, but if it is higher than the maximum premium, then policy holders will not be willing to purchase insurance. The specific amount is related to competition of insurance market. For example, if there is only one monopolistic insurance company, then premiums will be close to the maximum premium. If the insurance market is in a state of perfect competition, then premiums will be close to the minimum premium.

Now, we will examine the incomplete information situation. At this point, insurance companies do not know which people are high-risk and which are low-risk, they only know any policy holder has a 50% probability of being either type. From this we can calculate each policy holder's average probability of becoming ill within two years as 63%. Under this condition, if insurance coverage is maintained at ¥100,000, then each person's premiums cannot be less than ¥63,000. This will lead to an adverse selection consequence because low-risk people will not be willing to purchase insurance, but high-risk people will be. For low-risk people, a ¥63,000 insurance premium is much higher than the ¥54,000 maximum insurance premium they are willing to pay. However, this insurance premium is much lower than the ¥80,000 maximum insurance premium that high-risk people are willing to pay. Since only high-risk people purchase insurance, the insurance companies will certainly lose money (if 100 people purchase insurance, expected losses will be ¥7.5 million − ¥6.3 million = ¥1.2 million).

Can insurance companies design a mechanism that guarantees both types of people will purchase some insurance? In this example, the key issue is guaranteeing low-risk people are willing to purchase insurance. In other words, we want to satisfy the low-risk policy holders' participation constraint. One possibility is to have the two-year insurance policy make the insurance company not liable when the policy holder becomes ill in the first year. If there is no coverage in the first year, then the rate of coverage will change. In the first year, high-risk policy holders have a 50% chance of becoming ill, so their probability of sustaining to the second year is only 50%. Based on their 50% probability of becoming ill each year, high-risk people only have a 25% change of receiving compensation.

Similarly, there is only a 21% probability of low-risk policy holders receiving compensation. Therefore, if both types of people purchase insurance, then the average coverage rate is 23%, as shown in Table 10.2.

If insurance coverage is still ¥100,000, then insurance premiums will be based on insurance companies' minimum insurance premium of ¥23,000 to avoid losses. At this insurance premium level, high-risk people are still willing to purchase insurance, because for a ¥23,000 premium they obtain ¥25,000 expected coverage while the contract is valid. If we assume that low-risk people are willing to pay a risk premium not less than ¥2,000, then low-risk policy holders are also willing to purchase insurance, because their expected income plus risk premium would not be lower than ¥23,000.

This is actually a "pooling equilibrium". In this pooling equilibrium, both types of people purchase insurance. However, because information is asymmetric, we still have not reached the Pareto optimum since first-year risk was not insured for either type of person.

The reason this pooling equilibrium can appear is of course related to our numeric value assumptions. For example, if we assume that low-risk people are willing to pay a risk premium lower than ¥2,000 for a 21% coverage rate, or the probability that low-risk people become ill is 10% instead of 30% (and the probability for high-risk people is still 50%), then a market that only provides second-year coverage will not exist. Under these two circumstances, low-risk people will still not purchase insurance, but high-risk people will. Then insurance premiums based on average probabilities cannot compensate for insurance claim expenditures.

However, if we assume that high-risk people have a 90% probability of becoming ill each year, instead of 50% (and low-risk people still have a 30% probability), then there could be a second-year compensation contract that only low-risk people purchase. At this point, second-year coverage means the probability of high-risk people obtaining coverage is only 9%. Assuming insurance companies collect ¥21,000 in insurance premiums, then purchasing insurance is worthwhile for low-risk people. With a 21% chance of coverage, expected compensation is ¥21,000. However, purchasing insurance is not worthwhile for high-risk people, because their expected compensation is only ¥9,000.

This is actually a "separating equilibrium": Low-risk people purchase insurance and high-risk people do not. In real life, we see this characteristic of insurance contract for diseases like cancer. Insurance companies implemented a policy

Table 10.2 Insurance Contract No Compensation in the First Year

	probability of getting covered	*insurance coverage (ten thousand)*	*premium (ten thousand)*	*expected coverage (ten thousand)*
high-risk group	0.25	10	2.5	2.5
low-risk group	0.21	10	2.1	2.1
average	0.23	10	2.3	2.3

so that they are not liable for compensation if a policy-holder is diagnosed with cancer in the first year. In this case those who are highly likely to have a cancer within the first year will not buy insurance.

In reality, in the previous example, we can still have another "separating equilibrium" where only high-risk people purchase insurance. For example, imagine insurance companies provide a two-year insurance policy that charges a ¥75,000 insurance premium. At this point, although only high-risk people will purchase insurance, insurance companies can still balance revenue with expenditures, so there is equilibrium.

From the analysis described above, we can come to this type of conclusion: The greater the difference in risk and the lower the risk premium people are willing to pay, the lower the probability is that a pooling equilibrium will exist.

Now, we will consider the separating equilibrium with both risk groups purchasing insurance.

We will still assume that the probability of becoming ill each year for the two groups is 50% and 30%, respectively, and coverage is ¥100,000. Further, we assume that policy holders are willing to pay a ¥1,000 risk premium for every ten basis point reduction in risk. In this way, if compensation is paid in both years, then high-risk people are willing to pay a ¥7,500 risk premium and low-risk people are willing to pay a ¥5,100 risk premium. If compensation is only paid in the second year, then high-risk people will pay a ¥2,500 risk premium and low-risk people will pay a ¥2,100 risk premium. Consider the two insurance contracts below:

> Contract #1: A ¥23,000 premium for coverage of ¥100,000 for the second year only.
> Contract #2: A ¥75,000 premium for coverage of ¥100,000 for two years.

Given these two contracts, what choice will policy holders make? For a high-risk person, if he chooses Contract #1, the value of his expected coverage will be ¥25,000, which is higher than the ¥23,000 insurance premium, plus a ¥2,500 risk premium income, so his net benefit is ¥4,500 yuan. If he chooses Contract #2, then the value of his expected coverage will be ¥75,000, which is equal to the insurance premium, but he gains a ¥7,500 risk premium. Obviously, choosing Contract #2 is better than choosing Contract #1 (satisfying the incentive compatibility constraint) and is also preferable to not purchasing insurance (satisfying the participation constraint). For a low-risk person, if he chooses Contract #1, the value of his expected coverage will be ¥21,000, which is lower than the ¥23,000 insurance premium, but his risk premium income is ¥2,100, so the total gain from purchasing insurance is ¥100. If he chooses Contract #2, even if he obtains a ¥5,100 risk premium income, the value of his expected coverage is ¥51,000, which is less than the ¥75,000 insurance premium, so his net gain is −¥18,900. Obviously, choosing Contract #1 is better than Contract #2 (satisfying the incentive compatibility constraint) and is also better than not purchasing insurance (satisfying the participation constraint).

In the example described above, insurance companies designed Contract #1 for low-risk people and Contract #2 for high-risk people. Even if insurance companies do not know which specific person is high-risk or low-risk, given this contract menu, each type of person will self-select to reveal their private information. People that choose Contract #1 are certainly low-risk and people that choose Contract #2 are certainly high-risk. This partially resolves the adverse selection problem through incentive compatibility constraint.

However, this insurance for low-risk people is imperfect, because these people are not covered in the first year. The reason for this imperfect insurance is to prevent high-risk people from imitating low-risk people. A general conclusion is that under asymmetric information, there is only the second best, not the first best.

In reality, as to whether insurance companies provide insurance for low-risk people only, high-risk people only, or different policies for both depends on market conditions. Regardless, insurance contracts under asymmetric information are different than under symmetric information.

1.3 Partial insurance and full insurance

We will further consider the design of an automobile insurance policy. Imagine there are two types of drivers: High-risk drivers and low-risk drivers, each accounting for 50% of the total population. Assume the first type of person has a 30% probability of having an accident and the second type of person has a 10% probability of having an accident. Assume the value of the car is ¥100,000 and the insured amount is calculated based on the value of the car. If insurance companies know which type of person the policy holders are, they will charge the high-risk people (the first type) a ¥30,000 insurance premium and charge the low-risk people (the second type) a ¥10,000 insurance premium. If there is an accident within the term of the insurance, both types of people will be compensated ¥100,000. This is shown in Table 10.3.

If insurance companies cannot differentiate between the types of policy holders, then they can only charge a ¥20,000 premium for everyone based on the same standard. However, if the insurance premium is ¥20,000, then low-risk people might not purchase insurance. Assume that the risk premium for low-risk people is ¥7,000 (meaning the risk premium for each ¥10,000 worth of insurance is ¥700) and the risk premium for high risk people is ¥21,000 (meaning the risk premium for each ¥10,000 worth of insurance is ¥2,100). Here, because the risk of the

Table 10.3 Two Types of Automobile Insurance

	probability of having an accident	insurance coverage (ten thousand)	premium (ten thousand)	certain gain for insured person (ten thousand)
type I	0.3	10	3	7
type II	0.1	10	1	9
average	0.2	10	2	

first type is three times of the second type, we assume that the risk premium is also three times. For a second type of person (low-risk type), if he does not purchase insurance, then the expected payoff is ¥90,000, or a certainty-equivalent of ¥83,000. Here the certainty-equivalent is defined as the expected payoff minus the risk premium. After purchasing insurance, the certain payoff is only ¥80,000. Naturally, he prefers to not purchase insurance. However, high-risk people are still willing to purchase insurance. If they choose to not purchase insurance, then the expected payoff is ¥70,000 and the certainty-equivalent is ¥49,000. By purchasing insurance, the certain payoff is ¥80,000. Insurance increases his utility, so naturally he is willing to purchase insurance. However, if only high-risk people do purchase insurance, not low-risk people, then the expected payoff of insurance companies are negative. Thus insurance companies will lose money.

Now, we face a problem similar to the one in the previous section. In order for automobile insurance to exist, we must design a mechanism so that both types of people purchase insurance. One point must be explained: Information about policy holders' social groups, professions, and age can be obtained. The issue is that even within the same social groups, profession, and age there are still high-risk and low-risk people. How can we differentiate between these types? Below, we will design a proposal and see if it will work.

Now, we will assume insurance companies provide two contracts for policy holders to freely choose. Then, we will see which proposal each type of people accept.

Contract #1: ¥30,000 insurance premium for ¥100,000 coverage.
Contract #2: ¥2,000 insurance premium for ¥20,000 coverage.

Between these two contracts, who will choose the first and who will choose the second?

First, we will examine high-risk policy holders' options (as shown in Table 10.4).

The expected payoff and certainty-equivalent for not purchasing insurance and Contract #1 shown in Table 10.4 were already calculated. Now, we will examine the expected payoff and certainty-equivalent in Contract #2. Under Contract #2, if an accident does not happen (a probability of 0.7), then a policy holder's payoff is ¥98,000, but if an accident does happen (a probability of 0.3), then the payoff is ¥18,000. This means a policy holder's expected payoff is ¥74,000 (= 9.8 × 0.7 + 1.8 × 0.3) and the certainty-equivalent is ¥57,500 (the reader can calculate this assuming a high-risk driver's risk premium is ¥2,100 for every ¥10,000 of

Table 10.4 High-Risk Policy Holders' Options

	not purchasing insurance	Contract I	Contract II
expected gain (10,000)	7	7	7.4
certainty-equivalent (10,000)	4.9	7	5.75

insurance). So, between the two contracts, Contract #1 is optimal for a high-risk person, so he will choose Contract #1.

Next, we will examine low-risk policy holders' options (as shown in Table 10.5).

Similar to above, we can quickly calculate the certainty-equivalent for not purchasing insurance and Contract 1 as ¥83,000 and ¥70,000, respectively. Now, we will examine the expected payoff and certainty-equivalent in Contract #2. If an accident does not happen (a probability of 0.9), then the payoff is ¥98,000, but if an accident does happen (a probability of 0.1), then the payoff is ¥18,000. This means the expected gain is ¥90,000 (= $9.8 \times 0.9 + 1.8 \times 0.1$) and the certainty-equivalent is about ¥84,400 (the reader can calculate this assuming a low-risk driver's risk premium is ¥700 for every ¥10,000 of insurance). Between the two contracts, Contract #2 is optimal for a low-risk person, so he will choose Contract #2.

Therefore, if insurance companies design these two types of contracts, then high-risk people will choose Contract #1 and low-risk people will choose Contract #2. Might high-risk people imitate low-risk people and choose Contract #2? No. Similarly, low-risk people do not have an incentive to choose Contract #1, which was intended specifically for high-risk people. The incentive compatible constraints are met. This type of mechanism causes each type of person to have an incentive to tell the truth and undertake self-selection to choose the contract specifically designed for them. Insurance contracts actually separated low-risk people from high-risk people.

Note that these two contracts have a special characteristic: The first is full insurance and the second is partial insurance. In general, If the insurance covers full value of insured objects, it is called the full insurance; otherwise, if the insurance will only cover part of the value, it is called the partial insurance. Why would only a portion be insured? Because if full insurance is offered, then high-risk people will imitate low-risk people, thus causing information to be difficult to differentiate. The reader can test giving low-risk people full insurance and will find that high-risk people would certainly prefer the contract for the low-risk type. To inhibit high-risk people from imitating low-risk people, we can only provide partial insurance for low-risk people. Under complete information, it is optimal to fully insure all types of risks, but now insurance companies can only provide low-risk type with a partial insurance. This is a basic model proposed by Rothschild and Stiglitz (1976).

Are contracts like this in reality? Overall, yes. For example, in China's auto-insurance business, standard insurance contract will only insure 80% of the price

Table 10.5 Low-Risk Policy Holders' Options

	not purchasing insurance	*Contract I*	*Contract II*
expected gain (10,000)	9	7	9
certainty-equivalent (10,000)	8.3	7	8.44

of the car. Assuming your ¥400,000 car is stolen, the insurance company will only cover ¥320,000 and you are responsible for the remaining ¥80,000. However, you have also an option to cover the remaining 20% by paying additional insurance premium which is much higher than the standard rate. Using our previous example, the standard contract is a ¥2,000 premium for covering ¥20,000 (or 20% of the price of the car). However, if you want to insure the remaining ¥80,000 (80% of the price of the car), then the additional premium would be ¥28,000.[4] Of course, the result is still that the type of person that each contract is intended for will choose that contract. Our observations show that high-risk people will pay additional premiums to obtain full insurance and low-risk people will choose standard contracts.

Section two: price discrimination

2.1 Seller's ignorance

In the market, it is often the case that the seller of a good knows the quality of a product, but the buyer does not. This requires reputations and brands to display product quality information. We have already discussed this point previously.

Actually, there is another type of information asymmetry in the market: The buyer knows information that the seller does not. For example, for a specific product, the amount a buyer is willing to pay is often the buyer's private information unknown to the seller of a good. For a painting like *Along the River During the Qingming Festival*, some people are willing to spend tens of millions of yuan, whereas others are only willing to spend tens of thousands of yuan. This will lead to the bargaining problem discussed previously. As we discussed previously, an important reason bargaining takes place is because this type of information asymmetry exists on the market. From the seller's perspective, the higher the price, the better; but the buyer's perspective is precisely the opposite. Under asymmetric information, the buyer has an incentive to conceal his own information, such as pretending to not like something desired. At this point, the seller must think of a way to know the buyer's true preferences so that the buyer pays the highest price he is willing to pay. From the seller's perspective, the clearer his understanding of the buyer's needs, the more likely he is to obtain greater profit.

The seller must design a type of mechanism to separate consumers with different preferences. This is related to the various price-setting methods that exist in the market. For example, at a public swimming pool, a consumer can purchase an annual membership for a fixed period with a lower price each visit, or pay a higher price for each visit. This is actually a mechanism designed by the owner of the swimming pool to separate different consumers. What type of person will purchase an annual membership? The type of person that swims more frequently will purchase an annual membership. The person that does not go to the swimming pool often will not purchase an annual membership, but instead pay an entry fee each visit. In this way, even if the swimming pool owner does not know each person's preference, he will indirectly obtain information related to consumers' preferences through their selection of payment methods. If the owner had directly asked consumers how much they are willing to pay each time and from this set pricing standards, consumers might not tell him the truth. There are many similar examples. Certain products (or services) appear different, but are essentially a price mechanism design, such as first class, business class, and economy class airplane tickets.

This is known as "price discrimination" in economics.[5] Price discrimination refers to producers selling products with equivalent costs at different prices to different types of consumers. Even if costs are different, different consumers will pay price variances greater than production costs variances. Even though first class is more comfortable than economy class and the cost is higher, the variance between service and cost is much less than the price variance. Some people prefer to use the term "pricing differentiation", since they feel the word discrimination is too strong.

2.2 The two-part tariff and information rent

A monopolist seller implements price discrimination to obtain greater profits. When the seller perfectly knows consumer's demand information, this is easy to do. However, with asymmetric information, to obtain maximum profits, the seller must design a mechanism under which high-demand consumers would not imitate low-demand consumers.

To explain this point, let us consider an example. Assume the unit product cost of a product is 6 and there are two potential consumers: High-demand and low-demand consumers. As shown in Table 10.6, for the low-demand consumer, the utility from consuming one unit is 10, two units is 16, three units is 20, and four units is 23. For the high-demand consumer, the utility from consuming one unit is 20, two units is 32, three units is 40, and four units is 46. Note that here we assume that utility of high-demand consumer is twice that of low-demand consumer for equivalent levels of numeric consumption, and marginal utility decreases as consumption increases for both types of consumers.[6]

Given a production cost of 6, the social optimal arrangement is the low-demand consumer consumes 2 units and the high-demand consumer consumes 4 units. With complete information, the seller could sell 2 units to the low-demand consumer for a total price of 16 and 4 units to the high-demand consumer for a total price of 46.[7] This is so-called "perfect price discrimination". The seller's total sales volume is 6 units; the total sales revenue is 62, and the profit is 26. The total consumption amount is also socially optimal.

Table 10.6 A Comparison of Changes in Utility for Two Types of Consumers

consumption amount (unit)	1	2	3	4
utility for low-demand consumer	10	16	20	23
utility for high-demand consumer	20	32	40	46
marginal utility	6	6	6	6

However, if the seller does not know who is a high-demand consumer and who is a low-demand consumer, this outcome is unobtainable. For example, if consumers can only choose between buying 2 units for a total price of 16 or buying four units for 46, then both types of consumers will choose to buy 2 units. For high-demand consumers, buying two units brings about a consumer surplus of 16, but buying 4 units brings about a consumer surplus of 0. Therefore, he will imitate a low-demand consumer. The seller's total sales revenue would be 32, and the profit would be 8.

Alternatively, imagine the seller sells at a uniform price of 10 per unit. The low-demand consumer's optimal choice is to only buy 1 unit (for a consumer surplus of 0), and the high-demand consumer's optimal choice is to buy 2 units (for a consumer surplus of 12). The producer's total income would be 30 and profit would be 12. This is actually the maximum profit the producer would obtain under a unified price. The reader can verify this conclusion.

Now, we will consider the seller's optimal tariff system design. Imagine the seller provides consumers with the two proposals below to choose:

> **Proposal #1:** If the consumer does not buy a "shopping card", then the unit price is 10.
>
> **Proposal #2:** If the consumer buys a "shopping card" for a price of 9.9, then the unit price is 6.

How should the consumer choose? For the low-demand consumer, by choosing Proposal #1, the optimal purchase quantity is 1 and consumer surplus is 0. By choosing Proposal #2, consumer surplus is negative. Therefore, Proposal #1 is optimal (assuming the consumer always buys when so doing not worse than not buying.) For the high-demand consumer, by choosing Proposal #1, the optimal purchase quantity is 2 and consumer surplus is 12. By choosing Proposal #2, the optimal purchase quantity is 4 and consumer surplus is 12.1. Therefore, Proposal #2 is the optimal choice.

In this way, the seller uses two different sales proposals to differentiate between high-demand and low-demand consumers and obtain total profits of 13.9 (earning 4 from low-demand consumers and 9.9 from high-demand consumers), which is greater than the profit of 12 with a uniform price. Each type of consumer will choose the proposal the seller intended for him so neither one will imitate the other type.

This is a so-called "two-part tariff".[8] Compared to perfect price discrimination under symmetric information, this price system has two important characteristics. First, the low-demand consumer's consumption is not socially optimal, because given the margin cost is 6, the socially optimal consumption is 2 units for him. This is efficiency loss caused by asymmetric information. Second, high-demand consumers obtain consumer surplus of 12.1. Under perfect price discrimination, the high-demand consumer also does not obtain consumer surplus.

The purpose of these two characteristics is satisfying the incentive compatibility constraint. To make the low-demand consumer choose to buy 2 units, the unit price in Proposal #1 can only be set at 6. However, at this point, the high-demand consumer does not have an incentive to choose Proposal #2 (because a consumer surplus of 22 can be obtained by choosing Proposal #1). Similarly, if the high-demand consumer obtains a consumer surplus less than 12 from choosing Proposal #2, then he will choose Proposal #1 (to obtain a consumer surplus of 12 from purchasing two units). At this point, the seller's total profit is only 12 (= 30 − 18). Therefore, the price of the shopping card in Proposal #2 cannot be greater than 10 (and we assumed it was set at 9.9).

The consumer surplus of 12.1 obtained by the high-demand consumer can be understood as "information rent". A general conclusion is that under information asymmetry, in order to make people tell the truth, the party with "good" information must obtain a sufficiently high information rent. Here, the lower limit of "sufficiently high" is the surplus that can be obtained by pretending to have "bad" information. In this example, it was 12.

There is a broad application of the two-part tariff in reality, so this model became the standard model for researching the ways in which producers with incomplete information differentiate between consumers.[9] The swimming pool at the beginning of this section had a two-part tariff. Most clubs (such as golf clubs) implement two-part tariffs (a membership fee and a single-use fee). Most telecommunication services implement a two-part tariff: A fixed monthly fee (perhaps including a certain amount of free call) in addition to a fee per minute. For telecommunications providers with a dominant market power, this type of two-part tariff is an ideal method for appropriating consumer surplus and attaining profit maximization. A well-designed two-part tariff mechanism can attain the effect of perfect price discrimination.

2.3 Punishing the poor to scare the rich

In mid-nineteenth-century France, trains had first-class, second-class, and third-class seats with relatively large price discrepancies. First class was extremely comfortable. The biggest difference between second class and third class was that the former had a carriage roof, whereas the latter did not. Passengers in third class had to suffer the sun and rain. It stands to reason that the cost of a carriage roof would not be that high, so why did the railroad companies do this? Did the railroad companies have something against the people in third class? Of course not. The reason was related to asymmetric information.[10]

The railroad companies were always thinking of ways to earn more money from each customer. The trouble for them was that they did not know how much each passenger was willing to pay to ride the train. If the passengers affording to ride in the second class carriage chose the third class carriage, then the railroad company would be at a loss. Therefore, they decided to not give the third-class carriage a roof. In this way, the people affording to ride in the second-class carriage would not choose the third-class carriage, because they could not bear the third-class suffering. Only truly poor people would choose the third-class carriage. In other words, the railroad companies let the poor people suffer in order to frighten the rich people.

This explanation sounds absurd, but it is not too far from reality. For example, airplane seats in economy class are very narrow. By adding a few centimeters, the passengers could be much more comfortable. Why do airplane companies not do this? Since full airplanes are not common, reducing the number of seats by 10% would not impact economy class ticket revenue. The real problem is that if the airline companies make economy class comfortable, then passengers with the means to take first class or business class would switch to economy class. In order to inhibit rich people from mixing with the people without money in economy class, it is necessary to make passengers in economy a little uncomfortable.

For the same reasoning, the price difference between first class and economy class for international (or long distance) flights is much greater than the price difference for domestic (or short distance) flights. The longer flight time is, the more passengers suffer. If the price difference for domestic flights was as great as for international flights, then perhaps very few people would be willing to take a first class domestic flight. Even for rich people, being uncomfortable for one or two hours in economy class to reduce the cost by 80% is also worth it.

Similarly, when the Beijing-Tongzhou Expressway was completed in the 1990s, the government was not willing to repair the old route that ran parallel. Because there was a toll on the expressway, but the old route was free, no one would be willing to pay the toll if the two roads were in similar conditions. In order to make the people with relatively more money or more precious time to pay the expressway toll, the people that took the alternative route had to have an unpleasant, slower drive.[11]

These various pricing strategies are all designed by the seller to maximize profits by making different customers pay different prices. If the seller wants to directly charge different customers different prices, then the seller must know in advance different needs and tastes of customers. Ancient doctors would charge the wealthy a high amount, but charge the poor a low amount, or nothing at all. They could do this because they knew who was wealthy and who was poor. Today, hospitals do not know how much money patients have, so they provide different types of facilities to separate different patients so wealthy people pay more for medical care. Of course, some types of identification can resolve the asymmetric information problem. Student identification, for example, plays a role in providing information, so railroad companies can charge students lower prices.

Of course, from the perspective of income distribution, this type of price discrimination is not necessarily bad. For example, when hospitals charge wealthy people more, they make it possible to reduce medical fees for poor people. Cross subsidization between consumers is an important channel for wealth redistribution.

Section three: auction mechanism design and public good preferences

3.1 Four basic types of auctions

Many commodities are transacted through auctions or bidding. Antiques, paintings, and land are auctioned whereas projects and procurement rely on bidding.

Why is this system common? Stated simply, it helps to resolve two issues. The first issue is the principal-agent problem.[12] Transactions for many products are not truly negotiated between the buyer and the seller, but instead are done through an agent. This led to the principal-agent problem. Within a firm, the interests of a purchasing agent are different from the interests of the firm's owners, which might lead to kickbacks. At this point, using auctions or bids might reduce the agent's corrupt behavior.[13] Another example would be government land transfers in which government officials in power might seek personal gain. A piece of land originally worth ¥5 million might be sold for ¥3 million after the buyer bribes the official responsible for the sale. This would reduce the government's revenues. One way to resolve this issue is to implement an auction. In China, the government does not obtain a lot of the funds that it should because auctions or bids are not used. Instead, this money flows into the hands of the relevant administrators. These administrators dislike auctions because it would take away their opportunity for corruption. This is the first problem.

Another problem is asymmetric information between the transacting parties. For any item you want to sell, you hope to sell it for the best price, but you do not know how much each potential buyer is willing to pay. If you were to directly ask, no one would tell you the truth. An auction is a good mechanism design to resolve this kind of asymmetric information problem. The design of the auction mechanism is extremely important. If the mechanism is not designed well, the item being bid on might not be sold for very much or the bidders might collude or conspire. This is also a moral hazard problem. However, good mechanism design can prevent this type of moral hazard and sell the product for a good price.

Roughly speaking, there are four basic types of auctions.[14] They are all direct mechanisms in which bidders report their types.

The first type is the "English-style open-cry auction". This is the form we often see in films and on television. When the China Guardian Auction House auctions off a painting, it starts with a minimum price, then higher prices are called out. If the starting price is ¥2,000, then people that accept this price will raise their hands. If more than one person raises their hands, then the auctioneer will increase the price to ¥2,100 or so. If there are still a lot of people that accept the price, then the auctioneer will continue to increase the price until only one person has a hand raised. Then the item goes to the person that accepted the last called price. The last called price is the transaction price. This is the English-style auction.

The second type is the "Dutch-style auction", which is also an open-cry method. However, the Dutch-style auction is precisely the opposite of the English-style auction because it starts from a high price and comes down. For example, the price of an item will start at ¥90,000 and be called out multiple times. If no one is interested, then the price will be reduced to ¥85,000 and called out multiple times. If still no one is interested, the price will reduce further. Assume that if when the price drops to ¥32,000, a person raises his hand, then the deal is made.

The English-style auction is generally used for items whose value increases or are relatively stable over time. The Dutch-style auction is generally used for items whose value decreases over time, such as fresh flowers. Any mention of Dutch will make us think of its flower markets and famous tulips. The fresh flower market opens very early every day and operates as an auction. A characteristic of flowers is that the more time passes the cheaper they become. If certain flowers are not sold in the early morning, their quality will decline significantly, so the price will come down. Perhaps this is the reason this type of product utilizes a high-to-low price auction. Many products with similar characteristics are sold the same way, such as fashion.

The third type is "the first-price sealed auction". Bids for television advertising time belong to this category. For example, to auction off the ten seconds before the news broadcast, bidders write down the amount they are willing to pay for this time and place it in an envelope. After all participants have placed their bids, the auctioneer opens the envelopes and the highest bidder wins. Project bidding in essence belongs to this auction category, but "bidding" is multi-dimensional (including price, design, and timing), so the inviter of the bids must weigh multiple factors to determine the winner.

The price you bid will certainly not exceed the maximum amount you are willing to pay. Within this limit, should you bid a bit high or a bit low? By bidding a bit high, your chances of winning increase, but you gain less after winning. By bidding a bit low, your chances of winning are reduced, but you gain more after winning. Therefore, you must balance the two. Generally speaking, each bidder has his own maximum price, and will not write down that price. However, you must guess others' bidding prices in order to judge your own chance of winning. Here, there is more asymmetric information. Not only is there asymmetric information between the buyer and the seller, there is asymmetric information between buyers. If there was no asymmetric information between buyers, it would be simpler.

The fourth type is "the second-price sealed auction". Its basic operation is identical to the first-price sealed auction, where the highest (or lowest) price bidder wins offers, but the only difference is that the actual payment amount by the winner is the second-place quote.

The major difference between the second-price sealed auction and other three is that under the second-price sealed auction, telling the truth is the optimal strategy regardless of types.

3.2 The truth-telling auction mechanism

Below, we will have a more detailed discussion of the second-price sealed auction. It was designed by American economist William Vickery (1961). For this contribution, he was awarded the 1996 Nobel Memorial Prize in Economic Sciences.

Image you have an antique to sell. Certain potential buyers might be willing to pay more, and others might be willing to pay less, but you are not clear on the details. How can you obtain truthful information? If you were to walk up to each potential customer and directly ask, the customer that might be willing to pay ¥10,000 might claim to only be willing to pay ¥8,000. Vickrey proved that the second-price auction can resolve this issue.

Imagine there are ten people bidding, and their final bids, ranked from highest to lowest, are as follows: ¥100,000, ¥95,000, ¥90,000, ¥85,000, etc. According to the rules, the person that bid ¥100,000 will receive the antique, but he pays only ¥95,000 (the second highest bid price), which is ¥5,000 lower than his own bid. Why under this type of mechanism will people bid according to their true valuation? Stated simply, it is because your bid only influences whether or not you win, but does not influence the actual price you need to pay after you win. In other words, telling the truth is only beneficial whereas lying is only disadvantageous.

Assume that you value this item at ¥100,000. How much should you bid for it? Assume that in order to spend less, you bid ¥90,000. At this point, if the second highest bid is ¥95,000, you will lose the bid and your net gain is zero. However, if you bid ¥100,000, you will receive the item, and then pay ¥95,000. Your net gain is ¥5,000. Therefore, a true-value bid is better than a low bid. If the second highest bid is ¥80,000 and you bid ¥90,000, then you will pay ¥80,000. Your net gain is ¥20,000. If you bid ¥100,000, you still win, and the price you pay is still ¥80,000. Your net gain is also ¥20,000. Therefore, a true-value bid at least is not worse than a lower bid.

What happens to higher bids? Imagine you bid ¥110,000 in order to win an item. If another person's second highest bid is ¥105,000, then you win and pay ¥105,000. Your net gain is a loss of ¥5,000. If you bid ¥100,000, you will not lose this ¥5,000. This proves that a true-value bid is better than a higher bid. If another person's highest bid is ¥95,000 and you bid ¥110,000, then you will win and your net gain is ¥5,000. However, under this condition, even if your bid had been ¥100,000, then you would have also won and your net gain still would have been ¥5,000. This proves that a true-value bid is not worse than a higher bid.

Therefore, neither lower bids nor higher bids are better than true-value bids. In other words, telling the truth is your best option. In this way, under a second-price sealed auction, each person will tell the truth. In the previous discussion, we did not assume other people tell the truth. Actually, regardless if other people tell the truth, telling the truth is the best choice for you. This is a basic characteristic of the Vickrey auction mechanism. The reasoning behind this is similar to our discussion in the previous section: To make the person with private information truthfully reveal his own information, he must be given sufficient incentive. The net gain from winning the auction (the true value minus the paid price) is the "information rent" that entices a person to tell the truth.

By comparison, under the other three types of auction mechanisms, people generally will not tell the truth. Under a first-price sealed auction, if your true value is ¥100,000 and you bid ¥100,000, then the best situation is you win, and your net gain is 0. However, if you bid ¥90,000, but the other highest bid is lower than ¥90,000, then you will win and pay ¥90,000 for a net gain of ¥10,000. Under the worst situation, another person bids higher than you, so your net gain is zero. Because telling the truth does not create information rent, then of course you do not have an incentive to tell the truth.

Similarly, with open-cry, people generally will not tell the truth. In an English-style auction, if you are the only person left after the price reaches ¥90,000, and then you certainly will not say you are willing to bid ¥100,000. In a Dutch-style auction, even if the price falls to ¥100,000, you will not make an offer. If you made an offer, you would win, but by paying ¥100,000, your net gain would be zero. If you waited until the price dropped to ¥95,000 before making an offer, then your net gain would be ¥5,000. The longer you wait, the greater the benefit of winning is, but also the probability of winning declines. Should you make an offer when the price drops to ¥95,000? If you make an offer, you obtain a net gain of ¥5,000, but perhaps if you waited until the price drops to ¥90,000 there is still an opportunity to make an offer for a net gain of ¥10,000. Of course, when you are waiting until the price drops to ¥90,000, someone else may make an offer and you are left with nothing.

Of course, in these three types of auctions where the truth is not told, the more bidders there are, the closer each person's bid will be to the true value. This is the reason the auctioning party always hopes to have more bidders.

It must be pointed out that even if bidders tell the truth in the second-price sealed auction and do not tell the truth in the other three types of auctions, from the resource allocation perspective, with certain conditions satisfied, these four methods are "equivalent". Under any mechanism, the winner values the item the highest and produces equivalent expected revenue for the seller.[15]

3.3 Revealed preferences for public goods

One application of the second-price sealed auction mechanism for public goods is called the "Groves-Clarke-Vickrey mechanism".[16] Imagine the Beijing Municipal Government will invest in a project. There are multiple projects to choose from, such as a hospital or a freeway. However, because of limited funds, only one project can be chosen. Which project should the government invest in? This is a public goods selection problem. Similarly, if classmates want to have a meal together, selecting a restaurant is also a public good. Some people like Cantonese cuisine and some people like Sichuan cuisine, but everyone believes eating is better than not eating. How should we choose?

We will use the example of classmates having a meal to explain the Groves-Clarke-Vickrey mechanism. Assume that Person A, Person B, Person C, and Person D all want to have a meal together and they can choose between Cantonese cuisine and Sichuan cuisine. The goal is to maximize the total utility of the four people. To do this, each person must report the utility or value that Cantonese cuisine or Sichuan cuisine will bring to him. For example, Person A likes spicy food, so he believes Cantonese cuisine provides 10 units of utility and Sichuan cuisine provides 30 units of utility. Person B is precisely the opposite, with 30 and 10, respectively. Person C believes Cantonese cuisine provides 15 units of utility and Sichuan cuisine provides 20 units of utility. Person D believes Cantonese cuisine is worth 25 units and Sichuan cuisine is worth 10 units. After each person reports their own preferences, we can add them up, and then the classmates eat whichever cuisine has a highest total value.

The question is whether or not the person that prefers Sichuan cuisine will over report. Originally, Person A believed Sichuan cuisine was worth 30 units, but he might report 300 units. This will increase the total reported value of

Sichuan cuisine, but this is false information. How can we make each person tell the truth?

In regards to this issue, the Groves-Clarke-Vickrey mechanism allows each person to report their own preferences at will, but must pay a "tax" to do so. How is this tax calculated? First, add together the values reported by every other person, which in this example would be Person B, Person C, and Person D, to see if the value for Cantonese cuisine or Sichuan cuisine is higher. Then, add the value reported by Player A to see if the value for Cantonese cuisine or Sichuan cuisine is higher. If Person A's reporting does not change the overall result, then Person A does not need to pay a tax. However, if Person A's reporting changes the overall result, then he must pay a tax. In this case, changing the result means the other three people preferred Cantonese cuisine (in term of the total reported value of these three persons), but adding the value reported by Person A caused the total value of Sichuan cuisine to exceed Cantonese cuisine. How much tax should be paid? The tax paid by Person A must equal the loss that Person A brings about to others. Assume that for the other three people, Cantonese cuisine was worth 100 units and Sichuan cuisine was worth 90 units. Now that Person A's valuation causes Sichuan cuisine to be chosen, then Person A causes a loss of 10 units to the other three. This means that Person A must pay a 10-unit tax. We give the detailed calculations in Table 10.7.

As shown in Table 10.7, the total value for Cantonese cuisine is 80 units and the total value for Sichuan cuisine is 70 units. Obviously, they should eat Cantonese cuisine. Now, we will consider the tax issue. Excluding Person A, the total value for Cantonese cuisine is 70 and the total value for Sichuan cuisine is 40, so they should still eat Cantonese cuisine. In other words, Person A's reported value is not crucial because it does not influence the outcome. There is no need for Person A to pay a tax. Excluding Person B, the total value for Cantonese cuisine is 50 units and the total value for Sichuan cuisine is 60 units. B's reported value is crucial. In other words, without Person B, Sichuan cuisine is preferred over Cantonese cuisine, but with Person B, Cantonese cuisine will be selected. For this reason, Person B causes others a loss of 10 units, so Person B should pay a 10-unit tax. For the same reasoning, Person C does not need to pay a tax, but Person D does need to pay a 5-unit tax.

Why will each person tell the truth under this mechanism? Assume that Person A prefers to eat Sichuan cuisine, so in order to select Sichuan cuisine, he will

Table 10.7 The Groves-Clarke-Vickrey Mechanism Application Choosing a Restaurant

player	Cantonese cuisine value	Sichuan cuisine value	total value for Cantonese cuisine for others	total value for Sichuan cuisine for others	crucial or not	tax
A	10	30	70	40	no	0
B	30	10	50	60	yes	10
C	15	20	65	50	no	0
D	25	10	55	60	yes	5
total	80	70				

intentionally over-report the value of Sichuan cuisine for him. For his reporting to influence the final selection, he must report 40 units or higher. Assume that he reports 41 units, meaning he over reported 11 units (the value of Sichuan cuisine for Person A is 30 units). This would successfully influence the final outcome. Without him, the total value of Cantonese cuisine is 70 units and the total value of Sichuan cuisine is 40 units. Due to Person A over reporting the value of Sichuan cuisine, the final outcome becomes a total value of 81 units for Sichuan cuisine, whereas the total value for Cantonese cuisine is only 80 units. In the end, Sichuan cuisine will be selected. Because Person A brought about a 30-unit loss to everyone else, he must pay a 30-unit tax. Is this worthwhile for Person A? If Person A tells the truth and goes to eat Cantonese cuisine, he obtains 10 units of utility. Now that Person A lied in order to eat Sichuan cuisine, he obtains 30 units of utility. The utility gap between these two outcomes is 20 units. However, Person A must pay 30 units of tax, so of course it is not worthwhile. Similarly, Person A has no incentive to under-report the value either. At what point would under-reporting the value influence the final selection? Only when under reporting the value to a certain degree changes the weight of these two outcomes. As long as you change the outcome, you bring about losses to other people, so you must pay a tax.

So, we have proved that under the Groves-Clarke-Vickrey mechanism, telling the truth is the best choice for each person. If you tell a lie, you run the risk of being punished. Here, the "tax" is a punishment for telling a lie.[17]

Section four: equality and efficiency

The relationship between equality and efficiency in society is a topic people often discuss. The reader might ask: At what point can equality and efficiency be separated? The simple answer is: If information is perfect, then equality and efficiency can be separated. In other words, under conditions of complete information, society can both realize maximum efficiency while also reaching desired equality. The reason efficiency sometimes harms equality or equality sometimes harms efficiency is because information is incomplete.

4.1 The source of contradictions between equality and efficiency

Government taxation and income transfer policies are considered important means to realize equality. Absolute equality means each person in the end obtains the same utility. However, some people are high ability, and some people are low ability. In order to make each person obtain the same utility in the end, high-ability people must pay more taxes and low-ability people must pay less (or even be subsidized). Imagine a society composed of two people. One person can produce a 1-unit product for every hour of work, and the other can produce 2 units for every hour of work. Assume that the degree of suffering for one hour of work is the same. Assuming that the government requires 1 unit of taxation revenue, then the government should collect taxes from the second person, but not the first. In this way, the final outcome is: The first person keeps 1 unit of product, the second person is left with 1 unit of product after paying 1 unit of tax, and the government receives 1 unit of tax revenue. Alternatively, if the objective of government taxation is to maintain equality through transfer payments, then it should collect half a unit in taxes and subsidize the first person. The outcome would be each person has 1.5 units of production, which resolves the equality and efficiency issue. Even if the second person thinks this is a bad idea, he should still work because the government will still collect tax regardless if he works or not. So, when information about productivity is complete, there is no contradiction between equality and efficiency.

When information is asymmetric or incomplete, however, then there will be a contradiction between equality and efficiency. In the above example, if the government does not have information about each person's ability, then the government cannot collect taxes according to ability. Instead, it can only collect taxes according to output, such as collecting 1 unit of tax for every 2 units of production, but not levying tax on 1 unit of product. However, if output is the standard for taxation, then the second person has the choice either to work one hour to produce 2 units and pay 1 unit in taxes or work half an hour to produce 1 unit and not pay taxes. If he chooses the latter, other half hour could be used for leisure, which brings him positive utility. Therefore, that person's best option is to only work for half hour. In this way, because the high-ability person pretends to be low ability, not only does the government not have tax revenue, but there is also a contradiction between equality and efficiency. Note that even though the two people now have the same income (1 unit each), but they are unequal from the individual welfare perspective. Because the high-ability person only works half an hour, but the low-ability person works for a full hour, this means the high-ability person obtains more utility. At the same time, society suffers efficiency loss, because the high-ability person produces one unit less.

Therefore, under incomplete information, even if we are willing to sacrifice efficiency, there is no way to obtain absolute equality. High-ability people can always be a little better off than low-ability people.

What method of tax collection should the government implement so that high-ability people do not pretend to be low-ability? This is a question that the Mirrlees' Theory of Optimum Income Taxation attempted to answer (Mirrlees, 1971).

4.2 Mirrlees' Theory of Optimum Income Taxation

In reality, most countries implement a progressive tax system, meaning marginal tax rates increase as income increases. However, according to Mirrlees' Theory of Optimum Income Taxation, when the government cannot observe individual abilities, the marginal tax rate for the highest incomes should be zero. His research had a significant impact on information economics, in both methodological aspects and policy aspects. Later research proved that to make a person with private information tell the truth, he must obtain a benefit for telling the truth. Alternatively, if he tells a lie, he must be punished. We have already discussed this conclusion previously.

We will use a simple model to explain the basic contents of the Theory of Optimum Income Taxation.[18] Assume there are two people who have different production efficiencies for the same amount of time or effort. However, their costs of work are the same. Specifically, we assume that the first person's production function is $y_1 = x_1$ and the second person's production function is $y_2 = 2x_2$. The cost function for both of them is $C(x) = \frac{1}{2} x^2$. Here, x represents labor inputs, or how much time or effort a person spent, and y represents output. The subscripts represent the first and second person.

The first person's output equals x, meaning 1 unit can be produced in one hour or 2 units can be produced in two hours. The second person's output equals $2x$, meaning 2 units can be produced in one hour or 4 units can be produced in two hours. We assume that the marginal cost of work increases proportionally, meaning the longer work time is, the greater the additional suffering. For example, the total suffering from one hour of work is 0.5 units, but the total suffering from two hours of work is 2 units. This means the marginal cost of the first hour of work is 0.5 units, but the marginal cost of the second hour of work is 1.5 units, and so on. Assuming that one unit of consumption brings about one unit of utility, then social efficiency maximization means marginal output must equal marginal cost. It is easy to calculate that the first person (of low ability) should work one hour and the second person (of high ability) should work two hours. High-ability people should work more because given their marginal cost curve is the same as low-ability, their marginal productivity is relatively larger than the latter.

Without government taxation, each person will certainly choose this way. At this point, the first person's output is 1 unit, cost is 0.5 units, and net welfare is 0.5 units. The second person's output is 4 units, cost is 2 units, and net welfare is 2 units. Obviously, there is inequality because the second person is better off than the first.

Now, we will consider the ways government resolves the equality issue through taxation and subsidies. As was discussed previously, if the government knows the abilities of each person, then it could attain equality of outcome without harming efficiency. For example, if the government collected 0.75 units of tax from the second person and subsidizes the first person, then each person's level of welfare would be 1.25 units. However, after-tax income is still different, because the second person worked one hour more than the first person. This also means that if the government collects 1.5 units of tax from the second person and subsidizes the first person, then both would have the same 2.5-unit income. Actually, this is unfair, because the first person's welfare is 2 units, and the second person's welfare is only 0.5 units after income redistribution. This welfare distribution pattern is the same as before collecting the tax, but their respective positions have changed. This kind of situation could happen in reality, as shown in China's people's commune system where lazy people were better off than hard-working people.

When information about ability is asymmetric, taxes must be output-based. The government might implement this type of policy: If you produce 4 units, then you will pay 2 units of tax; if you produce 2 units or less, then you will not pay tax.

At this point, from the second person's perspective, when he works two hours to produce 4 units, then the government will take away 2 units and there will be only 2 unit left to him. Because his cost of work is also 2 units, the overall net gain is 0. However, assuming that he works one hour and produces 2 units, then he does not have to pay taxes. His cost of work is 0.5 units, so his gain is 1.5 units. Thus, high-ability people do not have an incentive to choose the socially optimal state.

Under this type of taxation policy, the second person (high ability) is still better off than the first person (low ability). So, it is impossible to have an equality even if we are willing to scarify the efficiency. We can further prove that under any circumstances, if we want the high-ability person to have an incentive to work more, then his life must be better than the low-ability person. Otherwise, he will not be incentivized. Of course, this is not the case if information is symmetric. However, because information is asymmetric, the contradiction between equality and efficiency cannot be resolved. As long as asymmetric information exists, the person with private information and high ability must be better off than the person with lower ability. In other words, the high-ability must obtain his "information rent".

Looking back, in this example, assuming that the government wants to collect taxes on the second (high-ability) person, as well as wants him to work two hours, then what conditions must be met? Because the second person can obtain a 1.5-unit surplus without paying taxes by only working one hour, then in order to incentivize him to work two hours, then his after-tax surplus cannot be less than 1.5 units. The cost of a high-ability person working two hours is 2 units for a 4-unit output. This means that taxes cannot exceed 0.5 units. As long as taxes are less than 0.5 units, then he might still have an incentive to work for two hours. As soon as taxes are greater than 0.5 units, then he will not have an incentive to work that long. Assume that the government transfers the entire 0.5-unit tax revenue to the low-ability person as a subsidy. At this point, the low-ability person worked for 1 hour for a 1-unit output. His cost of work is 0.5 units, and his subsidy is 0.5 units. His income is 1.5 units, and the net surplus is 1 unit. In this situation, a high-ability person has a 3.5-unit income, but a low-ability person only has a 1.5-unit income. The high-ability person is twice as capable as the low-ability person, but the income gap is more than double.

However, this type of redistribution is only one possibility, whether it can be realized depends on how the government collects that 0.5-unit tax. Assume the government collects 0.5 units of tax on the last 1 unit of output. In other words, the first 3 units of output are not taxed, but the last 1 unit of output is taxed at 50%. At this point, if the high-ability person only works for 1.5 hours to produce 3 units, he does not have to pay tax. His net utility is $3 - 1.125 = 1.875$ units. However, if he works two hours, he has to pay 0.5 units in tax. His net utility is $4 - 0.5 - 2 = 1.5$ units. Therefore, he still does not have an incentive to work two hours. Now, assume the government imposes the 0.5 unit tax on the second unit of outcome. In other words, the first 1 unit of output is not taxed, the second 1 unit of output is taxed at 50%, the third 1 unit and the fourth 1 unit of output are not taxed (so the marginal tax rate for the highest is 0%). If the high-ability person works two hours, his net utility is 1.5 units. If he works 1.5 hours, his net utility is 3 − 0.5 − 1.125 = 1.375 units. If he works one hour, his net utility is 2 − 0.5 − 0.5 = 1 unit. If he works one-half hour, then he does not pay tax, so his net utility is 1 − 0.125 = 0.875 units. Therefore, he will choose to work two hours. This is the meaning of the optimal marginal tax rate of 0% for the highest-income earners proven by James Mirrlees.

In summary, asymmetric information causes the contradiction between equality and efficiency. As long as asymmetric information exists, the owner of private information will obtain information rent. Even if we are willing to take a loss on efficiency, we cannot realize complete equality.

4.3 The loss of high-quality employees in state-owned enterprises

Below, we will analyze a major phenomenon during China's process of economic transition: The loss of high-quality employees in traditional state-owned enterprises. This phenomenon was especially prevalent in the 1990s. A large quantity of high-quality employees (including technicians and managers) left state-owned enterprises and joined foreign-owned enterprises or private enterprises. This phenomenon can be understood as the labor market's process of transition from a "(compulsory) pooling equilibrium" to a "separating equilibrium" as the wage system changed.

In Figure 10.2, the horizontal axis represents the degree of employee effort and the vertical axis represents output or wages. We have drawn separate production curves and utility indifference curves for high-quality employees and low-quality employees. The production curve is upward sloping because output increases as the degree of employee effort increases. However, given the same level of effort, high-quality employees produce more than low-quality employees. Therefore, the production curve of high-quality employees is steeper than that for low-quality

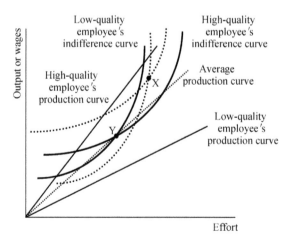

Figure 10.2 The Loss of High-Quality Employees in State-Owned Enterprises

employees. The indifference curve is also upward sloping because given that the greater effort causes more negative utility, in order to keep employees' utility constant, wages must increase accordingly. A higher indifference curve represents a higher utility level. However, to do the same work or produce the same output, high-quality employees spend less time and effort. Therefore, the wage compensation to sustain the same utility level is also smaller. For the low-ability person, higher compensation is required to do even a little work. Therefore, the high-quality employee's indifference curve is relatively flat and the low-ability person's indifference curve is relatively steep.

Under the planned economy, state-owned enterprises implemented an egalitarian wage system. Regardless of your ability or effort, you received the same wages, just as Point Y corresponds to this wage level on the vertical axis. Because there are no incentives, employees will only choose the smallest effort, just as Point Y corresponds to this level of effort on the horizontal axis. The average production curve passes through Point Y, meaning output just cover wage so that the state enterprise makes no profit and no loss. This is called a (coercive) "pooling equilibrium". The planned economy can attain "equality", but it comes at the expense of efficiency. The optimal point required by efficiency is the point where the indifference curve is tangent on the production curve.

Actually, this type of so-called "equality" is only equality in terms of income. From the utility perspective, it is inequality. We can see from Figure 10.2 that the high-quality employee's indifference curve that passes through Point Y intercepts the vertical axis at a greater level than for the low-quality employee's indifference curve. Because the corresponding intercept point for the level of effort is zero, the relatively high intercept is equivalent to the relatively high wage level. This means that the actual utility level obtained by the high-quality employee is higher than the low-quality employee. Therefore, this is unequal. The distance between the two intercept-points is the high-quality employee's "information rent" that we spoke of previously.

The reason this "pooling equilibrium" can be sustained is because employees under the planned economy did not have the freedom to leave. Actually, because all state-owned enterprises implemented a unified wage system, even if mobility was allowed, it would not make a difference. However, as Reform and Opening promoted non-state sectors (including private firms and China-foreign joint-ventures) which pay wages according to workers' productivities, once employee mobility was allowed, this pooling equilibrium could not be sustained. Assume that state-owned enterprises still provided a wage system like Point Y, but foreign-invested enterprises or private enterprises selected a different type of wage contract like Point X. At Point X, employees obtain higher wages, but must also work harder. Who is willing to choose contract X? Obviously, high-ability people will. Choosing contract X increases the utility level of a high-ability person (his dotted indifference curve that passes through Point X is higher than the original indifference curve passing Point Y). Low-ability people will not choose Point X because the utility at Point X is lower than for Point Y (his dotted indifference curve that passes through Point X is lower than the original indifference curve passing

Point Y). While working in a foreign-invested enterprise or a private enterprise is more demanding than in a state-owned enterprise, but wages are much higher, so high-ability people are willing to move from the state sector to non-state sector. But low-ability people are unwilling to join foreign-invested enterprise or private enterprise. They still prefer to remain in a state-owned enterprise. This separates high-ability people and low-ability people, so the labor market transitions from a "pooling equilibrium" to a "separating equilibrium".

What influence does this have on firm operations? For state-owned enterprises, after high-ability people leave, the production function is no longer the average production function. Instead, it becomes the low-ability production function (because only low-ability people are left in state-owned enterprises). At this point, Point Y is above the production function line. State-owned enterprise output can no longer cover wage expenditures, so they begin to make loss. By comparison, even though foreign-invested enterprises and private enterprises pay higher wages, because high-ability people's production function line is even high, they still make a profit.

The loss of high-quality employees in the 1990s was an important reason for state-owned enterprise to get into financial difficulty. Stated simply, under the original planned economy, low-ability people exploited high-ability people or high-ability people subsidized low-ability people because there was no choice for high ability people. As soon as foreign and private enterprises are established, everyone had a choice, so high-ability people went to places with higher wages to avoid the exploitation.

A simple example can explain this point. Assume that originally a high-ability person produces 200 units of output, and a low-ability person produces 100 units. If the proportion of high-ability employees is 20%, then as long as the average wage does not exceed 120 units, the enterprise will not lose money. Assume the actually paid wage at state-owned enterprises is 120 units. Now, suppose that non-state-owned enterprise appears that pays high-ability people a wage of 180 units. Although the high-quality people that join the new non-state owned firm work harder for the 180 units' wage, it is still better than receiving a 120-unit wage in the state sector. The low-ability people will choose to remain in the state-owned enterprise. The people employed by foreign and private firms have higher wages and higher output. They can produce 200 units of value, so the company still makes 20 units of profit. Previously, state-owned enterprises could have maintained balance between revenue and expenses. Now that only low-ability people remain, each employee produces 100 units of value while still receiving a wage of 120 units. How could state-owned enterprises not lose money? We saw during the process of marketization that the income gap expanded and society's income distribution became unequal.

Section five: the university faculty selection mechanism

5.1 Good-bad pooling and self-selection

Below, we will discuss the selection of university professors. Only a small portion of the population is qualified to be university professors. These people must have a strong preference for scholarship, and academic creativity. Who belongs to this group? This is an asymmetric information problem. We must have a way to identify people that satisfy the conditions described above. The hiring and promotion system is actually a classic mechanism design issue.

If we can design a mechanism so that people with true ability and an interest in scholarship are willing to become professors, whereas people without ability and an interest in scholarship do not choose to be professors, then this issue is resolved. We call this mechanism "self-selection".

For simplicity, we will discuss this mechanism design from the two measurements of "compensation" and "academic standards" for promotions. Assume that all candidates can be separated into two types: Qualified and unqualified. A qualified person truly has ability and is interested in scholarship. An unqualified person does not have ability and is unsuitable for scholarship. In Figure 10.3, the horizontal axis represents academic standards, and the vertical axis represents wage levels. Both of them are ranked from lowest to highest.

The upward sloping curves represents the indifference curves of two different types of candidates. The indifference curve for both is upward sloping because attaining relatively high academic standards means a professor must put in more effort and work longer, so the same utility level can only be maintained with higher wages. For each individual, a relatively high indifference curve represents a relatively high utility level.

However, the qualified person's indifference curve is flatter than the unqualified person's indifference curve. The reason is that attaining the same academic standard requires relatively less effort and thus lower wage compensation for the former than the latter. An intelligent person writes a good paper more easily than a stupid person. For a low-ability person, writing even a short essay is unbearable suffering that requires significant compensation. To write the same essay, a high-ability person requires much less compensation.

First, assume the reservation utility (or opportunity cost of utility provided by doing other jobs) for both types of people is the same. We will standardize each individual's reservation utility as zero, which is the origin point that the

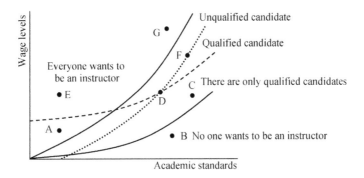

Figure 10.3 The Self-Selection Mechanism for University Instructors

corresponding indifference curves pass through. Consider the mechanisms below (each mechanism corresponds to a point on the graph):

Mechanism A: Very low academic standards and very low wages;
Mechanism B: Very high academic standards but very low wages;
Mechanism C: Very high academic standards and relatively high wages;
Mechanism D: Relatively high academic standards and relatively high wages.

Obviously, under Mechanism A, both qualified and unqualified people are willing to be a professor, because each type will obtain a utility greater than the reservation utility. Under Mechanism B, no one is willing to be a professor, because the utility obtained is smaller than the reservation utility. Under both Mechanism C and Mechanism D, qualified people will choose to be a professor and unqualified people will choose to not be a professor, because the former will obtain a utility greater than the reservation utility and the latter will not. In this way, Mechanism C and Mechanism D can automatically separate qualified people and unqualified people, whereas Mechanism A and Mechanism B cannot.

We can now use this framework to analyze the change in quality of China's university professors since Reform. Before the 1990s, wages for university professor were very low, but standards for promotions were also very low. Promotions was mainly seniority-based, so it was similar to Point A in the graph. Therefore, a high number of graduates were willing to remain on campus as teachers, regardless of whether or not they were actually suitable for the job. The result was that professors were a mixture of qualified and unqualified.

From the beginning of the 1990s, especially after Deng Xiaoping's Southern Tour speech, people had more choices. High-ability people had entrepreneurial opportunities and foreign-invested enterprises were hiring large quantities of local employees. At this point, the opportunity cost of a high-ability person being a professor increased dramatically, but the opportunity cost for low-ability people did not change much. Therefore, we can rationally assume that in Figure 10.3, the qualified person's reservation utility determined by external opportunity costs increased from the original solid indifference curve to the now dashed curve. The unqualified person's indifference curve remains at the original level. However, neither universities' standards for promotion nor professors' wages changed (or have changed very slightly). In other words, we are still operating under Mechanism A. Under this condition, among new advanced degree graduates, who were willing to join faculty? From Figure 10.3, we can see that people unqualified are still willing to be professors, whereas qualified people are not willing to join faculty. Among existing professors, the unqualified hope to remain on campus because they do not have better external options, whereas the qualified choose to leave campus because their outside opportunities are too attractive for them to stay. Even those who do not quit have part-time jobs outside of campus. The result is a decrease in the overall quality of faculty.

Of course, by saying this, I am speaking in absolutes. Certain outstanding scholars have such a strong preference for scholarship that even for very low compensation they will remain on campus to be a professor. These people played an important role in maintaining university standards after the 1990s. Today, they are the academic backbone of many universities.

In the late 1990s, the quality of professors was an issue that gained attention both inside and outside of universities. One method to resolve the issue was to increase academic standards for promotions, which many universities did. However, as shown in Figure 10.3, increasing academic standards alone cannot resolve the issue. For example, even if academic standards are increased to Point B, but faculty compensation is not increased sufficiently, then although unqualified will not be willing to be professors (because it is too hard), qualified people also do not have an incentive to be professors. It will still be difficult to raise faculty quality. Similarly, increased compensation alone will also not resolve the issue. As shown in Figure 10.3, if compensation is increased from Point A to Point E, but academic standards are not increased, then although qualified people are enticed to be professors, there is no way to stop unqualified people from choosing to be professors.

If we now want qualified people to willingly be professors as their careers and unqualified people not to choose being professors, what should we do? Raise the academic standards and increase compensation at the same time. If Point F, or even Point D is implemented, then academic standards will increase, and compensation will also have a corresponding increase. Under this condition, who is willing to be a professor? Low-ability people will be unwilling to be professors, because their utility will be lower than it would be for other jobs. For high-ability people, being a professor is now better than other jobs. This way, people suited to be professors choose to be instructors and people unsuited to be professors choose other work. We attain a separating equilibrium and the faculty quality is guaranteed.

However, compensation cannot increase too much. For example, if Point G is implemented, meaning academic standards are high, but compensation increased too much, then we are back to the original state where everyone was willing to be a professor.

Of course, the selection of university faculty is a complex process. Generally speaking, each university has certain basic requirements for professors, such as having a Ph.D., relevant recommendation letters, and successful interviews, etc. Regardless, having a suitable self-selection mechanism is extremely important. If the mechanism is not right, unsuitable people will be interested to be a professor. Solely relying on procedures will not guarantee faculty quality. Not only is this the case because it is difficult to evaluate the true level of candidates, but also personal relationships, or even corruption, are unavoidable. If academic requirements for faculty are very low, then people will try to pass themselves off as something they are not. Only with high requirements will we be able to recruit truly qualified and passionate people.

5.2 The incentive problem of the selector

Of course, we previously only discussed one aspect of the issue. The other aspect of the issue is how to give selectors an incentive to tell the truth. Because knowledge specialization leads to information asymmetry, the duty to select new faculty members can only be given to experts in the related field, mostly incumbent professors. However, even if these incumbent professors have the ability to judge the quality of applicants, there is still an issue of whether or not they have an incentive to tell the truth. In other words, we face a problem similar to the recruiting policy of Wu Dalang, a character in the novel *The Plum in the Golden Vase*. Wu Dalang was short man, so he refused to hire anyone taller than himself for his restaurant. How can incumbent professors be inhibited from intentionally making bad selections?

To resolve this issue, American universities designed two important systems: The tenure system and an academic bottom-out system.[19]

The tenure system rules that those who have been promoted to a tenured rank (normally full professor) can work until retirement. As long as certain rules are not violated, the school cannot fire a tenured professor. It is generally believed that the goal of the tenure system is to protect academic freedom.[20] However, it may also serve the purpose of selecting talented faculty members.

Imagine you are a professor in some department that can evaluate any new applicants, or are even on the hiring committee. You have the final vote, so your opinion of the candidate is key. Now, assume there is an exceptional candidate that is even above your level. Would you be willing to recruit him? Alternatively, assuming this person is mediocre or even a bad candidate, should you oppose him? Without the tenure system, each new fellow is your competitor that might replace you on some day in future. Expecting this possibility, you are more likely to select a person that is not as good as you and reject a person stronger than you. As each incumbent professor chooses someone worse than himself, the quality of the school becomes worse and worse. However, with the tenure system, you have no worry that newly recruited exceptional people will drive you out, so your incentive to tell a lie decreases significantly. Therefore, the tenure system is advantageous for the selection of exceptional talents.

The second system is the bottom-out system. The tenure system alone might be insufficient. After all, comparing relative performance is also a type of competition. Even if you do not need to leave, a more outstanding professor in the department will reduce your relative status. However, under the bottom-out system, if the academic success of your department ranks poorly over the years, then the whole department will be eliminated. If this happened, you must find new job somewhere else (in this case, the tenure system does not guarantee your job security). In this way, the higher the performance of the new fellow is, the more secure your position is. You have an interest in selecting exceptionally talented people.

In aggregate, the faculty system is designed with two primary goals: First, making applicants tell the truth; second, make the selectors tell the truth. Only when both goals are achieved can universities have outstanding faculty.[21]

Notes

1 Many scholars have contributed to this field. In 2007, Hurwicz (University of Minnesota), Maskin (Princeton Institute for Advanced Study), and Myerson (University of

Chicago) received the Nobel Memorial Prize in Economics for their innovative work in this field. Their contributions appeared in Hurwicz (1960, 1972); Maskin (1999); Laffont and Maskin (1979); Maskin and Riley (1984, 1985); Myerson (1979, 1983); Myerson and Satterthwaite (1983); etc. Vickery (1961); and Mirrlees (1971) was the earliest literature on mechanism design theory. For this contribution, they both received the 1997 Nobel Memorial Prize in Economics. See Garg, Narahari, and Gujar (2008).

2 For the classical literature, see Myerson (1979).

3 Our assumption about the probability people get ill is obviously excessive. We made this assumption only to explain the issue.

4 Because the previous example was only used to explain the problem, the disparity between the numbers in this assumption is greater.

5 The reader can find analysis of price discrimination in any microeconomics textbook.

6 The marginal utilities for low-demand consumers are 10, 6, 4, and 3; and the marginal utilities for high-demand consumers are 20, 12, 8, and 6.

7 Because the seller is a monopolist, there is no surplus left to consumers.

8 For a more detailed discussion of the two-part tariff, see Tirole (1988). The two-part tariff is a special case of more general non-linear price determination. The whole book of Wilson (1993) is devoted to non-linear price determination.

9 See Varian (1989).

10 This example is taken from Tirole (1988).

11 This method is also common in today's Internet Age. For example, IBM intentionally reduced the speed of the Laser Printer E from ten pages per minute to five pages per minute so that people who want a faster printer have to pay more money. Intel's 386SX microprocessor was a scaled-down version of an existing microprocessor. The China Postal Service is so slow for standard service that people have to use its EMS for urgent shipments. Shapiro and Varian (1998) provided various examples of this type pricing policy in information industry.

12 Chapter 11 will be devoted to the principal-agent model.

13 When the dual-track price system was implemented in China in the middle of 1980s, the market price of steel was about ¥1,000 per ton, much higher than the official price of ¥600. Sales representatives were not willing to sell at the market price. If they sold steel according to the market price, they lost their opportunities for kickbacks. If they sold at the planned price of ¥600, then they could charge a fee for the favor.

14 Of course, these four types of auctions can have different variations and combinations. See Klemperer (2004); Milgrom (2004); and Rasmusen (2006).

15 See Klemperer (2004, Chapter 2) and the related cited literature.

16 See Clarke (1971) and Groves (1973). Mueller (2003, Chapter 8) has detailed discussion about preference revelation mechanisms for public goods.

17 Under this mechanism, the tax for public goods is purely designed to make people tell the truth, so it is an "incentive tax". To this end, distribution of the gains from taxation cannot influence the incentive to tell the truth. The simplest method is to throw away these tax revenues, but this means the outcome is not a Pareto optimal (Groves and Ledyard, 1977). Luckily, the amount of these types of incentive taxes decrease as the number of voters increases (Tideman and Tullock, 1976). In other words, the more voters there are, the less incentive taxes must be collected. See Mueller (2003, Chapter 8).

18 Weiying Zhang (1997) has a simple but systematic introduction to Mirrlees' Theory of Optimum Income Taxation.

19 See Weiying Zhang (2012).

20 Traditionally, the tenure system is believed to protect academic freedom. Carmichael (1988) believed the tenure system provided incumbent professors an incentive to tell the truth when selecting new faculty members. For more discussion related to the tenure system, see McPherson and Schapiro (1999) and Chen and Lee (2009).

21 This is one of the primary goals of Peking University's faculty system reforms in 2003, of which the author of this book was one of major designers. See Weiying Zhang (2012).

11 Moral hazard and corruption

The most basic reason corruption occurs is asymmetric information about relevant actions. Theoretical research on asymmetric information of actions is called "principal-agent theory" or moral hazard theory.

In Economics, any relationship where the behavior of one person influences the interests of another person can be called a principal-agent relationship. The person with private information is called the agent, and the person without private information is called the principal.

There are four causes of the principal-agent issue: (1) A conflict exists between the interest of the principal and the agent; (2) there is asymmetric information and the principal has difficulty observing the agent's behavior; (3) the agent is risk-averse; or (4) the agent's capacity for liability is limited.

Conflicts of interest alone might not be sufficient to cause the principal-agent problem. If the principal can fully observe the agent's behavior, the agent is risk-neutral, or the agent's capacity for responsibility is not limited, then the principal-agent problem can also easily be resolved.

The primary issue in principal-agent theory research is the design of incentive contracts for the agent. Incentive contracts face a dilemma between incentives and insurance. The optimal contract must balance incentives and insurance.

The optimal intensity of incentives is determined by four factors: (1) The degree output depending on the agent's effort; (2) the degree of output uncertainty; (3) the degree of the agent's risk aversion; and (4) the agent's responsiveness to incentives.

Comparisons of relative performance improve incentive contracts, but might also lead to agents colluding with or undermining each other.

The contradiction between performance-based rewards and meritocracy means that incentive methods must be diversified. The "official standard" was actually homogenization of incentives. Not only did it severely distort resource allocation, it also harmed social harmony.

When an agent assumes multiple duties, the incentives for one must not come at the expense of incentives for another. This is the most difficult problem faced by incentive mechanism design in real life. This problem is especially serious in university and government organizations.

When it is difficult to effectively incentivize government officials, supervision is the only option. However, if government officials have excessive power, supervision will also not be effective. Therefore, to resolve the source of the corruption problem, government power must be reduced by establishing the rule of law and a democratic system.

Section one: speaking on corruption

Corruption is currently a very common phenomenon and is an issue most people care about strongly. What exactly is corruption? Simply stated, corruption can be defined as misuse of public or delegated power for private gain. From ancient times to the present, in places that public power has existed, so too has corruption. There are many famous corrupt officials in Chinese history, such as Liu Jin, Yan Song, Wei Zhongxian, Heshen, etc., of which Heshen's family wealth was worth 230,000 silver taels.[1] This corruption all happened within government, and can be considered political corruption. Political corruption takes many forms. The bribes taken by officials in government organizations every day is one form. In electoral politics, political contributions are also corrupt behavior. Corruption is not specifically an individual receiving some type of direct benefit. When a bureaucrat exercises public power that favors certain people that have special relationships with him, instead of exercising power according to legal procedures, it is political corruption.[2]

In addition to politics, public power is also misused in commercial relationships. For public companies that are listed, shareholders are dispersed, so without strong supervision, managers will commit corrupt behavior. In the process of operating a company, managers may steal assets or serve their own personal interests through false accounts or insider trading. The 2002 "Enron Affair" in America was a case of listed company management corruption. In China, corrupt behavior related to listed companies can be considered a given, such as false accounts, packaged listings, power-money transactions, etc., without even considering corrupt behavior within the company. Internal corruption may occur as a small detail or link, such as a purchasing agent for a supermarket taking a kickback or the sales person suppressing the price and taking the difference. These are all commercial corruption.

Behavior that misuses public power also occurs in academic circles. For example, in the process of evaluating academic credentials, relationships determine professor and assistant professor promotions, article publication in academic journals, and the distribution of research funding, instead of output quality or applicant's performance. These types of behavior are all academic corruption.

In smaller scales, such as within a household, corruption will also exist. As soon as a household exceeds two people, some type of public power will exist. If one person occupies an excessive amount of household funds, it can count as household corruption.

Of course, the most serious corruption occurs within government organizations. The more public power an organization has, the more serious the corruption problem will be. Transparency International is a global anti-corruption nongovernmental organization headquartered in Berlin specialized in researching corruption issues in world politics.[3] In its 2004 report, it listed modern examples of relatively large cases of corruption related to heads of government. The relevant data are reproduced in Table 11.1.

From the table, we can see that former Indonesian President Suharto, in office for 31 years, was accused of embezzling between $15 billion and $35 billion, while Indonesia's 2001 per capita GDP was only $695. Former Philippine President Marcos, in office for 14 years, embezzled between $5 billion and $10 billion. Former president of Zaire, Mobutu Sese Seko, in office for 32 years, embezzled $5 billion. Nigeria's former president, Sani Abacha, in office only five years, is reported to have embezzled between $2billion and $5 billion. Serbia/ Yugoslavia's former president, Slobodan Milosevic, ruling only ten years, embezzled $1 billion. Haitian President Jean-Claude Duvalier, in office for 15 years, embezzled between $300 million and $800 million. Former Peruvian President Alberto Fujimori, in office for 10 years, embezzled $600 million. Former Ukrainian Prime Minister Pavlo Lazarenko, only in office for one year, embezzled between $114 million and $200 million. Former Nicaraguan President Arnoldo Alemán embezzled $100 million. Former Philippine President Estrada embezzled between $78 million and $80 million. The evidence for these figures has been verified. From these examples, we can see how significant political corruption is.

What has been the most core root cause of various types of corruption? Stated simply, it is information asymmetry. The reader may ask: Why is the degree of

Table 11.1 A List of Corruption Amounts of Government Heads

head of government	Presidency	accused amount of corruption (USD)	domestic per capita GDP of 2001 (USD)
Suharto	President of Indonesia 1967–1998	15 billion– 35 billion	695
Ferdinand Marcos	President of Philippines 1972–1986	5 billion– 10 billion	912
Mobutu	President of Zaire 1965–1997	5 billion	99
Sani Abacha	President of Nigeria 1983–1998	2 billion– 5 billion	319
Slobodan Milosevic	President of Serbia/ Yugoslavia 1989–2000	1 billion	N/A
Jean-Claude Duvalier	President of Haiti 1971–1986	300 million– 800 million	460
Fujimori	President of Peru 1990–2000	600 million	2051
Lazarenko	President of Ukraine 1996–1997	114 million– 200 million	766
Arnoldo Aleman	President of Nicaragua 1997–2002	100 million	490
Joseph Estrada	President of the Philippines 1998–2001	78 million– 80 million	912

Source: *Global Corruption Report* 2004, p. 13.

corruption different in different countries? There are many reasons, such as the degree of economic development, culture, morals, political systems, etc., but the underlying reason is differences in information asymmetry. Different countries have designed different systems to resolve this issue. The degree of political transparency is very important, but actually the significance of political transparency is that it resolves the issue of information asymmetry. The democratic system helps to increase the degree of political transparency. Similarly, the freedom of the press is also very important, because if the press is free, the transmission of information will be rapid, and the restraints on officials will be relatively strong.

As pointed out in Chapter 8, informational asymmetry can be differentiated by time into ex-ante information asymmetry and ex-post information asymmetry. In the previous three chapters, we analyzed ex-ante information asymmetry. Ex-post information asymmetry refers to the behavior of one party being unobservable by another party. Ex-post information asymmetry can easily lead to corrupt behavior (moral hazard).[4] In the course of public affairs, certain behavior of the people that hold or exercise public power cannot be effectively observed by beneficiaries – such as the general public, stakeholders, or someone else related to the behavior – which causes serious information asymmetry. We can use the principal-agent theory to analyze this problem.[5]

Section two: the principal-agent problem

2.1 The definitions

We will first discuss the legal meaning of principals and agents. The laws related to principals and agents refer to a type of contractual relationship.[6] Assume that Party A signs a contract with Party B authorizing Party B to exercise some power or engage in some type of activity in the name of Party A. At that point, they have formed a type of principal-agent relationship, with Party A being the principal and Party B being the agent. If you want to litigate and hire a lawyer, the lawyer is your agent and will represent you in court. The most basic legal quality of this type of principal-agent relationship is that the principal must take responsibility for the actions of the agent. In other words, the costs or benefits of the results caused by the agent's behavior to a large degree belong to the principal. When litigating, if the ruling is not in favor of the plaintiff or defender, it is the principal that loses, not the lawyer acting as agent. If the court decides that the defendant is guilty and must serve prison time, it is the defendant that goes to prison, not the lawyer. The consequence of the agent's behavior is important to the principal. Both form a type of liability relationship.[7]

The concept of principals and agents in Economics is much broader than in the legal sense. In Economics, as long as there is any type of relationship in which the actions of one party influences interests of another party, it forms a principal-agent relationship. For example, after you purchase automobile insurance, the degree you take care of your car influences the interests of the insurance company. If you park your car without locking your door, the probability of car theft increases, so the likelihood of payment by the insurance company increases, which influences the interests of the insurance company. Your relationship with the insurance company is called a principal-agent relationship in which you are the agent and the insurance company is the principal. In an enterprise, the behavior of employees may influence the interests of the owner. When employees slack off, the profitability will decrease, so the interests of the owner will suffer. There is a principal-agent relationship between employees and owners. Further, the reason that the actions of one party will influence the interests of another party is related to information asymmetry. If information was symmetric, in theory each party could sign a complete contract that stipulate every possible action for every circumstance. Each action would be compensated accordingly, so all issues could be resolved by this complete contract. Because of this, when there is information asymmetry, the informed party is called an agent and the uninformed party is called the principal.

From this perspective, principal-agent relationships are common in society and throughout government, companies, and personal relationships. The government can be understood as an agent of the people, similar to how we often say that government is the servant of the people. The actions of any government official will influence the interests of the common people, but it is difficult for the common people to monitor the officials. So there is a type of principal-agent relationship between the common people and government officials.

The principal-agent relationship within companies is one of the most researched issues in Economics. When ownership and management are separate, the shareholders are principals. They elect the director, who in relation to the shareholder is the agent. The Board of Directors appoints the General Manager and the CEO, who become agents of the Board of Directors. The General Manager and CEO are responsible to the Board of Directors and the Board of Directors is responsible to the shareholders.

A principal-agent relationship also exists between instructors and students. If students do not study hard during the school and not perform well after graduation, they will damage the instructor's reputation. Similarly, if the instructor does not teach effectively, the students time will be wasted, and their interests will be harmed. From this perspective, they are a mutual principal-agent relationship, similar to a partnership.

The causes of principal-agent problems can be summed up in four types. The first cause is the existence of conflicts of interest between the principal and the agent. The most optimal choice for the agent may not be the most optimal choice for the principal, such as an action that is good for the manager but not good for the stakeholder. The second cause is information asymmetry. It is difficult for the principal to observe the actions of the agent. The third cause is that the agent may be risk-averse. The fourth cause is that the agent's liability capacity is limited. Conflicts of interest may not be the only cause of principal-agent problems. If the principal can fully observe the actions of the agent, the agent is not risk averse, or the agent has an unlimited capacity for liability, then principal-agent problems can be resolved easily.

We study the principal-agent issue in order to understand the reasons these conflicts happen and how to resolve them. Simply put, we want to know how to make the agent be willing to serve the interests of the principal. We want to know how to make politicians serve the people and which incentive mechanisms will guarantee that they do not abuse power or how to make managers serve the interests of shareholders and not misuse their powers. This is an issue of incentive mechanism design. Tests and student evaluations are a type of incentive mechanism in this principal-agent relationship. Instructors use tests as a means to make students have an interest in and motivation to study. Student evaluations of instructors are a constraint on the instructor to teach well.

2.2 Conflicts of interest

Conflicts of interest between principals and agents is a primary reason for principal-agent problems to occur. Without conflicts of interest problems would not occur. Let us take a simple example, as shown in Table 11.2(a). The agent has two choices. If the first choice is taken, the principal receives payoff of 100 units, and the agent receives payoff of 20 units. If the second choice is taken, the principal receives 200 units, and the agent receives 50. Added together, the total payoffs from both choices is 120 and 250 units, respectively.

According to Table 11.2(a), from the social optimum perspective, the second choice brings about the greatest gain. Gain can be understood as the profit of the principal and the benefits brought to the agent by control rights. In this example, the best choice for the principal is also best choice for the agent. If the agent was allowed to choose, he would choose the second option, which also brings about the greatest benefit for the principal. Therefore, a conflict of interest does not exist, nor is there an incentive problem.

Next, we will examine a different example, as shown in Table 11.2(b). The principal's gain is still 100 units in the first option and 200 units in the second option, but the agent will gain 50 units from the first option and 20 units from the second option. At this point, the agent's best choice is the first option, but the second option is a better choice for the principal. In this situation, we need to design a mechanism to give the agent an incentive to choose the second option instead of the first.

Table 11.2(a) No Conflict of Interest

	option I	*option II*
principal's gains	100	200
agent's gains	20	50
total	120	250

Table 11.2(b) With Conflict of Interest

	option I	*option II*
principal's gains	100	200
agent's gains	50	20
total	150	220

This type of conflict can explain many different phenomena. For example, when the government wants to build an expressway, the route the expressway takes is a selection issue. From an economic viewpoint, if the whole people are the principal – meaning we will use central government finances to fund the project, we must consider the path this expressway will follow and the best option for the whole people, assuming that we can define the interests of the whole people. As shown in Figure 11.1, between Point A and Point B, the best choice is Path (a) because the distance is the shortest, the cost is lowest, and the construction period is also the shortest.

However, from the viewpoint of an official, another path may be better. For example, the official responsible for this project may be from a town in Point C, which Path (a) will bypass. People from his hometown will persuade him to choose Path (b) because it is best for his hometown. By implementing Path (b), the public investment will increase, which harm the majority of the whole people. Actually, any affair involving the minority taking advantage of power granted by the majority is in essence corruption.

This type of conflict of interest could be called an overt conflict. Another type of conflict of interest is hidden conflict, in which the effort of the agent is a variable controlled by the agent and the principal has no way of observing the agent's effort. For example, a manager could slack off or work hard, and the enterprise's expected profit will decrease or increase accordingly. At this point, there is a conflict. From the shareholder's perspective, or from the principal's perspective, of course the manager should put in effort. However, the manager's effort is costly, so if there is not enough incentive, he may not be willing to work hard. This is a classic example of hidden conflict.

In the United States, people buy and sell houses through a real estate broker because a real estate agent has specialized knowledge and understands market conditions. The seller is the principal and the real estate broker is the agent. The research of Levitt and Syverson (2005) showed that for $300,000 homes, if the house belongs to the broker, the sales price will be $50,000 higher. We can see that the interests of the agent and principal are not completely aligned. The broker's commission is 2%, so for each $50,000 sold by the principal, the broker only receives $1,000, but this requires the broker to advertise more and wait longer for a better buyer. Waiting for better buyers is a costly activity for the broker that cannot be justified by $1,000, so the broker will help the principal sell the house at the first acceptable price.[8]

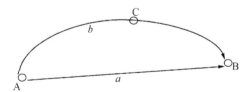

Figure 11.1 Road Construction Map

2.2 Information asymmetry

We previously discussed that conflicts of interest alone will not necessarily lead to the agency problem. Assume that the principal can observe the behavior of the agent. The optimal choice for the principal or society could be enforced with enforceable contracts. In our prior example, assume that the principal could observe the agent's choice. In that case, there is an easy solution. The principal could require the agent choose the second option, and if the agent chooses the first option, he will be punished severely. So, for the best of his interest, the agent will certainly choose the second option. At this point, there is no conflict of interest. This also means that as long as the asymmetric information problem does not exist, conflicts do not constitute a serious threat.

This entails the second major reason for principal-agent problems: Information asymmetry.

Generally speaking, principals can only observe results, not behavior of the agent. The observed results are not an accurate measure of behavior. Our previous example was very simple because actions and results correspond with each other, but this is not always the case in reality. The reason is that any type of result is caused by many different factors, of which the action of an agent is only one. In addition to subjective factors, many objective factors outside the control of the agent play a role. The Chinese often say, "Man proposes, God disposes". We can use a simply mathematical formula to represent this: $y = a + \varepsilon$.

Here, the result of actions is y. In addition to the agent's effort a, y also depends of another external factor ε; thus, this "luck" is not completely controlled by the agent. A farmer's output not only relies on the work of the farmer, but also the weather. A farmer might work harder to make the crops grow higher, but if at harvest time there are suddenly multiple days of rainy weather, the whole year's harvest is gone. On the contrary, some people may be lazy, but because of favorable weather throughout the year, the harvest may still be good. If we only look at output, we cannot determine if the farmer is hardworking or not. In other words, if we can only see the result, we cannot always infer the actions. When a large state-owned enterprise reports high profits, can we conclude that the manager did a good job? No. It may have been that a huge amount of infrastructure construction took place in the last year, and this enterprise, which produces steel, made money on rapidly rising prices. The high profits are not due to the manager's efforts, but instead were influenced by macro-economic factors. If there was only one factor, then y would equal a, or there was a certain relationship between them so that given y we could infer a accurately. It would not matter if we knew a, because as long as we knew y, we could naturally know the value of a. From this perspective, the reason that behavior is difficult to observe is because the results we observe are caused by many comprehensive factors.

We can depict the relationship between actions and results in Figure 11.2.

In Figure 11.2, the horizontal axis represents the agent's effort (which here is taken as a continuous variable). The vertical axis represents the results, which we call outputs. The upward sloping solid line is the expected output which increases

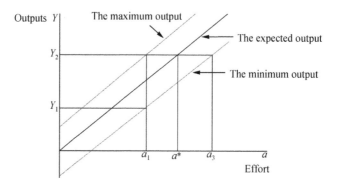

Figure 11.2 Output and Effort

along with effort. In our previous example, ε is an exogenous variable. Its average value is zero, but its variance is greater than zero. Even if the average value of output equals a, meaning it is equal to effort, actual output is influenced by external factor ε; thus, it falls between the two dotted lines. The two dotted lines represent the range of ε. Assume that the principal observes output y_2. The agent could have possibly chosen either effort a_1 or a_3, or any level of effort in between. The principal does not know exactly if the agent was lazy or hardworking.

2.3 Risk attitudes

Even if information is asymmetric, but the agent is risk neutral, then resolving the principal-agent problem is very easy. Contracting is one method. Contracting involves the agent paying a fixed fee to the principal and then claiming any surplus output. In this point, it is like the agent is working for himself, so a conflict of interest does not exist. This specific mechanism is explained in Figure 11.3.

Figure 11.3 is similar to 11.2, but here we have added the cost curve of the agent's effort. According to this curve, the higher the agent's effort, the higher the cost is also. In the contractor system, the principal obtains a fixed gain b_0 as shown in Figure 11.3, and the surplus is claimed by the agent. The agent's expected income is the expected output minus b_0. We can see that a^* represents the social optimal effort level because at this point the distance between the cost curve and the expected output curve is the greatest. The greatest distance also means the greatest profit. In mathematical terms, the slope of the expected output curve is precisely equal to the slope of the cost curve at that point, meaning marginal cost equals marginal gain. Under a full contractor system, the agent's expected gain equals $a - b_0$, with the optimal choice being a^*. This means that the individual optimal effort level for a manager under the contractor system also maximizes society's total profit. The optimal choice for the individual is also the optimal choice for society. However, if we assume that the manager dislikes risk, then our above conclusion does not stand. Later, we will further analyze this point.[9]

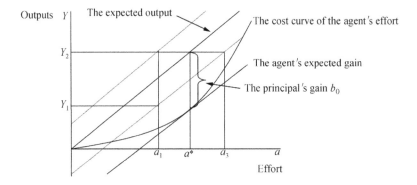

Figure 11.3 Effort and Output Under the Contractor System

2.4 Limited liability

In situations where the agent is risk neutral, the contractor system can resolve the incentive issue in principal-agent relationships. However, this is conditional. If the agent's capacity of liability is limited, the contractor system is unworkable. For instance, during state-owned enterprise reform, even if a person was willing to contract with a large enterprise and guarantee ¥500 million in profit, the government still did not dare to contract out the enterprise. The reason was that if the enterprise was not able to earn ¥500 million, he did not have enough wealth to pay compensation.

In general, when agents do not have the capacity for being fully accountable, a full contractor system cannot be implemented, and agents cannot assume complete liability. This point is very important. We can imagine that if each of us had an unlimited capacity to assume liability, society would be very simple. For example, when signing an employment contract, if the agent had the capacity to assume any liability, then the contract could state that only after profit (or some other indicator the principal cared about) reached a certain point would the principal pay the agent a certain amount. If the target was not hit, the agent would compensate the principal for a certain amount. In this case, the agent would be fully motivated. However, not everyone in society is wealthy enough to assume unlimited liability, so many systems and rules are necessary to restrict behavior. For example, why is a passenger not allowed to take firecrackers onto the train? Because he does not have the capacity to assume this liability for potential damage. If firecrackers exploded, the carrier would die as well, so how would he be able to assume liability? Alternatively, even if the carrier survived, his wealth was not enough to cover all losses. Therefore, this type of behavior is prohibited.[10]

Capacity for liability is actually related to risk attitudes. As a person's wealth increases, his capacity for liability increases. His risk attitude will change with his wealth. He may not detest risk as much. According to Optimal Risk Sharing Theory,[11] without incentive problems, if both the principal and the agent are risk-averse, risk should be shared between the principal and agent. If the principal is risk neutral and the agent is risk averse, the risk should be assumed entirely by the principal and the agent should receive fixed compensation. Optimal risk sharing means that wealthy business owners should assume the full risk and employees should receive fixed compensation.

Certain systems in our society are designed to allocate risk. Mutual assistance organizations in rural areas are based on this kind of principle. Imagine the two of us hunt rabbits, with two possible results: (1) With good luck, we capture six rabbits; or (2) with bad luck, we do not capture anything. If the probability of these two situations is equal, then the average result is three rabbits. The actual situation may be that we capture six rabbits and each of us gets three, or with bad luck, each person would get nothing. If we always split the result fifty-fifty, each individual's expected payoff is 1.5 rabbits. Assume that I am poor and you are wealthy. If today we do not capture any rabbits, I have nothing to eat, but you still have numerous rabbits in your home. At this point, I would bargain to make an offer with you that regardless if we capture a rabbit or not, you would guarantee me one rabbit. If no rabbit is captured, you would give me one of the rabbits in your home, but if we captured six rabbits, you would give me one, and the remaining five would be yours entirely. I would be willing to do this because as a poor person, I am risk averse, so I prefer to be insured: Regardless of luck or not, I will have a rabbit to eat. You will also accept my proposal, because as a wealthy person, you do not fear risk. On average, you will receive two rabbits per day, instead of only 1.5 rabbits. With this arrangement, the wealthy person provides the poor person with insurance. The 0.5 rabbits paid per day on average is the insurance premium. This simple example explains optimal risk sharing. According to this theory, the most risk-averse person should be insured by the least risk-averse person.

Section three: incentive mechanism design

3.1 The conflict between incentives and insurance

Insurance can increase each person's welfare, but if information is asymmetric, optimal risk allocation will lead to new issues. In our rabbit hunting exercise, if both parties agreed to the poor person receiving one rabbit regardless if rabbits were captured or not, there would be an optimal allocation of risk. The intelligent reader may have realized that if hunting rabbits requires the efforts of both parties, perhaps the poor person may no longer be willing to put in as much effort. His degree of effort is unrelated to his gains, so he has no incentive. With fully insurance, incentives do not exist.

The strongest incentive is for the agent to assume full risk, because when the liability is assumed entirely by the agent, the agent will put forth the most effort. From the perspective of risk allocation, however, this may not be the optimal arrangement. This creates a conflict between insurance and incentives. The more insurance there is, the less incentives there are; in order to increase incentives, insurance must be reduced. The optimal incentivized contractual arrangement is to find a balance between insurance and incentives. If risk is assumed entirely by the agent, incentives are high, but the cost of assuming that risk is too high. On the contrary, if he is given a fixed wage, he has insurance but no incentive. This is an issue that exists in all organizations.

We can use car insurance as an example to analyze the conflict between incentives and insurance. We can rationally assume that insurance companies are risk-neutral, because they have multiple customers, so according to the Law of Large Numbers they can have a certain income.[12] The optimal insurance between any individual and an insurance company is 100% insurance. This means that if you spend ¥100,000 on a car and lose it, the insurance company should compensate you fully so that you can buy a new car without suffering any loss. What is the optimal incentive? The optimal incentive is to not provide you with any insurance. If you lose the car, the loss is yours entirely, so you have an incentive to take good care of it, to the point where you may watch it from the window every night instead of sleeping. Neither of these proposals is optimal. The actual incentive mechanism must be designed to only provide partial insurance. Of course, actual insurance contracts also use many other incentive mechanisms. One type of incentive mechanism is to match each year's insurance premium with prior settlements. If there are no claims this year, next year your premiums will go down. If in the next year there are no claims, premiums will decrease further. However, as soon as there is a claim, your insurance premium will increase. This is actually an incentive mechanism because the more you take care of your car, the less insurance premiums you will pay over the long term.

The difficult choice between insurance and incentives also exists for liability in medical accidents. The probability of medical accidents occurring is related to the effort and ability of the doctor. From the perspective of insurance, it is best if the doctor as an individual does not assume liability for medical accidents. However, the doctor would not be driven to reduce the probability of medical accident occurrences. From the incentive perspective, it is best if the doctor assumes complete liability for accidents. However, the risk for the doctor would be too great, causing him to be unwilling to do risky operations, or in serious circumstances, be unwilling to be a doctor. Therefore, the way in which accident liability is split between the doctor, patient, hospital, and insurance company is an important issue.

From here, our discussions of principal-agent relationships have entered into the incentive mechanism design issue. The principal designs a contract for the agent to incentivize and restrict the actions of the agent so that the agent and principal's interests are aligned to the greatest extent possible. The rules and limitations that make up the content of this contract are an issue of incentive mechanism design. Agents have their own interests, so the incentive mechanism is like a policy and the agent's behavior is like a countermeasure. When designing an incentive mechanism, the principal must predict the type of action the agent will implement given a certain policy. Although the principal cannot directly observe the agent's behavior, the principal can use indirect methods to guide the agent to choose the behavior that the principal desires.

An incentive mechanism's design is actually a dynamic game process. First, the principal designs a contract, then the agent can choose to accept the contract or not. If the contract is accepted, he again chooses his actions. The final result is allocated according to the rules of the initial contract. According to the dynamic game theory that we learned previously, we can use backward induction to analyze this game. When designing this mechanism, the principal can predict the agent's choice of behavior given certain conditions, and then determine the best contract. Figure 11.4 displays contract design's game process.

The contract designed by the principal must be effective in the end, but this is conditional. If after designing the contract, no one has an incentive to respect it, the incentive mechanism is ineffective. First, the principal must make a credible commitment. Because contracts are enforced after the fact, if the principal does not have a reputation and the contract is unenforceable, naturally the agent will not choose his own behavior according to the requirements of the contract. Next, the agent must be willing to accept this contract. Now, for simplicity, we will assume that these conditions have already been satisfied.

Figure 11.5 is the example we used to analyze conflicts of interest (Table 11.2(b)). We will use it to analyze contract design by the principal. Temporarily, we will not consider the issue of risk. The agent has two types of choices. Incentivized contract design is limited to the option that shares profit between the principal and agent. Assume that x represents the share of monetary income that the agent will receive according to the contract. Every proportion x that the principal proposes is a contract. For the agent, if he accepts this contract, he must decide between the first or second type of action. If he chooses the first action, as the

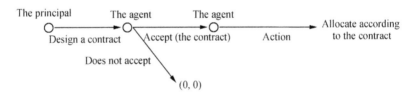

Figure 11.4 The Contract Design Flow

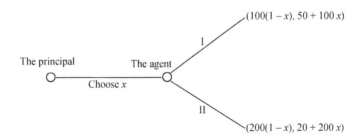

Figure 11.5 The Principal-Agent Game

agent he will receive 50 units of control benefit and $100x$ units' worth of monetary income. The principal's final income is $100(1 - x)$. Similarly, the diagram shows the payout if the agent chooses the second action.

We can use backwards induction to solve this dynamic game. First, we will examine the agent. Given contract x, how will the agent determine his action? If he chooses the first option, he will receive $50 + 100x$; if he chooses the second option, he will receive $20 + 200x$. It is easy to calculate that when $x \geq 0.3$, the agent has an incentive to choose the second action.[13] However, if $x < 0.3$, the agent will choose the first option and not the second. Next, we will examine the principal's choice. How should he determine x? The principal wants to design the contract in a way that will maximize his interests. According to our previous analysis, the principal hopes that the agent will choose the second option. This means that the contract must be designed in a way that the agent's gain from choosing the first option is less than the gain from choosing the second option. Naturally, $x = 0.3$ is the principal's optimal choice. This is the perfect equilibrium of this game's subgame.

3.2 Incentive intensity

Below, we will discuss a more complex example to explain the principles that the optimal incentive contract must follow. Assume that the output depends on the agent's action a as well as a random factor ε, thus $Y = a + \varepsilon$. Further assume that the distribution of ε is $N(0, \sigma^2)$, thus ε is a normal distribution with mean zero and variance σ^2. The monetary equivalent cost function of the agent's effort is $\frac{b}{2}a^2$, with b representing the coefficient of effort's degree of difficulty. The agent is risk-averse. His utility function is $u = -\exp(-\rho x)$, with ρ being his absolute risk aversion parameter. The larger ρ is, the more the agent dislikes risk. The principal provides the agent with a linear incentive contract $c = m + xY$, with m being a fixed wage and x being the agent's share of output. Optimal contract design is the selection of parameters m and x.

In this contract, x can be understood as the incentive intensity. If x equals 1, it is a contractor system with the strongest incentive (at this point, m is negative representing the contractor fee paid by the agent.) If x equals zero, it is a fixed wage system, so incentives are absent. What factors should x rely on? Through mathematical calculation, we can determine the optimal incentive as a mathematical expression:[14]

$$x = \frac{1}{\left(1 + b\rho\sigma^2\right)}$$

This formula includes the four factors that influence the intensity of incentives.

The first factor is the degree that output depends on the agent's efforts (because we assume that the marginal output of effort is 1, this factor is not reflected in the formula). The greater the agent's marginal contribution, the greater the share he should share, so the related incentive should be stronger. This explains why in many large organizations, incentives for management are much stronger than incentives for ordinary employees. The success or failure of an enterprise is impacted by the actions of management much more than ordinary employees.

The second factor is output's uncertainty factor σ^2. The more uncertain output is, or the more difficult it is to predict, the weaker incentives are. The third factor is the agent's degree of risk aversion ρ. The more an agent dislike risk, the weaker incentives should be. From the incentive formula, we can see that if the agent is risk neutral (meaning ρ equals zero), the optimal incentive is $x = 1$, which is a full contractor system. If ρ is greater than zero, the full contractor system is not the optimal choice. The fourth and final factor is b, the agent's degree of reaction to incentives. The agent's degree of reaction is the converse of the pain coefficient. The smaller b is, the stronger reactions are.[15]

We can use the above formula to analyze the insurance contracts. A characteristic of insurance contracts is that the more your behavior influences the occurrence of an accident, the stronger the insurance company incentivizes you, meaning the coverage ratio of insurance should be lower. Moral hazard does not exist for some behaviors. For example, a policy holder would take care of his eyes regardless of insured or not, so moral hazard does not exist for eye insurance. Car insurance is different. A car is not part of your body, so it has much less significance for the policy holder. Therefore, car insurance must include an incentive factor.

The basic conclusions we proposed of the incentive intensity is not only limited to individual incentives, but also organizational incentives. Incentive issues also exist between different organizations, such as an automobile factory incentivizing its component suppliers to reduce cost is an incentive issue. The cost of components is determined by the supplier's efforts, but also is impacted by external factors outside of the supplier's control (such as changes in raw materials prices or technological improvements). Contracts between automobile manufacturers and component suppliers often stipulate basic prices and the degree that prices increase with costs. If prices are entirely fixed, component suppliers assume full risk in the raw materials market, but have the greatest incentive to reduce cost. Alternatively, if prices adjust fully with costs, component suppliers do not face any risk (because the risk is assumed by the automobile factory), so they have no incentive to reduce costs. In Japan, the smaller a component supplier is, the higher the ratio of product prices changing with costs. The reason is that smaller suppliers are more risk-averse than larger suppliers do not. Supplier contracts embody the balance between incentives and insurance.[16]

We know that the reason incentives are an issue is because the principal cannot observe the agent's behavior. Naturally, if there are other signals that allow the principal to better predict the agent's behavior, then the incentive mechanism can be improved. If this type of information exists, using this type of information can both reduce the risk assumed by the agent and increase incentives at the same time.

Optimal incentive contracts depend on observable information. This is a general conclusion. In our previous analysis, the principal's contract compensation relied on output Y, not because output itself is important, but because it reveals certain information about effort *a*. We can see from an example that high performance does not necessarily mean compensation should be high. Assume that the agent has two types of effort. The output of high effort could be 100 or 500 and the output of low effort could be 0 or 200. When output is 200, should the agent's income be higher than when the output is 100? The answer is no. An output of 200 tells the principal that the agent certainly slacked off, because an output of 200 would only occur when the agent's effort is low. When output is 100, it means that the agent put in high effort. This example explains that incentivizing employees or an agent depends on the information included in observable variables. In this example, the output variable information can clearly tell the principal whether or not the agent slacked off or not. The optimal incentive contract should be that if the output is 100 or 500, the principal should pay the agent higher compensation, but if output is 200 or 0, the agent should receive less compensation.

3.3 Comparative performance evaluation

The design of incentive mechanisms requires effective information. The extension of this theory leads to the comparative performance evaluation.[17] For comparative performance evaluations, to determine the compensation scheme, the principal does not just look at the absolute value of the agent's output, but instead compare it to the output of other people in similar environments. The reason is that if two agents work in the same or similar environment, comparing two performances can provide more information about each agent's effort. If one person does well and the other does not, then this result is less likely to be an issue of luck. Instead, it is an issue of effort. Sports championships are a kind of comparative performance evaluation. For a specific candidate, the prize is not given based on the absolute speed of the athlete, but instead whether or not he ran faster than the others. Promotions within an organization are a similar mechanism. If there are two sales people, but one has had consistent better sales performance over the years than the other, the first one may be promoted. The key to entrance exams is not your score, but instead the ranking of your score against the scores of others. These actually are all comparative performance evaluations.

The comparative performance evaluation is also the essence of the entire market economy. The success or failure of an enterprise is not determined by the absolute production of a company, but instead it is determined by its relative competitive advantage. Therefore, if there is only one monopoly enterprise in an industry, it can still survive with low efficiency. Only after competition is introduced can the efficiency of the entire industry increase.

Of course, there may be errors during comparisons. If the environment that two people being evaluated is not entirely the same, a direct comparison may be difficult. Other factors may need to be taken into account. For example, if the company wants to promote sales people from various locations, it cannot only use sales revenue ranking as the only promotion metric. The sales revenue of each location is impacted by many factors like market size, culture and local competition, and the difference between different locations can be vast.

In addition to the above issue of scope, comparative performance evaluation may lead to incentive distortions. American Telephone and Telegraph Company (AT&T) had an unwritten rule before it broke up in 1984: The Chief Executive Officer of AT&T was not promoted among vice presidents, but instead was promoted among regional company general managers. This meant that a person that was a vice president could not become CEO. Only regional general managers had this opportunity. Why was the system designed in this way? The reason is that when two people can act in a way that mutually influences the other's performance, it may not be efficient to implement the comparative performance evaluation system. In this case, the comparative performance evaluation would lead agents to not only have an incentive to improve their own performance, but also sabotage their opponent's performance. An organization must inhibit this condition from occurring. One possible explanation of this example is that if vice presidents are promoted, there may be vicious competition between vice presidents, which will lead them to be unwilling to help each other. It would be difficult for regional general managers in New York, Washington, or California to harm each other, so their main priority is to improve their own performance. Generally speaking, if cooperation among agents is important, then in order to incentivize them to cooperate, the incentive mechanism based on comparative performance should not be used.[18]

Comparative performance evaluation also causes another type of distortion: Collusion among agents.[19] For instance, when bonuses were given in state-owned enterprises in the 1980s of China, workers must be ranked according to their performance into first-level, second-level, and third-level. Egalitarianism was not allowed. The actual situation was that members of working groups rotated themselves so that this time A received the first-level bonus and next time B received the first-level bonus until every person had the opportunity to receive the first-level bonus. On the surface it was not egalitarianism, but in reality, it was still egalitarianism. The design of an organization's incentive mechanism should inhibit this type of situation from happening. We know that the larger an organization is, the more difficult collusions are. If an organization only has six agents and bonuses are given monthly, the agents may conspire to rotate each month so that each person has an opportunity to receive a bonus without putting in high effort. However, if this organization had 60 people, would the person that was last in line be willing to wait? Perhaps not, because he would have to wait five years. Whether or not the enterprise or the current rewarding system will still be around after five years is unknown. This is why we say that the larger an organization is, the more difficult it is to conspire. A phenomenon we often see is that when an organization is small, the effect of appraisals is not very good. When there are only two people, determining the first place and second place winner will cause problems. Once an organization becomes larger, appraisals can be implemented. For example, when a real estate company has a few dozen sales people, it could implement a system that eliminates the lowest performer so that each person has an incentive to do his own work well. However, if there are only three of five sales people, the sales people may collude so that incentives will not play a role.

The occurrence of collusion is related to the principal's observability of information and the effectiveness of communication between agents. It may also be related to company culture, because small companies are like a family, so interpersonal relationships are important, whereas people in large enterprises are more distant, so non-interpersonal interaction may be more common.

3.4 Meritocracy and performance-based rewarding

In hierarchical organizations, monetary compensation is only one type of incentive. Another type of incentive mechanism is job promotion. Generally speaking, being in relatively high position not only means better material benefits, but also more power. Most people pursue power, so job promotions have a greater incentive and are a more important incentive mechanism. In reality, some people are more willing to have a lower paying job with more power.

Compared to monetary incentives, job promotions utilize comparative performance evaluation principle to a greater extent. Because positions are scarce, competition for positions is fiercer. The issue of agents "undermining" each other that was described previously is much more serious. I have never heard of anyone being murdered for a bonus, but murdering someone for a promotion in China's officialdom has happened multiple times. There is no need to mention the wars that were started over the right to rule.

Job promotion systems that are based on comparative performance evaluation is a type of reward system that most organizations use. Another principle in job promotions is to promote people based on merit (competence). Sometimes a performance-based rewards system and meritocracy are contradictory. Why? Because different positions require different levels of abilities and morals. Meritocracy promotes a suitable person into a suitable position, whereas a performance-based rewards system promotes the best performer in the current position into a higher position. However, a person that is good in one position may not be competent in a higher position. For example, Comrade Yonggui Chen may have been a good production brigade leader, and even a qualified county party chief, but he was not a qualified Vice Premier.[20] A rewards system often leads to something Management Studies calls the "Peter's principle." It states that in any hierarchical organization, each person will be promoted to his level of incompetence.

The contradiction between performance-based rewards and meritocracy is a big issue faced by many organizations. Diversification of incentives is a means to resolve this issue.[21] In universities, faculty rank is separated from administrative rank. Business enterprises have dual ranks of compensation and management. In this aspect, there are many good examples in Chinese history. As demonstrated by Professor Buke Yan of Peking University in his book *Grade and Position*, the coexistence of grade and position in dynastic China's bureaucratic structure was mainly motivated by solving the contradiction between rewards and meritocracy, with grades rewarding performance, contributions and morality by material compensations and honors, and positions being offered to those who are most suitable and competent.[22] For instance, when a general was victorious in battle, his grade could be raised and he could be given more land, but he may not necessarily be promoted to a higher position.

3.5 *Multi-task and incentives of university faculty*

Now we will examine an issue in the Ivory Tower: Incentives for university professors. We will first look at the characteristics of university faculty. The first characteristic is that they have multiple responsibilities. In our previous analysis, one person did only one thing, so we could use one metric to measure his performance. In reality, many agents have multiple responsibilities. This is also the nature of the work of university faculty. University faculty must teach as well as research, so they have two types of work. Although these two activities complement each other to some extent, they also compete with each other. They complement each other because good research will improve the quality of instruction. They compete with each other because the more time spent on teaching, the less time can be spent on research work. If they were not competitive, and instead only complementary, this issue would be much easier because only one task needs being incentivized and the other would come automatically. Regardless if teaching was incentivized or research was incentivized, both issues could be resolved at the same time. The substitutive relationship between teaching and research is a constraint on university faculty's incentive mechanism.

The second characteristic of university faculty is that not only is it difficult to supervise inputs, it is also difficult to observe outputs. Both rewarding and meritocracy face challenges. Universities require the creativity of faculty, but creativity not only relies on time inputs, but also is an issue of ability. Some research is done well because the researcher is hard-working, but also because the researcher is a genius. Often, the two factors of hard work and genius are not easy to separate. Even if we could fully supervise the time inputs of individual faculty on research and teaching, we still do not know the quality of his inputs, because there is no way to observe a person's thoughts. He may spend all day writing an article, but the quality of the article might be very low. He may also spend all day teaching, but may not have seriously prepared, so students do not enjoy his class. Thus, we cannot make evaluations based on inputs. University faculty must be evaluated on academic performance and output.

However, the next issue to come up is that academic performance and output measures are relatively difficult. It is difficult to establish an objective standard for instruction and research. Of course, in relation to research, instruction can at least be observed, but time must be spent to evaluate lecture syllabus or have students fill out surveys to measure it. You may say that research is also measurable based on the number of published articles. The problem is grasping the quality of articles. Who evaluates the quality of a professor's articles? One method is to track the impact factor of an article, but in many cases, the impact factor of an article is the same as the impact factor of the journal. An influential journal does not represent the influence of an article. There is a discrete phenomenon in the quality of articles in good journals, because not all articles in a good journal are good, just as not all articles in bad journals are bad. There is no correct measurement that can properly evaluate the output of university professors, and there are always some things that cannot be measured.

Whether to use the quantity or quality of academic works as a standard to evaluate research performance has long been a dispute. Although the two cannot be completely separated because there cannot possibly be quality without any quantity, but some people may make an outstanding contribution with only one article. Many Nobel Prize winners relied on one or two articles. Quality is of most importance, but sometimes, there is no way to measure quality.

Even if we were to only look at teaching performance, there are also two different categories. Do we teach knowledge based on text books or do we nurture student's creativity? It may be possible that a professor teaches knowledge very well, but cannot nurture creativity. For the issue of moral education, this is also not easy to measure. Tests can evaluate what a person has learnt – and to some extent can measure ability – but cannot evaluate his morality. Even if we use student's future accomplishments to evaluate faculty, this represents the performance of the whole faculty at a university, not its individual member, let alone the time period during which student achievements are evaluated must be determined. Measuring recent graduates and alumni ten years out of school is very different. Even if the accomplishments of students are a standard, it is not easy to measure. Which type of performance should be used to measure student success? Some students go overseas for further studies, some go into government, some go into business, and some go into academics. These accomplishments are not easily summed, so they cannot measure an instructor's performance. The success of students is also influenced by many other factors that are completely out of a faculty's control.

This issue is very general. In reality, many jobs involve multiple responsibilities. Even a factory worker's production involves quality and quantity. A manager must focus on both this year's profitability and the long-term competitiveness of the business. A salesperson must focus on the current sale as well as providing after-sales service. When one person does multiple things, the biggest challenge is the difference in the level of difficulty of measuring these things. If certain activities are easy to measure and others are not, in order to incentivize that person, only the easily measured aspects can be incentivized. However, sometimes this will cause incentive distortions. The person involved will focus energy on the things that are easily measured and have high incentives, but not on the things that are not easily measured. This may not be good, as shown by experiences of China's middle school education. In China, high school teachers are rewarded according to enrolment rate of their students, such as how many are enrolled by the top universities. As a result, school teachers have little incentive to do character education. This is a distortion of incentives.

At this point, if we want to incentivize agents to focus time and energy on a task that is not easy to measure, one method is to group jobs into positions according to the measurability. The activities that are easily measured should be separated from the activities that are not easily measured and two types should be allocated to different people. Examples would be separating sales and after sales support, day to day business operations and strategy, as well as instruction and research into different positions. Another method is to reduce the incentives for easily measurable tasks.[23] For university faculty, work quantity is relatively easy to measure, but work quality is harder to measure. If faculty compensation was determined by class time, many people would not do research. Alternatively, if we only gave bonuses according to research results, there may be no interest in instruction. If only quantity counted for research, then a professor may cut one article into three articles and publish it in a third-rate journal instead of a first-rate journal. If we want professors to split time evenly between instruction, research, quantity, and quality, then incentives cannot be too great for either one, otherwise the incentive to focus on the others will be damaged.

Because of the difficulty in observing and measuring performance, any obvious incentive cannot possibly be perfect. Perhaps for university professors, an incentive mechanism more important than wages and titles is the reputation mechanism among students and peers. Of course, an effective reputation mechanism cannot be separated from good academic norms and academic culture. Without good academic norms and a healthy academic culture, there will be adverse elimination, so the reputation mechanism cannot play a role.

Section four: the incentives of government officials

4.1 The difficulty of supervising government officials

There are many similarities between the activities of government officials and university faculty, but also considerable differences.

The first characteristic of government is that the people inside it are common agents.[24] They are given power by multiple principals, not just one. Different principals may demand the same government official to do competing or complementary (or even similar) affairs. Principals coordinate the agents' incentives, or individually incentivize the agents. In a large country like China, government bureaucrats have 1.3 billion principals. Having this many principals will lead to the free-rider problem. If an enterprise is owned by a single person, that person will supervise the manager, but if an enterprise is owned by 100 shareholders, then each shareholder will have less incentive to supervise the manager. The supervisor would only receive one percent of the benefit, but pay one hundred percent of the cost, so there will be free-riding among principals. If each person free-rides, then the manager can more easily misuse his power. The government has more principals, so this issue is even more serious. This is the reason that governments are not effectively supervised. Even worse, if there are contradictions between the interests of principals, or they have competing requirements for the agent, then there will be even more difficulties. At this point, each principal hopes that government officials will service their needs and not the needs of others.

The second characteristic of government officials is the same as university faculty in that their work has multiple responsibilities. Government officials do not act on a single task, so balancing each task is a big challenge. Assume we want to evaluate a government official, among the multiple indicators to consider, such as local economic development, environmental protection, sanitation, education, and culture, which is the most important? In the current evaluation system, a government bureaucrat must assume the burden for a shortcoming in any area. This is a reflection of multiple responsibilities.

Additionally, each aspect's performance is difficult to measure. For example, you may believe that gross domestic product is a firm measurement, but local officials may falsify records, which is quite common. Even something like grain output can be falsified. Actually, anything can be falsified by the government. As for the activities of an individual government official, it is difficult to supervise his output and effective input, because even if an official sits in an office all day, you cannot determine if he is thinking about ways to be corrupt or anti-corrupt. Actually, many of the things that consume the time of government bureaucrats are focused on spending more money and getting more power, not the needs of the citizens. This causes incentives for government officials to be very weak. Because there is no way to incentivize officials, supervision is more common. Incentives that are too strong and too weak will both distort government behavior. The difficulty of measurement will also cause incentives to be ineffective. For example, if we evaluate police performance based on the number of arrests, many innocents will end up in prison, but if we evaluate them on the crime rate, many criminal cases will not be recorded.

Without effective means to measure government official's inputs and outputs, there is no way to implement effective incentives. We can only implement procedural supervision and control so that they regulate fewer affairs in a way that clearly defines the things they can and cannot do. Of course, there are also departments within government that supervise officials. However, the question is: Why supervises the supervisors? In China, the Commission for Discipline Inspection supervises other government organs and officials, but who supervises the Commission for Discipline Inspection? You may say that they are supervised by a higher-level Commission for Discipline Inspection, but this chain of supervision always has a top. There is nothing above the central level. For this reason, restrictions on power are extremely important. This is a simple reason for the separation of political power. Governments cannot be supervised the way an enterprise can, so we can only rely on the separation of powers to create checks and balances.

4.2 The corruption equation

One major conclusion of Incentive Theory is: If you cannot supervise him, you can only "bribe" him. This is the so-called Efficiency Wage Theory. The efficiency wage was first proposed by Shapiro and Stiglitz (1984) in the 1980s originally to explain the unemployment issue. It had a major impact on Keynesian macroeconomics. Of course, "bribe" in this case does not refer to illegal bribery, instead it refers to reasonable compensation that incentivizes the agent to not do bad things. Therefore, we understand it as a type of incentive mechanism.

To better understand this theory, we will use some notations. Let us still use employment as an example. Assume that wages are represented by W. If the worker puts in effort, he pays personal cost C. The worker's gain is $W - C$ with normal effort. However, he can also be lazy so that he does not pay cost C and still receive wage W. In this case, his gain is greater than if he were to put in effort. However, laziness may be discovered. Assume that the probability of being discovered is p. Thus, there is only a probability of $1 - p$ that laziness will not be discovered and wage W will be received. As soon as the worker's laziness is discovered, his contract will be terminated. After being terminated, the worker will receive U, which is the market's reservation wage to be earned in an alternative job. Therefore, the expected utility of the worker's laziness is $pU + (1 - p)W$. How high should wages be to incentivize the worker to put in effort? The gain from effort must be greater than the expected gain from laziness, thus when $pU + (1 - p)W \leq W - C$. This means that wage levels must satisfy the inequality below:

$$W \geq U + C/p$$

The premise established by this simple formula is that a worker cannot be incentivized by work performance, and he can only occasionally be discovered being lazy or not. We can see that under this condition the minimum wage that guarantees workers are not lazy depends on the reservation wage U, the cost of effort C, and the probability of laziness being discovered p. In this inequation, the most important message is p. If there is 100% probability that laziness will be discovered, then his wages only have to account for his opportunity cost U plus his cost of effort C. However, if the probability of laziness being discovered is less than 1, you must pay him higher wages to "bribe" him not to be lazy. The lower the probability that laziness will be discovered, the higher the wage rate will be.

This reasoning has a tremendous impact on organizational design, because it means that the same character of person may receive different wages in different positions. Hard work may not be the reason for your higher wages, instead it may mean you become lazy too easily. For example, a person that works in finance and a person that works in a factory will put in the same effort but have different salary because the person in finance can be corrupt more easily. Similarly, a nanny in a wealthy household can be corrupt more easily than a nanny in a normal household, so wages should be higher.

Now, we will briefly analyze the incentive issue for government officials. In government bureaucratic organizations, different positions have different powers, deal with different affairs, and have different opportunities to accept bribes and illegal income from corruption. We use W to represent the wages of officials, and $B(q)$ to represent power rent. Power rent is the largest possible bribe that the official can receive while in the position, which can also be understood as the "opportunity cost" of not being corrupt. The size of this rent depends on the size of the official's power q. The relationship between the two is: The more power the official has, the higher is the opportunity cost of not being corrupt because the more power that person has, the more other people are willing to pay in bribes. As shown in Figure 11.6, the maximum power rent that can be obtained progressively increases with the official's power. This is different from a general production function because an increasing return to scale (or scope) exists, meaning the power rent increases faster than power. This is easy to understand because if you only have one type of power, you may only be able to help with one matter, but if you have two types of power, you may be able to help with three matters. At the beginning of this chapter, we saw a comparison between corrupt heads of state and per capita gross domestic product. It showed that even in very poor countries, national leaders can rake in huge bribes.

Of course, official corruption will be investigated or reported, so we use p to represent the probability that corruption will be discovered. Once corrupt officials are discovered, they will be punished to a certain degree. We use F to represent the punishment of discovered corruption. Similar to workers, government officials also have reserve the reservation utility U outside of government.

Given these variables, if we want to make government officials not corrupt, what conditions must we satisfy? Without corruption, a clean official will only receive wage W. If he is corrupt, in addition to his wages, he will receive bribe $B(q)$, so his gross income is $W + B(q)$. However, this is only one possibility. The other possibility is that his corruption is discovered, so he receives punishment F, then loses his job and must find a new job on the market for U. This punishment may be a fine, prison time or a loss of reputation. F represents an "objective" measure of punishment determined by the courts or the state. The psychological cost of the same punishment may be different for each individual, so we use aF to represent the punishment that the official actually feels. Here, coefficient a can be understood as "the thickness of the official's face". If coefficient a equals zero, it means that person has no shame and no punishment bothers him. If a is huge, it means that person has a strong sense of shamefulness so that even a small punishment will cause a large suffering. We will see that this coefficient is very important in determining if an official is corrupt or not.

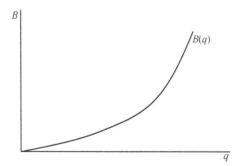

Figure 11.6 The Relationship Between Power and Rent

If an official is captured for corruption, his utility is $U - aF$. Therefore, the official's expected utility from corruption is $(1 - p)[W + B(q)] + p(U - aF)$. The required condition for an official to not be corrupt is when non-corrupt utility W is greater than the expected utility from corruption. From this, we can derive the corruption inequality below:

$$W \geq W^* = \frac{1-p}{p} B(q) + U - aF$$

Here, W^* is the minimum wage that guarantees an official is not corrupt. For convenience, we will call it the "clean government wage". If this inequality is not satisfied, officials will be corrupt.

Obviously, clean government wage W^* is related to power q because it increases as power increases. The more power there is, the higher is the opportunity cost of not being corrupt, so the higher the clean government wage is. We can also see that the same power under different systems of supervision will require a different clean government wage. If supervision is effective (meaning the probability of corruption being discovered is relatively large), the lower the required wages are. If supervision is ineffective, wages must be higher. Increasing the forcefulness of punishments or the probability of discovery can both decrease wage. Thus, there is a tradeoff between reducing corruption by supervisory means and "bribing" them with higher wages. We know that any supervision will fall short, and the government is especially difficult to supervise, so a third method is to reduce the power of government. Once power is reduced, wages can also be lowered.

4.3   The spread of corruption in China

People generally believe that corruption has increased in China over the last 30 years, and this judgment may be correct. The reasons for the increase in corruption and the measures to deal with corruption are both included in the above equation.

To analyze the ways in which corruption spreads, we will first make an extreme assumption that before Reform and Opening, this inequality held. (A more suitable assumption may be that this assumption was viable for the vast majority of officials.) After Reform and Opening, how was this inequality broken? First, we will examine the right side of the inequality. Assume that power did not change, but the rent from power increased. In other words, the corruption curve in Figure 11.6 moved upward. The reason is very simple. Under the planned economy, transactions were non-monetary, and individuals did not have the liberty to engage in commercial activities. The goal of bribing was non-commercial; it was done only to gain some type of consumable or work-related benefit. For example, it was useless to bribe the Ministry of Foreign Trade for an import or export license when you were not allowed to be engaged in foreign trade. This means that the commercial value of power was limited. In this situation, so-called corruption only involved a cigarette or bottle of alcohol to look after some hometown or alumni relations. However, as soon as the economy began to monetize, power had a market value. Even though power has not changed, rent from power has increased. The import and export licenses that no one wanted to buy previously are suddenly worth millions of yuan.

In reality, power has also changed. The command economy in the past was centralized management, so lower level officials were on a tight leash. Now, officials have a large degree of discretion. For example, investment projects and land appropriations were not allowed in the past, but now this power has been transferred to local governments.

Next, we will examine p, the possibility of corruption being discovered. This decreased after Reform and Opening. Why? Because as economic relationships become more complex and China's economy is in a state of transition, it becomes less and less clear as to what is legal and what is illegal. The forms of corruption are increasing and changing. Cash transactions and credit card payments are the main forms of bribes, and the number of banks to deposit money into is increasing. This has all caused the discovery of corruption to become more difficult. The more corruption spreads, the more difficult it is to discover any one act of corruption.

The reservation wage U outside of government has increased. In the past, when government officials were fired, they could only return to their hometowns to be peasants. The status of peasants in the Chinese economy caused the reservation utility outside of the government to be extremely low, so officials were most afraid of losing their positions. However, now this is different. Even if they cannot be a government official, they can still go into business and earn even higher incomes.

However, the punishment for corruption F has actually declined. Previously, embezzling ¥10,000 may have led to death by firing squad, but today embezzling up to ¥10 million may not even lead to death by firing squad. Even after considering the effects of inflation, the actual degree of punishments has decreased.

All of these factors added together caused the right side of this inequality to increase significantly. On the left side of the inequality, which represents wages, for the vast majority of officials, the degree of increase in wages has been far outpaced by the degree of increase in the right side of the inequality. In this way, this inequality was inverted. Not surprisingly, corruption began to spread.

The reader may ask why some officials are corrupt and others are not even if they hold the same power in the same level of government at the same position. The answer may be on the "shameless coefficient" a. When all other factors are equal, this inequality is invalid for shameless people with smaller a, but still valid for those with higher a. In this case, the former will be corrupt and the latter will remain clean. The size of this coefficient for each person is also related to the ratio of corrupt officials. If only a tiny minority of officials is corrupt, the vast majority of people will care about their reputations. However, as soon as the ratio of corrupt officials increases beyond a critical level, each person's shamelessness will increase because now corruption being discovered is not so shameful as before. This may be an important reason that the phenomenon of corruption increases so rapidly.[25]

4.4 Controlling corruption

How can we control corruption? According to the inequality above, anti-corruption measures can be summarized into a few points. First, increase wage W of officials. Second, further strengthen supervision so that the probability p of corruption being discovered increases. Third, reduce the power q of officials, which will also decrease rent $B(q)$ from power. Fourth, increase the degree of punishment F so punishments are more of a deterrent. Fifth, increase the shame coefficient a via moral education so that the psychological cost of punishments increases.

The reservation income U outside of government is determined by competition in the talent market and the overall condition of the economy, which on the micro level the government has a limited influence. Of course, the government can make certain changes, such as prohibiting corrupt officials from working in banks or financial institutions and from being appointed to general management or board member positions in companies.

Among all of these measures, reducing government power cures the disease, whereas other methods only cure the symptoms. Without power, there will not be corruption. The reason the citizenry is not corrupt is not because of higher morals, but instead because the citizenry does not have power. If the power of government is not reduced, the effects of other measures will be very limited. Some people advocate increasing wages in order to clean up government. However, if official's power is still as great as it is today, this "cleanliness" will not happen.[26] Official salaries in the millions of yuan would not only be something the treasury could not sustain, the citizenry would not agree to it. Recently, the strength of supervision has increased continuously, but corruption is still becoming a more and more serious problem. This proves that only relying on supervision will not have a big effect. As was asked before, "Who supervises the supervisors?" The ability to increase punishments has also a limit. The death penalty is already the extreme limit, and modern society cannot bring back the practice of family extermination.

Of course, under the current system of China, it is not easy to reduce power, even impossible. The only method that will truly cure the disease is to implement political to establish a rule of law society and democratic politics as well as allowing freedom of the press. International empirical research supports the following conclusions: (1) Countries with more regulations (such as restrictions on market entry) are more corrupt; and (2) countries with more political freedom are less corrupt (Djankov et al., 2002; Svenson, 2005).

Notes

1 According to *The Unofficial History of the Qing Dynasty (Heshan and His Family Wealth)* the total amount of Heshen's wealth was about two billion silver taels. While Xu Fucheng mentioned the wealth is 23 million silver taels in *Yongan Biji.*
2 Susan Rose-Ackerman discussed the corruption problem in developing countries in *Corruption and Government.* She analyzed the relationship between corruption and government, causes and consequences, and reform successes and failures in various countries. Glaeser and Goldin (2006) studied political corruption and reform. Svenson (2005) discussed eight questions related to public corruption: (1) What is corruption?

(2) Which countries are the most corrupt? (3) What are the Common Characteristics of Countries with High Corruption? (4) What is the Magnitude of Corruption? (5) Do Higher Wages for Bureaucrats Reduce Corruption? (6) Can Competition Reduce Corruption? (7) Why Have There Been So Few (Recent) Successful Attempts to Fight Corruption? (8) Does Corruption Adversely Affect Growth?

3 Readers that are interested in this organization can visit http://transparency.org.

4 Ex-ante information asymmetry is also a major reason for corruption. The reason many instances of corruption occur is because public officials have information that the public does not. A classic example is corrupt behavior in public infrastructure investment. This type of corruption occurs because public officials know the cost of a project, but the public does not. The public officials can wantonly increase the project's budget, then line their own pockets. Public officials' morals are also ex-ante asymmetric information, which leads to corruption in hiring practices.

5 The Principal Agent Theory was a branch of information economics developed in the 1970s. Innovative literature in this theory includes: Spence and Zechhauser (1971); Ross (1973); Mirrlees (1975); Holmstrom (1979); and Hart and Holmstrom (1987) is considered to be the best overview of principal-agent literature. Rees (1985) is an academic overview suitable for beginners. Jean-Jacques Laffont and David Martimort (2002) and Weiying Zhang (1996) are more detailed overall introductions to Principal-Agent Theory.

6 The law of agency is a part of commercial law; see Sealy and Hooley (2009). In law, the principal-agent relationship is very similar to the trust relationship. The biggest difference is that the principal-agent relationship is personal (a relationship between two people) but the trust relationship is proprietary. See Burn (1990, Chapter 1).

7 The relationship between the principal and trust is fiduciary. The law has stricter definitions of the rights and responsibilities of each party. Particularly, on the agent side, agent has to work for the best interest of the principal; without permission of the principal, the agent cannot re-delegate authorized power to another person; the agent cannot put himself into a conflict of interest with the principal; the agent has obligation of maintaining confidentiality to the principal. On the principal side, the principal must exempt the agent from liability within the legal limit, and compensate the agent according to the contract; if the principal has failed to compensate the agent, the agent holds a lien on the principal's asset.

8 For more information, refer to *Freakonomics* by Steven D. Levitt and Stephen J. Dubner (2005)

9 In addition to the risk attitude, there are other reasons that the contractor system cannot achieve the optimum in reality: (1) managers do not have enough assets to bear the liability for losses; and (2) the contractor system is short-term, but due to the continuity of firm asset values, short-term profit maximization is not necessarily optimal. The last point also means that the outcome of a longer contract period will be closer to the optimal, but the extension of a contract period is subject to risk attitude and liability constraints.

10 In fact, compulsory auto insurance was implemented due to the fear that people involved in a collision will be unable to bear the liability.

11 This is an application of general equilibrium theory when there is risk. Its mathematical proof and analysis can be found in microeconomics or finance textbooks.

12 The law of large numbers refers to the fact that although the result of each occurrence is different in randomized trials, but the average of the results of a large number of repetitive experiments is almost always close to a certain value.

13 Mathematically, if x happens to equal 0.3, his expected payoffs are the same, in which case, we will assume that he chooses one preferred by the principal.

14 We have omitted the detailed mathematical derivation here. Interested readers can refer to the classical paper by Holmstrom and Milgrom (1991), or to Chapter 6, *Game Theory and Information Economics* by Weiying Zhang.

15 For a more detailed discussion, see Milgrom and Roberts (1992, Chapter 7) or Weiying Zhang (2005, Chapter 7).
16 See Kawasaki and McMillan (1987).
17 For literature on comparative performance evaluation, see Lazear and Rosen (1981); Nalebuff and Stiglitz (1983); and Mookherjee (1984).
18 How to prevent political struggle within an organization is an important issue that needs to be considered in the design of an incentive mechanism. See Lazear (1989, 1997).
19 Collusion among the agents causes the principal's incentive mechanism to no longer play a role. Designing the mechanism to be collusion-proof is very important. Study of the collusion problem is the frontier of Principal-Agent Theory. For the collusion-proof design of comparative performance evaluation, see Shingo Ishiguro (2004).
20 Chen Yongui (1915–1986) was a peasant and brigade leader of Dazai Village of Shanxi Province, China. When Dazai was set up as a model village of agriculture, Chen was successively promoted until becoming a vice premier from 1975 to 1980. He was dismissed from the state leadership in 1980.
21 For a more detailed discussion of this issue, see Weiying Zhang (2005, Chapter 8, Section 6).
22 The full title of Buke Yan's (2002) book is *Grade and Position: Research on the System of Official Ranks During the Qin, Han, Wei, Jin, Southern, and Northern Dynasties.* Chinese version *Pinwei yu Zhiwei: Qinhanweijinnanbeichao Guanjie Zhidu Yanjiu.*
23 Holmstrom and Milgrom (1991) is a classic model of multi-task incentive theory.
24 Mathematical analysis and discussion of this issue can be found in Dixit (1996, 1997). Tirole (1994) also discussed the incentives of government organizations.
25 Xiang Feng, *Zhengfa Biji.* Nanjing: Jiangsu People's Press, 2004.
26 The conclusion of international empirical studies on whether or not higher official salaries can reduce corruption is uncertain (Svenson, 2005). Historically, Sweden is considered a model for high salaries reducing corruption. In the seventeenth and eighteenth centuries, Sweden was one of the most corrupt countries in Europe. Through increasing compensation for government officials and reducing regulation, a clean and efficient government emerged in Sweden by the beginning of the nineteenth century (Lindbeck, 1975). In transnational comparative research, Rauch and Evans (2000) and Treisman (2000) did not find strong evidence that high salaries can reduce corruption, but Van Rijckeghem and Weber (2001) found that the positive effect of high salaries on reducing corruption was evident. Di Tella and Schargrodsky (2003) found that under certain conditions, high salaries can indeed reduce corruption.

12 Evolutionary games and the spontaneous order

Since the 1990s, scholars of Game Theory and other social scientists have introduced evolutionary game theory into the study of social issues, especially to explain changes in social systems and the formation of social customs and norms. This gradually formed a new viewpoint in Game Theory.

Evolutionary game theory re-examined the game equilibrium concept from the "survival of the fittest" perspective and loosened the complete rationality assumption. It provided the Nash equilibrium and equilibrium selection with a different foundation.

In traditional game theory, rational people select a strategy that maximizes utility from a strategy set. However, in biological phenomenon, individual organisms do not select strategies. Instead, genes determine them.

Different from the biological world, in society, information and behavioral patterns do not only rely on genes for transmission. Instead, they also rely on communication, interaction, learning, and imitation to be transmitted. There are also numerous methods of transmission.

The most important concept in evolutionary games is the "evolutionarily stable strategy". An evolutionarily stable strategy can overcome the invasion of any variation by sustaining itself and continuously replicating itself.

Evolutionarily stable equilibriums are divided into monomorphic equilibrium and polymorphic equilibrium. If only one type of strategy or behavioral pattern can exist under an equilibrium state, then we call this type of equilibrium a "monomorphic equilibrium". If the equilibrium state includes multiple behavioral patterns, strategies, or genes that all have the same ability to survive, then we call this type of equilibrium a "polymorphic equilibrium".

The greatest difficulty faced by human cooperation is the Prisoner's Dilemma. Evolutionary games provided a new explanation for human society's escape from the Prisoner's Dilemma. In repeated games, "tit-for-tat" may be a type of evolutionarily stable strategy of survival that will lead to the appearance of cooperation. If a repeated game occurs a sufficient number of times, even if cooperation is not common in the original state, society will evolve towards a cooperative society. However, under certain conditions, a cooperative society might be destroyed. An example is the transformation in rural China after 1949.

The "first-on" rule in the property rights system is an evolutionarily stable equilibrium and a spontaneously formed social convention. A type of behavioral pattern evolves into a convention because people believe other people will respect it. In many situations, people respect social norms based on considerations of self-interest. A norm is a norm because it is an evolutionarily stable strategy. However, if a rule systematically favors a specific group of people, then this rule might not be widely accepted.

Section one: the basic factors of evolutionary games

1.1   From biological evolution to social evolution

Up to this point, our discussions of Game Theory have been within the scope of "traditional" Game Theory. A basic assumption that we have maintained throughout is the "individual rationality". In a game, each person has a well-defined preference and an unlimited ability to reason. The structure and rationality of the game is common knowledge to all players.[1] Rational people can understand and calculate all players' interactive strategies. Players choose the strategy that maximizes their own interests. Under this framework, as long as the basic structure of the game is known, such as the rules and information structure of the game, then rational people can calculate an equilibrium strategy.

However, in reality, this might not be the case. The structure of a game might be extremely complex, so reaching the equilibrium outcome requires a complex ability to reason. Any chess player might have had a similar experience. Although a subgame perfect equilibrium exists in chess, we have difficulty calculating it. Additionally, when there are multi-equilibriums in a game, which one is the most probable? As we have already pointed out, when multiple equilibriums exist, rationality is insufficient to tell us how people will act. Perhaps we must depend on "social norms" to coordinate people's actions, but in most circumstances we assume these social norms or customs are external.

This is the reason that many sociologists and other social scientists have had deep doubts about the rationality assumption. In many decisions, the decision-maker does not undertake detailed complex calculations. Instead, that person often impersonates others, relies on past experiences, or uses principles like the rule of thumb.[2] Examples include our use of cutlery or the side of the road we drive on. Further, if we examine the entire society as one, we know that systems are a type of rules of the game. People's behavior under the rules of the game and related systems were not designed by a central unified authority. People do not simply do something because there is a benefit from doing it or not do something because there is no benefit from doing it. The formation of the social order that we see, as was pointed out by Hayek (1960, 1979), was to a large degree a process of spontaneous evolution, not the outcome of meticulous design. Traditional Game Theory does not have a very good explanation for these phenomena and issues, so we use a new type of theoretical perspective to consider these issues. This new theoretical perspective is introduced from biology, also known as Evolutionary Game Theory.

Before the 1970s, biology rarely utilized Game Theory, but afterwards introduced certain concepts and analytical methods. Theories were proposed and applied to certain behaviors in specialized fields, mainly the animal world. The most classic and innovative was the evolutionarily stable strategy (abbreviated as ESS), proposed by John Maynard Smith and George R. Price in 1973.[3] Since the 1990s, Game Theorists, or it could be said all social scientists, introduced Biology's evolutionary game theory to the study of social issues, especially social institution change and the formation of social customs and social norms. This gradually formed a new perspective in Game Theory. Evolutionary game theory re-evaluated the game equilibrium concept from a new perspective, relaxed the assumption of complete rationality, and provided a different foundation for the Nash equilibrium and equilibrium selection. Evolutionary game theory is currently the cutting-edge of Game Theory research and is still in the process of development. This chapter uses examples to introduce the analytical methods of evolutionary games.[4]

Here, we will first introduce certain basic elements of Game Theory in biological evolution research. In Biology, the most influential theory is the Theory of Evolution. It has an important ability to explain the biological phenomena we observe. When Charles Darwin was researching biological evolution, he proposed the issue of competition for survival among populations. The animals that were most able to adapt to their environment continuously expanded and those that did not were eliminated. The modern Theory of Evolution was updated by the Theory of Genes proposed by Gregor Mendel, which stated that heredity was transmitted by genetics. Research in modern Biology also proposes that the deepest form of competition is the competition for survival between genes. Games in Biology are not games between individuals, but instead are games between genes. Each living thing that we observe is a carrier of genes. Oxford University Professor Richard Dawkins wrote *The Selfish Gene*. He believed that if each person's preference is to maximize utility, then the preference of a gene itself is to maximize its ability to reproduce and survive. If a gene has the ability to continuously reproduce itself and expand, then this type of gene can survive. If it cannot, then it will slowly be eliminated.[5]

Dawkins proposed the "selfish gene" theory to explain the phenomena of biological evolution. The selfish gene theory can provide a fresh explanation of many human behaviors, such as kinship. Half of our genes come from each of our parents. We also share common genes with our brothers, sisters, and cousins. Still, each person is but a gene carrier. Our close relationships represent a model for the maximum probability of survival of genes. In extreme situations, parents might be willing to die to save their children. From a biological perspective, this could be understood as the game outcome of genes increasing their ability to reproduce and survive.

1.2 Evolutionarily stable strategy

The "strategy" concept in the study of biological games refers to the behavioral patterns of organisms, especially animals, not the choices of individuals. In traditional game theory, rational people choose the strategy that maximizes their utility among a set of strategies. However, in biological game, strategies are not chosen, instead they are determined by genes. The individual will either do something one way or another, but there is no choice. The survival and reproduction of genes are determined by natural selection. Natural selection is the survival of the fittest, which means the adaptability of genes to the environment. In certain environments, the genes most suitable for survival will continuously reproduce from one generation to the next, but those that do not adapt will be eliminated. The process of biological evolution is a process of genes continuously reproducing and adapting. This is the process of natural selection. The final outcome of this selection process is a stable state. Of course, this is not stable at every moment in time, but in specific environments it is overall a stable state. The genes that exist in this type of stable state determine the behavioral methods of organisms. The behavior of organisms represents a stable pattern.

We call this type of stable behavioral pattern "evolutionarily stable strategy". This is an extremely important concept in evolutionary games. Dawkins believed the discovery of the evolutionarily stable strategy concept was one of the most important developments in the Theory of Evolution since Charles Darwin.[6]

The evolutionarily stable strategy concept can be formally defined both in dynamics and statics. From the static perspective, a behavior pattern, or what we previously called a strategy, is called evolutionarily stable if the group that implements this type of behavior cannot be invaded by some variation and any individual deviation from this pattern has a lower chance of survival. In other words, given a group's present behavior pattern, if after the occurrence of an alternative or mutated behavior the invader will be eliminated and the group resumes its original state, then this type of behavior pattern is called "evolutionarily stable strategy".

From the dynamic perspective, given that multiple behavioral patterns exist in the original state, such as some people in a population being selfish and some being altruistic, but with the passage of time, some specific behavioral pattern will gradually dominate the entire population, then this behavioral pattern is an evolutionarily stable strategy. The stable states in these two perspectives are interrelated, but not entirely equivalent.

There is an important relationship between the evolutionarily stable strategy and the Nash equilibrium concept discussed in the previous text. Simply stated, if a strategy in an evolutionary game is an evolutionarily stable strategy, then it certainly is also a Nash equilibrium in traditional game. However, not all Nash equilibriums are evolutionarily stable strategies. Evolutionarily stable strategies must meet stricter conditions than Nash equilibriums.[7] At the same time, we also see that when a game has multiple equilibriums, the process of evolution itself can assist us in choosing a specific equilibrium.

1.3 The difference between biological evolution and social evolution

One point worth emphasizing is that there is a significant difference between biological evolution and social evolution. The concept of evolutionarily stable strategy came out of biology, so when we apply it to the study of social evolution or the formation of the social order, we must take note of the major differences between the two.

The first difference is the definition of strategy. As was described previously, in biology, strategy refers to a behavioral pattern determined by genes, much like a computer program, not the choices of individuals. However, as we know, people's social behavior is not completely determined by genes. Instead, it is related to factors such as social relationships, social environment, cultural background, education level, and past experiences. The behavior pattern or action of each individual, even if not completely rational, to a certain degree is chosen by concerned individuals. For example, because of culture and customs, the behavioral patterns of people from different regions will be slightly different. The behavioral patterns of people from the same region but with different education backgrounds will also be different. Under these circumstances, the individual has certain choice freedom. The same person will also behave differently in different areas. He might choose a strategy that is more "survivable".

The second difference is the definition of fitness. In biology, fitness refers to genes' reproductive ability. In social games, fitness refers to the size of players' expected payoff. Payoff is the total or average compensation you can receive in a game from a given strategy profile. A higher payoff means a stronger ability to survive in society. This compensation has different definitions in different environments and changes according to the issue being analyzed. An example would be Firm A choosing Strategy A and Firm B choosing Strategy B. Given the strategies the players choose, if Strategy A brings about 20% profit rate for Firm A and Strategy B brings about 15% profit rate for Firm B, then the survivability of Firm A is higher than that of Firm B. Further, this also means that the firms that choose Strategy A will continuously increase and the firms that choose Strategy B will continuously decrease. The payoff can also be market share. If two enterprises are competing and the growth in market share of one firm is obviously faster than another firm, then the firm that is growing slower will be eliminated and the faster-growing firm will dominate the market.

The third difference is the issue of how behavior patterns are transmitted from one generation to the next. We know that in biology, the transmission of behavioral patterns relies on genetic heredity. In other words, within genes, DNA holds certain information that is continuously reproduced and split in order to multiply. However, in society, much of information and many behavioral patterns do not rely on genetic inheritance for transmission. Instead, they rely on communication, learning, and imitation for transmission, and the methods of transmission are numerous. A successful person could transmit information on his methods for success to his friends and colleagues. After his friends and colleagues observe this behavior, they will imitate him in order to succeed. Unsuccessful people will always learn from successful people and adjust their behaviors accordingly. This is a type of fitness-led imitation transmission. Of course, humans will also consciously use trial and error to learn how to choose a better strategy. You might choose one type of strategy to see if it works, then choose another if it does not. Before making this choice, you will also obtain additional information that informs you which choice is most likely to succeed. Therefore, society's education system plays an important role in the transmission of people's behavioral patterns. This method of transmission does hardly exist in biology. Although culture is not genetic, it does have a certain hereditary nature, called social heredity. This does not mean that a person is influenced by culture as soon as he is born, but certain culture will become ingrained in his behavior while growing up among his parents, siblings, friends, and neighbors. Therefore, social evolution and biological evolution are not entirely the same.[8]

1.4 Monomorphic equilibrium and polymorphic equilibrium

There are two categories of evolutionarily stable equilibriums: Monomorphic equilibriums and polymorphic equilibrium. In an evolutionarily stable state, if only one type of strategy or behavioral pattern can exist under the equilibrium state, then we call this type of equilibrium "monomorphic equilibrium". Alternatively, if the stable state includes multiple behavioral pattern, strategies, or genes with the same level of fitness, we call this type of equilibrium "polymorphic equilibrium".

Note that the polymorphic equilibrium is different from the multiple equilibrium that we discussed previously. The multiple equilibrium refers to that the game has multiple optimal strategy profiles, whereas a polymorphic equilibrium refers to the coexistence of multiple behavioral patterns in a group under a steady state. In our Traffic Game, "everyone keeping to the left" and "everyone keeping to the right" are both Nash equilibriums, so we say that this game has multiple equilibriums and from the evolutionary game perspective each equilibrium is evolutionarily stable. However, each equilibrium is a monomorphic equilibrium, because "some people keep to the left and some people keep to the right" cannot coexist in a steady state. Another example would be an organization where only people that tell the truth (or tell lies) can survive. This would be a monomorphic equilibrium. If both types of people could survive in the organization, then it would be a polymorphic equilibrium. In this way, monomorphic equilibrium is similar to a monolithic society or monolithic culture, whereas polymorphic equilibrium is similar to a pluralistic society or pluralistic culture.

Section two: examples of evolutionary games

2.1 Coordination games

Imagine a large-scale group of people. Within the population, there are two types of people or organisms with different behavioral patterns. The first group of people are accustomed to using their left hand and the second group of people are accustomed to using their right hand. This is the similar to having two different strategies. It must be noted that when we say "strategy" here, we do not mean two types of choices that people have, but instead are each person's established customs. The format of this game appears to be similar to the coordination game that we discussed previously, but actually is completely different. In the previous game examples, a person, such as Player A, has two choices, either choosing the left hand or the right hand. Similarly, Player B could choose between using the left hand or the right hand. However, in the current game, strategy is determined by "genetics", not the choices of an individual. Within a population, when any two people randomly meet to undertake a game (such as working together or eating side by side), there are four types of possible profiles, with the payoffs for each profile shown in Figure 12.1.

Assume that for these two people, when a lefty interacts with a lefty (or a righty interacts with a righty), then each person obtains a 1-unit payoff. If a lefty interacts with a righty, then each person receives 0 payoff.

The question is: Which type of strategy will be more fit and able to survive? Intuitively, the answer depends on the proportion of the people that use this strategy within the total population. If the majority of people are right-handed, then it is easier for right-handed people to survive; whereas if the majority of people are left-handed, then it is easier for left-handed people to survive. Here, the ability survive is actually a higher expected or average payoff.

For the convenience of analysis, we assume that x proportion of the people in the total population are left-handed and $1 - x$ proportion of the people are right-handed. We will examine the expected payoff for each type. Because the proportion of left-handed people in a population is x, random encounters means that a left-handed person has x probability of receiving 1 and $1 - x$ probability of receiving 0. His average payoff is x. For the same reason, the expected payoff for a right-handed person is $1 - x$. Will lefties or righties survive? If x is greater than $1 - x$, then left-handed people have an advantage, otherwise right-handed people have an advantage. Therefore, $x = 1/2$ is the critical value. If x is greater than $1/2$, then left-handed people are more able to survive because their expected payoff is higher. Because of this, when games go on from one generation to another, more and more people will imitate other left-handed people, or because of hereditary factors, less and less people will be right-handed. In the end, this will evolve into all people being left-handed. This is a monomorphic equilibrium. In this equilibrium, only one type or one strategy can survive. Alternatively, if in the original state, x was less than $1/2$, meaning the proportion of left-handed people is less than $1/2$, then right-handed people have the advantage. The proportion of

	Left handed	Right handed
Left handed	1, 1	0, 0
Right handed	0, 0	1, 1

Figure 12.1 The Coordination Game Payoff Structure

right-handed people will gradually increase until finally reaching one hundred percent. This is also a monomorphic equilibrium. Under these two types of equilibrium circumstances, only one type of strategy can survive. If x equals $1/2$, then the expected payoff of both strategies is the same, so their fitness for survival is equivalent. At this point, both types of people can survive. This type of situation is called binary equilibrium.

Thus, this simple game has three possible equilibriums. These three different equilibriums are not the outcomes of individual choices, but instead are strategies that survived natural selection. In the first circumstance, left-handed people survive. In the second circumstance, right-handed people survive. In the third circumstance, both types survive. However, among these three equilibriums, the former two equilibriums are evolutionarily stable, whereas the latter one is not. We previously said that in evolutionarily stable equilibriums, any slight deviation can return to the original state. To understand the differences between these equilibriums, we will use the left-handed equilibrium as an example. Assume that our example society has already entered a stable state in which everyone is left-handed. Now, a variation occurs. The organisms with this variance are a very small proportion, for example, just one percent of the population. After this one percent variable invades, the payoff for mutating individuals will be less than the left-handed individuals. Because of natural selection, this variation will be eliminated and the population will resume the equilibrium state where everyone is left-handed.

Similarly, if everyone is right handed in the original population state, but a very small proportion of the population becomes left handed, this type of person will also be eliminated by natural selection. Their behavioral pattern cannot successfully invade, so the final state return to everyone being right handed. Therefore, these two types of behavioral patterns states are evolutionarily stable strategies.

Now, we will examine the third equilibrium in which precisely half the population is right-handed and half the population is left-handed. If a variation occurs, causing the proportion of left-handed people to increase slightly, what will the outcome be? From the above analysis we know that from this point the fitness for survival will be stronger for left-handed people than right-handed people. Thus, the proportion of left-handed people will continuously increase over time, until in the end right-handed people disappear. Alternatively, if the variance causes the number of right-handed people to increase, then right-handed people will have an advantage. This will cause the number of right-handed people to gradually increase until everyone is right-handed. This is the reason we say this equilibrium is unstable.

We can use Figure 12.2 to describe the stable equilibrium and the unstable equilibrium. The horizontal axis represents the proportion of left-handed people, from 0 to 1. The vertical axis represents fitness or the expected payoff. We see that the payoff for righties reduces as x increases, and the payoff for left-handed people increases as x increases. The cut-off point is $x = 1/2$. At that point, the payoff for both patterns is equal, but it is not stable. As soon as a variation appears, it will either evolve towards the righty equilibrium ($x = 0$) or the lefty equilibrium ($x = 1$), depending on which direction the variation takes. From the figure, we can see that as soon as a variation appears, because the difference between the expected payoffs from the different behaviors increase, the process of evolution speeds up.

We can further compare this type of game equilibrium with the traditional game Nash equilibrium that we discussed previously. If it was a traditional game (where strategies represent the choices of individuals), then this game would have three Nash equilibriums: Both people use the left hand; both people use the right hand; and a mixed strategy equilibrium where each person has a one-half probability of using the left hand and one-half probability of using the right hand. The former two (pure strategy) equilibriums provide each player with a payoff of 1, whereas the payoff for each person in the mixed strategy equilibrium is 0.5. The payoff for the mixed strategy equilibrium is less than the payoff for the pure strategy equilibriums. Our previous analysis also gives three equilibriums, of which two were monomorphic (unitary) equilibriums, and one was a polymorphic equilibrium with two strategies coexisting at the same time.

The binary equilibrium and the mixed strategy equilibrium are similar in form, but the meanings are completely different. Under the current circumstances, each person uses a pure strategy, but it is only half the people using the left hand and half the people using the right hand. In traditional game theory, mixed strategies seem not reasonable, because they mean each person must implement random selection. However, from the evolutionary game perspective, the mixed strategy corresponds to a type of strategy profile for the proportion of people using different strategies. This is reasonable. As we discussed previously, an evolutionarily stable equilibrium is certainly a Nash equilibrium, but not all Nash equilibriums are evolutionarily stable equilibriums. We can see this in our example. If it is a unitary equilibrium under which there is only one type of behavioral pattern, then the stable strategy is the optimal response to itself. In other words, given that other people use the left hand, then it is best for you to use your left hand. This is actually the definition of a Nash equilibrium. Two unitary equilibrium ($x = 0$ and $x = 1$) are Nash equilibriums and evolutionarily stable. A binary equilibrium ($x = 1/2$) is a Nash equilibrium, but it is not evolutionarily stable.

We know that handedness is affected by both innate and postnatal factors. People that are innately left-handed may become right-handed after practice. In society, we find that lefties are a minority. Lefties are generally very intelligent,

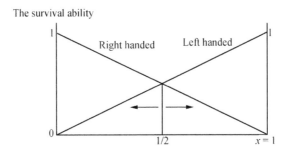

Figure 12.2 The Handedness Equilibrium

but they are a tiny minority. As soon as right-handedness became dominant, even if left-handed people are very intelligent, there is no way to change the outcome. The vast majority of us are right handed, so using the left hand has a certain disadvantage. If parents care about their children, they will teach their children to be right-handed. Not only do we see this from the heritage perspective, but also the social perspective. Even if the parents are accustomed to using their left hands, but left handedness is disadvantageous in the group, then their children will be raised to be right-handed. This is a classic example of social behavior. Many of our customs and behavioral patterns are either passed down from our parents, the outcome of their upbringing to make us more fit in society, or are the outcome of our own conscious decision to "fit in". If we do not fit in, we will not be able to cooperate well with others, so we continuously learn from and imitate others. For instance, as a left-handed person you might feel strange in a right-handed world and doubt yourself, so you will gradually accustom yourself to using your right hand. This is a classic characteristic of social evolution and social games. Many social behaviors are the combined outcome of the innate and postnatal factors.

Here, we will revisit the Traffic Game discussed in Chapter Three. As shown in Figure 12.3, this game and the Left-Right Hand Coordination Game are very similar.[9] Traffic rules require us to either keep left or keep right while driving. We can understand traffic rules as the outcome of long-term evolution. Imagine that in the beginning, society does not have any traffic rules. Some people keep to the left and some people keep to the right, but it is completely random. However, as long as more than half the people keep to the right, then the probability of an accident, and death, are higher for people that keep to the left. This way, you will also tend to keep to the right. With the passage of time, the number of people that keep to the left will decline and the number of people that keep to the right will increase. As this process slowly evolves, it will lead everyone to keep to the right. Alternatively, perhaps for chance reasons in the beginning, people that keep to the left are more numerous. People that keep to the right (more accurately: the behavioral pattern of keeping to the right) will slowly be eliminated. The final stable equilibrium outcome would be either everyone keeps to the right or keeps to the left. As soon as a stable equilibrium state is reached, then one or more new drivers that violate traffic rules are certain to have an accident. In other words, this equilibrium cannot be broken by small variations.

	Travel on the left	Travel on the right
Travel on the left	1, 1	−1, −1
Travel on the right	−1, −1	1, 1

Figure 12.3 The Transportation Game

Unlike the Left-Right hand game, the traffic game does not involve genes. Instead, behavioral patterns are transmitted through learning and imitation. For example, in Great Britain, cars and pedestrians keep to the left. If a British person goes to China, will he be able to adapt to China's driving customs? He must certainly change the customs from his British upbringing, and he must do so quickly! Of course, there are some technical factors that can assist him in changing his customs. For example, in places that keep to the left, the steering wheel is designed on the right, so it is natural to keep to the left. In China, steering wheels are on the left, so it is easier to keep to the right. In this instance, the change of customs and the technological environment are related. If he takes his British car to China, then his steering wheel would still be on the right. The adjustment may be slower than if he were to drive a car with the steering wheel on the left. This point shows that the speed of changing behavior and adapting to the environment is related to the environment itself.

2.2 The marriage game

In the previous games, everyone was in the same group, and two people within the group were selected at random to undertake a game. We analyzed the evolution of behavioral patterns within the same group. It was a direct application of biological analysis. The biological game studies the collective patterns of a group. In social life, more often parties to a game belong to different groups, such as buyers and sellers. Here, we are still analyzing a coordination game. This coordination game is called the assurance game.[10] We will use the marriage game in Figure 12.4 to explain it.

Imagine a society with a large scale population split half and half between men and women. Both men and women have two types: materialism or emotionalism. The first type prefers material life, such as more wealth and income, and better housing; and the other prefers spiritual life, such love, interest sharing, knowledge communication and contemplation.

The basic issue in this game is to match up one man and one woman randomly for marriage. If they are both materialistic, their payoff is 1 for each. If they are both emotional, their payoff is 2 each. We can understand this as two emotional people being together having a relatively higher utility. However, if a materialistic-type and an emotional-type are married, neither of them will feel

		Woman	
		Materialistic	Spiritual
Man	Materialistic	1, 1	0, 0
	Spiritual	0, 0	2, 2

Figure 12.4 The Marriage Game

comfortable, they will not speak a common language, and they will have difficulty living together. Therefore, we assume each person's payoff is 0.

What type of marriage will be mainstream in a free-choice society? For the convenience of discussion, we will assume that the ratio of materialistic-type people is the
same for both men and women.[11] This ratio is x, so the ratio of emotional-type people
is $1 - x$. For any individual person that is materialistic-type, the expected payoff is x
times 1, plus $1 - x$ times 0, or x. If an individual is emotional type, the expected payoff is x times 0, plus $1 - x$ times 2, or $2(1 - x)$. Therefore, if $x > 2(1 - x)$, thus $x > 2/3$,
then materialistic people survive more easily. Alternatively, emotional-type people
survive more easily if $x < 2/3$. In this way, if the total population of both male or
female, is more than two-thirds materialistic, then this society will evolve into everyone being materialistic and the emotional people will be eliminated. Alternatively,
if emotional-type people exceed one-third of society, then they are more suited for
survival and society will evolve into everyone being emotional and the materialistic
people will be eliminated. Thus, the stable equilibriums are: Either all people are
emotional or all people are materialistic.

If society is precisely two-thirds materialist-type people and one-third emotional-
type people, their expected payoffs are the same and both types of people can survive. However, this is not a stable equilibrium. For instance, if originally the ratio
of emotional-type people is one-third, but suddenly a few more emotional people
are added, then the ratio of emotional-type people exceeds one-third. Thus, they
can survive more easily than materialist-type people, so the whole society will
become emotional-type and the materialist-type will be eliminated. The above
analysis can be summarized in Figure 12.5.

Figure 12.5 is similar to Figure 12.2. The horizontal axis is the proportion of
the materialist-type, and the vertical axis is the expected payoffs. Here, the cut-off
point is not half population, because payoffs of different type matching are asymmetric. We can see that when x is equal to two-thirds, it is also an equilibrium,
but it is not a stable equilibrium. As long as a variation occurs, this type of equilibrium state will migrate towards either side until everyone is emotional-type or
materialist-type. Of course, here we are describing the direction, but not the speed
towards the equilibrium state. This process might be very short or very long.

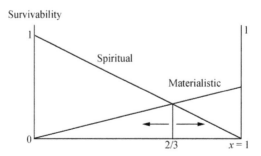

Figure 12.5 The Marriage Evolution Game

Complete materialist-type and complete emotional type are both evolutionarily stable equilibrium. However, comparatively speaking, the emotional-type equilibrium is Pareto optimal to the materialist-type equilibrium. Thus, in evolutionary games, the stable state is not necessarily the Pareto optimal equilibrium. If too many people in society are materialist-type in the initial stage, then it might become a society where everyone only pursues material interests. If we could design it, then of course we will design a society where everyone is emotional-type, but the reality is this outcome is not designed, but instead evolved. Thus, the actual equilibrium might be everyone is materialist-type.

The evolution of people's preferences in marriage is also a process of learning and imitation. Different from the traffic game, people's marriage preferences have relatively innate factors. However, there are social and customary aspects of marriage that will influence each individual's choices. Individual behavioral models are influenced by the social mainstream, so sometimes individuals can only "go with the flow". If most people are materialistic, it is best that you be a bit more materialistic like other people are. Not only does this apply to before marriage, but people also adjust their preferences after marriage. For example, you might have originally been an emotional-type person, but after marrying a materialist-type person, you might slowly become materialist-type. Of course, the opposite circumstance might occur. From the social perspective, a society's mainstream values will influence each individual's behavior in society, and sometimes an isolated individual might be unable to resist this factor.

Of course, our conclusion is a bit extreme. In reality, even in a society where materialism is prevalent, there are always certain people that put more weight on spiritual life, and live well. In other words, the state of marriage in reality is more like a "polymorphic equilibrium" that is stable, not a monomorphic equilibrium. The reason our theoretical conclusion is different from reality is that we assumed marriage pairing is completely random. In reality, marriage is not completely random, instead it is a search process.[12] At this point, still looking at our example, even if the ratio of materialist-type people exceeds two-thirds, emotional-type people can also survive in equilibrium. The reason is that emotional-type people can specifically search for people that also put weight on emotion, then both of them can obtain a payoff of 2. This is called "positive assortment" in the evolutional game theory.[13] The next generation raised by them is more likely to be emotional-type and also seek out to marry emotional-type people. In this way, emotion-types have an opportunity to survive from one generation to the next. Even though from ancient times to the present, people that pursue material interests have been in the majority, there has still not been a lack of emotional-type people that put weight on love. Of course, because the probability of search success is related to the distribution of different types of people in the population, our basic conclusion is still relevant. Obviously, when the vast majority of people in society are materialist-type, it is relatively difficulty for emotional-type people to find a suitable partner. At this point, changing preferences might be the best option.

The above analysis also tells us one point: There is a certain degree of path dependency in social evolution. In the previous examples, one equilibrium is Pareto optimal, and the other is not. Evolutionary equilibrium analysis means that our technology and social system might be locked in a non-Pareto optimal state for a long time. In the example above, if everyone becomes emotional-type, then everyone can live more happily. However, because each individual acts independently, when society's dominant values are set as materialist-type, then it is extremely difficult for an independent individual to change it. Therefore, social evolution does not always lead to the most efficient institutional arrangements.

However, one point that must be emphasized is that this society is assumed a being closed society. In a closed society, an inefficient equilibrium can survive for a long time. As soon as this society opens up, different social systems will compete. This type of competition might cause the institutional arrangements that originally were non-Pareto optimal to have no ability to survive. Assume that there are two societies: One that is purely emotional-type and one that is purely materialist-type. If these two societies are separated, then neither society will change. Now, if we combine these two societies into one, what new equilibrium will occur? This depends on the population size of the different societies. If originally both societies have a population of two million people, then in the new society, the emotional-type ratio is one-half. This exceeds the one-third critical value, so emotional-type people will have an advantage and the materialist-type society will no longer survive. However, if originally the materialist-type society has a population that exceeds three million, but the emotional-type society only has a population of one million, then the new society will be more likely to evolve into materialist-type.

Of course, this is only a mechanical example. The most important characteristic of humanity is our ability to learn and change our behavioral methods. This is the basic reason that social evolution is much faster than biological evolution. Because of this point, if the advantages of Pareto optimal states are great enough, and there is sufficient competition between different cultures and institutions, then high efficiency institutions will gradually eliminate low-efficiency institutions. There are many examples of this in real life. Competition between the Soviet Union and the United States is a classic example. Although there are many problems with the American system, it is still the most efficient and suitable for human nature in today's world. If each country was closed off from competition, the Soviet Union's planned economy system might have existed for a longer period of time. However, as soon as there was sufficient competition, the Soviet Union system, which was too inefficient and too anti-human nature, fell apart. Similarly, when we examine corporate governance structures across the globe, there are significant differences among countries in the relationship between the board of directors and management, incentive systems, ownership arrangements, voting systems, etc. Academia has separated corporate governance structures into two overall categories: The Anglo-American model, with a dominant equity market; and the Japanese-German model, where the equity market does not play a big role, but there is strict insider control of the corporation. Now that capital markets are globalizing, both Germany and Japan are moving closer to the American model, otherwise they will not be able to survive. Because of globalization, the entire world's corporate governance is converging.[14]

2.3 The hawk-dove game

The previous three examples of evolutionarily stable equilibrium are all mono-morphic equilibriums, meaning there is only one type of behavioral pattern in the stable state. Below, we will see an example of polymorphic stable equilibrium.

Imagine there are two types of people in a society: Aggressive type and temperate type. For convenience, we will refer to the former as "hawks" and the latter as "doves". Individuals interact randomly to undertake one-on-one games.[15] If a hawk and a hawk interact, they both obtain −1. If a hawk and a dove interact, then the hawk obtains 1 and the dove obtains 0. If a dove and a dove interact, both obtain 0.5.[16] The structure of the game is shown in Figure 12.6.

If in the population the proportion of hawks is x and the proportion of doves is $1 - x$, then the expected payoff for hawks is $-x + (1 - x) = 1-2x$ and the expected payoff for doves is $0.5(1 - x)$. From this we can see that if $x > 1/3$, then doves have the advantage. If $x < 1/3$, then hawks have the advantage. If $x = 1/3$, then neither hawks nor doves have an advantage over the other. Imagine that in the beginning $x > 1/3$. Because doves have a survival advantage, the proportion of doves will gradually increase and the proportion of doves will gradually decrease until $x = 1/3$.

Similarly, if in the beginning $x < 1/3$, because hawks have survival advantage, the proportion of hawks will gradually increase and the proportion of doves will gradually decrease until $x = 1/3$. When $x = 1/3$, after any small-scale invasion of hawks or doves, the population will quickly return to the $x = 1/3$ state. Therefore, $x = 1/3$ is the only evolutionarily stable equilibrium, as shown in Figure 12.7.

	Hawk	Dove
Hawk	−1, −1	1, 0
Dove	0, 1	0.5, 0.5

Figure 12.6 The Hawk and Dove Game

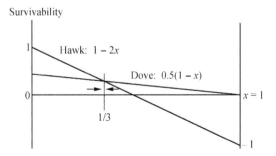

Figure 12.7 A Polymorphic Equilibrium

This evolutionarily stable equilibrium is polymorphic, meaning hawks and doves coexist in equilibrium. The reason for this is the relative minority in this game to the contrary have a relative advantage. This is similar to the situation in many organizations in real life. Even though within an organization there are overbearing people and modest people, both types of people can peacefully coexist. However, if the proportion of overbearing people is excessive, they will have a negative effect on each other, which is beneficial to the survival of modest people. Alternatively, if there are too many modest people, overbearing people can take advantage of them, which will attract the entry of more overbearing people.

Section three: the Prisoner's Dilemma and the evolution of cooperative culture

3.1 The survival of tit for tat

Now we will analyze the formation of social cooperative culture from the perspective of evolutionary games. As we know, human progress comes from human mutual cooperation, but the biggest difficulty faced by cooperation is the "Prisoner's Dilemma". Therefore, our discussion will begin with resolving the Prisoner's Dilemma.[17]

Imagine there are two types of people in society: One type that is innately cooperative and another that is innately non-cooperative. When two people interact at random, if both people are cooperative type, then both of them receive 4. If both people are non-cooperative type, both receive 0. If one person is cooperative type and the other is non-cooperative type, then the cooperative-type person's payoff is −1 and the non-cooperative-type person's payoff is 6. The payoff structure is shown in Figure 12.8.

If this is a one-shot game between two people, it is easy to see that regardless of the proportion of cooperative-type people, from the perspective of a cooperative-type individual, his payoff is inferior to the non-cooperative-type payoff. Therefore, in one-shot game situations, the evolved final equilibrium outcome is only one type of person in society, all of which are swindlers. This conclusion is a generality. In one-shot games, if only a dominant strategy exists, then this equilibrium is certainly an evolutionarily stable equilibrium. Specifically for this example, non-cooperation is an evolutionarily stable equilibrium.

	Cooperative	Non-cooperative
Cooperative	4, 4	−1, 6
Non-cooperative	6, −1	0, 0

Figure 12.8 The Prisoner's Dilemma

Assume this game repeats twice, what will the outcome be? A pair of players would be chosen at random from a group, and this fixed pair would undertake the game twice. As we know from Chapter 6, when the game repeats a second time, individual choices might be different from before. Now, each player's strategies have increased. In one-shot game, their strategies only were to cooperate or not cooperate. Now, we will assume an additional strategy called "tit for tat" (or TFT).

We will use different notations to represent different strategies. ALL-C represents always cooperating, meaning regardless of what the other person does, an individual will cooperate in both the first and second round. ALL-D represents always not cooperating. TFT represents cooperating in the first round, but then choosing the action that the opponent chose in the first round. If the opponent cooperates in the first round, then you will also cooperate in the second round, but if the opponent does not cooperate in the first round, you will not cooperate in the second round. Assume that in the overall population, there are three types of people: People that implement the ALL-C strategy, people that implement the TFT strategy, and people that implement the ALL-D strategy. Here, we will not consider discounting; instead we will calculate payoffs by simply adding them together.

If both people are cooperative type, then they will cooperate in the first and second rounds, so their payoff from both rounds is 8. If a cooperative type interacts with an opponent that implements the TFT strategy, then both people will cooperate in the first round and both will also cooperate in the second round, so the payoff is also 8. If a cooperative-type person interacts with a person that always does not cooperate, then the cooperative-type person will be cheated in both rounds for a combined payoff of −2, but his opponent will receive a payoff of 12 for not cooperating in both rounds. When a TFT-type person interacts with an ALL-C-type or another TFT-type person, then there is cooperation in both rounds for a payoff of 8. When a TFT-type person plays a game with an opponent that implements an ALL-D strategy, he cooperates in the first round for a payoff of −1, but he does not cooperate in the second round, with the payoff is 0. The total payoff for both rounds would be −1. The opponent that implemented an ALL-D strategy had a total payoff from both rounds of 6. If two ALL-D strategy players interact, neither one cooperates in either round, so the total payoff is 0. The payoffs for the entire game are shown in Figure 12.9.

In an evolutionary game structured like this, which type of person can survive best? First, we will examine people that use the ALL-C strategy. Obviously, this type of person will not survive best, because even under the best circumstances, that person is only as well off as the person that uses the TFT strategy. The other possibility is that this person will do worse than the person that uses the TFT

	ALL-C	TFT	ALL-D
ALL-C	8, 8	8, 8	−2, 12
TFT	8, 8	8, 8	−1, 6
ALL-D	12, −2	6, −1	0, 0

Figure 12.9 Two Repetitive Games

strategy, since the TFT person will only be swindled once, whereas the person that uses the ALL-C strategy will be swindled twice. Compared to the player that uses the ALL-D strategy, his situation is worse. Thus, we can conclude that the person that uses the ALL-C strategy has the lowest fitness to survive.

If the initial population is composed of two groups of people, one group cooperative type and the other group non-cooperative type, then a person that uses the TFT strategy could invade and replace the people that use the ALL-C strategy. If the initial population is either composed entirely of ALL-C-type people or ALL-C and TFT-type people, then ALL-D-type people could also invade because payoff for ALL-D-type people are better than for ALL-C-type people. Therefore, ALL-C is not an evolutionarily stable strategy. Stated simply, in a society, the type of person that naively cooperates has no means to survive in an evolutionarily stable equilibrium.

Now, assume that the process of evolution has already eliminated the group of naively cooperative people, so now all that is left is one group of ALL-D people that never cooperate and another group of TFT people. Under these circumstances, we come to the payoff structure shown in Figure 12.10.

We will examine which of these two types of people are fitter for survival. Assuming that the proportion of people in the original population that implements the TFT strategy is x, and the proportion of the population that implements the ALL-D strategy is $1 - x$. At this point, for an individual that implements the TFT strategy, his expected payoff is $8x - (1 - x) = 9x - 1$. The expected payoff for a person that uses the ALL-D strategy is $6x$. If $9x - 1 > 6x$, then it is easier for people that implement the TFT strategy to survive. Alternatively, if $9x - 1 < 6x$, then it is easier for people that implement the ALL-D strategy to survive. The cut-off is $x = 1/3$. If $x > 1/3$, meaning at least one-third of the people in the beginning are not swindlers but take revenge on people that swindle, then this type of person has a better ability to survive and can reach a stable equilibrium state. Alternatively, if $x < 1/3$, the non-cooperative-type people can survive more easily, so under the stable state everyone will become non-cooperative type. If x is precisely equal to one-third, then both types of people can survive, but this type of state is unstable. Similar to the previous analysis, we can use Figure 12.11 to represent the above conclusion.

Figure 12.11 shows how the expected payoff from each strategy changes as the proportion of people implementing the TFT strategy increases. When $x = 0$, the payoff for people that use the ALL-D strategy is higher than for the people that use the TFT strategy. As x increases from zero, the payoff for both strategies increases, but

	TFT	ALL-D
TFT	8, 8	−1, 6
ALL-D	6, −1	0, 0

Figure 12.10 TFT and ALL-D

the payoff for people using the TFT strategy increases faster. The two curves intersect at $x = 1/3$, above which the payoff for the TFT strategy is higher than the payoff for the ALL-D strategy. Any proportion higher or lower than $x = 1/3$ will lead to either the TFT strategy equilibrium or the ALL-D strategy equilibrium. Both of these two equilibriums are evolutionarily stable equilibriums. As we can see, depending on the initial state, society might converge towards the cooperative equilibrium or towards the non-cooperative equilibrium. However, in the cooperative equilibrium society, each person implements the TFT strategy. Precisely because of TFT will the society maintain a cooperative state under which any invading swindler will be eliminated.

More generally, let us consider a repeated game taking n times between a fixed pair of two people, but the initial matching of each pair is random. Similar to our above analysis, it is easy to show that entirely using the ALL-C strategy is not an evolutionarily stable strategy. Figure 12.12 shows the payoffs in a game from other two types of strategies.

Similar to before, we assume that the proportion of people in society implementing the TFT strategy is x. For the person implementing the TFT strategy, he has a probability x of interacting with a same type person for a payoff of $4n$ and a probability $1 - x$ of interacting with a swindler for a payoff of -1. His expected payoff is $4nx + x - 1$. For the person that utilizes the ALL-D strategy, he only has one chance to take advantage of the swindling, so his expected payoff is $6x$. Thus, if $(4n + 1)x - 1 > 6x$, or when $x > 1 / (4n - 5)$, then people that implement the

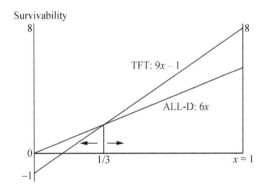

Figure 12.11 The Evolutionarily Stable Equilibrium

	TFT	ALL-D
TFT	$4n, 4n$	$-1, 6$
ALL-D	$6, -1$	$0, 0$

Figure 12.12 The Nth Game

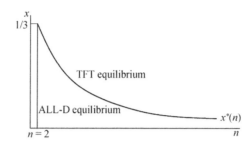

Figure 12.13 The Relationship Between the Cooperation Threshold X and the Number of Game Repetitions

TFT strategy have a survival advantage. In the end, the equilibrium will converge towards everyone implementing the TFT strategy and cooperative relationships will emerge throughout society. Otherwise, it will converge towards everyone implementing the ALL-D strategy. From this we can see that the critical proportion x^* (the proportion of people in society that implement the TFT strategy) that lead to cooperative society is related to the number of times the game repeats. This relationship is shown in Figure 12.13.

In Figure 12.13, the horizontal axis represents the number (n) of times the game repeats. The vertical axis represents the critical proportion (x) of the population that implements the TFT strategy. The curve shows the critical proportion x^* decreases as n increases. If the game is only undertaken twice, then only when x surpasses 1/3 will this society evolve into a cooperative society. However, as long as the number of repetitions is great enough, even if originally, the proportion x of people that implements the TFT strategy is tiny, in the end, the society will evolve towards a cooperative equilibrium. (We assumed here that the discount factor is 1. If the discount factor is 0.9, then the curve would move upwards slightly, but the basic conclusion is the same.). The curve $x^*(n)$ in the figure is a cut-off curve. If the original proportion is above this curve, then society will evolve into a cooperative equilibrium in which everyone implements the TFT strategy and everyone cooperates. If the original proportion is below this curve, then the equilibrium will become an ALL-D equilibrium in which no one will cooperate.

Let us specifically examine the relationship between n and the critical value of x^*. If $n = 2$, then x being greater than one-third is sufficient to cause cooperation to appear, as we saw earlier. If $n = 4$, then as long as $x > 0.1$ or so, it will be sufficient to bring about the cooperation equilibrium. Compared with the one-third required when $n = 2$, this critical value is much smaller. In other words, if we have two societies both of which have slightly less than 90% of people being non-cooperative type in the initial stage, then the society with the game repeating four times or more will slowly evolve to a cooperative-society, whereas the other society with the game repeating twice will evolve to a non-cooperative society.

As for research on Prisoner's Dilemma cooperation, we have already mentioned Robert Axelrod's well-known computer-run experiment studies conducted in 1981 and 1984. He reported that in the first experiment, among 14 types of strategies, the TFT strategy was the most successful and had the highest score. In the second group of 62 strategies, the TFT strategy was also the most successful.[18] Our previous discussion of the evolutionary game model may provide an explanation for this.[19]

3.2 The weak stable strategy and the strong stable strategy

Whether or not a type of behavioral pattern in society is evolutionarily stable depends on the type of variation strategy. Assume that there can only be two possible types of strategies: One type is the ALL_C and the other type is the TFT. If the original population of this society consists of pure All-C people, now a few people that implement the TFT strategy invade, will cooperation be broken? No. The ALL-C type people will continue to exist because no cheating will emerge. Therefore, this cooperation is still stable, but becoming a polymorphic equilibrium with both ALL-C and TFT types coexisting. Another situation is that the original population is entirely composed of TFT-type people. If a variation occurs with invaders that implement the ALL-C strategy, cooperation can still sustain. We will find that this is different from the evolutionarily stable state that we discussed previously. According to the previous definition, if a strategy equilibrium is an evolutionarily stable state, then after a variation, the invaders will be eliminated and the original equilibrium will resume. In the TFT society, if about one percent of the population becomes the ALL-C type, then this proportion will always be maintained. In this society, the ALL-C type people are as fit as the TFT type for survival. Under the equilibrium state, these two types of people can coexist forever.

In order to differentiate between the two states, we must define the concepts of strong stability and weak stability. An equilibrium is called a strong stable equilibrium, if after an intrusion the proportion of people that use the original strategy increases until the variation is eliminated. For example, if a group of people that implement the ALL-D strategy intrude into a society that is originally entirely composed of TFT-type people, then this small group of intruders will gradually be eliminated and this society will return to a complete TFT-type strategy. For the ALL-D variation, TFT is a strong stable equilibrium. Alternatively, an equilibrium is called weak stable equilibrium if after a variation intrudes the proportion of variants does not change, but instead continues forever. In the previous example, after one percent of people implement the ALL-C strategy, the proportion of people that implement the TFT strategy will sustain at 99% and the proportion of the ALL-C will sustain at 1%, so TFT is a weak stable equilibrium with the ALL-C variation. This type of variation is called a neutral variation, meaning that after it intrudes an equilibrium, it can survive but will not drive out the original behavioral pattern.

Thus, whether or not a strategy equilibrium is evolutionarily stable depends on the type of variation. There are numerous possible types of variations we can consider. We previously discussed the TFT strategy. Similarly, we can discuss the tit-for-two-tat strategy (thereafter, TF2T). Here, the TF2T strategy refers to cooperating in the beginning, continuing cooperation even after one occurrence of cheating from the opponent, but then taking revenge if being cheated second time, and returning to cooperation once the opponent stops cheating. We can understand this as the TF2T people being more tolerant than TFT people. Another strategy is the STFT strategy which stipulates the player does not cooperate in the first round and then takes the TFT strategy if the opponent cooperated previously. Examples of these two types of behavioral patterns can be found in real life. When joining a social group, some people will start off by viewing others as good people, even if they are swindled once. Others will start off by viewing others as bad people, but if they find the opponent to not be bad, they will start to cooperate. This created the TF2T and the STFT strategies.

We already know that ALL-C is a neutral variation of TFT. We can use similar methods to show that TF2T is also a neutral variation of TFT.

Imagine that a population is originally composed of TFT-and TF2T-type people and the entire society is in a state of cooperation. Now, a variation emerges with the intrusion of STFT-type people. At this point, the TFT strategy will not continue to exist, but the TF2T strategy will. The reason is that after the STFT strategy enters it will begin with a swindle, so naturally the TFT strategy will take revenge. The outcome will be a vicious cycle. For the people that implement the TF2T strategy, they will be swindled once after the STFT strategy intrudes, but from then on they will cooperate forever. If the future is important enough, meaning the discount factor is great enough and the game repeats enough times, then TFT-type people are less fit for survival than TF2T-type people. From this perspective, the TFT strategy is not even a weak stable equilibrium.

3.3 The destruction of cooperative culture

Above, we assumed that an individual's behavioral pattern is innate and the process of evolution is a continuous process of eliminating people with unfit behavioral patterns, therefore evolution is a long term process. However, as we have already pointed out, human behavior is both innate and influenced by learning. Human behavioral patterns are transmittable. Social evolution is a process of mutual learning and influence. If an individual finds his original strategy disadvantageous to himself, then he will learn to adopt a new strategy. Generally speaking, many people in social life imitate the behavior of successful people. This is the so-called "power of role models." This way, during social evolution, what will be eliminated may not be specific people, but instead certain types of behavioral patterns.

Assuming that a society is originally a cooperative society, will cooperation be destroyed in a short time period? Our previous analysis showed that under certain conditions a cooperative society might be destroyed. Assume that from the beginning everyone in this society implements the TFT strategy. This society will always be in a cooperative state. Assume that this cooperative state has been maintained for hundreds of years, perhaps even shorter than that, say a few decades. Because swindlers have never appeared, people in this society will rationally expect that cooperation is natural. They believe that everyone will forever be cooperative type (because swindlers have never appeared, no one knows if others are ALL-C type or TFT type.) In this situation, people that implemented the TFT strategy might implement the ALL-C strategy. At this point, ALL-D-type intruders could make their way in. In the first game after the intrusion, the payoff for other types of players will be -1, but ALL-D-type players will receive a payoff of 6.

Because the survivability of the variation is greater, certain people that were originally TFT type will also transform into ALL-D type. Within a short period of time, all of society will become non-cooperative, and cooperation will be destroyed. Of course, this explanation may be a bit extreme. If TFT-type people in the end all become ALL-C-type people, after a period of time they realize there are swindlers among them, then they may revert back to the TFT strategy. This will drive out the ALL-D strategy. The key point is that if one percent of society becomes swindlers, then it may cause thirty percent of society to gradually become swindlers. Only by this point of time, will people realize that the ALL-C strategy is incorrect and implement a new strategy such as reviving the TFT strategy. In other words, the evolution of behavioral patterns is not necessarily monotonous.

The above is a theoretical possible. If we look at the changes in Chinese society over the last sixty years, this possibility has really happened. For a long time, successful Chinese peasants had two characteristics: honesty and industriousness. In traditional agricultural society, people with these two characteristics were the fittest for survival. However, after collectivization and people's communes were implemented in the countryside in the 1950s, the rules of the game changed. Peasants soon found that lying and laziness brought about the most benefit, whereas honest and diligence could subject a person to struggle sessions or repression. Within the span of a few years, people that were originally honest became dishonest and people that were originally diligent became lazy. When I was little, the older peasants were still relatively hard working and looked down on the good-for-nothing young people, but when I grew up, this type of old peasant was a rarity. This is not to say that these people died (of course some of them did), but instead their behavior changed. Within one generation, customs changed and hard work was not one of them. By the late 1970s, after almost every peasant had become a deadbeat, people had no way to survive. This led to the household contract responsibility system and individual work on designated land. After this was implemented, lazy people could not survive, so the work ethic returned. Of course, the return of honesty required longer time.

If this was the case in the countryside, how could this not be the case in the cities? When those that lied and did bad things lived better than other people, more and more people eventually learned to imitate the former. If successful people become successful by saying "1 + 1 = 3", how could you doubt the correctness of "1 + 1 = 3"? This is the reason we see fewer and fewer government officials telling the truth. Parents raise their children very differently than before. In the past, parents cultivated their children to be honest and cooperate with others. Today, parents warn their children against being cheated.[20] Of course, similar to how it was thirty years ago in the countryside, more and more people believe that society cannot continue on like this.

Changes in society are often caused by population movements. The reason for this is that the evolutionarily stable strategies differ from region to region and country to country. When migration occurs, newcomers become a type of variation. Newcomers might transform the behavioral pattern of the local people, or they may assimilate. For example, in America, making connections with the government or bribing government officials is not good commercial practice, but in China, it is difficult to succeed without doing this. Therefore, we see that after American firms enter China, they slowly begin to "do as the locals do".

Whether or not a variation can change the original equilibrium depends on the scale of the variation. So far we have always assumed that variation emerge on a small scale. If the variation is large scale, the original stable state might not be stable any longer. China has a huge population, so when China interacts with the world, will China change the world or will the world change China? This issue merits our consideration.

Our analysis shows that spontaneous evolution might lead to inefficient equilibriums. Diego Gambetta (1993) analyzed the evolution of the Sicilian Mafia. This is an example of a cultural and institutional evolution that did not necessarily lead to efficient cooperation.[21] Over a long period of history, the south of Italy was occupied by Spain and France, which implanted a culture of untrustworthiness to rule the area. The entire judicial system was unreliable, while at the same time lack of trust between all sections of society suppressed economic activity, so the outcome of exchange could not be predicted. There was high social mobility, so trust was very limited to small circles. The above reasons in common led to the emergence of mafia-type organizations.

Section four: the spontaneous order and property rights

4.1 The spontaneous order

The property rights system is the most important system for the promotion of human cooperation (North, 1990). In today's world, many laws are related to the definition and protection of property rights. Many international agreements and treaties were also created to define property rights (such as sovereignty). However, the basic rules of property rights were not created by law. In the first half of the eighteenth century, David Hume (1740) pointed out that rules on property rights evolved spontaneously. A large amount of historical research and observations prove that Hume was correct.[22]

The most important rule for the property rights system is the "first-on rule". This rule is generally applicable from the ancient times to the present, from East to West, and from territorial sovereignty to forming a line to buy tickets. After the Second World War, the division of the Soviet and American spheres of influence also respected the first-on rule. In the dispute between China, the Philippines, and Vietnam in the South China Sea and in the dispute between China and Japan over the Diaoyu Islands, Chinese arguments are also based on the first-on rule. Which seats students sit in during class also respects the first-on rule.

Therefore, it is better to say that the first-on rule is a custom than a law. During my childhood in Wubao County, Shanxi Province, the Yellow River would flood every summer and leave behind large amounts of coal on banks (now I know that it came from surface coal fields in areas around Fugu County). In the places where the river curved, there would be a large amount of different sized pieces of coal on the river shore that was unclaimed property. At the time, this was the primary means of earning a living for residents by the river. The rule was that as long as someone put something they own on a piece of coal (such as a basket, a bag, or even pants), it was theirs and others could not dispute it. Once the river coal had been divided up in this way, the residents would take it home and sell it. Even without any legal protections, this rule was respected by all residents. This is a custom.[23]

We can also prove that property rights are the product of spontaneous evolution with a contrary example. In most countries, narcotics and prostitution are illegal. Not only are participants' behavior not protected by the law, they are strictly repressed once discovered. Why do these two markets still exist? Because both parties to the transaction respect the property rights they define and have historically formed. Similarly, even prisoners have their own rules for property rights.

How are rules for property rights formed? Economists are accustomed to explaining the formation of property rights from the perspective of "efficiency". For example, the reason people respect the "first-on rule" is because people will be more incentivized to develop new resources while at the same time reducing the costs of disputes. If rules are set through collective choice, then perhaps this explanation is correct (although it must also resolve the issue of the Prisoner's Dilemma in collective action). However, if rules are spontaneously formed without centralized design, then this explanation may not always be convincing. In the previous example of river coal, the first-on rule means residents must be one step faster than someone else, which is costly and can even be dangerous. If "equal distribution" or "drawing lots" were implemented, then these costs would be reduced. Therefore, in this example, the efficiency standard is not convincing.

Sugden (1989) explained the spontaneous formation of rules for property rights from the perspective of evolutionary games. Below, we will give a brief explanation of his theories.

4.2 The property rights game

We will us the "Hawk and Dove Game" discussed in Section Two to explain this issue.

First, we will consider a two-person game using traditional game theory. Imagine a piece of unclaimed property (such as river coal) valued at one unit. Both people want to obtain this property, and they have two strategies to choose from: The hawk strategy or the dove strategy. If both people choose the hawk strategy, each of them will receive -1. If one player chooses the hawk strategy and one player chooses the dove strategy, then the former will receive 1 and the latter will receive 0. If both people choose the dove strategy, then the property will be split evenly, and each will receive 0.5.

From Chapter 3, we know that this game has two pure strategy Nash equilibriums and one mixed strategy Nash equilibrium. The two pure strategy Nash equilibriums are either one player choosing the hawk strategy and the other player choosing the dove strategy. The mixed strategy Nash equilibrium is each person choosing the hawk strategy with a one-third probability and choosing the dove strategy with a two-thirds probability.

As we know, because there are multiple Nash equilibriums, when there are no other devices (such as some type of norm) to differentiate the two people, the outcome of the two people's choices is not necessarily a Nash equilibrium.

To resolve this issue, we will use some type of clear mechanism to differentiate between the two people. Imagine there are two signals: A and B. Each person has one-half probability of receiving either signal A or B. The two signals are negatively correlated, meaning if one person receives signal A, he knows that the other player certainly received signal B. (The reader can think of signal A indicating a "first-comer" and signal B indicating a "late-comer". We can understand one-half probability as meaning both players are equal and have an equal probability of coming first or last.). In this way, we can consider the following three evolutionary game strategies (behavioral patterns): (1) When signal A is received, choose the hawk strategy and when signal B is received, choose the dove strategy; (2) when signal A is received, choose the dove strategy, and when signal B is received, choose the hawk strategy; or (3) regardless of which signal is received, choose the hawk strategy at one-third probability and choose the dove strategy at two-thirds probability. (If A indicates first-comer, then Strategy (1) is the "first-on rule" of property rights.). Obviously, all of these three strategies are Nash equilibriums (although we are only using labels to differentiate the two people).

These three types of strategies are actually three types of different behavioral rules. Which type will become the "custom"? To answer this question, we must transition to evolutionary game analysis. From the perspective of the issue we care about, this is natural because customs do evolve.

Imagine a large population where any two people randomly interact to undertake the repeated Hawk-Dove Game that we discussed previously. Each person has an equal probability of being labeled A or B (a complete negative correlation), and each person acts according to a certain rule. First, we must note that Rule (3) (the mixed strategy) is not evolutionarily stable. To explain this point, imagine a population where almost everyone chooses Rule (3), but a small number of people choose Rule (1). Regardless if you choose Rule (1) or Rule (3), as long as your opponent chooses Rule (3), your expected payoff is 1/3. This means that there is no loss from choosing Rule (1). However, if your opponent also chooses Rule (1), then the two of you can coordinate. Therefore, people that choose Rule (1) are better off than everyone else that chooses Rule (3). With the passage of time, more and more people will imitate Rule (1). Therefore, Rule (3) is unstable.

Now imagine that everyone respected Rule (1). In this round of the game, you are labeled B and your opponent is labeled A. According to Rule (1), he will choose the hawk strategy and you should choose the dove strategy, so his payoff is 1 and your payoff is 0. If you choose Rule (2), you will receive −1. Therefore, given that others respect Rule (1), no one has an incentive to violate this rule, proving that Rule (1) is evolutionarily stable. Similarly, it is easy to show that Rule (2) is evolutionarily stable.

The above analysis shows that both Rule (1) and Rule (2) are evolutionarily stable. It is easy to prove that if the number of people that implement Rule (1) are greater than one half of the total population, then Rule (1) has a survival advantage. With the passage of time, everyone will convert to Rule (1), so it will become a custom. Alternatively, if the number of people that implement Rule (2) are greater than one half of the total population, then Rule (2) will become a custom.

4.3 The emergence of convention

If we explain the previous labels as the point of time at which a player arrives at the property, such as the A refers to the first comer and B refers to the second comer, then Rule (1) refers to the "first on rule", and Rule (2) could refer to a "last on rule." We proved that these two rules are evolutionarily stable and can become conventions, but we only observe the "first on rule", not the "last on rule". Why?

It first must be noted that conventions have evolved, they are not the outcome of collectively designing. The appearance of a convention does not necessarily mean it is Pareto optimal. To explain this point, let us assume that the value of this piece of property is asymmetric, where A values it at 0.9 and B values it at 1.1. When both people choose the dove strategy, A obtains 0.45 and B obtains 0.55. The other aspects of the game are completely the same as before. Because each person has an equal probability of being A or B, the expected payoff for both A and B under Rule (1) is 0.45 and the expected payoff for both A and B of Rule (2) is 0.55. In other words, Rule (2) is Pareto optimal to Rule (1). However, as soon as Rule (1) becomes a convention, no one will violate it.

The reason a type of behavioral pattern evolves into a convention is because people believe other people will respect it. As soon as most people respect it, a convention has the power to strengthen itself. The issue is: Where did people's initial belief come from? One possibility is that people accumulated some type of method to coordinate action from common experiences, then applied this method to other similar situations. If common experiences tell us that some type of established custom will be generally accepted in certain situations, then it will be imitated in similar situations.

Speaking for the first-on rule of property rights, the extent that it is so widely accepted proves that it necessarily is related to humanity's basic behavioral pattern. Actually, this rule is even common in the animal kingdom, so this should be related to human biology, but unrelated to culture.[24] One possible explanation is that humans, similar to animals, in the beginning, had to bodily occupy space to survive. As soon as a specific group began to live in an area (be they hunter gathers or otherwise), late comers that wanted to live in that area had to drive out the current occupiers, which necessarily led to conflict. From the late comer's perspective, the best option was to start in an area that had not yet been bodily occupied by others. At that ancient time, there were still a lot of unoccupied areas. This created the original "first-on rule" of usage rights. Slowly, perhaps as land became more precious, bodily occupation began "markingization": As soon as some group put some type of marking (including facilities built on it), this showed that the land belonged to someone and other people would acknowledge this. The first-on rule for ownership rights emerged from this. The next development is "symbolization" of occupation: marking was transformed into written records (or common memories), such as legal documents. This process is similar to seating in a crowding classroom. In the beginning, a seat belongs to whoever sits there. Then, seats are claimed by leaving a personal belonging, such as a bag, books on them. Later, people can expect the seating by allotting before anyone arrives. By this stage, ownership is created (animals only have a first-on rule for usage rights, but not for ownership rights). Another possibility is that biological characteristics determined that humans (and animals) can survive and flourish only when parents take care of the children and the children obeys the parents. The parents are the "first comer" and the children are the "late comer". Perhaps this is the original form of the first-on rule. Gradually, this type of rule slowly spread to other aspects. Of course, this is only my guess.

Regardless, precisely as Sugden pointed out, "imitation" are humanity's basic methods for learning and selecting behavior, and conventions may spread by "analogy" from one context to another. Therefore, we observe a "family relationship" between conventions. One such "family" is the "first come, first served" principle. The person in front of the line gets served first, the person closest to the door enters first, and the people hired last get laid off first, etc. The first-on rule in the property rights system is also a member of this family.

Confucius started from the behavioral norms within family relationships and then introduced "etiquette" to govern a nation. Perhaps this is the most convincing example of conventions forming by analogy. In Confucian academics, the relationship between the monarch and his subjects is comparable to the relationship between fathers and sons and the relationship between upper and lower classes is comparable to the relationship between brothers. This point also proves that "norm entrepreneurs" like Confucius have an important role in creating conventions and social behavioral norms. We will discuss this issue again in Chapter 14.

4.4 From conventions to norms

Conventions and norms are different. Conventions are behavioral rules that spontaneously evolved, referring to what people actually do. Norms refer to what people should do. When people believe each person should behave according to a convention, then that convention becomes a norm.

In many situations, people respect norms based on considerations for self-interest. The reason a norm is a norm is it is an evolutionarily stable strategy. Here, "interest" should be broadly understood to include each person's desire to be acknowledged by others. This desire for acknowledgement is at least as important as people's material desires. When we are despised for violating a norm, internally we will feel strongly displeased. Sometimes this type of displeasure exceeds material losses. It is easy to understand this point, because each of us lives in society. Our ability to survive depends on others' willingness to interact with us. Because of this reason, even though violating norms in certain circumstances will bring about material benefits, people are still willing to respect norms.

As soon as property rights rules were established, each person will expect others will also respect this rule. Given this expectation, each person has an interest in respect it. Given one's own respect, each person hopes others will also respect it. Any behavior that violates the rule will be considered a threat, causing fear and dissatisfaction. This type of dissatisfaction comes not only from the victim. The other beneficiaries of the rule will also indirectly feel threatened, because they also expect to rely on this rule to protect their own interests. They will sympathize with the victim.

Imagine you are the tenth person in line at the hospital. When I arrive, the line is already very long. I worry that I will not be able to see the doctor, so I cut in line between you and the ninth person in line. How will you react? Of course you will be angry, because not only do you now have to wait longer, but also because you expect that as soon as the rules are broken, more late-comers will cut in line, so you will never be seen. You might worry about retribution from physically pulling me back, but you still have total freedom to despise me. For the same reasons, everyone lined up behind you will be angry at me. What about the people before the ninth person? Their interests have not been directly harmed by my behavior, but they know that precisely because the "first-on rule" exists are they able to see the doctor before the people behind them in line. My behavior threatens their expectations. They will worry that without restraints, more others might cut in front of them. This will harm their interests. For this reason, they will speak up and denounce my behavior, or at least display contempt. With this many people upset at me, how will I feel?

Of course, there are always a few people that do not respect the rules, but occasional disrespect for the rules cannot change people's expectations towards the rules. As soon as a rule is established, occasional violations will not cause it to collapse. Actually, the people that occasionally violate a rule also hope that the rule will continue to exist, otherwise their own future interests are not guaranteed.

It must be pointed out that previously we assumed each person had an equivalent probability of being labeled a first-comer or a late-comer, so this rule treats everyone fairly. If a rule systematically favors one group, then this rule might not be commonly respected, because disadvantageous groups will not condemn delinquent behavior. In 1960s America, when black Americans rose up against racial discrimination policies, black Americans and white Americans opposed to racial discrimination commended their behavior instead of condemning it. This is an important driver of people within human societies becoming more and more equal. The reason racial, gender, and other discrimination based on innate factors are accepted less and less is because they systematically favor certain groups. In the property rights rules we discussed earlier, if people with a certain lineage were always labeled as "first comers", then the first-on rule might not be enforceable.[25]

Notes

1 Recall that something is called common knowledge when you know, I know, you know I know, I know you know, and so on. Aumann (1976a) was the first to provide a strict common knowledge model.
2 The rule of thumb is also known as the rule of experience or experience workability method.
3 John Maynard Smith and George R. Price, "The Logic of Animal Conflict." *Nature.* 1973, Volume 246, pp. 15–18; John Maynard Smith, *Evolution and Theory of Games.* Cambridge: Cambridge University Press, 1982.
4 Actually, evolutionary games are changing the entire research scope of economics. See these four papers published in the *Journal of Economic Perspectives* (2002, Volume II): (1) Richard Nelson and Sidney Winter, "*Evolutionary Theorizing in Economics*"; (2) Larry Samuelson, "*Evolution and Game Theory*"; (3) Theodore C. Bergstrom, "*Evolution of Social Behavior: Individual and Group Selection*"; (4) Arthur J. Robson,

"*Evolution and Human Nature*". Samuelson's *Evolutionary Games and Equilibrium* (1997) is outstanding research on evolutionary games. Also see Friedman (1998), Schmidt (2004), and Sugden (2001).

5 Richard Dawkins, *The Selfish Gene*. Oxford: Oxford University Press, 1976.

6 Richard Dawkins, *The Selfish Gene*. Oxford: Oxford University Press, 1976.

7 Nash equilibriums always exist in finite games, but evolutionarily stable strategies might not. See Vega-Redondo (2003) for a standard definition.

8 See Kenneth Binmore's *Game Theory and the Social Contract* for a discussion on social evolution methods and transmission factors. See also Axelrod (1984); Boyd and Richerson (1985); and Gale, Binmore, and Samuelson (1995).

9 We discussed in Chapter 3 the ways of coordinating expectations of the Traffic Game. Evolutionary games provide an explanation for the formation of traffic rules. See Young (1996).

10 The assurance game refers to both parties involved preferring to cooperate while engaged in some common matter.

11 Of course, we could make this more complex, such as defining x as the proportion for men and y for the proportion of women so that the two proportions are different. However, this will not influence the basic results of the analysis. Therefore, for simplicity, we will assume they are the same.

12 See Roth and Sotomayor (1990) for marriage pairing theoretical models. Gale and Shapley (1962) broadly applied this pairing model to the labor market and auction market. For their contributions to pairing market theory, they shared the 2012 Nobel Memorial Prize in Economics.

13 See Samuel Bowles and Herbert Gintis (2013): A Cooperative Species: Human Reciprocity and It Evolution. Chapter 4.

14 See Gilson (2001); Gordon and Roe (2004); and Yoshikawa and Rasheed (2009) for theories and empirical research on corporate governance structure convergence.

15 Maynard Smith (1982) started his book with the "Hawk-Dove Game". This game has become the standard model for discussions of evolutionary stability in biology.

16 The reader can take this game as territorial disputes between nations, power disputes between politicians, or market disputes between competing firms. In Chapter 3, we discussed a similar game. In Section Four, we will use this game to analyze the evolution of the property rights system.

17 Bendor and Swistak (2001) used evolutionary games to explain how to escape the Prisoner's Dilemma. Our discussions to a large degree were inspired by them.

18 Robert Axelrod, *The Evolution of Cooperation*. New York: Basic Books, 1984.

19 Linster (1992, 1994) and Nachbar (1992) expanded upon Axelrod's work. Their research shows that repeated Prisoner's Dilemma games are complex situations where the most successful strategy depends on the strategy pool (thus the total variations of behavioral patterns). Although "tit-for-tat" is sometimes most successful, it is not always the most successful. For example, if there is sustained obstruction during the process of evolution, then the "trigger strategy" is most successful. Later research simulated the Prisoner's Dilemma evolutionary model. See Samuelson (1997, Chapter 1) and the literature cited in Footnote 23.

20 See Yefu Zheng, *Xinren Lun*. Beijing: China Radio and Television Press, 2006.

21 Diego Gambetta, *The Sicilian Mafia: The Business of Private Protection*. Cambridge, MA: Harvard University Press, 1993.

22 See Sugden (1989) for detailed discussions.

23 Interestingly, Sugden (1989) began with a story about fishermen collecting wood after a flood in York, England. The rules those fishermen respected are very similar to the rules respected in my home town. I believe that kind of rule exists universally.

24 The below explanation is entirely my own conjecture.

25 This point is similar to our discussion in Chapter 1 of whether or not the Pareto efficiency standard is reasonable.

13 Laws and social norms

Laws and social norms are two basic rules of the game of human society. Two aspects embody the differences between the two. The first aspect is the different enforcement mechanism. Laws are enforced through governments, courts, or specialized enforcement organs as third parties. Social norms have diverse, non-government enforcement mechanisms. The second aspect is their respect formation. Laws are set and promulgated by specialized organs (the legislature), whereas social norms evolve spontaneously.

Laws and social norms are both substitutes and compliments. If laws are incompatible with social norms, then effective enforcement will be difficult.

Laws and social norms have three functions in common. First, they incentivize cooperation. Second, they coordinate expectations. Third, they transmit signals. Some laws and social norms might have three functions at the same time, or two of the three, or even just one. The three are interconnected, but their roles are not always aligned.

The reason people respect social norms is because they are common knowledge attained over a long period of mutual games. Some social norms are self-enforcing. Some social norms depend on the emotional behavior of other people for enforcement. Some social norms are enforced through social recognition, ridicule, or expulsion. Some social norms are internalized as individual morals.

The reasons people violate social norms includes: (1) The importance of internal short-term gain exceeded the importance of reputation; (2) other people do not have a means to punish people that violate social norms; (3) a group governed by different norms exists, or norms change too quickly; and (4) sometimes, violating social norms expresses loyalty to a specific group or organization.

The factors that influence the relative effectiveness of laws and social norms include: (1) Social scale; (2) private costs of social norm enforcement; (3) the speed and means of information flow; (4) the speed of social transformation; and (5) the degree of power separation in social governance.

The relationship between laws and social norms is similar to the relationship between firms and the market. Historically speaking, the expansion of the scope of the law's role is indisputable. However, the development of laws did not replace social norms. Instead, it made social norms have a more important role. A country that lacks effective social norms cannot possibly be a true rule-of-law country.

Section one: the effectiveness of laws

Laws and social norms are the two types of fundamental rules of the game for human society. They are the outcome of evolution over a long period. They serve as the premise for each game between people and jointly determine room for strategy, usable information, payoffs, and equilibrium outcomes for each person in a game. Taxation law, for example, will cause firms with the same output but under different tax rates to have different after-tax income. Similarly, in places where the law has prohibited smoking or people commonly believe smoking should not happen (such as meeting rooms), smokers will obtain different actual utility than otherwise. Because of this, laws and social norms influence people's behavior.

In previous chapters, we have many times touched upon the issue of law and social norms. In this chapter, we will more systematically discuss the relationship between the two.[1]

It is first necessary to point out that laws are adopted and enforced by the state as rules for social interactions and, and do, in consequence, possess great importance for regulating personal conducts, maintaining social order and promoting social cooperation. However, research conducted in jurisprudence, economics, and other social science academic circles over the past three decades has demonstrated that the efficacy of law has been greatly over-estimated by traditional literature. It is social norms, rather than law, that is the mainstay of social order.[2] If a disparity exists between generally accepted social norms and the law, then the efficacy of the law will be very limited (of course, law can alter social norms, as will be discussed later). Recognition of this point is very important for a country advancing toward the rule of law like China.

Roughly speaking, the effectiveness of a law to a large degree is determined by the support provided by social norms. If a law deviates from social norms, the costs of enforcement will greatly increase, to the extent even of preventing enforcement.[3] "The law cannot punish mass offenders" phenomenon in most situations is created by the conflict between the law and the social norms accepted by most of the people. In modern society, law has become more and more a substitute for other methods of governance, including force, violence, superstition, religion, and morality. However, law is not without limits. Law, or more correctly speaking, written law, in solving problems, can occupy only a part of society. Moreover, judges and enforcement officials will, consciously or unconsciously, take into account local customs, conventions and values when they make their judgments. This illustrates that directing social behavior cannot solely rely on law. Rather, it requires social norms, morality, customs, faith, etc.

Section two: the difference between laws and social norms

In terms of function, both social norms and law are the primary manifestation of an institution, that is, both are in essence a type of norm. They coordinate behavior between people through rules to achieve a certain degree of social order and common social consciousness, as well as maintain mainstream values. Before discussing the function of laws and social norms, we will first discuss the differences between the two.[4]

The most important difference between laws and social norms is in respect to the enforcement mechanism. Enforcement of law comes from the third-part y, such as the government, the courts, and specialized enforcement organs. Social norms are rules of behavior broadly accepted and respected by society. Their enforcement mechanisms are diverse, so we refer to it as "multi-party enforcement". When social norms are internalized into being considered moral personal behavior, there is "first-party enforcement", such as when a physician on a train voluntarily and boldly comes to the aid of a person who has taken sick, even when no one was aware that he was a physician. When social norms are maintained by the reputations of the persons involved, it may be termed second-party enforcement, such as, the faithful performance of commitments in commercial transactions or polite manners in everyday interactions. When social norms are enforced by acceptance, disdain, banishment, or humiliation from people not directly involved, it may be termed third part enforcement. Of course, in practice, these three types of enforcement can occur simultaneously. For example, when a person faithfully honors a commitment, it could be from his personal moral self-cultivation; and it could also be that he fears that if he fails to honor his commitment, his counterparty may not again deal with him, and he will lose opportunities for future cooperation; or, he fears that if he is viewed as untrustworthy, he will be unable to make new friends and find business partners. Of course, all three considerations could be at work. Unlike with the law, even in the case of third-party enforcement of social norms, enforcers do not carry the force of law, nor are their specially established enforcement organs.

The difference between the enforcement mechanism of laws and social norms is that (theoretically) laws must also possess coercive force and be enforced without stint or compromise. This is the so-called "rule rigidity" of the law. Otherwise, the authority of law would be undermined. As we know, even when a judge declares that you only need to apologize to a plaintiff, but you do not apologize, many countries would treat this as "contempt of court." A misdemeanor would become a felony, because you had defied the authority of the court. Social norms have no such coercive force.

The degree of coercion informing habits, social norms, and law is perhaps slightly more clearly gleaned from English expressions. Habits convey "do it", social norms "ought to do it" or "ought not to do it", while law says "must do it" or "must not do it". The tone in which these words are uttered is somewhat different. The habits referred to here are not social habits, but personal habits, hence "habit" rather than "convention" or "mores". There are many reasons for the development of personal habits, but individual will act according to his personal habits, without thinking more about it. For example, some people are habitually early risers, some night owls; no one interferes with these behaviors. Social norms differ from habits in that they constitute rules for interactions between people, as such with some rules that constrain personal behaviors ("ought not to do"), and some rules that appeal for certain kinds of behavior ("ought to do"). When personal habits affect the interests of others, these habits will be constrained by social norms. For example, people's taste in the clothes they wear may be different, but in a workplace or public place every person should dress and make themselves up in accordance with common norms. However, social norms lack coercive force because there is no specialized institution requiring that such norms are enforced.

However, that social norms lack coercive force does not mean there are no sanctions, even less that they lack the power to constrain. We can even say that to some degree the constraints imposed by social norms are more severe. Assume you steal 500 yuan from somebody and are discovered by the police. The police give you two options: The first is to be beaten by the police, who will however keep the matter secret; the second is to be sent home by the police, who will however then inform your entire neighborhood and your work unit of your theft. Which would you choose? It is conceivable that most people would choose to receive the beating because of the overwhelming importance of maintaining their reputations. To a great degree we cannot draw parallels between physical pain and reputational damage, but reputational damage is far greater than short term physical pain. Thus, the sanctions of social norms are not necessarily light, and the sanctions of law are not necessarily more severe than those of social norms. This reasoning is really nothing new. Several hundred years ago, the Chinese scholar Dai Zhen said: "We empathize with those that are killed by the law, but who empathizes with those that are killed by moral constraints (if we take a broad view of the meaning)?" It is clear that under many circumstances, the consequences of violating social norms are more serious.

The second difference between law and social norms is in how they came about. To a large degree, social norms constitute what Hayek termed "spontaneous order," that is, having taken shape and evolved from the bottom up, rather than being set, promulgated, and implemented by some institution.[5] Law is different. It is the product of drafting and adoption by specialized organs (the legislature) and implemented by specialized organs (the executive and judiciary), even including specialized institutions dedicated to research (law schools and legal scholars). A particular feature of all legal systems is that laws made by subordinate (lower) level state organs cannot be in conflict with laws made by superior state organs. When there is a conflict, lower level court judgments will be subject to "judicial review" through which higher courts can rectify the lower court judgment on appeal; previous legal norms will conform to newer legal norms and lose efficacy. This is a manifestation of the "centralized authority" characteristic of law.

Of course, law is not produced from nothing, a great amount of it finds its origins in social norms. Many laws constitute the recognition and acceptance of social norms. Much of modern contract law and commercial law originated from accepted rules for transactions between private individuals among traders around the Mediterranean Sea during the Middle Ages. (As a consequence, disparities existed between continental civil law based on Roman law and commercial law with origins in the commercial culture and practices of Mediterranean traders.) Over time, these gradually became national laws.[6] Many ancient Chinese laws were based on social conventions and customs, even Confucian doctrine.

Hayek differentiated between *thesis* (law of legislation) and *nomos* (law of liberty). The former was a top-down coercive process; the latter was a bottom-up spontaneous process. The former reflected the interest of rulers; the latter arose out of cooperative interactions and conflict resolution. He considered English common law and customary law to belong in the second category.[7]

The spontaneous nature of social norms determined that disparities could exist among social norms. Different people seek support for personal interests in different social norms. For example, each person might favor the income distribution norm that most benefits himself. Highly capable individuals consider distribution according to productivity to be the fairest norm, whereas relatively incapable individuals regard "equalitarianism" to be the best approach. In wage negotiations between labor and capital, when enterprise profits rise, workers could base their demand for wage increases on a norm of "fair sharing"; when the enterprise loses money, they would generally not accept this norm, while capitalists would see matters exactly opposite.[8]

Laws and social norms might be substitutable, and might also be complimentary. Theoretically speaking, substitutability suggests that when social norms can solve a problem, there is no need for law. Conversely, if law can effectively solve a problem, social norms are not needed. To some degree, the Confucian critique of the Legalist School was the hope of being able to use social norms and personal discipline as a substitute for law. Law is nothing more than a way of determining settlements and stopping disputes. If every person were capable of being a "humble man of virtue," prepared to "give and take in moderation", there would be no need for coercive law. Thus, a "nation of virtuous men" is the Confucian ideal.

If law and social norms are complementary, then enforcement for each one would support enforcement of the other. A good example is enforcement differences between the ban on public spitting and the ban on fireworks and firecrackers in Beijing Municipality, China, in the 1990s. Social norms supported the ban on public spitting because it was unhygienic and polluted the environment, but not the ban on fireworks and firecrackers because fireworks and firecrackers during the Spring Festive are the long tradition of Chinese people. As a result, the enforcement effectiveness of the first law was much more effective than that of the second law. In fact, after considerable hesitation, in 2006, Beijing began to lift the ban on fireworks and firecrackers.[9]

The difference in the way in which law and social norms have come about is related to the differences in their enforcement mechanisms. The reason we say that mutually complementary social norms and laws can improve enforcement of laws is because differences exist in enforcement of the two. Enforcement of social norms depends on a majority of members of a community because social norms are fundamentally underpinned by the commonly held values of the community. Where group understanding is lacking, the so-called community is no more than an agglomeration of individuals and is without significance. Rules, common understanding, a common value system, and the maintenance of necessary order are the core of what constitutes a community.[10] It is precisely the imperative of a value system and common order that causes enforcement of social norms to become enforcement of the community majority. Enforcement through monitoring of a minority of people by the majority will greatly increase the degree to which violations of the rules are discovered. The cost of supervising the minority's behavior will be spread throughout the majority. Therefore, under certain circumstances, this is a type of low-cost social enforcement mechanism.

However, law is different. Because it is studied, drafted, promulgated, and enforced by specialized institutions, it becomes the imposition of the value judgments of a minority of people on the heads of the majority. There is an intimate relationship between the law's violence and authority. Maintaining authority necessarily requires rigidity of the law. From the standpoint of enforcement, law is enforced by a minority on the majority. Moreover, the law is enforced by a third party. It is thus evident that the enforcement of laws compared to social norms depends on more elements and sometimes has a higher cost.

If laws are based on the group understanding of the majority, then they will be compatible with social norms and enforcement of each will be compatible. If laws are based on the group understanding of a minority, then conflicts with social norms are more likely. We often say that law is conservative precisely because of this dependence on group understanding.

If law and social norms are not compatible, the enforcement of law will become extraordinarily expensive. As Gu Yanwu said in *Records of Daily Knowledge*: "The monarch should not govern a country alone, otherwise harsh criminal law will be required, but the subjects should not govern in common because the law will be abandoned".[11] In a country ruled by law, order is kept by punishing crimes; it is necessary to rely on assistance from social norms. This is precisely the reason for the Confucian School's emphasis on the system of social norms and customs. Otherwise, as we discussed previously in the case of the ban on fireworks and the public enjoying the sound of fireworks, there will be incompatibility.

For any law, when there is incompatibility or misalignment with social norms, the final result of the struggle will be defeat of the laws, not of social norms. This is not only the case in China. The ultimate failure of alcohol prohibition in the United States is also a classic example.

Section three: the fundamental functions of laws and social norms

3.1 Three kinds of social norms

Kaushik Basu, economist at Cornell University in the United States, divides social norms into three types:[12]

1) Rationality-Limiting Norms

   Rationality-limiting norms refer to norms that would constrain people's choices to certain specific actions, without regard to how much utility this action brings to the people involved. For example, you observe someone else's wallet has been dropped on the ground. To you, it would be "rational" to pick up the wallet and walk away. Most of us would, however, consider the action of taking a wallet belonging to someone else to be bad. We can understand this to be a norm that limits your rational choices. The effect of this type of rationality-limiting norm is to change the feasible selection set that the people involve face. It reduces the range of available choices. Why would this type of norm become common? In Game Theory, the evolutionarily stable equilibrium perspective provides the explanation. Speaking from the social evolution perspective, if everyone is stealing things belonging to others, the society will certainly not survive long; hence, everyone will concur when it is said that stealing things belonging to others is unacceptable behavior, even if there is no legal punishment. In reality, there are many situations in which we find opportunities to take advantage of other people, but people do not usually act in this way. We can explain such "self-restraint" from the perspective of social evolution. A society that failed to establish such a norm might very well face extinction.

2) Preference-Changing Norms

Preference-changing norms refer to norms that change people's preferences. This type of norm changes parts of people's preferences with the passage of time. For example, when you have just begun to accept and practice the religion of Islam, you may feel that you will be prevented from eating pork by a rationality-limiting norm, even though you have always enjoyed eating pork. However, after a long period of not eating pork, you may actually stop having any desire to eat pork, that is, your preference will have changed, such that you no longer like pork. In this way, the norm became a preference.

3) Equilibrium-Selection Norms

Equilibrium-selection norms refer to norms that coordinate people to choose a specific Nash equilibrium among many. However, the selection of equilibrium strategies and actions is entirely in the personal interests of the people involved. Therefore, this norm does not change the game itself, but changes the equilibrium outcome of the game. The effect of this norm is to allow people to coordinate between when making their selection among multiple Nash equilibriums.

Using Basu's classifications, we can also delineate three types of law: Rationality-limiting law, preference-changing law, and equilibrium-selection law. Various laws constrain us from choosing to engage in certain behaviors, for example, the law against smoking in public places, the law against capturing or killing endangered species of animals; and moreover, over time, these laws will change our preferences. Although laws that limit choices and change preferences do not directly select an equilibrium, they do, by influencing persons' behavior, indirectly influence the choice of equilibrium.

Notwithstanding the differences between the creation and enforcement mechanisms of laws and social norms, their basic functions as the "rules of the game" of society are identical. Based the existing literature, we can identify the functions of law and social norms as possessing three aspects: First, encouraging cooperation; second, coordinating and harmonizing expectations; and third, conveying signals. We discuss each of these facets below.

3.2 Laws and social norms as incentive mechanisms

The first function of law and social norms is to incentivize and induce people's mutual cooperation. Limiting rational choices and changing preferences are the most important functions of social norms and laws. We are aware that the biggest problem confronting social cooperation is the contradiction between individual rationality and collective rationality caused by the "Prisoner's Dilemma." Under such circumstances, laws and social norms can change the payoff structure of the game by providing an incentive that harmonizes personal efficiency and social efficiency, thereby realizing the Pareto optimum. Laws and social norms can also, by changing preferences, induce people to refrain from choosing certain actions that are unfavorable to cooperation. This is the fundamental significance of the social incentive mechanism.

The essence of the incentives issue is internalizing externalities such that they become personal costs and benefits, and thereupon that they cause individuals to accept full responsibility for the consequences of their actions. In Chapter 2, we analyzed how contract law, through punishing breach behavior, causes cooperation to become a Nash equilibrium. When the parties involved sign a legally binding contract, this means that they have made a commitment that serves their own interests. This commitment is itself a dynamic game Nash equilibrium. Contract law serves to safeguard the mutual benefit of cooperation of the two parties to a transaction, resolving the Prisoner's Dilemma, and ensuring the realization of social efficiency. From this perspective, we say that it is a type of incentive mechanism.

In fact, this is not limited to contract law. A number of other laws are adopted with a view toward resolving the Prisoner's Dilemma. We can take environmental protection law as an example. Because the atmosphere circulates, enterprises that emit pollution into the air do not fully bear the consequences. Hence, an enterprise's optimal choice would lead to excessive pollution. Environmental protection laws incentivize enterprises to reduce pollution emissions by levying a tax on emissions exceeding a certain level. Similarly, bankruptcy laws oblige creditors to act collectively and prohibit individual actions by creditors, when an enterprise enters bankruptcy. This is precisely to preclude individual actions leading to a Prisoner's Dilemma. If individual creditors were to race against each other to assert their claims, the valuation of the assets would be greatly reduced. Intellectual property law is intended to resolve the Prisoner's Dilemma involved in invention and innovation. If intellectual property does not receive protection, the motivation of enterprises and individuals to innovate will be greatly diminished, and the pace of societal progress will slow down. To speak more generally, the system of private property rights is the most important incentive system. If private property rights are not effectively protected in a society, this society would descend into the Prisoner's Dilemma, as we observed with people's communes and state-owned enterprises.[13]

Traffic laws are also an incentive mechanism. Assuming that traffic rules are reasonable, if every person were to obey the rules, traffic would flow more smoothly and everyone could move faster and more safely. But, if actions violating the law were not punished, everyone would have an incentive to cut in front of each other, resulting in traffic jams or even traffic accidents.

However, the effectiveness of law in resolving the Prisoner's Dilemma depends upon the expectations of the persons involved toward whether or not the law will be effectively enforced. If the persons involved expect that the law will not be effectively enforced, then the law will be irrelevant, and we return to the original Prisoner's Dilemma because not cooperating is the only Nash equilibrium. Moreover, the effectiveness of law is related to the cost of enforcing the law. The enforceability of a law requires not only that the behavior of persons involved can be observed by the other persons involved, it also requires that this type of behavior can be verified in a court of law. Proving whether or not a person has breached a contract requires gathering a large volume of evidence, at great cost. In some cases, it is even impossible. Because costs are a factor, it is impossible that all uncooperative behavior will be punished by the law. "The operating cost of a legal system" and the "cost of proof" against a person involved are thresholds that serve to screen out many disputes. The higher the cost of the law is, the lower the ability of the law will be to resolve problems in social cooperation (the Prisoner's Dilemma).[14] The cost of laws dictates that laws will not be able to resolve all problems of cooperation.

The difference between social norms and laws is that social norms are enforced through a decentralized method. Even when some kind of non-cooperative behavior manages to evade the sanction of law, it may still not be able to evade the imposition of sanctions of social norms. Assuming "cooperation" is a generally acknowledged social norm, when one party cooperates and the other does not, then the non-cooperating party will be punished by social norms. This punishment could take the form of a loss of reputation, of a loss of future opportunities to cooperate, of a decline in social position, or even merely of the psychological cost of being regarded with disdain by fellow people. The punishments of social norms are not coercive in nature. Therefore, their effectiveness depends to a large extent upon the "sensitivity" of the person involved to punishment, such as whether or not he has other external options. Obviously, the same social norm will exercise a disparate degree of restraint on different people.[15]

Figure 13.1 displays the change in payoffs brought about by social norms in the Prisoner's Dilemma. When Player A does not cooperate, but Player B does cooperate, Player A's payoff changes from 4 to $4 - ax$. When Player A cooperates, but Player B does not cooperate, Player B's payoff changes from 4 to $4 - by$.[16] Here, x and y represent the "objective" punishment of social norms against

	B	
	Cooperate	Does not cooperate
Cooperate	3, 3	$-1, 4-by$
Does not cooperate	$4-ax, -1$	0, 0

Figure 13.1 Social Norms Solve the Prisoner's Dilemma

non-cooperative behavior, or "objective" costs for the two persons involved. The variables a and b can be understood as the degree of psychological impact that the punishment has on the persons involved (the degree of "thickness of face" or "shamelessness"). Therefore, ax and by can be understood as perceived costs. Clearly, only when $ax > 1$ and $by > 1$ can social norms cause "cooperation" to become a Nash equilibrium.

For legal punishments, it is not necessary to consider a and b, because as long as a determination is made, it must be enforced. However, the enforcement of social norms to a large degree depends on a and b. For a person that is shameless, the value of a or b will be close to zero, so social norms will not function for this type of person. Alternatively, if a person cares about his face, then the value of a or b will be great, so any punishment (x and y) will be enlarged by a greater degree. In this situation, social norms will be effective. Therefore, the governance effect of social norms depends on sufficient ethics and customs in society. This is the reason that Confucian intellectuals in ancient China put so much focus on ethics and customs. Emperor Kangxi once said, "I took the ethics and customs as my own responsibility". Hence, we can see that emperors emphasized folk customs. It is a requirement for social governance.

Similar to laws, the effectiveness of social norms also depends on obtaining information of relevant individual behavior.[17] If individual behavior is difficult to observe, then the incentive effect of social norms will be greatly reduced. As we discussed in Chapter 6, one method of resolving the information problem is dividing society into different organizations and communities so that to a certain degree each member takes on joint liability for other members. In this way, social norms can function through community norms and professional norms.[18] For example, if members of some group are swindlers, but other members of society have no way of knowing which person is the swindler, then they will boycott all members of this group as punishment. Out of self-interest, members of this group have an incentive to establish certain rules to constrain the behavior on the group members. They also have the incentive and possibility to supervise enforcement of the rules. From this perspective, "identity" is not only a signal to coordinate expectations, it is also a means to incentivize cooperation. For example, IBM employees' behavior in social interactions is constrained by the IBM employee identity. Similarly, the behavior of Peking University alumni is constrained by the reputation of Peking University. If the behavior of a Peking University graduate does not align with social norms, then it will damage the reputation of Peking University and impact other alumni. Therefore, if he seeks the aid of Peking University alumni, he must keep his behavior in check. Out of self-interest, alumni have a certain incentive to supervise each other.

As incentive mechanisms, laws and social norms mutually influence each other. On the streets of Beijing, we can see drivers, bicyclists, and pedestrians violating traffic laws everywhere. This is a major cause of traffic troubles in Beijing. This is related to both lack of enforcement and a lack of behavioral norms. Very few people view bicyclist or pedestrian violations of traffic rules as dishonorable, and few police officers punish these behaviors. As time goes on, the situation becomes worse, which also leads to more tolerance of rule-breaking behavior from drivers.

3.3 Laws and social norms as expectation coordinators

As we know, there are often multiple equilibriums in a game, at which point rationality cannot help players to coordinate on a particular equilibrium. Our choice depends on expectations of other people's behavior, but other people's behavior also depends on their expectations of our own behavior. If people's expectations are not aligned, then an equilibrium will not appear. Under these circumstances, a major function of laws and social norms is to help people choose a specific equilibrium through coordinated expectations. This function of laws and social norms can reduce transaction costs. In Chapter 3, we used traffic rules to explain this point. Driving on the left and driving on the right are both Nash equilibriums. If this had to be negotiated between the drivers each time, costs would be extremely high. With traffic regulations or well-known traffic norms, people can easily predict the movements of others, so a specific Nash equilibrium will appear.

There are many similar circumstances, such as television systems, 3G telecommunication standards, railroad gauges, school start times, contract wording, forms of currency, police and military uniforms, component compatibility, and business centers, etc. In all of these examples, there are multiple Nash equilibriums. The appearance of one specific Nash equilibrium might be the outcome of spontaneously formed social norms, the outcome of legal coordination, or formed with both of them playing a role.[19] However, regardless if something is a law or a social norm, in terms of coordinating expectations, as long as the specified behavior is a Nash equilibrium, it will be consciously respected. Historically, which equilibrium appears is chance, as traffic rules have shown us. Precisely for this reason did Basu propose the Core Theorem: Whatever behavior and outcomes in society are legally enforceable are also enforceable through social norms.[20]

Even if this is the case, why do we still need laws to coordinate expectations? One possible reason is that the formation and transmission of laws are faster. Imagine automobiles appear in a place that originally did not have automobiles. If we depend on the continuous trial and error method to form aligned expectations, not only will this require a very long time period, it will also come at a bloody price. However, if from the beginning the government implements clear traffic rules as laws, then expectations can form quickly without coming at a bloody price. When there are large migrations of people, this advantage of law is more obvious. Clear language, central expression, and regular effectiveness of laws reduce individuals' cost of obtaining information on rules. When a person arrives at a place for the first time, it is relatively easy to understand legal rules through a book of laws. Without laws, the cost of obtaining information would be relatively higher. The establishment, revision, and elimination of laws is explicit and rapid, whereas social norms are slower and vaguer.

Another (perhaps more important) possible reason is that the government uses laws for rent-seeking. As we saw in Chapter 3, in many situations, different Nash equilibriums mean different distributions of interest. At this point, even if everyone desires a singular equilibrium outcome, but different people prefer different equilibriums, then the people that set the rules of the game can receive an outcome that benefits themselves more. Based on the government's self-interest, it is even more willing to set the rules of the game.

Take the selection of currency as an example. The primary function of currency is as a medium of exchange to provide convenience for transactions. A unified currency is a Nash equilibrium, but there are many kinds of commodities to choose from as currency. In other words, there are multiple Nash equilibriums. Historically, currency was not designed by some authoritative organization, instead it spontaneously evolved out of countless transactions between people. Many types of commodities have served as currency, such as shells, cows, wood, silk, corn, etc., but with the passage of time, precious metals (gold, silver, and copper) became primary currencies. The reasons for this were the high unit value of precious metals, ease of dividing, non-perishability, and convenience to carry. Karl Marx referred to them as "innate currency". Precious metals were originally transacted in units of weight. Gradually, for the convenience of transactions, precious metals were cast into standard shapes as coins and coinage became a profession. Later, symbols for currency appeared as paper money and alternative bank notes. In this process of evolution, the governments of certain countries monopolized coinage and prohibited the private minting of currency. Later, government currency became "fiat money", which did not have natural value, and the private production of currency was no longer legal.

Why did government monopolize the production of currency? The most basic reason is to obtain seigniorage.[21] When currency is privately produced, the type of currency used and who produces the currency is a social norm. Except for state-owned assets and direct expropriation, taxation is the only means by which the government can obtain revenues. However, taxation is often not received well by the people, and in serious cases leads to revolution. If the government monopolizes the currency, then revenue can be obtained through inflation. When precious metal coins were used, the government frequently reduced the metal content of coins or changed the shape or style of coins. With the passage of time, the difference between the nominal and actual value of currency became greater. With paper currency, the government can print money out of nothing and transform the people's wealth into government revenue. This is the benefit brought about by monopolizing the rules of the game. Of course, if inflation is excessive, trust in government currency will completely erode. The people will utilize their own currency according to their own norms, or return to barter, and the government will have no way to obtain revenue. For this reason, governments will often have some self-restraint.

In addition to monopoly of the currency, many other laws are set by the government in order to seek rent.[22] For example, industry technology standards are best formed by market competition, but if the government monopolizes the setting of standards, interest groups can lobby the government for their benefit. This gives bureaucrats that are responsible for setting and approving standards an opportunity to accept bribes. However, because any standard that is chosen is a Nash equilibrium, any standard set by the government can often be followed. Of course, if the government sets a standard that is too inefficient, it will be overturned by the market.

When the government sets laws and policies, sometimes the behavior of government will negatively impact people's expectations and cause coordination to be more difficult. For example, if laws are excessively vague and policies change too frequently, then people will not know what course to take. Language, like currency, evolved spontaneously, not through central design. Linguistic norms include the definition of nouns and grammatical structures. When everyone respects definite linguistic norms, interpersonal communication is more effective, similar to everyone driving on the right. Because of ideological and political reasons, China has experienced serious language corruption.[23] Certain departments of authority wantonly change the definition of terms, sometimes granting them a completely different meaning than originally. So, the same term has a different definition in the minds of different people. Language becomes a terminology game, which causes communication to become difficult.

Even if laws are established for "virtuous" reasons, the government should also acknowledge that the law cannot regulate every single human affair, and neither should it. The law should respect the normal social norms that people have already formed, and often must depend on social norms, but it should not negatively impact social norms. For thousands of years, private lending has been a tradition. Interest rates, repayment terms, and means of repayment have governed by custom. Not only is private lending effective, it is ethical. Even without a written contract, lending agreements are generally respected by both parties. If the government uses laws to regulate interest rates or even outlaw private lending in the name of maintaining financial order, it will befuddle people's expectations. Not only will it limit people's liberty to lend and borrow money, it will cause resource allocation to be inefficient and cause a chaotic financial order, even harming social trust. Central banks are considered an indispensable tool for the coordination of financial activity expectations and maintaining order in the financial market, but experience has shown that central banks are often the culprits of financial crises.[24] In China, not only in the financial field, but also many business fields, the law's excessive interference in social life has become a public nuisance.

3.4 Laws and social norms as signal transmission mechanisms

The third function of laws and social norms is signaling. As we discussed in Chapter 9, because the distribution of information between people in a game is asymmetric, the person with "good" private information (such as the high-ability person) is willing to transmit information through some action (such as undertaking an education) to the party without private information (such as an employer). The reason this action can transmit information is because there are different costs for different types of people implementing this action. The costs for people with "good" information are lower than for people with "bad" information. This causes the latter to be unwilling to imitate the former.

As Posner (2000) pointed out, social norms are a type of restriction on people's liberty and behavior that adds costs. Obviously, respecting social norms means transferring partial individual liberty to the collective, so respecting them displays a willingness to cooperate with others. If there was no cost, there also would be no signal value. Precisely because there is cost can they function as signaling. For example, people who act bravely for a just cause need to take certain risks. Only people who have very high morality will take the risk, so taking this risk can transmit information.

This is not only limited to social norms. An individual's respect for the law means acceptance of other's restrictions. It shows that a person is reliable. The most classic example of this is the Law Merchant in the Middle Ages. The Law Merchant were not backed up by state violence, but merchants trusted its judgment. When merchants wanted to investigate a potential partner's credit, they only had to consult the Law Merchant to see if that person had respected the judgments or not. This is an important signal mechanism. A trustworthy merchant might have disputes for various reasons, but had no reason to disrespect the court's judgment. Therefore, respecting the court's judgment became a signal that a person put weight on his own reputation and was willing to cooperate with others.[25]

In modern society, courts are part of the state, and taxpayers bear the salaries of judges and operational costs of the courts, so why do they also charge litigation fees? This is also related to signaling function. Legal resources are limited, and not all disputes are worth being resolved by the courts. As to which cases should go to court and which should not is something the people involved are often more clear on. Litigation fees can serve as a self-selection mechanism that cause disputes unworthy of the courts to not be taken to court by the people involved.

There are also many other signaling functions of laws. For example, in ancient China there were leapfrogged petitions, which meant lodging an appeal to a higher court. Any petitioner will be punished first, which usually physical beatings. Why? Because petitioners did not follow the normal procedure to seek help from the government. How can the government distinguish whether the petition is true or false? The petitioner who had a real case would be willing to bear the punishment cost. There were numerous similar examples in ancient China, such as false accusation sentencing. If a petitioner sues a person, how can the court know the petitioner will not frame others? If the law found out the petitioner sued the wrong person, that petitioner is guilty of the crime he appealed. Taking the risk means a petition is unlikely to be false.

There are many examples in modern law. Many countries accept immigrants, but they have choices. In order to select the immigrants they want, the law establishes many restrictions. For example, Chinese immigrants to Canada must invest a certain amount of money. Immigrants to America must wait a certain number of years to obtain a green card. These restrictions all have signaling functions. Guarantees in litigation law have the same justification. Creditors fear that debtors will transfer assets or disappear after receiving court notifications, so they request the court to freeze the debtor's assets before the litigation. However, the courts do not know if the creditor's claim is legitimate, so the court requires creditors to provide guarantees. This guarantee proves that the creditor will compensate for any harm caused by a misrepresentation. Alternatively, the debtor must show the court that he will carry out the judgment by providing a guarantee to have his assets unfrozen. Otherwise, how would the court know if a debtor is telling the truth or not? In United States, shareholders can litigate against inappropriate behavior by the board. In 1912, the New York Commercial Commission found that most were false charges. New York State passed a law requiring guarantees to institute legal proceedings.

The signaling function of social norms and laws, from society's perspective, may also cause inappropriate outcomes.[26] The shaming penalty is an example. In almost every society, people will implement the shaming penalty for certain behaviors that violate social norms, such as theft, fraud, domestic violence, extramarital affairs, illegitimate children, incest, and even some viewpoints that do not accord with traditional viewpoints that are considered heresy. Shaming penalties include ridicule, denunciation, public discussion, the silent treatment, or assault. In many cases, people do not implement shaming penalties to protect justice, but instead to show they are "just". For example, imagine in a public place you observe a thief. Should you expose his behavior (such as shouting "catch the thief")? The cost for you might be the retaliation from the thief. However, in order to show you are a courageous person, to improve your reputation, you might choose to expose him. After shouting "catch the thief", people will gather around. To show their "justness", some people will attack the thief, and the thief might be beaten to death.

When people beat up a thief, they consider individual costs and gains, not social costs and gains. Therefore, behavior based on signaling might not necessarily lead to the social optimal outcome. Theft is wrong, but should not be punished with death. Who should be responsible for the death of a thief? Sometimes, an innocent person might be mistaken by others for something difficult to explain and be subject to serious shaming penalties. In rural areas in the past of China, as soon as a girl's sexual behavior was considered to be unrestrained, many people that wanted to show they are righteous would denounce her. In the end, only suicide could prove her innocence.

In China, tragedies caused by "signaling" behavior are countless. From the "Anti-Rightist Campaign" to the "Cultural Revolution", many people denounced or even murdered those that were accused of being "rightists", "taking the capitalist road", or of being "counter-revolutionaries", in order to signal their "loyalty to the great leader" or "dedication to the revolution". It was not necessary that they did really believe those people were bad people that should be denounced.

This type of "mob rule" caused by signaling is still prevalent today. For example, as soon as someone is called a "traitor" or said to be "speaking for the special interests", they will be denounced by netizens. These netizens do this to show they are "patriotic" and represent "fairness" and "justice".

Recognizing this point, the government can pass laws to inhibit the negative effects caused by signaling. For example, the law prohibits assaulting a thief and protects privacy. Before the modern era, laws in many countries had shaming penalties, such as being paraded about, public flogging, public executions, or face tattoos. Because of public signaling behavior, these punishments cause criminals to be punished far in excess of the proper punishments for their crimes. Even their partners, children, and other family members will have shaming penalties placed upon them by social norms. Excessive punishments cause people that originally commit minor crimes to commit major crimes. Certain people that originally would not have violated the law (such as the children of criminals), take to crime or even criminal organizations. As soon as criminal organizations appear, in order to show their loyalty, certain people will commit murder. The social order will become less stable. Primarily for this reason, Western countries eliminated legal shaming penalties.[27] One reason some people commit crimes after serving out their sentences is shaming penalties society places on them. When most people cut them off in order to display their "justness", former criminals will have no way to provide for their families, so will again turn to crime.

The government must also acknowledge that certain laws might have the opposite effect as intended because of the signaling function. For example, punishments for political opponents provide political opponents a signal to transmit. Without government punishments, certain people that oppose the government might only oppose certain policies without attracting public attention. However, as soon as they are punished by the government, they make a name for themselves and might even become the leader of the opposition. For this reason, in order to increase their reputation among political opponents, some people will choose extreme behavior. When a person is willing to risk their own freedom, the signal he transmits is reliable.

Lastly, we must point out that Posner's signaling model faces a paradox. Only under a separating equilibrium will a certain behavior signal information. This means that under equilibrium, only "good type" people should be the ones in society to respect social norms. However, the reason a norm can be called a social norm is that it is respected by the majority of people. It is not likely that the vast majority of people are "good type" people. In this way, we see that society can only be a "pooling equilibrium", not a "separating equilibrium". In other words, some person respecting social norms cannot tell us if he is a "good person" or a "bad person". One method to resolve this paradox is to combine the reputation model discussed in Chapter 7 and the signaling model discussed in Chapter 9. In the reputation model, because information is asymmetric, "bad people" have an incentive to imitate "good people". In the signaling model, because information is asymmetric, "good people" want to differentiate themselves from "bad people". In this way, in a repeated game signaling model, "bad people" have an incentive to imitate "good people" by respecting social norms. Even though we obtain a pooling equilibrium, two types of people respect social norms for different reasons. "Good people" respect social norms to show they are "good people" and "bad people" respect social norms to show they want to become "good people". Only a small number of very "bad" people will not respect social norms.[28]

To summarize, providing incentives, coordinating expectations, and transmitting signals are the three basic functions of laws and social norms. Some laws and social norms might play all three functions simultaneously, or only one or two. As we saw, the three are interrelated, but the functions might not be aligned. Additionally, regardless of the type of function, sometimes laws play a greater role and other times social norms play a greater role.

Section four: respect for and violation of social norms

If any law or social norm is not respected by the majority, it cannot possibly function as it should. Why do people need to respect the law? It is generally believed that people respect the law based on a fear of legal sanctions, because laws are backed up by coercive state power. If the law is not respected, punishments follow. Disregarding a legal judgment is a crime on top of a crime. Gary Becker and other economists used positivism to find that changes in punishments play an obvious role in increasing or reducing crime. They believed the growing empirical study of crime literature has shown that criminals react to the following factors as if they were really rational calculators of economic models: Opportunity costs, arrest probability, severity of punishment, and other relevant variables.[29] However, recent research has shown that the issue is not that simple. State violence is not the necessary condition for respect of the law. Instead, the legitimacy of the law is the reason people respect the law.[30] If the law itself is not reasonable and does not align with basic justness and social norms that people acknowledge, it will not be commonly respected.

4.1 The reasons people respect social norms

Social norms are not backed up with state violence, so why would people respect social norms? Fundamentally, social norms are common knowledge reached among people in long-term mutual games. For a person to survive in society, he must obtain opportunities to cooperate with others by respecting basic social norms accepted by the majority of people. Richard A. Posner, in a 1997 paper, summarized four reasons people respect social norms.[31]

First, some social norms are self-enforcing. This means that these norms are enforced by people's self-interested behavior and does not need third-party coercion. Self-enforcement is actually a characteristic of Nash equilibriums. If a social norm is a Nash equilibrium, it will be self-enforced. Some social norms do not constitute a Nash equilibrium in a one-time game, but do constitute a Nash equilibrium in a repeated game, so it can also be self-enforced. No one enforces the rules of cards and chess, but if you do not follow the rules, no one will be willing to play with you. Therefore, based on considerations of self-interest, it is best to respect the rules of the game. Many professional norms have similar characteristics.

Second, some social norms depend on the emotional behavior of others for enforcement. Emotional behavior often occurs when observed behavior differs from expectations and causes anger. Emotional behavior is often considered irrational because they are not decisions based on individual cost-benefit comparisons and people often regret them after the fact. However, they have an important role in maintaining social norms. Social norms are the behavioral patterns that people expect each person to respect. If your behavior differs from other's expectations, the other party might implement emotional behavior as retaliation. Based on this fear of emotional behavior, people will behave according to expectations provided by rational social norms. In the last chapter, we discussed the queue issue. When everyone lines up in an orderly fashion, if one person does not respect the rules, he might be reprimanded by others. This is a powerful force for maintaining order in the queue. Dueling can be understood as emotional behavior, because this type of behavior does not conform to the rational person assumption, but many people undertook it.[32] Of course, from the reputation perspective, emotion might be an extremely rational choice, because in places where conflict is common, establishing a reputation for emotion is beneficial.

Third, some norms are enforced by social approval, ridicule, ostracism, or reputation. Ridicule and disapproval cause people to feel psychological pressure. A person that makes noise during a meeting will be distained by others. A person that does not wear suitable clothes during a solemn ceremony will elicit peculiar stares. A person that tries to take seats on public transportation from the elderly or small children will be considered uncouth. A person that does not speak according to norms will be ridiculed. Therefore, any self-respecting person will respect basic social norms.

Social ostracism or objection refers to rejection or removal from a group or community for not respecting certain rules of the game. This type of punishment is common. A serious example would be a family disowning a member. A lesser example would be parents favoring one child over another. Group rejection includes the ancient practice of exiling someone from a community and the modern practice of stripping an offending member of membership. In certain economically developed villages in Guangzhou, residents that do not follow the rules have their residency status changed. Ancient laws had similar punishments, such as banishing a person to the frontier.

Reputation constraints are very important for people's respect of social norms because people are often only willing to maintain long-term cooperative relationships with people that have a good reputation. A person that does not repay money has difficulty borrowing money again. The more a person cares about his reputation, the more he will respect rules. The more people in a society care about reputation, the better social norms will be respected. In academia, it is precisely scholar's focus on reputation that maintains academic norms.

Fourth, certain individual norms are internalized as individual morals, so people consciously respect them based on guilt and shame. Social norms start as external forces to constrain individuals, but as time passes these external constraints might become individual customs internalized as behavioral norms. When a person does something that does not conform to social norms, he will often feel guilty or shameful. At this point, social norms are internalized as a type of moral norms. So even without external supervision, individuals will still consciously respect them. Even if they will not be caught, in general people will not take other people's stuff to avoid a guilty conscience. Education has an important role in internalizing social norms. This is an important reason education has been emphasized from ancient times to the present. Because the formation of moral norms is the outcome of imperceptible influence, the personal example and verbal instruction of parents has an irreplaceable role in people's respect for social norms.

4.2 The reasons people violate social norms

Although there are many forces at work to make people respect social norms, we still observe people violating social norms. Why do people violate social norms? Eric Posner, of the University of Chicago, listed four reasons in his book *Law and Social Norms*.[33]

First, internal focus on short-term interests exceeds the focus on reputation. This is a basic conclusion we derive from the reputation model. If a person only pursues short-term interests and does not care about long-term cooperation, then he will be unwilling to respect social norms. Many immoral and rule-breaking behaviors occur because people do not care about the future.

In rural areas of China in the past, whether or not a person had children to a large degree determined if a person was or was not trustworthy. Having children proved a person put weight on the future, whereas not having children meant not having an "investment" in the future.

If the people involved do not put weight on their own reputation, then it is even difficult for laws to play a role. Zhang and Rongzhu (2002) analyzed more than 600 court cases in the Haidian District of Beijing, and found that the vast majority of the cases were extremely simple, and repeated frequently. Many debtors had no reason to not repay their debts, nor did they even appear in court. After the judgment, they refused enforcement.[34] The reason is that the people involved do not care at all about reputation. If the courts coercively enforced each judgment, how high would the social cost be? Obviously, without the reputation mechanism, the law's role is extremely limited.

Second, others have no means to punish people that violate social norms. For example, if a person that violates social norms has a relatively high status, is extremely wealthy, or is very powerful, it will be difficult to sanction that person. In rural areas in the past of China, if a woman behaved inappropriately before marriage and had a bad reputation, it would be difficult to get married later in life, so parents were relatively strict towards daughters. This kind of issue might not be very serious for wealthy families, because marriage to their daughters could still provide social mobility, so there were still willing partners. When some person has power that others do not, it is relatively difficult to expel him, so social norms have weak constraints on that person. Feudal lords were among this category.

This is a difficult issue in Confucian culture. Confucianism did not provide a good method for restraining people that cannot be expelled. Just as Legalist Shang Yang pointed out: "The benefactor can be benevolent, but cannot make people benevolent; the righteous can love people, and cannot make people love; it is known that benevolence and righteousness are not enough to rule the world".[35] The Confucian method was education to make people conscious virtuous men, but this could not guarantee "un-expellable people" become virtuous men. When this type of person becomes emperor, "virtue under the heavens" is just an empty saying. Social governance in Confucian culture lacks effective tools to deal with un-expellable people, thus causing the rulers to on the one hand maintain mainstream opinions and values while on the other hand violate social norms and laws even more. Therefore, public lies and private truth became a common phenomenon.

Unconstrained power will damage trust and social norms, while similarly damaging laws. In modern Chinese society, untrustworthy government behavior is common. It is the greatest injury to social morals, social norms, and laws. We say that there should be rule of law, not rule by law. If government bureaucrats are not constrained by laws, the common people have no means to expel them, so social norms and laws have difficulty becoming truly effective governance mechanisms.

Of course, from the perspective of social transformation, people that are unconstrained by norms might play a role in pushing forward the transformation of social norms. During the Renaissance, if wealthy merchants had not begun to pursue more secular lives and pleasures by violating religious norms and prohibitions, the spirit of liberal humanism would not have replaced religious ascetics and inhibitions as the mainstream social ideology. Obviously, it is society's inability to expel these powerful, wealthy merchants that led to the Renaissance, which actually was a cultural revolution.

Third, different norm governance groups coexist, or norms change too quickly. If a person that should be expelled from or sanctioned by a group can be accepted by another group, sanctions will not have much of an effect. If different norm governance groups coexist, it is easy for norm breakers to avoid suffering from sanction. If norms in a group change too quickly, it is difficult to implement sanction. Under these two situations, people that can most easily transfer to another group or have the most hope of gaining from a new norm are most likely to not respect the original social norms. This principle is also applicable to laws.

Women's Liberation in contemporary China was rejected in rural areas, but because new and urban social groups emerged, people that were originally rejected in rural areas could still find an accepting (or even encouraging) group in urban areas. Under these conditions, traditional social norms like the three obediences and four virtues were no longer enforced.

Similarly, as social norms change rapidly, violations of social norms will increase. Here, violators include both the people that violate the traditional social norms, who become the vanguard, and people that transition relatively slow and violate the new social norms. The significant social changes in twentieth-century China led to what the sociologist calls "absence of collective norms".

Fourth, sometimes violating social norms expresses loyalty to a certain group or organization. This is caused by different social norms among different organizations. Different social norms reflect different identities. Violating some group's norms expresses belonging to another group or is a commitment to belonging to a certain group.

For example, in order to align with the perception of overall rebelliousness, young people have to be different from the previous generation. During the "Cultural Revolution" in China, many people cut themselves off from their own family to express loyalty to "the revolution" in order to join the Red Guards.

4.3 The second-order Prisoner's Dilemma issue

Up to this point, this chapter has avoided one issue: The incentive problem for enforcers of social norms. In simple repeated games with a reputation mechanism, the reason one person cooperates is because non-cooperation will be punished by the other party. In other words, there is second-party enforcement. However, social norms by definition are enforced by third-parties. A person might respect social norms out of fear of other's ridicule, but ridicule comes at a cost. The ridiculer might face bodily harm. If each person is self-interested and overlooks any violators that do not directly harm his own interests, then social norms cannot truly gain respect. This is a "second-order Prisoner's Dilemma" that we discussed in Chapter 6.

Scholars that research laws and social norms have proposed various theories to resolve this issue. McAdams (1997) proposed the "Esteem Theory" of social norms. He believed that competition for esteem caused people to not only be willing to respect social norms, but also have an incentive to despise people that do not respect social norms. Because esteem is cost-free, a second-order Prisoner's Dilemma does not exist. Contrary to this, Posner's Signaling Theory that we previously discussed believed that precisely because respecting social norms is costly do people respect social norms to show they are cooperative-type people. People despise people that do not respect social norms in order to transmit a signal. Cooter (1995, 2000a) used social norm internalization as ethics to resolve the second-order Prisoner's Dilemma issue. He believed that violating social norms brings about harm to people that have internalized ethical forces, so even if there is a cost associated with punishment, they are still willing to punish violators. In Chapter 6, we introduced the "boycott rule" (or "def-for-dev") of Mahoney and Sanchirico (2003), as well as the "foe-friend rule" of Bendor and Swistak (2001). These two theories are the same as the theory proposed by Sugden (1989) in the previous chapter. When social norms are understood as a perfect Nash equilibrium or an evolutionarily stable equilibrium, as long as the majority of people are expected to respect them, then each person has an incentive to respect them (including punishing violators).

These theories are mutually complementary. Social life is extremely complicated. Different social norms exist in different environments, so enforcement mechanisms cannot also be completely similar.

Section five: the social conditions of social norms and laws

5.1 Factors that influence the relative effectiveness of laws and social norms

The reasons people respect or violate social norms can help us determine the social conditions that influence relative effectiveness of social norms and laws. In other words, under what conditions are social norms and laws more effective? Generally speaking, the social conditions listed below directly influence the relative effectiveness of social norms and laws:

First, social scale. Social scale is actually the territory and population of a relevant group. Social norms and laws to a certain degree are the connected rules of these organizations, communities, or groups. The effectiveness of social norms and social scale are closely related. The smaller social scale is, the more a role social norms will play and the more effective they will be. If social scale is very large, then only relying on social norms will not be very effective. The importance of formal rules (laws) increases.[36] For example, in a small firm, not very many formal rules are required. Informal rules and organizational culture are sufficient to constrain individual behavior to guarantee mutual cooperation. Occasional disputes can be resolved through consultation. However, when firms become organizations with hundreds of people, or even publicly listed companies, formal rules (or laws) cannot be lacking. Without formal institutional constraints, a large organization will have difficulty surviving, let alone developing. This is the reason we see that even though villages in ancient times did not have formal laws, governance that relied on local rules and regulations was still methodical, whereas modern society requires state laws.

The emergence of taxation institutions is also related to social scale. According to the current mainstream view, taxation facilitated state sovereignty, and must necessarily be coercive. However, taxation is nothing more than fees collected for public services.[37] For the public behavior of a few people, such as a banquet, splitting the check equally is enough. In relatively small groups, such as a village, certain public expenditures are distributed according to voluntary principles. Even without coercion, the wealthiest are often willing to pay more. However, a nation relying on voluntary taxation will not work, so it must implement tax law to coercively collect it.

There are three reasons for this. First, the probability of repeated games decreases as community scale increases. Second, as social scale increases, transmitting information about individual behavior becomes more difficult. Third, the cost and benefit of enforcing social norms becomes more asymmetric as community scale increases. In a small community, interpersonal interactions are frequent. Everyone is familiar with each other, and individual behavior easily becomes public information. The reputation mechanism of repeated games is enough to restrain individual behavior. For example, in a small work unit, if you always avoid paying for lunch, after a while, no one will be willing to have lunch with you. However, in large groups, the opportunity for repeated games decreases. Then individual uncooperative behavior does not become public information easily. In addition, the larger community scale is, the greater the individual cost of implementing punishments and the lower the benefit. The constraint that social norms can have on individual behavior decreases. To this point, a specialized mechanism to collect information and sanction uncooperative behavior is required.[38] Because laws are relatively formal, expressed relatively clearly, professionally enforced, and backed up with state violence, they are more effective as social scale increases.

Second, the cost of private enforcement. The discussion above was actually a free-rider problem in collective action. As was discussed previously, social norms are enforced by dispersed individuals. Even if a group of people might collectively sanction the non-cooperative behavior of a certain person, within a group the individual punishment of other's non-cooperative behavior is actually providing a type of public good. It often faces the difficulty of transferring the cost of enforcement into group costs. Additionally, the individual enforcer might face the risk of emotional retribution from the person that violated social norms. When you observe a thief stealing someone, due to fear of retaliation, you might turn your head and pretend you did not see anything. Precisely because retaliation increases the cost of private enforcement, we often see people turning a blind eye to violations of social norms.

For this reason, the cost of private enforcement has a major role in the effectiveness of social norms. Given the community scale, the higher the cost of private enforcement, the more difficult it will be for social norms to be effective. Thus, for serious violations of social norms, enforcement of social norms is often difficult. As soon as criminal organizations appear, only legal violence (such as the police and military) can correct it.

When social norms depend on private enforcement, another issue will emerge: Knights and heroes. If the private execution costs are high, there will be knights. When certain people cannot be excluded from a group by social norms, knights play an important role. The ancient Chinese Legalists absolutely rejected knights and individual heroes since Legalists stressed legal monopoly. Han Fei, a famous Legalist, condemned and categorized knights as one of the "five beetles", regarding them the pest of society. Knights and heroes are "entrepreneurs" of private enforcement, but Confucian intellectuals also opposed them since it is hard to judge a private enforcer's moral level. Nowadays, the conflict between private enforcers (knights and heroes) and laws and social norms is a subject of American films.

From this point of view, legal and social norms are not only substitutes, but also complementary. When legal and social norms are consistent, the costs of private enforcement (such as expulsion, exclusion, criticism, etc.) will be reduced, thereby increasing the effectiveness of social norms. If private enforcement can be legally supported, in the event of retaliation, retaliation for private enforcement can be turned into a crime, thus becoming an act prohibited by law. Even if the retaliation is relatively minor, and does not constitute a crime, the law can still reduce the possibility of retaliation. For example, when you criticize a person for spitting in public without a relevant law, he might berate you. However, with a law in place, the likelihood is lower. A similar issue exists with smoking bans. If someone smokes in front of a non-smoking sign, you are more likely to have the courage to criticize his behavior. Here, the major reason the law plays a role is the law's expressive function. The legal prohibition of certain behaviors is actually an expression of condemnation of those behaviors.[39]

The difference between private enforcement and state enforcement provides a key to our understanding of the differences between civil law and criminal law. Civil law follows the rule of "if people do not report, the official does not intervene". If there is a dispute or litigation, it is because one party to the litigation reported it to the government. Criminal law is different. Following the rule "even if people do not report, the official does intervene", criminal law cuts off the link to private retaliation through the state. If killing is retaliated against with more killing, the death rate will be very high. However, when the state brings about litigation and implements sanctions, the link to private retaliation is cut off.[40]

Third, the speed and method of information flows. The effectiveness of social norms and laws depends on the speed of information flows and information quality. The easier it is to observe behavior that violates laws and social norms, the more effective laws and social norms are. If a swindler can be discovered after the first swindle, then punishment can be administered immediately. If it takes two occurrences to be discovered, the restrictive power of social norms will decrease. If it takes multiple occurrences to be discovered, then swindling will be quite prevalent.

However, the method of information transmission is different for social norms and laws. Social-norm-related information transmission is often informal, such as gossip, whereas for laws, it is much more formal. Only specialized organs can promulgate laws and specialized organs (such as the police and courts) collect and transmit information on violators.

The difference between the creation and transmission of information means that social norms are more effective in restraining the public's easily observable behavior, whereas laws must be introduced to restrain the public's behavior that is not easily observed. This point also means that as individual privacy rights become more important, laws have a relative advantage in balancing privacy rights protection and obtaining necessary information.[41] Similar to the Law Merchant in the Middle Ages, modern courts are also an organ that centralizes and transmits information. Lawrence Friedman believed the legal organ also functioned as a type of record. It acts as a repository for millions of necessary transactions in the modern world. These archives allow the day-to-day work of transactions to be effective. This was the primary characteristic of modern and ancient legal systems.[42] The courts can collect only necessary information and transmit information only to the people that need it. This greatly reduces costs of information collection and distribution.

Fourth, the speed of social transformation. The faster social transformation is, the less effective social norms will be and the more effective laws will be. This is because the formation and transmission of social norms is a relatively slow process, whereas the formation and transmission of laws is relatively quick. This was already analyzed in the previous text. Therefore, when society needs to hasten the speed of transformation, laws can more effectively play a leading role. When social changes happen too fast, the government needs to "apply a heavy code during times of chaos". This is the reason ancient Chinese legal philosophy proposed that "the penalty should be determined according to the social situation at the time".[43]

This is reason that Legalism was dominant during the Spring and Autumn and Warring States periods, but Confucian philosophy replaced Legalism after the Western Han Dynasty. During time of war, the Legalists advocated the use of national laws to regulate behavior. This method helped the First Emperor of Qin to unify China. However, in peacetime, relying solely on state law to govern society is difficult, so the Confucian emphasis on moral norms to govern society naturally became the mainstream ideology.

Fifth, the social division of power. The unity of the law also means the rigidity of the law; thus, the law's cost of enforcement is quite high. In this case, a diverse social governance mechanism means social division of power.

The social division of power is an important component of democratization. The different components of society organize people's internal norms through various organizations such as firms, associations, universities, communities, families, and local organizations to transform external governance into internal governance. They cause social norms to be effectively enforced through information transmission and joint liability. The degree of intermediary organization development has an important impact on the degree of trust between people.[44] The less-developed a country's non-governmental organizations are, the harder it will be for social norms to play a role. If the central authority eliminates spontaneous private organizations, then social governance can only rely on so-called "laws", but society is no longer social.

China's ancient social governance made full use of the social division of power. We now call this the "patriarchal clan system". The power of the clan helped to maintain mainstream social norms. Many civil affairs were not regulated by the law, and most disputes were handled by the clan elders. Mr. Xiaotong Fei, a well-known Chinese sociologist referred to this as "elder governance". Under the patriarchal clan system, many local matters were governed by social norms. In recent years, more attention has been put on township rules.[45]

5.2 The rule of law state and the rule of state law

Laws and social norms are both substitutes and compliments. With the development of globalization and the continuous expansion of laws, will the role of social norms in social governance decline or even disappear? There are different viewpoints on this in academia. One viewpoint, represented by Richard Allen Posner, is that as social life develops, laws will become more and more important and social norms will become less and less important. This viewpoint is relatively prominent among scholars at the University of Chicago that emphasize the state's active role in changing social norms.[46] Another school of thought, represented by Professor Robert C. Ellickson at Yale University, believes that when social relationships become complex, the government will lack the ability to obtain and process sufficient information, so social norms will still play additional and better roles.[47] Over the last 30 years, as more and more countries deregulated the state control, which expanded economic democracy and economy freedom in the market, non-governmental organizations have played more of a role in providing public services. This means that the boundaries of laws are shrinking, while social and market norms are relied on more and more. Certain recent research has shown the new form of social norms in modern society.[48]

In my view, the different enforcement mechanisms and required information structures of laws and social norms means that they can play a role on different levels. The state cannot replace communities, and laws cannot eliminate social norms. The relationship between laws and social norms is similar to the relationship between firms and markets in economics. According to Ronald Harry Coase's theory of the firm, firms exist because transaction costs in the market are too high. This means that a decline in market transaction costs will cause firm scale to shrink, or even the disappearance of firms. However, we actually find that the lower market transaction costs are, the more efficient firms operate. Alternatively, the more efficiently firms are managed, the more orderly the operation of the market is, so large-scale firms often only exist in countries with highly developed market transactions. The relationship between laws and social norms is similar. Even though historically the scope of laws has increased, not only did the development of laws not replace social norms, instead it caused social norms to play a more important role. A country that lacks effective social norm governance cannot possibly be a truly rule of law country. The primary reason is that in many aspects laws and social norms are complementary. Rational laws might reduce costs of social norm implementation. Social norms might also aid in reducing the enforcement costs of laws.[49] Here, social intermediary organizations play a key role. If intermediary organizations are not developed, the reputation mechanism cannot be established, so people will not respect basic social norms and the law will also have difficulty playing a relevant role.[50]

Speaking on today's China, correctly understanding the relationship between laws and social norms has both practical significance and profound historical significance. Over the last thirty years, with the deepening of reform and opening, China has made considerable progress towards establishing a rule of law country. This progress has not only manifested itself in an increase in legal statutes and the raised status of lawyers, but also the strengthening of the public's legal concepts and court autonomy. However, we have reason to worry that when China's legal circles, economic circles, and government are emphasizing establishing the rule of law, they excessively satisfy the setting and enforcement of legal statutes while overlooking the importance of social norms. In my view, the essence of "the rule of law" is each person acting according to socially accepted, fair rules of the game. Here, rules of the game not only include formal legal statutes set by the state, but should also include commonly accepted and respected informal rules, which are social norms. Laws set by the state must align with society's requirements of basic justice and effectiveness, otherwise there is not much difference between this and "rule by man". I believe that compared with Legalism, classical Confucian culture is more aligned with the modern rule of law spirit. The Confucian etiquette is in essence the combination of social norms and state laws. Cooter (1996) differentiated between the "rule-of-law state" and the "rule of state law". In rule of law countries, the law is aligned with social norms based on the concept of fairness, people obey the law based on respect for the law itself, and the law can be effectively enforced. Under the rule of state law, the law is not aligned with social norms, people obey the law out of fear of punishment, and the law is often ineffectively enforced. We must also guard against intrusions of state legislation into areas that should be governed by social norms. The dominance of laws over everything is not a true rule of law society.

Notes

1 This chapter is a revised version of the paper with the same title published in Comparative Studies (*Bijiao Magazine*) in the 11th issue of 2004.

2 Representative research includes: Robert Axelrod (1986); Robert Ellickson (1991); James Coleman (1994); Jon Elster (1989b); H. Peyton Young (1996, 1998, 2008); Eric Posner (2000); Richard McAdams (1997); Paul Mahoney and Chris Sanchirico (2003); Avner Greif (1994); Kausik Basu (1998); L. Bernstein (1992); Robert Cooter (1996, 2000b); and Dixit (2004), etc. Friedrich A. Hayek was without a doubt a pioneer in this field (Hayek, 1960, 1979). Steven N. S. Cheung's *The Fable of the Bees*, published in (1973), was also innovative literature.

3 See Cooter (1996).

4 Of course, in jurisprudence, there is a debate on what counts as a law. Laws are composed of two components: Rules and violence. Legal scholars that emphasize rules, such as Grotius and L. L. Fuller (see Bodenheimer (1962) and Fuller (1964, 1981)), expand the law to include many social norms. Legal scholars that emphasize violence, such as Kelsen (2009) and Marxists, exclude social norms. In recent years, the so-called Norms School has emerged in American jurisprudence in an attempt to harmonize the relationship between legal systems and social norms. Many Chinese legal scholars have also begun to focus on this issue, such as Suli Zhu (1996).

5 See Hayek (1960, 1979); Sugden (1989); and Young (1998).

6 See Trakman (1983).

7 See Hayek's, *Law, Legislation, and Liberty* (1979) as well as Skoble (2006).

8 See Elster (1989a).

9 For detailed discussion of these two stories, see Weiying Zhang (2004).

10 See Honore (1987), page 33–38.

11 Gu Yanwu, *Rizhilv*, Volume VI.

12 Basu (1998, 2000).

13 For more discussions related to laws as incentive systems, see Weiying Zhang's, "Zuòwéi Jīlì Zhìdù de Fǎlǜ." In *Xìnxī, Xìnrèn yǔ Fǎlǜ (Information, Trust and Law)*. Beijing: Sanlian Shudian, 2003.

14 Weiying Zhang and Rongzhu Ke, "Sīfǎ Guòchéng Zhōng de Nìxiàng Xuǎnzé." *China Social Sciences*. 2002, Volume 2.

15 Obviously, strictly speaking, the cost of different legal sanctions will be different for different people.

16 If we understand ax and by to be legal punishments, or compensation that should be paid for violating an agreement, then the Prisoner's Dilemma can be resolved through legal liability. This is an expression of the previous incentive role of laws. The role social norms play in transforming a game and the role of laws are aligned. The payoff structure in Figure 13.1 could be understood as the reduced form of a larger or repeated game, such as ax and by being long-term losses caused by non-cooperative behavior. As we showed in Chapter 6, if the game repeats, based on considerations of long-term interests, the people involved might choose cooperation. There are numerous contributions to the discussion of social norm formation from repeated Prisoner's Dilemma games. Axelrod (1984) is a classic, but see also Mahoney and Sanchirico (2003).

17 Kandori (1992).

18 In regards to the incentive effect of joint liability in laws, see Weiying Zhang and Deng Feng's, "Xìnxī, Jīlì yǔ Liándài Zérèn." *Social Sciences in China*. 2003, Volume 3.

19 Sugden (1989); Young (1996); and Basu (1998, 2000).

20 Basu (1998, 2000)

21 Rothbard (2005) and Hulsmann (2008).

22 Tullock, Seldon, and Brady (2002) analyzed regulations in the telecommunication and Internet fields based on rent-seeking reasons.

23 Zhang (2012). The corruption of language concept was introduced by Orwell (1946).

24 In regards to the Federal Reserve's responsibility for the financial crisis, see Woods (2009) and Weiying Zhang (2015, Chapter 14).

25 Milgrom, North, and Weingast (1990).

26 Eric Posner (2000).

27 Eric Posner (2000, Chapter 6).

28 Here, we assume that social norms themselves are good. If social norms themselves are not good, then perhaps violating norms is valuable behavior to society. This means that "the worst people" and "the best people" are often the same type of people, because from the perspective of old norms, they are "bad", but from the perspective of new norms, they are "good". Perhaps this type of person is an "institutional entrepreneur" that we discuss in the next chapter.

29 Cited from Richard A. Posner (1992), Economic Analysis of Law (the 4th edition), page 293.

30 Tyler (1990).

31 Richard Posner (1997).

32 Social norms also require people to maintain individual compliance. If you are cheated by someone, but do nothing about it, you will be looked down upon. See discussion related to the code of honor in Elster (1989a, Chapter 3). Additionally, emotional behavior also has biological reasons, because organisms that do not maintain individual privileges have difficulty surviving in competition. See Trivers (1971).

33 Eric Posner (2000).

34 Weiying Zhang and Rongzhu Ke, "Sīfǎ Guòchéng Zhōng de Nìxiàng Xuǎnzé." *Social Sciences in China*. 2002, Volume 2.

35 *The Book of Lord Shang, Rewards and Punishments*.

36 Richard Posner (1997) and Ellickson (1991).

37 Of course, in modern society, taxation is also a redistribution mechanism. The income redistribution can also be voluntarily done in a small communication.

38 Milgrom, North, and Weingast (1990).

39 See McAdams (1997), page 397–408.

40 See Weiying Zhang's, "Zuòwéi Jīlì Zhìdù de Fǎlǜ." In *Xìnxī, Xìnrèn yǔ Fǎlǜ (Information, Trust and Law)*. Beijing: Sanlian Shudian, 2003.

41 Richard Posner (1997) believed that the more the law protects private rights, the greater the need for laws to replace social norms. The reason is that more privacy rights protections means enforcers of social norms have more difficulty observing individual behavior, thus reducing the cost of violating social norms.

42 Lawrence Friedman, *The Legal System: A Social Science Perspective*. New York: Russell Sage Foundation, 1975.

43 See *The Book of Documents, Marquis Lu on Punishments*.

44 Putnam (1993) and Tocqueville (1835).

45 Zhiping Liang, *Qīngdài Xíguàn Fǎ: Shèhuì yǔ Guójiā*. Beijing: China University of Political Science and Law Press, 1996.

46 See Sunstein (1996) and Eric Posner (1999).

47 See Ellickson (1998) and Cooter (1997b).

48 See Benson (1990).

49 The relationship between laws and norms in social governance is like the relationship between rebar and concrete in construction. The taller the building is, the higher the quality requirements are for both.

50 Weiying Zhang, "Fǎlǜ Zhìdù de Xìnyù Jīchǔ." *Jīngjì Yánjiū*. 2002, Volume 1.

14 Institutional entrepreneurs and the rules of the game

The rules of the game in human society games are the result of long-term historical evolution, not the product of planning and design. However, certain people had a pivotal impact on the formation and creation of social norms and laws. These people can be called "institutional entrepreneurs".

The entrepreneur's most important role is innovation! For institutional entrepreneurs, innovation means making people use new values to replace old values and use new behavioral patterns to replace old behavioral methods. This means we must acknowledge things we might not acknowledge originally or no longer acknowledge the things we originally acknowledged.

The standard for measuring the success of institutional entrepreneurs is the number of followers the ideas and behavioral norms they proposed have.

Institutional entrepreneurs primarily face the mass market, not the niche market. Their innovations must undergo longer market tests. The behavioral norms they propose must constitute an "evolutionarily stable equilibrium" to become broadly accepted. Therefore, institutional entrepreneurs must have a more thorough and fundamental understanding of human nature than commercial entrepreneurs.

Institutional entrepreneurs take on tremendous risk. Sometimes they pay the ultimate price. The first reason for this is that their judgment of society's needs might be incorrect. There is significant uncertainty in social life. Second, they face the risks brought about by the second-order Prisoner's Dilemma. They must challenge the existing rules. Third, there is fierce competition between them.

The reason great institutional entrepreneurs are willing to take on the risk of innovating social rules of the game is based on their love for humanity. They want to improve the fate of mankind with their distinct lofty ideas and sacred mission. Therefore, we say they are saints.

During the "Axial Age" of human civilization, some of the greatest institutional entrepreneurs appeared. They established the cornerstones of human civilization. Their ideas became pillars of later thought, and even today are influencing our behavioral patterns.

Confucius was one of the most successful Axial Age institutional entrepreneurs. Confucian culture constituted a guiding system of social governance because it provided society with a normative model. In Chinese history, this emerged as the "etiquette" system.

An important function of the Confucian system is coordinating expectations and settling disputes. Rules for coordinated expectations further evolve into national governance.

The hierarchy is both a coordination mechanism and an incentive mechanism. "Virtuous men" are the standard for social governance accomplished through a hierarchy.

Although Confucianism is "people-oriented", it does not have a democratic systemic framework, so it cannot restrain the monarch effectively. Historical development up to the present makes it clear that only constitutional government and democracy can restrain the monarch.

However, classical Confucian culture is not contradictory to the rule of law and democracy. Not only can Confucian culture adapt to modern democracy and rule of law constitutional government, it can also be a positive power in China's social system transformation.

The establishment of the rule of law and democratization is a long process. Haste makes waste.

Section one: institutional entrepreneurs

1.1 Innovators of the rules of the game

The rules of the game in human society are the outcome of evolution over a long period, not the product of planning or design. This conclusion is not only applicable to social norms and culture, but is also applicable to most laws set by governments. However, we must also acknowledge that in this long process of history, certain people had a great influence on the formation of social norms and laws. Without thinkers or religious leaders like Socrates, Plato, Aristotle, Jesus Christ, St. Augustine, Aquinas, Luther, Calvin, Locke, Hume, Voltaire, Montesquieu, Rousseau, Adam Smith, John Mill, etc. contemporary Western society's mainstream social norms and laws would certainly be different than they are now. Similarly, behavioral norms in Chinese society were to a large degree shaped by Confucius, Laocius, Chuang Tzu, Mencius, Hsun Tzu, Chu Hsi, Wang Yangming, and so on. Without these types of great figures, we might live in a completely different world.

We refer to these people that created and changed the rules of the game as "institutional entrepreneurs".[1] This can include people like Deng Xiaoping, but in this text we will primarily focus on non-politician social norm innovators, although historically many politicians not only had a major impact on the formation of laws, but also the formation of social norms.[2]

Business entrepreneurs in the commercial field include outstanding leaders that have influenced history such as Henry Ford, Bill Gates, and Steve Jobs, but also lesser-known proprietors of retail stores. Similarly, institutional entrepreneurs include historical figures we just mentioned, such as Confucius, Jesus, or Chu Hsi, but also people whose names did not make the history books. For example, the transition of marriage norms in rural areas from parental selection to free choice in marriage was often started by individual rebellious youth. We must also acknowledge that many outstanding business entrepreneurs played the role of institutional entrepreneurs. At the same time that their new products and technologies transformed our way of life, they also had an impact on the transformation of our behavioral norms. For instance, with the advent of the Internet, electronic mail became a commonly accepted norm for the exchange of information. The promises someone makes in an email are a type of commitment, and violating this commitment is unethical behavior.

What is the most important function of entrepreneurs? Innovation! This point applies to both business entrepreneurs as well as institutional entrepreneurs. As Joseph Schumpeter pointed out, innovation is "creative destruction".[3] For business entrepreneurs, innovation means using new products to replace old products, new methods of production to replace old methods of production, new business models to replace old business models, and new management methods to replace old management methods. For institutional entrepreneurs, innovation means making people use new values to replace old values, new behavioral patterns to replace old behavioral patterns, and new standards of right and wrong or good and evil to replace old standards of right and wrong or good and evil. It means accepting things we originally did not accept or not accepting things we originally did accept. For instance, starting in the Northern Song Dynasty, foot-binding was a mainstream custom in Chinese society. After the Republic of China began, with the rise of the Women's Liberation Movement, the foot-binding custom was gradually eliminated. This is the outcome of institutional entrepreneur innovation.

For both business entrepreneurs and institutional entrepreneurs, whether or not their innovation can succeed or not is determined by the product or behavioral norm they propose being accepted by the "market". They must satisfy society's needs. Therefore, both types of entrepreneurs must have a thorough understanding of human nature. People that do not understand human nature cannot possibly become true entrepreneurs, either business or institutional.

In contrast with business entrepreneurs, institutional entrepreneurs primarily face the mass market, not a niche market.[4] Their innovations must pass the test over a much longer period of time. For the behavioral norms that they propose to be broadly accepted as social norms, they must form an "evolutionarily stable equilibrium" (see Chapter 12). Therefore, institutional entrepreneurs' understanding of human nature must be more thorough and foundational than commercial entrepreneurs'. Commercial entrepreneurs only need to understand what people like. Institutional entrepreneurs must understand the essence of humanity. Therefore, it is not surprising that great thinkers from the ancient times to the present throughout the world have described their thoughts using human nature as the starting point. The reason different institutional entrepreneurs from the same time period will propose different behavioral norms to a large degree is their different understanding of human nature. This was the reason for the debate on good and evil among philosophers in the Spring and Autumn and Warring States periods of China. The thoughts of Moh Tzu did not become institutionalized to a large degree because of errors in his understanding of human nature. The success of

Confucian scholars is to a large degree related to their basically correct understanding of human nature. Moh Tzu scholars believed that each person should love everyone equally, whereas Confucius believed that love is ranked by closeness. Modern biologists have proven that there is a genetic foundation for different levels of love. The more genes two people share, the higher the degree of love between them (see Chapter 12). Therefore, this type of "universal love" that Moh Tzu advocated is impossible. (Jesus Christ and Sakyamuni similarly advocated universal love, but the difference between them and Moh Tzu was that their thought system had a supernatural power.) Similarly, today's environmentalists are institutional entrepreneurs based on their understanding of human nature, human pursuits, and determinants of human happiness. Whether or not the specific behavioral norms they propose can become actual behavioral norms is to a large degree determined by these norms' conformance to human nature. Of course, because of human complexity, besides the pursuit of happiness, human nature is difficult to define in one-dimensional terms. Certain viewpoints that might appear to be conflicting might actually be complimentary. It is even difficult to say whether people are good by nature or evil by nature. Therefore, even if different institutional entrepreneurs have different understandings of human nature, they might still propose similar behavioral norms. Different behavioral norms proposed based on different judgments of human nature might also coexist, because different norms might satisfy the different attributes of human nature.

Human nature remains the same, but in different environments it might have different needs. Recognizing this need at the right time is a prerequisite of entrepreneurial innovation. Producing products that satisfy this type of demand is the key to entrepreneurial success. From this perspective, I classify business entrepreneurs into three categories. The first category can see demand that the consumer does not. The second category can satisfy demand that has already appeared on the market. The third category produces according to customer orders.[5] The first type of entrepreneur is the industry-creating entrepreneur, such as Henry Ford, Bill Gates, and Steve Jobs. By utilizing this categorical method based on ability to innovate and level of innovation, the institutional entrepreneur can at least be classified into two categories. The first category creates rules of the game that most people need but do not yet understand. The second type creates rules of the game when demand for them have already appeared, but not yet fulfilled. Confucius, Jesus Christ, and Socrates are the first category of institutional entrepreneur. They lived in a time where new rules of the game were required, but most people were not clear as to what the new rules of the game should be. Advocates of new norms and those that rebelled against old traditions were the second type of institutional entrepreneur.

In the next section, we will focus our discussion on the first type of institutional entrepreneur, but here we will first discuss the second type of institutional entrepreneur. We know that as soon as any social norm is formed, regardless if it is Pareto optimal or not, it is very difficult to change. However, certain social norms place too many limits on individual liberty and are detrimental to the majority's happiness. With the passage of time, it will be difficult for many people to tolerate it and most people will acknowledge the need for change. However, just as we discussed a "second order Prisoner's Dilemma" issue existing for the enforcement of social rules, so too might a similar issue exist for changing social norms. Changing the old norms might be good for everyone, but individual rationality may cause no one to be willing to violate the old norms first.[6] The reason is that as soon as a social norm is formed, individuals will worry about the punishment from a third party for violating the norm. For instance, as soon as arranged marriage becomes a custom, men and women that make their own choices will be looked down upon. Similarly, as soon as foot-binding became common, females that did not bind their feet had difficulty finding a partner later in life. Because of information transmission reasons, even if most people personally do not support the current norms, in order to show that they respect social norms, they will still openly admonish those that do not. However, after people's dissatisfaction towards the current norms accumulates to a certain degree, the second type of institutional entrepreneur will emerge to either be the first to violate the current norm or call on others to change old viewpoints. Gradually, old norms will be replaced by new norms, just as we saw with changing marriage concepts and the elimination of foot binding.[7]

Another classic example is dueling in pre-contemporary Europe. Dueling came about to protect the "honor" of nobility. The offended party would be mocked if a duel was not proposed. The other party would be considered shameless if the duel was not accepted. In this way, dueling became a norm that both parties had no option but to respect, even though both parties might pay a high price over an insignificant issue (such as a comment about a lady). Because noble people care more about "honor" and desire to show a spirit of nobility, dueling was much more prevalent between noble people. The United Kingdom had four prime ministers participate in a duel. Alexander Hamilton, of the American Federalist Party, died after a duel with the sitting vice president Alan Burr. Andrew Jackson, the seventh U.S. president, was also known for dueling. Russian poet Alexander Puskin was fatally wounded in a duel with his wife's lover. Joseph Schumpeter, a famous economist, also participated in a duel over something minor. The first institutional entrepreneurs to denounce the dueling custom were the Roman Catholic Church and certain other political leaders. Benjamin Franklin, an American politician, denounced it. George Washington encouraged military officials to reject dueling during the American War for Independence. Dueling was not common after the eighteenth century. Some US states explicitly abolished dueling. Although some states have not explicitly prohibited it, the winning party in a duel might be charged with other crimes. During the middle of the nineteenth century, British society generally did not support dueling, so from that point on it was very rare. By the end of the nineteenth century, legal dueling basically disappeared throughout the world. The international society has basically agreed that dueling is a barbaric way to resolve conflicts, and many countries have explicitly banned it.[8]

The second type of institutional entrepreneur also played a major role in the transformation of mainstream ideology and political systems. The drastic changes in Eastern Europe in 1989 are an example. By the end of the 1980s, the Romanian people's dissatisfaction towards Nicolae Ceausescu's tyrannical rule had reached an intolerable point, but because "respecting" him was a basic "social norm",[9] the vast majority of people did not dare to say anything. In December, 1989, people were still chanting "long live Ceausescu!" until suddenly someone shouted "down with Ceausescu!" When "long live" was replaced by "down with", norms changed completely. What was originally correct was now wrong, and what was originally wrong was now correct. Those people that shouted "down with" the earliest were the second type of institutional entrepreneur. They satisfied a need that already existed but was not expressed. Actually, many political opponents under despotic systems are this type of institutional entrepreneur. They say the things that most people think but are not willing to say. Eventually, this changes society's rules of the game.

1.2 Risk and beliefs

Any innovation is a type of exploration and faces uncertainty. Similar to commercial entrepreneurs, institutional entrepreneurs also have to take risks. Sometimes, they pay the ultimate price. There are three primary reasons for this. The first reason is that their judgment of social demand might be inaccurate. There are too many uncertainties in life. The second reason is the risk brought about by the second-order Prisoner's Dilemma that we previously discussed. They must challenge existing rules. The third reason is that intense competition exists between institutional entrepreneurs. It is not easy to determine the market demands of products, and it is even harder to determine great trends in social development. Even if institutional entrepreneurs have correct judgment, they also face the short-term disagreements of people accustomed to the old rules. This disagreement might be based on vested interests, or beliefs, or even the inert dictates of human nature. We are familiar with the persecution of different opinions, but those first type of entrepreneurs that established "big rules" throughout history paid a personal price that was often ignored by the common people. The later generations remembered their names, but often forgot their sufferings. Throughout history, not many of the great institutional entrepreneurs were lucky during their lifetimes. Confucius lived a miserable life as he roamed about the various kingdoms. Socrates displeased the citizens of Athens and was put to death by a democratic government. Pontius Pilate, a prefect of the Judaea province of the Roman Empire, sentenced Jesus Christ to death by crucifixion. Chu Hsi (a famous philosopher in the Song Dynasty) was dismissed as a "pseudo teacher", his ideas were dismissed as "pseudo-science", and his students were dismissed as "pseudo apprentices". Chu Hsi died at the age of 71 with sorrow. For these reasons, being an institutional entrepreneur is much less appealing than being a commercial entrepreneur.

An another major reason for the risk of being an institutional entrepreneur is the competition among them. The standard for measuring the success of institutional entrepreneurs is the number of followers for the thought and behavioral norms that they proposed. This is similar to the standard for measuring the success of commercial entrepreneurs, which is the number of consumers for their products.

However, there are two major differences between the market for rules and the market for products. First, in the market for rules, "winner-take-all" is standard, whereas in the market for product, "winner-take-all" is the exception. Competition between institutional entrepreneurs is similar to competition between the Microsoft and Android platforms or competition between different 3G standards. It is more win-lose than the product market. This is even more so under authoritarian systems. Second, competition in the market for rules goes over a long period of time. The "customers" of institutional entrepreneurs often only emerge hundreds of years after an institutional entrepreneur's lifetime. For example, the philosophers during the Spring and Autumn and Warring States Dynasties did not see the outcome of their competition. By the time of the First Emperor of Qin, the Legalists were dominant. By the early Western Han dynasty, Daoists were dominant. Only after Emperor Wu of Han "rejected all schools of thought but Confucianism" did Confucianism achieve a decisive victory, but by that time Confucius himself had already passed away 350 years prior. During the Wei, Jin, Southern-Northern, Sui, and Tang dynasties, Buddhism became a major competitor, and sometimes was even dominant. After the Northern Song dynasty, due to the efforts of Chu Hsi, Confucianism reclaimed its dominant position until the May Fourth Movement of 1919. From the perspective of the political system, since the First Emperor of Qin, rules have always been "externally Confucian and internally Legalist". By the time of the "Cultural Revolution", China was externally and internally Legalist. About one hundred years after people began chanting "down with Confucius!", there is now renewed interest in Confucianism. The Chinese government has opened "Confucius Institutes" throughout the world. No further mention of academia's respect for Confucianism is needed.

For this reason, perhaps the greatest difference between institutional entrepreneurs and commercial entrepreneurs is that institutional entrepreneurs absolutely cannot take "profit" as an objective. Even if a person is only motivated by money, he perhaps can become an outstanding commercial entrepreneur. However, if that person's goal is "gain", then he cannot become an institutional entrepreneur, especially not an outstanding one, although, as we have already discussed, certain commercial entrepreneurs also play the role of institutional entrepreneurs.

The reason great institutional entrepreneurs are willing to take such risks with society's rules of the game innovation is certainly based on their tremendous love for humanity and desire to improve the fate of mankind. They have unique noble ideas and a sense of mission. Perhaps they were born with this love and sense of purpose, which they may not be consciously aware of, so we call them "sages". Even if they are not sages, they must be different. They must care more about their future fame (the fame after death) than their present fame and fortune. Otherwise, they could not bear the pain experienced for their ideas during their life. For example, if Confucius was willing to give up his own ideas, he could find a senior position in any of the states he lives in. As long as Socrates confessed, glory, wealth, and rank would have followed him. According to the Athens law at that time, he could have paid fines or be exiled to avoid the death penalty. However, Socrates refused. He chose to drink poison because he believed sticking to his conscience and reason was more important than life. As long as Jesus had admitted guilt, he could have also avoided death. Other institutional entrepreneurs who are less known also need to have more perseverance than ordinary people in order to "take the responsibility to shape our world". As Mencius said, "Only Sages can have perseverance with little property."

It must be pointed out that the "winner-take-all" competition in the market for rules that we discussed previously does not mean the rules proposed by the "loser" and the ideas these rules are established on do not have an influence on the later world. In reality, all successful innovation involves both ideas accumulated in the past and contemporary ideas. Similar to bankrupt enterprises, the "assets" of "losers" are often absorbed by the "winners" and become a part of the latter. In India, for example, the Buddhism established by Sakyamuni in the end failed to compete with Hinduism. However, because its basic beliefs were assimilated by Hinduism through the Anti-Reform Movement, it still exists today. Similarly, in China, not only did later generations of Confucian scholars absorb aspects of Buddhism and Daoism, they even absorbed certain aspects of Legalism. Chu Hsi used Buddhism and Daoism to reform Confucianism to create Neo-Confucianism. Additionally, because humanity is widely dispersed and societies are diverse, rules that fail in one area can succeed in another area. Buddhism failed in India but succeeded in China and Southeast Asia. The mobility of humanity means that people that respect equivalent or similar social norms can form relatively independent societies. In this way, different institutional entrepreneurs can obtain equivalent success in different societies, such as Christianity in Europe, Islam in the Middle East, and Confucianism in East Asia. When humanity learns to be more tolerant, even in the same society, different social norms can peacefully coexist, as shown by the "Three Teachings" in China. Therefore, overall, we can say that human society is a "polymorphic evolutionarily stable equilibrium".

Section two: institutional entrepreneurs in the Axial Age

2.1 Establishing the rule for the public

An innumerable amount of people throughout human history could be called institutional entrepreneurs. A small portion of them will be known throughout the ages, but the vast majority was not even well-known during their own lifetimes. It is generally acknowledged that the about five-hundred year period starting in the middle of the sixth century before Christ was the "Axial Age" of human civilization.[10] Some of the world's greatest thinkers emerged during this period. They set the cornerstone of human civilization. Their ideas became the core ideas of later ages, and even today are influencing our behavioral patterns and way of life. Therefore, they could be called the greatest institutional entrepreneurs.[11] These outstanding figures include:

China: Confucius (551–479 BC), Mencius (372–289 BC), and Chu Hsi (313–238 B.C.) established and developed Confucianism. Laocius (about 300 years before Christ) and Chuang Tzu (368–286 BC) established and developed Daoism. Moh Tzu (468–376 BC) established and developed Mohism;

India: Mahavira (about 559 BC) established Jainism and Sakyamuni (about 560 BC) established Buddhism;

South West Asia: Jewish rabbi established Judaism (700– 500 BC), Zarathustra established Zoroastrianism (about 600 BC), Jesus established Christianity (circa 30 AD);

Ancient Greece: Parmenides (515–late fifth century BC), Socrates (469–399 BC), Plato (427–347 BC), Aristotle (384–322 BC), and so on.

Why did the Axial Age happen? Why did so many men of virtue emerge in this era? Perhaps, the simplest answer is that it was an era that required outstanding institutional entrepreneurs. It was an era that required new rules of the game for human civilization.

In the first 500 years of the first millennium BC, in both the West (primarily Southwest Asia) and the East, humanity was transitioning from the low-end society to the high-end society.[12] In the low-end society, religion and state were combined and rulers were the supernatural representatives of god. Rulers used their own moral orders to manage the people. "Witchcraft" was their basic method for managing society. They relied on local nobility (often their family) to provide armies and reimbursed them with the spoils of war. For these reasons, they did not need tax revenue. In the high-end society, rulers changed from "the chosen ones" to "chief executive officers". Rulers no longer pretended to have a direct connection with god. They required revenues to maintain an army and professional bureaucracy, so they required a large amount of taxes to maintain operations. With the transition from the low-end society to the high-end society, both East and West had continuous wars of subjugation, battles between rulers, and social chaos. If a new social order could not be established, the suffering of humanity would worsen. At this point, from the coast of the Aegean Sea to the Yellow River Basin, a group of outstanding thinkers answered the call. From the perspective of social status and geographic position, these people basically all (with a few exceptions) came from the fringe. However, they believed that humanity should take hold of its own destiny. God-like kings were not needed to redeem this tarnished world. Saving humanity could only depend on oneself, not corrupt and brutal rulers. Institutional entrepreneurs wanted to understand how the world worked. They wanted to establish new rules of the game for society in order to rescue humanity from its suffering.

During the Spring and Autumn and Warring States Dynasty, the philosophers came out of the traditional society and were given the title "*shi*", a low-level status in the nobility. These people lived in the era of church and state as one, so because of the limits of power on their position, they could only consider specific issues. They did not have the consciousness to discuss "ethics" above and beyond their position. After the separation of church and state, they had the consciousness and sense of duty to seek out "ethics" that transcended the world.[13] Although the philosophers had different viewpoints, they had a common desire to establish "ethics"(*dao*) for the public by discovering people's correct behavioral norms. The differences among them were due to each school of thought's understanding of "*dao*". Of course, similar to commercial entrepreneurs, each person utilizes a differentiation strategy to emphasize the difference between their own ideas and those of others.

Actually, in China, India, Southeast Asia, and the Greek peninsula, the great thinkers of the time faced similar issues. They were all seeking to discover "ethics" to save the world. Precisely because of concerns over corruption in Athens politics and the lack of any clear principles for daily life did Socrates attempt to use the "ask-and-answer" method of dialog to discover concepts of absolute truth, absolute virtue, and absolute beauty to provide permanent guidance for individual behavior. Plato sought to implement a "harmonious society" that could both maintain the special status of the nobility while at the same time be acceptable to the lower classes. He proposed a "republic" composed of four classes. Aristotle attempted to discover aspects of order in the natural world and human life.

Different thinkers in the Axial Age provided different types of ethics, but in terms of basic principles to guide human life, there were many commonalities. In the past, we were accustomed to talk of the differences between classical thought in the East and West. Although there were differences, we now can see that this disparity has been greatly exaggerated. Actually, the differences among Chinese philosophers might not be less than the differences between East and West. For example, the difference between the Confucian ideal state and the Daoist ideal state is not less than the difference between the Confucian ideal state and Plato's Republic. The commonalities between the Sophism in Ancient Greece and the Daoism in China are much greater than the similarities between Confucianism and Daoism. The difference between Moh Tzu and Jesus Christ might not be greater than the difference between Moh Tzu and Mencius. Perhaps the greatest difference between different schools of thought is whether or not there is a god or heaven. Another popular opinion is that Western classical thinkers defended democracy, whereas Chinese classical thinkers defended dictatorship. Actually, the true contribution of Ancient Greece to the Axial Age was not praise for democracy, but instead was criticism of the democratic system. Socrates, Plato, and Aristotle were all resolutely opposed to the democratic system.[14]

2.2 Principles of human behavior

What common values and norms did the outstanding institutional entrepreneurs of the Axial Age propose human behavior should respect? I summarize them as the following five points:

1) **Human-Centric Philosophy:** The vast majority of thinkers in the Axial Age believed that humans were the most precious of all organisms. Only humans are rational animals, so the goal of the social order is human happiness. Aristotle established rankings for all beings, with humans simultaneously possessing "mechanical growth", the ability to feel, and the ability to be rational.

Therefore, the soul of humans was superior to animals and plants. Humans were the center of Confucian teachings. Hsun Tzu said: "Man possesses energy, life, intelligence, and in addition, a sense of duty. Therefore he is the noblest being on earth". Mohist scholars were even more human-centric. They advocated universal love and innate equality. Jesus Christ believed that god created people in his image and endowed humans with reason. God loves all of humanity, not just certain groups. Buddhism preached love towards all creatures, but based on the objective of reincarnation, humans are the highest-ranking living creature.

Since humans are the lords of all things, all institutions and behavioral norms must have advancing human happiness as a starting point. They cannot have maintaining one group of people's interests as a starting point, nor can they sacrifice one group of people for the interests of another. This should be the standard for ethics and also the standard for judging good and evil. Confucian scholars spoke of the goal of virtuous government to be the people's happiness. The Legalists' goal was a rich nation and a strong army, so they often designed rules of the game contrary to human nature.

Humanity is both a group concept and an individual concept. Rodney Stark (2005) believed that among all the ideas of the Axial Age, perhaps only Christianity emphasized individualism and liberty, whereas other thinkers emphasized collectivism. There is no concept of "the individual" in Greek philosophy in the sense we speak of today. When Plato wrote *The Republic*, he put focus on the city-state polity, not individual citizens. He believed the happiness of the city-state as a whole was more important than the happiness of individuals. However, from the beginning, Christianity taught people that sin is an individual affair, not the fixed characteristic of a collective. Humanity has the ability and responsibility to determine our own actions. Each person has free will and the opportunity to choose. Therefore, we must take responsibility for our behavior. We make the choice between good and evil. God is only a judge that rewards good and punishes evil. However, Stark's view is only that of one scholar. Mr. Tsung-san Mou believed that Confucian scholars also advocated individualism. Respect for individual life is the basic spirit of benevolence, although Confucian individualism did not have concepts of liberty, equality, human rights, or rights.[15] Perhaps we could supplement this by saying Daoist scholars emphasized individuality and liberty. Chapter 57 of the *Tao Te Ching* reads: "I take no action and people are reformed. I enjoy peace and people become honest. I do nothing and people become rich. I have no desires and people return to the good and simple life."

2) **Reciprocity:** People form society, and each person has his own preferences and interests. This is the source of conflicts among people. What basic rules should people respect when interacting with each other? Confucius believed that benevolence was interpersonal relationship's highest principle. This means people treat each other as though we see others as ourselves. Two principles came out of this: "What you do not want done to yourself, do not

do to others" and "The man of perfect virtue, wishing to be established himself, seeks also to establish others; wishing to be enlarged himself, he seeks also to enlarge others".

The "reciprocity ethics" proposed by Confucius is now called the Golden Rule.[16] It was certainly a great accomplishment for Confucius to propose this basic rule for dealing with interpersonal relationships, but this was a basic rule for many other great thinkers during the Axial Age, and perhaps they proposed it earlier. It could be said that this was common sense for the great thinkers of the Axial Age. Almost every culture or religion included this rule. Greek philosopher Pittacus (640–568 BC) said: "Do not to your neighbor what you would take ill from him". Thales (624–546 BC), another Greek philosopher, said: "Avoid doing what you would blame others for doing". Buddhist teachings have similar sayings, such as: "Treat others as you treat yourself", or "hurt not others in ways that you yourself would find hurtful". Jesus Christ said: "Do unto others as you would have them do unto you". All of these could be translated as the Chinese saying "*jǐ suǒ bù yù, wù shī yú rén*". Actually, Christianity believes that the Golden Rule came from Jesus Christ. If we are not strict with our interpretations, we can find many similar meanings in *Moh Tzu* and *Tao Te Ching*.

The "Golden Rule" means that people are equal, because only equal people will consider issues from another person's perspective. This is equality in an ethical sense. Christianity advocates everyone being equal in front of god. Although people are unequal, in the eyes of god, everyone is equal. Mohist scholars believed that everyone was born equal and there should be equality of opportunity. Although Confucianism emphasized classes, these classes were career designations and status arrangements established on innate equality. If a person believes he is innately a higher level than another person, how could he possibly consider issues from another person's perspective? How could he hope others will treat him the same as he treats others? Therefore, it was not likely that Legalism or Plato would propose this type of rule.

The core of the "Golden Rule" is that each person should respect the preferences and rights of others. This type of respect is reciprocal. This aligns with contemporary principles of liberty and property rights. Respect for the preferences of others is the respect for the liberty of others. Since you do not like other people to deprive you of liberty, you should not deprive others of their liberty. Because you do not like other people interfering with your life at will, you should not interfere with the lives of others at will. Theft of your property will make you unhappy, so you should not steal the property of others. Precisely for this reason did seventeenth-century English philosopher Thomas Hobbes make this the general principle of natural law, which, he said, even the most ordinary person could understand.[17]

Some people believe that "What you do not want done to yourself, do not do to others" is insufficient. We should add "What you do want done to yourself, also do not do to others". If we understand "want done" as "material" preference or a specific behavior, then "What you do not want done to yourself, do not do to others" becomes "I do not like cars, so I should not require others to like cars". Naturally, we should add "Even though I like cars, I cannot require others to like cars". However, if we understand "want done" as preferences for liberty and rights, then this issue does not exist. Considering I dislike things I do not like forced upon me, then of course I should not force things others do not like on to them. Therefore, under any circumstances, I should respect the liberty and rights of other people, but I can still give others things that they like. If I like cars, but another person does not, and I force him to like them, then this itself violates the rule "What you do not want done to yourself, do not do to others". However, even if I do not like cars, but another person does, what is wrong about me giving him one? (However, if he does not like my gift and prefers to buy one himself, then I should not gift one.)

3) **Mutual Support and Love:** As one of the basic principles of interpersonal relations, mutual support and love not only requires people to "mutually respect each other", but also requires people to "love each other". Everyone who lives in society needs the help of others, and is eager to get other people's love. Hatred leads to conflict. In conflict, no one can live a happy life. You should treat people in a way that you want to be treated. If you want to get help from others, you should help others. If you want to get others' love, you should love others. If you want to live a happy life, you have to let other people live a happy life. Hence "mutual support and love" is a common proposal of many great thinkers during the Axial Age. They wanted to save the world with "love". The core concept of Confucianism is "*ren*" (benevolence). Confucius defined "benevolence" as "love for people". In Confucius's eyes, "Now the man of perfect virtue with benevolence, wishing to be established himself, seeks also to establish others; wishing to be enlarged himself, he seeks also to enlarge others".

Although the love concept in Confucianism is ranked (the closer people are, the deeper of their love is, and *vice versa*), it is still universal. Mencius believed that people should "expend the respect of the aged in one's family to that of other families and expend the love of the young ones in one's family to that of other families". Even between different social classes, the love should be mutual rather than one way. In an ideal Confucianism world, the emperor employs his ministers with propriety; the ministers serve their rulers with good faith. Sons behave filially, and fathers paternally. In this ideal concept, people's obligations are mutual. Rulers, ministers, sons, and fathers all have their own obligations. In Chapter 9 of *The Book of Rites*, it mentioned "there are ten righteous rules to follow. A father should love his children and children should behave filially. Older brothers should be genuine to younger siblings and younger ones should respect older siblings. Husbands should be a good partner and wives should support and love husbands. The elders should teach the young generation and the young generation should respect the elders. Emperors should be benevolent and his ministers should be loyal". Moh Tzu advocated universal love and innate equality. "We should regard other people's nation as our own, other people's family as ours, and other people's body as ours, too". Laocius also mentioned "the sage does not accumulate (for himself). The more that he expends for others, the more does he possess of his own; the more that he gives to others, the more does he have himself. With all the sharpness of the Way of Heaven, it injures not; with all the doing in the way of the sage he does not strive" (*Tao Te Ching*, Chapter 81).

Buddha wants us to be merciful because loving others will make a person closer to happiness. People should not only love their friends and other people, but also love their enemies; not only love human beings, but also love all creatures. Followers of Jesus Christ shared the same precepts with Buddha and Moh Tzu: "Love your enemies and pray for those who persecute you" (Matthew 5:44); "Love suffers long and is kind; love does not envy; love does not parade itself, is not puffed up; does not behave rudely, does not seek its own, is not provoked, thinks no evil; does not rejoice in iniquity, but rejoices in the truth; bears all things, believes all things, hopes all things, endures all things" (1 Corinthians 13). Kwang Tzu believed: "When the springs are dried up, the fishes collect together on the land. Than that they should moisten one another there by the damp about them, and keep one another wet by their slime, it would be better for them to forget one another in the rivers and lakes". He believed "mutual support" was important, although he believed liberty and self-reliance were more important than relying on others.

I have said before that from ancient times to the present, there are only two types of means for humanity to pursue happiness: The logic of theft and the logic of the market.[18] The logic of theft makes us happy by making others unhappy. The logic of the market makes others happy to obtain happiness for ourselves. The logic of theft prevailed in the Axial Age. Thinkers at the time attempted to use "mutual love" to abolish the logic of theft. By replacing "an unethical world" with "an ethical world," a harmonious society could resume. "Mutual love" is actually a type of logic of the market. It does not oppose benefiting yourself as long as you achieve happiness by making others happy. For example, Moh Tzu made it very clear that some people were opposed to "universal love" because they "do not acknowledge the benefits of universal love". In fact, loving others is beneficial to ourselves. "If you love and benefit other people, people will love and benefit you. If you hate and try to harm other people, other people will hate and harm you too".[19]

Because productive capabilities were lacking, technological progress was slow, and the primary form of wealth was limited land, besides a tiny number of people like Sima Qian, thinkers at the time (including Plato and Aristotle), could not see the win-win result of market competition.[20] They did not understand the appeal of the "invisible hand". Therefore, their primary means for the pursuit of happiness were restraints on desire, not increases in production. They believed people who have the least desire are the happiest ones. When there is no desire, happiness appears. Only with a good "heart" could people can have good "actions", thus the world could be free of sin and humanity could be happy. On this point, the view of Confucius, Moh Tzu, Laocius, Sakyumani, and Jesus Christ were all aligned. However, two thousand years later, today we should acknowledge that the market institution is the most effective means of realizing "mutual support and love" (but, of course, it is not the only means). As long as everyone implements the Golden Rule, then a self-interested "heart" can lead to "actions" that benefit others.

4) **Honesty and Honoring Promise:** In social games, a person's choice of behavior to a large degree depends on his expectations for other's behavior. His expectation for other's behavior is related to other's "words" and "action". Words transmit information promising to do something; actions actually do something. Confucius said: "[H]ear their words, and look at their conduct". Alignment between words and actions is the foundation of human mutual cooperation. Only then will people have stable expectations and behave based on long-term interests. Only then will society be harmonious. Misalignment between words and actions will befuddle expectations and cause difficulties coordinating behavior. It will necessarily lead to social conflicts. Alignment between words and actions is saying what you mean and meaning what you say.

Most of the thinkers of the Axial Age regarded honesty and trustworthiness as the basic principle that people should follow. Confucianism regards "benevolence, righteousness, rituals, wisdom, and faith" as the most important five virtues. The *Commentary on the Words* in the *Ten Writings* stressed "By working on his words, so that they rest firmly on truth, he makes his work enduring". Confucius said, "I do not know how a man without truthfulness is to get on. How can a large carriage be made to go without the crossbar for yoking the oxen to, or a small carriage without the arrangement for yoking the horses?" (*The Analects: Book II: Wei Chang*). Mencius said: "[S]incerity is the way of Heaven. To think how to be sincere is the way of man. Never has there been one possessed of complete sincerity, who did not move others. Never has there been one who had not sincerity who was able to move others" (*The Works of Mencius, Book IV, Part I*). Moh Tzu said: "His wisdom will not be far-reaching whose purpose is not firm. His action will not be effective whose promises are not kept" (*The Ethical and Political Works of Motse, Book I, Self-Cultivation*). Laocius said, "Sincere words are not fine; fine words are not sincere" (*Tao Te Ching*). Chuang Tzu said: "[W]ithout this pure sincerity one cannot move others" (*The Works of Chuang Tzu, The Old Fisherman*). The Five Precepts of Buddhism call on followers to abstain from killing, theft, sexual misconduct, lying, and intoxication, among which "lying" and Confucian "honesty" are interlinked. The rabbi of Judea warned that "Lying lips are abomination to the Lord: but they that deal truly are his delight" (*The Old Testament, Proverbs, 12:22*). The Ninth Commandment is "Thou shalt not bear false witness against thy neighbor". *Luke 16:10* reads: "He that is faithful in that which is least is faithful also in much: and he that is unjust in the least is unjust also in much". Socrates suggests that people should live an honest life. Honor is more important than wealth and other superficial things. In his view, people have the responsibility to pursue perfect character, to behave gracefully, and work to build a just society.

Perhaps it should be pointed out that honesty in Christianity is different from our general honesty. Jesus Christ emphasized honesty to God. As long as individuals were honest to God, then people would be honest to each other. In other words, honesty is guaranteed by God as an agent. Only in this way can honesty appear. To a faithful person, there are stronger requirements for this type of honesty. A person that hides the truth or tells a lie might not be discovered by another person, but God is all-knowing. Each word and every action can be seen clearly by God, so any swindle will be seen by God. Therefore, true Christians in any situation should be honest (unless telling a lie is done out of love, such as protecting another's life).

Honesty is not only a rule for average people, but also a basic rule that rulers must respect. In *The Analects*, Zigong asked Confucius about governance. Confucius said: "The requisites of government are that there be sufficiency of food, sufficiency of military equipment, and the confidence of the people in their ruler". Zigong asked: "If it cannot be helped, and one of these must be dispensed with, which of the three should be foregone first?" Confucius replied: "The military equipment". Zigong again asked: "If it cannot be helped, and one of the remaining two must be dispensed with, which of them should be foregone?" Confucius again replied: "Part with the food. From of old, death has been the lot of men; but if the people have no faith in their rulers, there is no standing for the state". Honesty is also emphasized by the Legalists. Shang Yang, a famous legalist and statesman of the State of Qin during the Warring States period, put a piece of wood at the south gate of the capital and told the public anyone who moves the wood to the north gate will be rewarded. People doubted him at first. When one person finally did it, Shang Yang gave the reward to that person. In this way, people believed Shang Yang's word. Shang Yang's reforms were successful in the State of Qin because people trusted Shang Yang's honesty. Han Fei, another Legalist, proposed "a person honest in small things can gain people's trust on big things".

"Honesty" as a behavioral principle is actually the repeated game's reputation mechanism in Game Theory. The difference is Axial Age thinkers saw it as a behavioral principle, whereas modern Game Theory has proven that it is the reason for individual's long-term interests. Only can a credible person obtain the trust of others. Only when people value trust can they escape the "Prisoner's Dilemma" and realize win-win cooperation.

5) **Reward Good and Punish Evil:** Although the Axial Age thinkers believed that humanity could be saved from sin with mutual love and honesty, they also understand that doing so would not be easy. The teachings (or theories) that they proposed were "normative", meaning people should act in that way, not "positive", meaning people will actually act in the way. They understood that people are self-interested, or even selfish, and choose to do or not do something based on self-interest. Precisely for this reason was there no morality on earth. The so-called debate on good and evil was nothing more than a semantic misunderstanding. Human nature is neither good nor evil. Mencius said "humans are virtuous" meaning human nature could "become

virtuous", as long as they were in the correct environment. He meant to say to those people that were committing evil acts "you are not people". If human nature is virtuous, how could there be that much evil? How could they still need his guidance? Hsun Tzu said "humans are evil" meaning they could be "morally cultivated" to become virtuous.[21] If human nature is evil, what is the point in reforming it? How can human nature be reformed? Therefore, for both Mencius and Hsun Tzu, "virtue" was nothing more than a behavioral standard set for members of society. Precisely because human nature is neither virtuous nor evil, did many Axial Age thinkers believe people's "hearts" could be reformed and therefore advocate their teachings. However, people's hearts cannot be reformed entirely through teachings, so they all proposed incentive mechanisms to change people's hearts and actions.

The incentive mechanism proposed by Axial Age thinkers was basically the same: Reward good and punish evil. Confucian scholars advocated "respect for and assignment to important roles for virtuous people". Hsun Tzu proposed "do not make the people who do not have virtue be rich, do not let the people who do not have talent be an official, do not reward the people who do not have credit". Confucianism tried to distinguish between gentlemen and villains so that the fame and fortune of gentleman was tempting enough to make people behave well. In fact, one of the important reasons why Confucianism emphasizes hierarchy is the incentive mechanism to "reward virtue and punish vice" (discussed in detail in the next section). Moh Tzu advocated "universal love", but he designed an incentive mechanism similar to the type people advocate for today. Mr. Zhongtian Yi summarized Moh Tzu's idea as "self-reliance, to each according to his contribution, from each according to his ability, and equality of opportunity".[22] Moh Tzu stated "the good will be discovered and rewarded and the bad will be discovered and punished" and "If a person is capable promote him, if incapable, lower his rank". Moh Tzu firmly opposed to the idea of "getting something for nothing" (or "the rich without merit"). Among Chinese classical thinkers, the Taoist school of Laocius seems to oppose the idea of "rewarding good and punishing evil". He said: "Not to value and employ men of superior ability is the way to keep the people from rivalry among themselves; not to prize articles which are difficult to procure is the way to keep them from becoming thieves; not to show them what is likely to excite their desires is the way to keep their minds from disorder" (*Tao Te Ching, Chapter 3*). However, Laocius opposed arbitrary rewards and punishments by the rulers and he was against of the idea that the means of controlling rewards and punishments are in the hands of the rulers, but he did not oppose natural rewards and punishments under the efficient ruler that does not exert himself.

Buddha designed a mechanism for benefiting virtue and punishing evil through reincarnation of the spirit. Buddha taught that good will be rewarded with good and bad will be rewarded with bad. Each interconnected life will be granted a "high-level" or "low-level" life based on the degree of morality in the previous life. Only the most virtuous will enter nirvana. People that believe these teachings naturally do not dare to be evil. Jesus Christ was similar to Buddha in that he said to "love your enemy" and advocated against "an eye for an eye and a tooth for a tooth". However, he used Heaven and Hell as a means of reward and punishment that was determined by a just god with the final say.

Rewards and punishments from God and the Kingdom of Heaven were much more powerful and effective than rewards and punishments in earthly life. "Heaven's vengeance is slow, but sure". A person can do bad things behind the backs of others, but is still seen by God. Further, because the contract between God and humans is long-term, anyone that wishes to obtain the final reward from God (immortality in the afterlife) must maintain a virtuous heart and act in a virtuous way at all times. Therefore, if a person truly believes in the existence of God, then the necessity of personal supervision declines dramatically. Of course, God also knows that humans will make mistakes due to temptation. God is tolerant, benevolent, and forgiving of certain mistakes, providing people with the opportunity to repent. However, a prerequisite is that people truly acknowledge their own mistakes, repent, and atone with virtuous behavior. Therefore, in most religions, repentance became a basic rule to request forgiveness from God (or God's representatives). This is similar in real life to apologizing to another person for a mistake and then obtaining forgiveness.

For most Axial Age thinkers, "rewarding virtue and punishing evil" is a critical component of justness and fairness. If virtuous and evil people all receive the same outcome, then obviously this kind of society is unjust and immoral. Therefore, everyone should know right and wrong, but not take the preferences of an individual as a way to judge standards of good and evil.

If we mechanically apply the previously discussed Game Theory, the above five basic ideas could be summarized as: Humans have the right to pursue their own happiness, but if an individual only considers his own short-term interests, it will lead to the "Prisoner's Dilemma". In order to resolve this issue, people are required to respect certain basic behavioral norms. In order to effectively enforce these behavioral norms, not only must people have virtuous hearts, there also must be an incentive mechanism that "rewards good and punishes evil". When people acknowledge their own long term interests and the mechanism for "rewarding good and punishing evil" is justly enforced, then humanity can escape the Prisoner's Dilemma to enjoy a harmonious and happy life.

2.3 Trajectory of success

All Axial Age thinkers undertook a personal duty to bring morality to the earth. However, as institutional entrepreneurs, some of them succeeded, others were not so successful, and some failed completely. The reason the successful ones succeeded is because the rules of the game that they proposed constituted evolutionarily stable strategies for human society. With the passage of time, as the number of followers increased, in the end they became society's behavioral norms, or what we call "culture". If they proposed rules of the game that were not evolutionarily stable, then their proposals would have been eliminated in the process of evolution. However, the reason the failures failed might be more complex.

Perhaps they proposed rules of the game that were not evolutionarily stable (such as Mohism), or perhaps there were other chance historical reasons, such as the British choosing to drive on the left. Of course, as we have already pointed out, certain thinkers appear to have not succeeded, but their ideas have been incorporated by others and still influence your lives.

From the perspective of 2,000 years later, the most successful Axial Age institutional entrepreneurs were sages such as Plato, Aristotle, the rabbi of Judea, Confucius, Laocius, Sakyumuni, and Jesus Christ. Plato's influence on the Western World has been so great that Rogers says that all proceeding thought has been a series of footnotes to Plato's thought.[23] Christian scholars in the Middle Ages referred to Aristotle as the "Father of Knowledge". The rules of the game for scientific research that Aristotle proposed have ruled the Western academic world for two thousand years. His theories on politics and ethics are still used today. Sakyamuni established Buddhism, Jesus Christ established Christianity, and in the seventh century, Mohammed established Islam (with the latter two stemming from the Hebrew *Bible*). These are referred to as the world's big three religions. Confucius established the Confucian School. Although it is not considered a religion, it has dominated the culture in East Asian societies. Taoism, established by Laocius, was considered a "national religion" in the beginning of the Western Han dynasty, but even today it has a major impact on Chinese society.

However, success has never come easy. History shows that the social behavioral norms established by Axial Age institutional entrepreneurs often had to endure centuries of struggle between the time they were proposed to the time they became the dominant culture in society. When these behavioral norms were first proposed, they were often considered anti-social forces. The initiators and their followers were brutally prosecuted by society and the authorities. Only after the number of followers reached a critical point were they tolerated, or in some cases established as the "national religion" by the rulers. For Christianity, over 360 years passed between the crucifixion of Jesus Christ and Emperor Theodosius's decree that Christianity was the state church of the Roman Empire. A similar amount of time passed between the death of Confucius and the Emperor Wu of Han's decision to only respect Confucianism. During this period, not only did Christianity have to compete with other religions and philosophies, it also had to struggle against anti-Christian powers. The Roman Empire was the largest anti-Christian power. Christians' refusal to worship the emperor was considered harmful to political stability, which led to attempts by the Roman authorities to eradicate it. In 64 AD, Emperor Nero blamed the Great Fire of Rome on Christian arsonists. In 250 AD, Emperor Decius initiated the first organized persecution of Christians in the Roman Empire. In 257 AD, Emperor Valerian initiated another persecution of Christians and executed Pope Sixtus II a year later. From 303 AD to 311 AD, Emperor Diocletian began a persecution of Christians throughout the empire that had yet to be seen in terms of passion, severity, and length. He stripped Christians of social honor and status, then ordered them tortured with no right of appeal. He stripped them of their liberty and right to self-defense. This was also the last persecution of Christians in the history of the Roman Empire. In 313 AD,

Constantine the Great issued the Edict of Milan, which respected the status of Christians. He also transferred a large amount of wealth to the church, did not tax churches, and accepted the hierarchy of the church. In 337 AD, Constantine the Great was baptized on his death bed. In 360 AD, Emperor Julian attempted to reinstate paganism, but failed. In 392 AD, under the rule of Theodosius, Christianity formally became the state church of the Roman Empire.[24]

The spread of Buddhism in China also followed a similar process. Buddhism entered China during the Eastern and Western Han Dynasties, but only developed significantly during the Northern and Southern Dynasty. By 400 AD, there were about one million Buddhists throughout China. In the north, Buddhists were primarily concentrated in the large cities, causing them to be in a fragile position in the face of imperial power. The strongest kingdom in the north at the time established a government department specifically to monitor Buddhists. Both Emperor Taiwu of Northern Wei and Emperor Wu of Northern Zhou prohibited or persecuted Buddhists. During the Southern Dynasty, Buddhists were spread throughout the Yangtze Basin, not concentrated in the capital Jiankang (present-day Nanjing). This allowed them to resist the rulers with help from local nobility, sometimes forcing the emperor to make concessions (such as in 402 AD, monks were allowed to not bow to the emperor). By 500 AD, the number of Buddhists had already reached 10 million people. In both the north and south, the rulers implemented policies similar to the ones Constantine the Great did for Christians, such as giving wealth to temples and reducing taxes on temples. Emperor Wu of Liang (464– 549 BC) believed in Buddhism and claimed to be "a slave to the triad of Buddha, Dharma, and Sangha". He became a monk four times, however, each time the state paid to get him back. He set up a large number of temples, personally preached, and held grand ceremonies. The two emperors of the Sui Dynasty supported Buddhism. After Emperor Wen of Sui unified the Northern and Southern Dynasties, he ordered the construction of temples in Buddhism's five holy mountains and restored temples that were destroyed during the Northern Zhou Dynasty. The Tang Dynasty was the heyday of Chinese Buddhism. Although the emperors of the Tang Dynasty claimed to be descendants of Laocius, the founder of Taoism, and respect Taoism, they actually implemented policies that combined Taoism and Buddhism. During Emperor Wuzong of Tang's reign (A.D. 840–846), due to social, economic, and other reasons, Buddhism was considered to be a threat to the regime, so a large-scale ban on Buddhism was implemented. The emperor ordered the confiscation or destruction of temple land and property and ordered monks and nuns to return to secular life. According to the *Institutional History of the Tang Dynasty*, more than 4,600 temples were demolished, more than 40,000 Buddhist temple artifacts were confiscated, and 260,500 monks and nuns were forced to return to civilian life. Buddhism was dealt a serious blow.[25] Only after the Song Dynasty was the status of Buddhism in China stable, until a large-scale ban on Buddhism and an anti-Buddhism movement began between the 1950s and the 1970s.

In terms of the evolutionary game that we discussed in Chapter 12, the ideas and social norms that Axial Age institutional entrepreneurs proposed were originally "variations" that invaded society. However, in the long-term survival-of-the-fittest process, not only were they not eliminated, instead they expanded as time went on. In the end, they became the mainstream in society, proving that they constituted evolutionarily stable strategies. However, here we must have a new understanding of "fitness". In biological games, "fitness" refers to a gene having a stronger reproductive ability. In the social game discussed in Chapter 12, "fitness" refers to the behavioral pattern that has the maximum payoff over the long-term. Now, we must understand "payoff" as "happiness" more generally. The degree of human happiness is not only related to material enjoyment, but the influence of beliefs.[26] The average person might suffer by not eating meat over a long period of time, but the opposite is the case for a true Buddhist. Many Christians and Buddhists (as well as followers of other religions) are willing to become martyrs. This means that giving up their faith is more unbearable than death.[27] Many people in the Communist Party died for their beliefs during the revolution for the same reasons. This is also the case for people's pursuit of liberty. Sandor Petofi wrote: "Life is dear. Love is dearer. Both can be given up for freedom". In human social competition, those with faith are more able to survive than those that do not. For this reason, not only did government persecution of religion throughout history not eradicate it, but instead made it stronger.

We know from management studies that when a commercial entrepreneur introduces a new product, in the beginning market scale is limited and growth is slow. However, once the market scale exceeds a certain critical point, the number of consumers grows rapidly until saturation. This is called the "S-shaped life cycle curve". The beliefs and social behavioral norms proposed by successful institutional entrepreneurs all have a similar S-shaped curve. In the beginning, there are a limited number of followers, but they gradually increase. When the number of followers exceeds a certain critical value, it will rapidly increase until this type of belief or behavioral pattern becomes society's mainstream culture. This aligns with the convergence of evolutionarily stable equilibrium we discussed in Chapter 12. The more people there are that follow a behavioral pattern, the faster it will spread.

Figure 14.1 is the log-linear graph showing the spread of Christians in the Roman Empire from 50 to 350 AD and Buddhists in China from 100 to 550 AD The horizontal axis represents years (in fifty-year increments) and the vertical axis represents the number of followers. Note that the number of followers is in log units of ten, so the next unit is ten times larger than the previous unit. From bottom to top, the population is one, ten, 100, 1,000, 10,000, etc.

Overall, the annual growth rate of Christians in the Roman Empire was 3.4%, meaning it doubled every 20 years. The annual growth rate of Buddhists in China was 2.3%, meaning it doubled every 30 years. These growth rates may not seem like much, but because of compounding, tiny numbers of followers can become the majority after three or four hundred years. In 50 AD, there were probably 1,400 Christians in the Roman Empire (0.0023% of the total population). By 200 AD, it was about 218,000 (0.36% of the total population). However, by 350 AD, the number of Christians had already reached 33.8 million (56.5% of the total population).[28] Similarly, in 100 AD, China had less than 1,000 Buddhists. By 400

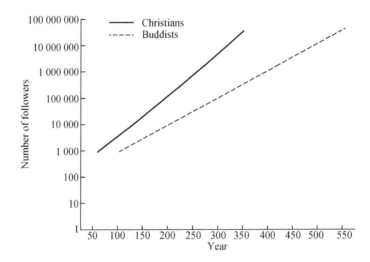

Figure 14.1 The Growth of Roman Christians and Chinese Buddhists
Source: Ian Morris (2010), page 327.

AD, this number had reached one million people. In 500 AD, the number of Buddhists exceeded 10 million people. By 550 AD, it had exceeded 30 million people.

Section three: Confucian social norms

3.1 Etiquette as a mixture of social norms and laws

Similar to Sakyamuni and Jesus Christ, Confucius was one of the most successful Axial Age institutional entrepreneurs. In the first few centuries, Confucianism also faced competition from other philosophies and was suppressed by the rulers. After Emperor Wu of Han, Confucian culture became mainstream Chinese culture. It has dominated Chinese society for more than 2,000 years. Confucianism has been broadly accepted by people in China and other East Asian countries. Today, there is renewed interest, and scholars speak of a Confucian Revival.[29]

Confucian culture constituted a dominant system for social governance because it provided society with a norm and formulae, which emerged as the "etiquette" system in Chinese history. As we analyzed previously, as social scale increases, in relation to social norms, laws will play a greater role in social governance. However, perhaps China is an exception. Over a very long period of history, China has always been the largest entity in the world. Confucian culture has always been the dominant force of social governance, or at least appeared to be. The reason responsible for this is, in essence, the rules of the game set by Confucianism are a mixture of social norms and laws.

What is the core of Confucian culture? There are different viewpoints in academia. Scholars that study Confucius might believe that "benevolence" is the core of Confucian culture. However, when we speak of Confucian culture, it is the core norms that constitute the governance mechanisms of Chinese society. It is a systematic thought process; therefore, "rule by rites" is the core. "Benevolence" is the soul of "rule by rites". Confucian thought formed Chinese institutions, and even the Qin Dynasty was no exception.

Recent archeological discoveries have indirectly proved the major influence Confucian thought had on the Qin Dynasty. Mr. Yinque Chen summarized this best. He said: "In the ancient times, Confucian scholars were experts of decrees and regulations. Li Si, a prime minister in the Qin Dynasty, reformed society based on the teachings of Hsun Tzu. The Qin Dynasty legal system was derived from Confucian teachings. Confucianism's ideal system had a unified transportation system, a unified writing system, and a unified ethical system. The First Emperor of Qin achieved this. The Han Dynasty succeeded the Qin Dynasty. The bureaucracy and legal system of the Han Dynasty were a continuation of the previous dynasty. Until the Jin Dynasty, law and ritual were often one in the same. Many Confucian doctrines were adopted in legal codes. Generally speaking, all political and social actions are related to legal codes, and the implementation of legal codes was influenced by Confucian culture. Confucian culture had the deepest impact on the institutions, laws, and public and private lives of the Chinese people over the last 2,000 years. Buddhism and Taoism played a part, but that is beyond our discussion here".[30] Although other ways of thinking existed, Confucian culture was still the systemic nucleus of the Chinese Empire, even the Chinese people.

What is the difference between the core of this type of system and the core of other systems? In other words, what is the core governance characteristic of the Confucian system? The social order advocated by Confucianism is one in which each person's way of life and behavior conforms to his role, identity, and status in society, the community, or the group. It is a combined behavioral norm for the family and the state. Different statuses have different behavioral norms, and thus different etiquette. Confucianism believes that as long as each person respects the behavioral norms of his status, then an ideal society can be maintained and the nation can have long-term stability. Confucianism advocates the rule of virtue. It believes sages are the ideal type of person, and people can be enlightened. Enlightenment plays a core role in obedience to social norms. Legalism sets law from the "rich nation and strong army" perspective, whereas Confucianism sets rules of the game from the harmonious interpersonal relationship perspective. This is the fundamental difference between the two.

During 2,000 years of Chinese legal development, Confucian thought directly transformed ethical norms based on status and moral reasoning into laws. This formed a unique system of governance where social norms and laws are combined to regulate each other. Under Confucian culture, social governance relies on social norms based on the patriarchal clan division of power to regulate most behavior in society. Law is punishment in the people's eyes. Most disputes are not escalated to the local authorities, but instead are resolved by the patriarchal clan or elders.

Of course, Confucian thought makes a distinction between social norms and laws. No Confucian intellectuals believed punishments (laws)[31] were unnecessary, but no Confucian intellectuals believed the law was superior. The relationship between dominant ethics and subordinate punishments could not be overturned. Confucius firmly believed, "If the people be led by laws, and uniformity sought to be given them by punishments, they will try to avoid the punishment, but have no sense of shame. If they be led by virtue, and uniformity sought to be given them by the rules of propriety, they will have the sense of shame, and moreover will become good" (*The Analects, Wei Zheng*). Therefore, from Confucianism's perspective, laws conform to social norms or morals.

3.2 Expectation coordination and dispute resolution

As was analyzed previously, the Chinese Empire under Confucian culture was a governance mechanism dominated by social norms or morals, and Confucius was a great "norm entrepreneur". However, the formation of Confucian norms was not the objective design of sages, but was instead deduced by Confucius and others based on actual life at the time. They are the outcome of social evolution formed over a long period of trial and error. This is the primary reason the Confucian School was competitive.

Similar to the role modern legal systems play in society, the major functions of the Confucian system were the coordination of expectations and resolution of disputes.

Where does Confucian "etiquette" come from? There are different viewpoints in academia, but one point in common is: Original social customs were the source of etiquette. *The Book of Rites* explains that "At the first use of ceremonies, they began with meat and drink". Mr. Dengyuan Chen's research on this utilized citations from *The Spring and Autumn Rhetoric*.[32] Etiquette came out of dispute resolution. At the same time, "from the perspective of the process of social division, so-called etiquette was between local customs and laws.[33] Social development is a gradual process of institutional evolution from "customs" to "etiquette" to "laws".

From the origin of etiquette, we can see that etiquette was originally related to the sequence of food and drink. Using our example from Chapter 3, it is resolving the issue of who goes first when two people need to enter a door at the same time by coordinating a Nash equilibrium. "Respect the old and cherish the young" is also a type of etiquette.

Therefore, the major functions of Confucian "etiquette" are the coordination of expectations and the resolution of disputes. Hsun Tzu explained this very clearly: "Desires are innate. When these desires are not satisfied, man will seek their satisfaction. If there is no limit to the desire, there can only be contention. Contention leads to disorder. Disorder leads to poverty. The first kings believed this disorder was evil, so they established etiquette and righteousness. The combination of the two over a long period of time was the origin of etiquette" (*The Works of Hsun Tzu, Li Yun*). In a society, everyone has desires, so conflicts will appear. The coordination of conflicts requires a series of norms. Divisions, or boundaries, are the core of etiquette. They are used to eliminate conflicts and maintain order.[34]

When these rules for coordinating expectation further evolve, they escalate into statecraft. "The course (of duty), virtue, benevolence, and righteousness cannot be fully carried out without the rules of propriety; nor are training and oral lessons for the rectification of manners complete; nor can the clearing up of quarrels and discriminating in disputes be accomplished; nor can (the duties between) ruler and minister, high and low, father and son, elder brother and younger, be determined; nor can students for office and (other) learners, in serving their masters, have an attachment for them; nor can majesty and dignity be shown in assigning the different places at court, in the government of the armies, and in discharging the duties of office so as to secure the operation of the laws; nor can there be the (proper) sincerity and gravity in presenting the offerings to spiritual Beings on occasions of supplication, thanksgiving, and the various sacrifices" (*The Book of Rites, Summary of the Rules of Propriety, Part I*). "In the right government of a state, the Rules of Propriety serve the same purpose as the steelyard in determining what is light and what is heavy; or as the carpenter's line in determining what is crooked and what is straight; or as the circle and square in determining what is square and what is round" (*The Book of Rights, The Different Teachings of the Different Kings*). "These rules (set forth) the way of reverence and courtesy; and therefore when the services in the ancestral temple are performed according to them, there is reverence; when they are observed in the court, the noble and the mean have their proper positions; when the family is regulated by them, there is affection between father and son, and harmony among brothers; and when they are honored in the country districts and villages, there is the proper order between old and young. There is the verification of what was said by Confucius, 'For giving security to superiors and good government. Of the people, there is nothing more excellent than the Rules of Propriety'" (*The Book of Rights, The Different Teachings of the Different Kings*). For etiquette to elevate to a system's highest level, each person in society must have rules to follow.

This idea was clearly expressed in *The Analects* when the Duke Jing of Qi asked Confucius about government. Confucius replied: "There is government, when the prince is prince, and the minister is minister; when the father is father, and the son is son" (*The Analects, Yan Yuan*). When emperors follow the norms of princes, ministers follow the norms of ministers, fathers follow the norms of fathers, and sons follow the norms of sons, then each will receive what is due to their status.

For a long time, people have mistakenly believed that Confucius' talk of "princes, ministers, fathers, and sons" meant he advocated inequality, especially absolute obedience to superiors. Rulers throughout the ages have also liked to explain Confucian thought in this way. Actually, Confucius emphasized reciprocity between people of different status. Regardless of people's status, they all must respect the same ethics. A prince's benevolence and the ministers' loyalty are mutual precepts. A father's love and a son's filial duty are mutual precepts. As long as each person acts according to the rules of their position, others will have stable expectations and know how to behave, so society will be harmonious. Unbenevolent princes, disloyal ministers, unloving fathers, and non-filial sons will lead to a chaotic social order. This is similar to the relationship principles that we emphasize between employers and employees. Employers must treat their employees well, and employees must strictly abide by professional ethics. Only then can a firm do well.

In many cases, in order for "etiquette" to become a rule that coordinates expectations and resolves disputes, it must have a "difference" premise. This relates to our discussion of property rights in Chapter 12. For example, people of different status dress in different ways to assist in the coordination of behavior. This is the major reason that etiquette must be formalized. Different etiquette exists for people of different status.

3.3 Virtuous men and the incentive mechanism

The Confucian system is also a type of incentive mechanism. It relies on the ranking system for social governance. A "virtuous man" (*jun zi*) is not born with his status, but instead is a standard for action. It is a symbol for merit, or a role model. A person with a benevolent heart, self-restraint, and noble ethics is seen as a virtuous man, whereas a person that harms others for his own benefit is seen as a villain. In the eyes of Confucius, a virtuous man can overcome opportunistic behavior in the Prisoner's Dilemma.

In *The Analects*, the phrase "virtuous man" appeared 106 times, and most of the times it was spoken by Confucius. Some of it dealt with virtuous men's training and learning, but it mostly focused on the expectations of virtuous men's morals.

First, virtuous men respect social ethics, ranks, and norms: "The superior man thinks of virtue; the small man thinks of comfort. The superior man thinks of the sanctions of law; the small man thinks of favors which he may receive" (*The Analects, Li Ren*); "The Master said of Zi Chan that he had four of the characteristics of a superior man – in his conduct of himself, he was humble; in serving his superior, he was respectful; in nourishing the people, he was kind; in ordering the people, he was just" (*The Analects, Gong Ye Chang*). "The superior man, extensively studying all learning, and keeping himself under the restraint of the rules of propriety, may thus likewise not overstep what is right" (*The Analects, Yong Ye*). "The men of former times in the matters of ceremonies and music were rustics, it is said, while the men of these latter times, in ceremonies and music, are accomplished gentlemen. If I have occasion to use those things, I follow the men of former times" (*The Analects, Xian Jin*). "The superior man in everything considers righteousness to be essential. He performs it according to the rules of propriety. He brings it forth in humility. He completes it with sincerity. This is indeed a superior man" (*The Analects, Wei Ling Gong*). "There are three things of which the superior man stands in awe. He stands in awe of the ordinances of Heaven. He stands in awe of great men. He stands in awe of the words of sages" (*The Analects, Ji Shi*).

Next, virtuous men are altruists, meaning they consider the long-term over short-term interests: "The accomplished scholar is not a utensil" (*The Analects, Wei Zheng*). "The mind of the superior man is conversant with righteousness; the mind of the mean man is conversant with gain" (*The Analects, Li Ren*). "The superior man seeks to perfect the admirable qualities of men, and does not seek to perfect their bad qualities. The mean man does the opposite of this" (*The Analects, Yan Yuan*). "The superior man dislikes the thought of his name not being mentioned after his death" (*The Analects, Wei Ling Gong*). "The object of the superior man is truth. Food is not his object. There is plowing – even in that there is sometimes want. So with learning – emolument may be found in it. The superior man is anxious lest he should not get truth; he is not anxious lest poverty should come upon him" (*The Analects, Wei Ling Gong*). "The superior man holds righteousness to be of highest importance" (*The Analects, Yang Huo*).

Further, a virtuous man is humble: "The student of virtue has no contentions. If it be said he cannot avoid them, shall this be in archery? But he bows complaisantly to his competitors; thus he ascends the hall, descends, and exacts the forfeit of drinking. In his contention, he is still the Junzi" (*The Analects, Ba Yi*). "The superior man is dignified, but does not wrangle. He is sociable, but not a partisan" (*The Analects, Wei Ling Gong*).

Finally, a virtuous man is cooperative: "The superior man is affable, but not adulatory; the mean man is adulatory, but not affable" (*The Analects, Zi Lu*).

We can see from the points above that the "virtuous man" is a behavioral standard a person should respect in social games. By acting according to this standard, people can escape the Prisoner's Dilemma. Mencius and Hsun Tzu developed the "virtuous man" further into a reward. Through the design of a system of social hierarchy, not only did the "virtuous man" have a higher social status, but was also materially better off. This incentivized people to be a "virtuous man" to realize social progress. In later dynasties, the "Nine Rank System" nominated virtuous men of various regions to be imperial officials. This system still existed on a large scale after the imperial examination system was implemented. Therefore, the design of the Confucian incentive mechanism nurtured virtuous men through social selection and social hierarchy that ensured rewards for them to escape the Prisoner's Dilemma.

We can use the game shown in Figure 14.2 to summarize the basic thought process of the Confucian incentive system.

The game on the left side of Figure 14.2 is a Prisoner's Dilemma game, and the game on the right is a coordination game. The payoff for each person in a coordination game depends on their order of movement. The person that moves first receives a higher compensation (similar to a hierarchical system). Therefore, if society can determine the order of movement in a coordination game based on an individual's performance in a Prisoner's Dilemma game, then an incentive mechanism is achieved.

Specifically, we turn the "cooperative person" in the Prisoner's Dilemma game into the "virtuous man" and the "uncooperative person" into the "unvirtuous

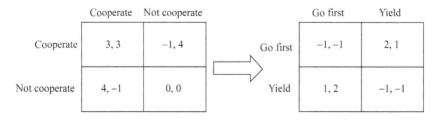

Figure 14.2 Hierarchy as an Incentive Mechanism

man". We can explain the "first-mover" in the coordination game as a "higher rank" and the "late-mover" as a "lower rank". Imagine a social game is a two-stage game. The first stage is a Prisoner's Dilemma game and the second stage is a coordination game. Imagine that a person's performance in the first stage of the game determines his status in the second stage of the game, meaning performing as a virtuous man in the first stage will lead to a higher rank in the second stage, and performing as an unvirtuous man in the first stage will lead to a lower rank in the second stage. Obviously, given this type of incentive mechanism, each person has an incentive to cooperate in the first stage of the game, so society can escape the Prisoner's Dilemma.

This is the reason Confucian scholars advocate a hierarchical system as an incentive mechanism. A hierarchical system is both a coordination mechanism and an incentive mechanism. The emphasis by Confucian scholars on a hierarchical system is often misunderstood to be Confucian scholars advocating inequality. Actually, a virtuous man is not born that way, but instead achieves that status through hard work. The Confucian social hierarchy is an incentive mechanism that rewards good and punishes evil. In today's market economy, monetary compensation is the most important incentive mechanism. However, in ancient society, when markets were not developed, solely relying on monetary compensation for rewards and punishments was insufficient, so social hierarchy was the most important method of rewards and punishments. Therefore, the best way to reward virtuous men was to combine "throne, riches, and fame" so that "having such great virtue, it could not but be that he should obtain the throne, that he should obtain those riches, that he should obtain his fame, that he should attain to his long life" (*The Book of Rites, Zhong Yong*), and "only the benevolent ought to be in high stations" (*The Works of Mencius, Li Lou, Part I*). This is the reason Confucian scholars have advocated rewards according to merit and promotions according to ability.

The use of hierarchical systems to resolve the Prisoner's Dilemma was analyzed early on in theories of the firm. As we discussed in Chapter 2, American economists Armen Alchian and Harold Demsetz published *Production, Information Costs, and Economic Organizations* in 1972. They believed that the way to resolve laziness in a team was to turn one person into a monitor and grant him the team's property rights. The situation is similar in society, where free-rider behavior is common. If one group of people have a higher status than others, or are endowed with property rights to allow them to lead society, then the free-rider problem can be resolved. However, how will the high-status people be restrained? In addition to property rights, there is also the reputation mechanism. We use the virtuous man's focus on reputation to restrain him.

Compensation and rewards not only appear as virtuous men obtaining a good reputation and respect from others, but also be guaranteed by a series of systems, especially laws as a complement to morality. Therefore, in ancient China, different classes of people had different privileges and duties. From the laws throughout the ages, we can see that housing, clothing, utensils, wedding ceremonies, funerals, sacrifices to the gods, and even the type of paint used on the front door were different. If a person of low-standing harmed a person of high-standing, the punishment was relatively heavy, but relatively light if the other way around. When virtuous men were selected to become officials and the nobility, they had even more legal privileges. When a crime was committed, arrest, trial, and punishment were not done according to the general judicial procedures.[35] The Han Dynasty had the First Privileges System and the Wei Dynasty had the Eight Deliberations System. During the Qing Dynasty, advanced scholars, recommended men, tribute scholars, officials, and student members could pay different amounts of money to avoid flogging or caning. In procedural law, officials were not confronted in court like commoners, but instead could send family members to appear in court. *The Rites of Zhou* decreed that men and women with titles could not be taken to court for lawsuits. These systems both showed that law was a means of governance based on etiquette and reflected the importance that Confucian scholars put on the reputation mechanism and hierarchy as an incentive mechanism. If the same punishments had been used for both virtuous and non-virtuous men, the incentive effect of the hierarchical system would decrease dramatically.

This is fundamentally different than Legalism. Shang Yang believed

> The way in which a sage administers a state is by unifying rewards, unifying punishments, and unifying education. . . . What I mean by the unifying of rewards is that profits and emoluments, office and rank, should be determined exclusively by military merit, and that there should not be different reasons for distributing them. . . . What I mean by the unification of punishments is that punishments should know no degree or grade, but that from ministers of state and generals down to great officers and ordinary folk, whosoever does not obey the king's commands, violates the interdicts of the state, or rebels against the statutes fixed by the ruler, should be guilty of death and should not be pardoned. . . . What I mean by the unification of education is that all those partisans of wide scholarship, sophistry, cleverness, good faith, integrity, rites and music, and moral culture, whether their reputations are unsullied or foul, should for these reasons not become rich or honored, should not discuss punishments, and should not compose their private views independently and memorialize their superiors.
>
> (The Book of Lord Shang, Rewards and Punishments)

This was opposition to different punishments and education. Han Fei believed:

> The law does not fawn on the noble; the string does not yield to the crooked. Whatever the law applies to, the wise cannot reject nor can the brave defy. Punishment for fault never skips ministers, reward for good never misses commoners. Therefore, to correct the faults of the high, to rebuke the vices of the low, to suppress disorders, to decide against mistakes, to subdue the arrogant, to straighten the crooked, and to unify the folkways of the masses, nothing could match the law. To warn the officials and overawe the people, to rebuke obscenity and danger, and to forbid falsehood and deceit, nothing

could match penalty. If penalty is severe, the noble cannot discriminate against the humble. If law is definite, the superiors are esteemed and not violated.

(The Works of Han Fei Tzu, Having Regulations)

Therefore, even though all along China had the concept that the emperor could be guilty of the same crimes as commoners and Legalists advocated unified punishments, in terms of overcoming social issues, such as the Prisoner's Dilemma and free riding, social governance under the Confucian system still had its relative advantage. Of course, this system basically did not allow for error, nor did it propose how to correct these problems when they occurred. However, if we do not consider the effective role of social norms and simply criticize Confucianism for being backwards, we would obviously be underrating the creative and cognitive abilities of Confucian intellectuals.

3.4 The value of Confucian culture as rules of the game in ancient society

Confucian culture was advanced in traditional society because it avoided the high costs of modern legal system while resolving the governance issue of a huge empire using social norms. A few aspects reflected its efficiency.

First, the system of rules and laws for the social separation of power are only used to support the system of social authority and dominant social norms. It does not attempt to resolve all issues. The best explanation of the relationship between etiquette and law in Confucian culture came from Du Yu (a Legalist in Ancient China), who advocated "introducing etiquette into laws". He believed that laws should be simple and clear.[36]

Jia Yi, an official in the Western Han Dynasty, differentiated between the benefits of etiquette as governance and "legal governance" (which is not the "rule of law" in the modern constitutional sense).[37]

The law as an ethical code secondary to social norms has been the primary characteristic of social governance in the Chinese Empire over the last two thousand years. Gongsun Hong, a Confucian scholar in the Han Dynasty, first proposed that rewards and punishments should be based on etiquette. Chen Chong in the Eastern Han Dynasty and Qiu Jun in the Ming Dynasty also had similar ideas.[38] Simian Lv is a contemporary scholar that has studied China's ancient systems.[39]

Through virtuous men spread throughout society, Confucianism established a self-governance mechanism in the base level of society. Most disputes were resolved before they occurred. This is the basic starting point for Confucian governance rules. It avoided the high costs of implementing the law by implementing "majority supervision". This type of low-cost governance model became more adaptable as the boundaries of the Chinese Empire expanded.

Second, governance should focus on people rather than rules. The diversity of rules should be established, providing room for rules to play a role in the spontaneous formation of social ethics. This avoided the issue of "internal conflicts between systems of rules" as the boundaries of the Chinese Empire expanded. Because the Chinese Empire has always been so large, only by replacing unified and rigid rules with hierarchical control of the social separation of power could the unity of the Chinese Empire be effectively maintained. The law only regulates certain relatively serious crimes and supports social classifications.

Third, social norms are established over a long period of time, and destroying social norms also require a long time. Rule of etiquette is ingrained in the Chinese Empire, and to a large degree is determined by this type of governance model. In contrast, legal governance is relatively easy to form, but also relatively easy to destroy.

After the collapse of the autocratic monarchy, China's laws have constantly changed. From the capitalist legal system in the Republican Era to Communism, Socialism, and Socialism with Chinese Characteristics, even the legal systems that currently exist in Chinese Hong Kong, Macau, and Taiwan, we can see that rule systems maintained by laws are relatively easy to destroy.

Fourth, the etiquette law system focused on the authority of the law, not the specific regulations in the law. By implementing the "virtuous man" political system, the primary function of the social system was the selection of virtuous men. Relying on virtuous men to rule the country is also a type of elite politics.

Confucian culture focuses more on the governance and restraint of officials and the authority they should have, not the specific duties of officials. This is a very important revelation. After society is a ranked system, restraints on officials are more important than restraints on the people. This could be seen in the Ming Dynasty, where "the emperor governed the officials, not the people". As a third party enforcement mechanism, if the law does not focus on the creation of authority, but instead only deals with disputes after the fact, then the law cannot possibly be carried out in a way that effectively guides the people.

We previously focused our analysis on "etiquette-law", whereas Professor Buke Yan proposed the importance of "rituals".[40] This confirms the relationship between ethics and education that we analyzed previously. It develops the ordinary people's compliance with social norms. At the same time, rituals are an external form that reminds people to respect norms and invite others to better supervise themselves. An official should look like an official. When people see a person dressed like an official, they will be able to expect his behavior. From the perspective of people participating in a game, obeying a certain ritual or social norm will transmit a signal that indicates a willingness to cooperate. More importantly, rituals are a means to create authority. A person that behaves in a way in accordance with a higher standard will have more authority. Because authority guarantees this type of authority can be displayed, it will be obeyed more greatly. Laws coordinate this series of behaviors.

3.5 The spirit of the rule of law in classical Confucianism and the future of China

Understanding the incentive mechanisms and mutual relationship between laws and social norms, as well as their conditions and boundaries, has a major significance for our understanding of social governance today. China must establish a system of constitutional governance and must transition to a rule of law society. However, the establishment of constitutional governance and the rule of law must both absorb Western culture and legal systems and connect with China's traditional culture and rules of the game.

From this chapter's analysis of Confucian culture, one conclusion is that classical Confucianism focused more on the *ex-ante* efficiency and fairness of rules, the "will of the people", and the authority of law. In our opinion, classical Confucian culture aligns more closely with the modern rule of law, whereas Legalism aligns more closely with the rule by law. Confucianism is closer to a type of natural law spirit, unlike the positivism of Legalism.[41]

From the beginning, Chinese Civilization formed a concept similar to the West's natural law. In *The Consultations of Gao Yao* chapter of *The Book of Documents*, China's first supreme judicial officer said: "The Heavens has its code, listing five types of rewards and five types of punishments". Gao Yao asserted that the world has rules which have their ultimate origin in the Heavens. The will of the people to a large degree is the will of Heaven. One basic principle in natural law is that the law is the will of god, and thus is the will of the people. Only laws that align with the will of the people are just laws and should be respected. The Confucian requirement for the ruling classes is higher than the "Mandate of Heaven" of the ruling class, and in essence is the will of the people. For any ruling class to have true legitimacy, it must act in accordance with the will of the people and look after their welfare, otherwise they do not have legitimacy. Although Mencius spoke of "heavenly appointments", his "heaven" was a deification of "the people". As *The Great Declaration* of *The Book of Zhou* stated: "Heaven sees according as my people see; Heaven hears according as my people hear". Therefore, the monarch's right to rule is formally "appointed by heaven" but essentially "authorized by the people". Confucians absolutely do not believe the rulers have a natural right to rule forever. Mencius said that if a monarch is incompetent, then he should be advised. If advising him three times is insufficient, then he should be deposed. At that point, it is legal to depose him. In Confucian culture, if an emperor does not look after the welfare of the people over the long term, then he is illegitimate. As soon as the ruler loses legitimacy, then overthrowing him becomes legitimate.[42] For this reason, many later rulers did not appreciate Mencius. The Hongwu Emperor, the first emperor of the Ming Dynasty, is a classic example.

The problem is that in reality it is difficult to determine under which circumstances legitimacy no longer exists. Different groups may have different judgments. The cost of revolt is also huge, and there are too many free riders (it is also a Prisoner's Dilemma), so it cannot be used frequently. This allows rulers that have lost legitimacy to extend their rule for a relatively long period of time through the use of weapons and dictatorship.

For two thousand years, Confucians have searched for a "Heavenly Sword" to discipline monarchs, but have been unsuccessful. Dong Zhongshu used "heavenly" behaviors as a standard for the legality of a monarch. Natural disasters,

s, pestilence, and famine, were warnings to the mon-
nere is no direct relationship between natural disasters
lers, so the authority of "heaven" declined significantly.
lely relying on the self-reflection of the rulers is difficult.
nism had no means to inhibit the emergence of self-indulgent
'ersuasion" was another method used by Confucianism. Confu-
believed giving guidance to the emperor was the most important
means ᴄ ᴠ nteeing the rulers serve the people. Confucian scholars view the
relationship between Emperor Taizong and Chancellor Wei as ideal. We see in history certain scholar-officials risking their lives to give feedback. However, rulers will often demote or sentence to death the chancellors that do so. Another method of restraint on the rulers that Confucian intellectuals have is "scholarly political criticism". During the latter part of the Ming Dynasty, the Donglin Movement made criticisms from outside the political authority. Other methods of restraint were lackluster.

As history has developed, we have clearly seen that although Confucianism has "people-oriented" thought, it does not have the systemic framework for democracy. The "Heavenly Sword" to deal with the monarch can only be constitutional government and democracy. Only when the government is restrained by the law can the government truly "rule for the people". Mr. Tsung-san Mou, a representative of contemporary neo-Confucianism, said: "Before, China only had 'democracy of governmental power' but not 'democracy of political power'. From the imperial examinations, we can see that governmental power was very democratic. However, true democracy is "democracy of political power". Only with democracy of political power can democracy of governmental power be truly guaranteed. Without democracy of political power, democracy of governmental power depends on the emergence of sage monarchs and virtuous ministers. This is a very unreliable condition.[43]

However, as we saw with previous analysis, there is no contradiction between classical Confucian culture, the rule of law, and democracy. From the transformation to modernity in Chinese Taiwan and other countries (and regions) in East Asia, we can see that not only can Confucian culture adapt to a system of modern democracy and rule-of-law constitutional government, but can also become a positive force for the transformation of China's social systems. Using Confucian culture to negate democracy and the rule of law is incorrect. Using democracy and the rule of law to negate Confucian culture is similarly incorrect. Many people see the contemporary culture that formed over the last half century as traditional Chinese culture. This is a huge misunderstanding. Putting the mistakes of modern people on the shoulders of sages from two thousand years ago is both ignorant and shameless.

We must acknowledge that the establishment of constitutional rule of law and democratization is a long and slow process. There were three pillars of Chinese traditional society: The imperial power system, the imperial examinations, and Confucian culture. However, within the first two decades of the twentieth century, the three pillars all collapsed. Imperial examinations were abolished in 1905. The Xinhai Revolution overthrew the emperor in 1911. Fourth of May Movement smashed Confucianism. This brought about dec of social chaos. Many issues in China's modernization might require further consideration and a deeper understanding of the governance doctrines ingrained in China. We must respect and utilize the wisdom that the Chinese have accumulated over thousands of years. The process of transformation cannot rush, and more haste, less speed. Chinese of today do not have a rule-of-law concept like Westerners, but also lost the sense of honor that previous generations had. We neither have a monarch, nor have we established a true democracy. We can imagine that if the people leading China's social transformation 100 years ago had a little more patience, then China's progress towards the rule of law and democratization would have been quicker. If we had not moved for the sake of movement, would we have had to take so many detours?

Notes

1 S. N. Eisenstadt introduced the word "institutional entrepreneur" in an article published in 1980. P. J. DiMaggio published a paper in 1988 that was a systematic analysis of the role institutional entrepreneurs play in system transformation. In the last thirty years, there have been more than one hundred English-language articles about institutional entrepreneurs. See Battilana, Leca, and Boxebaum (2008) for a general summary of this literature. Cass Sunstein (1996) and Richard Posner (2000), law professors at the University of Chicago, introduced the norm entrepreneur concept.

2 Zhongqiu Yao proposed the "legislation entrepreneur" in a paper titled *Yǐ Zuòwéi yī Zhǒng Zhìdù Biànqiān Móshì de "Zhuǎnxíng"*. It might be suitable to use this concept when we discuss the first type of institutional entrepreneur later.

3 See Joseph Schumpeter's, *Capitalism, Socialism, and Democracy*, Part II. New York: Routledge, 1994 (1942).

4 Of course, there are also institutional entrepreneurs oriented towards niche markets, such as tattoos and other ornaments that are only popular among some people.

5 See Weiying Zhang's, "The Two Essential Capabilities an Enterprise Must Foster." In Weiying Zhang's *The Road Leading to the Market*. London and New York: Routledge, 2017, pp. 130–133.

6 Sunstein (1996) discussed this issue.

7 See Appiah (2010), Chapter 2 for a discussion on abolishing foot binding.

8 See Appiah (2010), Chapter 2.

9 Here, I place "social norms" in quotation marks because they are the result of dictatorship, not the natural formation of social norms, so strictly speaking they do not count as social norms. This type of "respect" for a dictator is actually fear, and is entirely maintained through perception. The reason I respect you is that I mistakenly believe others fear you. As soon as I know that others no longer fear you, I no longer respect you. For this reason, change for this type of "norm" is often rapid.

10 The Axial Age was a term proposed by German philosophy Karl Jaspers at the end of World War II. See Morris (2010), page 254–255.

11 Using Zhongqiu Yao's concept, they are "legislation entrepreneurs".

12 I utilized a concept from Morris (2010).

13 See Yingshi Yu's, *Zhōngguó Wénhuà Tōngshì*, page 11. Church and state were combined during the Western Zhou Feudal Era. There is a detailed discussion of "heaven, god, and man" in Zhongqiu Yao's, *Fēngjiàn*, Chapter 7.

14 See Morris (2010), page 260.

15 See Tsung-san Mou's, *Zhèngdào yǔ Zhìdào* (2006), Chapter 7.
16 This concept appeared in the 1770s. See Anthony Flew's, *A Dictionary of Philosophy* (1979), page 134.
17 See Thomas Hobbes (1996), *Leviathan*.
18 See Weiying Zhang's, *The Logic of the Market* (2015).
19 See Zhongtian Yi's, *Wǒ Shān Zhī Shí* (2009), page 63.
20 It should be said that Confucian scholars acknowledge the role of the market. Zi Gong, one of Confucius' favored disciples, is the most famous entrepreneur in Chinese history. Sima Qian mentioned Tao Zhu and Zi Gong in The *Biography of Usurers*. In *The Analects*, Confucius and Zi Gong's dialog used the contemporary language of the market to discuss ethics. Mencius acknowledged market division of labor in *The Works of Mencius, Teng Wen Gong, Part I*. See Yingshi Yu's *Jìndài Zhōngguó Rújiào Lúnlǐ yǔ Shāngrén Jīngshén* (in *Zhōngguó Wénhuà Shǐ Tōngshì*, 2012).
21 See Zhongtian Yi's, *Wǒ Shān Zhī Shí* (2009), Chapter 17.
22 See Zhongtian Yi's, *Wǒ Shān Zhī Shí* (2009), Chapter 5.
23 See Perry Rogers, *Aspects of Western Civilization: Problems and Sources* (2008).
24 See Perry Rogers, *Aspects of Western Civilization: Problems and Sources* (2008), Chapter 3.
25 See Morris (2010), page 326–329.
26 From 2005 to 2009, Gallup researched the relationship between religious feelings, degree of life satisfaction, social support, and joy in 150 countries. Researchers found that in societies that lack food, employment, and a focus on health, people with religious faith are actually happier than those without. At the same time, the religious people in those countries feel that they receive more public support. However, in countries with sufficient social support, the relationship between religious beliefs and happiness is more complex. On the one hand, in wealthier countries, both believers and non-believers are happier than the people that live in environments that lack sufficient support. However, interestingly, in wealthier countries, the believers are less happy than their non-believer neighbors. Researchers found a similar disparity in American society. In poorer states, more people have faith. In those poorer states, religious people are happier than non-religious people. This research was published in *The Journal of Personality and Social Psychology* (2011), Volume Six. See Diener, Tayand, and Myers (2011).
27 Stark believed martyrdom is a rational choice. See Stark (1996), Chapter 8.
28 See Stark (1996), page 7.
29 Many later rulers and scholars intentionally and unintentionally distorted the Confucian thought of Confucius. In this chapter, we are discussing classical Confucian thought from before the Han Dynasty.
30 See Chen , Y., 1961, *shencha baogao* 3 (Review Report 3) in Youlan Feng's, *A History of Chinese Philosophy* (1983, trans. Derk Bodde).
31 Mr. Dengyuan Chen believed that pre-Qin philosophers all emphasized laws, but hand different foundational principles. See Dengyuan Chen's (2000), *Guó Shǐ Jiù Wén*, page 289–291.
32 See Dengyuan Chen's, *Guó Shǐ Jiù Wén* (2000), page 29.
33 See Buke Yan's, *Shìdàfū Zhèngzhì Yǎnshēng Shǐgǎo* (1996), page 79.
34 See Dengyuan Chen's, *Guó Shǐ Jiù Wén* (2000), page 152.
35 In Chapter 7, it is more effective to explain this as the reputation mechanism for people in high positions of power, so it is not a contradiction here.
36 See *The Book of Jin, Biography of Du Yu*.
37 See *The Book of Han, Biography of Jia Yi*.
38 See Tongzu Ju's, *Fǎlù zài Zhōngguó Shèhuì zhōng de Zuòyòng: Lìshǐ de Kǎochá* in *Zhōngwài Fǎxué* (1998, Volume Four).
39 See Simian Lv's, *Zhōngguó Zhìdù Shǐ* (2002), page 644.
40 See Buke Yan's, *Shìdàfū Zhèngzhì Yǎnshēng Shǐgǎo* (1996).

41 Sir Joseph Needham perhaps was the first scholar to propose the Confucian natural law idea. See *Science and Civilisation in China*, Volume One.
42 John Locke proposed a similar idea in 1689 and had a major impact on the formation of Western democracy.
43 See Tsung-san Mou's, *Zhèngdào yǔ Zhìdào* (2006), page 18.

References

Abreu, D., 1986, "External Equilibria of Oligopolistic Supergame." *Journal of Economic Theory*, 39: 191–225.

Acemoglu, D. and J. A. Robinson, 2006, *Economic Origins of Dictatorship and Democracy*. Cambridge: Cambridge University Press.

Akerlof, G., 1970, "The Market for Lemons: Quality Uncertainty and the Market Mechanism." *Quarterly Journal of Economics*, 84(3): 488–500.

Alchian, A. and H. Demsetz, 1972, "Production, Information Costs and Economic Organization." *American Economic Review*, 62: 777–795.

Appiah, K. A., 2010, *The Honor Code: How Moral Revolutions Happen*. New York: W.W. Norton & Company, Inc.

Armstrong, M., S. Cowan and J. Vickers, 1995, *Regulatory Reform*. Cambridge, MA: MIT Press.

Arrow, K., 1963, *Social Choice and Individual Values* (Revised edition). New York: John Wiley and Sons.

Arthur, W. B., 1990, "Positive Feedback in the Economy." *Scientific American*, 262: 92–99.

Arthur, W. B., 1994, *Increasing Returns and Path Dependence in the Economy*. Ann Arbor, MI: University of Michigan Press.

Aumann, R., 1976a, "Agreeing to Disagree." *Annals of Statistics*, 4: 1236–1239.

Aumann, R., 1976b, "An Elementary Proof That Integration Preserves Uppersemicontinuity." *Journal of Mathematical Economics*, Elsevier, 3(1): 15–18.

Aumann, R. and S. Hart, 1992, *Handbook of Game Theory with Economic Applications*. Amsterdam: North-Holland.

Axelrod, R., 1984, *The Evolution of Cooperation*. New York: Basic Books.

Axelrod, R., 1986, "An Evolutionary Approach to Norms." *American Political Science Review*, 80(4): 1095–1111.

Axelrod, R. and W. D. Hamilton, 1981, "The Evolution of Cooperation." *Science, New Series*, 211(4489): 1390–1396.

Barnett, T. P. M., 2009, *Great Power: America and the World after Bush*. New York: G.P. Putnam's Sons Publisher.

Baro, R., 1986, "Reputation in a Model of Monetary Policy with Incomplete Information." *Journal of Monetary Economics*, 17: 3–20.

Basu, K., 1998, "Social Norms and the Law." Published in P. Newman (ed.), *The New Palgrave Dictionary of Economics and Law*. London: Macmillan Press.

Basu, K., 2000, "The Role of Norms and Law in Economics: An Essay on Political Economy." Working Paper, Department of Economics, Cornell University, Ithaca, NY.

Battilana, J., B. Leca, and E. Boxenbaum. "Agency and Institutions: A Review of Institutional Entrepreneurship." Harvard Business School Working Paper, No. 08–096, May 2008, Cambridge, MA.

Bendor, J. and P. Swistak, 2001, "The Evolution of Norms." *American Journal of Sociology*, 106(6): 1493–1545.

Benson, B., 1990, *The Enterprise of Law: Justice without the State*. San Francisco: Pacific Research Institute for Public Policy.

Bergstrom, T. C., 2002, "Evolution of Social Behaviour: Individual and Group Selection." *Journal of Economic Perspectives*, 16(2): 67–88.

Bernheim, D. D. and M. Whinston, 1990, "Multimarket Contact and Collusive Behavior." *Rand Journal of Economics*, 21(1): 1–26.

Bernstein, L., 1992, "Opting Out of the Legal System: Extralegal Contractual Relation in the Diamond Industry." *Journal of Legal Studies*, 21: 115–157.

Binmore, K., 1987a, "Modelling Rational Players." *Economics and Philosophy*, 3: 179–214.

Binmore, K., 1987b, "Nash Bargaining Theory I, II." In K. Binmore and P. Dasgupta (eds.), *The Economics of Bargaining*. Cambridge: Basic Blackwell.

Binmore, K., 1997, "Introduction." In J. F. Nash, Jr. (ed.), *Essays on Game Theory*. Chetenham: Edward Elgar.

Binmore, K., 1998, *Game Theory and the Social Contract*. Cambridge, MA: MIT Press.

Bodenheimer, E., 1962, *Jurisprudence: The Philosophy and Method of the Law* (Revised edition). Cambridge, MA: Harvard University Press.

Bowles, Samuel and Herbert Gintis, 2013, *A Cooperative Species: Human Reciprocity and Its Evolution*. Princeton: Princeton University Press (reprinted edition.)

Boyd, R. and P. J. Richerson, 1985, *Culture and the Evolutionary Process*. Chicago: University of Chicago Press.

Brealey, R. A. and S. C. Myers, 2000, *Principles of Corporate Finance* (Sixth edition). New York: Irwin McGraw-Hill.

Burn, E. H., 1990, *Maudsley & Burn's Trusts & Trustees: Cases and Materials*. London: Butterworths.

Carmichael, H. L., 1988, "Incentives in Academics: Why Is There Tenure." *Journal of Political Economy*, 96: 453–472.

Chen, D., 2000, *guoshi jiuwen* (The Old Story of Chinese History). Beijing: Zhonghua Book Company.

Chen, Y., 1961, *shencha baogao* 3 (Review Report 3), collected in Feng Youlan: *zhongguo zhexue jianshi* (A History of Chinese Philosophy, Part Two). Beijing: Zhonghua Book Company.

Chen, Z. and S.-H. Lee, 2009, "Incentives in Academic Tenure under Asymmetric Information." *Economic Modelling*, 26: 300–308.

Cheung, S., 1973, "The Fable of the Bees: An Economic Investigation." *Journal of Law and Economics*, 16: 11–33.

Clarke, E. H., 1971, "Multipart Pricing of Public Goods." *Public Choice*, 11: 17–33.

Coase, R., 1960, "The Problem of Social Cost." *Journal of Law and Economics*, 3: 1–44.

Coase, R., 1972, "Durability and Monopoly." *Journal of Law and Economics*, 15(1): 143–149.

Coase, R., 1974, "The Lighthouse in Economics." *Journal of Law and Economics*, 17: 357–376.

Coleman, J., 1994, *Foundations of Social Theory*. Cambridge, MA and London: Harvard University Press, second Printing.

Cooter, R., 1991, "Coase Theorem." In J. Eatwell, M. Milgate, and P. Newman (eds.), *The New Palgrave Dictionary of Economics*, Vol. 1. London: The Macmillan Press.

Cooter, R., 1995, "Law and Unified Social Theory." *Journal of Law and Society*, 22(1): 50–67.

Cooter, R., 1996, "The Rule of State Law Versus the Rule-of-Law State: Economic Analysis of the Legal Foundations of Development." The Paper for the Annual Bank Conference on Development Economics, World Bank, April 25–26, 1996, Washington, DC.

Cooter, R., 1997a, "Law from order: Economic development and the jurisprudence of social norms." John M. Olin Working Papers in Law, Economics, and Institutions 96/97–4, University of California Berkeley, Berkeley. Available at: http://works.bepress.com/robert_cooter/61/

Cooter, R., 1997b, "Normative Failure Theory of Law." *Cornell Law Review*, 82(5): 947–979.

Cooter, R., 2000a, "Do Good Laws Make Good Citizens? An Economic Analysis of Internalized Norms." *Virginia Law Review*, 50(8): 1577–1601.

Cooter, R., 2000b, "Three Effects of Social Norms on Law: Expression, Deterrence, and Internalization." *Oregon Law Review*, 79(1): 1–22.

Crawford, V. and J. Sobel, 1982, "Strategic Information Transmission." *Econometrica*, 50(6): 1431–1451.

David, P., 1985, "Clio and the Economics of QWERTY." *American Economic Review*, 75(2): 332–337.

Dawkins, R., 2006 (1976), *The Selfish Gene: 30th Anniversary Edition*. Oxford: Oxford University Press. (First published in 1976).

Delong, B., 1991, "Did J. P. Mogan's Man Add Value? An Economist's Perspective on Financial Capitalism." In P. Temin (ed.), *Inside the Business Enterprise: Historical Perspectives on the Use of Information*. Chicago: University of Chicago Press.

De Soto, J. H., 2010, *Socialism, Economic Calculation and Entrepreneurship*. Cheltenham, UK: Edward Elgar Publishing Limited.

Diener, E., L. Tayand and D. G. Myers, 2011, "The Religion Paradox: If Religion Makes People Happy, Why Are so Many Dropping Out?" *Journal of Personality and Social Psychology*, 101(6): 1278–1290.

DiMaggio, P. J., 1988, "Interest and Agency in Institutional Theory." In L. Zucker (ed.), *Institutional Patterns and Organizations*. Cambridge, MA: Ballinger.

Di Tella, R. and E. Schargrodsky, 2003, "The Role of Wages and Auditing during a Crackdown on Corruption in the City of Buenos Ares." *Journal of Law and Economics*, 46(1): 269–292.

Dixit, A., 1996, *The Making of Economic Policy*. Cambridge, MA: MIT Press.

Dixit, A., 1997, "Power of Incentives in Private Versus Public Organizations." *The American Economic Review: Papers and Proceedings*, 87: 378–382.

Dixit, A., 2004, *Lawlessness and Economics: Alternative Models of Governance*. Princeton, NJ: Princeton University Press.

Djankov, S., R. La Porta, F. Lopez-De-Silanes and A. Shleifer, 2002, "The Regulation of Entry." *The Quarterly Journal of Economics*, 117(1): 1–37.

Eisenstadt, S. N., 1980, "Cultural Orientations, Institutional Entrepreneurs and Social Change: Comparative Analyses of Traditional Civilizations." *American Journal of Sociology*, 85: 840–869.

Ellickson, R., 1991, *Order without Law, How Neighbors Settle Disputes*. Cambridge, MA: Harvard University Press.

Ellickson, R., 1998, "Law and Economics Discovers Social Norms." *Journal of Legal Studies*, 27: 537–552.

Ellickson, R., 1999, "The Evolution of Social Norms: A Perspective from the Legal Academy." Working Paper No. 230, Yale Law School, Program for Studies in Law, Economics and Public Policy, Yale University, CT.

Elster, J., 1978, *Logic and Society*. New York: Wiley.

Elster, J., 1989a, *The Cement of Society: A Survey of Social Order*. Cambridge: Cambridge University Press.

Elster, J., 1989b, "Social Norms and Economic Theory." *Journal of Economic Perspectives*, 3(4): 99–117.

Feng, X., 2004, *fubai huibuhui chengwei yi xiang quanli* ("Will Corruption become a Right?"). In X. Feng (ed.), *Dairy on Zhengfa*. Nanjing: Jiangsu People's Publishing House.

Feng, Y., *zhongguo zhexue jianshi* (A History of Chinese Philosophy, Part Two) (1961 edition). Beijing: Zhonghua Book Company.

Fisher, R., W. Ury and B. Patton, 1991, *Getting to Yes: Negotiating Agreement without Giving in* (2nd edition). New York: Penguin.

Fisman, R. and T. Khanna, 1999, "Is trust a historical residue? Information flows and trust levels." *Journal of Economic Behavior & Organization*, 38: 79–92.

Friedman, D., 1998, "On Economic Applications of Evolutionary Game Theory." *Journal of Evolutionary Economics*, 8(1): 15–29.

Friedman, J., 1971, "A Non-Cooperative Equilibrium for Supergame." *Review of Economic Studies*, 38: 1–12.

Friedman, J., 1991, *Game Theory with Applications to Economics*. Oxford: Oxford University Press.

Friedman, L., 1975, *The Legal System: A Social Science Perspective*. New York: Russell Sage Foundation.

Fudenberg, D. and J. Tirole, 1991, *Game Theory*. Cambridge, MA: MIT Press.

Fukuyama, F., 1996, *Trust: The Social Virtues and the Creation of Prosperity*. New York: Free Press.

Fuller, L., 1964, *The Morality of Law*. New Haven, CT: Yale University Press.

Fuller, L., 1981, *The Principles of Social Order*. Durham, NC: Duke University Press.

Gale, D. and L. Shapley, 1962, "College Admissions and the Stability of Marriage." *American Mathematical Monthly*, 69: 9–15.

Gale, J., K. Binmore and L. Samuelson, 1995, "Learning to be Imperfect: The Ultimatum Game." *Games and Economic Behavior*, 8: 56–90.

Gambetta, D., 1993, *The Sicilian Mafia: The Business of Private Protection*. Cambridge, MA: Harvard University Press.

Garg, D., Y. Narahari and S. Gujar, 2008, "Foundations of Mechanism Design: A Tutorial Part 1 – Key Concepts and Classical Results." Sadhana, 33(2): 83–130. Indian Academy of Sciences, Bangalore, India.

Gibbons, R., 1992, *A Primer in Game Theory*. New York: Harvester Wheatsheaf.

Gilson, R. J., 2001, "Globalizing Corporate Governance: Convergence of Form or Function." *The American Journal of Comparative Law*, 49(2): 329–357.

Glaeser, E. and C. Goldin (eds.), 2006, *Corruption and Reform: Lessons from America's Economic History*. Chicago: University of Chicago Press.

Gordon, J. and M. Roe, 2004, *Convergence and Persistence in Corporate Governance*. Cambridge: Cambridge University Press.

Green, E. and R. Porter, 1984, "Noncooperative Collusion under Imperfect Price Information." *Econometrica*, 52: 87–100.

Greif, A., 1994, "Cultural Beliefs and the Organization of Society: A Historical and Theoretical Reflection on Collectivist and Individualist Societies." *The Journal of Political Economy*, 102(5): 912–950.

Grossman, S. and O. Hart, 1986, "The Costs and Benefits of Ownership: A Theory of Vertical and Lateral Integration." *Journal of Political Economy*, 94: 691–719.

Groves, T., 1973, "Incentives in Teams." *Econometrica*, 41: 617–631.

Groves, T. and J. Ledyard, 1977, "Optimal Allocation of Public Goods: A Solution to the 'Free-Rider' Problem." *Econometrica*, 45: 783–809.

Güth, W., R. Schmittberger and B. Schwarze, 1982, "An Experimental Analysis of Ultimatum Bargaining." *Journal of Economic Behavior and Organization*, 3(4): 367–388.

Hansmann, H., 1999a, "Higher Education as an Associative Good." Yale Law and Economics Working Paper No. 231; Yale ICF Working Paper No. 99–15, Yale Law School, Yale University, CT.

Hansmann, H., 1999b, "The State and Market in Higher Education." Working Paper, Yale Law School, Yale University, CT.

Hardin, G., 1968, "The Tragedy of the Commons." *Science*, 162(13): 1243–1248.

Harsanyi, J., 1973, "Games with Randomly Distributed Payoffs: A New Rationale for Mixed Strategic Equilibrium Points." *International Journal of Game Theory*, 2: 1–23.

Hart, O. and B. Holmstrom, 1987, "Theory of Contract." In T. Bewley (ed.), *Advances in Economic Theory: Fifth World Congress*. Cambridge: Cambridge University Press.

Hayek, F. A., 1935, "The Present State of the Debate." In F. A. Hayke (ed.), *Collectivist Economic Planning*. Clifton: Augustus M. Kelly, 201–243, 1975; reprinted as "Socialist Calculation II: The State of the Debate", In F. A. Hayek (ed.), *Individualism and Economic Order*. Chicago: Gateway Edition, 1972.

Hayek, F. A., 1937, "Economics and Knowledge." *Economica*, 4: 33–54.

Hayek, F. A., 1945, "The Use of Knowledge in Society." *American Economic Review*, 35(4): 519–530.

Hayek, F. A., 1960, *The Constitution of Liberty*. London: Routledge and Kegan Paul.

Hayek, F. A., 1979, *Law, Legislation and Liberty* (3 vol.). London: Routledge and Kegan Paul.

He, H., 2011, *xuanze xin shehui* (A Selective Society). Peking University Press.

Heap, S. P. Hargreaves and Y. Varoufakis, 1995, *Game Theory: A Critical Introduction*. London and New York: Routledge.

Held, D., 2006, *Models of Democracy* (3rd edition). Polity Press.

Hobbes, T., 1996 (1651), *Leviathan*. New York: Oxford University Press.

Holmstrom, B., 1979, "Moral Hazard and Observability." *Bell Journal of Economics*, 10: 74–91.

Holmstrom, B. and P. Milgrom, 1991, "Multi-Task Principal-Agent Analyses: Incentive Contract, Asset Ownership and Job Design." *Journal of Law, Economics and Organization*, 7: 24–52.

Honore, T., 1987, *Making Law Bind: Essays Legal and Philosophical*. Oxford: Clarendon Press.

Houba, H. and W. Bolt, 2002, *Credible Threats in Negotiation – a Game Theoretical Approach*. Boston: Kluwer Academic Publishers.

Hulsmann, J. G., 2008, *The Ethics of Money Production*. Auburn, AL: Ludwig Mises Institute.

Hume, D., 1740, *A Treatise of Human Nature* (2nd edition), L. A. Selby-Bigge (ed.). Oxford: Clarendon Press, 1978.

Hurwicz, L., 1960, "Optimality and Informational Efficiency in Resource Allocation Processes." In K. Arrow, S. Karlin, and P. Suppes (eds.), *Mathematical Methods in the Social Sciences*. Stanford, CA: Stanford University Press.

Hurwicz, L., 1972, "On Informationally Decentralized System." In M. Mcguire, R. Radner, and K. Arrow (eds.), *Decision and Organization: A Volume in Honor of Jacob Marschak*. Amsterdam: North Holland.

Ishiguro, S., 2004, "Collusion and Discrimination in Organizations." *Journal of Economic Theory*, 116: 357–369.

Jolls, C., C. R. Sunstein and R. Thaler, 1998, "A Behavioral Approach to Law and Economics." *Stanford Law Review*, 50: 1471–1550.

Jussim, L., 1986, "Self-Fulfilling Prophecies: A Theoretical and Integrative Review." *Psychological Review*, 93(4): 429–445.

Kahn, C. and G. Huberman, 1988, "The Two-Sided Uncertainty and 'Up-or-Out' Contract." *Journal of Labor Economics*, 6: 423–444.

Kahneman, D. and A. Tversky, 1979, "Prospect Theory: An Analysis of Decision under Risk." *Econometrica*, 47: 263–291.

Kahneman, D. and A. Tversky, 2000, *Choices, Values and Frames*. Cambridge: Cambridge University Press.

Kandori, M., 1992, "Social Norms and Community Enforcement." *Review of Economic Studies*, 59: 61–80.

Kawasaki, S. and J. McMillan, 1987, "The Design of Contracts: Evidence from Japanese Subcontracting." *Journal of Japanese and International Economics*, 1: 1327–1349.

Kelsen, H., 2009, *Pure Theory of Law*. Clark, NJ: The Lawbook Exchange Ltd.

Klein, B. and K. Leffler, 1981, "The Role of Market Forces in Assuring Contractual Performance." *Journal of Political Economy*, 81: 615–641.

Klein, D., 1990, "The Voluntary Provision of Public Goods? The Turnpike Companies of Early American Economy." *Economic Enquiry*, 28(4): 788–812.

Klein, D. (ed.), 1997a, *Reputation: Studies in the Voluntary Elicitation of Good Conduct*. Ann Arbor, MI: University of Michigan Press.

Klein, D., 1997b, "Trust for Hire: Voluntary Remedies for Quality and Safety." In D. Klein (ed.), *Reputation*. Ann Arbor, MI: University of Michigan Press.

Klemperer, P., 2004, *Auction: Theory and Practice*. Princeton, NJ: Princeton University Press.

Knack, S. and P. Keefer, 1997, "Does Social Capital Have an Economic Payoff? A Cross-Country Investigation." *Quarterly Journal of Economics*, 112(4): 1251–1288.

Kreps, D., 1986, "Corporate Culture and Economic Theory." In M. Tsuchiya (ed.), *Technological Innovation and Business Strategy*. Nippon Keizai Shimbuunsha Press. Also, in J. Alt and K. Shepsle (eds.), *Rational Perspective on Political Science*. Cambridge, MA: Harvard University Press, 1999.

Kreps, D., 1990, *A Course in Microeconomics*. Cambridge, MA: MIT Press.

Kreps, D., R. Milgrom, J. Roberts and R. Wilson, 1982, "Rational Cooperation in the Finitely Repeated Prisoner's dilemma." *Journal of Economic Theory*, 27: 245–252.

Kreps, D. and R. Wilson, 1982, "Sequential Equilibrium." *Econometrica*, 50: 863–894.

Kuran, T., 1997, *Private Truths, Public Lies: The Social Consequences of Preference Falsification*. Cambridge, MA: Harvard University Press.

Laffont, J. and D. Martimort, 2002, *The Theory of Incentives: The Principal-Agent Model*. Princeton, NJ: Princeton University Press.

Laffont, J. and E. Maskin, 1979, "A Differentiable Approach to Expected Utility Maximizing Mechanism." In J. Laffont (ed.), *Aggregation and Revelation of Preferences*. Amsterdam: North Holland.

Lazear, E., 1989, "Pay Equality and Industrial Politics." *Journal of Political Economy*, 97: 561–580.

Lazear, E., 1997, *Personnel Economics*. Cambridge, MA and London: MIT Press.

Lazear, E. and S. Rosen, 1981, "Rank-Order Tournaments as Optimum Labor Contracts." *Journal of Political Economy*, 89(5): 841–864.

Levitt, S. D. and S. J. Dubner, 2005, *Freakonomics: A Rogue Economist Explores the Hidden Side of Everything*. New York: William Morrow/HarperCollins.

Levitt, S. D. and C. Syverson, 2005, "Market Distortions When Agents are Better Informed: The Value of Information in Real Estate Transactions." NBER Working Paper Series No. 11053, National Bureau of Economic Research, Cambridge, MA.

Liang, Z., 1996, *qingdai xueguanfa* (Customary Law of Qing Dynasty). Beijing: China University of Political Science and Law Press.

Liebowitz, S. J. and S. E. Margolis, 1990, "The Fable of Keys." *Journal of Law and Economics*, 33(1): 1–25.

Liebowitz, S. J. and S. E. Margolis, 1999, "Beta, Macintosh and Other Famous Tales." Chapter 6 in S. J. Liebowitz and S. E. Margolis (eds.), *Winners, Losers and Microsoft.* Oakland. CA: The Independent Institute, 199–234.

Lindbeck, A., 1975, *Swedish Economic Policy*. London: MacMillan Press.

Linster, B. G., 1992, "Evolutionary Stability in the Infinitely Repeated Prisoner's dilemma Played by Two-State Moore Machines." *Southern Economic Journal*, 58: 880–903.

Linster, B. G., 1994, "Stochastic Evolutionary Dynamics in the Repeated Prisoner's dilemma." *Economic Inquiry*, 32: 342–357.

Locke, J., 1956 (1689), *Second Treatise of Government*. Cambridge, MA: Hackett Publishing Company, Inc.

Mahoney, P. G. and C. W. Sanchirico, 2003, "Norms, Repeated Games and the Role of Law." *California Law Review*, 1: 1281–1329.

Maskin, E., 1999, "Nash Equilibrium and Welfare Optimality." *Review of Economic Studies*, 66: 23–38.

Maskin, E. and J. Riley, 1984, "Optimal Auction with Risk Averse Buyers." *Econometrica*, 52: 1473–1518.

Maskin, E. and J. Riley, 1985, "Auction Theory with Private Value." *American Economic Review*, 75: 150–155.

Maslow, A. H., 1943, "A Theory of Human Motivation." *Psychological Review*, 50(4): 370–396.

Maslow, A. H., 1954, *Motivation and Personality*. New York: Harper.

Maynard Smith, J., 1982, *Evolution and Theory of Games*. Cambridge: Cambridge University Press.

Maynard Smith, J. and G. R. Price, 1973, "The Logic of Animal Conflict." *Nature*, 246(5427): 15–18.

McAdams, R., 1997, "The Origin, Development and Regulation of Norms." *Michigan Law Review*, 96(2): 238–433.

McPherson, M. S. and M. O. Schapiro, 1999, "Tenure Issues in Higher Education." *Journal of Economic Perspectives*, 13(1): 85–98.

Milgrom, P., 2004, *Putting Auction Theory to Work*. Cambridge: Cambridge University Press.

Milgrom, P., D. North and B. R. Weingast, 1990, "The Role of Institutions in the Revival of Trade: The Law Merchant, Private Judges, and the Champagne Fairs." *Economics and Politics*, 2: 1–23.

Milgrom, P. and J. Roberts, 1982, "Limit Pricing and Entry under Incomplete Information: An Equilibrium Analysis." *Econometrica*, 40: 433–459.

Milgrom, P. and J. Roberts, 1992, *Economics, Organization and Management*. Englewood Cliffs, NJ: Prentice Hall, Inc.

Mill, J., 2002 (1850), *On Liberty*. Mineola, New York: Dover Publications.

Mirrlees, J., 1971, "An Exploration in the Theory of Optimum Income Taxation." *Review of Economic Studies*, 38: 175–208.

Mirrlees, J., 1999 (1975), "The Theory of Moral Hazard and Unobservable Behaviour: Part I." *Review of Economic Studies*, 66(1): 3–21.

Mookherjee, D., 1984, "Optimal Incentive Schemes with Many Agents." *Review of Economic Studies*, 51(3): 433–446.

Morris, I., 2010, *Why the West Rules for Now: The Patterns of History and What They Reveal about the Future*. London: Profile Books.

Mou, Z., 2006, *zhengdao yu zhidao* (Political System and Governance). Guilin, China: Guangxi Normal University Press.

Mueller, D. C., 2003, *Public Choice III*. Cambridge: Cambridge University Press.

Myers, S. C. and N. Majluf, 1984, "Corporate Financing and Investment Decisions When Firms Have Information That Investors Do Not Have." *Journal of Financial Economics*, 13: 187–222.

Myerson, R., 1979, "Incentive Compatibility and the Bargaining Problem." *Econometrica*, 47: 61–73.

Myerson, R., 1983, "Mechanism Design by Informed Principal." *Econometrica*, 51: 1767–1797.

Myerson, R., 1999, "Nash Equilibrium and the History of Economic Theory." *Journal of Economic Literature*, 37(3): 1067–1082.

Myerson, R. and M. Satterthwaite, 1983, "Efficient Mechanism for Bilateral Trading." *Journal of Economic Theory*, 28: 265–281.

Nachbar, J. H., 1992, "Evolution in the Infinitely Repeated Prisoner's dilemma." *Journal of Economic Behavior and Organization*, 19: 307–326.

Nalebuff, B. and J. Stiglitz, 1983, "Prizes and Incentives: Towards a General Theory of Compensation and Competition." *The Bell Journal of Economics*, 14(1): 21–43.

Nash, J., 1950, "The Bargaining Problem." *Econometrica*, 18: 155–162.

Nash, J., 1951, "Non-Cooperative Games." *Annals of Mathematics*, 54: 286–295.

Nash, J., 1953, "Two-Person Cooperative Games." *Econometrica*, 21: 128–140.

Needham, J., 1981, *The Shorter Science and Civilization of China*, Vol. 1. Cambridge: Cambridge University Press.

Nelson, P., 1974, "Advertising as Information." *Journal of Political Economy*, 81: 729–754.

Nelson, R. and S. Winter, 1982, *An Evolutionary Theory of Economic Change*. Cambridge, MA: Harvard University Press.

Nelson, R. and S. Winter, 2002, "Evolutionary Theorizing in Economics." *Journal of Economic Perspectives*, 16(2): 23–46.

Newman, J. W., 1997 (1956), "Dun and Bradstreet: For the Promotion and Protection of Trade." Reprinted in D. Klein (ed.), *Reputation*. Ann Arbor, MI: University of Michigan Press.

North, D. C., 1990, *Institutions, Institutional Change and Economic Performance*. Cambridge: Cambridge University Press.

North, D. C. and B. R. Weingast, 1989, "Constitutions and Commitment: The Evolution of Institutions Governing Public Choices in Seventeenth-Century England." *Journal of Economic History*, 49: 803–832.

Oosterbeek, H., R. Sloof and G. van de Kuilen, 2004, "Cultural Differences in Ultimatum Game Experiments: Evidence from a Meta-Analysis." *Experimental Economics*, 7(2): 171–188.

Orwell, G., 1946, *Politics and the English Language*. First published: Horizon. London: GB.

Ostrom, E., 1990, *Governing the Commons*. Cambridge: Cambridge University Press.

Posner, E., 1999, "A Theory of Contract Law under Conditions of Radical Judicial Error." John M. Olin Law and Economic Working Paper No. 80, Chicago University, Chicago, IL.

Posner, E., 2000, *Law and Social Norms*. Cambridge, MA: Harvard University Press.

Posner, R., 1980, "The Ethical and Political Basis of the Efficiency Norm in Common Law Adjudication." *Hofstra Law Review*, 8: 487–507.

Posner, R., 1992, *Economic Analysis of Law* (4th edition). Boston: Little, Brown.

Posner, R., 1997, "Social Norms and the Law: An Economic Approach." *American Economic Review*, 87(2): 365–369.

Prelec, D. and D. Simester, 2001, "Always Leave Home without It: A Further Investigation of the Credit-Card Effect on Willingness to Pay." *Marketing Letters*, 12(1): 5–12.

Putnam, R., 1993, *Making Democracy Work: Civic Traditions in Modern Italy*. Princeton, NJ: Princeton University Press.

Rasmusen, E., 1994, *Game and Information: An Introduction to Game Theory*. Cambridge: Blackwell Publisher.

Rasmusen, E., 2006, *Games and Information* (4th edition). Oxford: Blackwell Publishers.

Rauch, J. and P. Evans, 2000, "Bureaucratic Structure and Bureaucratic Performance in Less Developed Countries." *Journal of Public Economics*, 75(1): 49–71.

Rawls, J., 1971, *A Theory of Justice*. Cambridge, MA: The Belknap Press of Harvard University Press.

Rees, R., 1985, "The Theory of Principal and Agent: Part I." *Bulletin of Economic Research*, 37(1): 3–26.

Robson, A. J., 2002, "Evolution and Human Nature." *Journal of Economic Perspectives*, 16(2): 89–107.

Rogers, P., 2008, *Aspects of Western Civilization: Problems and Sources in History*. London: Pearson Education Inc.

Rose-Ackerman, S., 2016, *Corruption and Government: Causes, Consequences, and Reform* (2nd edition). Cambridge: Cambridge University Press.

Ross, S., 1973, "The Economic Theory of Agency: The Principal's Problem." American Economic Review, 63(2): 134–139.

Ross, S. A., 1977, "The Determination of Financial Structure: The Incentive Signaling Approach." *The Bell Journal of Economics*, 8: 23–40.

Roth, A. E., 1979, *Axiomatic Models of Bargaining, Lecture Notes in Economics and Mathematical Systems*. Berlin Heidelberg: Springer Verlag.

Roth, A. E., 1985, *Game-Theoretic Models of Bargaining*. Cambridge: Cambridge University Press.

Roth, A. E. and M. Sotomayor, 1990, *Two-Sided Matching: A Study in Game-Theoretic Modeling and Analysis*. Cambridge: Cambridge University Press.

Rothbard, M. N., 1970, *Power and Market*. Auburn, AL: Ludwig Mises Institute.

Rothbard, M. N., 2005, *What Has Government Done for Our Money?* (5th edition). Auburn, AL: Ludwig von Mises Institute.

Rothschild, M. and J. Stiglitz, 1976, "Equilibrium in Competitive Insurance Markets." *Quarterly Journal of Economics*, 90: 629–649.

Rubinstein, A., 1982, "Perfect Equilibrium in a Bargaining Model." *Econometrica*, 50: 97–109.

Samuelson, L., 1997, *Evolutionary Games and Equilibrium Selection*. Cambridge, MA: MIT Press.

Samuelson, L., 2002, "Evolution and Game Theory." *Journal of Economic Perspectives*, 16(2): 47–66.

Schelling, T., 1960, *Strategy of Conflict*. Oxford: Oxford University Press.

Schelling, T., 2006, *Strategies of Commitment and Other Essays*. Cambridge, MA: Harvard University Press.

Schmalensee, R., 1978, "A Model of Advertising and Product Quality." *Journal of Political Economy*, 6: 485–503.

Schmidt, C., 2004, "Are Evolutionary Games Another Way of Thinking about Game Theory? Some Historical Considerations." *Journal of Evolutionary Economics*, 14(2): 249–262.

Schumpeter, J., 1994 (1942), *Capitalism, Socialism and Democracy*. New York: Routledge.

Sealy, L. and R. Hooley, 2009, *Commercial Law: Text, Cases and Materials* (4th edition). Oxford: Oxford University Press.

Selten, R., 1965, "Spieltheoretiche Behandlung eines Oligopolmodells mit Nachfragetragheit." *Zeitschrift fur Gesamte Staatswissenschaft*, 121: 301–324.

Selten, R., 1975, "Re-Examination of the Perfectness Concept for Equilibrium Points in Extensive Games." *International Journal of Game*, 4: 25–55.

Selten, R., 1978, "The Chain-Store Paradox." *Theory and Decision*, 9: 127–129.

Shapiro, C., A. Shaked and J. Sutton, 1984, "Involuntary Unemployment as a Perfect Equilibrium in a Bargaining Model." *Econometrica*, 52(6): 1351–1364.

Shapiro, C. and J. Stiglitz, 1984, "Equilibrium Unemployment as a Worker Discipline Device." *American Economic Review*, 74(3) 433–444.

Shapiro, C. and H. R. Varian, 1998, *Information Rules: A Strategic Guide to the Network Economy*. Cambridge, MA: Harvard Business Press.

Shearmur, J. and D. Klein, 1997, "Good Conduct in the Great Society: Adam Smith and the Role of Reputation." In D. Klein (ed.), *Reputation: Studies in the Voluntary Elicitation of Good Conduct*. Ann Arbor, MI: University of Michigan Press.

Shen, Y., 2003, *yanyuan bianfa* (Reform within Peking University Campus). Shanghai: Shanghai Culture Publishing House.

Shleifer, A. and R. Vishny, 1998, *Grabbing Hand: Government Pathologies and Their Cures*. Cambridge, MA: Harvard University Press.

Simon, H., 1951, "A Formal Theory of Employment Relationship." *Econometrica*, 19: 293–305.

Skoble, A., 2006, "Hayek the Philosopher of Law." In E. Feser (ed.), *The Cambridge Companion to Hayek*. Cambridge: Cambridge University Press.

Smith, C. R., 1998, "Moon Cakes: Gifts That Keep on Giving and Giving . . ." *Wall Street Journal*, Sept. 30, p. 1.

Sorkin, A. R., 2009, *Too Big to Fail: The Inside Story of How Wall Street and Washington Fought to Save the Financial System from Crisis*. New York: Viking Adult Press.

Spence, A. M., 1973, "Job Market Signalling." *Quarterly Journal of Economics*, 87: 355–374.

Spence, A. M., 1974, *Market Signaling*. Cambridge, MA: Harvard University Press.

Spence, M. and R. Zechhauser, 1971, "Insurance, Information and Individual Action." *American Economic Review (Papers and Proceedings)*, 61: 380–387.

Spulber, D., 2001, *Famous Fables of Economics: Myths of Market Failures*. Oxford: Wiley-Blackwell.

Stark, R., 1996, *The Rise of Christianity*. New York: Harper One.

Stark, R., 2005, *The Victory of Reason: How Christianity Led to Freedom, Capitalism and Western Success*. New York: Random House Trade Paperback.

Stigler, G., 1971, "The Theory of Economic Regulation." *Bell Journal of Economics*, 6: 417–429.

Stiglitz, J., 1994, *Whither Socialism?* Cambridge, MA: MIT Press.

Stiglitz, J. and A. Weiss, 1981, "Credit Rationing in Markets with Incomplete Information." *American Economic Review*, 71: 393–410.

Sugden, R., 1989, "Spontaneous Order." *Journal of Economic Perspective*, 3(4): 85–97.

Sugden, R., 2001, "The Evolutionary Turn in Game Theory." *Journal of Economic Methodology*, 8(1): 113–130.

Sunstein, C., 1996, "Social Norms and Social Roles." *Columbia Law Review*, 96(4): 903–968.

Svenson, K., 2005, "Eight Questions about Corruption." *Journal of Economic Perspectives*, 9(3): 19–42.

Tadelis, S., 1999, "What's in a Name? Reputation as a Tradeable Asset." *American Economic Review*, 89(3): 549–563.

Thaler, R. H., 1988, "Anomalies: The Ultimatum Game." *Journal of Economic Perspective*, 2: 195–206.

Tideman, T. N. and G. Tullock, 1976, "A New and Superior Process for Making Social Choices." *Journal of Political Economy*, 84: 1145–1159.

Tirole, J., 1988, *Theory of Industrial Organization*. Cambridge, MA: MIT Press.

Tirole, J., 1994, "The Internal Organization of Government." *Oxford Economic Papers*, 46(1): 1–29.

Tocqueville, A., 2003 (1835), *Democracy in America*. London and New York: Penguin Book.

Tompkinson, P. and J. Bethwaite, 1995, "The Ultimatum Game: Raising Stakes." *Journal of Economic Organization and Behaviour*, 27: 439–451.

Trakman, L. F., 1983, *The Law Merchant: The Evolution of Commercial Law*. Littleton, CO: Fred B. Rothman Co.

Treisman, D., 2000, "The causes of corruption: a cross-national study." Journal of Public Economics, 76(3): 399–457.

Trivers, R., 1971, "The Evolution of Reciprocal Altruism." *Quarterly Review of Biology*, 46(1): 35–57.

Tullock, G., A. Seldon and G. Brady, 2002, *Government Failure: A Primer in Public Choice*. Washington: Cato Institute.

Tyler, T., 1990, *Why People Obey the Law*. New Haven, CT: Yale University Press.

Van Rijckeghem, C. and B. Weder, 2001, "Bureaucratic Corruption and the Rate of Temptation: Do Wages in the Civil Service Affect Corruption, and by How Much?" *Journal of Development Economics*, 65(2): 307–331.

Varian, H., 1989, "Price Discrimination." Chapter 10 in R. Schmalensee and R. Willig (eds.), *The Handbook of Industrial Organization*, Vol. 1. Amsterdam and New York: Elsevier Science Publishers B.V. (North-Holland), 597–654.

Vega-Redondo, F., 2003, *Economics and the Theory of Games*. Cambridge: Cambridge University Press.

Vickers, J., 1986, "Signaling in a Model of Monetary Policy with Incomplete Information." *Oxford Economic Papers*, 38: 443–455.

Vickery, W., 1961, "Counterspeculation, Auctions and Completely Sealed Tenders." *Journal of Finance*, 16: 8–37.

von Neumann, J. and O. Morgenstern, 1947, *The Theory of Games and Economic Behaviour* (2nd edition). Princeton, NJ: Princeton University Press.

Walter, B., 2003, "Explaining the Intractability of Territorial Conflict." *International Studies Review*, 5(4): 137–153.

Wang, C., 2002, *qinquanfa de jingjixue fenxi* (An Economic Analysis of Tort Law). Beijing: China Renmin University Press.

Watson, B. (trans.), (1961). *Records of the Grand Historian of China*. New York: Columbia University Press.

Weber, M., 2002 (1904), *The Protestant Ethic and the Spirit of Capitalism: And Other Writings*. New York: Penguin Classics.

Wilson, E., 2000, *Sociobiology: The New Synthesis* (25th Anniversary edition). Cambridge, MA: Harvard University Press.

Wilson, R., 1993, *Nonlinear Pricing*. New York and Oxford: Oxford University Press.

Woods, T. E., Jr., 2009, *Meltdown*. Washington, DC: Regnery Publisher, Inc.

Wu, S., 2004, *yinbi de zhixu* (A Hidden Order). Haikou: Hainan Publishing House.

Yan, B., 1996, *shidafu yanshengshi* (A Study on Evolutionary History of Scholar-Officials). Beijing: Peking University Press.

Yan, B., 2002, *pinwei yu zhiwei: qinhanweijinnanbeichao guanjie zhidu yanjiu* (Grade and Position: Research on the System of Official Ranks During the Qin, Han, Wei, Jin, Southern, and Northern Dynasties). Beijing: Zhonghua Book Company.

Yao, Z., 1998, "yi zuowei yizhong zhidu bianqian mushi de zhuanxing" ("Transformation as a Model of Institutional Change"). In Z. Yao, *A Theoretical Analysis of China's*

Transition: A Austrian School Perspective (2009 edition). Hangzhou, China: Zhejiang University Press.

Yao, Z., 2012, *fengjian* (Federal System). Hanzhou, China: Hainan Publishing House.

Yi, Z., 2009, *tashan zhi shi* (Stone from Other Mountain). Guilin, China: Guangxi Normal University Press.

Yoshikawa, T. and A. Rasheed, 2009, "Convergence of Corporate Governance: Critical Review and Future Directions." *Corporate Governance: An International Review*, 17(3): 388–404.

Young, H. P., 1996, "The Economics of Convention." *Journal of Economic Perspective*, 10(2): 105–122.

Young, H. P., 1998, *Individual Strategy and Social Structure*. Princeton, NJ: Princeton University Press.

Young, H. P., 2008, "Social Norms." In S. N. Durlauf and L. E. Blume (eds.), *The New Palgrave Dictionary of Economics* (2nd edition). London: Palgrave Macmillan.

Yu, Y.-S., 2012a, "shishuo keju zai zhongguo shi shang de gongneng yu yiyi" ("On Functions and Implications of Imperial Examination in Chinese History"). In *zhonghua wenhua tongshi* (A General Explanation of Chinese Culture) (2012 edition). Beijing: Joint Publishing.

Yu, Y.-S., 2012b, *zhonghua wenhua tongshi* (A General Explanation of Chinese Culture). Beijing: Joint Publishing.

Zahavi, A., 1975, "Mate Election – a Selection for a Handicap." *Journal of Theoretical Biology*, 53: 205–214.

Zahavi, A., 1997, *The Handicap Principle: A Missing Piece of Darwin's Puzzle*. Oxford: Oxford University Press.

Zhang, W., 1996, *boyilun yu xinx jinjixue* (Game Theory and Information Economics). Shanghai: Shanghai People's Publishing House.

Zhang, W., 1997, "James Mirrlees's Contributions to Information Economics." In W. Zhang (ed.), *Collections of James Mirrlees's Essays*. Beijing: The Commercial Press.

Zhang, W., 1998, "kongzhiquan de buke buchangxing yu guoyou qiye jianbing zhong de chanquan zhangai" ("Un-Compensability of Control Rights and Barriers to Merge and Acquisition of SOEs"). *Economic Research Journal*, (1998–7): 21–22.

Zhang, W., 2001, "Reputational Foundation of the Legal System." *Economic Research Journal*, (2001–1): 3–13.

Zhang, W., 2003, "Entrepreneurs and Professional Managers: How to Build Trust." *Journal of Peking University (Philosophy and Social Sciences)*, (10): 29–39.

Zhang, W., 2004, *daxue de luoji* (The Logic of the University) (2004 edition, 2005 edition, 2012 edition). Beijing: Peking University Press.

Zhang, W., 2005, *chanquan, jili yu gongsi zhili* (Property Rights, Incentive and Governance). Beijing: Economic Science Press.

Zhang, W., 2006, *jingzhnegli yu qiye chengzhang* (Competitiveness and the Growth of the Firm). Beijing: Peking University Press.

Zhang, W., 2012, *shima gaibina zhongguo* (What Has Changed China?). Beijing: CITIC Press.

Zhang, W., 2015, *The Logic of the Market: An Insider's View of Chinese Economic Reform*. Washington, DC: Cato Institute Press. (The first and second Chinese edition was published in 2010 and 2012 by Shanghai People's Publishing House).

Zhang, W., 2017a (1995), *The Origin of the Capitalist Firm: An Entrepreneurial/Contractual Theory of the Firm*. Singapore: Springer. (The first Chinese edition was published by Shanghai People's Publishing House, 1995).

Zhang, W., 2017b, *The Road Leading to the Market*. London and New York: Routledge.

Zhang, W. and F. Deng, 2003, "xinxi, jli yu liandai zeren: dui zhongguo gudai lianzuo, baojia zhidu de fa jingjixue fenx" ("Information, Incentive and Joint Liability: A Law and Economic Analysis of Ancient China's Joint Liability"). *Chinese Social Sciences*, (3): 99–112.

Zhang, W. and K. Rongzhu, 2002a, "sifa guocheng zhong de nixiang xuanze" ("Adverse Selection in Legal Procedure"). *Chinese Social Sciences*, (2): 31–43.

Zhang, W. and K. Rongzhu, 2002b, "Xinren jiqi Jieshi: laizi zhongguo de kua sheng diaocha fenxi" ("Trust and Explanation: From China's Cross-Regional Data"). *Economic Research Journal*, (10): 59–70.

Zheng, Y., 2001, *xiren lun* (On Trust). Beijing: China Radio and Television Press.

Zhu, S., 1996, *fazhi jiqi bentu ziyuan* (The Rule of Law and Local Legal Resources). Beijing: China University of Political Science and Law Press.

Index

For Product Safety Concerns and Information please contact our EU
representative GPSR@taylorandfrancis.com
Taylor & Francis Verlag GmbH, Kaufingerstraße 24, 80331 München, Germany